SCOTT, FORESMAN AND COMPANY

CHICAGO
ATLANTA
DALLAS
NEW YORK
SAN FRANCISCO

SCOTT, FORESMAN AND COMPANY

CHICAGO
ATLANTA
DALLAS
NEW YORK
SAN FRANCISCO

MODERN AMERICAN NARRATION

MARK TWAIN

ERNEST HEMINGWAY

WILLIAM FAULKNER

EDITED BY

RANDALL STEWART, BROWN UNIVERSITY

DOROTHY BETHURUM, CONNECTICUT COLLEGE

Modern American Narration *is one of four books constituting* Living Masterpieces of American Literature: *Book One*, Concord Idealism, *Emerson and Thoreau; Book Two,* Classic American Fiction, *Poe, Hawthorne, Melville, and James; Book Three,* Modern American Narration, *Mark Twain, Hemingway, and Faulkner; Book Four,* American Poetry, *Poe, Emerson, Whitman, Dickinson, Frost, and Eliot.*

FOREWORD

The bringing together in the same volume of these three writers—Mark Twain, Hemingway, and Faulkner—will suggest to the teacher and student a number of stimulating opportunities for analysis and comparison.

The appropriateness of the grouping, the editors believe, will be generally acknowledged. All three are "modern" writers, and are connected in significant ways. Hemingway, for example, has confessed his debt to Mark Twain's prose; and the strain of frontier realism and humor in Faulkner, as Malcolm Cowley has pointed out, owes much to Mark Twain. If Hemingway and Faulkner are the two chief writers of prose fiction in twentieth-century America (and agreement seems pretty general now that they are), Mark Twain is their chief forerunner in the nineteenth century.

They have certain stylistic resemblances. Although Mark Twain is sometimes too "literary" to be quite colloquial, Hemingway too stylized or mannered, and Faulkner too involved, all three, nevertheless, have caught the basic speech rhythms of America. Their writings show that they have studied the American rhythms and locutions attentively. All three, moreover, are both realists and romanticists, for they demonstrate in their writings that the truth about human life embraces both the commonplace and the exceptional, the low and the high, the sordid and the heroic. It would be interesting to compare the "heroes" of these authors displayed in the present selections: Bixby, Garcia, Francis, Sam Fathers.

All three, once more, belong by origin to the Mississippi Valley: Mark Twain to Missouri, Hemingway to Michigan, and Faulkner to Mississippi. Faulkner has stayed in Mississippi. Mark Twain, though he moved to New England and dealt with a variety of times and places, wrote his best books about his native habitat, the river and the river town. Hemingway wrote some of his best pieces about his boyhood days in Michigan, though he traveled to Europe and Africa and located many of his famous stories in foreign places. But regardless of geographical variations, these writers are American in an especially indigenous sense. Their work has made American literature distinctively and autochthonously American. They have given to America a new kind of literary fame throughout the world.

Randall Stewart
Dorothy Bethurum

CONTENTS ■■■■■■■■■■■■■■■■■■■■■■■■

MODERN AMERICAN NARRATION

MARK TWAIN

ERNEST HEMINGWAY

WILLIAM FAULKNER

MARK TWAIN

OLD TIMES ON THE MISSISSIPPI

MODERN AMERICAN NARRATION

MARK TWAIN

ERNEST HEMINGWAY

WILLIAM FAULKNER

THE RIVER

Mark Twain (Samuel Langhorne Clemens) spent his boyhood days in Hannibal, Missouri, on the Mississippi River. His boyhood ambition to be a river pilot prompted him to take advantage of an opportunity in 1857—when he was twenty-two—to apprentice himself to Horace Bixby, a master pilot. After seventeen months, he received his pilot's license—in September 1858—and became Bixby's partner. He practiced his profession with distinguished success until the spring of 1861, when the outbreak of the Civil War put an end, temporarily, to steamboating on the Mississippi. After the war, the competition of the railroads prevented the steamboats from regaining their former importance and glory. Mark Twain, meanwhile, after sojourns in the Far West and in Europe, had become a writer.

In 1874 Mark Twain was living in Hartford, Connecticut, and his friend William Dean Howells was editor of the *Atlantic Monthly*. When he was urged by Howells to write something for the magazine, he at first said he had nothing in mind at the moment, but later, after a stimulating and encouraging conversation with his Hartford friend and neighbor, Reverend Joseph Twitchell, he wrote to Howells as follows:

> I take back the remark that I can't write for the January number, for Twitchell and I have had a long walk in the woods, and I got to telling him about old Mississippi days of steamboating glory and grandeur as I saw them (during four years) *from the pilot-house*. He said, "What a virgin subject to hurl into a magazine!" I hadn't thought of that before. Would you like a series of papers to run through three months or six or nine— or about four months, say?

Howells was delighted. He replied: "I want the sketches, if you can make them, *every month*." Mark Twain set to work at once with a will, and the copy that he sent to Editor Howells appeared in seven installments of the *Atlantic,* in 1875, under the title *Old Times on the Mississippi.*

The author of the monumental, four-volume biography of Mark Twain, Albert Bigelow Paine, says of this work:

> Those piloting chapters are so convincing, so real, and at the same time of such extraordinary charm and interest, that if the English language should survive a thousand years, or ten times as long, they would be as fresh and vivid at the end of that period as the day they were penned. In them the atmosphere of the river and its environment—its pictures, its thousand aspects of life—are reproduced with what is no less than literary necromancy. Not only does he make you smell the river, you can fairly hear it breathe.

Mark Twain revisited the river in 1882, and by adding new material gathered at that time, enlarged the original work into a book three times as long, which was published in 1883 as *Life on the Mississippi.* The added material is of considerable interest; it points up the contrast between prewar and postwar scenes and shows the author in a more critical mood. But the longer work is a potpourri; it lacks the unity and sustained excellence that make *Old Times on the Mississippi* a great classic.

Mark Twain's strength depended in a very special sense upon the river. His origins were there. It entered into the substance of his earliest recollections. His knowledge of the river—and this of course is the kind of knowledge that is most useful to a writer—was unconscious and instinctive. The river was not a subject that he had to "work up"; he merely drew upon a great fund of accumulated experience. This he did supremely well in *Huckleberry Finn* and *Old Times on the Mississippi,* where the action is entirely concerned with the river, the river traffic, and the settlements along the river banks. It is no accident that these two, by common consent, are Mark Twain's best books. *Tom Sawyer* and *Pudd'nhead Wilson* are river books too, though to a lesser degree, the action taking place in St. Petersburg and Dawson's Landing, both of which are river towns. Certain chapters of *The Gilded Age* have to do with the river. Portions of these works likewise show us Mark Twain at his best. When he separates himself from the river—as in *A Connecticut Yankee*—he can still be amusing and forceful, but his work loses a certain authority. He is no longer at home. The same point can be made about Hawthorne and New England, Melville and seafaring life, Faulkner and Mississippi.

Mark Twain never wrote before or again with such high and unflagging enthusiasm as in *Old Times on the Mississippi.* "If I have seemed to love my subject," he confessed in Chapter 6, "it is no surprising thing, for I loved the profession [of steamboat piloting] far better than any I have followed since, and I took a measureless pride in it." The river was a world in itself. Its population was a microcosm of humanity, and in his fictional creations Mark Twain often drew upon his piloting days and his knowledge of the river folk. "In that brief, sharp schooling," he said, "I got personally and familiarly acquainted with all the different types of human nature that are to be found in fiction, biography, or history. When I find a well-drawn character in fiction or biography, I generally take a warm personal interest in him, for the reason that I have known him before—met him on the river."

Similarities between characters and incidents in *Old Times on the Mississippi* and characters and incidents in the author's fictional works emphasize the centrality of the river in his whole creative life. The night watchman is an adumbration of the King, or the Duke, in *Huckleberry Finn*. Stephen W.'s gift of gab recalls Colonel Beriah Sellers of *The Gilded Age*. The anecdote of the rivalry between the young cubs for the attention of the "pretty girl of sixteen" reads like something out of *Tom Sawyer*. *Old Times on the Mississippi* is a rich collection of embryonic materials. Or to put it another way, it is a remarkable compendium of Mark Twain and his world.

It has been objected that the book romanticizes its subject too much. Bernard DeVoto (in *Mark Twain's America*) speaks of two historical aspects of the subject in particular, of which there is no hint in Mark Twain: the unregulated, cutthroat competition in the river traffic, which resulted in jerry-built boats and fraudulent practices generally; and "the squalid venery of the steamboats, which were consistently a habitation for the loves of travelers, river rats, and frontiersmen." The objection, historically speaking, is doubtless valid. But it should be remembered that the description of sexual immorality was not permitted in American literature in Mark Twain's time. It should be noted, too, that *Old Times on the Mississippi* was written with complete consistency from the standpoint of the pilot, particularly the young pilot absorbed in his profession, who in his professional capacity had nothing to do with, and no inclination to attend to, the shenanigans of the passengers or the chicanery of the boat's owners. Given the point of view from which the story is told, the exclusion of certain matters (the inclusion of which the historian rightly insists upon for a complete picture) becomes an artistic necessity. *Old Times on the Mississippi*, in short, is not a history but a work of art.

MARK TWAIN AND THE MODERN

It has often been observed that modern American prose began with Mark Twain. Other great American writers of the nineteenth century —Poe, Hawthorne, Melville, James—used a literary English, a bookish style, which more often than not had little relation to American speech. Mark Twain was the first of our great writers to catch the

American language, the American speech rhythms, the American idiom. At his best he achieves a perfect naturalness. Consider the following passage, for example, from *Old Times on the Mississippi:*

> And the boat *is* rather a handsome sight, too. She is long and sharp and trim and pretty; she has two tall, fancy-topped chimneys, with a gilded device of some kind swung between them; a fanciful pilot-house, all glass and "gingerbread," perched on top of the "texas" deck behind them; the paddle-boxes are gorgeous with a picture or with gilded rays above the boat's name; the boiler-deck, the hurricane-deck, and the texas deck are fenced and ornamented with clean white railings; there is a flag gallantly flying from the jack-staff; the furnace doors are open and the fires glaring bravely; the upper decks are black with passengers; the captain stands by the big bell, calm, imposing, the envy of all; great volumes of the blackest smoke are rolling and tumbling out of the chimneys—a husbanded grandeur created with a bit of pitchpine just before arriving at a town; the crew are grouped on the forecastle; the broad stage is run far out over the port bow, and an envied deck-hand stands picturesquely on the end of it with a coil of rope in his hand; the pent steam is screaming through the gauge-cocks; the captain lifts his hand, a bell rings, the wheels stop; then they turn back, churning the water to foam, and the steamer is at rest.

The student should practice reading this passage aloud to see how well it meets the tests of idiom, word order, and oral rhythm.

Hemingway, among other moderns, has paid special tribute to Mark Twain's use of language and the "modernness" of his style. It would indeed be possible to juxtapose passages from Hemingway and Mark Twain that would reveal remarkable stylistic similarities: colloquial ease, coordinate syntax, sharpness and accuracy of detail. And there are striking aesthetic and spiritual resemblances between these two writers, also: a democratic approach that selects subjects from uncommon common life; an emphasis upon an "aristocracy" of talent and skill—the professional talent and skill, for example, of a bullfighter or a steamboat pilot; the concept of the disciplined life, the life lived according to rule or code, as a means of achieving order—one's private order, perhaps—in a chaotic world.

LARGER MEANINGS

Speaking of his early life in Hannibal, Mark Twain once said, "You can hardly imagine what it meant to a boy in those days, shut in as we were, to see those steamboats pass up and down." Van Wyck Brooks (in *The Ordeal of Mark Twain*) sees in the character of the steamboat pilot "a sort of channel for all the aesthetic idealism of the Mississippi region." Brooks continues this thought in a now classic passage:

> Think of the squalor of those villages, their moral and material squalor, their dim and ice-bound horizon, their petty taboos: repression at one extreme, eruption at the other, and shiftlessness for a golden mean. . . . Those steamboats were indeed "floating enchantments," beautiful, comely, clean. . . . And what an air they had of *going* somewhere. . . . And the pilot! Mark Twain tells how he longed to be a cabin boy, to do any menial work about the decks in order to serve the majestic boats and their worthy sovereigns. Of what are we reminded but the breathless, the fructifying adoration of a young apprentice in the atelier of some great master of the Renaissance? And we are right. Mark Twain's soul is that of the artist, and what we see unfolding itself is indeed the natural passion of the novice lavished, for love of the métier, upon the only creative . . . the only purposive figure in all his experience.

Old Times on the Mississippi is one of the great narratives of modern literature. It is interesting biographically for the light it throws on Sam Clemens. It is important historically, despite certain omissions, for the light it throws on the Mississippi Valley in the 1850's. But it is even more interesting and important as a work of art, which is to say that the book has values that transcend its author and its locale. The book has larger meanings, and these larger meanings constitute its chief importance as literature.

The river is richly symbolic and stands for many things—for adventure, for mystery and endless change, for the arterial life-giving stream, for the Stream of Time, or of Consciousness. The ship is a traditional symbol both of the individual life and of the collective life of community or state. And the pilot has a rich tradition of symbolic meaning. It would be interesting to inquire into Mark Twain's enlargement of this particular tradition. He obviously stresses in his portrait of the pilot the labor and difficulty involved in his mastery of the profession, the authority and prestige, or "status," once the mastery is achieved, and withal a certain humor and nonchalance, and relaxation even, in the carriage of a great pilot. This last characteristic, especially, seems distinctively a trait of the American hero.

As one reads and rereads *Old Times on the Mississippi*, the book takes on the marks of a saga. Characters and incidents expand into the typical and legendary. Mark Twain was right, after all, in viewing his subject in a heroic light, just as Thoreau was right in viewing the Fitchburg Line in a heroic light. Trainmen and steamboatmen, from one angle of vision, can be heroic, even Homeric. Mark Twain's "lightning pilot," Horace Bixby, could stand watch with Columbus or Ulysses or any other celebrated water-traveler without derogation. Great writers always make us aware of the human potential, the value of the human element, the capacity for heroism.

LIFE AND WORKS

Mark Twain (Samuel Langhorne Clemens) was born in Florida, Missouri, in 1835; four years later the family moved to Hannibal. From 1848 to 1857 he worked a good deal on newspapers—as typesetter, printer, and reporter—first for the paper of his brother Orion in Hannibal, and later in New York, Cincinnati, Keokuk, and elsewhere. He was a pilot on the Mississippi from 1857 to 1861, when the Civil War closed the river to steamboats. In the 1860's he was a newspaper man in Nevada and California and a traveler in Europe. In 1869 he published *Innocents Abroad,* and in 1870 he married Olivia Langdon of Elmira, New York. The Clemenses moved to Hartford, Connecticut, in 1872. His more important works are: *Roughing It* (1871), *The Gilded Age* (1873), *Old Times on the Mississippi* (1875), *Tom Sawyer* (1876), *Life on the Mississippi* (1883), *Huckleberry Finn* (1884), *A Connecticut Yankee in King Arthur's Court* (1889), *Pudd'nhead Wilson* (1894), *Joan of Arc* (1896), and *The Mysterious Stranger* (1916). He lectured much in the United States and abroad and received honorary degrees from Yale and Oxford. He died in 1910.

Some very useful books about Mark Twain are: William Dean Howells, *My Mark Twain* (1910); Albert Bigelow Paine, *Mark Twain, a Biography* (1912); Van Wyck Brooks, *The Ordeal of Mark Twain* (1920); Bernard DeVoto, *Mark Twain's America* (1932); Dixon Wecter, *Sam Clemens of Hannibal* (1952).

OLD TIMES ON THE MISSISSIPPI

CHAPTER 1

When I was a boy, there was but one permanent ambition among my comrades in our village on the west bank of the Mississippi River. That was, to be a steamboatman. We had transient ambitions of other sorts, but they were only transient. When a circus came and went, it left us all burning to become clowns; the first negro minstrel show that came to our section left us all suffering to try that kind of life; now and then we had a hope that, if we lived and were good, God would permit us to be pirates. These ambitions faded out, each in its turn; but the ambition to be a steamboatman always remained.

Once a day a cheap, gaudy packet arrived upward from St. Louis, and another downward from Keokuk. Before these events had transpired, the day was glorious with expectancy; after they had transpired, the day was a dead and empty thing. Not only the boys, but the whole village, felt this. After all these years I can picture that old time to myself now, just as it was then: the white town drowsing in the sunshine of a summer's morning; the streets empty, or pretty nearly so; one or two clerks sitting in front of the Water Street stores, with their splint-bottomed chairs tilted back against the wall, chins on breasts, hats slouched over their faces, asleep—with shingle-shavings enough around to show what broke them down; a sow and a litter of pigs loafing along the sidewalk, doing a good business in water-melon rinds and seeds; two or three lonely little freight piles scattered about the "levee"; a pile of "skids" on the slope of the stone-paved wharf, and the fragrant town drunkard asleep in the shadow of them; two or three wood flats at the head of the wharf, but nobody to listen to the peaceful lapping of the wavelets against them; the great Mississippi, the majestic, the magnificent Mississippi, rolling its mile-wide tide along, shining in the sun; the dense forest away on the other side; the "point" above the town, and the "point" below, bounding the river-glimpse and turning it into a sort of sea, and withal a very still and brilliant and lonely one. Presently a film of dark smoke appears above one of those remote "points"; instantly a negro drayman, famous for his quick eye and prodigious voice, lifts up the cry, "S-t-e-a-m-boat a-comin'!" and the scene changes! The town drunkard stirs, the clerks wake up, a furious clatter of drays follows, every house and store pours out a human contribution, and all in a twinkling the dead town is alive and moving. Drays, carts, men, boys, all go hurrying from many quarters to a common center, the wharf. Assembled there, the people fasten their eyes upon the coming boat as upon a wonder they are seeing for the first time. And the boat is rather a handsome sight, too. She is long and sharp and trim and pretty; she has two tall, fancy-topped chimneys, with a gilded device of some kind swung between them; a fanciful pilot-house, all glass and "gingerbread," perched on top of the "texas" deck behind them; the paddle-boxes are gorgeous with a picture or with gilded rays above the boat's name; the boiler-deck, the hurricane-deck, and the texas deck are fenced and ornamented with clean white railings; there is a flag gallantly flying from the jack-staff; the furnace doors are open and the fires glaring bravely; the upper decks are black with passengers; the captain stands by the big bell, calm, imposing, the envy of all; great volumes of the blackest smoke are rolling and tumbling out of the chimneys—a husbanded grandeur created with a bit of pitchpine just before arriving at a town; the crew are grouped on the forecastle; the broad stage is run far out over the port bow, and an envied deck-hand stands picturesquely on the end of it with a coil of rope in his hand; the pent steam is screaming through the gauge-cocks; the captain lifts his hand, a bell rings, the wheels stop; then they turn back, churning the water to foam, and the steamer is at rest. Then such a scramble as there is to get aboard, and to get ashore, and to take in freight and to discharge freight, all at one and the same time; and such a yelling and cursing as the mates facilitate it all with! Ten minutes later the steamer is under way again, with no flag on the jack-staff and no black smoke issuing from the chimneys. After ten more minutes the town is dead again, and the town drunkard asleep by the skids once more.

My father was a justice of the peace, and I supposed he possessed the power of life and death over all men, and could hang anybody that offended him. This was distinction enough for me as a general thing; but the desire to be a steamboatman kept intruding, nevertheless. I first wanted to be a cabin-boy, so that I could come out with a white apron on and shake a tablecloth over the side, where all my old comrades could see me; later I thought I would rather be the deckhand who stood on the end of the stage-plank with the coil of rope in his hand, because he was particularly conspicuous. But these were only day-dreams—they were too heavenly to be contemplated as real possibilities. By and by one of our boys went away. He was not heard of for a long time. At last he turned up as apprentice engineer or "striker" on a steamboat. This thing shook the bottom out of all my Sunday-school teachings. That boy had been notoriously worldly, and I just the reverse; yet he was exalted to this eminence, and I left in obscurity and misery. There was nothing generous about this fellow in his greatness. He would always manage to have a rusty bolt to scrub while his boat tarried at our town, and he would sit on the inside guard and scrub it, where we all could see him and envy him and loathe him. And whenever his boat was laid up he would come home and swell around the town in his blackest and greasiest clothes, so that nobody could help remembering that he was a steamboatman; and he used all sorts of steamboat technicalities in his talk, as if he were so used to them that he forgot common people could not understand them. He would speak of the "labboard" side of a horse in an easy, natural way that would make one wish he was dead. And he was always talking about "St. Looy" like an old citizen; he would refer casually to occasions when he was "coming down Fourth Street," or when he was "passing by the Planters' House," or when there was a fire and he took a turn on the brakes of "the old Big Missouri"; and then he would go on and lie about how many towns the size of ours were burned down there that day. Two or three of the boys had long been persons of consideration among us because they had been to St. Louis once and had a vague general knowledge of its wonders, but the day of their glory was over now. They lapsed into a humble silence, and learned to disappear when the ruthless "cub"-engineer approached. This fellow had money, too, and hair-oil. Also an ignorant silver watch and a showy brass watch-chain. He wore a leather belt and used no suspenders. If ever a youth was cordially admired and hated by his comrades, this one was. No girl could withstand his charms. He "cut out" every boy in the village. When his boat blew up at last, it diffused a tranquil contentment among us such as we had not known for months. But when he came home the next week, alive, renowned, and appeared in church all battered up and bandaged, a shining hero, stared at and wondered over by everybody, it seemed to us that the partiality of Providence for an undeserving reptile had reached a point where it was open to criticism.

This creature's career could produce but one result, and it speedily followed. Boy after boy managed to get on the river. The minister's son became an engineer. The doctor's and the postmaster's sons became "mud clerks"; the wholesale liquor dealer's son became a barkeeper on a boat; four sons of the chief merchant, and two sons of the county judge, became pilots. Pilot was the grandest position of all. The pilot, even in those days of trivial wages, had a princely salary—from a hundred and fifty to two hundred and fifty dollars a month, and no board to pay. Two months of his wages would pay a preacher's salary for a year. Now some of us were left disconsolate. We could not get on the river—at least our parents would not let us.

So, by and by, I ran away. I said I would never come home again till I was a pilot and could come in glory. But somehow I could not manage it. I went meekly aboard a few of the boats that lay packed together like sardines at the long St.

Louis wharf, and humbly inquired for the pilots, but got only a cold shoulder and short words from mates and clerks. I had to make the best of this sort of treatment for the time being, but I had comforting day-dreams of a future when I should be a great and honored pilot, with plenty of money, and could kill some of these mates and clerks and pay for them.

Months afterward the hope within me struggled to a reluctant death, and I found myself without an ambition. But I was ashamed to go home. I was in Cincinnati, and I set to work to map out a new career. I had been reading about the recent exploration of the river Amazon by an expedition sent out by our government. It was said that the expedition, owing to difficulties, had not thoroughly explored a part of the country lying about the headwaters, some four thousand miles from the mouth of the river. It was only about fifteen hundred miles from Cincinnati to New Orleans, where I could doubtless get a ship. I had thirty dollars left; I would go and complete the exploration of the Amazon. This was all the thought I gave to the subject. I never was great in matters of detail. I packed my valise, and took passage on an ancient tub called the *Paul Jones*, for New Orleans. For the sum of sixteen dollars I had the scarred and tarnished splendors of "her" main saloon principally to myself, for she was not a creature to attract the eye of wiser travelers.

When we presently got under way and went poking down the broad Ohio, I became a new being, and the subject of my own admiration. I was a traveler! A word never had tasted so good in my mouth before. I had an exultant sense of being bound for mysterious lands and distant climes which I never have felt in so uplifting a degree since. I was in such a glorified condition that all ignoble feelings departed out of me, and I was able to look down and pity the untraveled with a compassion that had hardly a trace of contempt in it. Still, when we stopped at villages and wood-yards, I could not help lolling carelessly upon the railings of the boiler-deck to enjoy the envy of the country boys on the bank. If they did not seem to discover me, I presently sneezed to attract their attention, or moved to a position where they could not help seeing me. And as soon as I knew they saw me I gaped and stretched, and gave other signs of being mightily bored with traveling.

I kept my hat off all the time, and stayed where the wind and the sun could strike me, because I wanted to get the bronzed and weather-beaten look of an old traveler. Before the second day was half gone I experienced a joy which filled me with the purest gratitude; for I saw that the skin had begun to blister and peel off my face and neck. I wished that the boys and girls at home could see me now.

We reached Louisville in time—at least the neighborhood of it. We stuck hard and fast on the rocks in the middle of the river, and lay there four days. I was now beginning to feel a strong sense of being a part of the boat's family, a sort of infant son to the captain and younger brother to the officers. There is no estimating the pride I took in this grandeur, or the affection that began to swell and grow in me for those people. I could not know how the lordly steamboatman scorns that sort of presumption in a mere landsman. I particularly longed to acquire the least trifle of notice from the big stormy mate, and I was on the alert for an opportunity to do him a service to that end. It came at last. The riotous pow-wow of setting a spar was going on down on the forecastle, and I went down there and stood around in the way—or mostly skipping out of it—till the mate suddenly roared a general order for somebody to bring him a capstan bar. I sprang to his side and said: "Tell me where it is—I'll fetch it!"

If a rag-picker had offered to do a diplomatic service for the Emperor of Russia, the monarch could not have been more astounded than the mate was. He even stopped swearing. He stood and stared down at me. It took him ten seconds to scrape his disjointed remains together again. Then he said impressively: "Well, if this don't beat hell!" and turned to his work with the air of a man who had been confronted with a problem too abstruse for solution.

I crept away, and courted solitude for the rest of the day. I did not go to dinner; I stayed away from supper until everybody else had finished. I did not feel so much like a member of the boat's family now as before. However, my spirits returned, in instalments, as we pursued our way down the river. I was sorry I hated the mate so, because it was not in (young) human nature not to admire him. He was huge and muscular, his face was bearded and whiskered all over; he had a red woman and a blue woman tattooed on his right arm—one on each side of a blue anchor with a red rope to it; and in the matter of profanity he was sublime. When he was getting out cargo at a landing, I was always where I could see and hear. He felt all the majesty of his great position, and made the world feel it, too. When he gave even the simplest order, he discharged it like a blast of lightning, and sent a long, reverberating peal of profanity thundering after it. I could not help contrasting the way in which the average landsman would give an order with the mate's way of doing it. If the landsman should wish the gang-plank moved a foot farther forward, he would probably say: "James, or William, one of you push that plank forward, please"; but put the mate in his place, and he would roar out: "Here, now, start that gang-plank for'ard! Lively, now! *What*'re you about! Snatch it! *snatch* it! There! there! Aft again! aft again! Don't you hear me? Dash it to dash! are you going to *sleep* over it! *'Vast* heaving. 'Vast heaving, I tell you! Going to heave it clear astern? WHERE're you going with that barrel! *for'ard* with it 'fore I make you swallow it, you dash-dash-dash-*dashed* split between a tired mud-turtle and a crippled hearse-horse!"

I wished I could talk like that.

When the soreness of my adventure with the mate had somewhat worn off, I began timidly to make up to the humblest official connected with the boat—the night watchman. He snubbed my advances at first, but I presently ventured to offer him a new chalk pipe, and that softened him. So he allowed me to sit with him by the big bell on the hurricane-deck, and in time he melted into conversation. He could not well have helped it, I hung with such homage on his words and so plainly showed that I felt honored by his notice. He told me the names of dim capes and shadowy islands as we glided by them in the solemnity of the night, under the winking stars, and by and by got to talking about himself. He seemed over-sentimental for a man whose salary was six dollars a week—or rather he might have seemed so to an older person than I. But I drank in his words hungrily, and with a faith that might have moved mountains if it had been applied judiciously. What was it to me that he was soiled and seedy and fragrant with gin? What was it to me that his grammar was bad, his construction worse, and his profanity so void of art that it was an element of weakness rather than strength in his conversation? He was a wronged man, a man who had seen trouble, and that was enough for me. As he mellowed into his plaintive history his tears dripped upon the lantern in his lap, and I cried, too, from sympathy. He said he was the son of an English nobleman—either an earl or an alderman, he could not remember which, but believed was both; his father, the nobleman, loved him, but his mother hated him from the cradle; and so while he was still a little boy he was sent to "one of them old, ancient colleges"—he couldn't remember which; and by and by his father died and his mother seized the property and "shook" him, as he phrased it. After his mother shook him, members of the nobility with whom he was acquainted used their influence to get him the position of "loblolly-boy in a ship"; and from that point my watchman threw off all trammels of date and locality and branched out into a narrative that bristled all along with incredible adventures; a narrative that was so reeking with blood-shed, and so crammed with hair-breadth escapes and the most engaging and unconscious personal villainies, that I sat speechless, enjoying, shuddering, wondering, worshiping.

It was a sore blight to find out afterward that he was a low, vulgar, ignorant, sentimental, half-witted humbug, an untraveled native of the wilds of Illinois, who had absorbed wildcat literature and appropriated its marvels, until in time he had woven odds and ends of the mess into this yarn, and then gone on telling it to fledglings like me, until he had come to believe it himself.

CHAPTER 2

What with lying on the rocks four days at Louisville, and some other delays, the poor old *Paul Jones* fooled away about two weeks in making the voyage from Cincinnati to New Orleans. This gave me a chance to get acquainted with one of the pilots, and he taught me how to steer the boat, and thus made the fascination of river life more potent than ever for me.

It also gave me a chance to get acquainted with a youth who had taken deck passage—more's the pity; for he easily borrowed six dollars of me on a promise to return to the boat and pay it back to me the day after we should arrive. But he probably died or forgot, for he never came. It was doubtless the former, since he had said his parents were wealthy, and he only traveled deck passage because it was cooler.[1]

I soon discovered two things. One was that a vessel would not be likely to sail for the mouth of the Amazon under ten or twelve years; and the other was that the nine or ten dollars still left in my pocket would not suffice for so impossible an exploration as I had planned, even if I could afford to wait for a ship. Therefore it followed that I must contrive a new career. The *Paul Jones* was now bound for St. Louis. I planned a siege against my pilot, and at the end of three hard days he surrendered. He agreed to teach me the Mississippi River from New Orleans to St. Louis for five hundred dollars, payable out of the first wages I should receive after graduating. I entered upon the small enterprise of "learning" twelve or thirteen hundred miles of the great Mississippi River with the easy confidence of my time of life. If I had really known what I was about to require of my fac-

---

1. **Deck passage:** steerage passage. [Mark Twain's note.]

ulties, I should not have had the courage to begin. I supposed that all a pilot had to do was to keep his boat in the river, and I did not consider that that could be much of a trick, since it was so wide.

The boat backed out from New Orleans at four in the afternoon, and it was "our watch" until eight. Mr. Bixby, my chief, "straightened her up," plowed her along past the sterns of the other boats that lay at the Levee, and then said, "Here, take her; shave those steamships as close as you'd peel an apple." I took the wheel, and my heartbeat fluttered up into the hundreds; for it seemed to me that we were about to scrape the side off every ship in the line, we were so close. I held my breath and began to claw the boat away from the danger; and I had my own opinion of the pilot who had known no better than to get us into such peril, but I was too wise to express it. In half a minute I had a wide margin of safety intervening between the *Paul Jones* and the ships; and within ten seconds more I was set aside in disgrace, and Mr. Bixby was going into danger again and flaying me alive with abuse of my cowardice. I was stung, but I was obliged to admire the easy confidence with which my chief loafed from side to side of his wheel, and trimmed the ships so closely that disaster seemed ceaselessly imminent. When he had cooled a little he told me that the easy water was close ashore and the current outside, and therefore we must hug the bank, up-stream, to get the benefit of the former, and stay well out, down-stream, to take advantage of the latter. In my own mind I resolved to be a down-stream pilot and leave the up-streaming to people dead to prudence.

Now and then Mr. Bixby called my attention to certain things. Said he, "This is Six-Mile Point." I assented. It was pleasant enough information, but I could not see the bearing of it. I was not conscious that it was a matter of any interest to me. Another time he said, "This is Nine-Mile Point." Later he said, "This is Twelve-Mile Point." They were all about level with the water's edge; they all looked about alike to me; they were monotonously unpicturesque. I hoped Mr. Bixby would change the subject. But no; he would crowd up around a point, hugging the shore with affection, and then say: "The slack water ends here, abreast this bunch of China trees; now we cross over." So he crossed over. He gave me the wheel once or twice, but I had no luck. I either came near chipping off the edge of a sugar-plantation, or I yawed too far from shore, and so dropped back into disgrace again and got abused.

The watch was ended at last, and we took supper and went to bed. At midnight the glare of a lantern shone in my eyes, and the night watchman said:

"Come, turn out!"

And then he left. I could not understand this extraordinary procedure; so I presently gave up trying to, and dozed off to sleep. Pretty soon the watchman was back again, and this time he was gruff. I was annoyed. I said:

"What do you want to come bothering around here in the middle of the night for? Now, as like as not, I'll not get to sleep again to-night."

The watchman said:

"Well, if this ain't good, I'm blessed."

The "off-watch" was just turning in, and I heard some brutal laughter from them, and such remarks as "Hello, watchman! ain't the new cub turned out yet? He's delicate, likely. Give him some sugar in a rag, and send for the chambermaid to sing 'Rock-a-by Baby,' to him."

About this time Mr. Bixby appeared on the scene. Something like a minute later I was climbing the pilot-house steps with some of my clothes on and the rest in my arms. Mr. Bixby was close behind, commenting. Here was something fresh —this thing of getting up in the middle of the night to go to work. It was a detail in piloting that had never occurred to me at all. I knew that boats ran all night, but somehow I had never happened to reflect that somebody had to get up out of a warm bed to run them. I began to fear that piloting was not quite so romantic as I had imagined it was; there was something very real and worklike about this new phase of it.

It was a rather dingy night, although a fair number of stars were out. The big mate was at the wheel, and he had the old tub pointed at a star and was holding her straight up the middle of the river. The shores on either hand were not much more than half a mile apart, but they seemed wonderfully far away and ever so vague and indistinct. The mate said:

"We've got to land at Jones's plantation, sir."

The vengeful spirit in me exulted. I said to myself, "I wish you joy of your job, Mr. Bixby; you'll have a good time finding Mr. Jones's plantation such a night as this; and I hope you never *will* find it as long as you live."

Mr. Bixby said to the mate:

"Upper end of the plantation, or the lower?"

"Upper."

"I can't do it. The stumps there are out of water at this stage. It's no great distance to the lower, and you'll have to get along with that."

"All right, sir. If Jones don't like it, he'll have to lump it, I reckon."

And then the mate left. My exultation began to cool and my wonder to come up. Here was a man who not only proposed to find this plantation on such a night, but to find either end of it you preferred. I dreadfully wanted to ask a question, but I was carrying about as many short answers as my cargo-room would admit of, so I held my peace. All I desired to ask Mr. Bixby was the simple question whether he was ass enough to really imagine he was going to find that plantation on a night when all plantations were exactly alike and all of the same color. But I held in. I used to have fine inspirations of prudence in those days.

Mr. Bixby made for the shore and soon was scraping it, just the same as if it had been daylight. And not only that, but singing:

"Father in heaven, the day is declining," etc.

It seemed to me that I had put my life in the keeping of a peculiarly reckless outcast. Presently he turned on me and said:

"What's the name of the first point above New Orleans?"

I was gratified to be able to answer promptly, and I did. I said I didn't know.

"Don't *know*?"

This manner jolted me. I was down at the foot again, in a moment. But I had to say just what I had said before.

"Well, you're a smart one!" said Mr. Bixby. "What's the name of the *next* point?"

Once more I didn't know.

"Well, this beats anything. Tell me the name of *any* point or place I told you."

I studied awhile and decided that I couldn't.

"Look here! What do you start out from, above Twelve-Mile Point, to cross over?"

"I—I—don't know."

"You—you—don't know?" mimicking my drawling manner of speech. "What *do* you know?"

"I—I—nothing, for certain."

"By the great Caesar's ghost, I believe you! You're the stupidest dunderhead I ever saw or ever heard of, so help me Moses! The idea of *you* being a pilot—*you!* Why, you don't know enough to pilot a cow down a lane."

Oh, but his wrath was up! He was a nervous man, and he shuffled from one side of his wheel to the other as if the floor was hot. He would boil awhile to himself, and then overflow and scald me again.

"Look here! What do you suppose I told you the names of those points for?"

I tremblingly considered a moment, and then the devil of temptation provoked me to say:

"Well to—to—be entertaining, I thought."

This was a red rag to the bull. He raged and stormed so (he was crossing the river at the time) that I judged it made him blind, because he ran over the steering-oar of a trading-scow. Of course the traders sent up a volley of red-hot profanity. Never was a man so grateful as Mr. Bixby was; because he was brimful, and here were subjects who could *talk back*. He threw open a window, thrust his head out, and such an irruption followed as I never had heard before. The fainter and farther away the scowmen's curses drifted, the higher Mr. Bixby lifted his voice and the weightier his adjectives grew. When he closed the window he was empty. You could have drawn a seine through his system and not caught curses enough to disturb your mother with. Presently he said to me in the gentlest way:

"My boy, you must get a little memorandum-book; and every time I tell you a thing, put it down right away. There's only one way to be a pilot, and that is to get this entire river by heart. You have to know it just like A B C."

That was a dismal revelation to me; for my memory was never loaded with anything but blank cartridges. However, I did not feel discouraged long. I judged that it was best to make some allowances, for doubtless Mr. Bixby was "stretching." Presently he pulled a rope and struck a few strokes on the big bell. The stars were all gone now, and the night was as black as ink. I could hear the wheels churn along the bank, but I was not entirely certain that I could see the shore. The voice of the invisible watchman called up from the hurricane-deck:

"What's this, sir?"

"Jones's plantation."

I said to myself, "I wish I might venture to offer a small bet that it isn't." But I did not chirp. I only waited to see. Mr. Bixby handled the engine-bells, and in due time the boat's nose came to the land, a torch glowed from the forecastle, a man skipped ashore, a darky's voice on the bank said: "Gimme de k'yarpet-bag, Mass' Jones," and the next moment we were standing up the river again, all serene. I reflected deeply awhile, and then said—but not aloud—"Well, the finding of that plantation was the luckiest accident that ever happened; but it couldn't happen again in a hundred years." And I fully believed it *was* an accident, too.

By the time we had gone seven or eight hundred miles up the river, I had learned to be a tolerably plucky up-stream steersman, in daylight; and before we reached St. Louis I had made a trifle of progress in night work, but only a trifle. I had a note-book that fairly bristled with the names of towns, "points," bars, islands, bends, reaches, etc.; but the information was to be found only in the note-book—none of it was in my head. It made my heart ache to think I had only got half of the river set down; for as our watch was four hours off and four hours on, day and night, there was a long four-hour gap in my book for every time I had slept since the voyage began.

My chief was presently hired to go on a big New Orleans boat, and I packed my satchel and went with him. She was a grand affair. When I stood in her pilot-house I was so far above the water that I seemed perched on a mountain; and her decks stretched so far away, fore and aft, below me, that I wondered how I could ever have considered the little *Paul Jones* a large craft. There were other differences, too. The *Paul Jones's* pilot-house was a cheap, dingy, battered rattle trap, cramped for room; but here was a sumptuous glass temple; room enough to have a dance in; showy red and gold window-curtains; an imposing sofa; leather cushions and a back to the high bench where visiting pilots sit, to spin yarns and "look at the river"; bright, fanciful "cuspidores," instead of a broad wooden box filled with sawdust; nice new oilcloth on the floor; a hospitable big stove for winter; a wheel as high as my head, costly with inlaid work; a wire tiller-rope; bright brass knobs for the bells; and a tidy, white-aproned, black "texas-tender," to bring up tarts and ices and coffee during mid-watch, day and night. Now this was "something like"; and so I began to take heart once more to believe that piloting was a romantic sort of occupation after all. The moment we were under way I began to prowl about the great steamer and fill myself with joy. She was as clean and as dainty as a drawing-room; when I looked down her long, gilded saloon, it was like gazing through a splendid tunnel; she had an oil-picture, by some gifted sign-painter, on every stateroom door; she glittered with no end of prism-fringed chandeliers; the clerk's office was elegant, the bar was marvelous, and the bar-keeper had been barbered and upholstered at incredible cost. The boiler-deck (*i.e.*, the second story of the boat, so to speak) was as spacious as a church, it seemed to me; so with the forecastle; and there was no pitiful handful of deck-hands, firemen, and roustabouts down there, but a whole battalion of men. The fires were fiercely glaring from a long row of furnaces, and over them were eight huge boilers! This was unutterable pomp. The mighty engines—but enough of this. I had never felt so fine before. And when I found that the regiment of natty servants respectfully "sir'd" me, my satisfaction was complete.

When I returned to the pilot-house St. Louis was gone, and I was lost. Here was a piece of river which was all down in my book, but I could make neither head nor tail of it: you understand, it was turned around. I had seen it when coming up-stream, but I had never faced about to see how it looked when it was behind me. My heart broke again, for it was plain that I had got to learn this troublesome river *both ways*.

The pilot-house was full of pilots, going down to "look at the river." What is called the "upper river" (the two hundred miles between St. Louis and Cairo, where the Ohio comes in) was low; and the Mississippi changes its channel so constantly that the pilots used to always find it necessary to run down to Cairo to take a fresh look, when their boats were to lie in a port a week; that is, when the water was at a low stage. A deal of this "looking at the river" was done by poor fellows who seldom had a berth, and whose only hope of getting one lay in their being always freshly posted and therefore ready to drop into the shoes of some reputable pilot, for a single trip, on account of such pilot's sudden illness, or some other necessity. And a good many of them constantly ran up and down inspecting the river, not because they ever really hoped to get a berth, but because (they being guests of the boat) it was cheaper to "look at the river" than stay ashore and pay board. In time these fellows grew dainty in their tastes, and only infested boats that had an established reputation for setting good tables. All visiting pilots were useful, for they were always ready and willing, winter or summer, night or day, to go out in the yawl and help buoy the channel or assist the boat's pilots in any way they could. They were likewise welcomed because all pilots are tireless talkers, when gathered together, and as they talk only about the river they are always understood and are always interesting. Your true pilot cares nothing about anything on earth but the river, and his pride in his occupation surpasses the pride of kings.

We had a fine company of these river inspectors along, this trip. There were eight or ten, and there was abundance of room for them in our great pilot-house. Two or three of them wore polished silk hats, elaborate shirt-fronts, diamond breastpins, kid gloves, and patent-leather boots. They were choice in their English, and bore themselves with a dignity proper to men of solid means and prodigious reputation as pilots. The others were more or less loosely clad, and wore upon their heads tall felt cones that were suggestive of the days of the Commonwealth.

I was a cipher in this august company, and felt subdued, not to say torpid. I was not even of sufficient consequence to assist at the wheel when it was necessary to put the tiller hard down in a hurry; the guest that stood nearest did that when occasion required—and this was pretty much all the time, because of the crookedness of the channel and the scant water. I stood in a corner; and the talk I listened to took the hope all out of me. One visitor said to another:

"Jim, how did you run Plum Point, coming up?"

"It was in the night, there, and I ran it the way one of the boys on the *Diana* told me; started out about fifty yards above the wood-pile on the false point, and held on the cabin under Plum Point till I raised the reef—quarter less twain— then straightened up for the middle bar till I got well abreast the old one-limbed cottonwood in the bend, then got my stern on the cottonwood, and head on the low place above the point, and came through a-booming—nine and a half."

"Pretty square crossing, an't it?"

"Yes, but the upper bar's working down fast."

Another pilot spoke up and said:

"I had better water than that, and ran it lower down; started out from the false point—mark twain—raised the second reef abreast the big snag in the bend, and had quarter less twain."

One of the gorgeous ones remarked:

"I don't want to find fault with your leadsmen, but that's a good deal of water for Plum Point, it seems to me."

There was an approving nod all around as this quiet snub dropped on the boaster and "settled" him. And so they went on talk-talk-talking. Meantime, the thing that was running in my mind was, "Now, if my ears hear aright, I have not only to get the names of all the towns and islands and bends and so on, by heart, but I must even get up a warm personal acquaintanceship with every old snag and one-limbed cottonwood and obscure wood-pile that ornaments the banks of this river for twelve hundred miles; and more than that, I must actually know where these things are in the dark, unless these guests are gifted with eyes that can pierce through two miles of solid blackness. I wish the piloting business was in Jericho and I had never thought of it."

At dusk Mr. Bixby tapped the big bell three times (the signal to land), and the captain emerged from his drawing-room in the forward end of the "texas," and looked up inquiringly. Mr. Bixby said:

"We will lay up here all night, captain."

"Very well, sir."

That was all. The boat came to shore and tied up for the night. It seemed to me a fine thing that the pilot could do as he pleased, without asking so grand a captain's permission. I took my supper and went immediately to bed, discouraged by my day's observations and experiences. My late voyage's note-booking was but a confusion of meaningless names. It had tangled me all up in a knot every time I had looked at it in the daytime. I now hoped for respite in sleep; but no, it reveled all through my head till sunrise again, a frantic and tireless nightmare.

Next morning I felt pretty rusty and low-spirited. We went booming along, taking a good many chances, for we were anxious to "get out of the river" (as getting out to Cairo was called) before night should overtake us. But Mr. Bixby's partner, the other pilot, presently grounded the boat, and we lost so much time getting her off that it was plain the darkness would overtake us a good long way above the mouth. This was a great misfortune, especially to certain of our visiting pilots, whose boats would have to wait for their return, no matter how long that might be. It sobered the pilot-house talk a good deal. Coming up-stream, pilots did not mind low water or any kind of darkness; nothing stopped them but fog. But down-stream work was different; a boat was too nearly helpless, with a stiff current pushing behind her; so it was not customary to run down-stream at night in low water.

There seemed to be one small hope, however: if we could get through the intricate and dangerous Hat Island crossing before night, we could venture the rest, for we would have plainer sailing and better water. But it would be insanity to attempt Hat Island at night. So there was a deal of looking at watches all the rest of the day, and a constant ciphering upon the speed we were making; Hat Island was the eternal subject; sometimes hope was high and sometimes we were delayed in a bad crossing, and down it went again. For hours all hands lay under the burden of this suppressed excitement; it was even communicated to me, and I got to feeling so solicitous about Hat Island, and under such an awful pressure of responsibility, that I wished I might have five minutes on shore to draw a good, full, relieving breath, and start over again. We were standing no regular watches. Each of our pilots ran such portions of the river as he had run when coming up-stream, because of his greater familiarity with it; but both remained in the pilot-house constantly.

An hour before sunset Mr. Bixby took the wheel, and Mr. W— stepped aside.

For the next thirty minutes every man held his watch in his hand and was restless, silent, and uneasy. At last somebody said, with a doomful sigh:

"Well, yonder's Hat Island—and we can't make it."

All the watches closed with a snap, everybody sighed and muttered something about its being "too bad, too bad—ah, if we could *only* have got there half an hour sooner!" and the place was thick with the atmosphere of disappointment. Some started to go out, but loitered, hearing no bell-tap to land. The sun dipped behind the horizon, the boat went on. Inquiring looks passed from one guest to another; and one who had his hand on the door-knob and had turned it, waited, then presently took away his hand and let the knob turn back again. We bore steadily down the bend. More looks were exchanged, and nods of surprised admiration—but no words. Insensibly the men drew together behind Mr. Bixby, as the sky darkened and one or two dim stars came out. The dead silence and sense of waiting became oppressive. Mr. Bixby pulled the cord, and two deep, mellow notes from the big bell floated off on the night. Then a pause, and one more note was struck. The watchman's voice followed, from the hurricane-deck:

"Labboard lead, there! Stabboard lead!"

The cries of the leadsmen began to rise out of the distance, and were gruffly repeated by the word-passers on the hurricane-deck.

"M-a-r-k three! M-a-r-k three! Quarter-less-three! Half twain! Quarter twain! M-a-r-k twain! Quarter-less—"

Mr. Bixby pulled two bell-ropes, and was answered by faint jinglings far below in the engine-room, and our speed slackened. The steam began to whistle through the gauge-cocks. The cries of the leadsmen went on—and it is a weird sound, always, in the night. Every pilot in the lot was watching now, with fixed eyes, and talking under his breath. Nobody was calm and easy but Mr. Bixby. He would put his wheel down and stand on a spoke, and as the steamer swung into her (to me) utterly invisible marks—for we seemed to be in the midst of a wide and gloomy sea—he would meet and fasten her there. Out of the murmur of half-audible talk, one caught a coherent sentence now and then—such as:

"There; she's over the first reef all right!"

After a pause, another subdued voice:

"Her stern's coming down just *exactly* right, by *George!*"

"Now she's in the marks; over she goes!"

Somebody else muttered:

"Oh, it was done beautiful—*beautiful!*"

Now the engines were stopped altogether, and we drifted with the current. Not that I could see the boat drift, for I could not, the stars being all gone by this time. This drifting was the dismalest work; it held one's heart still. Presently I discovered a blacker gloom than that which surrounded us. It was the head of the island. We were closing right down upon it. We entered its deeper shadow, and so imminent seemed the peril that I was likely to suffocate; and I had the strongest impulse to do *something*, anything, to save the vessel. But still Mr. Bixby stood by his wheel, silent, intent as a cat, and all the pilots stood shoulder to shoulder at his back.

"She'll not make it!" somebody whispered.

The water grew shoaler and shoaler, by the leadsman's cries, till it was down to:

"Eight-and-a-half! E-i-g-h-t feet! E-i-g-h-t feet! Seven-and—"

Mr. Bixby said warningly through his speaking-tube to the engineer:

"Stand by, now!"

"Ay, ay, sir!"

"Seven-and-a-half! Seven feet! *Six*-and—"

We touched bottom! Instantly Mr. Bixby set a lot of bells ringing, shouted through the tube, "*Now*, let her have it—every ounce you've got!" then to his partner, "Put her hard down! snatch her! snatch her!" The boat rasped and ground her way through the sand, hung upon the apex of disaster a single tremendous instant, and then over she went! And such a shout as went up at Mr. Bixby's back never loosened the roof of a pilot-house before!

There was no more trouble after that. Mr. Bixby was a hero that night; and it was some little time, too, before his exploit ceased to be talked about by rivermen.

Fully to realize the marvelous precision required in laying the great steamer in her marks in that murky waste of water, one should know that not only must she pick her intricate way through snags and blind reefs, and then shave the head of the island so closely as to brush the overhanging foliage with her stern, but at one place she must pass almost within arm's reach of a sunken and invisible wreck that would snatch the hull timbers from under her if she should strike it, and destroy a quarter of a million dollars' worth of steamboat and cargo in five minutes, and maybe a hundred and fifty human lives into the bargain.

The last remark I heard that night was a compliment to Mr. Bixby, uttered in soliloquy and with unction by one of our guests. He said:

"By the Shadow of Death, but he's a lightning pilot!"

CHAPTER 3

At the end of what seemed a tedious while, I had managed to pack my head full of islands, towns, bars, "points," and bends; and a curiously inanimate mass of lumber it was, too. However, inasmuch as I could shut my eyes and reel off a good long string of these names without leaving out more than ten miles of river in every fifty, I began to feel that I could take a boat down to New Orleans if I could make her skip those little gaps. But of course my complacency could hardly get start enough to lift my nose a trifle into the air, before Mr. Bixby would think of something to fetch it down again. One day he turned on me suddenly with this settler:—

"What is the shape of Walnut Bend?"

He might as well have asked me my grandmother's opinion of protoplasm. I reflected respectfully, and then said I didn't know it had any particular shape. My gun powdery chief went off with a bang, of course, and then went on loading and firing until he was out of adjectives.

I had learned long ago that he only carried just so many rounds of ammunition, and was sure to subside into a very placable and even remorseful old smooth-bore as soon as they were all gone. That word "old" is merely affectionate; he was not more than thirty-four. I waited. By and by he said,—

"My boy, you've got to know the *shape* of the river perfectly. It is all there is left to steer by on a very dark night. Everything else is blotted out and gone. But mind you, it hasn't the same shape in the night that it has in the daytime."

"How on earth am I ever going to learn it, then?"

"How do you follow a hall at home in the dark? Because you know the shape of it. You can't see it."

"Do you mean to say that I've got to know all the million trifling variations of shape in the banks of this interminable river as well as I know the shape of the front hall at home?"

"On my honor, you've got to know them *better* than any man ever did know the shapes of the halls in his own house."

"I wish I was dead!"

"Now I don't want to discourage you, but—"

"Well, pile it on me; I might as well have it now as another time."

"You see, this has got to be learned; there isn't any getting around it. A clear starlight night throws such heavy shadows that if you didn't know the shape of a shore perfectly you would claw away from every bunch of timber, because you would take the black shadow of it for a solid cape; and you see you would be getting scared to death every fifteen minutes by the watch. You would be fifty yards from shore all the time when you ought to be within twenty feet of it. You can't see a snag in one of those shadows, but you know exactly where it is, and the shape of the river tells you when you are coming to it. Then there's your pitch dark night; the river is a very different shape on a pitch dark night from what it is on a starlight night. All shores seem to be straight lines, then, and mighty dim ones, too; and you'd *run* them for straight lines, only you know better. You boldly drive your boat into what seems to be a solid, straight wall (you knowing very well that in reality there is a curve there), and that wall falls back and makes way for you. Then there's your gray mist. You take a night when there's one of these grisly, drizzly, gray mists, and then there isn't *any* particular shape to a shore. A gray mist would tangle the head of the oldest man that ever lived. Well, then, different kinds of *moonlight* change the shape of the river in different ways. You see—"

"Oh, don't say any more, please! Have I got to learn the shape of the river according to all these five hundred thousand different ways? If I tried to carry all that cargo in my head it would make me stoop-shouldered."

"No! you only learn *the* shape of the river; and you learn it with such absolute certainty that you can always steer by the shape that's *in your head*, and never mind the one that's before your eyes."

"Very well, I'll try it; but, after I have learned it, can I depend on it? Will it keep the same form and not go fooling around?"

Before Mr. Bixby could answer, Mr. W— came in to take the watch, and he said:

"Bixby, you'll have to look out for President's Island, and all that country clear away up above the Old Hen and Chickens. The banks are caving and the shape of the shores changing like everything. Why, you wouldn't know the point above 40. You can go up inside the old sycamore snag, now."

So that question was answered. Here were leagues of shore changing shape. My spirits were down in the mud again. Two things seemed pretty apparent to me. One was, that in order to be a pilot a man had got to learn more than any one man ought to be allowed to know; and the other was, that he must learn it all over again in a different way every twenty-four hours.

That night we had the watch until twelve. Now it was an ancient river custom for the two pilots to chat a bit when the watch changed. While the relieving pilot put on his gloves and lit his cigar, his partner, the retiring pilot, would say something like this:

"I judge the upper bar is making down a little at Hale's Point; had quarter twain with the lower lead and mark twain with the other."

"Yes, I thought it was making down a little last trip. Meet any boats?"

"Met one abreast the head of 21, but she was away over hugging the bar, and I couldn't make her out entirely. I took her for the Sunny South—hadn't any skylights forward of the chimneys."

And so on. And as the relieving pilot took the wheel his partner would mention that we were in such-and-such a bend, and say we were abreast of such-and-such a man's woodyard or plantation. This was courtesy; I supposed it was *necessity*. But Mr. W— came on watch full twelve minutes late on this particular night—a tremendous breach of etiquette; in fact, it is the unpardonable sin among pilots. So Mr. Bixby gave him no greeting whatever, but simply surrendered the wheel and marched out of the pilot-house without a word. I was appalled; it was a villainous night for blackness, we were in a particularly wide and blind part of the river, where there was no shape or substance to anything, and it seemed incredible that Mr. Bixby should have left that poor fellow to kill the boat, trying to find out where he was. But I resolved that I would stand by him anyway. He should find that he was not wholly friendless. So I stood around, and waited to be asked where we were. But Mr. W— plunged on serenely through the solid firmament of black cats that stood for an atmosphere, and never opened his mouth. "Here is a proud devil!" thought I; "here is a limb of Satan that would rather send us all to destruction than put himself under obligations to me, because I am not yet one of the salt of the earth and privileged to snub captains and lord it over everything dead and alive in a steamboat." I presently climbed up on the bench; I did not think it was safe to go to sleep while this lunatic was on watch.

However, I must have gone to sleep in the course of time, because the next thing I was aware of was the fact that day was breaking, Mr. W— gone, and Mr. Bixby at the wheel again. So it was four o'clock and all well—but me; I felt like a skinful of dry bones, and all of them trying to ache at once.

Mr. Bixby asked me what I had stayed up there for. I confessed that it was to do Mr. W— a benevolence—tell him where he was. It took five minutes for the entire preposterousness of the thing to filter into Mr. Bixby's system, and then I judge it filled him nearly up to the chin; because he paid me a compliment—and not much of a one either. He said:

"Well, taking you by and large, you do seem to be more different kinds of an ass than any creature I ever saw before. What did you suppose he wanted to know for?"

I said I thought it might be a convenience to him.

"Convenience! Dash! Didn't I tell you that a man's got to know the river in the night the same as he'd know his own front hall?"

"Well, I can follow the front hall in the dark if I know it *is* the front hall; but suppose you set me down in the middle of it in the dark and not tell me which hall it is, how am *I* to know?"

"Well, you've *got* to, on the river!"

"All right. Then I'm glad I never said anything to Mr. W——."

"I should say so! Why, he'd have slammed you through the window and utterly ruined a hundred dollars' worth of window-sash and stuff."

I was glad this damage had been saved, for it would have made me unpopular with the owners. They always hated anybody who had the name of being careless and injuring things.

I went to work now to learn the shape of the river; and of all the eluding and ungraspable objects that ever I tried to get mind or hands on, that was the chief. I would fasten my eyes upon a sharp, wooded point that projected far into the river some miles ahead of me, and go to laboriously photographing its shape in my brain; and just as I was beginning to succeed to my satisfaction, we would draw up toward it and the exasperating thing would begin to melt away and fold back into the bank! If there had been a conspicuous dead tree standing upon the very point of the cape, I would find that tree inconspicuously merged into the general forest, and occupying the middle of a straight shore, when I got abreast of it! No prominent hill would stick to its shape long enough for me to make up my mind what its form really was, but it was as dissolving and changeful as if it had been a mountain of butter in the hottest corner of the tropics. Nothing ever had the same shape when I was coming down-stream that it had borne when I went up. I mentioned these little difficulties to Mr. Bixby. He said:

"That's the very main virtue of the thing. If the shapes didn't change every three seconds they wouldn't be of any use. Take this place where we are now, for instance. As long as that hill over yonder is only one hill, I can boom right along the way I'm going; but the moment it splits at the top and forms a V, I know I've got to scratch to starboard in a hurry, or I'll bang this boat's brains out against a rock; and then the moment one of the prongs of the V swings behind the other, I've got to waltz to larboard again, or I'll have a misunderstanding with a snag that would snatch the keelson out of this steamboat as neatly as if it were a sliver in your hand. If that hill didn't change its shape on bad nights there would be an awful steamboat graveyard around here inside of a year."

It was plain that I had got to learn the shape of the river in all the different ways that could be thought of,—upside down, wrong end first, inside out, fore-and-aft, and "thort-ships,"—and then know what to do on gray nights when it hadn't any shape at all. So I set about it. In the course of time I began to get the best of this knotty lesson, and my self-complacency moved to the front once more. Mr. Bixby was all fixed and ready to start to the rear again. He opened on me after this fashion:

"How much water did we have in the middle crossing at Hole-in-the-Wall, trip before last?"

I considered this an outrage. I said:

"Every trip, down and up, the leadsmen are singing through that tangled place for three quarters of an hour on a stretch. How do you reckon I can remember such a mess as that?"

"My boy, you've got to remember it. You've got to remember the exact spot and the exact marks the boat lay in when we had the shoalest water, in every one of the two thousand shoal places between St. Louis and New Orleans; and you mustn't get the shoal soundings and marks of one trip mixed up with the shoal soundings and marks of another, either, for they're not often twice alike. You must keep them separate."

When I came to myself again, I said:

"When I get so that I can do that, I'll be able to raise the dead, and then I won't have to pilot a steamboat to make a living. I want to retire from this business. I want a slush-bucket and a brush; I'm only fit for a roustabout. I haven't got brains enough to be a pilot; and if I had I wouldn't have strength enough to carry them around, unless I went on crutches."

"Now drop that! When I say I'll learn a man the river, I mean it. And you can depend on it, I'll learn him or kill him."

There was no use in arguing with a person like this. I promptly put such a strain on my memory that by and by even the shoal water and the countless crossing-marks began to stay with me. But the result was just the same. I never could more than get one knotty thing learned before another presented itself. Now I had often seen pilots gazing at the water and pretending to read it as if it were a book; but it was a book that told me nothing. A time came at last, however, when Mr. Bixby seemed to think me far enough advanced to bear a lesson on water-reading. So he began:

"Do you see that long, slanting line on the face of the water? Now, that's a reef. Moreover, it's a bluff reef. There is a solid sand-bar under it that is nearly as straight up and down as the side of a house. There is plenty of water close up to it, but mighty little on top of it. If you were to hit it you would knock the boat's brains out. Do you see where the line fringes out at the upper end and begins to fade away?"

"Yes, sir."

"Well, that is a low place; that is the head of the reef. You can climb over there, and not hurt anything. Cross over, now, and follow along close under the reef—easy water there—not much current."

I followed the reef along till I approached the fringed end. Then Mr. Bixby said:

"Now get ready. Wait till I give the word. She won't want to mount the reef; a boat hates shoal water. Stand by—wait—*wait*—keep her well in hand. *Now* cramp her down! Snatch her! snatch her!"

He seized the other side of the wheel and helped to spin it around until it was hard down, and then we held it so. The boat resisted, and refused to answer for a while, and next she came surging to starboard, mounted the reef, and sent a long, angry ridge of water foaming away from her bows.

"Now watch her; watch her like a cat, or she'll get away from you. When she fights strong and the tiller slips a little, in a jerky, greasy sort of way, let up on her a trifle; it is the way she tells you at night that the water is too shoal; but keep edging her up, little by little, toward the point. You are well up on the bar now; there is a bar under every point, because the water that comes down around it forms an eddy and allows the sediment to sink. Do you see those fine lines on the face of the water that branch out like the ribs of a fan? Well, those are little reefs; you want to just miss the ends of them, but run them pretty close. Now look out—look out! Don't you crowd that slick, greasy-looking place; there ain't nine feet there; she won't stand it. She begins to smell it; look sharp, I tell you! Oh, blazes, there you go! Stop the starboard wheel! Quick! Ship up to back! Set her back!"

The engine bells jingled and the engines answered promptly, shooting white columns of steam far aloft out of the 'scape-pipes, but it was too late. The boat had "smelt" the bar in good earnest; the foamy ridges that radiated from her bows suddenly disappeared, a great dead swell came rolling forward, and swept ahead of her, she careened far over to larboard, and went tearing away toward the shore as if she were about scared to death. We were a good mile from where we ought to have been when we finally got the upper hand of her again.

During the afternoon watch the next day, Mr. Bixby asked me if I knew how to run the next few miles. I said:

"Go inside the first snag above the point, outside the next one, start out from the lower end of Higgins's woodyard, make a square crossing, and—"

"That's all right. I'll be back before you close up on the next point."

But he wasn't. He was still below when I rounded it and entered upon a piece of the river which I had some misgivings about. I did not know that he was hiding behind a chimney to see how I would perform. I went gayly along, getting prouder and prouder, for he had never left the boat in my sole charge such a length of time before. I even got to "setting" her and letting the wheel go entirely, while I vaingloriously turned my back and inspected the stern marks and hummed a tune, a sort of easy indifference which I had prodigiously admired in Bixby and other great pilots. Once I inspected rather long, and when I faced to the front again my heart flew into my mouth so suddenly that if I hadn't clapped my teeth together I should have lost it. One of those frightful bluff reefs was stretching its deadly length right across our bows! My head was gone in a moment; I did not know which end I stood on; I gasped and could not get my breath; I spun the wheel down with such rapidity that it wove itself together like a spider's web; the boat answered and turned square away from the reef, but the reef followed her! I fled, but still it followed, still it kept—right across my bows! I never looked to see where I was going, I only fled. The awful crash was imminent. Why didn't that villain come? If I committed the crime of ringing a bell I might get thrown overboard. But better that than kill the boat. So in blind desperation, I started such a rattling "shivaree" down below as never had astounded an engineer in this world before, I fancy. Amidst the frenzy of the bells the engines began to back and fill in a curious way, and my reason forsook its throne—we were about to crash into the woods on the other side of the river. Just then Mr. Bixby stepped calmly into view on the hurricane deck. My soul went out to him in gratitude. My distress vanished; I would have felt safe on the brink of Niagara with Mr. Bixby on the hurricane deck. He blandly and sweetly took his toothpick out of his mouth between his fingers, as if it were a cigar,—we were just in the act of climbing an overhanging big tree, and the passengers were scudding astern like rats,— and lifted up these commands to me ever so gently:

"Stop the starboard! Stop the larboard! Set her back on both!"

The boat hesitated, halted, pressed her nose among the boughs a critical instant, then reluctantly began to back away.

"Stop the larboard! Come ahead on it! Stop the starboard! Come ahead on it! Point her for the bar!"

I sailed away as serenely as a summer's morning. Mr. Bixby came in and said, with mock simplicity:

"When you have a hail, my boy, you ought to tap the big bell three times before you land, so that the engineers can get ready."

I blushed under the sarcasm, and said I hadn't had any hail.

"Ah! Then it was for wood, I suppose. The officer of the watch will tell you when he wants to wood up."

I went on consuming, and said I wasn't after wood.

"Indeed? Why, what could you want over here in the bend, then? Did you ever know of a boat following a bend up-stream at this stage of the river?"

"No, sir—and *I* wasn't trying to follow it. I was getting away from a bluff reef."

"No, it wasn't a bluff reef; there isn't one within three miles of where you were."

"But I saw it. It was as bluff as that one yonder."

"Just about. Run over it!"

"Do you give it as an order?"

"Yes. Run over it!"

"If I don't, I wish I may die."

"All right; I am taking the responsibility."

I was just as anxious to kill the boat, now, as I had been to save it before. I impressed my orders upon my memory, to be used at the inquest, and made a straight break for the reef. As it disappeared under our bows I held my breath; but we slid over it like oil.

"Now, don't you see the difference? It wasn't anything but a *wind* reef. The wind does that."

"So I see. But it is exactly like a bluff reef. How am I ever going to tell them apart?"

"I can't tell you. It is an instinct. By and by you will just naturally *know* one from the other, but you never will be able to explain why or how you know them apart."

It turned out to be true. The face of the water, in time, became a wonderful book—a book that was a dead language to the uneducated passenger, but which told its mind to me without reserve, delivering its most cherished secrets as clearly as if it uttered them with a voice. And it was not a book to be read once and thrown aside, for it had a new story to tell every day. Throughout the long twelve hundred miles there was never a page that was void of interest, never one that you could leave unread without loss, never one that you would want to skip, thinking you could find higher enjoyment in some other thing. There never was so wonderful a book written by man; never one whose interest was so absorbing, so unflagging, so sparklingly renewed with every re-perusal. The passenger who could not read it was charmed with a peculiar sort of faint dimple on its surface (on the rare occasions when he did not overlook it altogether); but to the pilot that was an *italicized* passage; indeed, it was more than that, it was a legend of the largest capitals, with a string of shouting exclamation points at the end of it, for it meant that a wreck or a rock was buried there that could tear the life out of the strongest vessel that ever floated. It is the faintest and simplest expression the water ever makes, and the most hideous to a pilot's eye. In truth, the passenger who could not read this book saw nothing but all manner of pretty pictures in it, painted by the sun and shaded by the clouds, whereas to the trained eye these were not pictures at all, but the grimmest and most dead-earnest of reading matter.

Now when I had mastered the language of this water, and had come to know every trifling feature that bordered the great river as familiarly as I knew the letters of the alphabet, I had made a valuable acquisition. But I had lost something, too. I had lost something which could never be restored to me while I lived. All the grace, the beauty, the poetry, had gone out of the majestic river! I still kept in mind a certain wonderful sunset which I witnessed when steamboating was new to me. A broad expanse of the river was turned to blood; in the middle distance the red hue brightened into gold, through which a solitary log came floating, black and conspicuous; in one place a long, slanting mark lay sparkling upon the water; in another the surface was broken by boiling, tumbling rings, that were as many-tinted as an opal; where the ruddy flush was faintest, was a smooth spot that was covered with graceful circles and radiating lines, ever so delicately traced; the shore on our left was densely wooded, and the somber shadow that fell from this forest was broken in one place by a long, ruffled trail that shone like silver; and high above the forest wall a clean-stemmed dead tree waved a single leafy bough that glowed like a flame in the unobstructed splendor that was flowing from the sun. There were graceful curves, reflected images, woody heights, soft distances; and over the whole scene, far and near, the dissolving lights drifted steadily, enriching it every passing moment with new marvels of coloring.

I stood like one bewitched. I drank it in, in a speechless rapture. The world was new to me, and I had never seen anything like this at home. But as I have said, a day came when I began to cease from noting the glories and the charms which the moon and the sun and the twilight wrought upon the river's face; another day came when I ceased altogether to note them. Then, if that sunset scene had been repeated, I should have looked upon it without rapture, and should have commented upon it, inwardly, after this fashion: "This sun means that we are going to have wind to-morrow; that floating log means that the river is rising, small thanks to it; that slanting mark on the water refers to a bluff reef which is going to kill somebody's steamboat one of these nights, if it keeps on stretching out like that; those tumbling 'boils' show a dissolving bar and a changing channel there; the lines and circles in the slick water over yonder are a warning that that troublesome place is shoaling up dangerously; that silver streak in the shadow of the forest is the 'break' from a new snag, and he has located himself in the very best place he could have found to fish for steamboats; that tall dead tree, with a single living branch, is not going to last long, and then how is a body ever going to get through this blind place at night without the friendly old landmark?"

No, the romance and the beauty were all gone from the river. All the value any feature of it had for me now was the amount of usefulness it could furnish toward compassing the safe piloting of a steamboat. Since those days, I have pitied doctors from my heart. What does the lovely flush in a beauty's cheek mean to a doctor but a "break" that ripples above some deadly disease? Are not all her visible charms sown thick with what are to him the signs and symbols of hidden decay? Does he ever see her beauty at all, or doesn't he simply view her professionally, and comment upon her unwholesome condition all to himself? And doesn't he sometimes wonder whether he has gained most or lost most by learning his trade?

CHAPTER 4

Whosoever has done me the courtesy to read my chapters which have preceded this may possibly wonder that I deal so minutely with piloting as a science. It was the prime purpose of those chapters; and I am not quite done yet. I wish to show, in the most patient and painstaking way, what a wonderful science it is. Ship channels are buoyed and lighted, and therefore it is a comparatively easy undertaking to learn to run them; clear water rivers, with gravel bottoms, change their channels very gradually, and therefore one needs to learn them but once; but piloting becomes another matter when you apply it to vast streams like the Mississippi and the Missouri, whose alluvial banks cave and change constantly, whose snags are always hunting up new quarters, whose sandbars are never at rest, whose channels are forever dodging and shirking, and whose obstructions must be confronted in all nights and all weathers without the aid of a single lighthouse or a single buoy; for there is neither light nor buoy to be found anywhere in all this three or four thousand miles of villainous river. I feel justified in enlarging upon this great science for the reason that I feel sure no one has ever yet written a paragraph about it who had piloted a steamboat himself, and so had a practical knowledge of the subject. If the theme were hackneyed, I should be obliged to deal gently with the reader; but since it is wholly new, I have felt at liberty to take up a considerable degree of room with it.

When I had learned the name and position of every visible feature of the river; when I had so mastered its shape that I could shut my eyes and trace it from St. Louis to New Orleans; when I had learned to read the face of the water as one would cull the news from the morning paper; and finally, when I had trained my dull memory to treasure up an endless array of soundings and crossing-marks, and keep fast hold of them, I judged that my education was complete; so I got to tilting my cap to the side of my head, and wearing a toothpick in my mouth at the wheel. Mr. Bixby had his eye on these airs. One day he said,—

"What is the height of that bank yonder, at Burgess's?"

"How can I tell, sir? It is three-quarters of a mile away."

"Very poor eye—very poor. Take the glass."

I took the glass and presently said—

"I can't tell. I suppose that that bank is about a foot and a half high."

"Foot and a half! That's a six-foot bank. How high was the bank along here, last trip?"

"I don't know; I never noticed."

"You didn't? Well, you must always do it hereafter."

"Why?"

"Because you'll have to know a good many things that it tells you. For one thing, it tells you the stage of the river—tells you whether there's more water or less in the river along here than there was last trip."

"The leads tell me that." I rather thought I had the advantage of him there.

"Yes, but suppose the leads lie? The bank would tell you so, and then you would stir those leadsmen up a bit. There was a ten-foot bank here last trip, and there is only a six-foot bank now. What does that signify?"

"That the river is four feet higher than it was last trip."

"Very good. Is the river rising or falling?"

"Rising."

"No, it ain't."

"I guess I am right, sir. Yonder is some drift-wood floating down the stream."

"A rise *starts* the drift-wood, but then it keeps on floating a while after the river is done rising. Now the bank will tell you about this. Wait till you come to a place where it shelves a little. Now here: do you see this narrow belt of fine sediment? That was deposited while the water was higher. You see the drift-wood begins to strand, too. The bank helps in other ways. Do you see that stump on the false point?"

"Ay, ay, sir."

"Well, the water is just up to the roots of it. You must make a note of that."

"Why?"

"Because that means that there's seven feet in the chute of 103."

"But 103 is a long way up the river yet."

"That's where the benefit of the bank comes in. There is water enough in 103 *now*, yet there may not be by the time we get there, but the bank will keep us posted all along. You don't run close chutes on a falling river, up-stream, and there are precious few of them that you are allowed to run at all downstream. There's a law of the United States against it. The river may be rising by the time we get to 103, and in that case we'll run it. We are drawing—how much?"

"Six feet aft—six and a half forward."

"Well, you do seem to know something."

"But what I particularly want to know is, if I have got to keep up an everlasting measuring of the banks of this river, twelve hundred miles, month in and month out?"

"Of course!"

My emotions were too deep for words for a while. Presently I said:

"And how about these chutes? Are there many of them?"

"I should say so! I fancy we shan't run any of the river this trip as you've ever seen it run before—so to speak. If the river begins to rise again, we'll go up behind bars that you've always seen standing out of the river, high and dry, like a roof of a house; we'll cut across low places that you've never noticed at all, right through the middle of bars that cover three hundred acres of river; we'll creep through cracks where you've always thought was solid land; we'll dart through the woods and leave twenty-five miles of river off to one side; we'll see the hind side of every island between New Orleans and Cairo."

"Then I've got to go to work and learn just as much more river as I already know."

"Just about twice as much more, as near as you can come at it."

"Well, one lives to find out. I think I was a fool when I went into this business."

"Yes, that is true. And you are yet. But you'll not be when you've learned it."

"Ah, I never can learn it!"

"I will see that you *do*."

By and by I ventured again:

"Have I got to learn all this thing just as I know the rest of the river—shapes and all—and so I can run it at night?"

"Yes. And you've got to have good fair marks from one end of the river to the other, that will help the bank tell you when there is water enough in each of these countless places—like that stump, you know. When the river first begins to rise, you can run half a dozen of the deepest of them; when it rises a foot more you can run another dozen; the next foot will add a couple of dozen, and so on: so you see you have to know your banks and marks to a dead moral certainty, and never get them mixed; for when you start through one of those cracks, there's no backing out again, as there is in the big river; you've got to go through, or stay there six months if you get caught on a falling river. There are about fifty of these cracks which you can't run at all except when the river is brimful and over the banks."

"This new lesson is a cheerful prospect."

"Cheerful enough. And mind what I've just told you; when you start into one of those places you've got to go through. They are too narrow to turn around in, too crooked to back out of, and the shoal water is always *up at the head*; never elsewhere. And the head of them is always likely to be filling up, little by little, so that the marks you reckon their depth by, this season, may not answer for next."

"Learn a new set, then, every year?"

"Exactly. Cramp her up to the bar! What are you standing up through the middle of the river for?"

The next few months showed me strange things. On the same day that we held the conversation above narrated we met a great rise coming down the river. The whole vast face of the stream was black with drifting dead logs, broken boughs, and great trees that had caved in and been washed away. It required the nicest steering to pick one's way through this rushing raft, even in the daytime, when crossing from point to point; and at night the difficulty was mightily increased; every now and then a huge log, lying deep in the water, would suddenly appear right under our bows, coming head-on; no use to try to avoid it then; we could only stop the engines, and one wheel would walk over that log from one end to the other, keeping up a thundering racket and careening the boat in a way that was very uncomfortable to passengers. Now and then we would hit one of these sunken logs a rattling bang, dead in the center, with a full head of steam, and it would stun the boat as if she had hit a continent. Sometimes this log would lodge and stay right across our nose, and back the Mississippi up before it; we would have to do a little crawfishing, then, to get away from the obstruction. We often hit *white* logs in the dark, for we could not see them until we were right on them, but a black log is a pretty distinct object at night. A white snag is an ugly customer when the daylight is gone.

Of course, on the great rise, down came a swarm of prodigious timber-rafts from the headwaters of the Mississippi, coal-barges from Pittsburg, little trading-scows from everywhere, and broadhorns from "Posey County," Indiana, freighted with "fruit and furniture"—the usual term for describing it, though in plain

English the freight thus aggrandized was hoop-poles and pumpkins. Pilots bore a mortal hatred to these craft, and it was returned with usury. The law required all such helpless traders to keep a light burning, but it was a law that was often broken. All of a sudden, on a murky night, a light would hop up, right under our bows, almost, and an agonized voice, with the backwoods "whang" to it, would wail out:

"Whar'n the —— you goin' to! Cain't you see nothin', you dash-dashed aig-suckin', sheep-stealin' one-eyed son of a stuffed monkey!"

Then for an instant, as we whistled by, the red glare from our furnaces would reveal the scow and the form of the gesticulating orator, as if under a lightning flash, and in that instant our firemen and deck-hands would send and receive a tempest of missiles and profanity, one of our wheels would walk off with the crashing fragments of a steering-oar, and down the dead blackness would shut again. And that flatboatman would be sure to go into New Orleans and sue our boat, swearing stoutly that he had a light burning all the time, when in truth his gang had the lantern down below to sing and lie and drink and gamble by, and no watch on deck. Once, at night, in one of those forest-bordered crevices (behind an island) which steamboatmen intensely describe with the phrase "as dark as the inside of a cow," we should have eaten up a Posey County family, fruit, furniture, and all, but that they happened to be fiddling down below and we just caught the sound of the music in time to sheer off, doing no serious damage, unfortunately, but coming so near it that we had good hopes for a moment. These people brought up their lantern, then, of course; and as we backed and filled to get away, the precious family stood in the light of it—both sexes and various ages—and cursed us till everything turned blue. Once a coalboatman sent a bullet through our pilot-house when we borrowed a steering-oar of him in a very narrow place.

During this big rise these small-fry craft were an intolerable nuisance. We were running chute after chute,—a new world to me,—and if there was a particularly cramped place in a chute, we would be pretty sure to meet a broadhorn there; and if he failed to be there, we would find him in a still worse locality, namely, the head of the chute, on the shoal water. And then there would be no end of profane cordialities exchanged.

Sometimes, in the big river, when we would be feeling our way cautiously along through a fog, the deep hush would suddenly be broken by yells and a clamor of tin pans, and all in an instant a log raft would appear vaguely through the webby veil, close upon us; and then we did not wait to swap knives, but snatched our engine-bells out by the roots and piled on all the steam we had, to scramble out of the way! One doesn't hit a rock or a solid log raft with a steamboat when he can get excused.

You will hardly believe it, but many steamboat clerks always carried a large assortment of religious tracts with them in those old departed steamboating days. Indeed they did! Twenty times a day we would be cramping up around a bar, while a string of these small-fry rascals were drifting down into the head of the bend away above and beyond us a couple of miles. Now a skiff would dart away from one of them, and come fighting its laborious way across the desert of water. It would "ease all" in the shadow of our forecastle, and the panting oarsmen would shout, "Gimme a pa-a-per!" as the skiff drifted swiftly astern. The clerk would throw over a file of New Orleans journals. If these were picked up *without comment,* you might notice that now a dozen other skiffs had been drifting down upon us without saying anything. You understand, they had been waiting to see how No. 1 was going to fare. No. 1 making no comment, all the rest would bend to their oars and come on, now; and as fast as they came the clerk would heave over neat bundles of religious tracts, tied to shingles. The amount of hard swearing which twelve packages of religious literature will command when impartially divided up among twelve raftsmen's crews, who have pulled a heavy skiff two miles on a hot day to get them, is simply incredible.

As I have said, the big rise brought a new world under my vision. By the time the river was over its banks we had forsaken our old paths and were hourly climbing over bars that had stood ten feet out of water before; we were shaving stumpy shores, like that at the foot of Madrid Bend, which I had always seen avoided before; we were clattering through chutes like that of 82, where the opening at the foot was an unbroken wall of timber till our nose was almost at the very spot. Some of these chutes were utter solitudes. The dense, untouched forest overhung both banks of the crooked little crack, and one could believe that human creatures had never intruded there before. The swinging grape-vines, the grassy nooks and vistas glimpsed as we swept by, the flowering creepers waving their red blossoms from the tops of dead trunks, and all the spendthrift richness of the forest foliage, were wasted and thrown away there. The chutes were lovely places to steer in; they were deep, except at the head; the current was gentle; under the "points" the water was absolutely dead, and the invisible banks so bluff that where the tender willow thickets projected you could bury your boat's broadside in them as you tore along, and then you seemed fairly to fly.

Behind other islands we found wretched little farms, and wretcheder little log-cabins; there were crazy rail fences sticking a foot or two above the water, with one or two jeans-clad, chills-racked, yellow-faced male miserables roosting on the top rail, elbows on knees, jaws in hands, grinding tobacco and discharging the result at floating chips through crevices left by lost teeth; while the rest of the family and the few farm-animals were huddled together in an empty wood-flat riding at her moorings close at hand. In this flatboat the family would have to cook and eat and sleep for a lesser or greater number of days (or possibly weeks), until the river should fall two or three feet and let them get back to their log-cabins and their chills again—chills being a merciful provision of an all-wise Providence to enable them to take exercise without exertion. And this sort of watery camping out was a thing which these people were rather liable to be treated to a couple of times a year: by the December rise out of the Ohio, and the June rise out of the Mississippi. And yet these were kindly dispensations, for they at least enabled the poor things to rise from the dead now and then, and look upon life when a steamboat went by. They appreciated the blessing, too, for they spread their mouths and eyes wide open and made the most of these occasions. Now what *could* these banished creatures find to do to keep from dying of the blues during the low-water season!

Once, in one of these lovely island chutes, we found our course completely bridged by a great fallen tree. This will serve to show how narrow some of the chutes were. The passengers had an hour's recreation in a virgin wilderness, while the boat-hands chopped the bridge away; for there was no such thing as turning back, you comprehend.

From Cairo to Baton Rouge, when the river is over its banks, you have no particular trouble in the night; for the thousand-mile wall of dense forest that guards the two banks all the way is only gapped with a farm or wood-yard opening at intervals, and so you can't "get out of the river" much easier than you could get out of a fenced lane; but from Baton Rouge to New Orleans it is a different matter. The river is more than a mile wide, and very deep—as much as two hundred feet, in places. Both banks, for a good deal over a hundred miles, are shorn of their timber and bordered by continuous sugar plantations, with only here and there a scattering sapling or row of ornamental China-trees. The timber is shorn off clear to the rear of the plantations, from two to four miles. When the first frost threatens to come, the planters snatch off their crops in a hurry. When they have finished grinding the cane, they form the refuse of the stalks (which they call "bagasse") into great piles and set fire to them, though in other sugar countries the bagasse is used for fuel in the furnaces of the sugar-mills. Now the piles of damp bagasse burn slowly, and smoke like Satan's own kitchen.

An embankment ten or fifteen feet high guards both banks of the Mississippi all the way down that lower end of the river, and this embankment is set back from the edge of the shore from ten to perhaps a hundred feet, according to circumstances; say thirty or forty feet, as a general thing. Fill that whole region with an impenetrable gloom of smoke from a hundred miles of burning bagasse piles, when the river is over the banks, and turn a steamboat loose along there at midnight and see how she will feel. And see how you will feel, too! You find yourself away out in the midst of a vague, dim sea that is shoreless, that fades out and loses itself in the murky distances; for you cannot discern the thin rib of embankment, and you are always imagining you see a straggling tree when you don't. The plantations themselves are transformed by the smoke, and look like a part of the sea. All through your watch you are tortured with the exquisite misery of uncertainty. You hope you are keeping in the river, but you do not know. All that you are sure about is that you are likely to be within six feet of the bank *and* destruction, when you think you are a good half-mile from shore. And you are sure, also, that if you chance suddenly to fetch up against the embankment and topple your chimneys overboard, you will have the small comfort of knowing that it is about what you were expecting to do. One of the great Vicksburg packets darted out into a sugar plantation one night, at such a time, and had to stay there a week. But there was no novelty about it; it had often been done before.

I thought I had finished this chapter, but I wish to add a curious thing, while it is in my mind. It is only relevant in that it is connected with piloting. There used to be an excellent pilot on the river, a Mr. X., who was a somnambulist. It was said that if his mind was troubled about a bad piece of river, he was pretty sure to get up and walk in his sleep and do strange things. He was once fellow-pilot for a trip or two with George Ealer, on a great New Orleans passenger packet. During a considerable part of the first trip George was uneasy, but got over it by and by, as X. seemed content to stay in his bed when asleep. Late one night the boat was approaching Helena, Ark.; the water was low, and the crossing above the town in a very blind and tangled condition. X. had seen the crossing since Ealer had, and as the night was particularly drizzly, sullen, and dark, Ealer was considering whether he had not better have X. called to assist in running the place, when the door opened and X. walked in. Now, on very dark nights, light is a deadly enemy to piloting; you are aware that if you stand in a lighted room, on such a night, you cannot see things in the street to any purpose; but if you put out the lights and stand in the gloom you can make out objects in the street pretty well. So, on very dark nights, pilots do not smoke; they allow no fire in the pilot-house stove, if there is a crack which can allow the least ray to escape; they order the furnaces to be curtained with huge tarpaulins and the skylights to be closely blinded. Then no light whatever issues from the boat. The undefinable shape that now entered the pilot-house had Mr. X.'s voice. This said:

"Let me take her, George; I've seen this place since you have, and it is so crooked that I reckon I can run it myself easier than I could tell you how to do it."

"It is kind of you, and I swear *I* am willing. I haven't got another drop of perspiration left in me. I have been spinning around and around the wheel like a squirrel. It is so dark I can't tell which way she is swinging till she is coming around like a whirligig."

So Ealer took a seat on the bench, panting and breathless. The black phantom assumed the wheel without saying anything, steadied the waltzing steamer with a turn or two, and then stood at ease, coaxing her a little to this side and then to that, as gently and as sweetly as if the time had been noonday. When Ealer observed this marvel of steering, he wished he had not confessed! He stared, and wondered, and finally said:

"Well, I thought I knew how to steer a steamboat, but that was another mistake of mine."

X. said nothing, but went serenely on with his work. He rang for the leads; he rang to slow down the steam; he worked the boat carefully and neatly into invisible marks, then stood at the center of the wheel and peered blandly out into the blackness, fore and aft, to verify his position; as the leads shoaled more and more, he stopped the engines entirely, and the dead silence and suspense of "drifting" followed; when the shoalest water was struck, he cracked on the steam, carried her handsomely over, and then began to work her warily into the next system of shoal marks; the same patient, heedful use of leads and engines followed, the boat slipped through without touching bottom, and entered upon the third and last intricacy of the crossing; imperceptibly she moved through the gloom, crept by inches into her marks, drifted tediously till the shoalest water was cried, and then, under a tremendous head of steam, went swinging over the reef and away into deep water and safety!

Ealer let his long-pent breath pour out in a great relieving sigh, and said:

"That's the sweetest piece of piloting that was ever done on the Mississippi River! I wouldn't believe it could be done, if I hadn't seen it."

There was no reply, and he added:

"Just hold her five minutes longer, partner, and let me run down and get a cup of coffee."

A minute later Ealer was biting into a pie, down in the "texas," and comforting himself with coffee. Just then the night watchman happened in, and was about to happen out again, when he noticed Ealer and exclaimed:

"Who is at the wheel, sir?"

"X."

"Dart for the pilot-house, quicker than lightning!"

The next moment both men were flying up the pilot-house companion-way, three steps at a jump! Nobody there! The great steamer was whistling down the middle of the river at her own sweet will! The watchman shot out of the place again; Ealer seized the wheel, set an engine back with power, and held his breath while the boat reluctantly swung away from a "towhead," which she was about to knock into the middle of the Gulf of Mexico!

By and by the watchman came back and said:

"Didn't that lunatic tell you he was asleep, when he first came up here?"

"No."

"Well, he was. I found him walking along on top of the railings, just as unconcerned as another man would walk a pavement; and I put him to bed; now just this minute there he was again, away astern, going through that sort of tight-rope deviltry the same as before."

"Well, I think I'll stay by next time he has one of those fits. But I hope he'll have them often. You just ought to have seen him take this boat through Helena crossing. *I* never saw anything so gaudy before. And if he can do such gold-leaf, kid-glove, diamond-breastpin piloting when he is sound asleep what *couldn't* he do if he was dead!"

CHAPTER 5

When the river is very low, and one's steamboat is "drawing all the water" there is in the channel,—or a few inches more, as was often the case in the old times,—one must be painfully circumspect in his piloting. We used to have to "sound" a number of particularly bad places almost every trip when the river was at a very low stage.

Sounding is done in this way: The boat ties up at the shore, just above the shoal crossing; the pilot not on watch takes his "cub" or steersman and a picked crew of men (sometimes an officer also), and goes out in the yawl—provided the boat has not that rare and sumptuous luxury, a regularly devised "sounding-boat"—and proceeds to hunt for the best water, the pilot on duty watching his movements through a spy-glass, meantime, and in some instances assisting by signals of the boat's whistle, signifying "try higher up" or "try lower down"; for the surface of the water, like an oil-painting, is more expressive and intelligible when inspected from a little distance than very close at hand. The whistle signals are seldom necessary, however; never, perhaps, except when the wind confuses the significant ripples upon the water's surface. When the yawl has reached the shoal place, the speed is slackened, the pilot begins to sound the depth with a pole ten or twelve feet long, and the steersman at the tiller obeys the order to "hold her up to starboard"; or "let her fall off to larboard"; or "steady—steady as you go."

When the measurements indicate that the yawl is approaching the shoalest part of the reef, the command is given to "Ease all!" Then the men stop rowing and the yawl drifts with the current. The next order is, "Stand by with the buoy!" The moment the shallowest point is reached, the pilot delivers the order, "Let go the buoy!" and over she goes. If the pilot is not satisfied, he sounds the place again; if he finds better water higher up or lower down, he removes the buoy to that place. Being finally satisfied, he gives the order, and all the men stand their oars straight up in the air, in line; a blast from the boat's whistle indicates that the signal has been seen; then the men "give way" on their oars and lay the yawl alongside the buoy; the steamer comes creeping carefully down, is pointed straight at the buoy, husbands her power for the coming struggle, and presently, at the critical moment, turns on all her steam and goes grinding and wallowing over the buoy and the sand, and gains the deep water beyond. Or maybe she doesn't; maybe she "strikes and swings." Then she has to while away several hours (or days) sparring herself off.

Sometimes a buoy is not laid at all, but the yawl goes ahead, hunting the best water, and the steamer follows along in its wake. Often there is a deal of fun and excitement about sounding, especially if it is a glorious summer day, or a blustering night. But in winter the cold and the peril take most of the fun out of it.

A buoy is nothing but a board four or five feet long, with one end turned up; it is a reversed school-house bench, with one of the supports left and the other removed. It is anchored on the shoalest part of the reef by a rope with a heavy stone made fast to the end of it. But for the resistance of the turned-up end of the reversed bench, the current would pull the buoy under water. At night, a paper lantern with a candle in it is fastened on top of the buoy, and this can be seen a mile or more, a little glimmering spark in the waste of blackness.

Nothing delights a cub so much as an opportunity to go out sounding. There is such an air of adventure about it; often there is danger; it is so gaudy and man-of-war-like to sit up in the stern-sheets and steer a swift yawl; there is something fine about the exultant spring of the boat when an experienced old sailor crew throw their souls into the oars; it is lovely to see the white foam stream away from the bows; there is music in the rush of the water; it is deliciously exhilarating, in summer, to go speeding over the breezy expanses of the river when the world of wavelets is dancing in the sun. It is such grandeur, too, to the cub, to get a chance to give an order; for often the pilot will simply say, "Let her go about!" and leave the rest to the cub, who instantly cries, in his sternest tone of command, "Ease, starboard! Strong on the larboard! Starboard, give way! With a will, men!" The cub enjoys sounding for the further reason that the eyes of the passengers are watching all the yawl's movements with absorbing interest, if the time be daylight; and if it be night, he knows that those same wondering eyes are fastened upon the yawl's lantern as it glides out into the gloom and dims away in the remote distance.

One trip a pretty girl of sixteen spent her time in our pilot-house with her uncle and aunt, every day and all day long. I fell in love with her. So did Mr. Thornburg's cub, Tom G. Tom and I had been bosom friends until this time; but now a coolness began to arise. I told the girl a good many of my river adventures, and made myself out a good deal of a hero; Tom tried to make himself appear to be a hero, too, and succeeded to some extent, but then he always had a way of embroidering. However, virtue is its own reward, so I was a barely perceptible trifle ahead in the contest. About this time something happened which promised handsomely for me: the pilots decided to sound the crossing at the head of 21. This would occur about nine or ten o'clock at night, when the passengers would be still up; it would be Mr. Thornburg's watch, therefore my chief would have to do the sounding. We had a perfect love of a sounding-boat—long, trim, graceful, and as fleet as a greyhound; her thwarts were cushioned; she carried twelve oarsmen; one of the mates was always sent in her to transmit orders to her crew, for ours was a steamer where no end of "style" was put on.

We tied up at the shore above 21, and got ready. It was a foul night, and the river was so wide, there, that a landsman's uneducated eyes could discern no opposite shore through such a gloom. The passengers were alert and interested; everything was satisfactory. As I hurried through the engine-room, picturesquely gotten up in storm toggery, I met Tom, and could not forbear delivering myself of a mean speech:

"Ain't you glad *you* don't have to go out sounding?"

Tom was passing on, but he quickly turned, and said:

"Now just for that, you can go and get the sounding-pole yourself. I was going after it, but I'd see you in Halifax, now, before I'd do it."

"Who wants you to get it? I don't. It's in the sounding-boat."

"It ain't, either. It's been new-painted; and it's been up on the ladies' cabin guards two days, drying."

I flew back, and shortly arrived among the crowd of watching and wondering ladies just in time to hear the command:

"Give way, men!"

I looked over, and there was the gallant sounding-boat booming away, the unprincipled Tom presiding at the tiller, and my chief sitting by him with the sounding-pole which I had been sent on a fool's errand to fetch. Then that young girl said to me:

"Oh, how awful to have to go out in that little boat on such a night! Do you think there is any danger?"

I would rather have been stabbed. I went off, full of venom, to help in the pilot-house. By and by the boat's lantern disappeared, and after an interval a wee spark glimmered upon the face of the water a mile away. Mr. Thornburg blew the whistle in acknowledgment, backed the steamer out, and made for it. We flew along for a while, then slackened steam and went cautiously gliding toward the spark. Presently Mr. Thornburg exclaimed:

"Hello, the buoy-lantern's out!"

He stopped the engines. A moment or two later he said:

"Why, there it is again!"

So he came ahead on the engines once more, and rang for the leads. Gradually the water shoaled up, and then began to deepen again! Mr. Thornburg muttered:

"Well, I don't understand this. I believe that buoy has drifted off the reef. Seems to be a little too far to the left. No matter, it is safest to run over it, anyhow."

So, in that solid world of darkness we went creeping down on the light. Just as our bows were in the act of ploughing over it, Mr. Thornburg seized the bell-ropes, rang a startling peal, and exclaimed:

"My soul, it's the sounding-boat!"

A sudden chorus of wild alarms burst out far below—a pause—and then a sound of grinding and crashing followed. Mr. Thornburg exclaimed:

"There! the paddle-wheel has ground the sounding-boat to lucifer matches! Run! See who is killed!"

I was on the main-deck in the twinkling of an eye. My chief and the third mate and nearly all the men were safe. They had discovered their danger when it was too late to pull out of the way; then, when the great guards overshadowed them a moment later, they were prepared and knew what to do; at my chief's order they sprang at the right instant, seized the guard, and were hauled aboard. The next moment the sounding-yawl swept aft to the wheel and was struck and splintered to atoms. Two of the men and the cub Tom were missing—a fact which spread like wild-fire over the boat. The passengers came flocking to the forward gangway, ladies and all, anxious-eyed, white-faced, and talked in awed voices of the dreadful thing. And often and again I heard them say, "Poor fellows! poor boy, poor boy!"

By this time the boat's yawl was manned and away, to search for the missing. Now a faint call was heard, off to the left. The yawl had disappeared in the other direction. Half the people rushed to one side to encourage the swimmer with their shouts; the other half rushed the other way to shriek to the yawl to turn about. By the callings the swimmer was approaching, but some said the sound showed failing strength. The crowd massed themselves against the boiler-deck railings, leaning over and staring into the gloom; and every faint and fainter cry wrung from them such words as "Ah, poor fellow, poor fellow! is there *no* way to save him?"

But still the cries held out, and drew nearer, and presently the voice said pluckily:

"I can make it! Stand by with a rope!"

What a rousing cheer they gave him! The chief mate took his stand in the glare of a torch-basket, a coil of rope in his hand, and his men grouped about him. The next moment the swimmer's face appeared in the circle of light, and in another one the owner of it was hauled aboard, limp and drenched, while cheer on cheer went up. It was that devil Tom.

The yawl crew searched everywhere, but found no sign of the two men. They probably failed to catch the guard, tumbled back, and were struck by the wheel and killed. Tom had never jumped for the guard at all, but had plunged head-first into the river and dived under the wheel. It was nothing; I could have done it easy enough, and I said so; but everybody went on just the same, making a wonderful to-do over that ass, as if he had done something great. That girl couldn't seem to have enough of that pitiful "hero" the rest of the trip; but little I cared; I loathed her, any way.

The way we came to mistake the sounding-boat's lantern for the buoy-light was this: My chief said that after laying the buoy he fell away and watched it till it seemed to be secure; then he took up a position a hundred yards below it and a little to one side of the steamer's course, headed the sounding-boat up-stream, and waited. Having to wait some time, he and the officer got to talking; he looked up when he judged that the steamer was about on the reef; saw that the buoy was gone, but supposed that the steamer had already run over it; he went on with his talk; he noticed that the steamer was getting very close down to him, but that was the correct thing; it was her business to shave him closely, for convenience in taking him aboard; he was expecting her to sheer off, until the last moment; then it flashed upon him that she was trying to run him down, mistaking his lantern for the buoy-light; so he sang out, "Stand by to spring for the guard, men!" and the next instant the jump was made.

But I am wandering from what I was intending to do; that is, make plainer than perhaps appears in the previous chapters some of the peculiar requirements of the science of piloting. First of all, there is one faculty which a pilot must incessantly cultivate until he has brought it to absolute perfection. Nothing short of perfection will do. That faculty is memory. He cannot stop with merely thinking a thing is so and so; he must *know* it; for this is eminently one of the "exact" sciences. With what scorn a pilot was looked upon, in the old times, if he ever ventured to deal in that feeble phrase "I think," instead of the vigorous one "I know!" One cannot easily realize what a tremendous thing it is to know every trivial detail of twelve hundred miles of river and know it with absolute exactness. If you will take the longest street in New York, and travel up and down it, conning its features patiently until you know every house and window and lamp-post and big and little sign by heart, and know them so accurately that you can instantly name the one you are abreast of when you are set down at random in that street in the middle of an inky black night, you will then have a tolerable notion of the amount and the exactness of a pilot's knowledge who carries the Mississippi River in his head. And then, if you will go on until you know every street crossing, the character, size, and position of the crossing-stones, and the varying depth of mud in each of those numberless places, you will have some idea of what the pilot must know in order to keep a Mississippi steamer out of trouble. Next, if you will take half of the signs in that long street, and *change their places* once a month, and still manage to know their positions accurately on dark nights, and keep up with these repeated changes without making any mistakes, you will understand what is required of a pilot's peerless memory by the fickle Mississippi.

I think a pilot's memory is about the most wonderful thing in the world. To know the Old and New Testaments by heart, and be able to recite them glibly, forward or backward, or begin at random anywhere in the book and recite both ways and never trip or make a mistake, is no extravagant mass of knowledge, and no marvellous facility, compared to a pilot's massed knowledge of the Mississippi and his marvellous facility in the handling of it. I make this comparison deliberately, and believe I am not expanding the truth when I do it. Many will think my figure too strong, but pilots will not.

And how easily and comfortably the pilot's memory does its work; how placidly effortless is its way; how *unconsciously* it lays up its vast stores, hour by hour, day by day, and never loses or mislays a single valuable package of them all! Take an instance. Let a leadsman cry, "Half twain! half twain! half twain! half twain! half twain!" until it becomes as monotonous as the ticking of a clock; let conversation be going on all the time, and the pilot be doing his share of the talking, and no longer consciously listening to the leadsman; and in the midst of this endless string of half twains let a single "quarter twain!" be interjected, without emphasis, and then the half twain cry go on again, just as before: two or three weeks later that pilot can describe with precision the boat's position in the river when that quarter twain was uttered, and give you such a lot of head-marks, stern-marks, and side-marks to guide you, that you ought to be able to take the boat there and put her in that same spot again yourself! The cry of "quarter twain" did not really take his mind from his talk, but his trained faculties instantly photographed the bearings, noted the change of depth, and laid up the important details for future reference without requiring any assistance from *him* in the matter. If you were walking and talking with a friend, and another friend at your side kept up a monotonous repetition of the vowel sound A, for a couple of blocks, and then in the midst interjected an R, thus, A, A, A, A, A, R, A, A, A, etc., and gave the R no emphasis, you would not be able to state, two or three weeks afterward, that the R had been put in, nor be able to tell what objects you were passing at the moment it was done. But you could if your memory had been patiently and laboriously trained to do that sort of thing mechanically.

Give a man a tolerably fair memory to start with, and piloting will develop it into a very colossus of capability. But *only in the matters it is daily drilled in.* A time would come when the man's faculties could not help noticing landmarks and soundings, and his memory could not help holding on to them with the grip of a vise; but if you asked that same man at noon what he had had for breakfast, it would be ten chances to one that he could not tell you. Astonishing things can be done with the human memory if you will devote it faithfully to one particular line of business.

At the time that wages soared so high on the Missouri River, my chief, Mr. Bixby, went up there and learned more than a thousand miles of that stream with an ease and rapidity that were astonishing. When he had seen each division *once* in the daytime and *once* at night, his education was so nearly complete that he took out a "daylight" license; a few trips later he took out a full license, and went to piloting day and night—and he ranked A 1, too.

Mr. Bixby placed me as steersman for a while under a pilot whose feats of memory were a constant marvel to me. However, his memory was born in him, I think, not built. For instance, somebody would mention a name. Instantly Mr. Brown would break in:

"Oh, I knew *him*. Sallow-faced, red-headed fellow, with a little scar on the side of his throat, like a splinter under the flesh. He was only in the Southern trade six months. That was thirteen years ago. I made a trip with him. There was five feet in the upper river then; the *Henry Blake* grounded at the foot of Tower Island drawing four and a half; the *George Elliott* unshipped her rudder on the wreck of the *Sunflower*——"

"Why, the *Sunflower* didn't sink until——"

"*I* know when she sunk; it was three years before that, on the 2d of December; Asa Hardy was captain of her, and his brother John was first clerk; and it was his first trip in her, too; Tom Jones told me these things a week afterward in New Orleans; he was first mate of the *Sunflower*. Captain Hardy stuck a nail in his foot the 6th of July of the next year, and died of the lockjaw on the 15th. His brother John died two years after,—3d of March,—erysipelas. I never saw either of the Hardys,—they were Alleghany River men,—but people who knew them told me all these things. And they said Captain Hardy wore yarn socks winter and summer just the same, and his first wife's name was Jane Shook,—she was from New England,—and his second one died in a lunatic asylum. It was in the blood. She was from Lexington, Kentucky. Name was Horton before she was married."

And so on, by the hour, the man's tongue would go. He could *not* forget any thing. It was simply impossible. The most trivial details remained as distinct and luminous in his head, after they had lain there for years, as the most memorable events. His was not simply a pilot's memory; its grasp was universal. If he were talking about a trifling letter he had received seven years before, he was pretty sure to deliver you the entire screed from memory. And then, without observing that he was departing from the true line of his talk, he was more than likely to hurl in a long-drawn parenthetical biography of the writer of that letter; and you were lucky indeed if he did not take up that writer's relatives, one by one, and give you their biographies, too.

Such a memory as that is a great misfortune. To it, all occurrences are of the same size. Its possessor cannot distinguish an interesting circumstance from an uninteresting one. As a talker, he is bound to clog his narrative with tiresome details and make himself an insufferable bore. Moreover, he cannot stick to his subject. He picks up every little grain of memory he discerns in his way, and so is led aside. Mr. Brown would start out with the honest intention of telling you a vastly funny anecdote about a dog. He would be "so full of laugh" that he could hardly begin; then his memory would start with the dog's breed and personal appearance; drift into a history of his owner; of his owner's family, with descriptions of weddings and burials that had occurred in it, together with recitals of congratulatory verses and obituary poetry provoked by the same; then his memory would recollect that one of these events occurred during the celebrated "hard winter" of such and such a year, and a minute description of that winter would follow, along with the names of people who were frozen to death, and statistics showing the high figures which pork and hay went up to. Pork and hay would suggest corn and fodder; corn and fodder would suggest cows and horses; cows and horses would suggest the circus and certain celebrated bare-back riders; the transition from the circus to the menagerie was easy and natural; from the elephant to equatorial Africa was but a step; then of course the heathen savages would suggest religion; and at the end of three or four hours' tedious jaw, the watch would change, and Brown would go out of the pilot-house muttering extracts from sermons he had heard years before about the efficacy of prayer as a means of grace. And the original first mention would be all you had learned about that dog, after all this waiting and hungering.

A pilot must have a memory; but there are two higher qualities which he must also have. He must have good and quick judgment and decision, and a cool, calm courage that no peril can shake. Give a man the merest trifle of pluck to start with, and by the time he has become a pilot he cannot be unmanned by any danger a steamboat can get into; but one cannot quite say the same for judgment. Judgment is a matter of brains, and a man must *start* with a good stock of that article or he will never succeed as a pilot.

The growth of courage in the pilot-house is steady all the time, but it does not reach a high and satisfactory condition until some time after the young pilot has been "standing his own watch" alone and under the staggering weight of all the responsibilities connected with the position. When an apprentice has become pretty thoroughly acquainted with the river, he goes clattering along so fearlessly with his steamboat, night or day, that he presently begins to imagine that it is *his* courage that animates him; but the first time the pilot steps out and leaves him to his own devices he finds out it was the other man's. He discovers that the article has been left out of his own cargo altogether. The whole river is bristling with exigencies in a moment; he is not prepared for them; he does not know how to meet them; all his knowledge forsakes him; and within fifteen minutes he is as white as a sheet and scared almost to death. Therefore pilots wisely train these cubs by various strategic tricks to look danger in the face a little more calmly. A favorite way of theirs is to play a friendly swindle upon the candidate.

Mr. Bixby served me in this fashion once, and for years afterward I used to blush, even in my sleep, when I thought of it. I had become a good steersman; so good, indeed, that I had all the work to do on our watch, night and day. Mr. Bixby seldom made a suggestion to me; all he ever did was to take the wheel on particularly bad nights or in particularly bad crossings, land the boat when she needed to be landed, play gentleman of leisure nine-tenths of the watch, and collect the wages. The lower river was about bank-full, and if any body had questioned my ability to run any crossing between Cairo and New Orleans without help or instruction, I should have felt irreparably hurt. The idea of being afraid of any crossing in the lot, in the *daytime*, was a thing too preposterous for contemplation. Well, one matchless summer's day I was bowling down the bend above Island 66, brimful of self-conceit and carrying my nose as high as a giraffe's when Mr. Bixby said:

"I am going below a while. I suppose you know the next crossing?"

This was almost an affront. It was about the plainest and simplest crossing in the whole river. One couldn't come to any harm, whether he ran it right or not; and as for depth, there never had been any bottom there. I knew all this, perfectly well.

"Know how to *run* it? Why, I can run it with my eyes shut."

"How much water is there in it?"

"Well, that is an odd question. I couldn't get bottom there with a church steeple."

"You think so, do you?"

The very tone of the question shook my confidence. That was what Mr. Bixby was expecting. He left, without saying anything more. I began to imagine all sorts of things. Mr. Bixby, unknown to me, of course, sent somebody down to the forecastle with some mysterious instructions to the leadsmen, another messenger was sent to whisper among the officers, and then Mr. Bixby went into hiding behind a smoke-stack where he could observe results. Presently the captain stepped out on the hurricane deck; next the chief mate appeared; then a clerk. Every moment or two a straggler was added to my audience; and before I got to the head of the island I had fifteen or twenty people assembled down there under my nose. I began to wonder what the trouble was. As I started across, the captain glanced aloft at me and said, with a sham uneasiness in his voice:

"Where is Mr. Bixby?"

"Gone below, sir."

But that did the business for me. My imagination began to construct dangers out of nothing, and they multiplied faster than I could keep the run of them. All at once I imagined I saw shoal water ahead! The wave of coward agony that surged through me then came near dislocating every joint in me. All my confidence in that crossing vanished. I seized the bell-rope; dropped it, ashamed; seized it again; dropped it once more; clutched it tremblingly once again, and pulled it so feebly that I could hardly hear the stroke myself. Captain and mate sang out instantly, and both together:

"Starboard lead there! and quick about it!"

This was another shock. I began to climb the wheel like a squirrel; but I would hardly get the boat started to port before I would see new dangers on that side, and away I would spin to the other; only to find perils accumulating to starboard, and be crazy to get to port again. Then came the leadsman's sepulchral cry:

"D-e-e-p four!"

Deep four in a bottomless crossing! The terror of it took my breath away.

"M-a-r-k three! M-a-r-k three! Quarter-less three! Half twain!"

This was frightful! I seized the bell-ropes and stopped the engines.

"Quarter twain! Quarter twain! *Mark* twain!"

I was helpless. I did not know what in the world to do. I was quaking from head to foot, and I could have hung my hat on my eyes, they stuck out so far.

"Quarter-*less*-twain! Nine-and-a-*half!*"

We were *drawing* nine! My hands were in a nerveless flutter. I could not ring a bell intelligibly with them. I flew to the speaking-tube and shouted to the engineer:

"Oh, Ben, if you love me, *back* her! Quick, Ben! Oh, back the immortal *soul* out of her!"

I heard the door close gently. I looked around, and there stood Mr. Bixby, smiling a bland, sweet smile. Then the audience on the hurricane deck sent up a thundergust of humiliating laughter. I saw it all, now, and I felt meaner than the meanest man in human history. I laid in the lead, set the boat in her marks, came ahead on the engines, and said:

"It was a fine trick to play on an orphan, *wasn't* it? I suppose I'll never hear the last of how I was ass enough to heave the lead at the head of 66."

"Well, no, you won't, maybe. In fact I hope you won't; for I want you to learn something by that experience. Didn't you *know* there was no bottom in that crossing?"

"Yes, sir, I did."

"Very well, then. You shouldn't have allowed me or anybody else to shake your confidence in that knowledge. Try to remember that. And another thing: when you get into a dangerous place, don't turn coward. That isn't going to help matters any."

It was a good enough lesson, but pretty hardly learned. Yet about the hardest part of it was that for months I so often had to hear a phrase which I had conceived a particular distaste for. It was, "Oh, Ben, if you love me, back her!"

CHAPTER 6

In my preceding chapters I have tried, by going into the minutiæ of the science of piloting, to carry the reader step by step to a comprehension of what the science consists of; and at the same time I have tried to show him that it is a very curious and wonderful science, too, and very worthy of his attention. If I have seemed to love my subject, it is no surprising thing, for I loved the profession far better than any I have followed since, and I took a measureless pride in it. The reason is plain: a pilot, in those days, was the only unfettered and entirely independent human being that lived in the earth. Kings are but the hampered servants of parliament and the people; parliaments sit in chains forged by their constituency; the editor of a newspaper cannot be independent, but must work with one hand tied behind him by party and patrons, and be content to utter only half or two-thirds of his mind; no clergyman is a free man and may speak the whole truth, regardless of his parish's opinions; writers of all kinds are manacled servants of the public. We write frankly and fearlessly, but then we "modify" before we print. In truth, every man and woman and child has a master, and worries and frets in servitude; but, in the day I write of, the Mississippi pilot had *none*. The captain could stand upon the hurricane deck, in the pomp of a very brief authority, and give him five or six orders while the vessel backed into the stream, and then that skipper's reign was over. The moment that the boat was under way in the river, she was under the sole and unquestioned control of the pilot. He could do with her exactly as he pleased, run her when and whither he chose, and tie her up to the bank whenever his judgment said that that course was best. His movements were entirely free; he consulted no one, he received commands from nobody, he promptly resented even the merest suggestions. Indeed, the law of the United States forbade him to listen to commands or suggestions, rightly considering that the pilot necessarily knew better how to handle the boat than anybody could tell him. So here was the novelty of a king without a keeper, an absolute monarch who was absolute in sober truth and not by a fiction of words. I have seen a boy of eighteen taking a great steamer serenely into what seemed almost certain destruction, and the aged captain standing mutely by, filled with apprehension but powerless to interfere. His interference, in that particular instance, might have been an excellent thing, but to permit it would have been to establish a most pernicious precedent. It will easily be guessed, considering the pilot's boundless authority, that he was a great personage in the old steamboating days. He was treated with marked courtesy by the captain and with marked deference by all the officers and servants; and this deferential spirit was quickly communicated to the passengers, too. I think pilots were about the only people I ever knew who failed to show, in some degree, embarrassment in the presence of travelling foreign princes. But then, people in one's own grade of life are not usually embarrassing objects.

By long habit, pilots came to put all their wishes in the form of commands. It "gravels" me, to this day, to put my will in the weak shape of a request, instead of launching it in the crisp language of an order.

In those old days, to load a steamboat at St. Louis, take her to New Orleans and back, and discharge cargo, consumed about twenty-five days, on an average.

Seven or eight of these days the boat spent at the wharves of St. Louis and New Orleans, and every soul on board was hard at work, except the two pilots; *they* did nothing but play gentleman up town, and receive the same wages for it as if they had been on duty. The moment the boat touched the wharf at either city they were ashore; and they were not likely to be seen again till the last bell was ringing and everything in readiness for another voyage.

When a captain got hold of a pilot of particularly high reputation, he took pains to keep him. When wages were four hundred dollars a month on the Upper Mississippi, I have known a captain to keep such a pilot in idleness, under full pay, three months at a time, while the river was frozen up. And one must remember that in those cheap times four hundred dollars was a salary of almost inconceivable splendor. Few men on shore got such pay as that, and when they did they were mightily looked up to. When pilots from either end of the river wandered into our small Missouri village, they were sought by the best and the fairest, and treated with exalted respect. Lying in port under wages was a thing which many pilots greatly enjoyed and appreciated; especially if they belonged in the Missouri River in the heyday of that trade (Kansas times), and got nine hundred dollars a trip, which was equivalent to about eighteen hundred dollars a month. Here is a conversation of that day. A chap out of the Illinois River, with a little sternwheel tub, accosts a couple of ornate and gilded Missouri River pilots:

"Gentlemen, I've got a pretty good trip for the up-country, and shall want you about a month. How much will it be?"

"Eighteen hundred dollars apiece."

"Heavens and earth! You take my boat, let me have your wages, and I'll divide!"

I will remark, in passing, that Mississippi steamboatmen were important in landsmen's eyes (and in their own, too, in a degree) according to the dignity of the boat they were on. For instance, it was a proud thing to be of the crew of such stately craft as the *Aleck Scott* or the *Grand Turk*. Negro firemen, deckhands, and barbers belonging to those boats were distinguished personages in their grade of life, and they were well aware of that fact, too. A stalwart darky once gave offence at a negro ball in New Orleans by putting on a good many airs. Finally one of the managers bustled up to him and said:

"Who *is* you, any way? Who *is* you? dat's what *I* wants to know!"

The offender was not disconcerted in the least, but swelled himself up and threw that into his voice which showed that he knew he was not putting on all those airs on a stinted capital.

"Who *is* I? Who *is* I? I let you know mighty quick who I is! I want you niggers to understan' dat I fires de middle do'[1] on de *Aleck Scott!*"

That was sufficient.

The barber of the *Grand Turk* was a spruce young negro, who aired his importance with balmy complacency, and was greatly courted by the circle in which he moved. The young colored population of New Orleans were much given to flirting, at twilight, on the pavements of the back streets. Somebody saw and heard something like the following, one evening, in one of those localities. A middle-aged negro woman projected her head through a broken pane and

1. **do':** door [Mark Twain's note]

shouted (very willing that the neighbors should hear and envy), "You Mary Ann, come in de house dis minute! Stannin' out dah foolin' 'long wid dat low trash, an' heah's de barber off'n de *Gran' Turk* wants to conwerse wid you!"

My reference, a moment ago, to the fact that a pilot's peculiar official position placed him out of the reach of criticism or command, brings Stephen W. naturally to my mind. He was a gifted pilot, a good fellow, a tireless talker, and had both wit and humor in him. He had a most irreverent independence, too, and was deliciously easy-going and comfortable in the presence of age, official dignity, and even the most august wealth. He always had work, he never saved a penny, he was a most persuasive borrower, he was in debt to every pilot on the river, and to the majority of the captains. He could throw a sort of splendor around a bit of harum-scarum, devil-may-care piloting, that made it almost fascinating—but not to everybody. He made a trip with good old Captain Y. once, and was "relieved" from duty when the boat got to New Orleans. Somebody expressed surprise at the discharge. Captain Y. shuddered at the mere mention of Stephen. Then his poor, thin old voice piped out something like this:

"Why, bless me! I wouldn't have such a wild creature on my boat for the world—not for the whole world! He swears, he sings, he whistles, he yells—I never saw such an Injun to yell. All times of the night—it never made any difference to him. He would just yell that way, not for anything in particular, but merely on account of a kind of devilish comfort he got out of it. I never could get into a sound sleep but he would fetch me out of bed, all in a cold sweat, with one of those dreadful war-whoops. A queer being—very queer being; no respect for anything or anybody. Sometimes he called me 'Johnny.' And he kept a fiddle and a cat. He played execrably. This seemed to distress the cat, and so the cat would howl. Nobody could sleep where that man—and his family—was. And reckless? There never was anything like it. Now you may believe it or not, but as sure as I am sitting here, he brought my boat a-tilting down through those awful snags at Chicot under a rattling head of steam, and the wind a-blowing like the very nation, at that! My officers will tell you so. They saw it. And, sir, while he was a-tearing right down through those snags, and I a-shaking in my shoes and praying, I wish I may never speak again if he didn't pucker up his mouth and go to *whistling!* Yes, sir; whistling 'Buffalo gals, can't you come out to-night, can't you come out to-night, can't you come out to-night;' and doing it as calmly as if we were attending a funeral and weren't related to the corpse. And when I remonstrated with him about it, he smiled down on me as if I was his child, and told me to run in the house and try to be good, and not be meddling with my superiors!"

Once a pretty mean captain caught Stephen in New Orleans out of work and as usual out of money. He laid steady siege to Stephen, who was in a very "close place," and finally persuaded him to hire with him at one hundred and twenty-five dollars per month, just half wages, the captain agreeing not to divulge the secret and so bring down the contempt of all the guild upon the poor fellow. But the boat was not more than a day out of New Orleans before Stephen discovered that the captain was boasting of his exploit, and that all the officers had been told. Stephen winced, but said nothing. About the middle of the afternoon the captain stepped out on the hurricane deck, cast his eye around, and looked a good deal surprised. He glanced enquiringly aloft at Stephen, but Stephen was whistling placidly and attending to business. The captain stood around a while in evident discomfort, and once or twice seemed about to make a suggestion; but the etiquette of the river taught him to avoid that sort of rashness, and so he managed to hold his peace. He chafed and puzzled a few minutes longer, then retired to his apartments. But soon he was out again, and apparently more perplexed than ever. Presently he ventured to remark, with deference:

"Pretty good stage of the river now, ain't it, sir?"

"Well, I should say so! Bank-full *is* a pretty liberal stage."

"Seems to be a good deal of current here."

"Good deal don't describe it! It's worse than a mill-race."

"Isn't it easier in toward shore than it is out here in the middle?"

"Yes, I reckon it is; but a body can't be too careful with a steamboat. It's pretty safe out here; can't strike any bottom here, you can depend on that."

The captain departed, looking rueful enough. At this rate, he would probably die of old age before his boat got to St. Louis. Next day he appeared on deck and again found Stephen faithfully standing up the middle of the river, fighting the whole vast force of the Mississippi, and whistling the same placid tune. This thing was becoming serious. In by the shore was a slower boat clipping along in the easy water and gaining steadily; she began to make for an island chute; Stephen stuck to the middle of the river. Speech was *wrung* from the captain. He said:

"Mr. W., don't that chute cut off a good deal of distance?"

"I think it does, but I don't know."

"Don't know! Well, isn't there water enough in it now to go through?"

"I expect there is, but I am not certain."

"Upon my word this is odd! Why, those pilots on that boat yonder are going to try it. Do you mean to say that you don't know as much as they do?"

"*They!* Why, *they* are two-hundred-and-fifty-dollar pilots! But don't you be uneasy; I know as much as any man can afford to know for a hundred and twenty-five!"

The captain surrendered.

Five minutes later Stephen was bowling through the chute and showing the rival boat a two-hundred-and-fifty-dollar pair of heels.

One day, on board the *Aleck Scott,* my chief, Mr. Bixby, was crawling carefully through a close place at Cat Island, both leads going, and everybody holding his breath. The captain, a nervous, apprehensive man, kept still as long as he could, but finally broke down and shouted from the hurricane deck:

"For gracious' sake, give her steam, Mr. Bixby! give her steam! She'll never raise the reef on this headway!"

For all the effect that was produced upon Mr. Bixby, one would have supposed that no remark had been made. But five minutes later, when the danger was past and the leads laid in, he burst instantly into a consuming fury, and gave the captain the most admirable cursing I ever listened to. No bloodshed ensued, but that was because the captain's cause was weak, for ordinarily he was not a man to take correction quietly.

Having now set forth in detail the nature of the science of piloting, and likewise described the rank which the pilot held among the fraternity of steamboatmen, this seems a fitting place to say a few words about an organization which the pilots once formed for the protection of their guild. It was curious and note-worthy in this, that it was perhaps the compactest, the completest, and the strong-est commercial organization ever formed among men.

For a long time wages had been two hundred and fifty dollars a month; but curiously enough, as steamboats multiplied and business increased, the wages began to fall little by little. It was easy to discover the reason of this. Too many pilots were being "made." It was nice to have a "cub," a steersman, to do all the hard work for a couple of years, gratis, while his master sat on a high bench and smoked; all pilots and captains had sons or nephews who wanted to be pilots. By and by it came to pass that nearly every pilot on the river had a steersman. When a steersman had made an amount of progress that was satisfactory to any two pilots in the trade, they could get a pilot's license for him by signing an applica-tion directed to the United States Inspector. Nothing further was needed; usually no questions were asked, no proofs of capacity required.

Very well, this growing swarm of new pilots presently began to undermine the wages in order to get berths. Too late—apparently—the knights of the tiller per-ceived their mistake. Plainly, something had to be done, and quickly, but what was to be the needful thing? A close organization. Nothing else would answer. To compass this seemed an impossibility; so it was talked and talked and then dropped. It was too likely to ruin whoever ventured to move in the matter. But at last about a dozen of the boldest—and some of them the best—pilots on the river launched themselves into the enterprise and took all the chances. They got a spe-cial charter from the legislature, with large powers, under the name of the Pilots' Benevolent Association; elected their officers, completed their organization, con-tributed capital, put "association" wages up to two hundred and fifty dollars at once—and then retired to their homes, for they were promptly discharged from employment. But there were two or three unnoticed trifles in their by-laws which had the seeds of propagation in them. For instance, all idle members of the asso-ciation, in good standing, were entitled to a pension of twenty-five dollars per month. This began to bring in one straggler after another from the ranks of the new-fledged pilots, in the dull (summer) season. Better have twenty-five dollars than starve; the initiation fee was only twelve dollars, and no dues required from the unemployed.

Also, the widows of deceased members in good standing could draw twenty-five dollars per month, and a certain sum for each of their children. Also, the said deceased would be buried at the association's expense. These things resurrected all the superannuated and forgotten pilots in the Mississippi Valley. They came from farms, they came from interior villages, they came from everywhere. They came on crutches, on drays, in ambulances,—any way, so they got there. They paid in their twelve dollars, and straightway began to draw out twenty-five dol-lars a month and calculate their burial bills.

By and by all the useless, helpless pilots, and a dozen first-class ones, were in the association, and nine-tenths of the best pilots out of it and laughing at it. It was the laughing-stock of the whole river. Everybody joked about the by-law re-quiring members to pay ten per cent. of their wages, every month, into the treas-ury for the support of the association, whereas all the members were outcast and tabooed, and no one would employ them. Everybody was derisively grateful to the association for taking all the worthless pilots out of the way and leaving the

whole field to the excellent and the deserving; and everybody was not only jocu-
larly grateful for that, but for a result which naturally followed, namely, the
gradual advance of wages as the busy season approached. Wages had gone up
from the low figure of one hundred dollars a month to one hundred and twenty-
five, and in some cases to one hundred and fifty; and it was great fun to enlarge
upon the fact that this charming thing had been accomplished by a body of men
not one of whom received a particle of benefit from it. Some of the jokers used
to call at the association rooms and have a good time chaffing the members and
offering them the charity of taking them as steersmen for a trip, so that they could
see what the forgotten river looked like. However, the association was content;
or at least gave no sign to the contrary. Now and then it captured a pilot who was
"out of luck," and added him to its list; and these later additions were very valuable, for they were good pilots; the incompetent ones had all been absorbed before. As business freshened, wages climbed gradually up to two hundred and fifty
dollars—the association figure—and became firmly fixed there; and still without
benefiting a member of that body, for no member was hired. The hilarity at the
association's expense burst all bounds, now. There was no end to the fun which
that poor martyr had to put up with.

However, it is a long lane that has no turning. Winter approached, business
doubled and trebled, and an avalanche of Missouri, Illinois, and Upper Mississippi River boats came pouring down to take a chance in the New Orleans trade.
All of a sudden pilots were in great demand, and were correspondingly scarce.
The time for revenge was come. It was a bitter pill to have to accept association
pilots at last, yet captains and owners agreed that there was no other way. But
none of these outcasts offered! So there was a still bitterer pill to be swallowed:
they must be sought out and asked for their services. Captain —— was the first
man who found it necessary to take the dose, and he had been the loudest derider
of the organization. He hunted up one of the best of the association pilots and
said:

"Well, you boys have rather got the best of us for a little while, so I'll give in
with as good a grace as I can. I've come to hire you; get your trunk aboard right
away. I want to leave at twelve o'clock."

"I don't know about that. Who is your other pilot?"

"I've got I. S. Why?"

"I can't go with him. He don't belong to the association."

"What?"

"It's so."

"Do you mean to tell me that you won't turn a wheel with one of the very best
and oldest pilots on the river because he don't belong to your association?"

"Yes, I do."

"Well, if this isn't putting on airs! I supposed I was doing you a benevolence;
but I begin to think that I am the party that wants a favor done. Are you acting
under a law of the concern?"

"Yes."

"Show it to me."

So they stepped into the association rooms, and the secretary soon satisfied the
captain, who said:

"Well, what am I to do? I have hired Mr. S. for the entire season."

"I will provide for you," said the secretary. "I will detail a pilot to go with you, and he shall be on board at twelve o'clock."

"But if I discharge S., he will come on me for the whole season's wages."

"Of course that is a matter between you and Mr. S., captain. We cannot meddle in your private affairs."

The captain stormed, but to no purpose. In the end he had to discharge S., pay him about a thousand dollars, and take an association pilot in his place. The laugh was beginning to turn the other way, now. Every day, thenceforward, a new victim fell; every day some outraged captain discharged a non-association pet, with tears and profanity, and installed a hated association man in his berth. In a very little while idle non-associationists began to be pretty plenty, brisk as business was, and much as their services were desired. The laugh was shifting to the other side of their mouths most palpably. These victims, together with the captains and owners, presently ceased to laugh altogether, and began to rage about the revenge they would take when the passing business "spurt" was over.

Soon all the laughers that were left were the owners and crews of boats that had two non-association pilots. But their triumph was not very long-lived. For this reason: It was a rigid rule of the association that its members should never, under any circumstances whatever, give information about the channel to any "outsider." By this time about half the boats had none but association pilots, and the other half had none but outsiders. At the first glance one would suppose that when it came to forbidding information about the river these two parties could play equally at that game; but this was not so. At every good-sized town from one end of the river to the other, there was a "wharf-boat" to land at, instead of a wharf or a pier. Freight was stored in it for transportation; waiting passengers slept in its cabins. Upon each of these wharf-boats the association's officers placed a strong box, fastened with a peculiar lock which was used in no other service but one—the United States mail service. It was the letter-bag lock, a sacred governmental thing. By dint of much beseeching the Government had been persuaded to allow the association to use this lock. Every association man carried a key which would open these boxes. That key, or rather a peculiar way of holding it in the hand when its owner was asked for river information by a stranger,—for the success of the St. Louis and New Orleans association had now bred tolerably thriving branches in a dozen neighboring steamboat trades,—was the association man's sign and diploma of membership; and if the stranger did not respond by producing a similar key and holding it in a certain manner duly prescribed, his question was politely ignored. From the association's secretary each member received a package of more or less gorgeous blanks, printed like a billhead, on handsome paper, properly ruled in columns; a billhead worded something like this:

STEAMER GREAT REPUBLIC.

John Smith, Master.
Pilots, John Jones and Thomas Brown.

CROSSINGS.	SOUNDINGS.	MARKS.	REMARKS.

These blanks were filled up, day by day, as the voyage progressed, and deposited in the several wharf-boat boxes. For instance, as soon as the first crossing out from St. Louis was completed, the items would be entered upon the blank, under the appropriate headings, thus:

"St. Louis. Nine and a half (feet). Stern on courthouse, head on dead cottonwood above wood-yard, until you raise the first reef, then pull up square." Then under head of Remarks: "Go just outside the wrecks; this is important. New snag just where you straighten down; go above it."

The pilot who deposited that blank in the Cairo box (after adding to it the details of every crossing all the way down from St. Louis) took out and read half a dozen fresh reports (from upward-bound steamers) concerning the river between Cairo and Memphis, posted himself thoroughly, returned them to the box, and went back aboard his boat again so armed against accident that he could not possibly get his boat into trouble without bringing the most ingenious carelessness to his aid.

Imagine the benefits of so admirable a system in a piece of river twelve or thirteen hundred miles long, whose channel was shifting every day! The pilot who had formerly been obliged to put up with seeing a shoal place once or possibly twice a month, had a hundred sharp eyes to watch it for him now, and bushels of intelligent brains to tell him how to run it. His information about it was seldom twenty-four hours old. If the reports in the last box chanced to leave any misgivings on his mind concerning a treacherous crossing, he had his remedy; he blew his steam whistle in a peculiar way as soon as he saw a boat approaching; the signal was answered in a peculiar way if that boat's pilots were association men; and then the two steamers ranged alongside and all uncertainties were swept away by fresh information furnished to the enquirer by word of mouth and in minute detail.

The first thing a pilot did when he reached New Orleans or St. Louis was to take his final and elaborate report to the association parlors and hang it up there —*after* which he was free to visit his family. In these parlors a crowd was always gathered together, discussing changes in the channel, and the moment there was a fresh arrival everybody stopped talking till this witness had told the newest news and settled the latest uncertainty. Other craftsmen can "sink the shop" sometimes, and interest themselves in other matters. Not so with a pilot; he must devote himself wholly to his profession and talk of nothing else; for it would be small gain to be perfect one day and imperfect the next. He has no time or words to waste if he would keep "posted."

But the outsiders had a hard time of it. No particular place to meet and exchange information, no wharf-boat reports, none but chance and unsatisfactory ways of getting news. The consequence was that a man sometimes had to run five hundred miles of river on information that was a week or ten days old. At a fair stage of the river that might have answered, but when the dead low water came it was destructive.

Now came another perfectly logical result. The outsiders began to ground steamboats, sink them, and get into all sorts of trouble, whereas accidents seemed to keep entirely away from the association men. Wherefore even the owners and captains of boats furnished exclusively with outsiders, and previously considered to be wholly independent of the association and free to comfort themselves with

brag and laughter, began to feel pretty uncomfortable. Still, they made a show of
keeping up the brag, until one black day when every captain of the lot was formally ordered to immediately discharge his outsiders and take association pilots
in their stead. And who was it that had the dashing presumption to do that?
Alas! it came from a power behind the throne that was greater than the throne
itself. It was the underwriters!

It was no time to "swap knives." Every outsider had to take his trunk ashore
at once. Of course it was supposed that there was collusion between the association and the underwriters, but this was not so. The latter had come to comprehend the excellence of the "report" system of the association and the safety it secured, and so they had made their decision among themselves and upon plain
business principles.

There was weeping and wailing and gnashing of teeth in the camp of the outsiders now. But no matter, there was but one course for them to pursue, and they
pursued it. They came forward in couples and groups, and proffered their twelve
dollars and asked for membership. They were surprised to learn that several new
by-laws had been long ago added. For instance, the initiation fee had been raised
to fifty dollars; that sum must be tendered, and also ten per cent. of the wages
which the applicant had received each and every month since the founding of the
association. In many cases this amounted to three or four hundred dollars. Still,
the association would not entertain the application until the money was present.
Even then a single adverse vote killed the application. Every member had to vote
yes or no in person and before witnesses; so it took weeks to decide a candidacy,
because many pilots were so long absent on voyages. However, the repentant sinners scraped their savings together, and one by one, by our tedious voting process, they were added to the fold. A time came, at last, when only about ten remained outside. They said they would starve before they would apply. They remained idle a long while, because of course nobody could venture to employ
them.

By and by the association published the fact that upon a certain date the wages
would be raised to five hundred dollars per month. All the branch associations
had grown strong now, and the Red River one had advanced wages to seven hundred dollars a month. Reluctantly the ten outsiders yielded, in view of these
things, and made application. There was *another* new by-law, by this time, which
required them to pay dues not only on all the wages they had received since the
association was born, but also on what they would have received if they had continued at work up to the time of their application, instead of going off to pout in
idleness. It turned out to be a difficult matter to elect them, but it was accomplished at last. The most virulent sinner of this batch had stayed out and allowed
"dues" to accumulate against him so long that he had to send in six hundred and
twenty-five dollars with his application.

The association had a good bank account now and was very strong. There was
no longer an outsider. A by-law was added forbidding the reception of any more
cubs or apprentices for five years; after which time a limited number would be
taken, not by individuals, but by the association, upon these terms: the applicant
must not be less than eighteen years old, and of respectable family and good
character; he must pass an examination as to education, pay a thousand dollars
in advance for the privilege of becoming an apprentice, and must remain under

the commands of the association until a great part of the membership (more than half, I think) should be willing to sign his application for a pilot's license.

All previously articled apprentices were now taken away from their masters and adopted by the association. The president and secretary detailed them for service on one boat or another, as they chose, and changed them from boat to boat according to certain rules. If a pilot could show that he was in infirm health and needed assistance, one of the cubs would be ordered to go with him.

The widow and orphan list grew, but so did the association's financial resources. The association attended its own funerals in state and paid for them. When occasion demanded, it sent members down the river upon searches for the bodies of brethren lost by steamboat accidents; a search of this kind sometimes cost a thousand dollars.

The association procured a charter and went into the insurance business also. It not only insured the lives of its members, but took risks on steamboats.

The organization seemed indestructible. It was the tightest monopoly in the world. By the United States law no man could become a pilot unless two duly licensed pilots signed his application, and now there was nobody outside of the association competent to sign. Consequently the making of pilots was at an end. Every year some would die and others become incapacitated by age and infirmity; there would be no new ones to take their places. In time the association could put wages up to any figure it chose; and as long as it should be wise enough not to carry the thing too far and provoke the national government into amending the licensing system, steamboat owners would have to submit, since there would be no help for it.

The owners and captains were the only obstruction that lay between the association and absolute power, and at last this one was removed. Incredible as it may seem, the owners and captains deliberately did it themselves. When the pilots' association announced, months beforehand, that on the first day of September, 1861, wages would be advanced to five hundred dollars per month, the owners and captains instantly put freights up a few cents, and explained to the farmers along the river the necessity of it, by calling their attention to the burdensome rate of wages about to be established. It was a rather slender argument, but the farmers did not seem to detect it. It looked reasonable to them that to add five cents freight on a bushel of corn was justifiable under the circumstances, overlooking the fact that this advance on a cargo of forty thousand sacks was a good deal more than necessary to cover the new wages.

So, straightway the captains and owners got up an association of their own, and proposed to put captains' wages up to five hundred dollars, too, and move for another advance in freights. It was a novel idea, but of course an effect which had been produced once could be produced again. The new association decreed (for this was before all the outsiders had been taken into the pilots' association) that if any captain employed a non-association pilot, he should be forced to discharge him, and also pay a fine of five hundred dollars. Several of these heavy fines were paid before the captains' organization grew strong enough to exercise full authority over its membership; but that all ceased, presently. The captains tried to get the pilots to decree that no member of their corporation should serve under a non-association captain; but this proposition was declined. The pilots saw that they would be backed up by the captains and the underwriters anyhow, and so they wisely refrained from entering into entangling alliances.

As I have remarked, the pilots' association was now the compactest monopoly in the world, perhaps, and seemed simply indestructible. And yet the days of its glory were numbered. First, the new railroad, stretching up through Mississippi, Tennessee, and Kentucky, to Northern railway centres, began to divert the passenger travel from the steamboats; next the war came and almost entirely annihilated the steamboating industry during several years, leaving most of the pilots idle and the cost of living advancing all the time; then the treasurer of the St. Louis association put his hand into the till and walked off with every dollar of the ample fund; and finally, the railroads intruding everywhere, there was little for steamers to do, when the war was over, but carry freights; so straightway some genius from the Atlantic coast introduced the plan of towing a dozen steamer cargoes down to New Orleans at the tail of a vulgar little tug-boat; and behold, in the twinkling of an eye, as it were, the association and the noble science of piloting were things of the dead and pathetic past!

CHAPTER 7

It was always the custom for the boats to leave New Orleans between four and five o'clock in the afternoon. From three o'clock onward they would be burning rosin and pitch-pine (the sign of preparation), and so one had the picturesque spectacle of a rank, some two or three miles long, of tall, ascending columns of coal-black smoke; a colonnade which supported a sable roof of the same smoke blended together and spreading abroad over the city. Every outward-bound boat had its flag flying at the jack-staff, and sometimes a duplicate on the verge staff astern. Two or three miles of mates were commanding and swearing with more than usual emphasis: countless processions of freight barrels and boxes were spinning athwart the levee and flying aboard the stage-planks; belated passengers were dodging and skipping among these frantic things, hoping to reach the forecastle companion-way alive, but having their doubts about it; women with reticules and bandboxes were trying to keep up with husbands freighted with carpet-sacks and crying babies, and making a failure of it by losing their heads in the whirl and roar and general distraction; drays and baggage-vans were clattering hither and thither in a wild hurry, every now and then getting blocked and jammed together, and then during ten seconds one could not see them for the profanity, except vaguely and dimly; every windlass connected with every fore-hatch, from one end of that long array of steamboats to the other, was keeping up a deafening whiz and whir, lowering freight into the hold, and the half-naked crews of perspiring negroes that worked them were roaring such songs as "De Las' Sack! De Las' Sack!"—inspired to unimaginable exaltation by the chaos of turmoil and racket that was driving everybody else mad. By this time the hurricane and boiler decks of the steamers would be packed black with passengers. The "last bells" would begin to clang, all down the line, and then the powwow seemed to double; in a moment or two the final warning came—a simultaneous din of Chinese gongs, with the cry, "All dat ain't goin', please to git asho'!"—and behold the powwow quadrupled! People came swarming ashore, overturning excited stragglers that were trying to swarm aboard. One more moment later a long array of stage-planks was being hauled in, each with its customary latest passenger clinging to the end of it with teeth, nails, and every thing else, and the customary latest procrastinator making a wild spring shoreward over his head.

Now a number of the boats slide backward into the stream, leaving wide gaps in the serried rank of steamers. Citizens crowd the decks of boats that are not to go, in order to see the sight. Steamer after steamer straightens herself up, gathers all her strength, and presently comes swinging by, under a tremendous head of steam, with flag flying, black smoke rolling, and her entire crew of firemen and deck-hands (usually swarthy negroes) massed together on the forecastle, the best "voice" in the lot towering from the midst (being mounted on the capstan), waving his hat or a flag, and all roaring a mighty chorus, while the parting cannons boom and the multitudinous spectators wave their hats and huzza! Steamer after steamer falls into line, and the stately procession goes winging its flight up the river.

In the old times, whenever two fast boats started out on a race, with a big crowd of people looking on, it was inspiring to hear the crews sing, especially if the time were night-fall, and the forecastle lit up with the red glare of the torch-baskets. Racing was royal fun. The public always had an idea that racing was dangerous; whereas the opposite was the case—that is, after the laws were passed which restricted each boat to just so many pounds of steam to the square inch. No engineer was ever sleepy or careless when his heart was in a race. He was constantly on the alert, trying gauge-cocks and watching things. The dangerous place was on slow, plodding boats, where the engineers drowsed around and allowed chips to get into the "doctor" and shut off the water supply from the boilers.

In the "flush times" of steamboating, a race between two notoriously fleet steamers was an event of vast importance. The date was set for it several weeks in advance, and from that time forward the whole Mississippi Valley was in a state of consuming excitement. Politics and the weather were dropped, and people talked only of the coming race. As the time approached, the two steamers "stripped" and got ready. Every incumbrance that added weight, or exposed a resisting surface to wind or water, was removed, if the boat could possibly do without it. The "spars," and sometimes even their supporting derricks, were sent ashore, and no means left to set the boat afloat in case she got aground. When the *Eclipse* and the *A. L. Shotwell* ran their great race many years ago, it was said that pains were taken to scrape the gilding off the fanciful device which hung between the *Eclipse's* chimneys, and that for that one trip the captain left off his kid gloves and had his head shaved. But I always doubted these things.

If the boat was known to make her best speed when drawing five and a half feet forward and five feet aft, she carefully loaded to that exact figure—she wouldn't enter a dose of homœopathic pills on her manifest after that. Hardly any passengers were taken, because they not only add weight but they never will "trim boat." They always run to the side when there is anything to see, whereas a conscientious and experienced steamboatman would stick to the centre of the boat and part his hair in the middle with a spirit level.

No way-freights and no way-passengers were allowed, for the racers would stop only at the largest towns, and then it would be only "touch and go." Coal-flats and wood-flats were contracted for beforehand, and these were kept ready to hitch on to the flying steamers at a moment's warning. Double crews were carried, so that all work could be quickly done.

The chosen date being come, and all things in readiness, the two great steamers back into the stream, and lie there jockeying a moment, apparently watching each other's slightest movement, like sentient creatures; flags drooping, the pent steam shrieking through safety-valves, the black smoke rolling and tumbling from the chimneys and darkening all the air. People, people everywhere; the shores, the house-tops, the steamboats, the ships, are packed with them, and you know that the borders of the broad Mississippi are going to be fringed with humanity thence northward twelve hundred miles, to welcome these racers.

Presently tall columns of steam burst from the 'scape-pipes of both steamers, two guns boom a good-by, two red-shirted heroes mounted on capstans wave their small flags above the massed crews on the forecastles, two plantive solos linger on the air a few waiting seconds, two mighty choruses burst forth—and here they come! Brass bands bray "Hail Columbia," huzza after huzza thunders from the shores, and the stately creatures go whistling by like the wind.

Those boats will never halt a moment between New Orleans and St. Louis, except for a second or two at large towns, or to hitch thirty-cord wood-boats alongside. You should be on board when they take a couple of those wood-boats in tow and turn a swarm of men into each; by the time you have wiped your glasses and put them on, you will be wondering what has become of that wood.

Two nicely matched steamers will stay in sight of each other day after day. They might even stay side by side, but for the fact that pilots are not all alike, and the smartest pilots will win the race. If one of the boats has a "lightning" pilot, whose "partner" is a trifle his inferior, you can tell which one is on watch by noting whether that boat has gained ground or lost some during each four-hour stretch. The shrewdest pilot can delay a boat if he has not a fine genius for steering. Steering is a very high art. One must not keep a rudder dragging across a boat's stern if he wants to get up the river fast.

There is a great difference in boats, of course. For a long time I was on a boat that was so slow we used to forget what year it was we left port in. But of course this was at rare intervals. Ferry-boats used to lose valuable trips because their passengers grew old and died, waiting for us to get by. This was at still rarer intervals. I had the documents for these occurrences, but through carelessness they have been mislaid. This boat, the *John J. Roe,* was so slow that when she finally sunk in Madrid Bend it was five years before the owners heard of it. That was always a confusing fact to me, but it is according to the record, anyway. She was dismally slow; still, we often had pretty exciting times racing with islands, and rafts, and such things. One trip, however, we did rather well. We went to St. Louis in sixteen days. But even at this rattling gait I think we changed watches three times in Fort Adams reach, which is five miles long. A "reach" is a piece of straight river, and of course the current drives through such a place in a pretty lively way.

That trip we went to Grand Gulf, from New Orleans, in four days (three hundred and forty miles) ; the *Eclipse* and *Shotwell* did it in one. We were nine days out, in the chute of 63 (seven hundred miles); the *Eclipse* and *Shotwell* went there in two days. Something over a generation ago, a boat called the *J. M. White* went from New Orleans to Cairo in three days, six hours, and forty-four minutes. In 1853 the *Eclipse* made the same trip in three days, three hours, and twenty minutes. In 1870 the *R. E. Lee* did it in three days and *one* hour. This last is called the fastest trip on record. I will try to show that it was not. For this reason: the distance between New Orleans and Cairo, when the *J. M. White* ran it, was about eleven hundred and six miles; consequently her average speed was a trifle over fourteen miles per hour. In the *Eclipse's* day the distance between the two ports had become reduced to one thousand and eighty miles; consequently her average speed was a shade under fourteen and three-eighths miles per hour. In the *R. E. Lee's* time the distance had diminished to about one thousand and thirty miles; consequently her average was about fourteen and one-eighth miles per hour. Therefore the *Eclipse's* was conspicuously the fastest time that has ever been made.

These dry details are of importance in one particular. They give me an opportunity of introducing one of the Mississippi's oddest peculiarities—that of shortening its length from time to time. If you will throw a long, pliant apple-paring over your shoulder, it will pretty fairly shape itself into an average section of the Mississippi River; that is, the nine or ten hundred miles stretching from Cairo, Ill., southward to New Orleans, the same being wonderfully crooked, with a brief straight bit here and there at wide intervals. The two-hundred-mile stretch from Cairo northward to St. Louis is by no means so crooked, that being a rocky country which the river cannot cut much.

The water cuts the alluvial banks of the "lower" river into deep horseshoe curves; so deep, indeed, that in some places if you were to get ashore at one extremity of the horseshoe and walk across the neck, half or three-quarters of a mile, you could sit down and rest a couple of hours while your steamer was coming around the long elbow at a speed of ten miles an hour to take you on board again. When the river is rising fast, some scoundrel whose plantation is back in the country, and therefore of inferior value, has only to watch his chance, cut a little gutter across the narrow neck of land some dark night, and turn the water into it, and in a wonderfully short time a miracle has happened: to wit, the whole Mississippi has taken possession of that little ditch, and placed the countryman's plantation on its bank (quadrupling its value), and that other party's formerly valuable plantation finds itself away out yonder on a big island; the old water-course around it will soon shoal up, boats cannot approach within ten miles of it, and down goes its value to a fourth of its former worth. Watches are kept on those narrow necks at needful times, and if a man happens to be caught cutting a ditch across them, the chances are all against his ever having another opportunity to cut a ditch.

Pray observe some of the effects of this ditching business. Once there was a neck opposite Port Hudson, La., which was only half a mile across in its narrowest place. You could walk across there in fifteen minutes; but if you made the journey around the cape on a raft, you travelled thirty-five miles to accomplish the same thing. In 1722 the river darted through that neck, deserted its old bed, and thus shortened itself thirty-five miles. In the same way it shortened itself twenty-five miles at Black Hawk Point in 1699. Below Red River Landing, Raccourci cut-off was made (forty or fifty years ago, I think). This shortened the river twenty-eight miles. In our day, if you travel by river from the southernmost of these three cut-offs to the northernmost, you go only seventy miles. To do the same thing a hundred and seventy-six years ago, one had to go a hundred and fifty-eight miles—a shortening of eighty-eight miles in that trifling distance. At some forgotten time in the past, cut-offs were made above Vidalia, La.; at Island 92, at Island 84, and at Hale's Point. These shortened the river, in the aggregate, seventy-seven miles.

Since my own day on the Mississippi, cut-offs have been made at Hurricane Island, at Island 100, at Napoleon, Ark.; at Walnut Bend, and at Council Bend. These shortened the river, in the aggregate, sixty-seven miles. In my own time a cut-off was made at American Bend, which shortened the river ten miles or more.

Therefore the Mississippi between Cairo and New Orleans was twelve hundred and fifteen miles long one hundred and seventy-six years ago. It was eleven hundred and eighty after the cut-off of 1722. It was one thousand and forty after the American Bend cut-off. It has lost sixty-seven miles since. Consequently, its length is only nine hundred and seventy-three miles at present.

Now, if I wanted to be one of those ponderous scientific people, and "let on" to prove what had occurred in the remote past by what had occurred in a given time in the recent past, or what will occur in the far future by what has occurred in late years, what an opportunity is here! Geology never had such a chance, nor such exact data to argue from! Nor "development of species," either! Glacial epochs are great things, but they are vague—vague. Please observe:

In the space of one hundred and seventy-six years the Lower Mississippi has shortened itself two hundred and forty-two miles. That is an average of a trifle over one mile and a third per year. Therefore, any calm person, who is not blind or idiotic, can see that in the Old Oölitic Silurian Period, just a million years ago next November, the Lower Mississippi River was upward of one million three hundred thousand miles long, and stuck out over the Gulf of Mexico like a fishing-rod. And by the same token any person can see that seven hundred and forty-two years from now the Lower Mississippi will be only a mile and three-quarters long, and Cairo and New Orleans will have joined their streets together, and be plodding comfortably along under a single mayor and a mutual board of aldermen. There is something fascinating about science. One gets such wholesale returns of conjecture out of such a trifling investment of fact.

When the water begins to flow through one of those ditches I have been speaking of, it is time for the people thereabouts to move. The water cleaves the banks away like a knife. By the time the ditch has become twelve or fifteen feet wide, the calamity is as good as accomplished, for no power on earth can stop it now. When the width has reached a hundred yards, the banks begin to peel off in slices half an acre wide. The current flowing around the bend travelled formerly only five miles an hour; now it is tremendously increased by the shortening of the distance. I was on board the first boat that tried to go through the cut-off at American Bend, but we did not get through. It was toward midnight, and a wild night it was—thunder, lightning, and torrents of rain. It was estimated that the current in the cut-off was making about fifteen or twenty miles an hour; twelve or thirteen was the best our boat could do, even in tolerably slack water, therefore perhaps we were foolish to try the cut-off. However, Mr. Brown was ambitious, and he kept on trying. The eddy running up the bank, under the "point," was about as swift as the current out in the middle; so we would go flying up the shore like a lightning express train, get on a big head of steam, and "stand by for a surge" when we struck the current that was whirling by the point. But all our preparations were useless. The instant the current hit us it spun us around like a top, the water deluged the forecastle, and the boat careened so far over that one could hardly keep his feet. The next instant we were away down the river, clawing with might and main to keep out of the woods. We tried the experiment four times. I stood on the forecastle companion-way to see. It was astonishing to observe how suddenly the boat would spin around and turn tail the moment she emerged from the eddy and the current struck her nose. The sounding concussion and the quivering would have been about the same if she had come full speed against a sandbank. Under the lightning flashes one could see the plantation cabins and the goodly acres tumble into the river, and the crash they made was not a bad effort at thunder. Once, when we spun around, we only missed a house about twenty feet that had a light burning in the window, and in the same instant that house went overboard. Nobody could stay on our forecastle; the water swept across it in a torrent every time we plunged athwart the current. At the end of our fourth effort we brought up in the woods two miles below the cut-off; all the country there was overflowed, of course. A day or two later the cut-off was three quarters of a mile wide, and boats passed up through it without much difficulty, and so saved ten miles.

The old Raccourci cut-off reduced the river's length twenty-eight miles. There used to be a tradition connected with it. It was said that a boat came along there in the night and went around the enormous elbow the usual way, the pilots not knowing that the cut-off had been made. It was a grisly, hideous night, and all shapes were vague and distorted. The old bend had already begun to fill up, and the boat got to running away from mysterious reefs, and occasionally hitting one. The perplexed pilots fell to swearing, and finally uttered the entirely unnecessary wish that they might never get out of that place. As always happens in such cases, that particular prayer was answered, and the others neglected. So to this day that phantom steamer is still butting around in that deserted river, trying to find her way out. More than one grave watchman has sworn to me that on drizzly, dismal nights, he has glanced fearfully down that forgotten river as he passed the head of the island, and seen the faint glow of the spectre steamer's lights drifting through the distant gloom, and heard the muffled cough of her 'scape-pipes and the plaintive cry of her leadsmen.

In the absence of further statistics, I beg to close this chapter with one more reminiscence of "Stephen."

Most of the captains and pilots held Stephen's note for borrowed sums, ranging from two hundred and fifty dollars upward. Stephen never paid one of these notes, but he was very prompt and very zealous about renewing them every twelve months.

Of course there came a time, at last, when Stephen could no longer borrow of his ancient creditors; so he was obliged to lie in wait for new men who did not know him. Such a victim was good-hearted, simple-natured young Yates (I use a fictitious name, but the real name began, as this one does, with a Y). Young Yates graduated as a pilot, got a berth, and when the month was ended and he stepped up to the clerk's office and received his two hundred and fifty dollars in crisp new bills, Stephen was there! His silvery tongue began to wag, and in a very little while Yates's two hundred and fifty dollars had changed hands. The fact was soon known at pilot headquarters, and the amusement and satisfaction of the old creditors were large and generous. But innocent Yates never suspected that Stephen's promise to pay promptly at the end of the week was a worthless one. Yates called for his money at the stipulated time; Stephen sweetened him up and put him off a week. He called then, according to agreement, and came away sugar-coated again, but suffering under another postponement. So the thing went on. Yates haunted Stephen week after week, to no purpose, and at last gave it up. And then straightway Stephen began to haunt Yates! Wherever Yates appeared, there was the inevitable Stephen. And not only there, but beaming with affection and gushing with apologies for not being able to pay. By and by, whenever poor Yates saw him coming, he would turn and fly, and drag his company with him, if he had company; but it was of no use; his debtor would run him down and corner him. Panting and red-faced, Stephen would come, with outstretched hands and eager eyes, invade the conversation, shake both of Yates's arms loose in their sockets, and begin:

"My, what a race I've had! I saw you didn't see me, and so I clapped on all steam for fear I'd miss you entirely. And here you are! there, just stand so, and let me look at you! Just the same old noble countenance. [To Yates's friend:] Just look at him! *Look* at him! Ain't it just *good* to look at him! *Ain't* it now? Ain't he just a picture! *Some* call him a picture; *I* call him a panorama! That's what he is—an entire panorama. And now I'm reminded! How I do wish I could have seen you an hour earlier! For twenty-four hours I've been saving up that two hundred and fifty dollars for you; been looking for you everywhere. I waited at the Planter's from six yesterday evening till two o'clock this morning, without rest or food. My wife says, 'Where have you been all night?' I said, 'This debt lies heavy on my mind.' She says, 'In all my days I never saw a man take a debt to heart the way you do.' I said, 'It's my nature; how can *I* change it?' She says, 'Well, do go to bed and get some rest.' I said, 'Not till that poor, noble young man has got his money.' So I set up all night, and this morning out I shot, and the first man I struck told me you had shipped on the *Grand Turk* and gone to New Orleans. Well, sir, I had to lean up against a building and cry. So help me goodness, I couldn't help it. The man that owned the place come out cleaning up with a rag, and said he didn't like to have people cry against his building, and then it seemed to me that the whole world had turned against me, and it wasn't any use to live any more; and coming along an hour ago, suffering no man knows what agony, I met Jim Wilson and paid him the two hundred and fifty dollars on account; and to think that here you are, now, and I haven't got a cent! But as sure as I am standing here on this ground on this particular brick,—there, I've scratched a mark on the brick to remember it by,—I'll borrow that money and pay it over to you at twelve o'clock sharp, to-morrow! Now, stand so; let me look at you just once more."

And so on. Yates's life became a burden to him. He could not escape his debtor and his debtor's awful sufferings on account of not being able to pay. He dreaded to show himself in the street, lest he should find Stephen lying in wait for him at the corner.

Bogart's billiard saloon was a great resort for pilots in those days. They met there about as much to exchange river news as to play. One morning Yates was there; Stephen was there, too, but kept out of sight. But by and by, when about all the pilots had arrived who were in town, Stephen suddenly appeared in the midst, and rushed for Yates as for a long-lost brother.

"*Oh*, I am so glad to see you! Oh my soul, the sight of you is such a comfort to my eyes! Gentlemen, I owe all of you money; among you I owe probably forty thousand dollars. I want to pay it; I intend to pay it—every last cent of it. You all know, without my telling you, what sorrow it has cost me to remain so long under such deep obligations to such patient and generous friends; but the sharpest pang I suffer—by far the sharpest—is from the debt I owe to this noble young man here; and I have come to this place this morning especially to make the announcement that I have at last found a method whereby I can pay off all my debts! And most especially I wanted *him* to be here when I announced it. Yes, my faithful friend, my benefactor, I've found the method! I've found the method to pay off *all* my debts, and you'll get your money!" Hope dawned in Yates's eye; then Stephen, beaming benignantly, and placing his hand upon Yates's head, added, "I am going to pay them off in alphabetical order!"

Then he turned and disappeared. The full significance of Stephen's "method" did not dawn upon the perplexed and musing crowd for some two minutes; and then Yates murmured with a sigh:

"Well, the Y's stand a gaudy chance. He won't get any further than the C's in *this* world, and I reckon that after a good deal of eternity has wasted away in the next one, I'll still be referred to up there as 'that poor, ragged pilot that came here from St. Louis in the early days!'"
1875

ERNEST HEMINGWAY ■■■■■■■■■■■■■■

THE BATTLER
THE UNDEFEATED
A CLEAN, WELL-LIGHTED PLACE

IN THE PUBLIC DOMAIN

When the editors of *Time* magazine addressed to Ernest Hemingway in 1947 the question "Has the 'Hemingway influence' declined?" he made the now famous reply, "Hemingway influence only a certain clarification of the language which is now in the public domain."[1]

There can be no doubt as to the magnitude and pervasiveness of the influence, and its incorporation in the public domain, long before 1947. *The Sun Also Rises*, which appeared in 1926, marked an epoch in American writing. Scores of young authors in the late 1920's and down through the 1930's tried to write like Hemingway. The influence extended to speech as well. The Hemingway style, in fact, may have contributed as much to American speech as it is reputed to have derived from it, for not long after *The Sun Also Rises* appeared, young people in bars began to talk like Jake and Brett, and before many years had passed, college students and even high-school youngsters had picked up certain superficial aspects of the Hemingway language and syntax.

The more imitable aspects can be seen in a passage of dialogue like the following from *The Sun Also Rises:*

> "You're a hell of a good guy," Bill said. "Anybody ever tell you you were a good guy?"
> "I'm not a good guy."
> "Listen. You're a hell of a good guy. . . ."

Another passage from the same work illustrates a kind of writing that was less imitable:

> We stayed five nights and had good fishing. The nights were cold and the days were hot, and there was always a breeze even in the heat of the day. It was hot enough so that it felt good to

1. *Time* magazine, August 4, 1947.

wade in a cold stream, and the sun dried you when you came
out and sat on the bank. We found a stream with a pool deep
enough to swim in. In the evenings we played three-handed
bridge with an Englishman named Harris. . . .

The plain, monosyllabic language, the repetition of key words and
phrases, the simple declarative sentence, and the coordinate construction were the more obvious devices. F. M. Ford has given us what
Edmund Wilson calls "the perfect simile" for the impression produced by Hemingway's writing at its best:

Hemingway's words [says Ford] strike you, each one, as if
they were pebbles fetched fresh from a brook. They live and
shine, each in its place. So one of his pages has the effect of a
brook-bottom into which you look down through the flowing
water. The words form a tessellation, each in order beside the
other.[2]

Freshness, clarity, naturalness—these are some of the qualities suggested by Ford's simile and illustrated brilliantly enough in the passage describing the wonderful fishing trip in Spain.

One of the more interesting and serious occupations of the student
should be an analysis of Hemingway's style. What are its effects, and
how are they produced? The simplicity may be deceptive; the writing is probably more calculated than it appears to be. Horace's famous adage, *Ars celare artem,* warns us that art achieves its ends by
unobtrusive means. How new was this kind of writing, after all, in
1926? Whitman in some respects was a forerunner: like Hemingway
after him, he employed coordination and eschewed stock phrases. Another forerunner was Mark Twain, for whose *Huckleberry Finn*
Hemingway has expressed great admiration.[3] But Hemingway's origi-
nality cannot be diminished by hypothetical debts to Whitman or
Mark Twain.

One must consider also the relation of the style to the subject matter, and the author's attitude toward the life he portrays. It is interesting to observe that two such influential prose writers as Hemingway and Henry James should be at the opposite poles of style: one
writing for the ear, the other for the eye; one giving us rhythms of
speech, the other literary convolutions found only on the printed
page; one elemental and sensuous, the other sophisticated and abstract; one simple and coordinate in style, the other complex and in-
finitely qualifying. Each style is admirably fitted for the purpose for
which it is intended. James is concerned primarily with the intellec-

2. Quoted in Edmund Wilson, "Hemingway: Gauge of Morale," in *Ernest Hemingway: the Man
and His Work,* edited by J. K. M. McCaffery, p. 238.
3. "All modern American literature comes out of one book by Mark Twain called 'Huckleberry
Finn.' All American writing comes from that. There was nothing before. There has been nothing
as good since." From *The Green Hills of Africa.*

tual analysis of experience. Hemingway's aim is the sensuous and emotional rendering of experience. These writers are perhaps the two great complements of our century. To be well-rounded, one's knowledge must take cognizance of each, the world of each, and the rendering of their worlds.

IN OUR TIME

The novels of Hemingway have struck a popular note. One associates them, memorably, with certain phases of the spiritual history of our time. *The Sun Also Rises* (1926) is the classic embodiment of "the lost generation"—those disillusioned expatriates who after the First World War sought a solace for their despair on the Left Bank. The sexual impotence of Jake symbolizes the spiritual impotence of that era. *A Farewell to Arms* (1929) showed the futility of war and the beauty and pathos of a love—Henry's and Catharine's—snatched out of the chaos around them. The background of *For Whom the Bell Tolls* (1940) is the Civil War in Spain in the 1930's. Hemingway's hero, Robert Jordan, fights bravely on the Loyalist side and, like Henry before him, experiences a brief, rapturous love. *Across the River and into the Trees* (1950) again shows us a soldier's affair of the heart, but the soldier this time, though enjoying the love of a young girl, is past middle age and stricken. He is not only the battered representative of those who have lived through two world wars, but a symbol of the dogged stoicism—stripped of foolish dreams—necessary to survival in our modern era. *Across the River and into the Trees* may prove to be as broadly symbolic of the 1950's as the earlier novels were of their respective times.

Hemingway's world, like our own, is a world that has suffered the ravages of war. His heroes have actually fought, and have been actually wounded, spiritually as well as physically. More than any other modern writer, perhaps, Hemingway understands war and what it means to the man in the fighting ranks. He gives to Jordan a political motive: "I have fought for what I believed in," Jordan says, referring to his support of the Loyalists against the Fascists in Spain. But the other heroes have no programs. This is a part of Hemingway's realism, for not many soldiers have entertained ambitious social and political programs since the collapse, long ago, of Woodrow Wilson's Fourteen Points.

Hemingway, then, is not primarily a political writer. He is, rather, an intensely personal one. Man's life, he seems to say, can be good, despite the chaos of war and the uncertainties of an armed truce. The life of the senses can be rich and vivid. Friends can enjoy convivial occasions together. Lovers can be true to one another. A man can be true to his own better self. Though living in a world "swept with confused alarms of struggle and flight, where ignorant armies clash by night," we can salvage something very precious from the general debacle—companionship, love, self-respect.

THREE STORIES

Hemingway is one of the not very many important writers of novels whose talent does not suffer by representation in the short story. Some indeed would claim an even greater excellence for his short fiction. But whether this be justified or not, his writing is so economical and sharp that he does not require long fiction for his best effects.

The three stories ("The Battler," from *In Our Time;* "The Undefeated," from *Men Without Women;* and "A Clean Well-Lighted Place," from *Winner Take Nothing*) chosen for this book from a total of forty-nine show many of the author's virtues. Each story is a kind of microcosm of the world as Hemingway sees and records it, and most of the things that can be said about the man and his work can be illustrated in these pieces.

The work is artful but not meretricious. There is not the manipulation of plot that one associates with the slick modern story. There are, for example, no surprise endings, and the author is, in general, closer to Sherwood Anderson than to O. Henry. There is, to be sure, a finality in "The Undefeated," but it is the finality of death. In the other two stories a state of mind, a condition, is portrayed, which antedates the story itself and continues indefinitely beyond the story's end. One feels that one is reading a transcript of reality, but with this difference, that selection and arrangement have imposed a certain form upon the confusion of real life. Art, as it should, has clarified experience.

Economy, sharpness, and accuracy are not the least of Hemingway's virtues. There is no superfluity or irrelevance of action or word. Repetition is frequent, but it is artfully used to underscore an important idea, as in the repetition of "light" in "A Clean, Well-Lighted Place." The accuracy and sharpness derive chiefly from the author's extraordinary powers of observation and especially from his talent for observing and recording physical detail. Hemingway's sense of terrain, for example, comes out in "The Battler," where the reader sees the railroad embankment clearly, and the well ballasted track, with sand and gravel packed between the ties, all of this being presented exactly as an actual walker along the track would see and feel it. One comes to have great confidence in the author's accounts of things; one comes to feel that here is a reliable author and no fake, whether the matter in hand is a railroad embankment, or the custom in a Paris café of reckoning the bill by the accumulated saucers, or the intricate and elaborate ritual of a bullfight in Madrid, for in each case the author's method is wonderfully meticulous. No writer in English can surpass Hemingway (and who indeed can quite equal him?) in accuracy and sharpness of detail. It is significant that he should speak of the danger lest "the instrument you write with" become "dull and blunt" and of the need "to put it on the grindstone again and hammer it into shape and put a whetstone to it."

The thoughtful reader of these stories will want to look beyond the tales themselves for larger meanings. What do the characters stand for? What does the action add up to? What is the author's view of life? The answers of no two readers to these questions will be identical because no two readers bring to the interpretation identical minds and experiences. The remarks that follow are intended to do no more than suggest some directions that speculation about these stories might take.

Life in these stories is a contest, a battle that requires skill and courage and in which man can win only a measure of victory. Manuel Garcia is, or has been, a good bullfighter. Ad Francis was a champion pugilist in his time. The old man, past eighty, in "A Clean, Well-Lighted Place" must have been something of a person in former years: his strong head for brandy, his ability, though a little drunk, to drink without spilling and at last to walk away "with dignity," though a bit unsteadily, all connote, in Hemingway, a certain distinction of character.

Life has its heroic aspects, but it is also pathetic. We see these men when they are past their prime. We have to infer their former stature and condition from that which remains. Francis has crazy spells, the result of his having taken "too many beatings." Formerly, he fought with cause; now, in his crazy moments, he fights without cause. His sanity can be preserved only when he is kept away from people. The world is at last too much for the individual, however plucky he may be.

The contest of life is one that requires not only strength and pluck but skill and presence of mind. One noteworthy characteristic of the men in these stories (and of Hemingway's heroes in general) is a careful attention to the details of the business in hand. In bullfighting, of course, the utmost precision is a matter of life and death, and perhaps that is why bullfighting is Hemingway's favorite symbol. But whether or not the action involves the hazards of the bull ring, carefulness is a significant behavior trait in these stories. In "The Battler," Nick "came up the track toward the fire carefully"; later, he "dropped carefully down the embankment and cut into the woods. . . ." Care and precision mark the manner in which the waiter, in "A Clean, Well-Lighted Place," serves his customer: "He put down the saucer and poured the glass full of brandy. . . . The old man motioned with his finger. 'A little more,' he said. The waiter poured on into the glass so that the brandy slopped over and ran down the stem into the top saucer of the pile." One can be sure that in the first instance the glass was filled in exactly the right amount, and that in the second, the excess was exactly measured also. Bullfighters, pugilists, bartenders—all favorite symbolic characters in Hemingway—

are careful and precise. Here—as at so many points—Hemingway holds the mirror up to his competitive American world. You must keep your mind on what you are doing, or you will be sorry.

Hemingway portrays not only our competitive American world but the neurotic state that it has helped to produce. Francis, as we have seen, is a little crazy from too many beatings. Manuel suffers from an anxiety neurosis: "The final stuff with the sword was all he worried over. He did not really worry. He did not even think about it. But standing there he had a heavy sense of apprehension." The older waiter in "A Clean, Well-Lighted Place" lacks "confidence": "What did he fear? It was not fear or dread. It was a nothing that he knew too well." The modern anxiety and some of its manifestations and causes are symbolically presented in these stories.

Despite the buffetings of the world, the Hemingway hero can achieve a certain dignity. The professional pride of Manuel is something to admire: "I'm going good now, I tell you . . . I've got the stuff." To the very end he refuses to resign, refuses to surrender his "coleta," the badge of his profession. A man can and must believe in himself. He must and can have professional standards, a tested procedure, a code, that he can adhere to. The bullfighter's ritual is Hemingway's most elaborate symbol of code. The old man's regular visits to the café and the mode of life of Francis and Bugs are examples of codified patterns that are not so much solutions of life's difficulties as ways of adjusting oneself to them.

It is significant that in all three stories the action takes place in a lighted area surrounded by darkness: the bull ring, the campfire, and the café. The lighted area seems pitifully small in comparison with the vast enveloping darkness. If the darkness stands for the disorder and chaos of a hostile world or universe, and the spot of light for the small amount of order and discipline and civilization and security that the individual has been able to wrest out of the surrounding chaos and old night, Hemingway seems to say that the small lighted area is enough, or at any rate must be made to do.

Not to be overlooked in these stories is the great asset of human sympathy. The Hemingway hero (unlike the Byronic hero) is never alone. Francis has as companion extraordinary the Negro Bugs; Manuel is supported by the loyal Zurito; the aged man in the café has an understanding friend in the older waiter. The café is, after all, a place where congenial souls may meet. Living in a clean, well-lighted place does not mean solitary withdrawal so long as there are others who also prefer such a place.

In the stories just considered, as in the novels mentioned earlier, Hemingway sees man as somewhat grimly and precariously situated in a world of hostile forces. Perhaps he is doomed to go down in defeat at last. But his life need not be joyless or ignoble. It is significant, finally, that one speaks naturally of Hemingway's *heroes*. Whatever their limitations, they exhibit virtues unknown to the ignorant, or the careless, or the mean.

LIFE AND WORKS

Ernest Hemingway was born in Oak Park, Illinois, in 1898 and graduated from the Oak Park High School in 1917. He served in Italy during the First World War as a member of a volunteer American ambulance unit, and later in an Italian combat unit; he was wounded, and decorated for valor by the Italian government. In the early 1920's he was identified (along with F. Scott Fitzgerald and Ezra Pound) with the American Colony in Paris to whom Gertrude Stein addressed the famous words: "You are all a lost generation." During the Spanish Civil War—in 1937–1938—he gave active support to the Loyalist cause in newspaper reports prepared for the North American Newspaper Alliance, in a public address before the League of American Writers, in the preparation of a film, *The Spanish Earth,* and in his antifascist play, *The Fifth Column.*

His works include two volumes of sketches: *Death in the Afternoon* (1932), a book about bullfighting, and *The Green Hills of Africa* (1935), an account of the author's travels; four collections of short stories: *In Our Time* (1925), *Men Without Women* (1927), *Winner Take Nothing* (1933), and *The Fifth Column and the First Forty-nine Stories* (1938); and six novels: *The Sun Also Rises* (1926), *A Farewell to Arms* (1929), *To Have and Have Not* (1937), *For Whom the Bell Tolls* (1940), *Across the River and into the Trees* (1950), and *The Old Man and the Sea* (1952).

Critical commentary is abundant, some of the better examples of which have been collected in *Ernest Hemingway: the Man and His Work,* edited by J. K. M. McCaffery (1950). Other illuminating criticism may be found in Malcolm Cowley, *The Portable Hemingway* (1944); Robert Penn Warren, "Hemingway," *The Kenyon Review* (Winter 1947); John W. Aldridge, *After the Lost Generation* (1951); Carlos H. Baker, *Hemingway; the Writer As Artist* (1952); and Philip Young, *Ernest Hemingway* (1952).

THE BATTLER

Nick stood up. He was all right. He looked up the track at the lights of the caboose going out of sight around the curve. There was water on both sides of the track, then tamarack swamp.

He felt of his knee. The pants were torn and the skin was barked. His hands were scraped and there were sand and cinders driven up under his nails. He went over to the edge of the track down the little slope to the water and washed his hands. He washed them carefully in the cold water, getting the dirt out from the nails. He squatted down and bathed his knee.

That lousy crut of a brakeman. He would get him some day. He would know him again. That was a fine way to act.

"Come here, kid," he said. "I got something for you."

He had fallen for it. What a lousy kid thing to have done. They would never suck him in that way again.

"Come here, kid, I got something for you." Then *wham* and he lit on his hands and knees beside the track.

Nick rubbed his eye. There was a big bump coming up. He would have a black eye, all right. It ached already. That son of a crutting brakeman.

He touched the bump over his eye with his fingers. Oh, well, it was only a black eye. That was all he had gotten out of it. Cheap at the price. He wished he could see it. Could not see it looking into the water, though. It was dark and he was a long way off from anywhere. He wiped his hands on his trousers and stood up, then climbed the embankment to the rails.

He started up the track. It was well ballasted and made easy walking, sand and gravel packed between the ties, solid walking. The smooth roadbed like a causeway went on ahead through the swamp. Nick walked along. He must get to somewhere.

Nick had swung on to the freight train when it slowed down for the yards outside of Walton Junction. The train, with Nick on it, had passed through Kalkaska as it started to get dark. Now he must be nearly to Mancelona. Three or four miles of swamp. He stepped along the track, walking so he kept on the ballast between the ties, the swamp ghostly in the rising mist. His eye ached and he was hungry. He kept on hiking, putting the miles of track back of him. The swamp was all the same on both sides of the track.

Ahead there was a bridge. Nick crossed it, his boots ringing hollow on the iron. Down below the water showed black between the slits of ties. Nick kicked a loose spike and it dropped into the water. Beyond the bridge were hills. It was high and dark on both sides of the track. Up the track Nick saw a fire.

He came up the track toward the fire carefully. It was off to one side of the track, below the railway embankment. He had only seen the light from it. The track came out through a cut and where the fire was burning the country opened out and fell away into woods. Nick dropped carefully down the embankment and cut into the woods to come up to the fire through the trees. It was a beechwood forest and the fallen beechnut burrs were under his shoes as he walked between the trees. The fire was bright now, just at the edge of the trees. There was a man sitting by it. Nick waited behind the tree and watched. The man looked to be alone. He was sitting there with his head in his hands looking at the fire. Nick stepped out and walked into the firelight.

The man sat there looking into the fire. When Nick stopped quite close to him he did not move.

"Hello!" Nick said.

The man looked up.

"Where did you get the shiner?" he said.

"A brakeman busted me."

"Off the through freight?"

"Yes."

"I saw the bastard," the man said. "He went through here 'bout an hour and a half ago. He was walking along the top of the cars slapping his arms and singing."

"The bastard!"

"It must have made him feel good to bust you," the man said seriously.

"I'll bust him."

"Get him with a rock sometime when he's going through," the man advised.

"I'll get him."

"You're a tough one, aren't you?"

"No," Nick answered.

"All you kids are tough."

"You got to be tough," Nick said.

"That's what I said."

The man looked at Nick and smiled. In the firelight Nick saw that his face was misshapen. His nose was sunken, his eyes were slits, he had queer-shaped lips. Nick did not perceive all this at once, he only saw the man's face was queerly formed and mutilated. It was like putty in color. Dead looking in the firelight.

"Don't you like my pan?" the man asked.

Nick was embarrassed.

"Sure," he said.

"Look here!" the man took off his cap.

He had only one ear. It was thickened and tight against the side of his head. Where the other ear should have been there was a stump.

"Ever see one like that?"

"No," said Nick. It made him a little sick.

"I could take it," the man said. "Don't you think I could take it, kid?"

"You bet!"

"They all bust their hands on me," the little man said. "They couldn't hurt me."

He looked at Nick. "Sit down," he said. "Want to eat?"

"Don't bother," Nick said. "I'm going on to the town."

"Listen!" the man said. "Call me Ad."

"Sure!"

"Listen," the little man said. "I'm not quite right."

"What's the matter?"

"I'm crazy."

He put on his cap. Nick felt like laughing.

"You're all right," he said.

"No, I'm not. I'm crazy. Listen, you ever been crazy?"

"No," Nick said. "How does it get you?"

"I don't know," Ad said. "When you got it you don't know about it. You know me, don't you?"

"No."

"I'm Ad Francis."

"Honest to God?"

"Don't you believe it?"

"Yes."

Nick knew it must be true.

"You know how I beat them?"

"No," Nick said.

"My heart's slow. It only beats forty a minute. Feel it."

Nick hesitated.

"Come on," the man took hold of his hand. "Take hold of my wrist. Put your fingers there."

The little man's wrist was thick and the muscles bulged above the bone. Nick felt the slow pumping under his fingers.

"Got a watch?"

"No."

"Neither have I," Ad said. "It ain't any good if you haven't got a watch."

Nick dropped his wrist.

"Listen," Ad Francis said. "Take ahold again. You count and I'll count up to sixty."

Feeling the slow hard throb under his fingers Nick started to count. He heard the little man counting slowly, one, two, three, four, five, and on—aloud.

"Sixty," Ad finished. "That's a minute. What did you make it?"

"Forty," Nick said.

"That's right," Ad said happily. "She never speeds up."

A man dropped down the railroad embankment and came across the clearing to the fire.

"Hello, Bugs!" Ad said.

"Hello!" Bugs answered. It was a negro's voice. Nick knew from the way he walked that he was a negro. He stood with his back to them, bending over the fire. He straightened up.

"This is my pal Bugs," Ad said. "He's crazy, too."

"Glad to meet you," Bugs said. "Where you say you're from?"

"Chicago," Nick said.

"That's a fine town," the negro said. "I didn't catch your name."

"Adams. Nick Adams."

"He says he's never been crazy, Bugs," Ad said.

"He's got a lot coming to him," the negro said. He was unwrapping a package by the fire.

"When are we going to eat, Bugs?" the prizefighter asked.

"Right away."

"Are you hungry, Nick?"

"Hungry as hell."

"Hear that, Bugs?"

"I hear most of what goes on."

"That ain't what I asked you."

"Yes, I heard what the gentleman said."

Into a skillet he was laying slices of ham. As the skillet grew hot the grease sputtered and Bugs, crouching on long nigger legs over the fire, turned the ham and broke eggs into the skillet, tipping it from side to side to baste the eggs with the hot fat.

"Will you cut some bread out of that bag, Mister Adams?" Bugs turned from the fire.

"Sure."

Nick reached in the bag and brought out a loaf of bread. He cut six slices. Ad watched him and leaned forward.

"Let me take your knife, Nick," he said.

"No, you don't," the negro said. "Hang onto your knife, Mister Adams."

The prizefighter sat back.

"Will you bring me the bread, Mister Adams?" Bugs asked. Nick brought it over.

"Do you like to dip your bread in the ham fat?" the negro asked.

"You bet!"

"Perhaps we'd better wait until later. It's better at the finish of the meal. Here."

The negro picked up a slice of ham and laid it on one of the pieces of bread, then slid an egg on top of it.

"Just close that sandwich, will you, please, and give it to Mister Francis."

Ad took the sandwich and started eating.

"Watch out how that egg runs," the negro warned. "This is for you, Mister Adams. The remainder for myself."

Nick bit into the sandwich. The negro was sitting opposite him beside Ad. The hot fried ham and eggs tasted wonderful.

"Mister Adams is right hungry," the negro said. The little man whom Nick knew by name as a former champion fighter was silent. He had said nothing since the negro had spoken about the knife.

"May I offer you a slice of bread dipped right in the hot ham fat?" Bugs said.

"Thanks a lot."

The little white man looked at Nick.

"Will you have some, Mister Adolph Francis?" Bugs offered from the skillet.

Ad did not answer. He was looking at Nick.

"Mister Francis?" came the nigger's soft voice.

Ad did not answer. He was looking at Nick.

"I spoke to you, Mister Francis," the nigger said softly.

Ad kept on looking at Nick. He had his cap down over his eyes. Nick felt nervous.

"How the hell do you get that way?" came out from under the cap sharply at Nick.

"Who the hell do you think you are? You're a snotty bastard. You come in here where nobody asks you and eat a man's food and when he asks to borrow a knife you get snotty."

He glared at Nick, his face was white and his eyes almost out of sight under the cap.

"You're a hot sketch. Who the hell asked you to butt in here?"

"Nobody."

"You're damn right nobody did. Nobody asked you to stay either. You come in here and act snotty about my face and smoke my cigars and drink my liquor and then talk snotty. Where the hell do you think you get off?"

Nick said nothing. Ad stood up.

"I'll tell you, you yellow-livered Chicago bastard. You're going to get your can knocked off. Do you get that?"

Nick stepped back. The little man came toward him slowly, stepping flat-footed forward, his left foot stepping forward, his right dragging up to it.

"Hit me," he moved his head. "Try and hit me."

"I don't want to hit you."

"You won't get out of it that way. You're going to take a beating, see? Come on and lead at me."

"Cut it out," Nick said.

"All right, then, you bastard."

The little man looked down at Nick's feet. As he looked down the negro, who had followed behind him as he moved away from the fire, set himself and tapped him across the base of the skull. He fell forward and Bugs dropped the cloth-wrapped blackjack on the grass. The little man lay there, his face in the grass. The negro picked him up, his head hanging, and carried him to the fire. His face looked bad, the eyes open. Bugs laid him down gently.

"Will you bring me the water in the bucket, Mister Adams," he said. "I'm afraid I hit him just a little hard."

The negro splashed water with his hand on the man's face and pulled his ears gently. The eyes closed.

Bugs stood up.

"He's all right," he said. "There's nothing to worry about. I'm sorry, Mister Adams."

"It's all right." Nick was looking down at the little man. He saw the blackjack on the grass and picked it up. It had a flexible handle and was limber in his hand. It was made of worn black leather with a handkerchief wrapped around the heavy end.

"That's a whalebone handle," the negro smiled. "They don't make them any more. I didn't know how well you could take care of yourself and, anyway, I didn't want you to hurt him or mark him up no more than he is."

The negro smiled again.

"You hurt him yourself."

"I know how to do it. He won't remember nothing of it. I have to do it to change him when he gets that way."

Nick was still looking down at the little man, lying, his eyes closed in the fire-light. Bugs put some wood on the fire.

"Don't you worry about him none, Mister Adams. I seen him like this plenty of times before."

"What made him crazy?" Nick asked.

"Oh, a lot of things," the negro answered from the fire. "Would you like a cup of this coffee, Mister Adams?"

He handed Nick the cup and smoothed the coat he had placed under the unconscious man's head.

"He took too many beatings, for one thing," the negro sipped the coffee. "But that just made him sort of simple. Then his sister was his manager and they was always being written up in the papers all about brothers and sisters and how she loved her brother and how he loved his sister, and then they got married in New York and that made a lot of unpleasantness."

"I remember about it."

"Sure. Of course they wasn't brother and sister no more than a rabbit, but there was a lot of people didn't like it either way and they commenced to have disagreements, and one day she just went off and never come back."

He drank the coffee and wiped his lips with the pink palm of his hand.

"He just went crazy. Will you have some more coffee, Mister Adams?"

"Thanks."

"I seen her a couple of times," the negro went on. "She was an awful good-looking woman. Looked enough like him to be twins. He wouldn't be bad-looking without his face all busted."

He stopped. The story seemed to be over.

"Where did you meet him?" asked Nick.

"I met him in jail," the negro said. "He was busting people all the time after she went away and they put him in jail. I was in for cuttin' a man."

He smiled, and went on soft-voiced:

"Right away I liked him and when I got out I looked him up. He likes to think I'm crazy and I don't mind. I like to be with him and I like seeing the country and I don't have to commit no larceny to do it. I like living like a gentleman."

"What do you all do?" Nick asked.

"Oh, nothing. Just move around. He's got money."

"He must have made a lot of money."

"Sure. He spent all his money, though. Or they took it away from him. She sends him money."

He poked up the fire.

"She's a mighty fine woman," he said. "She looks enough like him to be his own twin."

The negro looked over at the little man, lying breathing heavily. His blond hair was down over his forehead. His mutilated face looked childish in repose.

"I can wake him up any time now, Mister Adams. If you don't mind I wish you'd sort of pull out. I don't like to not be hospitable, but it might disturb him back again to see you. I hate to have to thump him and it's the only thing to do when he gets started. I have to sort of keep him away from people. You don't mind, do you, Mister Adams? No, don't thank me, Mister Adams. I'd have warned you about him but he seemed to have taken such a liking to you and I thought things were going to be all right. You'll hit a town about two miles up the track. Mancelona they call it. Good-bye. I wish we could ask you to stay the night but it's just out of the question. Would you like to take some of that ham and some bread with you? No? You better take a sandwich," all this in a low, smooth, polite nigger voice.

"Good. Well, good-bye, Mister Adams. Good-bye and good luck!"

Nick walked away from the fire across the clearing to the railway tracks. Out of the range of the fire he listened. The low soft voice of the negro was talking. Nick could not hear the words. Then he heard the little man say, "I got an awful headache, Bugs."

"You'll feel better, Mister Francis," the negro's voice soothed. "Just you drink a cup of this hot coffee."

Nick climbed the embankment and started up the track. He found he had a ham sandwich in his hand and put it in his pocket. Looking back from the mounting grade before the track curved into the hills he could see the firelight in the clearing.

1925

THE UNDEFEATED

Manuel Garcia climbed the stairs to Don Miguel Retana's office. He set down his suitcase and knocked on the door. There was no answer. Manuel, standing in the hallway, felt there was someone in the room. He felt it through the door.

"Retana," he said, listening.

There was no answer.

He's there, all right, Manuel thought.

"Retana," he said and banged the door.

"Who's there?" said someone in the office.

"Me, Manolo," Manuel said.

"What do you want?" asked the voice.

"I want to work," Manuel said.

Something in the door clicked several times and it swung open. Manuel went in, carrying his suitcase.

A little man sat behind a desk at the far side of the room. Over his head was a bull's head, stuffed by a Madrid taxidermist; on the walls were framed photographs and bull-fight posters.

The little man sat looking at Manuel.

"I thought they'd killed you," he said.

Manuel knocked with his knuckles on the desk. The little man sat looking at him across the desk.

"How many corridas[1] you had this year?" Retana asked.

"One," he answered.

"Just that one?" the little man asked.

"That's all."

"I read about it in the papers," Retana said. He leaned back in the chair and looked at Manuel.

Manuel looked up at the stuffed bull. He had seen it often before. He felt a certain family interest in it. It had killed his brother, the promising one, about nine years ago. Manuel remembered the day. There was a brass plate on the oak shield the bull's head was mounted on. Manuel could not read it, but he imagined it was in memory of his brother. Well, he had been a good kid.

The plate said: "The Bull 'Mariposa' of the Duke of Veragua, which accepted 9 varas for 7 caballos,[2] and caused the death of Antonio Garcia, Novillero, April 27, 1909."

Retana saw him looking at the stuffed bull's head.

1. **corridas:** bullfights.
2. **caballos:** horses.

"The lot the Duke sent me for Sunday will make a scandal," he said. "They're all bad in the legs. What do they say about them at the Café?"

"I don't know," Manuel said. "I just got in."

"Yes," Retana said. "You still have your bag."

He looked at Manuel, leaning back behind the big desk.

"Sit down," he said. "Take off your cap."

Manuel sat down; his cap off, his face was changed. He looked pale, and his coleta[1] pinned forward on his head, so that it would not show under the cap, gave him a strange look.

"You don't look well," Retana said.

"I just got out of the hospital," Manuel said.

"I heard they'd cut your leg off," Retana said.

"No," said Manuel. "It got all right."

Retana leaned forward across the desk and pushed a wooden box of cigarettes toward Manuel.

"Have a cigarette," he said.

"Thanks."

Manuel lit it.

"Smoke?" he said, offering the match to Retana.

"No," Retana waved his hand, "I never smoke."

Retana watched him smoking.

"Why don't you get a job and go to work?" he said.

"I don't want to work," Manuel said. "I am a bull-fighter."

"There aren't any bull-fighters any more," Retana said.

"I'm a bull-fighter," Manuel said.

"Yes, while you're in there," Retana said.

Manuel laughed.

Retana sat, saying nothing and looking at Manuel.

"I'll put you in a nocturnal if you want," Retana offered.

"When?" Manuel asked.

"To-morrow night."

"I don't like to substitute for anybody," Manuel said. That was the way they all got killed. That was the way Salvador got killed. He tapped with his knuckles on the table.

"It's all I've got," Retana said.

"Why don't you put me on next week?" Manuel suggested.

"You wouldn't draw," Retana said. "All they want is Litri and Rubito and La Torre. Those kids are good."

"They'd come to see me get it," Manuel said, hopefully.

"No, they wouldn't. They don't know who you are any more."

"I've got a lot of stuff," Manuel said.

"I'm offering to put you on to-morrow night," Retana said. "You can work with young Hernandez and kill two novillos[2] after the Charlots.[3]

"Whose novillos?" Manuel asked.

---

1. **coleta:** pigtail worn by the bullfighter, the badge of his profession.
2. **novillos:** bulls.
3. **Charlots:** comic performances preceding the fight.

"I don't know. Whatever stuff they've got in the corrals. What the veterinaries won't pass in the daytime."

"I don't like to substitute," Manuel said.

"You can take it or leave it," Retana said. He leaned forward over the papers. He was no longer interested. The appeal that Manuel had made to him for a moment when he thought of the old days was gone. He would like to get him to substitute for Larita because he could get him cheaply. He could get others cheaply too. He would like to help him though. Still he had given him the chance. It was up to him.

"How much do I get?" Manuel asked. He was still playing with the idea of refusing. But he knew he could not refuse.

"Two hundred and fifty pesetas," Retana said. He had thought of five hundred, but when he opened his mouth it said two hundred and fifty.

"You pay Villalta seven thousand," Manuel said.

"You're not Villalta," Retana said.

"I know it," Manuel said.

"He draws it, Manolo," Retana said in explanation.

"Sure," said Manuel. He stood up. "Give me three hundred, Retana."

"All right," Retana agreed. He reached in the drawer for a paper.

"Can I have fifty now?" Manuel asked.

"Sure," said Retana. He took a fifty peseta note out of his pocket-book and laid it, spread out flat, on the table.

Manuel picked it up and put it in his pocket.

"What about a cuadrilla?"[1] he asked.

"There's the boys that always work for me nights," Retana said. "They're all right."

"How about picadors?" Manuel asked.

"They're not much," Retana admitted.

"I've got to have one good pic," Manuel said.

"Get him then," Retana said. "Go and get him."

"Not out of this," Manuel said. "I'm not paying for any cuadrilla out of sixty duros."

Retana said nothing but looked at Manuel across the big desk.

"You know I've got to have one good pic," Manuel said.

Retana said nothing but looked at Manuel from a long way off.

"It isn't right," Manuel said.

Retana was still considering him, leaning back in his chair, considering him from a long way away.

"There're the regular pics," he offered.

"I know," Manuel said. "I know your regular pics."

Retana did not smile. Manuel knew it was over.

"All I want is an even break," Manuel said reasonably. "When I go out there I want to be able to call my shots on the bull. It only takes one good picador."

He was talking to a man who was no longer listening.

"If you want something extra," Retana said, "go and get it. There will be a regular cuadrilla out there. Bring as many of your own pics as you want. The charlotada is over by 10.30."

1. **cuadrilla:** fighter who assists the chief performer.

"All right," Manuel said. "If that's the way you feel about it."

"That's the way," Retana said.

"I'll see you to-morrow night," Manuel said.

"I'll be out there," Retana said.

Manuel picked up his suitcase and went out.

"Shut the door," Retana called.

Manuel looked back. Retana was sitting forward looking at some papers. Manuel pulled the door tight until it clicked.

He went down the stairs and out of the door into the hot brightness of the street. It was very hot in the street and the light on the white buildings was sudden and hard on his eyes. He walked down the shady side of the steep street toward the Puerto del Sol. The shade felt solid and cool as running water. The heat came suddenly as he crossed the intersecting streets. Manuel saw no one he knew in all the people he passed.

Just before the Puerto del Sol he turned into a café.

It was quiet in the café. There were a few men sitting at tables against the wall. At one table four men played cards. Most of the men sat against the wall smoking, empty coffee-cups and liqueur-glasses before them on the tables. Manuel went through the long room to a small room in back. A man sat at a table in the corner asleep. Manuel sat down at one of the tables.

A waiter came in and stood beside Manuel's table.

"Have you seen Zurito?" Manuel asked him.

"He was in before lunch," the waiter answered. "He won't be back before five o'clock."

"Bring me some coffee and milk and a shot of the ordinary," Manuel said.

The waiter came back into the room carrying a tray with a big coffee-glass and a liqueur-glass on it. In his left hand he held a bottle of brandy. He swung these down to the table and a boy who had followed him poured coffee and milk into the glass from two shiny, spouted pots with long handles.

Manuel took off his cap and the waiter noticed his pigtail pinned forward on his head. He winked at the coffee-boy as he poured out the brandy into the little glass beside Manuel's coffee. The coffee-boy looked at Manuel's pale face curiously.

"You fighting here?" asked the waiter, corking up the bottle.

"Yes," Manuel said. "To-morrow."

The waiter stood there, holding the bottle on one hip.

"You in the Charlie Chaplins?" he asked.

The coffee-boy looked away, embarrassed.

"No. In the ordinary."

"I thought they were going to have Chaves and Hernandez," the waiter said.

"No. Me and another."

"Who? Chaves or Hernandez?"

"Hernandez, I think."

"What's the matter with Chaves?"

"He got hurt."

"Where did you hear that?"

"Retana."

"Hey, Looie," the waiter called to the next room, "Chaves got cogida."

Manuel had taken the wrapper off the lumps of sugar and dropped them into his coffee. He stirred it and drank it down, sweet, hot, and warming in his empty stomach. He drank off the brandy.

"Give me another shot of that," he said to the waiter.

The waiter uncorked the bottle and poured the glass full, slopping another drink into the saucer. Another waiter had come up in front of the table. The coffee-boy was gone.

"Is Chaves hurt bad?" the second waiter asked Manuel.

"I don't know," Manuel said, "Retana didn't say."

"A hell of a lot he cares," the tall waiter said. Manuel had not seen him before. He must have just come up.

"If you stand in with Retana in this town, you're a made man," the tall waiter said. "If you aren't in with him, you might just as well go out and shoot yourself."

"You said it," the other waiter who had come in said. "You said it then."

"You're right I said it," said the tall waiter. "I know what I'm talking about when I talk about that bird."

"Look what he's done for Villalta," the first waiter said.

"And that ain't all," the tall waiter said. "Look what he's done for Marcial Lalanda. Look what he's done for Nacional."

"You said it, kid," agreed the short waiter.

Manuel looked at them, standing talking in front of his table. He had drunk his second brandy. They had forgotten about him. They were not interested in him.

"Look at that bunch of camels," the tall waiter went on. "Did you ever see this Nacional II?"

"I seen him last Sunday didn't I?" the original waiter said.

"He's a giraffe," the short waiter said.

"What did I tell you?" the tall waiter said. "Those are Retana's boys."

"Say, give me another shot of that," Manuel said. He had poured the brandy the waiter had slopped over in the saucer into his glass and drank it while they were talking.

The original waiter poured his glass full mechanically, and the three of them went out of the room talking.

In the far corner the man was still asleep, snoring slightly on the intaking breath, his head back against the wall.

Manuel drank his brandy. He felt sleepy himself. It was too hot to go out into the town. Besides there was nothing to do. He wanted to see Zurito. He would go to sleep while he waited. He kicked his suitcase under the table to be sure it was there. Perhaps it would be better to put it back under the seat, against the wall. He leaned down and shoved it under. Then he leaned forward on the table and went to sleep.

When he woke there was someone sitting across the table from him. It was a big man with a heavy brown face like an Indian. He had been sitting there some time. He had waved the waiter away and sat reading the paper and occasionally looking down at Manuel, asleep, his head on the table. He read the paper laboriously forming the words with his lips as he read. When it tired him he looked at Manuel. He sat heavily in the chair, his black Cordoba hat tipped forward.

Manuel sat up and looked at him.

"Hello, Zurito," he said.

"Hello, kid," the big man said.

"I've been asleep." Manuel rubbed his forehead with the back of his fist.

"I thought maybe you were."

"How's everything?"

"Good. How is everything with you?"

"Not so good."

They were both silent. Zurito, the picador, looked at Manuel's white face. Manuel looked down at the picador's enormous hands folding the paper to put away in his pocket.

"I got a favor to ask you, Manos," Manuel said.

Manosduros was Zurito's nickname. He never heard it without thinking of his huge hands. He put them forward on the table self-consciously.

"Let's have a drink," he said.

"Sure," said Manuel.

The waiter came and went and came again. He went out of the room looking back at the two men at the table.

"What's the matter, Manolo?" Zurito set down his glass.

"Would you pic two bulls for me to-morrow night?" Manuel asked, looking up at Zurito across the table.

"No," said Zurito. "I'm not pic-ing."

Manuel looked down at his glass. He had expected that answer; now he had it. Well, he had it.

"I'm sorry, Manolo, but I'm not pic-ing." Zurito looked at his hands.

"That's all right," Manuel said.

"I'm too old," Zurito said.

"I just asked you," Manuel said.

"Is it the nocturnal to-morrow?"

"That's it. I figured if I had just one good pic, I could get away with it."

"How much are you getting?"

"Three hundred pesetas."

"I get more than that for pic-ing."

"I know," said Manuel. "I didn't have any right to ask you."

"What do you keep on doing it for?" Zurito asked. "Why don't you cut off your coleta, Manolo?"

"I don't know," Manuel said.

"You're pretty near as old as I am," Zurito said.

"I don't know," Manuel said. "I got to do it. If I can fix it so that I get an even break, that's all I want. I got to stick with it, Manos."

"No, you don't."

"Yes, I do. I've tried keeping away from it."

"I know how you feel. But it isn't right. You ought to get out and stay out."

"I can't do it. Besides, I've been going good lately."

Zurito looked at his face.

"You've been in the hospital."

"But I was going great when I got hurt."

Zurito said nothing. He tipped the cognac out of his saucer into his glass.

"The papers said they never saw a better faena,"[1] Manuel said.

Zurito looked at him.

"You know when I get going I'm good," Manuel said.

"You're too old," the picador said.

"No," said Manuel. "You're ten years older than I am."

"With me it's different."

"I'm not too old," Manuel said.

They sat silent, Manuel watching the picador's face.

"I was going great till I got hurt," Manuel offered.

"You ought to have seen me, Manos," Manuel said, reproachfully.

"I don't want to see you," Zurito said. "It makes me nervous."

"You haven't seen me lately."

"I've seen you plenty."

Zurito looked at Manuel, avoiding his eyes.

"You ought to quit it, Manolo."

"I can't," Manuel said. "I'm going good now, I tell you."

Zurito leaned forward, his hands on the table.

"Listen. I'll pic for you and if you don't go big to-morrow night, you'll quit. See? Will you do that?"

"Sure."

Zurito leaned back, relieved.

"You got to quit," he said. "No monkey business. You got to cut the coleta."

"I won't have to quit," Manuel said. "You watch me. I've got the stuff."

Zurito stood up. He felt tired from arguing.

"You got to quit," he said. "I'll cut your coleta myself."

"No, you won't," Manuel said. "You won't have a chance."

Zurito called the waiter.

"Come on," said Zurito. "Come on up to the house."

Manuel reached under the seat for his suitcase. He was happy. He knew Zurito would pic for him. He was the best picador living. It was all simple now.

"Come on up to the house and we'll eat," Zurito said.

Manuel stood in the patio de caballos waiting for the Charlie Chaplins to be over. Zurito stood beside him. Where they stood it was dark. The high door that led into the bull-ring was shut. Above them they heard a shout, then another shout of laughter. Then there was silence. Manuel liked the smell of the stables about the patio de caballos. It smelt good in the dark. There was another roar from the arena and then applause, prolonged applause, going on and on.

"You ever seen these fellows?" Zurito asked, big and looming beside Manuel in the dark.

"No," Manuel said.

"They're pretty funny," Zurito said. He smiled to himself in the dark.

The high, double, tight-fitting door into the bull-ring swung open and Manuel saw the ring in the hard light of the arc-lights, the plaza, dark all the way around, rising high; around the edge of the ring were running and bowing two men dressed like tramps, followed by a third in the uniform of a hotel bell-boy who

---

1. **faena**: the final stages of a bullfight.

stooped and picked up the hats and canes thrown down onto the sand and tossed them back up into the darkness.

The electric light went on in the patio.

"I'll climb onto one of those ponies while you collect the kids," Zurito said.

Behind them came the jingle of the mules, coming out to go into the arena and be hitched onto the dead bull.

The members of the cuadrilla, who had been watching the burlesque from the runway between the barrera and the seats, came walking back and stood in a group talking, under the electric light in the patio. A good-looking lad in a silver-and-orange suit came up to Manuel and smiled.

"I'm Hernandez," he said and put out his hand.

Manuel shook it.

"They're regular elephants we've got to-night," the boy said cheerfully.

"They're big ones with horns," Manuel agreed.

"You drew the worst lot," the boy said.

"That's all right," Manuel said. "The bigger they are, the more meat for the poor."

"Where did you get that one?" Hernandez grinned.

"That's an old one," Manuel said. "You line up your cuadrilla, so I can see what I've got."

"You've got some good kids," Hernandez said. He was very cheerful. He had been on twice before in nocturnals and was beginning to get a following in Madrid. He was happy the fight would start in a few minutes.

"Where are the pics?" Manuel asked.

"They're back in the corrals fighting about who gets the beautiful horses," Hernandez grinned.

The mules came through the gate in a rush, the whips snapping, bells jangling and the young bull ploughing a furrow of sand.

They formed up for the paseo[1] as soon as the bull had gone through.

Manuel and Hernandez stood in front. The youths of the cuadrillas were behind, their heavy capes furled over their arms. In back, the four picadors, mounted, holding their steel-tipped push-poles erect in the half-dark of the corral.

"It's a wonder Retana wouldn't give us enough light to see the horses by," one picador said.

"He knows we'll be happier if we don't get too good a look at these skins," another pic answered.

"This thing I'm on barely keeps me off the ground," the first picador said.

"Well, they're horses."

"Sure, they're horses."

They talked, sitting their gaunt horses in the dark.

Zurito said nothing. He had the only steady horse of the lot. He had tried him, wheeling him in the corrals and he responded to the bit and the spurs. He had taken the bandage off his right eye and cut the strings where they had tied his ears tight shut at the base. He was a good, solid horse, solid on his legs. That was all he needed. He intended to ride him all through the corrida. He had already, since he had mounted, sitting in the half-dark in the big, quilted saddle, waiting

---

1. **paseo:** entering procession.

for the paseo, pic-ed through the whole corrida in his mind. The other picadors went on talking on both sides of him. He did not hear them.

The two matadors stood together in front of their three peones,[1] their capes furled over their left arms in the same fashion. Manuel was thinking about the three lads in back of him. They were all three Madrilenos, like Hernandez, boys about nineteen. One of them, a gypsy, serious, aloof, and dark-faced, he liked the look of. He turned.

"What's your name, kid?" he asked the gypsy.

"Fuentes," the gypsy said.

"That's a good name," Manuel said.

The gypsy smiled, showing his teeth.

"You take the bull and give him a little run when he comes out," Manuel said.

"All right," the gypsy said. His face was serious. He began to think about just what he would do.

"Here she goes," Manuel said to Hernandez.

"All right. We'll go."

Heads up, swinging with the music, their right arms swinging free, they stepped out, crossing the sanded arena under the arc-lights, the cuadrillas opening out behind, the picadors riding after, behind came the bull-ring servants and the jingling mules. The crowd applauded Hernandez as they marched across the arena. Arrogant, swinging, they looked straight ahead as they marched.

They bowed before the president, and the procession broke up into its component parts. The bull-fighters went over to the barrera and changed their heavy mantles for the light fighting capes. The mules went out. The picadors galloped jerkily around the ring, and two rode out the gate they had come in by. The servants swept the sand smooth.

Manuel drank a glass of water poured for him by one of Retana's deputies, who was acting as his manager and sword-handler. Hernandez came over from speaking with his own manager.

"You got a good hand, kid," Manuel complimented him.

"They like me," Hernandez said happily.

"How did the paseo go?" Manuel asked Retana's man.

"Like a wedding," said the handler. "Fine. You came out like Joselito and Belmonte."

Zurito rode by, a bulky equestrian statue. He wheeled his horse and faced him toward the toril on the far side of the ring where the bull would come out. It was strange under the arc-light. He pic-ed in the hot afternoon sun for big money. He didn't like this arc-light business. He wished they would get started.

Manuel went up to him.

"Pic him, Manos," he said. "Cut him down to size for me."

"I'll pic him, kid," Zurito spat on the sand. "I'll make him jump out of the ring."

"Lean on him, Manos," Manuel said.

"I'll lean on him," Zurito said. "What's holding it up?"

"He's coming now," Manuel said.

Zurito sat there, his feet in the box-stirrups, his great legs in the buckskin-covered armor gripping the horse, the reins in his left hand, the long pic held in

---

1. **peones:** the matadors' subordinates.

his right hand, his broad hat well down over his eyes to shade them from the lights, watching the distant door of the toril. His horse's ears quivered. Zurito patted him with his left hand.

The red door of the toril swung back and for a moment Zurito looked into the empty passageway far across the arena. Then the bull came out in a rush, skidding on his four legs as he came out under the lights, then charging in a gallop, moving softly in a fast gallop, silent except as he woofed through wide nostrils as he charged, glad to be free after the dark pen.

In the first row of seats, slightly bored, leaning forward to write on the cement wall in front of his knees, the substitute bull-fight critic of *El Heraldo* scribbled: "Campagnero, Negro, 42, came out at 90 miles an hour with plenty of gas—"

Manuel, leaning against the barrera, watching the bull, waved his hand and the gypsy ran out, trailing his cape. The bull, in full gallop, pivoted and charged the cape, his head down, his tail rising. The gypsy moved in a zigzag, and as he passed, the bull caught sight of him and abandoned the cape to charge the man. The gyp sprinted and vaulted the red fence of the barrera as the bull struck it with his horns. He tossed into it twice with his horns, banging into the wood blindly.

The critic of *El Heraldo* lit a cigarette and tossed the match at the bull, then wrote in his note-book, "large and with enough horns to satisfy the cash customers, Campagnero showed a tendency to cut into the terrane of the bull-fighters."

Manuel stepped out on the hard sand as the bull banged into the fence. Out of the corner of his eye he saw Zurito sitting the white horse close to the barrera, about a quarter of the way around the ring to the left. Manuel held the cape close in front of him, a fold in each hand, and shouted at the bull. "Huh! Huh!" The bull turned, seemed to brace against the fence as he charged in a scramble, driving into the cape as Manuel side-stepped, pivoted on his heels with the charge of the bull, and swung the cape just ahead of the horns. At the end of the swing he was facing the bull again and held the cape in the same position close in front of his body, and pivoted again as the bull recharged. Each time, as he swung, the crowd shouted.

Four times he swung with the bull, lifting the cape so it billowed full, and each time bringing the bull around to charge again. Then, at the end of the fifth swing, he held the cape against his hip and pivoted, so the cape swung out like a ballet dancer's skirt and wound the bull around himself like a belt, to step clear, leaving the bull facing Zurito on the white horse, come up and planted firm, the horse facing the bull, its ears forward, its lips nervous, Zurito, his hat over his eyes, leaning forward, the long pole sticking out before and behind in a sharp angle under his right arm, held halfway down, the triangular iron point facing the bull.

El Heraldo's second-string critic, drawing on his cigarette, his eyes on the bull, wrote: "the veteran Manolo designed a series of acceptable veronicas, ending in a very Belmontistic recorte[1] that earned applause from the regulars, and we entered the tercio of the cavalry."

Zurito sat his horse, measuring the distance between the bull and the end of the pic. As he looked, the bull gathered himself together and charged, his eyes on the horse's chest. As he lowered his head to hook, Zurito sunk the point of the

1. veronicas . . . recorte: flourishes of the cape. *Belmontistic* refers to Belmonte, a famous fighter.

pic in the swelling hump of muscle above the bull's shoulder, leaned all his weight on the shaft, and with his left hand pulled the white horse into the air, front hoofs pawing, and swung him to the right as he pushed the bull under and through so the horns passed safely under the horse's belly and the horse came down, quivering, the bull's tail brushing his chest as he charged the cape Hernandez offered him.

Hernandez ran sideways, taking the bull out and away with the cape, toward the other picador. He fixed him with a swing of the cape, squarely facing the horse and rider, and stepped back. As the bull saw the horse he charged. The picador's lance slid along his back, and as the shock of the charge lifted the horse, the picador was already half-way out of the saddle, lifting his right leg clear as he missed with the lance and falling to the left side to keep the horse between him and the bull. The horse, lifted and gored, crashed over with the bull driving into him, the picador gave a shove with his boots against the horse and lay clear, waiting to be lifted and hauled away and put on his feet.

Manuel let the bull drive into the fallen horse; he was in no hurry, the picador was safe; besides, it did a picador like that good to worry. He'd stay on longer next time. Lousy pics! He looked across the sand at Zurito a little way out from the barrera, his horse rigid, waiting.

"Huh!" he called to the bull, "Tomar!" holding the cape in both hands so it would catch his eye. The bull detached himself from the horse and charged the cape, and Manuel, running sideways and holding the cape spread wide, stopped, swung on his heels, and brought the bull sharply around facing Zurito.

"Campagnero accepted a pair of varas[1] for the death of one rosinante,[2] with Hernandez and Manolo at the quites,"[3] *El Heraldo's* critic wrote. "He pressed on the iron and clearly showed he was no horse-lover. The veteran Zurito resurrected some of his old stuff with the pike-pole, notably the suerte—"

"Olé! Olé!" the man sitting beside him shouted. The shout was lost in the roar of the crowd, and he slapped the critic on the back. The critic looked up to see Zurito, directly below him, leaning far out over his horse, the length of the pic rising in a sharp angle under his armpit, holding the pic almost by the point, bearing down with all his weight, holding the bull off, the bull pushing and driving to get at the horse, and Zurito, far out, on top of him, holding him, holding him, and slowly pivoting the horse against the pressure, so that at last he was clear. Zurito felt the moment when the horse was clear and the bull could come past, and relaxed the absolute steel lock of his resistance, and the triangular steel point of the pic ripped in the bull's hump of shoulder muscle as he tore loose to find Hernandez's cape before his muzzle. He charged blindly into the cape and the boy took him out into the open arena.

Zurito sat patting his horse and looking at the bull charging the cape that Hernandez swung for him out under the bright light while the crowd shouted.

"You see that one?" he said to Manuel.

"It was a wonder," Manuel said.

"I got him that time," Zurito said. "Look at him now."

1. varas: shafts.
2. rosinante: broken-down horse, so called from Don Quixote's steed.
3. quites: the point of the bull's diversion.

At the conclusion of a closely turned pass of the cape the bull slid to his knees. He was up at once, but far out across the sand Manuel and Zurito saw the shine of the pumping flow of blood, smooth against the black of the bull's shoulder.

"I got him that time," Zurito said.

"He's a good bull," Manuel said.

"If they gave me another shot at him, I'd kill him," Zurito said.

"They'll change the thirds on us," Manuel said.

"Look at him now," Zurito said.

"I got to go over there," Manuel said, and started on a run for the other side of the ring, where the monos[1] were leading a horse out by the bridle toward the bull, whacking him on the legs with rods and all, in a procession, trying to get him toward the bull, who stood, dropping his head, pawing, unable to make up his mind to charge.

Zurito, sitting his horse, walking him toward the scene, not missing any detail, scowled.

Finally the bull charged, the horse leaders ran for the barrera, the picador hit too far back, and the bull got under the horse, lifted him, threw him onto his back.

Zurito watched. The monos, in their red shirts, running out to drag the picador clear. The picador, now on his feet, swearing and flopping his arms. Manuel and Hernandez standing ready with their capes. And the bull, the great, black bull, with a horse on his back, hooves dangling, the bridle caught in the horns. Black bull with a horse on his back, staggering short-legged, then arching his neck and lifting, thrusting, charging to slide the horse off, horse sliding down. Then the bull into a lunging charge at the cape Manuel spread for him.

The bull was slower now, Manuel felt. He was bleeding badly. There was a sheen of blood all down his flank.

Manuel offered him the cape again. There he came, eyes open, ugly, watching the cape. Manuel stepped to the side and raised his arms, tightening the cape ahead of the bull for the veronica.

Now he was facing the bull. Yes, his head was going down a little. He was carrying it lower. That was Zurito.

Manuel flopped the cape; there he comes; he side-stepped and swung in another veronica. He's shooting awfully accurately, he thought. He's had enough fight, so he's watching now. He's hunting now. Got his eye on me. But I always give him the cape.

He shook the cape at the bull; there he comes; he side-stepped. Awful close that time. I don't want to work that close to him.

The edge of the cape was wet with blood where it had swept along the bull's back as he went by.

All right, here's the last one.

Manuel, facing the bull, having turned with him each charge, offered the cape with his two hands. The bull looked at him. Eyes watching, horns straight forward, the bull looked at him, watching.

"Huh!" Manuel said, "Toro!" and leaning back, swung the cape forward. Here he comes. He side-stepped, swung the cape in back of him, and pivoted, so

1. **monos:** attendants.

the bull followed a swirl of cape and then was left with nothing, fixed by the pass, dominated by the cape. Manuel swung the cape under his muzzle with one hand, to show the bull was fixed, and walked away.

There was no applause.

Manuel walked across the sand toward the barrera, while Zurito rode out of the ring. The trumpet had blown to change the act to the planting of the bande-rillos[1] while Manuel had been working with the bull. He had not consciously noticed it. The monos were spreading canvas over the two dead horses and sprinkling sawdust around them.

Manuel came up to the barrera for a drink of water. Retana's man handed him the heavy porous jug.

Fuentes, the tall gypsy, was standing holding a pair of banderillos, holding them together, slim, red sticks, fish-hook points out. He looked at Manuel.

"Go on out there," Manuel said.

The gypsy trotted out. Manuel set down the jug and watched. He wiped his face with his handkerchief.

The critic of *El Heraldo* reached for the bottle of warm champagne that stood between his feet, took a drink, and finished his paragraph.

"—the aged Manolo rated no applause for a vulgar series of lances with the cape and we entered the third of the palings."

Alone in the centre of the ring the bull stood, still fixed. Fuentes, tall, flat-backed, walking toward him arrogantly, his arms spread out, the two slim, red sticks, one in each hand, held by the fingers, points straight forward. Fuentes walked forward. Back of him and to one side was a peon with a cape. The bull looked at him and was no longer fixed.

His eyes watched Fuentes, now standing still. Now he leaned back, calling to him. Fuentes twitched the two banderillos and the light on the steel points caught the bull's eye.

His tail went up and he charged.

He came straight, his eyes on the man. Fuentes stood still, leaning back, the banderillos pointing forward. As the bull lowered his head to hook, Fuentes leaned backward, his arms came together and rose, his two hands touching, the banderillos two descending red lines, and leaning forward drove the points into the bull's shoulder, leaning far in over the bull's horns and pivoting on the two upright sticks, his legs tight together, his body curving to one side to let the bull pass.

"Olé!" from the crowd.

The bull was hooking wildly, jumping like a trout, all four feet off the ground. The red shafts of the banderillos tossed as he jumped.

Manuel standing at the barrera, noticed that he hooked always to the right.

"Tell him to drop the next pair on the right," he said to the kid who started to run out to Fuentes with the new banderillos.

A heavy hand fell on his shoulder. It was Zurito.

"How do you feel, kid?" he asked.

Manuel was watching the bull.

Zurito leaned forward on the barrera, leaning the weight of his body on his arms. Manuel turned to him.

1. **banderillos:** barbed darts.

"You're going good," Zurito said.

Manuel shook his head. He had nothing to do now until the next third. The gypsy was very good with the banderillos. The bull would come to him in the next third in good shape. He was a good bull. It had all been easy up to now. The final stuff with the sword was all he worried over. He did not really worry. He did not even think about it. But standing there he had a heavy sense of apprehension. He looked out at the bull, planning his faena, his work with the red cloth that was to reduce the bull, to make him manageable.

The gypsy was walking out toward the bull again, walking heel-and-toe, insultingly, like a ball-room dancer, the red shafts of the banderillos twitching with his walk. The bull watched him, not fixed now, hunting him, but waiting to get close enough so he could be sure of getting him, getting the horns into him.

As Fuentes walked forward the bull charged. Fuentes ran across the quarter of a circle as the bull charged and, as he passed running backward, stopped, swung forward, rose on his toes, arms straight out, and sunk the banderillos straight down into the tight of the big shoulder muscles as the bull missed him.

The crowd were wild about it.

"That kid won't stay in this night stuff long," Retana's man said to Zurito.

"He's good," Zurito said.

"Watch him now."

They watched.

Fuentes was standing with his back against the barrera. Two of the cuadrilla were back of him, with their capes ready to flop over the fence to distract the bull.

The bull, with his tongue out, his barrel heaving, was watching the gypsy. He thought he had him now. Back against the red planks. Only a short charge away. The bull watched him.

The gypsy bent back, drew back his arms, the banderillos pointing at the bull. He called to the bull, stamped one foot. The bull was suspicious. He wanted the man. No more barbs in the shoulder.

Fuentes walked a little closer to the bull. Bent back. Called again. Somebody in the crowd shouted a warning.

"He's too damn close," Zurito said.

"Watch him," Retana's man said.

Leaning back, inciting the bull with the banderillos, Fuentes jumped, both feet off the ground. As he jumped the bull's tail rose and he charged. Fuentes came down on his toes, arms straight out, whole body arching forward, and drove the shafts straight down as he swung his body clear of the right horn.

The bull crashed into the barrera where the flopping capes had attracted his eye as he lost the man.

The gypsy came running along the barrera toward Manuel, taking the applause of the crowd. His vest was ripped where he had not quite cleared the point of the horn. He was happy about it, showing it to the spectators. He made the tour of the ring. Zurito saw him go by, smiling, pointing at his vest. He smiled.

Somebody else was planting the last pair of banderillos. Nobody was paying any attention.

Retana's man tucked a baton inside the red cloth of a muleta,[1] folded the cloth

1. muleta: red flag.

over it, and handed it over the barrera to Manuel. He reached in the leather sword-case, took out a sword, and holding it by its leather scabbard, reached it over the fence to Manuel. Manuel pulled the blade out by the red hilt and the scabbard fell limp.

He looked at Zurito. The big man saw he was sweating.

"Now you get him, kid," Zurito said.

Manuel nodded.

"He's in good shape," Zurito said.

"Just like you want him," Retana's man assured him.

Manuel nodded.

The trumpeter, up under the roof, blew for the final act, and Manuel walked across the arena toward where, up in the dark boxes, the president must be.

In the front row seats the substitute bull-fight critic of *El Heraldo* took a long drink of the warm champagne. He had decided it was not worth while to write a running story and would write up the corrida back in the office. What the hell was it anyway? Only a nocturnal. If he missed anything he would get it out of the morning papers. He took another drink of the champagne. He had a date at Maxim's at twelve. Who were these bull-fighters anyway? Kids and bums. A bunch of bums. He put his pad of paper in his pocket and looked over toward Manuel, standing very much alone in the ring, gesturing with his hat in a salute toward a box he could not see high up in the dark plaza. Out in the ring the bull stood quiet, looking at nothing.

"I dedicate this bull to you, Mr. President, and to the public of Madrid, the most intelligent and generous of the world," was what Manuel was saying. It was a formula. He said it all. It was a little long for nocturnal use.

He bowed at the dark, straightened, tossed his hat over his shoulder, and, carrying the muleta in his left hand and the sword in his right, walked out toward the bull.

Manuel walked toward the bull. The bull looked at him; his eyes were quick. Manuel noticed the way the banderillos hung down on his left shoulder and the steady sheen of blood from Zurito's pic-ing. He noticed the way the bull's feet were. As he walked forward, holding the muleta in his left hand and the sword in his right, he watched the bull's feet. The bull could not charge without gathering his feet together. Now he stood square on them, dully.

Manuel walked toward him, watching his feet. This was all right. He could do this. He must work to get the bull's head down, so he could go in past the horns and kill him. He did not think about the sword, not about killing the bull. He thought about one thing at a time. The coming things oppressed him, though. Walking forward, watching the bull's feet, he saw successively his eyes, his wet muzzle, and the wide, forward-pointing spread of his horns. The bull had light circles about his eyes. His eyes watched Manuel. He felt he was going to get this little one with the white face.

Standing still now and spreading the red cloth of the muleta with the sword, pricking the point into the cloth so that the sword, now held in his left hand, spread the red flannel like the jib of a boat, Manuel noticed the points of the bull's horns. One of them was splintered from banging against the barrera. The other was sharp as a porcupine quill. Manuel noticed while spreading the muleta that the white base of the horn was stained red. While he noticed these things he did not lose sight of the bull's feet. The bull watched Manuel steadily.

He's on the defensive now, Manuel thought. He's reserving himself. I've got to bring him out of that and get his head down. Always get his head down. Zurito had his head down once, but he's come back. He'll bleed when I start him going and that will bring it down.

Holding the muleta, with the sword in his left hand widening it in front of him, he called to the bull.

The bull looked at him.

He leaned back insultingly and shook the wide-spread flannel.

The bull saw the muleta. It was a bright scarlet under the arc-light. The bull's legs tightened.

Here he comes. Whoosh! Manuel turned as the bull came and raised the muleta so that it passed over the bull's horns and swept down his broad back from head to tail. The bull had gone clean up in the air with the charge. Manuel had not moved.

At the end of the pass the bull turned like a cat coming around a corner and faced Manuel.

He was on the offensive again. His heaviness was gone. Manuel noted the fresh blood shining down the black shoulder and dripping down the bull's leg. He drew the sword out of the muleta and held it in his right hand. The muleta held low down in his left hand, leaning toward the left, he called to the bull. The bull's legs tightened, his eyes on the muleta. Here he comes, Manuel thought. Yuh!

He swung with the charge, sweeping the muleta ahead of the bull, his feet firm, the sword following the curve, a point of light under the arcs.

The bull recharged as the pase natural finished and Manuel raised the muleta for a pase de pecho. Firmly planted, the bull came by his chest under the raised muleta. Manuel leaned his head back to avoid the clattering banderillo shafts. The hot, black bull body touched his chest as it passed.

Too damn close, Manuel thought. Zurito, leaning on the barrera, spoke rapidly to the gypsy, who trotted out toward Manuel with a cape. Zurito pulled his hat down low and looked out across the arena at Manuel.

Manuel was facing the bull again, the muleta held low and to the left. The bull's head was down as he watched the muleta.

"If it was Belmonte doing that stuff, they'd go crazy," Retana's man said.

Zurito said nothing. He was watching Manuel out in the centre of the arena.

"Where did the boss dig this fellow up?" Retana's man asked.

"Out of the hospital," Zurito said.

"That's where he's going damn quick," Retana's man said.

Zurito turned on him.

"Knock on that," he said, pointing to the barrera.

"I was just kidding, man," Retana's man said.

"Knock on the wood."

Retana's man leaned forward and knocked three times on the barrera.

"Watch the faena," Zurito said.

Out in the centre of the ring, under the lights, Manuel was kneeling, facing the bull, and as he raised the muleta in both hands the bull charged, tail up.

Manuel swung his body clear and, as the bull recharged, brought around the muleta in a half-circle that pulled the bull to his knees.

"Why, that one's a great bull-fighter," Retana's man said.

"No, he's not," said Zurito.

Manuel stood up and, the muleta in his left hand, the sword in his right, acknowledged the applause from the dark plaza.

The bull had humped himself up from his knees and stood waiting, his head hung low.

Zurito spoke to two of the other lads of the cuadrilla and they ran out to stand back of Manuel with their capes. There were four men back of him now. Hernandez had followed him since he first came out with the muleta. Fuentes stood watching, his cape held against his body, tall, in repose, watching lazy-eyed. Now the two came up. Hernandez motioned them to stand one at each side. Manuel stood alone, facing the bull.

Manuel waved back the men with the capes. Stepping back cautiously, they saw his face was white and sweating.

Didn't they know enough to keep back? Did they want to catch the bull's eye with the capes after he was fixed and ready? He had enough to worry about without that kind of thing.

The bull was standing, his four feet square, looking at the muleta. Manuel furled the muleta in his left hand. The bull's eyes watched it. His body was heavy on his feet. He carried his head low, but not too low.

Manuel lifted the muleta at him. The bull did not move. Only his eyes watched.

He's all lead, Manuel thought. He's all square. He's framed right. He'll take it.

He thought in bull-fight terms. Sometimes he had a thought and the particular piece of slang would not come into his mind and he could not realize the thought. His instincts and his knowledge worked automatically, and his brain worked slowly and in words. He knew all about bulls. He did not have to think about them. He just did the right thing. His eyes noted things and his body performed the necessary measures without thought. If he thought about it, he would be gone.

Now, facing the bull, he was conscious of many things at the same time. There were the horns, the one splintered, the other smoothly sharp, the need to profile himself toward the left horn, lance himself short and straight, lower the muleta so the bull would follow it, and, going in over the horns, put the sword all the way into a little spot about as big as a five-peseta piece straight in back of the neck, between the sharp pitch of the bull's shoulders. He must do all this and must then come out from between the horns. He was conscious he must do all this, but his only thought was in words: "Corto y derecho."

"Corto y derecho," he thought, furling the muleta. Short and straight. Corto y derecho, he drew the sword out of the muleta, profiled on the splintered left horn, dropped the muleta across his body, so his right hand with the sword on the level with his eye made the sign of the cross, and, rising on his toes, sighted along the dipping blade of the sword at the spot high up between the bull's shoulders.

Corto y derecho he lanced himself on the bull.

There was a shock, and he felt himself go up in the air. He pushed on the sword as he went up and over, and it flew out of his hand. He hit the ground and the bull was on him. Manuel, lying on the ground, kicked at the bull's muzzle with his slippered feet. Kicking, kicking, the bull after him, missing him in his excitement, bumping him with his head, driving the horns into the sand. Kicking like a man keeping a ball in the air, Manuel kept the bull from getting a clean thrust at him.

Manuel felt the wind on his back from the capes flopping at the bull, and then the bull was gone, gone over him in a rush. Dark, as his belly went over. Not even stepped on.

Manuel stood up and picked up the muleta. Fuentes handed him the sword. It was bent where it had struck the shoulder blade. Manuel straightened it on his knee and ran toward the bull, standing now beside one of the dead horses. As he ran, his jacket flopped where it had been ripped under his armpit.

"Get him out of there," Manuel shouted to the gypsy. The bull had smelled the blood of the dead horse and ripped into the canvas cover with his horns. He charged Fuentes's cape, with the canvas hanging from his splintered horn, and the crowd laughed. Out in the ring, he tossed his head to rid himself of the canvas. Hernandez, running up from behind him, grabbed the end of the canvas and neatly lifted it off the horn.

The bull followed it in a half-charge and stopped still. He was on the defensive again. Manuel was walking toward him with the sword and muleta. Manuel swung the muleta before him. The bull would not charge.

Manuel profiled toward the bull, sighting along the dipping blade of the sword. The bull was motionless, seemingly dead on his feet, incapable of another charge. Manuel rose to his toes, sighting along the steel, and charged.

Again there was the shock and he felt himself being borne back in a rush, to strike hard on the sand. There was no chance of kicking this time. The bull was on top of him. Manuel lay as though dead, his head on his arms, and the bull bumped him. Bumped his back, bumped his face in the sand. He felt the horn go into the sand between his folded arms. The bull hit him in the small of the back. His face drove into the sand. The horn drove through one of his sleeves and the bull ripped it off. Manuel was tossed clear and the bull followed the capes.

Manuel got up, found the sword and muleta, tried the point of the sword with his thumb, and then ran toward the barrera for a new sword.

Retana's man handed him the sword over the edge of the barrera.

"Wipe off your face," he said.

Manuel, running again toward the bull, wiped his bloody face with his handkerchief. He had not seen Zurito. Where was Zurito?

The cuadrilla had stepped away from the bull and waited with their capes. The bull stood, heavy and dull again after the action.

Manuel walked toward him with the muleta. He stopped and shook it. The bull did not respond. He passed it right and left, left and right before the bull's muzzle. The bull's eyes watched it and turned with the swing, but he would not charge. He was waiting for Manuel.

Manuel was worried. There was nothing to do but go in. Corto y derecho. He profiled close to the bull, crossed the muleta in front of his body and charged. As he pushed in the sword, he jerked his body to the left to clear the horn. The bull passed him and the sword shot up in the air, twinkling under the arc-lights, to fall red-hilted on the sand.

Manuel ran over and picked it up. It was bent and he straightened it over his knee.

As he came running toward the bull, fixed again now, he passed Hernandez standing with his cape.

"He's all bone," the boy said encouragingly.

Manuel nodded, wiping his face. He put the bloody handkerchief in his pocket.

There was the bull. He was close to the barrera now. Damn him. Maybe he was all bone. Maybe there was not any place for the sword to go in. The hell there wasn't! He'd show them.

He tried a pass with the muleta and the bull did not move. Manuel chopped the muleta back and forth in front of the bull. Nothing doing.

He furled the muleta, drew the sword out, profiled and drove in on the bull. He felt the sword buckle as he shoved it in, leaning his weight on it, and then it shot high in the air, end-over-ending into the crowd. Manuel had jerked clear as the sword jumped.

The first cushions thrown down out of the dark missed him. Then one hit him in the face, his bloody face looking toward the crowd. They were coming down fast. Spotting the sand. Somebody threw an empty champagne-bottle from close range. It hit Manuel on the foot. He stood there watching the dark, where the things were coming from. Then something whished through the air and struck by him. Manuel leaned over and picked it up. It was his sword. He straightened it over his knee and gestured with it to the crowd.

"Thank you," he said. "Thank you."

Oh, the dirty bastards! Dirty bastards! Oh, the lousy, dirty bastards! He kicked into a cushion as he ran.

There was the bull. The same as ever. All right, you dirty, lousy bastard!

Manuel passed the muleta in front of the bull's black muzzle.

Nothing doing.

You won't! All right. He stepped close and jammed the sharp peak of the muleta into the bull's damp muzzle.

The bull was on him as he jumped back and as he tripped on a cushion he felt the horn go into him, into his side. He grabbed the horn with his two hands and rode backward, holding tight onto the place. The bull tossed him and he was clear. He lay still. It was all right. The bull was gone.

He got up coughing and feeling broken and gone. The dirty bastards!

"Give me the sword," he shouted. "Give me the stuff."

Fuentes came up with the muleta and the sword.

Hernandez put his arm around him.

"Go on to the infirmary, man," he said. "Don't be a damn fool."

"Get away from me," Manuel said. "Get to hell away from me."

He twisted free. Hernandez shrugged his shoulders. Manuel ran toward the bull.

There was the bull standing, heavy, firmly planted.

All right, you bastard! Manuel drew the sword out of the muleta, sighted with the same movement, and flung himself on to the bull. He felt the sword go in all the way. Right up to the guard. Four fingers and his thumb into the bull. The blood was hot on his knuckles, and he was on top of the bull.

The bull lurched with him as he lay on, and seemed to sink; then he was standing clear. He looked at the bull going down slowly over on his side, then suddenly four feet in the air.

Then he gestured at the crowd, his hand warm from the bull blood.

All right, you bastards! He wanted to say something, but he started to cough. It was hot and choking. He looked down for the muleta. He must go over and salute the president. President hell! He was sitting down looking at something. It was the bull. His four feet up. Thick tongue out. Things crawling around on his belly and under his legs. Crawling where the hair was thin. Dead bull. To hell with the bull! To hell with them all! He started to get to his feet and commenced to cough. He sat down again, coughing. Somebody came and pushed him up.

They carried him across the ring to the infirmary, running with him across the sand, standing blocked at the gate as the mules came in, then around under the dark passageway, men grunting as they took him up the stairway, and then laid him down.

The doctor and two men in white were waiting for him. They laid him out on the table. They were cutting away his shirt. Manuel felt tired. His whole chest felt scalding inside. He started to cough and they held something to his mouth. Everybody was very busy.

There was an electric light in his eyes. He shut his eyes.

He heard someone coming very heavily up the stairs. Then he did not hear it. Then he heard a noise far off. That was the crowd. Well, somebody would have to kill his other bull. They had cut away all his shirt. The doctor smiled at him. There was Retana.

"Hello, Retana!" Manuel said. He could not hear his voice.

Retana smiled at him and said something. Manuel could not hear it.

Zurito stood beside the table, bending over where the doctor was working. He was in his picador clothes, without his hat.

Zurito said something to him. Manuel could not hear it.

Zurito was speaking to Retana. One of the men in white smiled and handed Retana a pair of scissors. Retana gave them to Zurito. Zurito said something to Manuel. He could not hear it.

To hell with this operating-table! He'd been on plenty of operating-tables before. He was not going to die. There would be a priest if he was going to die.

Zurito was saying something to him. Holding up the scissors.

That was it. They were going to cut off his coleta. They were going to cut off his pigtail.

Manuel sat up on the operating-table. The doctor stepped back, angry. Someone grabbed him and held him.

"You couldn't do a thing like that, Manos," he said.

He heard suddenly, clearly, Zurito's voice.

"That's all right," Zurito said. "I won't do it. I was joking."

"I was going good," Manuel said. "I didn't have any luck. That was all."

Manuel lay back. They had put something over his face. It was all familiar. He inhaled deeply. He felt very tired. He was very, very tired. They took the thing away from his face.

"I was going good," Manuel said weakly. "I was going great."

Retana looked at Zurito and started for the door.

"I'll stay here with him," Zurito said.

Retana shrugged his shoulders.

Manuel opened his eyes and looked at Zurito.

"Wasn't I going good, Manos?" he asked, for confirmation.

"Sure," said Zurito. "You were going great."

The doctor's assistant put the cone over Manuel's face and he inhaled deeply. Zurito stood awkwardly, watching.

1927

A CLEAN, WELL-LIGHTED PLACE

It was late and every one had left the café except an old man who sat in the shadow the leaves of the tree made against the electric light. In the day time the street was dusty, but at night the dew settled the dust and the old man liked to sit late because he was deaf and now at night it was quiet and he felt the difference. The two waiters inside the café knew that the old man was a little drunk, and while he was a good client they knew that if he became too drunk he would leave without paying, so they kept watch on him.

"Last week he tried to commit suicide," one waiter said.

"Why?"

"He was in despair."

"What about?"

"Nothing."

"How do you know it was nothing?"

"He has plenty of money."

They sat together at a table that was close against the wall near the door of the café and looked at the terrace where the tables were all empty except where the old man sat in the shadow of the leaves of the tree that moved slightly in the wind. A girl and a soldier went by in the street. The street light shone on the brass number on his collar. The girl wore no head covering and hurried beside him.

"The guard will pick him up," one waiter said.

"What does it matter if he gets what he's after?"

"He had better get off the street now. The guard will get him. They went by five minutes ago."

The old man sitting in the shadow rapped on his saucer with his glass. The younger waiter went over to him.

"What do you want?"

The old man looked at him. "Another brandy," he said.

"You'll be drunk," the waiter said. The old man looked at him. The waiter went away.

"He'll stay all night," he said to his colleague. "I'm sleepy now. I never get into bed before three o'clock. He should have killed himself last week."

The waiter took the brandy bottle and another saucer from the counter inside the café and marched out to the old man's table. He put down the saucer and poured the glass full of brandy.

"You should have killed yourself last week," he said to the deaf man. The old man motioned with his finger. "A little more," he said. The waiter poured on into the glass so that the brandy slopped over and ran down the stem into the top saucer of the pile. "Thank you," the old man said. The waiter took the bottle back inside the café. He sat down at the table with his colleague again.

"He's drunk now," he said.

"He's drunk every night."

"What did he want to kill himself for?"

"How should I know."

"How did he do it?"

"He hung himself with a rope."

"Who cut him down?"

"His niece."

"Why did they do it?"

"Fear for his soul."

"How much money has he got?"

"He's got plenty."

"He must be eighty years old."

"Anyway I should say he was eighty."

"I wish he would go home. I never get to bed before three o'clock. What kind of hour is that to go to bed?"

"He stays up because he likes it."

"He's lonely. I'm not lonely. I have a wife waiting in bed for me."

"He had a wife once too."

"A wife would be no good to him now."

"You can't tell. He might be better with a wife."

"His niece looks after him."

"I know. You said she cut him down."

"I wouldn't want to be that old. An old man is a nasty thing."

"Not always. This old man is clean. He drinks without spilling. Even now, drunk. Look at him."

"I don't want to look at him. I wish he would go home. He has no regard for those who must work."

The old man looked from his glass across the square, then over at the waiters.

"Another brandy," he said, pointing to his glass. The waiter who was in a hurry came over.

"Finished," he said, speaking with that omission of syntax stupid people employ when talking to drunken people or foreigners. "No more tonight. Close now."

"Another," said the old man.

"No. Finished." The waiter wiped the edge of the table with a towel and shook his head.

The old man stood up, slowly counted the saucers, took a leather coin purse from his pocket and paid for the drinks, leaving half a peseta tip.

The waiter watched him go down the street, a very old man walking unsteadily but with dignity.

"Why didn't you let him stay and drink?" the unhurried waiter asked. They were putting up the shutters. "It is not half-past two."

"I want to go home to bed."

"What is an hour?"

"More to me than to him."

"An hour is the same."

"You talk like an old man yourself. He can buy a bottle and drink at home."

"It's not the same."

"No, it is not," agreed the waiter with a wife. He did not wish to be unjust. He was only in a hurry.

"And you? You have no fear of going home before your usual hour?"

"Are you trying to insult me?"

"No, hombre, only to make a joke."

"No," the waiter who was in a hurry said, rising from pulling down the metal shutters. "I have confidence. I am all confidence."

"You have youth, confidence, and a job," the older waiter said. "You have everything."

"And what do you lack?"

"Everything but work."

"You have everything I have."

"No. I have never had confidence and I am not young."

"Come on. Stop talking nonsense and lock up."

"I am of those who like to stay late at the café," the older waiter said. "With all those who do not want to go to bed. With all those who need a light for the night."

"I want to go home and into bed."

"We are of two different kinds," the older waiter said. He was now dressed to go home. "It is not only a question of youth and confidence although those things are very beautiful. Each night I am reluctant to close up because there may be some one who needs the café."

"Hombre, there are bodegas open all night long."

"You do not understand. This is a clean and pleasant café. It is well lighted. The light is very good and also, now, there are shadows of the leaves."

"Good night," said the younger waiter.

"Good night," the other said. Turning off the electric light he continued the conversation with himself. It is the light of course but it is necessary that the place be clean and pleasant. You do not want music. Certainly you do not want music. Nor can you stand before a bar with dignity although that is all that is provided for these hours. What did he fear? It was not fear or dread. It was a nothing that he knew too well. It was all a nothing and a man was nothing too. It was only that and light was all it needed and a certain cleanness and order. Some lived in it and never felt it but he knew it all was nada y pues nada[1] y nada y pues nada. Our nada who art in nada, nada be thy name thy kingdom nada thy will be nada in nada as it is in nada. Give us this nada our daily nada and nada us our nada as we nada our nadas and nada us not into nada but deliver us from nada; pues nada. Hail nothing full of nothing, nothing is with thee. He smiled and stood before a bar with a shining steam pressure coffee machine.

"What's yours?" asked the barman.

"Nada."

"Otro loco mas," said the barman and turned away.

1. **nada y pues nada:** nothing and after that nothing.

"A little cup," said the waiter.

The barman poured it for him.

"The light is very bright and pleasant but the bar is unpolished," the waiter said.

The barman looked at him but did not answer. It was too late at night for conversation.

"You want another copita?" the barman asked.

"No, thank you," said the waiter and went out. He disliked bars and bodegas. A clean, well-lighted café was a very different thing. Now, without thinking further, he would go home to his room. He would lie in the bed and finally, with daylight, he would go to sleep. After all, he said to himself, it is probably only insomnia. Many must have it.

1938

WILLIAM FAULKNER ■■■■■■■■■■■■■■■

THE BEAR

MID-CENTURY RECOGNITION

The award of the Nobel Prize to William Faulkner in 1950 dramatized his importance. It was an importance incompletely recognized hitherto by many readers, and the Nobel award served the useful purpose of sending them back to his works. No other contemporary novelist, consequently, has been so extensively and conscientiously *re*read in recent times as Faulkner. One result of this re-examination has been the enormous enhancement of his fame: he is seen more and more clearly as one of the great fiction writers in English in the twentieth century. If it is asked, Wherefore great? one can name categorically several marks of greatness present in Faulkner: a significant fable or myth (the fictional world that he has constructed), an idiomatic language that is original and eloquent, and a moral significance of cosmic proportions.

His remarks delivered in Stockholm upon receiving the Nobel Prize contributed much toward a new and more intelligent attitude toward the man and his work. In this memorable little speech (which is extraordinarily suggestive of Nathaniel Hawthorne), Faulkner said that "the problems of the human heart in conflict with itself . . . alone can make good writing because only that is worth writing about, worth the agony and the sweat." A writer, he said, should have "no room in his workshop for anything but the old verities and truths of the heart, the old universal truths, lacking which any story is ephemeral and doomed—love and honor and pity and pride and compassion and sacrifice." He refused "to accept the end of man." Man, he declared, is "immortal . . . because he has a soul, a spirit capable of compassion and sacrifice and endurance"; the writer's great function is to "help man endure by lifting up his heart"; the writer's works should be "not merely the record of man" but "one of the props, the pillars, to help him endure and prevail." Prompted by these words, readers of Faulkner remembered examples in his stories of remarkable human endurance and fidelity to principle. The determination of

Anse Bundren, in *As I Lay Dying*, to bury his wife in Jefferson in accordance with his promise to her; the persistent and finally successful endeavor of the nameless convict in *The Wild Palms* to return the boat and his female passenger to their rightful destination through the raging flood-waters of the Mississippi; the steady strength of Dilsey, the old Negress in *The Sound and the Fury*, who stands with heroic firmness amidst the wreckage of the Compson family—these are only three examples among the many in Faulkner's fiction of the moral ideas set forth in the Stockholm speech. Examples like these indeed show how a writer's work can help man endure and prevail.

THE SOUTH AND THE WORLD

Faulkner has absorbed the South more completely perhaps than any other Southern writer. All of his important fiction deals with the South and reflects a deep love of his native region as well as a criticism of certain aspects of its history and culture. It is significant that he has remained in the South in a century when so many important writers have preferred a migratory existence; his roots are in the South in very much the same way that Hawthorne's were in New England. Faulkner's statement (quoted in the newspapers) that he would give the Nobel Prize money to the public schools of Oxford, Mississippi (his place of residence), for the purchase of some much-needed educational equipment had an old-fashioned ring: it seemed to hark back to an earlier era in our history when (as in the ante-bellum South) local responsibilities were locally assumed.

Faulkner's South is a mythical community known in his stories as "Yoknapatawpha County." It is situated in northern Mississippi and populated with a rich assortment of Southern types. The Sartoris family represent the true aristocracy, with whom the author is mainly in sympathy. The Snopeses, whom the author dislikes, stand for the unscrupulous commercialism of modern times. The Sartorises were men of honor, though it was an honor that eventually became formalized —possibly too formalized—in a code. The Snopeses are men of low cunning, successful go-getters whose corrupting influence has been pervasive. Most of Faulkner's characters can be classified as either "Sartoris" or "Snopes," according to their quality and attitude, even though there may be no family connection. The character in Faulkner who remarked that "General Johnston or General Forrest wouldn't have took a Snopes into his army at all," was probably taking too romantic a view of the Southern military, but Faulkner clearly—and perhaps rightly—feels that the trend in the modern South has been away from the honor of the Sartorises and toward the cunning and go-gettism of the Snopeses. One of the most powerful chapters in all Faulkner is the section in *The Sound and the Fury* where Jason Compson is frantically and unsuccessfully playing the

New York stock market. The author intends to show here the corruption of the best Southern tradition by modern commercialism. He intends to suggest, no doubt, that the North is the chief source of these corrupting influences and that the Northern victory in the Civil War made this corruption inevitable. Jason's talk with the riffraff of the town, whom he now so closely resembles, shows how depraved his condition has become:

> . . . you can just bet I shut them up too. I says my people owned slaves here when you all were running little shirt tail country stores and farming land no nigger would look at on shares.

The Civil War to Faulkner is the chief event in Southern history. His characters allude to the war and relive it. His panorama of Southern history is long and impressive. It begins with the early settlements in the old Southwest (of which Mississippi was a part) about 1800 and continues beyond the Second World War, but the grand event of this cycle is the War of Secession. An incident in the story "Shall Not Perish" is symbolic of the author's view of Southern history: "Grandpap" wakes up in the picture show just as horses on the screen are careering toward the spectators; whereupon he rushes madly out of the building shouting "Forrest! Forrest! Here he comes! Get out of the way!" While he is being gradually pacified by a bottle of beer, "Mother" (the narrator is a nine-year-old boy) explains and justifies Grandpap's behavior by saying, "He wasn't running from anybody! He was running in front of them, hollering at all clods to look out because better men than they were coming, even seventy-five years afterwards, still powerful, still dangerous, still coming!" To Faulkner as to Grandpap, the Civil War heroes are heroes still, in comparison with whom too many of today's men are mere clods. Salvation can be found only in a rebirth of the older heroism. (If it is urged that the older heroism never really existed, Faulkner would perhaps reply that we must nevertheless believe that it did and that it is capable of being reborn; perhaps he would add that if it never existed, we should—to save ourselves—be under the necessity of inventing it.)

Faulkner writes about the South, and his works have value as a historical and social record. But like other great writers, he transcends his region. In his pages the South becomes a microcosm of the world, for the central conflict in Faulkner's South is not peculiar to that region but is essentially world-wide. One of his best critics has put the matter as follows:

> The Sartorises act traditionally; that is to say, they act always with an ethically responsible will. They represent vital morality, humanism. Being anti-traditional, the Snopeses are immoral from the Sartoris point-of-view. But the Snopeses do not recognize this point-of-view; acting only for self-interest, they

acknowledge no ethical duty. Really, then, they are a-moral; they represent naturalism or animalism. And the Sartoris-Snopes conflict is fundamentally a struggle between humanism and naturalism.[1]

The more one ponders this statement, the more clearly one is likely to see its application beyond the confines of the South. Viewed in this light, the fiction of Faulkner ceases to be sociology primarily and becomes an allegory of man.

The violence in Faulkner's stories can be taken both as social record and as symbol. One of the most interesting examples is *Sanctuary*, the most violent of his fictions and a work in which readers were slow to see more than a surface sensationalism. They were not helped by the author's perverse and perhaps intentionally misleading comment that *Sanctuary* was "a cheap idea . . . deliberately conceived to make money." In today's perspective (it is now more than twenty years since the book first appeared) the story can be read as a criticism of the mechanization of the South and of modern mechanical civilization wherever found. Malcolm Cowley has pointed out that Popeye, the chief symbolical character,

is always described in mechanical terms: his eyes "looked like rubber knobs"; . . . his tight suit and stiff hat were "all angles, like a modernistic lampshade"; and in general he had "that vicious depthless quality of stamped tin."[2]

Sanctuary, Cowley adds, is not "a mere accumulation of pointless horrors," as many readers once supposed. In this new reading, Popeye becomes a horrible symbol of the spiritual impotence of the Machine Age. Indeed, Faulkner's work as a whole is a trenchant and often violent criticism of the shortcomings of the modern world.

''THE BEAR''

Students of Faulkner have unanimously regarded "The Bear" as one of the best of his fictions. A long story of about fifty thousand words, it has certain advantages over both the short stories and the novels of the author: by its greater mass it produces a more appreciable effect than the former, and being of a more manageable size than the longer works, it has a tighter structure than most of Faulkner's novels. At the same time, it has the scope, the eloquence, and the overtones that are characteristic of the author's best work.

Isaac McCaslin, the chief character of the story, was born in 1867; the climactic event of the action, the killing of Old Ben, the bear, occurs in 1883, when Ike is sixteen. Parts 1, 2, and 3 tell an exciting

1. George Marion O'Donnell, "Faulkner's Mythology," *Kenyon Review*, Summer 1939, p. 286.
2. *The Portable Faulkner*, 1946.

story of the bear hunt, and Part 3 concludes with the deaths of the bear, the dog Lion (the bear's chief antagonist), and old Sam Fathers, the presiding genius of the hunt. Part 5 tells of young McCaslin's last visit to the woods about two years later; the woods are now "doomed," because their owner, Major de Spain, has leased them (excepting the burial site of Fathers and Lion) to a lumber company, and a planing mill has already been set up on the edge of the forest. Parts 1, 2, 3, and 5, then, tell a continuous and unified story.

The narration is managed from the point of view of Ike. (It would be interesting and curious to consider the large number of Faulkner's actions that are seen through the eyes of young boys and the possible reasons why this should be a favorite device of the author.) The narration, however, is not confined with strict realism to his perceptions and language. Here, as in other works, Faulkner gives an interpretation rather than a literal transcription of the boy's thoughts; the language, moreover, is for the most part the author's instead of the boy's. Such a method retains the advantages of the restricted point of view without sacrificing the "Faulknerian" scope and richness.

Faulkner glorifies the old hunters. Their talk was "the best of all talking." Sam Fathers, the son of a Negro slave and a Chickasaw chief, was the boy's principal mentor, though he learned, too, from Boon Hogganbeck (who was also part Indian), from the gentry— Major de Spain, General Compson, and cousin McCaslin—from Ash, the Negro cook, and even from Tennie's Jim. The animals, also, were his instructors: the lesser ones as well as Old Ben and Lion. In such a school the boy learned humility and patience and the conquest of fear, for Fathers told the boy, "Be scared. You can't help that. But don't be afraid. Ain't nothing in the woods going to hurt you if you don't corner it, or it don't smell that you are afraid." The crowning spiritual grace was a kind of surrender to the woods, which was achieved when the boy entered them alone and without gun, watch, or compass.

The hunting world of Parts 1–3 is a world of noble qualities. It is also a stable, traditional world. The men observe a long-established ritual. It is a society where every man has his place and knows it, where rank is respected, and where rank is likely to have a solid basis in merit: Boon's station, for example, is shown to be rightfully inferior to Sam Fathers', though Sam is part Negro. The boy's attitude toward this society of hunters is one of admiration and respect, and he feels great pride in their recognition of his worthiness. Hunting and other comparable forms of outdoor life were important elements in the older Southern tradition. The author seems to regard these things as wholesome and even heroic. We are to regard the inroads of the lumber industry, viewed sadly at the end of the story by Ike McCaslin, as marking a downward step in the South's culture.[3]

3. There are no "Snopes" characters (that is, antitraditional, naturalistic characters) in "The Bear." The planing mill, though, may symbolize the Snopes idea, and Major de Spain's sale of the timber rights to the lumber company presumably shows a degree of corruption in that strongly traditional figure.

Part 4, which is nearly as long as the other parts put together, is separate from them: it is concerned with the history of the McCaslin family from the time of Carothers McCaslin, Ike's grandfather, down to Ike's reaching the age of twenty-one (some five years after the hunting action) and perhaps somewhat beyond. The history is found chiefly in the old ledgers, which record

the whole plantation in its mazed and intricate entirety—the land, the fields, and what they represented in terms of cotton ginned and sold, the men and women whom they fed and clothed and even paid a little cash money at Christmas-time in return for the labor which planted and raised and picked and ginned the cotton, the machinery and mules and gear with which they raised it and their cost and upkeep and replacement —that whole edifice intricate and complex and founded upon injustice . . . yet solvent and efficient and . . . not only still intact but enlarged. . . .

The ledgers contain, also, and often by inference, more personal and intimate information about the McCaslins. Young Ike pores over these old records. They become almost an obsession, and the fourth part consists largely of his ruminations (aided somewhat by his cousin McCaslin) upon them and what they suggest.

The view of the Old South here presented seems ambivalent. A romantic view of the Confederacy is suggested, for example, in the following speech by Ike:

"Who else could have declared a war against a power with ten times the area and a hundred times the men and a thousand times the resources, except men who could believe that all necessary to conduct a successful war was not acumen nor shrewdness nor politics nor diplomacy nor money nor even integrity and simple arithmetic, but just love of land and courage?"

One must suppose that the young man feels this strongly, and that the author does too, despite cousin McCaslin's mock-heroic reply: "And an unblemished and gallant ancestry and the ability to ride a horse. . . . Don't leave that out." The South, moreover, was especially favored by the Creator, as shown in the following affectionate description:

". . . this land this South for which He had done so much with woods for game and streams for fish and deep rich soil for seed and lush springs to sprout it and long summers to mature it and serene falls to harvest it and short mild winters for men and animals. . . ."

Blessed with the bounties of nature and a heroic breed of men, the South would seem indeed fortunate among nations. (This more favorable aspect agrees in the main with the impression made by the hunting story.) But the South, being a part of mankind, illustrates the fall of man, a fall that is perhaps all the greater and more tragic because of the South's richer endowments. (Faulkner likes to intensify the high tragedy in his treatment of the South.) The plantation economy, as we have seen, was "founded upon injustice," the injustice, chiefly, of Negro slavery. "This whole land, the whole South," Ike McCaslin cries out (and the author cries out with him), "is cursed, and all of us who derive from it, whom it ever suckled, white and black both, lie under the curse." Evidence of the curse of slavery is plentiful among the family records presented in Part 4. Bedford Forrest, according to the records, had been a crooked slave dealer before he became a great general, and in one sale had cheated Ike's father. Ike's grandfather, when an old man, had a son by an unmarried slave girl and made the unjust and ironical provision in his will that the boy should receive one thousand dollars upon coming of age, thereby himself avoiding payment, and probably acknowledgment as well, and placing the obligation, where it obviously did not belong, upon his legitimate sons. Hubert Fitz-Hubert Beauchamp, Ike's uncle on his mother's side, was an aristocratic ne'er-do-well—a condition and type doubtless fostered by the institution of slavery—who gave his young nephew a handsome gift in pieces of gold and then proceeded to "borrow" piece by piece until, upon the boy's majority, there remained only "I.O.U.'s." These and other instances of moral decay revealed in the family annals support Isaac McCaslin's conviction that the land itself had been cursed by slavery. At the end of Part 4, Ike has renounced his landed inheritance and his marriage also (his wife having insisted upon the retention of the land) and is following the trade of a carpenter, "because if the Nazarene had found carpentering good for the life and ends He had assumed and elected to serve, it would be all right too for Isaac McCaslin. . . ."

The relation between Part 4 and the rest of "The Bear" poses an interesting question of structure. The two portions differ intrinsically: Parts 1, 2, 3, and 5 are story, which builds up to a magnificent climax in Part 3 and levels off in the nostalgic epilogue of Part 5; Part 4 is history, presented without the contrivance of plot. The hunting story is predominantly in the heroic or romantic vein; the family history seems in comparison realistic and factual. A line of connection and influence from one portion to the other is suggested in the statement (in Part 4) by Isaac McCaslin, who is about to give up the land, "Yes. Sam Fathers set me free." The meaning would seem to be, "free from material greed."

Possibly the only flaw in Faulkner's structure is that the secondary, enclosed portion (or "enclave," as it has been called) carries the protagonist to a point beyond that reached in the final section of the "story," to a point that the "story" even in its final phase—which comes after the enclave—scarcely seems to envisage. But regardless of whether this be a flaw, the two portions of "The Bear" supplement each other effectively, each being a commentary on the other. Here, as in most of his work, Faulkner is aiming at a truth too large to be encompassed by a single, simple narrative. The truth about the South is both sordid and heroic, and—by extension—the truth about the world. In the larger sense, "The Bear" is about the world, for the sin of slavery exists wherever man has suffered the abridgment of his freedom by whatever tyranny, and conversely, the humility, courage, and freedom learned by the boy in the company of the hunters are virtues in any time and place.

Faulkner is great both for his "content" and his "style." The two things are really inseparable, since one cannot exist without the other. The scope and richness of the content are made possible by the fluid, symbolical style. Faulkner has freed himself from the trammels of the conventional sentence, and by so doing has achieved a rapid, flexible prose that can render experience with a larger fidelity.

Symbolical interpretations may well be left to the individual reader, with perhaps the suggestion only that the symbolism in "The Bear" seems to have a religious connotation. With its ceremonials, its disciplines, its sudden revelations, and its heroic and perhaps atoning deaths, the hunting of the bear takes on the aspects of a religious quest. Old Ben, Lion, and Sam Fathers (all "taintless and incorrupt-ible") are a kind of sacred trinity, whose virtues become godlike and immortal.

LIFE AND WORKS

William Faulkner was born in Ripley, Mississippi, in 1897 and was educated at the University of Mississippi. During World War I he was a lieutenant with the Canadian Flying Corps; after the war he worked for a while on a newspaper in New Orleans. Subsequently he made his permanent residence in Oxford, Mississippi. His more important novels are *The Sound and the Fury* (1929), *As I Lay Dying* (1930), *Light in August* (1932), *Absalom, Absalom!* (1936), *The Wild Palms* (1939), and *Intruder in the Dust* (1948). The more important collections of shorter fictions are: *These 13* (1931), *The Unvanquished* (1938), and *Go Down, Moses*, which includes "The Bear" (1942). He was awarded the Nobel Prize for literature in 1950.

Among the more important critical commentaries are: G. M. O'Donnell, "Faulkner's Mythology," *Kenyon Review* (Summer 1939), I, 288–299; Malcolm Cowley, "William Faulkner's Legend of the South," *Sewanee Review* (Summer 1945), LIII, 343–361; Ward L. Miner, *The World of William Faulkner* (1952); and Irving Howe, *William Faulkner: a Critical Study* (1952).

THE BEAR

PART 1

There was a man and a dog too this time. Two beasts, counting Old Ben, the bear, and two men, counting Boon Hogganbeck, in whom some of the same blood ran which ran in Sam Fathers, even though Boon's was a plebeian strain of it and only Sam and Old Ben and the mongrel Lion were taintless and incorruptible.

Isaac McCaslin was sixteen. For six years now he had been a man's hunter. For six years now he had heard the best of all talking. It was of the wilderness, the big woods, bigger and older than any recorded document—of white man fatuous enough to believe he had bought any fragment of it, of Indian ruthless enough to pretend that any fragment of it had been his to convey; bigger than Major de Spain and the scrap he pretended to, knowing better; older than old Thomas Sutpen of whom Major de Spain had had it and who knew better; older even than old Ikkemotubbe, the Chickasaw chief, of whom old Sutpen had had it and who knew better in his turn. It was of the men, not white nor black nor red, but men, hunters, with the will and hardihood to endure and the humility and skill to survive, and the dogs and the bear and deer juxtaposed and reliefed against it, ordered and compelled by and within the wilderness in the ancient and unremitting contest according to the ancient and immitigable rules which voided all regrets and brooked no quarter;—the best game of all, the best of all breathing and forever the best of all listening, the voices quiet and weighty and deliberate for retrospection and recollection and exactitude among the concrete trophies—the racked guns and the heads and skins—in the libraries of town houses or the offices of plantation houses or (and best of all) in the camps themselves where the intact and still-warm meat yet hung, the men who had slain it sitting before the burning logs on hearths, when there were houses and hearths, or about the smoky blazing of piled wood in front of stretched tarpaulins when there were not. There was always a bottle present, so that it would seem to him that those fine fierce instants of heart and brain and courage and wiliness and speed were concentrated and distilled into that brown liquor which not women, not boys and children, but only hunters drank, drinking not of the blood they spilled but some condensation of the wild immortal spirit, drinking it moderately, humbly even, not with the pagan's base and baseless hope of acquiring thereby the virtues of cunning and strength and speed but in salute to them. Thus it seemed to him on this December morning not only natural but actually fitting that this should have begun with whiskey.

He realized later that it had begun long before that. It had already begun on that day when he first wrote his age in two ciphers and his cousin McCaslin brought him for the first time to the camp, the big woods, to earn for himself from the wilderness the name and state of hunter provided he in his turn were humble and enduring enough. He had already inherited then, without ever having seen it, the big old bear with one trap-ruined foot that in an area almost a hundred miles square had earned for himself a name, a definite designation like a living man:—the long legend of corn-cribs broken down and rifled, of shoats and grown pigs and even calves carried bodily into the woods and devoured, and traps and deadfalls overthrown and dogs mangled and slain, and shotgun and even rifle shots delivered at point-blank range yet with no more effect than so many peas blown through a tube by a child—a corridor of wreckage and destruction beginning back before the boy was born, through which sped, not fast but rather with the ruthless and irresistible deliberation of a locomotive, the shaggy tremendous shape. It ran in his knowledge before he ever saw it. It loomed and towered in his dreams before he even saw the unaxed woods where it left its crooked print, shaggy, tremendous, red-eyed, not malevolent but just big, too big for the dogs which tried to bay it, for the horses which tried to ride it down, for the men and the bullets they fired into it; too big for the very country which was its constricting scope. It was as if the boy had already divined what his senses and intellect had not encompassed yet: that doomed wilderness whose edges were being constantly and punily gnawed at by men with plows and axes who feared it because it was wilderness, men myriad and nameless even to one another in the land where the old bear had earned a name, and through which ran not even a mortal beast but an anachronism indomitable and invincible out of an old, dead time, a phantom, epitome and apotheosis of the old, wild life which the little puny humans swarmed and hacked at in a fury of abhorrence and fear, like pygmies about the ankles of a drowsing elephant;—the old bear, solitary, indomitable, and alone; widowered, childless, and absolved of mortality—old Priam reft of his old wife and outlived all his sons.

Still a child, with three years, then two years, then one year yet before he too could make one of them, each November he would watch the wagon containing the dogs and the bedding and food and guns and his cousin McCaslin and Tennie's Jim and Sam Fathers too, until Sam moved to the camp to live, depart for the Big Bottom, the big woods. To him, they were going not to hunt bear and deer but to keep yearly rendezvous with the bear which they did not even intend to kill. Two weeks later they would return, with no trophy, no skin. He had not expected it. He had not even feared that it might be in the wagon this time with the other skins and heads. He did not even tell himself that in three years or two years or one year more he would be present and that it might even be his gun. He believed that only after he had served his apprenticeship in the woods which would prove him worthy to be a hunter, would he even be permitted to distinguish the crooked print, and that even then for two November weeks he would merely make another minor one, along with his cousin and Major de Spain and General Compson and Walter Ewell and Boon and the dogs which feared to bay it, and the shotguns and rifles which failed even to bleed it, in the yearly pageant-rite of the old bear's furious immortality.

His day came at last. In the surrey with his cousin and Major de Spain and General Compson he saw the wilderness through a slow drizzle of November rain just above the ice point, as it seemed to him later he always saw it or at least always remembered it—the tall and endless wall of dense November woods under the dissolving afternoon and the year's death, sombre, impenetrable (he could not even discern yet how, at what point they could possibly hope to enter it even though he knew that Sam Fathers was waiting there with the wagon), the surrey moving through the skeleton stalks of cotton and corn in the last of open country, the last trace of man's puny gnawing at the immemorial flank, until, dwarfed by that perspective into an almost ridiculous diminishment, the surrey itself seemed to have ceased to move (this too to be completed later, years later, after he had grown to a man and had seen the sea) as a solitary small boat hangs in lonely immobility, merely tossing up and down, in the infinite waste of the ocean, while the water and then the apparently impenetrable land which it nears without appreciable progress, swings slowly and opens the widening inlet which is the anchorage. He entered it. Sam was waiting, wrapped in a quilt on the wagon seat behind the patient and steaming mules. He entered his novitiate to the true wilderness with Sam beside him as he had begun his apprenticeship in miniature to manhood after the rabbits and such with Sam beside him, the two of them wrapped in the damp, warm, Negro-rank quilt, while the wilderness closed behind his entrance as it had opened momentarily to accept him, opening before his advancement as it closed behind his progress, no fixed path the wagon followed but a channel nonexistent ten yards ahead of it and ceasing to exist ten yards after it had passed, the wagon progressing not by its own volition but by attrition of their intact yet fluid circumambience, drowsing, earless, almost lightless.

It seemed to him that at the age of ten he was witnessing his own birth. It was not even strange to him. He had experienced it all before, and not merely in dreams. He saw the camp—a paintless six-room bungalow set on piles above the spring high-water—and he knew already how it was going to look. He helped in the rapid orderly disorder of their establishment in it, and even his motions were familiar to him, foreknown. Then for two weeks he ate the coarse, rapid food— the shapeless sour bread, the wild strange meat, venison and bear and turkey and coon which he had never tasted before—which men ate, cooked by men who were hunters first and cooks afterward; he slept in harsh sheetless blankets as hunters slept. Each morning the gray of dawn found him and Sam Fathers on the stand, the crossing, which had been allotted him. It was the poorest one, the most barren. He had expected that; he had not dared yet to hope even to himself that he would even hear the running dogs this first time. But he did hear them. It was on the third morning—a murmur, sourceless, almost indistinguishable, yet he knew what it was although he had never before heard that many dogs running at once, the murmur swelling into separate and distinct voices until he could call the five dogs which his cousin owned from among the others. "Now," Sam said, "slant your gun up a little and draw back the hammers and then stand still."

But it was not for him, not yet. The humility was there; he had learned that. And he could learn the patience. He was only ten, only one week. The instant had passed. It seemed to him that he could actually see the deer, the buck, smoke-colored, elongated with speed, vanished, the woods, the gray solitude still ringing even when the voices of the dogs had died away; from far away across the sombre woods and the gray half-liquid morning there came two shots. "Now let your hammers down," Sam said.

He did so. "You knew it too," he said.

"Yes," Sam said. "I want you to learn how to do when you didn't shoot. It's after the chance for the bear or the deer has done already come and gone that men and dogs get killed."

"Anyway, it wasn't him," the boy said. "It wasn't even a bear. It was just a deer."

"Yes," Sam said, "it was just a deer."

Then one morning, it was in the second week, he heard the dogs again. This time before Sam even spoke he readied the too-long, too-heavy, man-size gun as Sam had taught him, even though this time he knew the dogs and the deer were coming less close than ever, hardly within hearing even. They didn't sound like any running dogs he had ever heard before even. Then he found that Sam, who had taught him first of all to cock the gun and take position where he could see best in all directions and then never to move again, had himself moved up beside him. "There," he said. "Listen." The boy listened, to no ringing chorus strong and fast on a free scent but, a moiling yapping an octave too high and with something more than indecision and even abjectness in it which he could not yet recognize, reluctant, not even moving very fast, taking a long time to pass out of hearing, leaving even then in the air that echo of thin and almost human hysteria, abject, almost humanly grieving, with this time nothing ahead of it, no sense of a fleeing unseen smoke-colored shape. He could hear Sam breathing at his shoulder. He saw the arched curve of the old man's inhaling nostrils.

"It's Old Ben!" he cried, whispering.

Sam didn't move save for the slow gradual turning of his head as the voices faded on and the faint steady rapid arch and collapse of his nostrils. "Hah," he said. "Not even running. Walking."

"But up here!" the boy cried. "Way up here!"

"He do it every year," Sam said. "Once. Ash and Boon say he comes up here to run the other little bears away. Tell them to get to hell out of here and stay out until the hunters are gone. Maybe." The boy no longer heard anything at all, yet still Sam's head continued to turn gradually and steadily until the back of it was toward him. Then it turned back and looked down at him—the same face, grave, familiar, expressionless until it smiled, the same old man's eyes from which as he watched there faded slowly a quality darkly and fiercely lambent, passionate and proud. "He don't care no more for bears than he does for dogs or men neither. He come to see who's here, who's new in camp this year, whether he can shoot or not, can stay or not. Whether we got the dog yet that can bay and hold him until a man gets there with a gun. Because he's the head bear. He's the man." It faded, was gone; again they were the eyes as he had known them all his life. "He'll let them follow him to the river. Then he'll send them home. We might as well go too; see how they look when they get back to camp."

The dogs were there first, ten of them huddled back under the kitchen, himself and Sam squatting to peer back into the obscurity where they crouched, quiet, the eyes rolling and luminous, vanishing, and no sound, only that effluvium which the boy could not quite place yet, of something more than dog, stronger than dog and not just animal, just beast even. Because there had been nothing in front of the abject and painful yapping except the solitude, the wilderness, so that when the eleventh hound got back about mid-afternoon and he and Tennie's Jim held the passive and still trembling bitch while Sam daubed her tattered ear and raked shoulder with turpentine and axle-grease, it was still no living creature but only the wilderness which, leaning for a moment, had patted lightly once her temerity. "Just like a man," Sam said. "Just like folks. Put off as long as she could having to be brave, knowing all the time that sooner or later she would have to be brave once so she could keep on calling herself a dog, and knowing before-hand what was going to happen when she done it."

He did not know just when Sam left. He only knew that he was gone. For the next three mornings he rose and ate breakfast and Sam was not waiting for him. He went to his stand alone; he found it without help now and stood on it as Sam had taught him. On the third morning he heard the dogs again, running strong and free on a true scent again, and he readied the gun as he had learned to do and heard the hunt sweep past on since he was not ready yet, had not deserved other yet in just one short period of two weeks as compared to all the long life which he had already dedicated to the wilderness with patience and humility; he heard the shot again, one shot, the single clapping report of Walter Ewell's rifle. By now he could not only find his stand and then return to camp without guid-ance, by using the compass his cousin had given him he reached Walter, waiting beside the buck and the moiling of dogs over the cast entrails, before any of the others except Major de Spain and Tennie's Jim on the horses, even before Uncle Ash arrived with the one-eyed wagon-mule which did not mind the smell of blood or even, so they said, of bear.

It was not Uncle Ash on the mule. It was Sam, returned. And Sam was waiting when he finished his dinner and, himself on the one-eyed mule and Sam on the other one of the wagon team, they rode for more than three hours through the rapid shortening sunless afternoon, following no path, no trail even that he could discern, into a section of country he had never seen before. Then he understood why Sam had made him ride the one-eyed mule which would not spook at the smell of blood, of wild animals. The other one, the sound one, stopped short and tried to whirl and bolt even as Sam got down, jerking and wrenching at the rein while Sam held it, coaxing it forward with his voice since he did not dare risk hitching it, drawing it forward while the boy dismounted from the marred one which would stand. Then, standing beside Sam in the thick great gloom of an-cient woods and the winter's dying afternoon, he looked quietly down at the rot-ted log scored and gutted with claw-marks and, in the wet earth beside it, the print of the enormous warped two-toed foot. Now he knew what he had heard in the hounds' voices in the woods that morning and what he had smelled when he peered under the kitchen where they huddled. It was in him too, a little different because they were brute beasts and he was not, but only a little different—an eagerness, passive; an abjectness, a sense of his own fragility and impotence against the timeless woods, yet without doubt or dread; a flavor like brass in the sudden run of saliva in his mouth, a hard sharp constriction either in his brain or his stomach, he could not tell which and it did not matter; he knew only that for the first time he realized that the bear which had run in his listening and loomed in his dreams since before he could remember and which therefore must have existed in the listening and the dreams of his cousin and Major de Spain and even old General Compson before they began to remember in their turn, was a mortal animal and that they had departed for the camp each November with no actual intention of slaying it, not because it could not be slain but because so far they had no actual hope of being able to. "It will be tomorrow," he said.

"You mean we will try tomorrow," Sam said. "We ain't got the dog yet."

"We've got eleven," he said. "They ran him Monday."

"And you heard them," Sam said. "Saw them too. We ain't got the dog yet. It won't take but one. But he ain't there. Maybe he ain't nowhere. The only other way will be for him to run by accident over somebody that had a gun and knowed how to shoot it."

"That wouldn't be me," the boy said. "It would be Walter or Major or——"

"It might," Sam said. "You watch close tomorrow. Because he's smart. That's how come he has lived this long. If he gets hemmed up and has got to pick out somebody to run over, he will pick out you."

"How?" he said. "How will he know. . . ." He ceased. "You mean he already knows me, that I ain't never been to the big bottom before, ain't had time to find out yet whether I . . ." He ceased again, staring at Sam; he said humbly, not even amazed: "It was me he was watching. I don't reckon he did need to come but once."

"You watch tomorrow," Sam said. "I reckon we better start back. It'll be long after dark now before we get to camp."

The next morning they started three hours earlier than they had ever done. Even Uncle Ash went, the cook, who called himself by profession a camp cook and who did little else save cook for Major de Spain's hunting and camping parties, yet who had been marked by the wilderness from simple juxtaposition to it until he responded as they all did, even the boy who until two weeks ago had never even seen the wilderness, to a hound's ripped ear and shoulder and the print of a crooked foot in a patch of wet earth. They rode. It was too far to walk: the boy and Sam and Uncle Ash in the wagon with the dogs, his cousin and Major de Spain and General Compson and Boon and Walter and Tennie's Jim riding double on the horses; again the first gray light found him, as on that first morning two weeks ago, on the stand where Sam had placed and left him. With the gun which was too big for him, the breech-loader which did not even belong to him but to Major de Spain and which he had fired only once, at a stump on the first day to learn the recoil and how to reload it with the paper shells, he stood against a big gum tree beside a little bayou whose black still water crept without motion out of a cane-brake, across a small clearing and into the cane again, where, invisible, a bird, the big woodpecker called Lord-to-God by Negroes, clattered at a dead trunk. It was a stand like any other stand, dissimilar only in incidentals to the one where he had stood each morning for two weeks; a territory new to him yet no less familiar than that other one which after two weeks he had come to believe he knew a little—the same solitude, the same loneliness through which frail and timorous man had merely passed without altering it, leaving no mark nor scar, which looked exactly as it must have looked when the first ancestor of Sam Fathers' Chickasaw predecessors crept into it and looked about him, club or stone axe or bone arrow drawn and ready, different only because, squatting at the edge of the kitchen, he had smelled the dogs huddled and cringing beneath it and saw the raked ear and side of the bitch that, as Sam had said, had to be brave once in order to keep on calling herself a dog, and saw yesterday in the earth beside the gutted log, the print of the living foot. He heard no dogs at all. He never did certainly hear them. He only heard the drumming of the woodpecker stop short off, and knew that the bear was looking at him. He never saw it. He did not know whether it was facing him from the cane or behind him. He did not move, holding the useless gun which he knew now he would never fire at it, now or ever, tasting in his saliva that taint of brass which he had smelled in the huddled dogs when he peered under the kitchen.

Then it was gone. As abruptly as it had stopped, the woodpecker's dry hammering set up again, and after a while he believed he even heard the dogs—a murmur, scarce a sound even, which he had probably been hearing for a time, perhaps a minute or two, before he remarked it, drifting into hearing and then out again, dying away. They came nowhere near him. If it was dogs he heard, he could not have sworn to it; if it was a bear they ran, it was another bear. It was Sam himself who emerged from the cane and crossed the bayou, the injured bitch following at heel as a bird dog is taught to walk. She came and crouched against his leg, trembling. "I didn't see him," he said. "I didn't, Sam."

"I know it," Sam said. "He done the looking. You didn't hear him neither, did you?"

"No," the boy said. "I——"

"He's smart," Sam said. "Too smart." Again the boy saw in his eyes that quality of dark and brooding lambence as Sam looked down at the bitch trembling faintly and steadily against the boy's leg. From her raked shoulder a few drops of fresh blood clung like bright berries. "Too big. We ain't got the dog yet. But maybe some day."

Because there would be a next time, after and after. He was only ten. It seemed to him that he could see them, the two of them, shadowy in the limbo from which time emerged and became time: the old bear absolved of mortality and himself who shared a little of it. Because he recognized now what he had smelled in the huddled dogs and tasted in his own saliva, recognized fear as a boy, a youth, recognizes the existence of love and passion and experience which is his heritage but not yet his patrimony, from entering by chance the presence or perhaps even merely the bedroom of a woman who has loved and been loved by many men. *So I will have to see him,* he thought, without dread or even hope. *I will have to look at him.* So it was in June of the next summer. They were at the camp again, celebrating Major de Spain's and General Compson's birthdays. Although the one had been born in September and the other in the depth of winter and almost thirty years earlier, each June the two of them and McCaslin and Boon and Walter Ewell (and the boy too from now on) spent two weeks at the camp, fishing and shooting squirrels and turkey and running coons and wildcats with the dogs at night. That is, Boon and the Negroes (and the boy too now) fished and shot squirrels and ran the coons and cats, because the proven hunters, not only Major de Spain and old General Compson (who spent those two weeks sitting in a rocking chair before a tremendous iron pot of Brunswick stew, stirring and tasting, with Uncle Ash to quarrel with about how he was making it and Tennie's Jim to pour whiskey into the tin dipper from which he drank it), but even McCaslin and Walter Ewell who were still young enough, scorned such, other than shooting the wild gobblers with pistols for wagers or to test their marksmanship.

That is, his cousin McCaslin and the others thought he was hunting squirrels. Until the third evening he believed that Sam Fathers thought so too. Each morning he would leave the camp right after breakfast. He had his own gun now, a new breech-loader, a Christmas gift; he would own and shoot it for almost seventy years, through two new pairs of barrels and locks and one new stock, until all that remained of the original gun was the silver-inlaid trigger-guard with his and McCaslin's engraved names and the date in 1878. He found the tree beside the little bayou where he had stood that morning. Using the compass he ranged from that point; he was teaching himself to be better than a fair woodsman without even knowing he was doing it. On the third day he even found the gutted log where he had first seen the print. It was almost completely crumbled now, healing with unbelievable speed, a passionate and almost visible relinquishment, back into the earth from which the tree had grown. He ranged the summer woods now, green with gloom, if anything actually dimmer than they had been in November's gray dissolution, where even at noon the sun fell only in windless dappling upon the earth which never completely dried and which crawled with snakes—moccasins and watersnakes and rattlers, themselves the color of the dappled gloom so that he would not always see them until they moved; returning to camp later and later and later, first day, second day, passing in the twilight of the third evening the little log pen enclosing the log barn where Sam was putting up the stock for the night. "You ain't looked right yet," Sam said.

He stopped. For a moment he didn't answer. Then he said peacefully, in a peaceful rushing burst, as when a boy's miniature dam in a little brook gives way: "All right. Yes. But how? I went to the bayou. I even found that log again. I——"

"I reckon that was all right. Likely he's been watching you. You never saw his foot?"

"I . . ." the boy said. "I didn't . . . I never thought . . ."

"It's the gun," Sam said. He stood beside the fence, motionless, the old man, son of a Negro slave and a Chickasaw chief, in the battered and faded overalls and the frayed five-cent straw hat which had been the badge of the Negro's slavery and was now the regalia of his freedom. The camp—the clearing, the house, the barn and its tiny lot with which Major de Spain in his turn had scratched punily and evanescently at the wilderness—faded in the dusk, back into the immemorial darkness of the woods. *The gun*, the boy thought. *The gun.* "You will have to choose," Sam said.

He left the next morning before light, without breakfast, long before Uncle Ash would wake in his quilts on the kitchen floor and start the fire. He had only the compass and a stick for the snakes. He could go almost a mile before he would need to see the compass. He sat on a log, the invisible compass in his hand, while the secret night-sounds which had ceased at his movements, scurried again and then fell still for good and the owls ceased and gave over to the waking day birds and there was light in the gray wet woods and he could see the compass. He went fast yet still quietly, becoming steadily better and better as a woodsman without yet having time to realize it; he jumped a doe and a fawn, walked them out of the bed, close enough to see them—the crash of undergrowth, the white scut, the fawn scudding along behind her, faster than he had known it could have run. He was hunting right, upwind, as Sam had taught him, but that didn't matter now. He had left the gun; by his own will and relinquishment he had accepted not a gambit, not a choice, but a condition in which not only the bear's heretofore inviolable anonymity but all the ancient rules and balances of hunter and hunted had been abrogated. He would not even be afraid, not even in the moment when the fear would take him completely: blood, skin, bowels, bones, memory from the long time before it even became his memory—all save that thin clear quenchless lucidity which alone differed him from this bear and from all the other bears and bucks he would follow during almost seventy years, to which Sam had said: "Be scared. You can't help that. But don't be afraid. Ain't nothing in the woods going to hurt you if you don't corner it or it don't smell that you are afraid. A bear or a deer has got to be scared of a coward the same as a brave man has got to be."

By noon he was far beyond the crossing on the little bayou, farther into the new and alien country than he had ever been, travelling now not only by the compass but by the old, heavy, biscuit-thick silver watch which had been his father's. He had left the camp nine hours ago; nine hours from now, dark would already have been an hour old. He stopped, for the first time since he had risen from the log when he could see the compass face at last, and looked about, mopping his sweating face on his sleeve. He had already relinquished, of his will, because of his need, in humility and peace and without regret, yet apparently that had not been enough, the leaving of the gun was not enough. He stood for a moment— a child, alien and lost in the green and soaring gloom of the markless wilderness. Then he relinquished completely to it. It was the watch and the compass. He was still tainted. He removed the linked chain of the one and the looped thong of the other from his overalls and hung them on a bush and leaned the stick beside them and entered it.

When he realized he was lost, he did as Sam had coached and drilled him: made a cast to cross his backtrack. He had not been going very fast for the last two or three hours, and he had gone even less fast since he left the compass and watch on the bush. So he went slower still now, since the tree could not be very far; in fact, he found it before he really expected to and turned and went to it. But there was no bush beneath it, no compass nor watch, so he did next as Sam had coached and drilled him: made this next circle in the opposite direction and much larger, so that the pattern of the two of them would bisect his track somewhere, but crossing no trace nor mark anywhere of his feet or any feet, and now he was going faster though still not panicked, his heart beating a little more rapidly but strong and steady enough, and this time it was not even the tree because there was a down log beside it which he had never seen before and beyond the log a little swamp, a seepage of moisture somewhere between earth and water, and he did what Sam had coached and drilled him as the next and the last, seeing as he sat down on the log the crooked print, the warped indentation in the wet ground which while he looked at it continued to fill with water until it was level full and the water began to overflow and the sides of the print began to dissolve away. Even as he looked up he saw the next one, and, moving, the one beyond it; moving, not hurrying, running, but merely keeping pace with them as they appeared before him as though they were being shaped out of thin air just one constant pace short of where he would lose them forever and be lost forever himself, tireless, eager, without doubt or dread, panting a little above the strong rapid little hammer of his heart, emerging suddenly into a little glade, and the wilderness coalesced. It rushed, soundless, and solidified—the tree, the bush, the compass and the watch glinting where a ray of sunlight touched them. Then he saw the bear. It did not emerge, appear: it was just there, immobile, fixed in the green and windless noon's hot dappling, not as big as he had dreamed it but as big as he had expected, bigger, dimensionless against the dappled obscurity, looking at him. Then it moved. It crossed the glade without haste, walking for an instant into the sun's full glare and out of it, and stopped again and looked back at him across one shoulder. Then it was gone. It didn't walk into the woods. It faded, sank back into the wilderness without motion as he had watched a fish, a huge old bass, sink back into the dark depths of its pool and vanish without even any movement of its fins.

PART 2

So he should have hated and feared Lion. He was thirteen then. He had killed his buck and Sam Fathers had marked his face with the hot blood, and in the next November he killed a bear. But before that accolade he had become as competent in the woods as many grown men with the same experience. By now he was a better woodsman than most grown men with more. There was no territory within twenty-five miles of the camp that he did not know—bayou, ridge, landmark trees and path; he could have led anyone direct to any spot in it and brought him back. He knew game trails that even Sam Fathers had never seen; in the third fall he found a buck's bedding-place by himself and unbeknown to his cousin he borrowed Walter Ewell's rifle and lay in wait for the buck at dawn and killed it when it walked back to the bed as Sam had told him how the old Chickasaw fathers did.

By now he knew the old bear's footprint better than he did his own, and not only the crooked one. He could see any one of the three sound prints and distinguish it at once from any other, and not only because of its size. There were other bears within that fifty miles which left tracks almost as large, or at least so near that the one would have appeared larger only by juxtaposition. It was more than that. If Sam Fathers had been his mentor and the backyard rabbits and squirrels his kindergarten, then the wilderness the old bear ran was his college and the old male bear itself, so long unwifed and childless as to have become its own ungendered progenitor, was his alma mater.

He could find the crooked print now whenever he wished, ten miles or five miles or sometimes closer than that, to the camp. Twice while on stand during the next three years he heard the dogs strike its trail and once even jump it by chance, the voices high, abject, almost human in their hysteria. Once, still-hunting with Walter Ewell's rifle, he saw it cross a long corridor of down timber where a tornado had passed. It rushed through rather than across the tangle of trunks and branches as a locomotive would, faster than he had ever believed it could have moved, almost as fast as a deer even because the deer would have spent most of that distance in the air; he realized then why it would take a dog not only of abnormal courage but size and speed too ever to bring it to bay. He had a little dog at home, a mongrel, of the sort called fyce by Negroes, a ratter, itself not much bigger than a rat and possessing that sort of courage which had long since stopped being bravery and had become foolhardiness. He brought it with him one June and, timing them as if they were meeting an appointment with another human being, himself carrying the fyce with a sack over its head and Sam Fathers with a brace of the hounds on a rope leash, they lay downwind of the trail and actually ambushed the bear. They were so close that it turned at bay although he realized later this might have been from surprise and amazement at the shrill and frantic uproar of the fyce. It turned at bay against the trunk of a big cypress, on its hind feet; it seemed to the boy that it would never stop rising, taller and taller, and even the two hounds seemed to have taken a kind of desperate and despairing courage from the fyce. Then he realized that the fyce was actually not going to stop. He flung the gun down and ran. When he overtook and grasped the shrill, frantically pinwheeling little dog, it seemed to him that he was directly under the bear. He could smell it, strong and hot and rank. Sprawling, he looked up where it loomed and towered over him like a thunderclap. It was quite familiar, until he remembered: this was the way he had used to dream about it.

Then it was gone. He didn't see it go. He knelt, holding the frantic fyce with both hands, hearing the abased wailing of the two hounds drawing further and further away, until Sam came up, carrying the gun. He laid it quietly down beside the boy and stood looking down at him. "You've done seed him twice now, with a gun in your hands," he said. "This time you couldn't have missed him."

The boy rose. He still held the fyce. Even in his arms it continued to yap frantically, surging and straining toward the fading sound of the hounds like a collection of live-wire springs. The boy was panting a little. "Neither could you," he said. "You had the gun. Why didn't you shoot him?"

Sam didn't seem to have heard. He put out his hand and touched the little dog in the boy's arms which still yapped and strained even though the two hounds were out of hearing now. "He's done gone," Sam said. "You can slack off and rest now, until next time." He stroked the little dog until it began to grow quiet under his hand. "You's almost the one we wants," he said. "You just ain't big enough. We ain't got that one yet. He will need to be just a little bigger than smart, and a little braver than either." He withdrew his hand from the fyce's head and stood looking into the woods where the bear and the hounds had vanished. "Somebody is going to, some day."

"I know it," the boy said. "That's why it must be one of us. So it won't be until the last day. When even he don't want it to last any longer."

So he should have hated and feared Lion. It was in the fourth summer, the fourth time he had made one in the celebration of Major de Spain's and General Compson's birthday. In the early spring Major de Spain's mare had foaled a horse colt. One evening when Sam brought the horses and mules up to stable them for the night, the colt was missing and it was all he could do to get the frantic mare into the lot. He had thought at first to let the mare lead him back to where she had become separated from the foal. But she would not do it. She would not even feint toward any particular part of the woods or even in any particular direction. She merely ran, as if she couldn't see, still frantic with terror. She whirled and ran at Sam once, as if to attack him in some ultimate desperation, as if she could not for the moment realize that he was a man and a long-familiar one. He got her into the lot at last. It was too dark by that time to back-track her, to unravel the erratic course she had doubtless pursued.

He came to the house and told Major de Spain. It was an animal, of course, a big one, and the colt was dead now, wherever it was. They all knew that. "It's a panther," General Compson said at once. "The same one. That doe and fawn last March." Sam had sent Major de Spain word of it when Boon Hoganbeck came to the camp on a routine visit to see how the stock had wintered—the doe's throat torn out, and the beast had run down the helpless fawn and killed it too.

"Sam never did say that was a panther," Major de Spain said. Sam said nothing now, standing behind Major de Spain where they sat at supper, inscrutable, as if he were just waiting for them to stop talking so he could go home. He didn't even seem to be looking at anything. "A panther might jump a doe, and he wouldn't have much trouble catching the fawn afterward. But no panther would have jumped that colt with the dam right there with it. It was Old Ben," Major de Spain said. "I'm disappointed in him. He has broken the rules. I didn't think he would have done that. He has killed mine and McCaslin's dogs, but that was all right. We gambled the dogs against him; we gave each other warning. But now he has come into my house and destroyed my property, out of season too. He broke the rules. It was Old Ben, Sam." Still Sam said nothing, standing there until Major de Spain should stop talking. "We'll back-track her tomorrow and see," Major de Spain said.

Sam departed. He would not live in the camp; he had built himself a little hut something like Joe Baker's, only stouter, tighter, on the bayou a quarter-mile away, and a stout log crib where he stored a little corn for the shoat he raised each year. The next morning he was waiting when they waked. He had already found the colt. They did not even wait for breakfast. It was not far, not five hundred yards from the stable—the three-months' colt lying on its side, its throat torn out and the entrails and one ham partly eaten. It lay not as if it had been dropped but as if it had been struck and hurled, and no cat-mark, no claw-mark where a panther would have gripped it while finding its throat. They read the tracks where the frantic mare had circled and at last rushed in with that same ultimate desperation with which she had whirled on Sam Fathers yesterday evening, and the long tracks of dead and terrified running and those of the beast which had not even rushed at her when she advanced but had merely walked three or four paces toward her until she broke, and General Compson said, "Good God, what a wolf!"

Still Sam said nothing. The boy watched him while the men knelt, measuring the tracks. There was something in Sam's face now. It was neither exultation nor joy nor hope. Later, a man, the boy realized what it had been, and that Sam had known all the time what had made the tracks and what had torn the throat out of the doe in the spring and killed the fawn. It had been foreknowledge in Sam's face that morning. *And he was glad*, he told himself. *He was old. He had no children, no people, none of his blood anywhere above earth that he would ever meet again. And even if he were to, he could not have touched it, spoken to it, because for seventy years now he had had to be a Negro. It was almost over now and he was glad.*

They returned to camp and had breakfast and came back with guns and the hounds. Afterward the boy realized that they also should have known then what killed the colt as well as Sam Fathers did. But that was neither the first nor the last time he had seen men rationalize from and even act upon their misconceptions. After Boon, standing astride the colt, had whipped the dogs away from it with his belt, they snuffed at the tracks. One of them, a young dog hound without judgment yet, bayed once, and they ran for a few feet on what seemed to be a trail. Then they stopped, looking back at the men, eager enough, not baffled, merely questioning, as if they were asking "Now what?" Then they rushed back to the colt, where Boon, still astride it, slashed at them with the belt.

"I never knew a trail to get cold that quick," General Compson said.

"Maybe a single wolf big enough to kill a colt with the dam right there beside it don't leave scent," Major de Spain said.

"Maybe it was a hant," Walter Ewell said. He looked at Tennie's Jim. "Hah, Jim?"

Because the hounds would not run it, Major de Spain had Sam hunt out and find the tracks a hundred yards farther on and they put the dogs on it again and again the young one bayed and not one of them realized then that the hound was not baying like a dog striking game but was merely bellowing like a country dog whose yard has been invaded. General Compson spoke to the boy and Boon and Tennie's Jim: to the squirrel hunters. "You boys keep the dogs with you this morning. He's probably hanging around somewhere, waiting to get his breakfast off the colt. You might strike him."

But they did not. The boy remembered how Sam stood watching them as they went into the woods with the leashed hounds—the Indian face in which he had never seen anything until it smiled, except that faint arching of the nostrils on that first morning when the hounds had found Old Ben. They took the hounds with them on the next day, though when they reached the place where they hoped to strike a fresh trail, the carcass of the colt was gone. Then on the third morning Sam was waiting again, this time until they had finished breakfast. He said, "Come." He led them to his house, his little hut, to the corn-crib beyond it. He had removed the corn and had made a deadfall of the door, baiting it with the colt's carcass; peering between the logs, they saw an animal almost the color of a gun or pistol barrel, what little time they had to examine its color or shape. It was not crouched nor even standing. It was in motion, in the air, coming toward them—a heavy body crashing with tremendous force against the door so that the thick door jumped and clattered in its frame, the animal, whatever it was, hurling itself against the door again seemingly before it could have touched the floor and got a new purchase to spring from. "Come away," Sam said, "fore he break his neck." Even when they retreated the heavy and measured crashes continued, the stout door jumping and clattering each time, and still no sound from the beast itself—no snarl, no cry.

"What in hell's name is it?" Major de Spain said.

"It's a dog," Sam said, his nostrils arching and collapsing faintly and steadily and that faint, fierce milkiness in his eyes again as on that first morning when the hounds had struck the old bear. "It's the dog."

"*The* dog?" Major de Spain said.

"That's gonter hold Old Ben."

"Dog the devil," Major de Spain said. "I'd rather have Old Ben himself in my pack than that brute. Shoot him."

"No," Sam said.

"You'll never tame him. How do you ever expect to make an animal like that afraid of you?"

"I don't want him tame," Sam said; again the boy watched his nostrils and the fierce milky light in his eyes. "But I almost rather he be tame than scared, of me or any man or any thing. But he won't be neither, of nothing."

"Then what are you going to do with it?"

"You can watch," Sam said.

Each morning through the second week they would go to Sam's crib. He had removed a few shingles from the roof and had put a rope on the colt's carcass and had drawn it out when the trap fell. Each morning they would watch him lower a pail of water into the crib while the dog hurled itself tirelessly against the door and dropped back and leaped again. It never made any sound and there was nothing frenzied in the act but only a cold and grim indomitable determination. Toward the end of the week it stopped jumping at the door. Yet it had not weakened appreciably and it was not as if it had rationalized the fact that the door was not going to give. It was as if for that time it simply disdained to jump any longer. It was not down. None of them had ever seen it down. It stood, and they could see it now—part mastiff, something of Airedale and something of a dozen other strains probably, better than thirty inches at the shoulders and weighing as they guessed almost ninety pounds, with cold yellow eyes and a tremendous chest and over all that strange color like a blued gun-barrel.

Then the two weeks were up. They prepared to break camp. The boy begged to remain and his cousin let him. He moved into the little hut with Sam Fathers. Each morning he watched Sam lower the pail of water into the crib. By the end of that week the dog was down. It would rise and half stagger, half crawl to the water and drink and collapse again. One morning it could not even reach the water, could not raise its forequarters even from the floor. Sam took a short stick and prepared to enter the crib. "Wait," the boy said. "Let me get the gun——"

"No," Sam said. "He can't move now." Nor could it. It lay on its side while Sam touched it, its head and the gaunted body, the dog lying motionless, the yellow eyes open. They were not fierce and there was nothing of petty malevolence in them, but a cold and almost impersonal malignance like some natural force. It was not even looking at Sam nor at the boy peering at it between the logs.

Sam began to feed it again. The first time he had to raise its head so it could lap the broth. That night he left a bowl of broth containing lumps of meat where the dog could reach it. The next morning the bowl was empty and the dog was lying on its belly, its head up, the cold yellow eyes watching the door as Sam entered, no change whatever in the cold yellow eyes and still no sound from it even when it sprang, its aim and coordination still bad from weakness so that Sam had time to strike it down with the stick and leap from the crib and slam the door as the dog, still without having had time to get its feet under it to jump again seemingly, hurled itself against the door as if the two weeks of starving had never been.

At noon that day someone came whooping through the woods from the direction of the camp. It was Boon. He came and looked for a while between the logs, at the tremendous dog lying again on its belly, its head up, the yellow eyes blinking sleepily at nothing: the indomitable and unbroken spirit. "What we better do," Boon said, "is to let that sonofabitch go and catch Old Ben and run him on the dog." He turned to the boy his weather-reddened and beetling face. "Get your traps together. Cass says for you to come on home. You been in here fooling with that horse-eating varmint long enough."

Boon had a borrowed mule at the camp; the buggy was waiting at the edge of the bottom. He was at home that night. He told McCaslin about it. "Sam's going to starve him again until he can go in and touch him. Then he will feed him again. Then he will starve him again, if he has to."

"But why?" McCaslin said. "What for? Even Sam will never tame that brute."

"We don't want him tame. We want him like he is. We just want him to find out at last that the only way he can get out of that crib and stay out of it is to do what Sam or somebody tells him to do. He's the dog that's going to stop Old Ben and hold him. We've already named him. His name is Lion."

Then November came at last. They returned to the camp. With General Compson and Major de Spain and his cousin and Walter and Boon he stood in the yard among the guns and bedding and boxes of food and watched Sam Fathers and Lion come up the lane from the lot—the Indian, the old man in battered overalls and rubber boots and a worn sheepskin coat and a hat which had belonged to the boy's father; the tremendous dog pacing gravely beside him. The hounds rushed out to meet them and stopped, except the young one which still had but little of judgment. It ran up to Lion, fawning. Lion didn't snap at it. He didn't even pause. He struck it rolling and yelping for five or six feet with a blow of one paw as a bear would have done and came on into the yard and stood, blinking sleepily at nothing, looking at no one, while Boon said, "Jesus. Jesus. —Will he let me touch him?"

"You can touch him," Sam said. "He don't care. He don't care about nothing or nobody."

The boy watched that too. He watched it for the next two years from that moment when Boon touched Lion's head and then knelt beside him, feeling the bones and muscles, the power. It was as if Lion were a woman—or perhaps Boon was the woman. That was more like it—the big, grave, sleepy-seeming dog which, as Sam Fathers said, cared about no man and no thing; and the violent, insensitive, hard-faced man with his touch of remote Indian blood and the mind almost of a child. He watched Boon take over Lion's feeding from Sam and Uncle Ash both. He would see Boon squatting in the cold rain beside the kitchen while Lion ate. Because Lion neither slept nor ate with the other dogs though none of them knew where he did sleep until in the second November, thinking until then that Lion slept in his kennel beside Sam Fathers' hut, when the boy's cousin McCaslin said something about it to Sam by sheer chance and Sam told him. And that night the boy and Major de Spain and McCaslin with a lamp entered the back room where Boon slept—the little, tight, airless room rank with the smell of Boon's unwashed body and his wet hunting-clothes—where Boon, snoring on his back, choked and waked and Lion raised his head beside him and looked back at them from his cold, slumbrous yellow eyes.

"Damn it, Boon," McCaslin said. "Get that dog out of here. He's got to run Old Ben tomorrow morning. How in hell do you expect him to smell anything fainter than a skunk after breathing you all night?"

"The way I smell ain't hurt my nose none that I ever noticed," Boon said.

"It wouldn't matter if it had," Major de Spain said. "We're not depending on you to trail a bear. Put him outside. Put him under the house with the other dogs."

Boon began to get up. "He'll kill the first one that happens to yawn or sneeze in his face or touches him."

"I reckon not," Major de Spain said. "None of them are going to risk yawning in his face or touching him either, even asleep. Put him outside. I want his nose right tomorrow. Old Ben fooled him last year. I don't think he will do it again."

Boon put on his shoes without lacing them; in his long soiled underwear, his hair still tousled from sleep, he and Lion went out. The others returned to the front room and the poker game where McCaslin's and Major de Spain's hands waited for them on the table. After a while McCaslin said, "Do you want me to go back and look again?"

"No," Major de Spain said. "I call," he said to Walter Ewell. He spoke to McCaslin again. "If you do, don't tell me. I am beginning to see the first sign of my increasing age: I don't like to know that my orders have been disobeyed, even when I knew when I gave them that they would be.—A small pair," he said to Walter Ewell.

"How small?" Walter said.

"Very small," Major de Spain said.

And the boy, lying beneath his piled quilts and blankets waiting for sleep, knew likewise that Lion was already back in Boon's bed, for the rest of that night and the next one and during all the nights of the next November and the next one. He thought then: *I wonder what Sam thinks. He could have Lion with him, even if Boon is a white man. He could ask Major or McCaslin either. And more than that. It was Sam's hand that touched Lion first and Lion knows it.* Then he became a man and he knew that too. It had been all right. That was the way it should have been. Sam was the chief, the prince; Boon, the plebeian, was his huntsman. Boon should have nursed the dogs.

On the first morning that Lion led the pack after Old Ben, seven strangers appeared in the camp. They were swampers: gaunt, malaria-ridden men appearing from nowhere, who ran trap-lines for coons or perhaps farmed little patches of cotton and corn along the edge of the bottom, in clothes but little better than Sam Fathers' and nowhere near as good as Tennie's Jim's, with worn shotguns and rifles, already squatting patiently in the cold drizzle in the side yard when day broke. They had a spokesman; afterward Sam Fathers told Major de Spain how all during the past summer and fall they had drifted into the camp singly or in pairs and threes, to look quietly at Lion for a while and then go away: "Mawnin, Major. We heerd you was aimin to put that ere blue dawg on that old two-toed bear this mawnin. We figgered we'd come up and watch, if you don't mind. We won't do no shooting, lessen he runs over us."

"You are welcome," Major de Spain said. "You are welcome to shoot. He's more your bear than ours."

"I reckon that ain't no lie. I done fed him enough cawn to have a sheer in him. Not to mention a shoat three years ago."

"I reckon I got a sheer too," another said. "Only it ain't in the bear." Major de Spain looked at him. He was chewing tobacco. He spat. "Hit was a heifer calf. Nice un too. Last year. When I finally found her, I reckon she looked about like that colt of yourn looked last June."

"Oh," Major de Spain said. "Be welcome. If you see game in front of my dogs, shoot it."

Nobody shot Old Ben that day. No man saw him. The dogs jumped him within a hundred yards of the glade where the boy had seen him that day in the summer of his eleventh year. The boy was less than a quarter-mile away. He heard the jump but he could distinguish no voice among the dogs that he did not know and therefore would be Lion's, and he thought, believed, that Lion was not among them. Even the fact that they were going much faster than he had ever heard them run behind Old Ben before and that the high thin note of hysteria was missing now from their voices was not enough to disabuse him. He didn't comprehend until that night, when Sam told him that Lion would never cry on a trail. "He gonter growl when he catches Old Ben's throat," Sam said. "But he ain't gonter never holler, no more than he ever done when he was jumping at that two-inch door. It's that blue dog in him. What you call it?"

"Airedale," the boy said.

Lion was there; the jump was just too close to the river. When Boon returned with Lion about eleven that night, he swore that Lion had stopped Old Ben once but that the hounds would not go in and Old Ben broke away and took to the river and swam for miles down it and he and Lion went down one bank for about ten miles and crossed and came up the other but it had begun to get dark before they struck any trail where Old Ben had come up out of the water, unless he was still in the water when he passed the ford where they crossed. Then he fell to cursing the hounds and ate the supper Uncle Ash had saved for him and went off to bed and after a while the boy opened the door of the little stale room thunderous with snoring and the great grave dog raised its head from Boon's pillow and blinked at him for a moment and lowered its head again.

When the next November came and the last day, the day which it was now becoming traditional to save for Old Ben, there were more than a dozen strangers waiting. They were not all swampers this time. Some of them were townsmen, from other county seats like Jefferson, who had heard about Lion and Old Ben and had come to watch the great blue dog keep his yearly rendezvous with the old two-toed bear. Some of them didn't even have guns and the hunting-clothes and boots they wore had been on a store shelf yesterday.

This time Lion jumped Old Ben more than five miles from the river and bayed and held him and this time the hounds went in, in a sort of desperate emulation. The boy heard them; he was that near. He heard Boon whooping; he heard the two shots when General Compson delivered both barrels, one containing five buckshot, the other a single ball, into the bear from as close as he could force his almost unmanageable horse. He heard the dogs when the bear broke free again. He was running now; panting, stumbling, his lungs bursting, he reached the place where General Compson had fired and where Old Ben had killed two of the hounds. He saw the blood from General Compson's shots, but he could go no further. He stopped, leaning against a tree for his breathing to ease and his heart to slow, hearing the sound of the dogs as it faded on and died away.

In camp that night—they had as guests five of the still terrified strangers in new hunting coats and boots who had been lost all day until Sam Fathers went out and got them—he heard the rest of it: how Lion had stopped and held the bear again but only the one-eyed mule which did not mind the smell of wild blood would approach and Boon was riding the mule and Boon had never been known to hit anything. He shot at the bear five times with his pump gun, touching nothing, and Old Ben killed another hound and broke free once more and reached the river and was gone. Again Boon and Lion hunted as far down one bank as they dared. Too far; they crossed in the first of dusk and dark overtook them within a mile. And this time Lion found the broken trail, the blood perhaps, in the darkness where Old Ben had come up out of the water, but Boon had him on a rope, luckily, and he got down from the mule and fought Lion hand-to-hand until he got him back to camp. This time Boon didn't even curse. He stood in the door, muddy, spent, his huge gargoyle's face tragic and still amazed. "I missed him," he said. "I was in twenty-five feet of him and I missed him five times."

"But we have drawn blood," Major de Spain said. "General Compson drew blood. We have never done that before."

"But I missed him," Boon said. "I missed him five times. With Lion looking right at me."

"Never mind," Major de Spain said. "It was a damned fine race. And we drew blood. Next year we'll let General Compson or Walter ride Katie, and we'll get him."

Then McCaslin said, "Where is Lion, Boon?"

"I left him at Sam's," Boon said. He was already turning away. "I ain't fit to sleep with him."

So he should have hated and feared Lion. Yet he did not. It seemed to him that there was a fatality in it. It seemed to him that something, he didn't know what, was beginning; had already begun. It was like the last act on a set stage. It was the beginning of the end of something, he didn't know what except that he would not grieve. He would be humble and proud that he had been found worthy to be a part of it too or even just to see it too.

PART 3

It was December. It was the coldest December he had ever remembered. They had been in camp four days over two weeks, waiting for the weather to soften so that Lion and Old Ben could run their yearly race. Then they would break camp and go home. Because of these unforeseen additional days which they had had to pass waiting on the weather, with nothing to do but play poker, the whiskey had given out and he and Boon were being sent to Memphis with a suitcase and a note from Major de Spain to Mr. Semmes, the distiller, to get more. That is, Major de Spain and McCaslin were sending Boon to get the whiskey and sending him to see that Boon got back with it or most of it or at least some of it.

Tennie's Jim waked him at three. He dressed rapidly, shivering, not so much from the cold because a fresh fire already boomed and roared on the hearth, but in that dead winter hour when the blood and the heart are slow and sleep is incomplete. He crossed the gap between house and kitchen, the gap of iron earth beneath the brilliant and rigid night where dawn would not begin for three hours yet, tasting, tongue, palate, and to the very bottom of his lungs, the searing dark, and entered the kitchen, the lamp-lit warmth where the stove glowed, fogging the windows, and where Boon already sat at the table at breakfast, hunched over his plate, almost in his plate, his working jaws blue with stubble and his face innocent of water and his coarse, horse-mane hair innocent of comb—the quarter Indian, grandson of a Chickasaw squaw, who on occasion resented with his hard and furious fists the intimation of one single drop of alien blood and on others, usually after whiskey, affirmed with the same fists and the same fury that his father had been the full-blood Chickasaw and even a chief and that even his mother had been only half white. He was four inches over six feet; he had the mind of a child, the heart of a horse, and little hard shoe-button eyes without depth or meanness or generosity or viciousness or gentleness or anything else, in the ugliest face the boy had ever seen. It looked like somebody had found a walnut a little larger than a football and with a machinist's hammer had shaped features into it and then painted it, mostly red; not Indian red but a fine bright ruddy color which whiskey might have had something to do with but which was mostly just happy and violent out-of-doors, the wrinkles in it not the residue of the forty years it had survived but from squinting into the sun or into the gloom of canebrakes where game had run, baked into it by the camp fires before which he had lain trying to sleep on the cold November or December ground while waiting for daylight so he could rise and hunt again, as though time were merely something he walked through as he did through air, aging him no more than air did. He was brave, faithful, improvident and unreliable; he had neither profession job nor trade and owned one vice and one virtue: whiskey, and that absolute and unquestioning fidelity to Major de Spain and the boy's cousin McCaslin. "Sometimes I'd call them both virtues," Major de Spain said once. "Or both vices," McCaslin said.

He ate his breakfast, hearing the dogs under the kitchen, wakened by the smell of frying meat or perhaps by the feet overhead. He heard Lion once, short and peremptory, as the best hunter in any camp has only to speak once to all save the fools, and none other of Major de Spain's and McCaslin's dogs were Lion's equal in size and strength and perhaps even in courage, but they were not fools; Old Ben had killed the last fool among them last year.

Tennie's Jim came in as they finished. The wagon was outside. Ash decided he would drive them over to the log-line where they would flag the outbound log-train and let Tennie's Jim wash the dishes. The boy knew why. It would not be the first time he had listened to old Ash badgering Boon.

It was cold. The wagon wheels banged and clattered on the frozen ground; the sky was fixed and brilliant. He was not shivering, he was shaking, slow and steady and hard, the food he had just eaten still warm and solid inside him while his outside shook slow and steady around it as though his stomach floated loose. "They won't run this morning," he said. "No dog will have any nose today."

"Cep Lion," Ash said. "Lion don't need no nose. All he need is a bear." He had wrapped his feet in towsacks and he had a quilt from his pallet bed on the kitchen floor drawn over his head and wrapped around him until in the thin brilliant starlight he looked like nothing at all that the boy had ever seen before. "He run a bear through a thousand-acre ice-house. Catch him too. Them other dogs don't matter because they ain't going to keep up with Lion nohow, long as he got a bear in front of him."

"What's wrong with the other dogs?" Boon said. "What the hell do you know about it anyway? This is the first time you've had your tail out of that kitchen since we got here except to chop a little wood."

"Ain't nothing wrong with them," Ash said. "And long as it's left up to them, ain't nothing going to be. I just wish I had knowed all my life how to take care of my health good as them hounds knows."

"Well, they ain't going to run this morning," Boon said. His voice was harsh and positive. "Major promised they wouldn't until me and Ike get back."

"Weather gonter break today. Gonter soft up. Rain by night." Then Ash laughed, chuckled, somewhere inside the quilt which concealed even his face. "Hum up here, mules!" he said, jerking the reins so that the mules leaped forward and snatched the lurching and banging wagon for several feet before they slowed again into their quick, short-paced, rapid plodding. "Sides, I like to know why Major need to wait on you. It's Lion he aiming to use. I ain't never heard tell of you bringing no bear nor no other kind of meat into this camp."

Now Boon's going to curse Ash or maybe even hit him, the boy thought. But Boon never did, never had; the boy knew he never would even though four years ago Boon had shot five times with a borrowed pistol at a Negro on the street in Jefferson, with the same result as when he had shot five times at Old Ben last fall. "By God," Boon said, "he ain't going to put Lion or no other dog on nothing until I get back tonight. Because he promised me. Whip up them mules and keep them whipped up. Do you want me to freeze to death?"

They reached the log-line and built a fire. After a while the log-train came up out of the woods under the paling east and Boon flagged it. Then in the warm caboose the boy slept again while Boon and the conductor and brakeman talked about Lion and Old Ben as people later would talk about Sullivan and Kilrain and, later still, about Dempsey and Tunney. Dozing, swaying as the springless caboose lurched and clattered, he would hear them still talking, about the shoats and calves Old Ben had killed and the cribs he had rifled and the traps and dead-falls he had wrecked and the lead he probably carried under his hide—Old Ben, the two-toed bear in a land where bears with trap-ruined feet had been called Two-Toe or Three-Toe or Cripple-Foot for fifty years, only Old Ben was an extra bear (the head bear, General Compson called him) and so had earned a name such as a human man could have worn and not been sorry.

They reached Hoke's at sunup. They emerged from the warm caboose in their hunting clothes, the muddy boots and stained khaki and Boon's blue unshaven jowls. But that was all right. Hoke's was a sawmill and commissary and two stores and a loading-chute on a sidetrack from the main line, and all the men in it wore boots and khaki too. Presently the Memphis train came. Boon bought three packages of popcorn-and-molasses and a bottle of beer from the news butch and the boy went to sleep again to the sound of his chewing.

But in Memphis it was not all right. It was as if the high buildings and the hard pavements, the fine carriages and the horse cars and the men in starched collars and neckties made their boots and khaki look a little rougher and a little muddier and made Boon's beard look worse and more unshaven and his face look more and more like he should never have brought it out of the woods at all or at least out of reach of Major de Spain or McCaslin or someone who knew it and could have said, "Don't be afraid. He won't hurt you." He walked through the station, on the slick floor, his face moving as he worked the popcorn out of his teeth with his tongue, his legs spraddled and stiff in the hips as if he were walking on buttered glass, and that blue stubble on his face like the filings from a new gun-barrel. They passed the first saloon. Even through the closed doors the boy could seem to smell the sawdust and the reek of old drink. Boon began to cough.

He coughed for something less than a minute. "Damn this cold," he said. "I'd sure like to know where I got it."

"Back there in the station," the boy said.

Boon had started to cough again. He stopped. He looked at the boy. "What?" he said.

"You never had it when we left camp nor on the train either." Boon looked at him, blinking. Then he stopped blinking. He didn't cough again. He said quietly:

"Lend me a dollar. Come on. You've got it. If you ever had one, you've still got it. I don't mean you are tight with your money because you ain't. You just don't never seem to ever think of nothing you want. When I was sixteen a dollar bill melted off of me before I even had time to read the name of the bank that issued it." He said quietly: "Let me have a dollar, Ike."

"You promised Major. You promised McCaslin. Not till we get back to camp."

"All right," Boon said in that quiet and patient voice. "What can I do on just one dollar? You ain't going to lend me another."

"You're damn right I ain't," the boy said, his voice quiet too, cold with rage which was not at Boon, remembering: Boon snoring in a hard chair in the kitchen so he could watch the clock and wake him and McCaslin and drive them the seventeen miles in to Jefferson to catch the train to Memphis; the wild, never-bridled Texas paint pony which he had persuaded McCaslin to let him buy and which he and Boon had bought at auction for four dollars and seventy-five cents and fetched home wired between two gentle old mares with pieces of barbed wire and which had never even seen shelled corn before and didn't even know what it was unless the grains were bugs maybe, and at last (he was ten and Boon had been ten all his life) Boon said the pony was gentled and with a towsack over its head and four Negroes to hold it they backed it into an old two-wheeled cart and hooked up the gear and he and Boon got up and Boon said, "All right, boys. Let him go" and one of the Negroes—it was Tennie's Jim—snatched the towsack off and leaped for his life and they lost the first wheel against a post of the open gate only at that moment Boon caught him by the scruff of the neck and flung him into the roadside ditch so he only saw the rest of it in fragments: the other wheel as it slammed through the side gate and crossed the back yard and leaped up onto the gallery and scraps of the cart here and there along the road and Boon vanishing rapidly on his stomach in the leaping and spurting dust and still holding the reins until they broke too and two days later they finally caught the pony seven miles away still wearing the hames and the headstall of the bridle around its neck like a duchess with two necklaces at one time. He gave Boon the dollar.

"All right," Boon said. "Come on in out of the cold."

"I ain't cold," he said.

"You can have some lemonade."

"I don't want any lemonade."

The door closed behind him. The sun was well up now. It was a brilliant day, though Ash had said it would rain before night. Already it was warmer; they could run tomorrow. He felt the old lift of the heart, as pristine as ever, as on the first day; he would never lose it, no matter how old in hunting and pursuit: the best, the best of all breathing, the humility and the pride. He must stop thinking about it. Already it seemed to him that he was running, back to the station, to the tracks themselves: the first train going south; he must stop thinking about it. The street was busy. He watched the big Norman draft horses, the Percherons; the trim carriages from which the men in the fine overcoats and the ladies rosy in furs descended and entered the station. (They were still next door to it but one.) Twenty years ago his father had ridden into Memphis as a member of Colonel Sartoris' horse in Forrest's command, up Main street and (the tale told) into the lobby of the Gayoso Hotel where the Yankee officers sat in the leather chairs spitting into the tall bright cuspidors and then out again, scot-free——

The door opened behind him. Boon was wiping his mouth on the back of his hand. "All right," he said. "Let's go tend to it and get the hell out of here."

They went and had the suitcase packed. He never knew where or when Boon got the other bottle. Doubtless Mr. Semmes gave it to him. When they reached Hoke's again at sundown, it was empty. They could get a return train to Hoke's in two hours; they went straight back to the station as Major de Spain and then McCaslin had told Boon to do and then ordered him to do and had sent the boy along to see that he did. Boon took the first drink from his bottle in the washroom. A man in a uniform cap came to tell him he couldn't drink there and looked at Boon's face once and said nothing. The next time he was pouring into his water glass beneath the edge of a table in a restaurant when the manager (she was a woman) did tell him he couldn't drink there and he went back to the washroom. He had been telling the Negro waiter and all the other people in the restaurant who couldn't help but hear him and who had never heard of Lion and didn't want to, about Lion and Old Ben. Then he happened to think of the zoo. He had found out that there was another train to Hoke's at three o'clock and so they would spend the time at the zoo and take the three o'clock train until he came back from the washroom for the third time. Then they would take the first train back to camp, get Lion and come back to the zoo where, he said, the bears were fed on ice cream and lady fingers and he would match Lion against them all.

So they missed the first train, the one they were supposed to take, but he got Boon onto the three o'clock train and they were all right again, with Boon not even going to the washroom now but drinking in the aisle and talking about Lion and the men he buttonholed no more daring to tell Boon he couldn't drink there than the man in the station had dared.

When they reached Hoke's at sundown, Boon was asleep. The boy waked him at last and got him and the suitcase off the train and he even persuaded him to eat some supper at the sawmill commissary. So he was all right when they got in the caboose of the log-train to go back into the woods, with the sun going down red and the sky already overcast and the ground would not freeze tonight. It was the boy who slept now, sitting behind the ruby stove while the springless caboose jumped and clattered and Boon and the brakeman and the conductor talked about Lion and Old Ben because they knew what Boon was talking about because this was home. "Overcast and already thawing," Boon said. "Lion will get him tomorrow."

It would have to be Lion, or somebody. It would not be Boon. He had never hit anything bigger than a squirrel that anybody ever knew, except the Negro woman that day when he was shooting at the Negro man. He was a big Negro and not ten feet away but Boon shot five times with the pistol he had borrowed from Major de Spain's Negro coachman and the Negro he was shooting at outed with a dollar-and-a-half mail-order pistol and would have burned Boon down with it only it never went off, it just went snicksnicksnicksnicksnick five times and Boon still blasting away and he broke a plate-glass window that cost McCaslin forty-five dollars and hit a Negro woman who happened to be passing in the leg only Major de Spain paid for that; he and McCaslin cut cards, the plate-glass window against the Negro woman's leg. And the first day on stand this year, the first morning in camp, the buck ran right over Boon; he heard Boon's old pump gun go whow. whow. whow. whow. whow. and then his voice: "God damn, here he comes! Head him! Head him!" and when he got there the buck's tracks and the five exploded shells were not twenty paces apart.

There were five guests in camp that night from Jefferson: Mr. Bayard Sartoris and his son and General Compson's son and two others. And the next morning he looked out the window, into the gray thin drizzle of daybreak which Ash had predicted, and there they were, standing and squatting beneath the thin rain, almost two dozen of them who had fed Old Ben corn and shoats and even calves for ten years, in their worn hats and hunting coats and overalls which any town Negro would have thrown away or burned and only the rubber boots strong and sound, and the worn and blueless guns, and some even without guns. While they ate breakfast a dozen more arrived, mounted and on foot: loggers from the camp thirteen miles below and sawmill men from Hoke's and the only gun among them that one which the log-train conductor carried: so that when they went into the woods this morning Major de Spain led a party almost as strong, excepting that some of them were not armed, as some he had led in the last darkening days of '64 and '65. The little yard would not hold them. They overflowed it, into the lane where Major de Spain sat his mare while Ash in his dirty apron thrust the greasy cartridges into his carbine and passed it up to him and the great grave blue dog stood at his stirrup not as a dog stands but as a horse stands, blinking his sleepy topaz eyes at nothing, deaf even to the yelling of the hounds which Boon and Tennie's Jim held on leash.

"We'll put General Compson on Katie this morning," Major de Spain said. "He drew blood last year; if he'd had a mule then that would have stood, he would have———"

"No," General Compson said. "I'm too old to go helling through the woods on a mule or a horse or anything else any more. Besides, I had my chance last year and missed it. I'm going on a stand this morning. I'm going to let that boy ride Katie."

"No, wait," McCaslin said. "Ike's got the rest of his life to hunt bears in. Let somebody else———"

"No," General Compson said. "I want Ike to ride Katie. He's already a better woodsman than you or me either and in another ten years he'll be as good as Walter."

At first he couldn't believe it, not until Major de Spain spoke to him. Then he was up, on the one-eyed mule which would not spook at wild blood, looking down at the dog motionless at Major de Spain's stirrup, looking in the gray streaming light bigger than a calf, bigger than he knew it actually was—the big head, the chest almost as big as his own, the blue hide beneath which the muscles flinched or quivered to no touch since the heart which drove blood to them loved no man and no thing, standing as a horse stands yet different from a horse which infers only weight and speed while Lion inferred not only courage and all else that went to make up the will and desire to pursue and kill, but endurance, the will and desire to endure beyond all imaginable limits of flesh in order to overtake and slay. Then the dog looked at him. It moved its head and looked at him across the trivial uproar of the hounds, out of the yellow eyes as depthless as Boon's, as free as Boon's of meanness or generosity or gentleness or viciousness. They were just cold and sleepy. Then it blinked, and he knew it was not looking at him and never had been, without even bothering to turn its head away.

That morning he heard the first cry. Lion had already vanished while Sam and Tennie's Jim were putting saddles on the mule and horse which had drawn the wagon and he watched the hounds as they crossed and cast, snuffing and whimpering, until they too disappeared. Then he and Major de Spain and Sam and Tennie's Jim rode after them and heard the first cry out of the wet and thawing woods not two hundred yards ahead, high, with that abject, almost human quality he had come to know, and the other hounds joining in until the gloomed woods rang and clamored. They rode then. It seemed to him that he could actually see the big blue dog boring on, silent, and the bear too: the thick, locomotive-like shape which he had seen that day four years ago crossing the blow-down, crashing on ahead of the dogs faster than he had believed it could have moved, drawing away even from the running mules. He heard a shotgun, once. The woods had opened, they were going fast, the clamor faint and fading on ahead; they passed the man who had fired—a swamper, a pointing arm, a gaunt face, the small black orifice of his yelling studded with rotten teeth.

He heard the changed note in the hounds' uproar and two hundred yards ahead he saw them. The bear had turned. He saw Lion drive in without pausing and saw the bear strike him aside and lunge into the yelling hounds and kill one of them almost in its tracks and whirl and run again. Then they were in a streaming tide of dogs. He heard Major de Spain and Tennie's Jim shouting and the pistol sound of Tennie's Jim's leather thong as he tried to turn them. Then he and Sam Fathers were riding alone. One of the hounds had kept on with Lion though. He recognized its voice. It was the young hound which even a year ago had had no judgment and which, by the lights of the other hounds anyway, still had none. *Maybe that's what courage is,* he thought. "Right," Sam said behind him. "Right. We got to turn him from the river if we can."

Now they were in cane: a brake. He knew the path through it as well as Sam did. They came out of the undergrowth and struck the entrance almost exactly. It would traverse the brake and come out onto a high open ridge above the river. He heard the flat clap of Walter Ewell's rifle, then two more. "No," Sam said. "I can hear the hound. Go on."

They emerged from the narrow roofless tunnel of snapping and hissing cane, still galloping, onto the open ridge below which the thick yellow river, reflectionless in the gray and streaming light, seemed not to move. Now he could hear the hound too. It was not running. The cry was a high frantic yapping and Boon was running along the edge of the bluff, his old gun leaping and jouncing against his back on its sling made of a piece of cotton plowline. He whirled and ran up to them, wild-faced, and flung himself onto the mule behind the boy. "That damn boat!" he cried. "It's on the other side! He went straight across! Lion was too close to him! That little hound too! Lion was so close I couldn't shoot! Go on!" he cried, beating his heels into the mule's flanks. "Go on!"

They plunged down the bank, slipping and sliding in the thawed earth, crashing through the willows and into the water. He felt no shock, no cold, he on one side of the swimming mule, grasping the pommel with one hand and holding his gun above the water with the other, Boon opposite him. Sam was behind them somewhere, and then the river, the water about them, was full of dogs. They swam faster than the mules; they were scrabbling up the bank before the mules touched bottom. Major de Spain was whooping from the bank they had just left and, looking back, he saw Tennie's Jim and the horse as they went into the water.

Now the woods ahead of them and the rain-heavy air were one uproar. It rang and clamored; it echoed and broke against the bank behind them and reformed and clamored and rang until it seemed to the boy that all the hounds which had ever bayed game in this land were yelling down at him. He got his leg over the mule as it came up out of the water. Boon didn't try to mount again. He grasped one stirrup as they went up the bank and crashed through the undergrowth which fringed the bluff and saw the bear, on its hind feet, its back against a tree while the bellowing hounds swirled around it and once more Lion drove in, leaping clear of the ground.

This time the bear didn't strike him down. It caught the dog in both arms, almost loverlike, and they both went down. He was off the mule now. He drew back both hammers of the gun but he could see nothing but moiling spotted hound-bodies until the bear surged up again. Boon was yelling something, he could not tell what; he could see Lion still clinging to the bear's throat and he saw the bear, half erect, strike one of the hounds with one paw and hurl it five or six feet and then, rising and rising as though it would never stop, stand erect again and begin to rake at Lion's belly with its forepaws. Then Boon was running. The boy saw the gleam of the blade in his hand and watched him leap among the hounds, hurdling them, kicking them aside as he ran, and fling himself astride the bear as he had hurled himself onto the mule, his legs locked around the bear's belly, his left arm under the bear's throat where Lion clung, and the glint of the knife as it rose and fell.

It fell just once. For an instant they almost resembled a piece of statuary: the clinging dog, the bear, the man astride its back, working and probing the buried blade. Then they went down, pulled over backward by Boon's weight, Boon underneath. It was the bear's back which reappeared first but at once Boon was astride it again. He had never released the knife and again the boy saw the almost infinitesimal movement of his arm and shoulder as he probed and sought; then the bear surged erect, raising with it the man and the dog too, and turned and still carrying the man and the dog it took two or three steps toward the woods on its hind feet as a man would have walked and crashed down. It didn't collapse, crumple. It fell all of a piece, as a tree falls, so that all three of them, man dog and bear, seemed to bounce once.

He and Tennie's Jim ran forward. Boon was kneeling at the bear's head. His left ear was shredded, his left coat sleeve was completely gone, his right boot had been ripped from knee to instep; the bright blood thinned in the thin rain down his leg and hand and arm and down the side of his face which was no longer wild but was quite calm. Together they prized Lion's jaws from the bear's throat. "Easy, goddamn it," Boon said. "Can't you see his guts are all out of him?" He began to remove his coat. He spoke to Tennie's Jim in that calm voice: "Bring the boat up. It's about a hundred yards down the bank there. I saw it." Tennie's Jim rose and went away. Then, and he could not remember if it had been a call or an exclamation from Tennie's Jim or if he had glanced up by chance, he saw Tennie's Jim stooping and saw Sam Fathers lying motionless on his face in the trampled mud.

The mule had not thrown him. He remembered that Sam was down too even before Boon began to run. There was no mark on him whatever and when he and Boon turned him over, his eyes were open and he said something in that tongue which he and Joe Baker had used to speak together. But he couldn't move. Tennie's Jim brought the skiff up; they could hear him shouting to Major de Spain across the river. Boon wrapped Lion in his hunting coat and carried him down to the skiff and they carried Sam down and returned and hitched the bear to the one-eyed mule's saddle-bow with Tennie's Jim's leash-thong and dragged him down to the skiff and got him into it and left Tennie's Jim to swim the horse and the two mules back across. Major de Spain caught the bow of the skiff as Boon jumped out and past him before it touched the bank. He looked at Old Ben and said quietly: "Well." Then he walked into the water and leaned down and touched Sam and Sam looked up at him and said something in that old tongue he and Joe Baker spoke. "You don't know what happened?" Major de Spain said.

"No, sir," the boy said. "It wasn't the mule. It wasn't anything. He was off the mule when Boon ran in on the bear. Then we looked up and he was lying on the ground." Boon was shouting at Tennie's Jim, still in the middle of the river.

"Come on, goddamn it!" he said. "Bring me that mule!"

"What do you want with a mule?" Major de Spain said.

Boon didn't even look at him. "I'm going to Hoke's to get the doctor," he said in that calm voice, his face quite calm beneath the steady thinning of the bright blood.

"You need a doctor yourself," Major de Spain said. "Tennie's Jim——"

"Damn that," Boon said. He turned on Major de Spain. His face was still calm, only his voice was a pitch higher. "Can't you see his goddamn guts are all out of him?"

"Boon!" Major de Spain said. They looked at one another. Boon was a good head taller than Major de Spain; even the boy was taller now than Major de Spain.

"I've got to get the doctor," Boon said. "His goddamn guts——"

"All right," Major de Spain said. Tennie's Jim came up out of the water. The horse and the sound mule had already scented Old Ben; they surged and plunged all the way up to the top of the bluff, dragging Tennie's Jim with them, before he could stop them and tie them and come back. Major de Spain unlooped the leather thong of his compass from his buttonhole and gave it to Tennie's Jim. "Go straight to Hoke's," he said. "Bring Doctor Crawford back with you. Tell him there are two men to be looked at. Take my mare. Can you find the road from here?"

"Yes, sir," Tennie's Jim said.

"All right," Major de Spain said. "Go on." He turned to the boy. "Take the mules and the horse and go back and get the wagon. We'll go on down the river in the boat to Coon bridge. Meet us there. Can you find it again?"

"Yes, sir," the boy said.

"All right. Get started."

He went back to the wagon. He realized then how far they had run. It was already afternoon when he put the mules into the traces and tied the horse's lead-rope to the tail-gate. He reached Coon bridge at dusk. The skiff was already there. Before he could see it and almost before he could see the water he had to leap from the tilting wagon, still holding the reins, and work around to where he could grasp the bit and then the ear of the plunging sound mule and dig his heels and hold it until Boon came up the bank. The rope of the led horse had already snapped and it had already disappeared up the road toward camp. They turned the wagon around and took the mules out and he led the sound mule a hundred yards up the road and tied it. Boon had already brought Lion up to the wagon and Sam was sitting up in the skiff now and when they raised him he tried to walk up the bank and to the wagon and he tried to climb into the wagon but Boon did not wait; he picked Sam up bodily and set him on the seat. Then they hitched Old Ben to the one-eyed mule's saddle again and dragged him up the bank and set two skid-poles into the open tail-gate and got him into the wagon and he went and got the sound mule and Boon fought it into the traces, striking it across its hard hollow-sounding face until it came into position and stood trembling. Then the rain came down, as though it had held off all day waiting on them.

They returned to camp through it, through the streaming and sightless dark, hearing long before they saw any light the horn and the spaced shots to guide them. When they came to Sam's dark little hut he tried to stand up. He spoke again in the tongue of the old fathers; then he said clearly: "Let me out. Let me out."

"He hasn't got any fire," Major said. "Go on!" he said sharply.

But Sam was struggling now, trying to stand up. "Let me out, master," he said. "Let me go home."

So he stopped the wagon and Boon got down and lifted Sam out. He did not wait to let Sam try to walk this time. He carried him into the hut and Major de Spain got light on a paper spill from the buried embers on the hearth and lit the lamp and Boon put Sam on his bunk and drew off his boots and Major de Spain covered him and the boy was not there, he was holding the mules, the sound one which was trying again to bolt since when the wagon stopped Old Ben's scent drifted forward again along the streaming blackness of air, but Sam's eyes were probably open again in that profound look which saw further than them or the hut, further than the death of a bear and the dying of a dog. Then they went on, toward the long wailing of the horn and the shots which seemed each to linger intact somewhere in the thick streaming air until the next spaced report joined and blended with it, to the lighted house, the bright streaming windows, the quiet faces as Boon entered, bloody and quite calm, carrying the bundled coat. He laid Lion, blood coat and all, on his stale sheetless pallet bed which not even Ash, as deft in the house as a woman, could ever make smooth.

The sawmill doctor from Hoke's was already there. Boon would not let the doctor touch him until he had seen to Lion. He wouldn't risk giving Lion chloroform. He put the entrails back and sewed him up without it while Major de Spain held his head and Boon his feet. But he never tried to move. He lay there, the yellow eyes open upon nothing while the quiet men in the new hunting clothes and in the old ones crowded into the little airless room rank with the smell of Boon's body and garments, and watched. Then the doctor cleaned and disinfected Boon's face and arm and leg and bandaged them and, the boy in front with a lantern and the doctor and McCaslin and Major de Spain and General Compson following, they went to Sam Fathers' hut. Tennie's Jim had built up the fire; he squatted before it, dozing. Sam had not moved since Boon had put him in the bunk and Major de Spain had covered him with the blankets, yet he opened his eyes and looked from one to another of the faces and when McCaslin touched his shoulder and said, "Sam. The doctor wants to look at you," he even drew his hands out of the blanket and began to fumble at his shirt buttons until McCaslin said, "Wait. We'll do it." They undressed him. He lay there—the copper-brown, almost hairless body, the old man's body, the old man, the wild man not even one generation from the woods, childless, kinless, peopleless—motionless, his eyes open but no longer looking at any of them, while the doctor examined him and drew the blankets up and put the stethoscope back into his bag and snapped the bag and only the boy knew that Sam too was going to die.

"Exhaustion," the doctor said. "Shock maybe. A man his age swimming rivers in December. He'll be all right. Just make him stay in bed for a day or two. Will there be somebody here with him?"

"There will be somebody here," Major de Spain said.

They went back to the house, to the rank little room where Boon still sat on the pallet bed with Lion's head under his hand while the men, the ones who had hunted behind Lion and the ones who had never seen him before today, came quietly in to look at him and went away. Then it was dawn and they all went out into the yard to look at Old Ben, with his eyes open too and his lips snarled back from his worn teeth and his mutilated foot and the little hard lumps under his skin which were the old bullets (there were fifty-two of them, buckshot rifle and ball) and the single almost invisible slit under his left shoulder where Boon's blade had finally found his life. Then Ash began to beat on the bottom of the dishpan with a heavy spoon to call them to breakfast and it was the first time he could remember hearing no sound from the dogs under the kitchen while they were eating. It was as if the old bear, even dead there in the yard, was a more potent terror still than they could face without Lion between them.

The rain had stopped during the night. By midmorning the thin sun appeared, rapidly burning away mist and cloud, warming the air and the earth; it would be one of those windless Mississippi December days which are a sort of Indian summer's Indian summer. They moved Lion out to the front gallery, into the sun. It was Boon's idea. "Goddamn it," he said, "he never did want to stay in the house until I made him. You know that." He took a crowbar and loosened the floor boards under his pallet bed so it could be raised, mattress and all, without disturbing Lion's position, and they carried him out to the gallery and put him down facing the woods.

Then he and the doctor and McCaslin and Major de Spain went to Sam's hut.

This time Sam didn't open his eyes and his breathing was so quiet, so peaceful that they could hardly see that he breathed. The doctor didn't even take out his stethoscope nor even touch him. "He's all right," the doctor said. "He didn't even catch cold. He just quit."

"Quit?" McCaslin said.

"Yes. Old people do that sometimes. Then they get a good night's sleep or maybe it's just a drink of whiskey, and they change their minds."

They returned to the house. And then they began to arrive—the swamp-dwellers, the gaunt men who ran trap-lines and lived on quinine and coons and river water, the farmers of little corn- and cotton-patches along the bottom's edge whose fields and cribs and pigpens the old bear had rifled, the loggers from the camp, and the sawmill men from Hoke's and the town men from further away than that, whose hounds the old bear had slain and whose traps and deadfalls he had wrecked and whose lead he carried. They came up mounted and on foot and in wagons, to enter the yard and look at him and then go on to the front where Lion lay, filling the little yard and overflowing it until there were almost a hundred of them squatting and standing in the warm and drowsing sunlight, talking quietly of hunting, of the game and the dogs which ran it, of hounds and bear and deer and men of yesterday vanished from the earth, while from time to time the great blue dog would open his eyes, not as if he were listening to them but as though to look at the woods for a moment before closing his eyes again, to remember the woods or to see that they were still there. He died at sundown.

Major de Spain broke camp that night. They carried Lion into the woods, or Boon carried him that is, wrapped in a quilt from his bed, just as he had refused to let anyone else touch Lion yesterday until the doctor got there; Boon carrying Lion, and the boy and General Compson and Walter and still almost fifty of them following with lanterns and lighted pine-knots—men from Hoke's and even further, who would have to ride out of the bottom in the dark, and swampers and trappers who would have to walk even, scattering toward the little hidden huts where they lived. And Boon would let nobody else dig the grave either and lay Lion in it and cover him, and then General Compson stood at the head of it while the blaze and smoke of the pine-knots streamed away among the winter branches and spoke as he would have spoken over a man. Then they returned to camp. Major de Spain and McCaslin and Ash had rolled and tied all the bedding. The mules were hitched to the wagon and pointed out of the bottom and the wagon was already loaded and the stove in the kitchen was cold and the table was set with scraps of cold food and bread and only the coffee was hot when the boy ran into the kitchen where Major de Spain and McCaslin had already eaten. "What?" he cried. "What? I'm not going."

"Yes," McCaslin said, "we're going out tonight. Major wants to get on back home."

"No!" he said. "I'm going to stay."

"You've got to be back in school Monday. You've already missed a week more than I intended. It will take you from now until Monday to catch up. Sam's all right. You heard Doctor Crawford. I'm going to leave Boon and Tennie's Jim both to stay with him until he feels like getting up."

He was panting. The others had come in. He looked rapidly and almost frantically around at the other faces. Boon had a fresh bottle. He upended it and started the cork by striking the bottom of the bottle with the heel of his hand and drew the cork with his teeth and spat it out and drank. "You're damn right you're going back to school," Boon said. "Or I'll burn the tail off of you myself if Cass don't, whether you are sixteen or sixty. Where in hell do you expect to get without education? Where would Cass be? Where in hell would I be if I hadn't never went to school?"

He looked at McCaslin again. He could feel his breath coming shorter and shorter and shallower and shallower, as if there were not enough air in the kitchen for that many to breathe. "This is just Thursday. I'll come home Sunday night on one of the horses. I'll come home Sunday, then. I'll make up the time I lost studying Sunday night, McCaslin," he said, without even despair.

"No, I tell you," McCaslin said. "Sit down here and eat your supper. We're going out to——"

"Hold up, Cass," General Compson said. The boy did not know General Compson had moved until he put his hand on his shoulder. "What is it, bud?" he said.

"I've got to stay," he said. "I've got to."

"All right," General Compson said. "You can stay. If missing an extra week of school is going to throw you so far behind you'll have to sweat to find out what some hired pedagogue put between the covers of a book, you better quit altogether.—And you shut up, Cass," he said, though McCaslin had not spoken. "You've got one foot straddled into a farm and the other foot straddled into a bank; you ain't even got a good hand-hold where this boy was already an old man long before you damned Sartorises and Edmondses invented farms and banks to keep yourselves from having to find out what this boy was born knowing, and fearing too maybe, but without being afraid, that could go ten miles on a compass because he wanted to look at a bear none of us had ever got near enough to put a bullet in and looked at the bear and came the ten miles back on the compass in the dark; maybe by God that's the why and the wherefore of farms and banks.—I reckon you still ain't going to tell what it is?"

But still he could not. "I've got to stay," he said.

"All right," General Compson said. "There's plenty of grub left. And you'll come home Sunday, like you promised McCaslin? Not Sunday night: Sunday."

"Yes, sir," he said.

"All right," General Compson said. "Sit down and eat, boys," he said. "Let's get started. It's going to be cold before we get home."

They ate. The wagon was already loaded and ready to depart; all they had to do was to get into it. Boon would drive them out to the road, to the farmer's stable where the surrey had been left. He stood beside the wagon, in silhouette on the sky, turbaned like a Paythan and taller than any there, the bottle tilted. Then he flung the bottle from his lips without even lowering it, spinning and glinting in the faint starlight, empty. "Them that's going," he said, "get in the goddamn wagon. Them that ain't, get out of the goddamn way." The others got in. Boon mounted to the seat beside General Compson and the wagon moved, on into the obscurity until the boy could no longer see it, even the moving density of it amid the greater night. But he could still hear it, for a long while: the slow, deliberate banging of the wooden frame as it lurched from rut to rut. And he could hear Boon even when he could no longer hear the wagon. He was singing, harsh, tuneless, loud.

That was Thursday. On Saturday morning Tennie's Jim left on McCaslin's woods-horse which had not been out of the bottom one time now in six years, and late that afternoon rode through the gate on the spent horse and on to the commissary where McCaslin was rationing the tenants and the wage-hands for the coming week, and this time McCaslin forestalled any necessity or risk of having to wait while Major de Spain's surrey was being horsed and harnessed. He took their own, and with Tennie's Jim already asleep in the back seat he drove in to Jefferson and waited while Major de Spain changed to boots and put on his overcoat, and they drove the thirty miles in the dark of that night and at daybreak on Sunday morning they swapped to the waiting mare and mule and as the sun rose they rode out of the jungle and onto the low ridge where they had buried Lion: the low mound of unannealed earth where Boon's spade-marks still showed, and beyond the grave the platform of freshly cut saplings bound between four posts and the blanket-wrapped bundle upon the platform and Boon and the boy squatting between the platform and the grave until Boon, the bandage removed, ripped from his head so that the long scoriations of Old Ben's claws resembled crusted tar in the sunlight, sprang up and threw down upon them with the old gun with which he had never been known to hit anything although McCaslin was already off the mule, kicked both feet free of the irons and vaulted down before the mule had stopped, walking toward Boon.

"Stand back," Boon said. "By God, you won't touch him. Stand back, McCaslin." Still McCaslin came on, fast yet without haste.

"Cass!" Major de Spain said. Then he said, "Boon! You, Boon!" and he was down too and the boy rose too, quickly, and still McCaslin came on not fast but steady and walked up to the grave and reached his hand steadily out, quickly yet still not fast, and took hold the gun by the middle so that he and Boon faced one another across Lion's grave, both holding the gun, Boon's spent indomitable amazed and frantic face almost a head higher than McCaslin's beneath the black scoriations of beast's claws and then Boon's chest began to heave as though there were not enough air in all the woods, in all the wilderness, for all of them, for him and anyone else, even for him alone.

"Turn it loose, Boon," McCaslin said.

"You damn little spindling—" Boon said. "Don't you know I can take it away from you? Don't you know I can tie it around your neck like a damn cravat?"

"Yes," McCaslin said. "Turn it loose, Boon."

"This is the way he wanted it. He told us. He told us exactly how to do it. And by God you ain't going to move him. So we did it like he said, and I been sitting here ever since to keep the damn wildcats and varmints away from him and by God—" Then McCaslin had the gun, downslanted while he pumped the slide, the five shells snicking out of it so fast that the last one was almost out before the first one touched the ground and McCaslin dropped the gun behind him without once having taken his eyes from Boon's.

"Did you kill him, Boon?" he said. Then Boon moved. He turned, he moved like he was still drunk and then for a moment blind too, one hand out as he blundered toward the big tree and seemed to stop walking before he reached the tree so that he plunged, fell toward it, flinging up both hands and catching himself against the tree and turning until his back was against it, backing with the tree's trunk his wild spent scoriated face and the tremendous heave and collapse of his chest, McCaslin following, facing him again, never once having moved his eyes from Boon's eyes. "Did you kill him, Boon?"

"No!" Boon said. "No!"

"Tell the truth," McCaslin said. "I would have done it if he had asked me to." Then the boy moved. He was between them, facing McCaslin; the water felt as if it had burst and sprung not from his eyes alone but from his whole face, like sweat.

"Leave him alone!" he cried. "Goddamn it! Leave him alone!"

PART 4

then he was twenty-one. He could say it, himself and his cousin juxtaposed not against the wilderness but against the tamed land which was to have been his heritage, the land which old Carothers McCaslin, his grandfather, had bought with white man's money from the wild men whose grandfathers without guns hunted it, and tamed and ordered, or believed he had tamed and ordered it, for the reason that the human beings he held in bondage and in the power of life and death had removed the forest from it and in their sweat scratched the surface of it to a depth of perhaps fourteen inches in order to grow something out of it which had not been there before, and which could be translated back into the money he who believed he had bought it had had to pay to get it and hold it, and a reasonable profit too: and for which reason old Carothers McCaslin, knowing better, could raise his children, his descendants and heirs, to believe the land was his to hold and bequeath, since the strong and ruthless man has a cynical foreknowledge of his own vanity and pride and strength and a contempt for all his get: just as, knowing better, Major de Spain had his fragment of that wilderness which was bigger and older than any recorded deed: just as, knowing better, old Thomas Sutpen, from whom Major de Spain had had his fragment for money: just as Ikkemotubbe, the Chickasaw chief, from whom Thomas Sutpen had had the fragment for money or rum or whatever it was, knew in his turn that not even a fragment of it had been his to relinquish or sell

not against the wilderness but against the land, not in pursuit and lust but in relinquishment; and in the commissary as it should have been, not the heart perhaps but certainly the solar-plexus of the repudiated and relinquished: the square, galleried, wooden building squatting like a portent above the fields whose laborers it still held in thrall, '65 or no, and placarded over with advertisements for snuff and cures for chills and salves and potions manufactured and sold by white men to bleach the pigment and straighten the hair of Negroes that they might resemble the very race which for two hundred years had held them in bondage and from which for another hundred years not even a bloody civil war would have set them completely free

himself and his cousin amid the old smells of cheese and salt meat and kerosene and harness, the ranked shelves of tobacco and overalls and bottled medicine and thread and plow-bolts, the barrels and kegs of flour and meal and molasses and nails, the wall pegs dependant with plowlines and plow-collars and hames and trace-chains, and the desk and the shelf above it on which rested the ledgers in which McCaslin recorded the slow outward trickle of food and supplies and equipment which returned each fall as cotton made and ginned and sold (two threads frail as truth and impalpable as equators yet cable-strong to bind for life them who made the cotton to the land their sweat fell on), and the older ledgers, clumsy and archaic in size and shape, on the yellowed pages of which were recorded in the faded hand of his father Theophilus and his uncle Amodeus during the two decades before the Civil War the manumission, in title at least, of Carothers McCaslin's slaves:

'Relinquish,' McCaslin said. 'Relinquish. You, the direct male descendant of him who saw the opportunity and took it, bought the land, took the land, got the land no matter how, held it to bequeath, no matter how, out of the old grant, the first patent, when it was a wilderness of wild beasts and wilder men, and cleared it, translated it into something to bequeath to his children, worthy of bequeathment for his descendants' ease and security and pride, and to perpetuate his name and accomplishments. Not only the male descendant but the only and last descendant in the male line and in the third generation, while I am not only four generations from old Carothers, I derived through a woman and the very McCaslin in my name is mine only by sufferance and courtesy and my grandmother's pride in what that man accomplished, whose legacy and monument you think you can repudiate.' and he

'I can't repudiate it. It was never mine to repudiate. It was never Father's and Uncle Buddy's to bequeath me to repudiate, because it was never Grandfather's to bequeath them to bequeath me to repudiate, because it was never old Ikkemotubbe's to sell to Grandfather for bequeathment and repudiation. Because it was never Ikkemotubbe's fathers' fathers' to bequeath Ikkemotubbe to sell to Grandfather or any man because on the instant when Ikkemotubbe discovered, realized, that he could sell it for money, on that instant it ceased ever to have been his forever, father to father to father, and the man who bought it bought nothing.'

'Bought nothing?' and he

'Bought nothing. Because He told in the Book how He created the earth, made it and looked at it and said it was all right, and then He made man. He made the earth first and peopled it with dumb creatures, and then He created man to be His overseer on the earth and to hold suzerainty over the earth and the animals on it in His name, not to hold for himself and his descendants inviolable title forever, generation after generation, to the oblongs and squares of the earth, but to hold the earth mutual and intact in the communal anonymity of brotherhood, and all the fee He asked was pity and humility and sufferance and endurance and the sweat of his face for bread. And I know what you are going to say,' he said: 'That nevertheless Grandfather—' and McCaslin

'—did own it. And not the first. Not alone and not the first since, as your Authority states, man was dispossessed of Eden. Nor yet the second and still not alone, on down through the tedious and shabby chronicle of His chosen sprung from Abraham; and of the sons of them who dispossessed Abraham, and of the five hundred years during which half the known world and all it contained was chattel to one city, as this plantation and all the life it contained was chattel and revokeless thrall to this commissary store and those ledgers yonder during your grandfather's life; and the next thousand years while men fought over the fragments of that collapse until at last even the fragments were exhausted and men snarled over the gnawed bones of the old world's worthless evening until an accidental egg discovered to them a new hemisphere. So let me say it: That nevertheless and notwithstanding old Carothers did own it. Bought it, got it, no matter; kept it, held it, no matter; bequeathed it: else why do you stand here relinquishing and repudiating? Held it, kept it for fifty years until you could repudiate it, while He—this Arbiter, this Architect, this Umpire—condoned—or did He? looked down and saw—or did He? Or at least did nothing: saw, and could not, or did not see; saw, and would not, or perhaps He would not see— perverse, impotent, or blind: which?' and he

'Dispossessed.' and McCaslin

'What?' and he

'Dispossessed. Not impotent: He didn't condone; not blind, because He watched it. And let me say it. Dispossessed of Eden. Dispossessed of Canaan, and those who dispossessed him dispossessed him dispossessed, and the five hundred years of absentee landlords in the Roman bagnios, and the thousand years of wild men from the northern woods who dispossessed them and devoured their ravished substance ravished in turn again and then snarled in what you call the old world's worthless twilight over the old world's gnawed bones, blasphemous in His name until He used a simple egg to discover to them a new world where a nation of people could be founded in humility and pity and sufferance and pride of one to another. And Grandfather did own the land nevertheless and notwithstanding because He permitted it, not impotent and not condoning and not blind, because He ordered and watched it. He saw the land already accursed even as Ikkemotubbe and Ikkemotubbe's father old Issetibbeha and old Issetibbeha's fathers too held it, already tainted even before any white man owned it by what Grandfather and his kind, his fathers, had brought into the new land which He had vouchsafed them out of pity and sufferance, on condition of pity and humility and sufferance and endurance, from that old world's corrupt and worthless twilight as though in the sailfuls of the old world's tainted wind which drove the ships—' and McCaslin

'Ah.'

'—and no hope for the land anywhere so long as Ikkemotubbe and Ikkemotubbe's descendants held it in unbroken succession. Maybe He saw that only by voiding the land for a time of Ikkemotubbe's blood and substituting for it another blood, could He accomplish His purpose. Maybe He knew already what that other blood would be, maybe it was more than justice that only the white man's blood was available and capable to raise the white man's curse, more than vengeance when—' and McCaslin

'Ah.'

'—when He used the blood which had brought in the evil to destroy the evil as doctors use fever to burn up fever, poison to slay poison. Maybe He chose Grandfather out of all of them He might have picked. Maybe He knew that Grandfather himself would not serve His purpose because Grandfather was born too soon too, but that Grandfather would have descendants, the right descendants; maybe He had foreseen already the descendants Grandfather would have, maybe He saw already in Grandfather the seed progenitive of the three generations He saw it would take to set at least some of His lowly people free—' and McCaslin

'The sons of Ham. You who quote the Book: the sons of Ham.' and he

'There are some things He said in the Book, and some things reported of Him that He did not say. And I know what you will say now: That if truth is one thing to me and another thing to you, how will we choose which is truth? You don't need to choose. The heart already knows. He didn't have His Book written to be read by what must elect and choose, but by the heart, not by the wise of the earth because maybe they don't need it or maybe the wise no longer have any heart, but by the doomed and lowly of the earth who have nothing else to read with but the heart. Because the men who wrote His Book for Him were writing about truth and there is only one truth and it covers all things that touch the heart.' and McCaslin

'So these men who transcribed His Book for Him were sometime liars.' and he

'Yes. Because they were human men. They were trying to write down the heart's truth out of the heart's driving complexity, for all the complex and troubled hearts which would beat after them. What they were trying to tell, what He wanted said, was too simple. Those for whom they transcribed His words could not have believed them. It had to be expounded in the everyday terms which they were familiar with and could comprehend, not only those who listened but those who told it too, because if they who were that near to Him as to have been elected from among all who breathed and spoke language to transcribe and relay His words, could comprehend truth only through the complexity of passion and lust and hate and fear which drives the heart, what distance back to truth must they traverse whom truth could only reach by word-of-mouth?' and McCaslin

'I might answer that, since you have taken to proving your points and disproving mine by the same text, I don't know. But I don't say that, because you have answered yourself: No time at all if, as you say, the heart knows truth, the infallible and unerring heart. And perhaps you are right, since although you admitted three generations from old Carothers to you, there were not three. There were not even completely two. Uncle Buck and Uncle Buddy. And they not the first and not alone. A thousand other Bucks and Buddies in less than two generations and sometimes less than one in this land which so you claim God created and man himself cursed and tainted. Not to mention 1865.' and he

'Yes. More men than Father and Uncle Buddy,' not even glancing toward the shelf above the desk, nor did McCaslin. They did not need to. To him it was as though the ledgers in their scarred cracked leather bindings were being lifted down one by one in their fading sequence and spread open on the desk or perhaps upon some apocryphal Bench, or even Altar, or perhaps before the Throne Itself for a last perusal and contemplation and refreshment of the Allknowledgeable, before the yellowed pages and the brown thin ink in which was recorded the injustice and a little at least of its amelioration and restitution faded back forever into the anonymous communal original dust

the yellowed pages scrawled in fading ink by the hand first of his grandfather and then of his father and uncle, bachelors up to and past fifty and then sixty, the one who ran the plantation and the farming of it, and the other who did the housework and the cooking and continued to do it even after his twin married and the boy himself was born the two brothers who as soon as their father was buried moved out of the tremendously-conceived, the almost barnlike edifice which he had not even completed, into a one-room log cabin which the two of them built themselves and added other rooms to while they lived in it, refusing to allow any slave to touch any timber of it other than the actual raising into place the logs which two men alone could not handle, and domiciled all the slaves in the big house some of the windows of which were still merely boarded up with odds and ends of plank or with the skins of bear and deer nailed over the empty frames: each sundown the brother who superintended the farming would parade the Negroes as a first sergeant dismisses a company, and herd them willynilly, man woman and child, without question protest or recourse, into the tremendous abortive edifice scarcely yet out of embryo, as if even old Carothers McCaslin had paused aghast at the concrete indication of his own vanity's boundless conceiving: he would call his mental roll and herd them in and with a hand-wrought nail as long as a flenching-knife and suspended from a short deer-hide thong attached to the door-jamb for that purpose, he would nail to the door of that house which lacked half its windows and had no hinged back door at all, so that presently, and for fifty years afterward, when the boy himself was big enough to hear and remember it, there was in the land a sort of folk-tale: of the countryside all night long full of skulking McCaslin slaves dodging the moonlit roads and the Patrol-riders to visit other plantations, and of the unspoken gentlemen's agreement between the two white men and the two dozen black ones that, after the white man had counted them and driven the home-made nail into the front door at sundown, neither of the white men would go around behind the house and look at the back door, provided that all the Negroes were behind the front one when the brother who drove it drew out the nail again at daybreak

the twins who were identical even in their handwriting, unless you had specimens side by side to compare, and even when both hands appeared on the same page (as often happened, as if, long since past any oral intercourse, they had used the diurnally advancing pages to conduct the unavoidable business of the compulsion which had traversed all the waste wilderness of North Mississippi in 1830 and '40 and singled them out to drive) they both looked as though they had been written by the same perfectly normal ten-year-old boy, even to the spelling, except that the spelling did not improve as one by one the slaves which Carothers McCaslin had inherited and purchased—Roscius and Phoebe and Thucydides and Eunice and their descendants, and Sam Fathers and his mother for both of whom he had swapped an underbred trotting gelding to old Ikkemotubbe, the Chickasaw chief, from whom he had likewise bought the land, and Tennie Beauchamp whom the twin Amodeus had won from a neighbor in a poker-game, and the anomaly calling itself Percival Brownlee which the twin Theophilus had purchased, neither he nor his brother ever knew why apparently, from Bedford Forrest while he was still only a slave-dealer and not yet a general (It was a single page, not long and covering less than a year, not seven months in fact, begun in the hand which the boy had learned to distinguish as that of his father:

Percavil Brownly 26yr Old. cleark @ Bookepper. bought from N.B.Forest at Cold Water 3 Mar 1856 $265. dolars

and beneath that, in the same hand:

*5 mar 1856 No bookepper any way Cant read. Can write his Name but I
already put that down My self Says he can Plough but dont look like it to
Me. sent to Feild to day Mar 5 1856*

and the same hand:

*6 Mar 1856 Cant plough either Says he aims to be a Precher so may be he
can lead live stock to Crick to Drink*

and this time it was the other, the hand which he now recognized as his uncle's
when he could see them both on the same page:

Mar 23th 1856 Cant do that either Except one at a Time Get shut of him

then the first again:

24 Mar 1856 Who in hell would buy him

then the second:

*19th of Apr 1856 Nobody You put yourself out of Market at Cold Water
two months ago I never said sell him Free him*

the first:

22 Apr 1856 Ill get it out of him

the second:

Jun 13th 1856 How $1 per yr 265$ 265 yrs Wholl sign his Free paper

then the first again:

*1 Oct 1856 Mule josephine Broke Leg @ shot Wrong stall wrong niger
wrong everything $100. dolars*

and the same:

2 Oct 1856 Freed Debit McCaslin @ McCaslin $265. dolars

then the second again:

*Oct 3th Debit Theophilus McCaslin Niger 265$ Mule 100$ 365$ He hasnt
gone yet Father should be here*

then the first:

3 Oct 1856 Son of a bitch wont leave What would father done

the second:

29th of Oct 1856 Renamed him

the first:

31 Oct 1856 Renamed him what

the second:

Chrstms 1856 Spintrius

) took substance and even a sort of shadowy life with their passions and complexities too, as page followed page and year year; all there, not only the general
and condoned injustice and its slow amortization but the specific tragedy which
had not been condoned and could never be amortized; the new page and the new
ledger, the hand which he could now recognize at first glance as his father's:

> Father dide Lucius Quintus Carothers McCaslin, Callina 1772 Missippy
> 1837. Dide and burid 27 June 1837
> Roskus. rased by Granfather in Callina Dont know how old. Freed 27 June
> 1837 Dont want to leave. Dide and Burid 12 Jan 1841
> Fibby Roskus Wife. bought by granfather in Callina says Fifty Freed 27
> June 1837 Dont want to leave. Dide and burd 1 Aug 1849
> Thucydus Roskus @ Fibby Son born in Callina 1779. Refused 10acre peace
> fathers Will 28 Jun 1837 Refused Cash offer $200. dolars from A. @ T.
> McCaslin 28 Jun 1837 Wants to stay and work it out

and beneath this and covering the next five pages and almost that many years,
the slow, day-by-day accrument of the wages allowed him and the food and
clothing—the molasses and meat and meal, the cheap durable shirts and jeans
and shoes, and now and then a coat against rain and cold—charged against the
slowly yet steadily mounting sum of balance (and it would seem to the boy that
he could actually see the black man, the slave whom his white owner had forever
manumitted by the very act from which the black man could never be free so
long as memory lasted, entering the commissary, asking permission perhaps of
the white man's son to see the ledger-page which he could not even read, not even
asking for the white man's word, which he would have had to accept for the reason that there was absolutely no way under the sun for him to test it, as to how
the account stood, how much longer before he could go and never return, even if
only as far as Jefferson seventeen miles away), on to the double pen-stroke closing
the final entry:

> 3 Nov 1841 By Cash to Thucydus McCaslin $200. dolars Set Up blaksmith
> in J. Dec 1841 Dide and burid in J. 17 feb 1854
> Eunice Bought by Father in New Orleans 1807 $650. dolars. Marrid to
> Thucydus 1809 Drownd in Crick Cristmas Day 1832

and then the other hand appeared, the first time he had seen it in the ledger to
distinguish it as his uncle's, the cook and housekeeper whom even McCaslin, who
had known him and the boy's father for sixteen years before the boy was born,
remembered as sitting all day long in the rocking chair from which he cooked
the food, before the kitchen fire on which he cooked it:

> June 21th 1833 Drownd herself

and the first:

> 23 Jun 1833 Who in hell ever heard of a niger drownding him self

and the second, unhurried, with a complete finality; the two identical entries
might have been made with a rubber stamp save for the date:

> Aug 13th 1833 Drownd herself

and he thought *But why? But why?* He was sixteen then. It was neither the first time he had been alone in the commissary nor the first time he had taken down the old ledgers familiar on their shelf above the desk ever since he could remember. As a child and even after nine and ten and eleven, when he had learned to read, he would look up at the scarred and cracked backs and ends but with no particular desire to open them, and though he intended to examine them someday because he realized that they probably contained a chronological and much more comprehensive though doubtless tedious record than he would ever get from any other source, not alone of his own flesh and blood but of all his people, not only the whites but the black ones too, who were as much a part of his ancestry as his white progenitors, and of the land which they had all held and used in common and fed from and on and would continue to use in common without regard to color or titular ownership, it would only be on some idle day when he was old and perhaps even bored a little, since what the old books contained would be after all these years fixed immutably, finished, unalterable, harmless. Then he was sixteen. He knew what he was going to find before he found it. He got the commissary key from McCaslin's room after midnight while McCaslin was asleep and with the commissary door shut and locked behind him and the forgotten lantern stinking anew the rank dead icy air, he leaned above the yellowed page and thought not Why drowned herself, but thinking what he believed his father had thought when he found his brother's first comment: Why did Uncle Buddy think she had drowned herself? finding, beginning to find on the next succeeding page what he knew he would find, only this was still not it because he already knew this:

> *Tomasina called Tomy Daughter of Thucydus @ Eunice Born 1810 dide in Child bed June 1833 and Burd. Yr stars fell*

nor the next:

> *Turl Son of Thucydus @ Eunice Tomy born Jun 1833 yr stars fell Fathers will*

and nothing more, no tedious recording filling this page of wages, day by day, and food and clothing charged against them, no entry of his death and burial because he had outlived his white half-brothers and the books which McCaslin kept did not include obituaries: just *Fathers will* and he had seen that too: old Carothers' bold cramped hand far less legible than his sons' even and not much better in spelling, who while capitalizing almost every noun and verb, made no effort to punctuate or construct whatever, just as he made no effort either to explain or obfuscate the thousand-dollar legacy to the son of an unmarried slave-girl, to be paid only at the child's coming-of-age, bearing the consequence of the act of which there was still no definite incontrovertible proof that he acknowledged, not out of his own substance, but penalizing his sons with it, charging them a cash forfeit on the accident of their own paternity; not even a bribe for silence toward his own fame since his fame would suffer only after he was no longer present to defend it, flinging almost contemptuously, as he might a cast-off hat or pair of shoes, the thousand dollars which could have had no more reality to him under those conditions than it would have to the Negro, the slave who would not even see it until he came of age, twenty-one years too late to begin to learn what money was. *So I reckon that was cheaper than saying My son to a nigger,* he thought. *Even if My son wasn't but just two words. But there must have been love,* he thought. *Some sort of love. Even what he would have called love: not just an afternoon's or a night's spittoon.* There was the old man, old, within five years of his life's end, long a widower and, since his sons were not only bachelors but were approaching middleage, lonely in the house and doubtless even bored, since his plantation was established now and functioning and there was enough money now, too much of it probably for a man whose vices even apparently remained below his means; there was the girl, husbandless and young, only twenty-three when the child was born: perhaps he had sent for her at first out of loneliness, to have a young voice and movement in the house, summoned her, bade her mother send her each morning to sweep the floors and make the beds and the mother acquiescing since that was probably already understood, already planned: the only child of a couple who were not field hands and who held themselves something above the other slaves, not alone for that reason but because the husband and his father and mother too had been inherited by the white man from his father, and the white man himself had travelled three hundred miles and better to New Orleans in a day when men travelled by horseback or steamboat, and bought the girl's mother as a wife for him

and that was all. The old frail pages seemed to turn of their own accord even while he thought, *His own daughter His own daughter. No. No Not even him,* back to that one where the white man (not even a widower then) who never went anywhere, any more than his sons in their time ever did, and who did not need another slave, had gone all the way to New Orleans and bought one. And Tomey's Terrel was still alive when the boy was ten years old and he knew from his own observation and memory that there had already been some white in Tomey's Terrel's blood before his father gave him the rest of it; and looking down at the yellowed page spread beneath the yellow glow of the lantern smoking and stinking in that rank chill midnight room fifty years later, he seemed to see her actually walking into the icy creek on that Christmas day six months before her daughter's and her lover's (*Her first lover's,* he thought. *Her first*) child was born, solitary, inflexible, griefless, ceremonial, in formal and succinct repudiation of grief and despair, who had already had to repudiate belief and hope

that was all. He would never need look at the ledgers again nor did he; the yellowed pages in their fading and implacable succession were as much a part of his consciousness and would remain so forever, as the fact of his own nativity:

> *Tennie Beauchamp 21yrs Won by Amodeus McCaslin from Hubert Beauchamp Esqre Possible Strait against three Treys in sigt Not called 1859 Marrid to Tomys Turl 1859*

and no date of freedom because her freedom, as well as that of her first surviving child, derived not from Buck and Buddy McCaslin in the commissary but from a stranger in Washington, and no date of death and burial, not only because McCaslin kept no obituaries in his books, but because in this year 1883 she was still alive and would remain so to see a grandson by her last surviving child:

> *Amodeus McCaslin Beauchamp Son of tomys Turl @ Tennie Beauchamp 1859 dide 1859*

then his uncle's hand entire, because his father was now a member of the cavalry command of that man whose name as a slave-dealer he could not even spell: and not even a page and not even a full line:

> *Dauter Tomes Turl and tenny 1862*

and not even a line and not even a sex and no cause given though the boy could guess it because McCaslin was thirteen then and he remembered how there was not always enough to eat in more places than Vicksburg:

> *Child of tomes Turl and Tenny 1863*

and the same hand again and this one lived, as though Tennie's perseverance and the fading and diluted ghost of old Carothers' ruthlessness had at last conquered even starvation: and clearer, fuller, more carefully written and spelled than the boy had yet seen it, as if the old man, who should have been a woman to begin with, trying to run what was left of the plantation in his brother's absence in the intervals of cooking and caring for himself and the fourteen-year-old orphan, had taken as an omen for renewed hope the fact that this nameless inheritor of slaves was at least remaining alive along enough to receive a name:

> *James Thucydus Beauchamp Son of Tomes Turl and Tenny Beauchamp Born 29th december 1864 and both Well Wanted to call him Theophilus but Tride Amodeus McCaslin and Callina McCaslin and both dide so Disswaded Them Born at Two clock A,m, both Well*

but no more, nothing; it would be another two years yet before the boy, almost a man now, would return from the abortive trip into Tennessee with the still-intact third of old Carothers' legacy to his Negro son and his descendants, which as the three surviving children established at last one by one their apparent intention of surviving, their white half-uncles had increased to a thousand dollars each, conditions permitting, as they came of age, and completed the page himself as far as it would even be completed when that day was long passed beyond which a man born in 1864 (or 1867 either, when he himself saw light) could have expected or himself hoped or even wanted to be still alive; his own hand now, queerly enough resembling neither his father's nor his uncle's nor even McCaslin's, but like that of his grandfather's save for the spelling:

> *Vanished sometime on night of his twenty-first birthday Dec 29 1885. Traced by Isaac McCaslin to Jackson Tenn. and there lost. His third of legacy $1000.00 returned to McCaslin Edmonds Trustee this day Jan 12 1886*

but not yet: that would be two years yet, and now his father's again, whose old commander was now quit of soldiering and slave-trading both; once more in the ledger and then not again, and more illegible than ever, almost indecipherable at all from the rheumatism which now crippled him, and almost completely innocent now even of any sort of spelling as well as punctuation, as if the four years during which he had followed the sword of the only man ever breathing who ever sold him a Negro, let alone beat him in a trade, had convinced him not only of the vanity of faith and hope, but of orthography too:

> *Miss sophonsiba b dtr t t @ t 1869*

but not of belief and will because it was there, written, as McCaslin had told him, with the left hand, but there in the ledger one time more and then not again, for the boy himself was a year old, and when Lucas was born six years later, his father and uncle had been dead inside the same twelve-months almost five years; his own hand again, who was there and saw it, 1886, she was just seventeen, two years younger than himself, and he was in the commissary when McCaslin entered out of the first of dusk and said, 'He wants to marry Fonsiba,' like that: and he looked past McCaslin and saw the man, the stranger, taller than McCaslin and wearing better clothes than McCaslin and most of the other white men the boy knew habitually wore, who entered the room like a white man and stood in it like a white man, as though he had let McCaslin precede him into it not because McCaslin's skin was white but simply because McCaslin lived there and knew the way, and who talked like a white man too, looking at him past McCaslin's shoulder rapidly and keenly once and then no more, without further interest, as a mature and contained white man not impatient but just pressed for time might have looked. 'Marry Fonsiba?' he cried. 'Marry Fonsiba?' and then no more either, just watching and listening while McCaslin and the Negro talked:

'To live in Arkansas, I believe you said.'
'Yes. I have property there. A farm.'
'Property? A farm? You own it?'
'Yes.'
'You don't say Sir, do you?'
'To my elders, yes.'
'I see. You are from the North.'
'Yes. Since a child.'
'Then your father was a slave.'
'Yes. Once.'
'Then how do you own a farm in Arkansas?'
'I have a grant. It was my father's. From the United States. For military service.'
'I see,' McCaslin said. 'The Yankee army.'
'The United States army,' the stranger said; and then himself again, crying it at McCaslin's back:
'Call aunt Tennie! I'll go get her! I'll——' But McCaslin was not even including him; the stranger did not even glance back toward his voice, the two of them speaking to one another again as if he were not even there:
'Since you seem to have it all settled,' McCaslin said, 'why have you bothered to consult my authority at all?'
'I don't,' the stranger said. 'I acknowledge your authority only so far as you admit your responsibility toward her as a female member of the family of which you are the head. I don't ask your permission. I——'
'That will do!' McCaslin said. But the stranger did not falter. It was neither as if he were ignoring McCaslin nor as if he had failed to hear him. It was as though he were making, not at all an excuse and not exactly a justification, but simply a statement which the situation absolutely required and demanded should be made in McCaslin's hearing whether McCaslin listened to it or not. It was as if he were talking to himself, for himself to hear the words spoken aloud. They

faced one another, not close yet at slightly less than foils' distance, erect, their voices not raised, not impactive, just succinct:

'—I inform you, notify you in advance as chief of her family. No man of honor could do less. Besides, you have, in your way, according to your lights and upbringing——'

'That's enough, I said,' McCaslin said. 'Be off this place by full dark. Go.' But for another moment the other did not move, contemplating McCaslin with that detached and heatless look, as if he were watching reflected in McCaslin's pupils the tiny image of the figure he was sustaining.

'Yes,' he said. 'After all, this is your house. And in your fashion you have. . . . But no matter. You are right. This is enough.' He turned back toward the door; he paused again but only for a second, already moving while he spoke: 'Be easy. I will be good to her.' Then he was gone.

'But how did she ever know him?' the boy cried. 'I never even heard of him before! And Fonsiba, that's never been off this place except to go to church since she was born——'

'Ha,' McCaslin said. 'Even their parents don't know until too late how seventeen-year-old girls ever met the men who marry them too, if they are lucky.' And the next morning they were both gone, Fonsiba too. McCaslin never saw her again, nor did he, because the woman he found at last, five months later, was no one he had ever known. He carried a third of the three-thousand-dollar fund in gold in a money-belt, as when he had vainly traced Tennie's Jim into Tennessee a year ago. They—the man—had left an address of some sort with Tennie, and three months later a letter came, written by the man although McCaslin's wife, Alice, had taught Fonsiba to read and write too a little. But it bore a different postmark from the address the man had left with Tennie, and he travelled by rail as far as he could and then by contracted stage and then by a hired livery rig and then by rail again for a distance: an experienced traveller by now and an experienced bloodhound too, and a successful one this time because he would have to be; as the slow interminable empty muddy December miles crawled and crawled and night followed night in hotels, in roadside taverns of rough logs and containing little else but a bar, and in the cabins of strangers, and the hay of lonely barns, in none of which he dared undress because of his secret golden girdle like that of a disguised one of the Magi travelling incognito and not even hope to draw him, but only determination and desperation, he would tell himself: *I will have to find her. I will have to. We have already lost one of them. I will have to find her this time.* He did. Hunched in the slow and icy rain, on a spent hired horse splashed to the chest and higher, he saw it—a single log edifice with a clay chimney, which seemed in process of being flattened by the rain to a nameless and valueless rubble of dissolution in that roadless and even pathless waste of unfenced fallow and wilderness jungle—no barn, no stable, not so much as a hen-coop: just a log cabin built by hand and no clever hand either, a meagre pile of clumsily-cut firewood sufficient for about one day and not even a gaunt hound to come bellowing out from under the house when he rode up—a farm only in embryo, perhaps a good farm, maybe even a plantation someday, but not now, not for years yet and only then with labor, hard and enduring and unflagging work and sacrifice; he shoved open the crazy kitchen door in its awry frame and entered an icy gloom where not even a fire for cooking burned, and after another moment saw, crouched into the wall's angle behind a crude table, the coffee-colored face which he had known all his life but knew no more, the body which had been born within a hundred yards of the room that he was born in and in which some of his own blood ran, but which was now completely inheritor of generation after generation to whom an unannounced white man on a horse was a white man's hired Patroller wearing a pistol sometimes and a blacksnake whip always; he entered the next room, the only other room the cabin owned, and found, sitting in a rocking chair before the hearth, the man himself, reading —sitting there in the only chair in the house, before that miserable fire for which there was not wood sufficient to last twenty-four hours, in the same ministerial clothing in which he had entered the commissary five months ago and a pair of gold-framed spectacles which, when he looked up and then rose to his feet, the boy saw did not even contain lenses, reading a book in the midst of that desolation, that muddy waste, fenceless and even pathless and without even a walled shed for stock to stand beneath: and over all, permeant, clinging to the man's very clothing and exuding from his skin itself, that rank stink of baseless and imbecile delusion, that boundless rapacity and folly, of the carpet-bagger followers of victorious armies.

'Don't you see?' he cried. 'Don't you see? This whole land, the whole South, is cursed, and all of us who derive from it, whom it ever suckled, white and black both, lie under the curse? Granted that my people brought the curse onto the land: maybe for that reason their descendants alone can—not resist it, not combat it—maybe just endure and outlast it until the curse is lifted. Then your peoples' turn will come because we have forfeited ours. But not now. Not yet. Don't you see?'

The other stood now, the unfrayed garments still ministerial even if not quite so fine, the book closed upon one finger to keep the place, the lenseless spectacles held like a music master's wand in the other workless hand while the owner of it spoke his measured and sonorous imbecility of the boundless folly and the baseless hope: 'You're wrong. The curse you whites brought into this land has been lifted. It has been voided and discharged. We are seeing a new era, an era dedicated, as our founders intended it, to freedom, liberty and equality for all, to which this country will be the new Canaan——'

'Freedom from what? From work? Canaan?' He jerked his arm, comprehensive, almost violent: whereupon it all seemed to stand there about them, intact and complete and visible in the drafty, damp, heatless, Negro-stale Negro-rank sorry room—the empty fields without plow or seed to work them, fenceless against the stock which did not exist within or without the walled stable which likewise was not there. 'What corner of Canaan is this?'

'You are seeing it at a bad time. This is winter. No man farms this time of year.'

'I see. And of course her need for food and clothing will stand still while the land lies fallow.'

'I have a pension,' the other said. He said it as a man might say *I have grace* or *I own a gold mine.* 'I have my father's pension too. It will arrive on the first of the month. What day is this?'

'The eleventh,' he said. 'Twenty days more. And until then?'

'I have a few groceries in the house from my credit account with the merchant in Midnight who banks my pension check for me. I have executed to him a power of attorney to handle it for me as a matter of mutual—'

'I see. And if the groceries don't last the twenty days?'

'I still have one more hog.'

'Where?'

'Outside,' the other said. 'It is customary in this country to allow stock to range free during the winter for food. It comes up from time to time. But no matter if it doesn't; I can probably trace its footprints when the need——'

'Yes!' he cried. 'Because no matter: you still have the pension check. And the man in Midnight will cash it and pay himself out of it for what you have already eaten and if there is any left over, it is yours. And the hog will be eaten by then or you still can't catch it, and then what will you do?'

'It will be almost spring then,' the other said. 'I am planning in the spring——'

'It will be January,' he said. 'And then February. And then more than half of March—' and when he stopped again in the kitchen she had not moved, she did not even seem to breathe or to be alive except her eyes watching him; when he took a step toward her it was still not movement because she could have retreated no further: only the tremendous, fathomless, ink-colored eyes in the narrow, thin, too thin, coffee-colored face watching him without alarm, without recognition, without hope. 'Fonsiba,' he said. 'Fonsiba. Are you all right?'

'I'm free,' she said. Midnight was a tavern, a livery stable, a big store (that would be where the pension check banked itself as a matter of mutual elimination of bother and fret, he thought) and a little one, a saloon and a blacksmith shop. But there was a bank there too. The president (the owner, for all practical purposes) of it was a translated Mississippian who had been one of Forrest's men too: and his body lightened of the golden belt for the first time since he left home eight days ago, with pencil and paper he multiplied three dollars by twelve months and divided it into one thousand dollars; it would stretch that way over almost twenty-eight years and for twenty-eight years at least she would not starve, the banker promising to send the three dollars himself by a trusty messenger on the fifteenth of each month and put it into her actual hand, and he returned home and that was all because in 1874 his father and his uncle were both dead and the old ledgers never again came down from the shelf above the desk to which his father had returned them for the last time that day in 1869. But he could have completed it:

> *Lucas Quintus Carothers McCaslin Beauchamp. Last surviving son and child of Tomey's Terrel and Tennie Beauchamp. March 17, 1874*

except that there was no need: not *Lucius Quintus @c @c @c*, but *Lucas Quintus*, not refusing to be called Lucius, because he simply eliminated that word from the name; not denying, declining the name itself, because he used three quarters of it; but simply taking the name and changing, altering it, making it no longer the white man's but his own, by himself composed, himself self-progenitive and nominate, by himself ancestored, as, for all the old ledgers recorded to the contrary, old Carothers himself was

and that was all: 1874 the boy; 1888 the man, repudiated denied and free; 1895 and husband but no father, unwidowered but without a wife, and found long since that no man is ever free and probably could not bear it if he were; married then and living in Jefferson in the little new jerrybuilt bungalow which his wife's father had given them: and one morning Lucas stood suddenly in the doorway of the room where he was reading the Memphis paper and he looked at the paper's dateline and thought *It's his birthday. He's twenty-one today* and Lucas said: 'Whar's the rest of that money old Carothers left? I wants it. All of it.'

that was all: and McCaslin

'More men than that one Buck and Buddy to fumble-heed that truth so mazed for them that spoke it and so confused for them that heard yet still there was 1865:' and he

'But not enough. Not enough of even Father and Uncle Buddy to fumble-heed in even three generations not even three generations fathered by Grandfather not even if there had been nowhere beneath His sight any but Grandfather and so He would not even have needed to elect and choose. But He tried and I know what you will say. That having Himself created them He could have known no more of hope than He could have pride and grief, but He didn't hope He just waited because He had made them: not just because He had set them alive and in motion but because He had already worried with them so long: worried with them so long because He had seen how in individual cases they were capable of anything, any height or depth remembered in mazed incomprehension out of heaven where hell was created too, and so He must admit them or else admit his equal somewhere and so be no longer God and therefore must accept responsibility for what He Himself had done in order to live with Himself in His lonely and paramount heaven. And He probably knew it was vain but He had created them and knew them capable of all things because He had shaped them out of the primal Absolute which contained all and had watched them since in their individual exaltation and baseness, and they themselves not knowing why nor how nor even when: until at last He saw that they were all Grandfather all of them and that even from them the elected and chosen the best the very best He could expect (not hope mind: not hope) would be Bucks and Buddies and not even enough of them and in the third generation not even Bucks and Buddies but—' and McCaslin

'Ah:' and he

'Yes. If He could see Father and Uncle Buddy in Grandfather He must have seen me too. —an Isaac born into a later life than Abraham's and repudiating immolation: fatherless and therefore safe declining the altar because maybe this time the exasperated Hand might not supply the kid—' and McCaslin

'Escape:' and he

'All right. Escape.—Until one day He said what you told Fonsiba's husband that afternoon here in this room: *This will do. This is enough:* not in exasperation or rage or even just sick to death as you were sick that day: just *This is enough* and looked about for one last time, for one time more since He had created them, upon this land this South for which He had done so much with woods for game and streams for fish and deep rich soil for seed and lush springs to sprout it and long summers to mature it and serene falls to harvest it and short mild winters for men and animals, and saw no hope anywhere and looked beyond it where hope should have been, where to East North and West lay illimitable that whole hopeful continent dedicated as a refuge and sanctuary of liberty and freedom from what you called the old world's worthless evening, and saw the rich descendants of slavers, females of both sexes, to whom the black they shrieked of was another specimen another example like the Brazilian macaw brought home in a cage by a traveller, passing resolutions about horror and outrage in warm and air-proof halls: and the thundering cannonade of politicians earning votes and the medicine-shows of pulpiteers earning Chatauqua fees, to whom the outrage and the injustice were as much abstractions as Tariff or Silver or Immortality and who employed the very shackles of its servitude and the sorry rags of its regalia as they did the other beer and banners and mottoes, redfire and brimstone and sleight-of-hand and musical handsaws: and the whirling wheels which manufactured for a profit the pristine replacements of the shackles and shoddy garments as they wore out, and spun the cotton and made the gins which ginned it and the cars and ships which hauled it, and the men who ran the wheels for that profit and established and collected the taxes it was taxed with and the rates for hauling it and the commissions for selling it: and He could have repudiated them since they were his creation now and forever more throughout all their generations, until not only that old world from which He had rescued them but this new one too which He had revealed and led them to as a sanctuary and refuge were become the same worthless tideless rock cooling in the last crimson evening, except that out of all that empty sound and bootless fury one silence, among that loud and moiling all of them just one simple enough to believe that horror and outrage were first and last simply horror and outrage and crude enough to act upon that, illiterate and had no words for talking or perhaps was just busy and had no time to, one out of them all who did not bother Him with cajolery and adjuration then pleading then threat, and had not even bothered to inform Him in advance what he was about so that a lesser than He might have even missed the simple act of lifting the long ancestral musket down from the deerhorns above the door, whereupon He said *My name is Brown too* and the other *So is mine* and He *Then mine or yours can't be because I am against it* and the other *So am I* and He triumphantly *Then where are you going with that gun?* and the other told him in one sentence one word and He: amazed: Who knew neither hope nor pride nor grief *But your Association, your Committee, your Officers. Where are your Minutes, your Motions, your Parliamentary Procedures?* and the other *I ain't against them. They are all right I reckon for them that have the time. I am just against the weak because they are niggers being held in bondage by the strong just because they are white.* So He turned once more to this land which He still intended to save because He had done so much for it—' and McCaslin

'What?' and he

'—to these people He was still committed to because they were his creations—' and McCaslin

'Turned back to us? His face to us?' and he

'—whose wives and daughters at least made soups and jellies for them when they were sick, and carried the trays through the mud and the winter too into the stinking cabins, and sat in the stinking cabins and kept fires going until crises came and passed, but that was not enough: and when they were very sick had them carried into the big house itself into the company room itself maybe and nursed them there, which the white man would have done too for any other of his cattle that was sick but at least the man who hired one from a livery wouldn't have, and still that was not enough: so that He said and not in grief either, Who had made them and so could know no more of grief than He could of pride or hope: *Apparently they can learn nothing save through suffering, remember nothing save when underlined in blood*—' and McCaslin

'Ashby on an afternoon's ride, to call on some remote maiden cousins of his mother or maybe just acquaintances of hers, comes by chance upon a minor engagement of outposts and dismounts and with his crimson-lined cloak for target leads a handful of troops he never saw before against an entrenched position of backwoods-trained riflemen. Lee's battle-order, wrapped maybe about a handful of cigars and doubtless thrown away when the last cigar was smoked, found by a Yankee Intelligence officer on the floor of a saloon behind the Yankee lines after Lee had already divided his forces before Sharpsburg. Jackson on the Plank Road, already rolled up the flank which Hooker believed could not be turned and, waiting only for night to pass to continue the brutal and incessant slogging which would fling that whole wing back into Hooker's lap where he sat on a front gallery in Chancellorsville drinking rum toddies and telegraphing Lincoln that he had defeated Lee, is shot from among a whole covey of minor officers and in the blind night by one of his own patrols, leaving as next by seniority Stuart, that gallant man born apparently already horsed and sabred and already knowing all there was to know about war except the slogging and brutal stupidity of it: and that same Stuart off raiding Pennsylvania hen-roosts when Lee should have known of all of Meade just where Hancock was on Cemetery Ridge: and Longstreet too at Gettysburg and that same Longstreet shot out of saddle by his own men in the dark by mistake just as Jackson was. His face to us? His face to us?' and he

'How else have made them fight? Who else but Jacksons and Stuarts and Ashbys and Morgans and Forrests?—the farmers of the central and middle-west, holding land by the acre instead of the tens or maybe even the hundreds, farming it themselves and to no single crop of cotton or tobacco or cane, owning no slaves and needing and wanting none, and already looking toward the Pacific coast, not always as long as two generations there and having stopped where they did stop only through the fortuitous mischance that an ox died or a wagon-axle broke. And the New England mechanics who didn't even own land and measured all things by the weight of water and the cost of turning wheels, and the narrow fringe of traders and shipowners still looking backward across the Atlantic and attached to the continent only by their counting-houses. And those who should have had the alertness to see: the wildcat manipulators of mythical wilderness townsites; and the astuteness to rationalize: the bankers who held the mortgages on the land which the first were only waiting to abandon, and on the railroads and steamboats to carry them still further west, and on the factories and the wheels and the rented tenements those who ran them lived in; and the leisure and scope to comprehend and fear in time and even anticipate: the Boston-bred (even when not born in Boston) spinster, descendants of long lines of similarly-bred and likewise spinster aunts and uncles whose hands knew no callus except that of the indicting pen, to whom the wilderness itself began at the top of tide and who looked, if at anything other than Beacon Hill, only toward heaven —not to mention all the loud rabble of the camp-followers of pioneers: the bellowing of politicians, the mellifluous choiring of self-styled men of God, the—' and McCaslin

'Here, here. Wait a minute:' And he

'Let me talk now. I'm trying to explain to the head of my family something which I have got to do which I don't quite understand myself, not in justification of it but to explain it if I can. I could say I don't know why I must do it but that I do know I have got to because I have got myself to have to live with for the rest of my life and all I want is peace to do it in. But you are the head of my family. More. I knew a long time ago that I would never have to miss my father, even if you are just finding out that you have missed your son—the drawers of bills and the shavers of notes and the schoolmasters and the self-ordained to teach and lead and all that horde of the semi-literate with a white shirt but no change for it, with one eye on themselves and watching each other with the other one. Who else could have made them fight: could have struck them so aghast with fear and dread as to turn shoulder to shoulder and face one way and even stop talking for a while and even after two years of it keep them still so wrung with terror that some among them would seriously propose moving their very capital into a foreign country lest it be ravaged and pillaged by a people whose entire white male population would have little more than filled any one of their larger cities: except Jackson in the Valley and three separate armies trying to catch him and none of them ever knowing whether they were just retreating from a battle or just running into one, and Stuart riding his whole command entirely around the biggest single armed force this continent ever saw in order to see what it looked like from behind, and Morgan leading a cavalry charge against a stranded man-of-war. Who else could have declared a war against a power with ten times the area and a hundred times the men and a thousand times the resources, except men who could believe that all necessary to conduct a successful war was not acumen nor shrewdness nor politics nor diplomacy nor money nor even integrity and simple arithmetic, but just love of land and courage——'

'And an unblemished and gallant ancestry and the ability to ride a horse,' McCaslin said. 'Don't leave that out.' It was evening now, the tranquil sunset of October mazy with windless woodsmoke. The cotton was long since picked and ginned, and all day now the wagons loaded with gathered corn moved between field and crib, processional across the enduring land. 'Well, maybe that's what He wanted. At least, that's what He got.' This time there was no yellowed procession of fading and harmless ledger-pages. This was chronicled in a harsher book, and McCaslin, fourteen and fifteen and sixteen, had seen it and the boy himself had inherited it as Noah's grandchildren had inherited the Flood although they had not been there to see the deluge: that dark corrupt and bloody time while three separate peoples had tried to adjust not only to one another but to the new land which they had created and inherited too and must live in for the reason that those who had lost it were no less free to quit it than those who had gained it were:—those upon whom freedom and equality had been dumped overnight and without warning or preparation or any training in how to employ it or even just endure it and who misused it, not as children would nor yet because they had been so long in bondage and then so suddenly freed, but misused it as human beings always misuse freedom, so that he thought *Apparently there is a wisdom beyond even that learned through suffering necessary for a man to distinguish between liberty and license;* those who had fought for four years and lost to preserve a condition under which that franchisement was anomaly and

paradox, not because they were opposed to freedom as freedom but for the old
reasons for which man (not the generals and politicians but man) has always
fought and died in wars: to preserve a status quo or to establish a better future
one to endure for his children; and lastly, as if that were not enough for bitterness and hatred and fear, that third race even more alien to the people whom
they resembled in pigment and in whom even the same blood ran, than to the people whom they did not,—that race threefold in one and alien even among themselves save for a single fierce will for rapine and pillage, composed of the sons of
middleaged Quartermaster lieutenants and Army sutlers and contractors in military blankets and shoes and transport mules, who followed the battles they themselves had not fought and inherited the conquest they themselves had not helped
to gain, sanctioned and protected even if not blessed, and left their bones and in
another generation would be engaged in a fierce economic competition of small
sloven farms with the black men they were supposed to have freed and the white
descendants of fathers who had owned no slaves anyway whom they were supposed to have disinherited, and in the third generation would be back once more
in the little lost county seats as barbers and garage mechanics and deputy sheriffs
and mill- and gin-hands and power-plant firemen, leading, first in mufti then
later in an actual formalized regalia of hooded sheets and passwords and fiery
Christian symbols, lynching mobs against the race their ancestors had come to
save: and of all that other nameless horde of speculators in human misery, manipulators of money and politics and land, who follow catastrophe and are their
own protection as grasshoppers are and need no blessing and sweat no plow or
axe-helve and batten and vanish and leave no bones, just as they derived apparently from no ancestry, no mortal flesh, no act even of passion or even of lust:
and the Jew who came without protection too, since after two thousand years he
had got out of the habit of being or needing it, and solitary, without even the solidarity of the locusts, and in this a sort of courage since he had come thinking
not in terms of simple pillage but in terms of his great-grandchildren, seeking
yet some place to establish them to endure even though forever alien: and un-
blessed: a pariah about the face of the Western earth which twenty centuries later
was still taking revenge on him for the fairy tale with which he had conquered
it. McCaslin had actually seen it, and the boy even at almost eighty would never
be able to distinguish certainly between what he had seen and what had been
told him: a lightless and gutted and empty land where women crouched with the
huddled children behind locked doors and men armed in sheets and masks rode
the silent roads and the bodies of white and black both, victims not so much of
hate as of desperation and despair, swung from lonely limbs: and men shot dead
in polling-booths with the still wet pen in one hand and the unblotted ballot in
the other: and a United States marshal in Jefferson who signed his official papers
with a crude cross, an ex-slave called Sickymo, not at all because his ex-owner
was a doctor and apothecary but because, still a slave, he would steal his master's grain alcohol and dilute it with water and peddle it in pint bottles from a
cache beneath the roots of a big sycamore tree behind the drug store, who had
attained his high office because his half-white sister was the concubine of the
Federal A.P.M.: and this time McCaslin did not even say Look but merely lifted
one hand, not even pointing, not even specifically toward the shelf of ledgers
but toward the desk, toward the corner where it sat beside the scuffed patch on

the floor where two decades of heavy shoes had stood while the white man at the desk added and multiplied and subtracted. And again he did not need to look because he had seen this himself and, twenty-three years after the Surrender and twenty-four after the Proclamation, was still watching it: the ledgers, new ones now and filled rapidly, succeeding one another rapidly and containing more names than old Carothers or even his father and Uncle Buddy had ever dreamed of; new names and new faces to go with them, among which the old names and faces that even his father and uncle would have recognized, were lost, vanished— Tomey's Terrel dead, and even the tragic and miscast Percival Brownlee, who couldn't keep books and couldn't farm either, found his true niche at last, reappeared in 1862 during the boy's father's absence and had apparently been living on the plantation for at least a month before his uncle found out about it, conducting impromptu revival meetings among Negroes, preaching and leading the singing also in his high sweet true soprano voice and disappeared again on foot and at top speed, not behind but ahead of a body of raiding Federal horse and reappeared for the third and last time in the entourage of a travelling Army paymaster, the two of them passing through Jefferson in a surrey at the exact moment when the boy's father (it was 1866) also happened to be crossing the Square, the surrey and its occupants traversing rapidly that quiet and bucolic scene and even in that fleeting moment, and to others beside the boy's father, giving an illusion of flight and illicit holiday like a man on an excursion during his wife's absence with his wife's personal maid, until Brownlee glanced up and saw his late co-master and gave him one defiant female glance and then broke again, leaped from the surrey and disappeared this time for good, and it was only by chance that McCaslin, twenty years later, heard of him again, an old man now and quite fat, as the well-to-do proprietor of a select New Orleans brothel; and Tennie's Jim gone, nobody knew where, and Fonsiba in Arkansas with her three dollars each month and the scholar-husband with his lenseless spectacles and frock coat and his plans for the spring; and only Lucas was left, the baby, the last save himself of old Carothers' doomed and fatal blood which in the male derivation seemed to destroy all it touched, and even he was repudiating and at least hoping to escape it;—Lucas, the boy of fourteen whose name would not even appear for six years yet among those rapid pages in the bindings new and dustless too since McCaslin lifted them down daily now to write into them the continuation of that record which two hundred years had not been enough to complete, and another hundred would not be enough to discharge; that chronicle which was a whole land in miniature, which multiplied and compounded was the entire South, twenty-three years after surrender and twenty-four from emancipation—that slow trickle of molasses and meal and meat, of shoes and straw hats and overalls, of plowlines and collars and heel-bolts and buckheads and clevises, which returned each fall as cotton—the two threads frail as truth and impalpable as equators yet cable-strong to bind for life them who made the cotton to the land their sweat fell on: and he

'Yes. Binding them for a while yet, a little while yet. Through and beyond that life and maybe through and beyond the life of that life's sons and maybe even through and beyond that of the sons of those sons. But not always, because they will endure. They will outlast us because they are—' it was not a pause, barely a falter even, possibly appreciable only to himself, as if he couldn't speak even to McCaslin, even to explain his repudiation, that which to him too, even in the act of escaping (and maybe this was the reality and the truth of his need to escape), was heresy: so that even in escaping he was taking with him more of that evil and unregenerate old man who could summon, because she was his property, a human being because she was old enough and female, to his widower's house and get a child on her and then dismiss her because she was of an inferior race, and then bequeath a thousand dollars to the infant because he would be dead then and wouldn't have to pay it, than even he had feared. 'Yes. He didn't want to. He had to. Because they will endure. They are better than we are. Stronger than we are. Their vices are vices aped from white men or that white men and bondage have taught them: improvidence and intemperance and evasion—not laziness: evasion: of what white men had set them to, not for their aggrandizement or even comfort but his own—' and McCaslin

'All right. Go on: Promiscuity. Violence. Instability and lack of control. Inability to distinguish between mine and thine—' and he

'How distinguish, when for two hundred years mine did not even exist for them?' and McCaslin

'All right. Go on. And their virtues—' and he

'Yes. Their own. Endurance—' and McCaslin

'So have mules:' and he

'—and pity and tolerance and forbearance and fidelity and love of children—' and McCaslin

'So have dogs:' and he

'—whether their own or not or black or not. And more: what they got not only not from white people but not even despite white people because they had it already from the old free fathers a longer time free than us because we have never been free—' and it was in McCaslin's eyes too, he had only to look at McCaslin's eyes and it was there, that summer twilight seven years ago, almost a week after they had returned from the camp before he discovered that Sam Fathers had told McCaslin: an old bear, fierce and ruthless not just to stay alive but ruthless with the fierce pride of liberty and freedom, jealous and proud enough of liberty and freedom to see it threatened not with fear nor even alarm but almost with joy, seeming deliberately to put it into jeopardy in order to savor it and keep his old strong bones and flesh supple and quick to defend and preserve it; an old man, son of a Negro slave and an Indian king, inheritor on the one hand of the long chronicle of a people who had learned humility through suffering and learned pride through the endurance which survived the suffering, and on the other side the chronicle of a people even longer in the land than the first, yet who now existed there only in the solitary brotherhood of an old and childless Negro's alien blood and the wild and invincible spirit of an old bear; a boy who wished to learn humility and pride in order to become skillful and worthy in the woods but found himself becoming so skillful so fast that he feared he would never become worthy, because he had not learned humility and pride though he had tried, until one day an old man, who could not have defined either, led him as though by the hand to where an old bear and a little mongrel dog showed him that, by possessing one thing other, he would possess them both; and a little dog, nameless and mongrel and many-fathered, grown yet weighing less than six pounds, who couldn't be dangerous because there was nothing anywhere much smaller, not fierce because that would have been called just noise, not humble because it was already too near the ground to genuflect, and not proud because it would not have been close enough for anyone to discern what was casting that shadow, and which didn't even know it was not going to heaven since they had already decided it had no immortal soul, so that all it could be was brave, even though they would probably call that too just noise. *'And you didn't shoot,'* McCaslin said. *'How close were you?'*

'I don't know,' he said. *'There was a big wood tick just inside his off hind leg. I saw that. But I didn't have the gun then.'*

'But you didn't shoot when you had the gun,' McCaslin said. *'Why?'* But McCaslin didn't wait, rising and crossing the room, across the pelt of the bear he had killed two years ago and the bigger one McCaslin had killed before he was born, to the bookcase beneath the mounted head of his first buck, and returned with the book and sat down again and opened it. *'Listen,'* he said. He read the five stanzas aloud and closed the book on his finger and looked up. *'All right,'* he said. *'Listen,'* and read again, but only one stanza this time and closed the book and laid it on the table. *'She cannot fade, though thou hast not thy bliss,'* McCaslin said: *'Forever wilt thou love, and she be fair.'*

'He's talking about a girl,' he said.

'He had to talk about something,' McCaslin said. Then he said, *'He was talking about truth. Truth is one. It doesn't change. It covers all things which touch the heart—honor and pride and pity and justice and courage and love. Do you see now?'* He didn't know. Somehow it had seemed simpler than that, simpler than somebody talking in a book about a young man and a girl he would never need to grieve over because he could never approach any nearer and would never have to get any further away. He had heard about an old bear and finally got big enough to hunt it and he hunted it four years and at last met it with a gun in his hands and he didn't shoot. Because a little dog—But he could have shot long before the fyce covered the twenty yards to where the bear waited, and Sam Fathers could have shot at any time during the interminable minute while Old Ben stood on his hind legs over them. . . . He ceased. McCaslin watched him, still speaking, the voice, the words as quiet as the twilight itself was: *'Courage and honor and pride, and pity and love of justice and of liberty. They all touch the heart, and what the heart holds to becomes truth, as far as we know truth. Do you see now?'*

and he could still hear them, intact in this twilight as in that one seven years ago, no louder still because they did not need to be because they would endure: and he had only to look at McCaslin's eyes beyond the thin and bitter smiling, the faint lip-lift which would have had to be called smiling;—his kinsman, his father almost, who had been born too late into the old time and too soon for the new, the two of them juxtaposed and alien now to each other against their ravaged patrimony, the dark and ravaged fatherland still prone and panting from its etherless operation:

'Habet then.—So this land is, indubitably, of and by itself cursed:' and he

'Cursed:' and again McCaslin merely lifted one hand, not even speaking and not even toward the ledgers: so that, as the stereopticon condenses into one instantaneous field the myriad minutiae of its scope, so did that slight and rapid gesture establish in the small cramped and cluttered twilit room not only the

ledgers but the whole plantation in its mazed and intricate entirety—the land, the fields and what they represented in terms of cotton ginned and sold, the men and women whom they fed and clothed and even paid a little cash money at Christmas-time in return for the labor which planted and raised and picked and ginned the cotton, the machinery and mules and gear with which they raised it and their cost and upkeep and replacement—that whole edifice intricate and complex and founded upon injustice and erected by ruthless rapacity and carried on even yet with at times downright savagery not only to the human beings but the valuable animals too, yet solvent and efficient and, more than that: not only still intact but enlarged, increased; brought still intact by McCaslin, himself little more than a child then, through and out of the debacle and chaos of twenty years ago where hardly one in ten survived, and enlarged and increased and would continue so, solvent and efficient and intact and still increasing so long as McCaslin and his McCaslin successors lasted, even though their surnames might not even be Edmonds then: and he

'Habet too. Because that's it: not the land, but us. Not only the blood, but the name too; not only its color but its designation: Edmonds, white, but, a female line, could have no other but the name his father bore; Beauchamp, the elder line and the male one, but, black, could have had any name he liked and no man would have cared, except the name his father bore who had no name—' and McCaslin

'And since I know too what you know I will say now, once more let me say it: And one other, and in the third generation too, and the male, the eldest, the direct and sole and white and still McCaslin even, father to son to son—' and he

'I am free:' and this time McCaslin did not even gesture, no inference of fading pages, no postulation of the stereoptic whole, but the frail and iron thread strong as truth and impervious as evil and longer than life itself and reaching beyond record and patrimony both to join him with the lusts and passions, the hopes and dreams and griefs, of bones whose names while still fleshed and capable even old Carothers' grandfather had never heard: and he:

'And of that too:' and McCaslin

'Chosen, I suppose (I will concede it) out of all your time by Him, as you say Buck and Buddy were from theirs. And it took Him a bear and an old man and four years just for you. And it took you fourteen years to reach that point and about that many, maybe more, for Old Ben, and more than seventy for Sam Fathers. And you are just one. How long then? How long?' and he

'It will be long. I have never said otherwise. But it will be all right because they will endure—' and McCaslin

'And anyway, you will be free.—No, not now nor ever, we from them nor they from us. So I repudiate too. I would deny even if I knew it were true. I would have to. Even you can see that I could do no else. I am what I am; I will be always what I was born and have always been. And more than me. More than me, just as there were more than Buck and Buddy in what you called His first plan which failed:' and he

'And more than me:' and McCaslin

'No. Not even you. Because mark. You said how on that instant when Ikkemotubbe realized that he could sell the land to Grandfather, it ceased forever to have been his. All right; go on: Then it belonged to Sam Fathers, old Ikkemotubbe's son. And who inherited from Sam Fathers, if not you? co-heir perhaps with Boon, if not of his life maybe, at least of his quitting it?' and he

'Yes. Sam Fathers set me free.'

and Isaac McCaslin, not yet Uncle Ike, a long time yet before he would be uncle to half a county and still father to none, living in one small cramped fireless rented room in a Jefferson boardinghouse where petit juries were domiciled during court terms and itinerant horse- and mule-traders stayed, with his kit of brand-new carpenter's tools and the shotgun McCaslin had given him with his name engraved in silver and old General Compson's compass (and, when the General died, his silver-mounted horn too) and the iron cot and mattress and the blankets which he would take each fall into the woods for more than sixty years and the bright tin coffee-pot

there had been a legacy, from his Uncle Hubert Beauchamp, his godfather, that bluff burly roaring childlike man from whom Uncle Buddy had won Tomey's Terrel's wife Tennie in the poker-game in 1859—'posible strait against three Treys in sigt Not called'—; no pale sentence or paragraph scrawled in cringing fear of death by a weak and trembling hand as a last desperate sop flung backward at retribution, but a Legacy, a Thing, possessing weight to the hand and bulk to the eye and even audible: a silver cup filled with gold pieces and wrapped in burlap and sealed with his godfather's ring in the hot wax, which (intact still) even before his Uncle Hubert's death and long before his own majority, when it would be his, had become not only a legend but one of the family lares. After his father's and his Uncle Hubert's sister's marriage they moved back into the big house, the tremendous cavern which old Carothers had started and never finished, cleared the remaining Negroes out of it and with his mother's dowry completed it, at least the rest of the windows and doors and moved into it, all of them save Uncle Buddy who declined to leave the cabin he and his twin had built, the move being the bride's notion and more than just a notion, and none ever to know if she really wanted to live in the big house or if she knew beforehand that Uncle Buddy would refuse to move: and two weeks after his birth in 1867, the first time he and his mother came down stairs one night, and the silver cup sitting on the cleared dining-room table beneath the bright lamp, and while his mother and his father and McCaslin and Tennie (his nurse: carrying him)—all of them again but Uncle Buddy—watched, his Uncle Hubert rang one by one into the cup the bright and glinting mintage and wrapped it into the burlap envelope and heated the wax and sealed it and carried it back home with him where he lived alone now without even his sister either to hold him down as McCaslin said or to try to raise him up as Uncle Buddy said, and (dark times then in Mississippi) Uncle Buddy said most of the niggers gone and the ones that didn't go even Hub Beauchamp could not have wanted: but the dogs remained and Uncle Buddy said Beauchamp fiddled while Nero fox-hunted

they would go and see it there; at last his mother would prevail and they would depart in the surrey, once more all save Uncle Buddy and McCaslin to keep Uncle Buddy company, until one winter Uncle Buddy began to fail and from then on it was himself, beginning to remember now, and his mother and Tennie and Tomey's Terrel to drive: the twenty-two miles into the next county, the twin gateposts on one of which McCaslin could remember the half-grown boy blowing a fox-horn at breakfast, dinner, and supper-time and jumping down to open to any passer who happened to hear it, but where there were no gates at all now, the shabby and overgrown entrance to what his mother still insisted that people call Warwick because her brother was, if truth but triumphed and justice but prevailed, the rightful earl of it, the paintless house which outwardly did not change but which on the inside seemed each time larger because he was too little to realize then that there was less and less in it of the fine furnishings, the rosewood and mahogany and walnut, which for him had never existed anywhere anyway save in his mother's tearful lamentations, and the occasional piece small enough to be roped somehow onto the rear or the top of the carriage on their return (And he remembered this, he had seen it: an instant, a flash, his mother's soprano 'Even my dress! Even my dress!' loud and outraged in the barren unswept hall; a face young and female and even lighter in color than Tomey's Terrel's for an instant in a closing door; a swirl, a glimpse of the silk gown and the flick and glint of an ear-ring: an apparition rapid and tawdry and illicit, yet somehow even to the child, the infant still almost, breathless and exciting and evocative: as though, like two limpid and pellucid streams meeting, the child which he still was had made serene and absolute and perfect rapport and contact through that glimpsed nameless illicit hybrid female flesh with the boy which had existed at that stage of inviolable and immortal adolescence in his uncle for almost sixty years; the dress, the face, the ear-rings gone in that same aghast flash and his uncle's voice: 'She's my cook! She's my new cook! I had to have a cook, didn't I?' then the uncle himself, the face alarmed and aghast too yet still innocently and somehow even indomitably of a boy, they retreating in their turn now, back to the front gallery, and his uncle again, pained and still amazed, in a sort of desperate resurgence if not of courage at least of self-assertion: 'They're free now; They're folks too just like we are!' and his mother: 'That's why! That's why! My mother's house! Defiled! Defiled!' and his uncle: 'Damn it, Sibbey, at least give her time to pack her grip:' then over, finished, the loud uproar and all, himself and Tennie and he remembered Tennie's inscrutable face at the broken shutterless window of the bare room which had once been the parlor while they watched, hurrying down the lane at a stumbling trot, the routed compounder of his uncle's uxory: the back, the nameless face which he had seen only for a moment, the once-hooped dress ballooning and flapping below a man's overcoat, the worn heavy carpet-bag jouncing and banging against her knee, routed and in retreat true enough and in the empty lane, solitary, young-looking, and forlorn, yet withal still exciting and evocative and wearing still the silken banner captured inside the very citadel of respectability, and unforgettable.)

the cup, the sealed inscrutable burlap, sitting on the shelf in the locked closet, Uncle Hubert unlocking the door and lifting it down and passing it from hand to hand: his mother, his father, McCaslin and even Tennie, insisting that each take it in turn and heft it for weight and shake it again to prove the sound, Uncle Hubert himself standing spraddled before the cold unswept hearth in which the very bricks themselves were crumbling into a litter of soot and dust and mortar and the droppings of chimney-sweeps, still roaring and still innocent and still indomitable: and for a long time he believed nobody but himself had noticed that his uncle now put the cup only into his hands, unlocked the door and lifted it down and put it into his hands and stood over him until he had shaken it obediently until it sounded then took it from him and locked it back into the closet before anyone else could have offered to touch it, and even later, when competent not only to remember but to rationalize, he could not say what it was or even if it had been anything because the parcel was still heavy and still rattled, not even when, Uncle Buddy dead and his father, at last and after almost seventy-five years in bed after the sun rose, said: 'Go get that damn cup. Bring that damn Hub Beauchamp too if you have to:' because it still rattled though his uncle no longer put it even into his hands now but carried it himself from one to the other, his mother, McCaslin, Tennie, shaking it before each in turn, saying: 'Hear it? Hear it?' his face still innocent, not quite baffled but only amazed and not very amazed and still indomitable:

and, his father and Uncle Buddy both gone now, one day without reason or any warning the almost completely empty house in which his uncle and Tennie's ancient and quarrelsome great-grandfather (who claimed to have seen Lafayette and McCaslin said in another ten years would be remembering God) lived, cooked and slept in one single room, burst into peaceful conflagration, a tranquil instantaneous sourceless unanimity of combustion, walls floors and roof: at sunup it stood where his uncle's father had built it sixty years ago, at sundown the four blackened and smokeless chimneys rose from a light white powder of ashes and a few charred ends of planks which did not even appear to have been very hot: and out of the last of evening, the last one of the twenty-two miles, on the old white mare which was the last of that stable which McCaslin remembered, the two old men riding double up to the sister's door, the one wearing his fox-horn on its braided deerhide thong and the other carrying the burlap parcel wrapped in a shirt, the tawny wax-daubed shapeless lump sitting again and on an almost identical shelf and his uncle holding the half-opened door now, his hand not only on the knob but one foot against it and the key waiting in the other hand, the face urgent and still not baffled but still and even indomitably not very amazed and himself standing in the half-opened door looking quietly up at the burlap shape, become almost three times its original height and a good half less than its original thickness, and turning away, and he would remember not his mother's look this time nor yet Tennie's inscrutable expression but McCaslin's dark and aquiline face grave insufferable and bemused:

then one night they waked him and fetched him still half-asleep into the lamp light, the smell of medicine which was familiar by now in that room and the smell of something else which he had not smelled before and knew at once and would never forget, the pillow, the worn and ravaged face from which looked out still the boy innocent and immortal and amazed and urgent, looking at him and trying to tell him until McCaslin moved and leaned over the bed and drew from the top of the night shirt the big iron key on the greasy cord which suspended it, the eyes saying Yes Yes Yes now, and cut the cord and unlocked the closet and brought the parcel to the bed, the eyes still trying to tell him even when he took the parcel so that was still not it, the hands still clinging to the parcel even while relinquishing it, the eyes more urgent than ever trying to tell him but they never did; and he was ten and his mother was dead too and McCaslin said, 'You are almost halfway now. You might as well open it:' and he: 'No. He said twenty-one:' and he was twenty-one and McCaslin shifted the bright lamp to the center of the cleared dining-room table and set the parcel beside it and laid his open knife beside the parcel and stood back with that expression of old grave intolerant and repudiating and he lifted it, the burlap lump which fifteen years ago had changed its shape completely overnight, which shaken gave forth a thin weightless not-quite-musical curiously muffled clatter, the bright knife-blade hunting amid the mazed intricacy of string, the knobby gouts of wax bearing his uncle's Beauchamp seal rattling onto the table's polished top and, standing amid the collapse of burlap folds, the unstained tin coffee-pot still brand new, the handful of copper coins and now he knew what had given them the muffled sound: a collection of minutely folded scraps of paper sufficient almost for a rat's nest, of good linen bond, of the crude ruled paper such as Negroes use, of raggedly-torn ledger-pages and the margins of newspapers and once the paper label from a new pair of overalls, all dated and all signed, beginning with the first one not six months after they had watched him seal the silver cup into the burlap on this same table in this same room by the light even of this same lamp almost twenty-one years ago:

I owe my Nephew Isaac Beauchamp McCaslin five (5) pieces Gold which I,O.U constitues My note of hand with Interest at 5 percent.
Hubert Fitz-Hubert Beauchamp
at Warwick 27 Nov 1867

and he: 'Anyway he called it Warwick:' once at least, even if no more. But there was more:

Isaac 24 Dec 1867 I.O.U. 2 pieces Gold H.Fh.B. I.O.U. Isaac 1 piece Gold 1 Jan 1868 H.Fh.B.

then five again then three then one then one then a long time and what dream, what dreamed splendid recoup, not of any injury or betrayal of trust because it had been merely a loan: nay, a partnership:

I.O.U. Beauchamp McCaslin or his heirs twenty-five (25) pieces Gold This & All preceeding constituting My notes of hand at twenty (20) percentum compounded annually. This date of 19th January 1873
Beauchamp

no location save that in time and signed by the single not name but word as the old proud earl himself might have scrawled Nevile: and that made forty-three and he could not remember himself of course but the legend had it at fifty, which balanced: one: then one: then one: then one and then the last three and then the last chit, dated after he came to live in the house with them and written in the shaky hand not of a beaten old man because he had never been beaten to know it but of a tired old man maybe and even at that tired only on the outside and still indomitable, the simplicity of the last one the simplicity not of resignation but merely of amazement, like a simple comment or remark, and not very much of that:

One silver cup. Hubert Beauchamp

and McCaslin: 'So you have plenty of coppers anyway. But they are still not old enough yet to be either rarities or heirlooms. So you will have to take the money:' except that he didn't hear McCaslin, standing quietly beside the table and looking peacefully at the coffee-pot and the pot sitting one night later on the mantel above what was not even a fireplace in the little cramped ice-like room in Jefferson as McCaslin tossed the folded banknotes onto the bed and, still standing (there was nowhere to sit save on the bed) did not even remove his hat and overcoat: and he

'As a loan. From you. This one:' and McCaslin

'You can't. I have no money that I can lend to you. And you will have to go to the bank and get it next month because I won't bring it to you:' and he could not hear McCaslin now either, looking peacefully at McCaslin, his kinsman, his father almost yet no kin now as, at the last, even fathers and sons are no kin: and he

'It's seventeen miles, horseback and in the cold. We could both sleep here:' and McCaslin

'Why should I sleep here in my house when you won't sleep yonder in yours?' and gone, and he looking at the bright rustless unstained tin and thinking, and not for the first time, how much it takes to compound a man (Isaac McCaslin for instance) and of the devious intricate choosing yet unerring path that man's (Isaac McCaslin's for instance) spirit takes among all that mass to make him at last what he is to be, not only to the astonishment of them (the ones who sired the McCaslin who sired his father and Uncle Buddy and their sister, and the ones who sired the Beauchamp who sired his Uncle Hubert and his Uncle Hubert's sister) who believed they had shaped him, but to Isaac McCaslin too

as a loan and used it though he would not have had to: Major de Spain offered him a room in his house as long as he wanted it and asked nor would ever ask any question, and old General Compson more than that, to take him into his own room, to sleep in half of his own bed and more than Major de Spain because he told him baldly why: 'You sleep with me and before this winter is out, I'll know the reason. You'll tell me. Because I don't believe you just quit. It looks like you just quit but I have watched you in the woods too much and I don't believe you just quit even if it does look damn like it:' using it as a loan, paid his board and rent for a month and bought the tools, not simply because he was good with his hands because he had intended to use his hands and it could have been with horses, and not in mere static and hopeful emulation of the Nazarene, as the young gambler buys a spotted shirt because the old gambler won in one yesterday, but (without the arrogance of false humility and without the false humbleness of pride, who intended to earn his bread, didn't especially want to earn it but had to earn it and for more than just bread) because if the Nazarene had found carpentering good for the life and ends He had assumed and elected to serve, it would be all right too for Isaac McCaslin even though Isaac McCaslin's ends, although simple enough in their apparent motivation, were and would be always incomprehensible to him, and his life, invincible enough in its needs, if he could have helped himself, not being the Nazarene, he would not have chosen it: and paid it back. He had forgotten the thirty dollars which McCaslin put into the bank in his name each month, fetched it in to him and flung it onto the bed that first one time but no more; he had a partner now or rather he was the partner: a blasphemous profane clever old dipsomaniac who had built blockade-runners in Charleston in '62 and '63 and had been a ship's carpenter since and appeared in Jefferson two years ago, nobody knew from where nor why, and spent a good part of his time since recovering from delirium tremens in the jail; they had put a new roof on the stable of the bank's president and (the old man in jail again still celebrating that job) he went to the bank to collect for it and the president said, 'I should borrow from you instead of paying you:' and it had been seven months now and he remembered for the first time, two-hundred-and-ten dollars, and this was the first job of any size and when he left the bank the account stood at two-twenty, two-forty to balance, only twenty dollars more to go, then it did balance though by then the total had increased to three hundred and thirty and he said, 'I will transfer it now:' and the president said, 'I can't do that. McCaslin told me not to. Haven't you got another initial you could use and open another account?' but that was all right, the coins the silver and the bills as they accumulated knotted into a handkerchief and the coffee-pot wrapped in an old shirt as when Tennie's great-grandfather had fetched it from Warwick eighteen years ago, in the bottom of the iron-bound trunk which old Carothers had brought from Carolina and his landlady said, 'Not even a lock! And you don't even lock your door, not even when you leave!' and himself looking at her as peacefully as he had looked at McCaslin that first night in this same room, no kin to him at all yet more than kin as those who serve you even for pay are your kin and those who injure you are more than brother or wife

and he had the wife now; got the old man out of jail and fetched him to the rented room and sobered him by superior strength, did not even remove his own shoes for twenty-four hours, got him up and got food into him and they built the barn this time from the ground up and he married her: an only child, a small girl yet curiously bigger than she seemed at first, solider perhaps, with dark eyes and a passionate heart-shaped face, who had time even on that farm to watch most of the day while he sawed timbers to the old man's measurements: and she: 'Papa told me about you. That farm is really yours, isn't it?' and he

'And McCaslin's:' and she

'Was there a will leaving half of it to him?' and he

'There didn't need to be a will. His grandmother was my father's sister. We were the same as brothers:' and she

'You are the same as second cousins and that's all you ever will be. But I don't suppose it matters:' and they were married, they were married and it was the new country, his heritage too as it was the heritage of all, out of the earth, beyond the earth yet of the earth because his too was of the earth's long chronicle, his too because each must share with another in order to come into it, and in the sharing they become one: for that while, one: for that little while at least, one: indivisible, that while at least irrevocable and unrecoverable, living in a rented room still but for just a little while and that room wall-less and topless and floorless in glory for him to leave each morning and return to at night; her father already owned the lot in town and furnished the material and he and his partner would build it, her dowry from one: her wedding-present from three, she not to know it until the bungalow was finished and ready to be moved into and he never knew who told her, not her father and not his partner and not even in drink though for a while he believed that, himself coming home from work and just time to wash and rest a moment before going down to supper, entering no rented cubicle since it would still partake of glory even after they would have grown old and lost it: and he saw her face then, just before she spoke: 'Sit down:' the two of them sitting on the bed's edge, not even touching yet, her face strained and terrible, her voice a passionate and expiring whisper of immeasurable promise: 'I love you. You know I love you. When are we going to move?' and he

'I didn't—I didn't know—Who told you—' the hot fierce palm clapped over his mouth, crushing his lips into his teeth, the fierce curve of fingers digging into his cheek and only the palm slacked off enough for him to answer:

'The farm. Our farm. Your farm:' and he

'I——' then the hand again, finger and palm, the whole enveloping weight of her although she still was not touching him save the hand, the voice: 'No! No!' and the fingers themselves seeming to follow through the cheek the impulse to speech as it died in his mouth, then the whisper, the breath again, of love and of incredible promise, the palm slackening again to let him answer:

'When?' and he

'I——' then she was gone, the hand too, standing, her back to him and her head bent, the voice so calm now that for an instant it seemed no voice of hers that he ever remembered: 'Stand up and turn your back and shut your eyes:' and repeated before he understood and stood himself with his eyes shut and heard the bell ring for supper below stairs, and the calm voice again: 'Lock the door:' and he did so and leaned his forehead against the cold wood, his eyes closed, hearing his heart and the sound he had begun to hear before he moved until it ceased and the bell rang again below stairs and he knew it was for them this time, and he heard the bed and turned and he had never seen her naked before, he had asked her to once, and why: that he wanted to see her naked because he loved her and he wanted to see her looking at him naked because he loved her, but after that he never mentioned it again, even turning his face when she put the nightgown on over her dress to undress at night and putting the dress on over the gown to re-move it in the morning, and she would not let him get into bed beside her until the lamp was out and even in the heat of summer she would draw the sheet up over them both before she would let him turn to her: and the landlady came up the stairs up the hall and rapped on the door and then called their names but she didn't move, lying still on the bed outside the covers, her face turned away on the pillow, listening to nothing, thinking of nothing, not of him anyway he thought: then the landlady went away and she said, 'Take off your clothes:' her head still turned away, looking at nothing, thinking of nothing, waiting for nothing, not even him, her hand moving as though with volition and vision of its own, catch-ing his wrist at the exact moment when he paused beside the bed so that he never paused but merely changed the direction of moving, downward now, the hand drawing him and she moved at last, shifted, a movement one single complete in-herent not practiced and one time older than man, looking at him now, drawing him still downward with the one hand down and down and he neither saw nor felt it shift, palm flat against his chest now and holding him away with the same apparent lack of any effort or any need for strength, and not looking at him now, she didn't need to, the chaste woman, the wife, already looked upon all the men who ever rutted and now her whole body had changed, altered, he had never seen it but once and now it was not even the one he had seen but composite of all woman-flesh since man that ever of its own will reclined on its back and opened, and out of it somewhere, without any movement of lips even, the dying and in-vincible whisper: 'Promise:' and he

'Promise?'

'The farm.' He moved. He had moved, the hand shifting from his chest once more to his wrist, grasping it, the arm still lax and only the light increasing pressure of the fingers as though arm and hand were a piece of wire cable with one looped end, only the hand tightening as he pulled against it. 'No,' he said. 'No:' and she was not looking at him still but not like the other, but still the hand: 'No, I tell you. I won't. I can't. Never:' and still the hand and he said, for the last time, he tried to speak clearly and he knew it was still gently and he thought, *She already knows more than I with all the man-listening in camps where there was nothing to read ever even heard of. They are born already bored with what a boy approaches only at fourteen and fifteen with blundering and aghast trembling:* 'I can't. Not ever. Remember:' and still the steady and invincible hand and he said 'Yes' and he thought, *She is lost. She was born lost. We were all born lost* then he stopped thinking and even saying Yes, it was like nothing he had ever dreamed, let alone heard in mere man-talking until after a no-time he returned and lay spent on the insatiate immemorial beach and again with a movement one time more, older than man, she turned and freed herself and on their wedding night she had cried and he thought she was crying now at first, into the tossed and wadded pillow, the voice coming from somewhere between the pillow and the cachinnation: 'And that's all. That's all from me. If this don't get you that son you talk about, it won't be mine:' lying on her side, her back to the empty rented room, laughing and laughing

PART 5

He went back to the camp one more time before the lumber company moved in and began to cut the timber. Major de Spain himself never saw it again. But he made them welcome to use the house and hunt the land whenever they liked, and in the winter following the last hunt when Sam Fathers and Lion died, General Compson and Walter Ewell invented a plan to corporate themselves, the old group, into a club and lease the camp and the hunting privileges of the woods— an invention doubtless of the somewhat childish old General but actually worthy of Boon Hogganbeck himself. Even the boy, listening, recognized it for the subterfuge it was: to change the leopard's spots when they could not alter the leopard, a baseless and illusory hope to which even McCaslin seemed to subscribe for a while, that once they had persuaded Major de Spain to return to the camp he might revoke himself, which even the boy knew he would not do. And he did not. The boy never knew what occurred when Major de Spain declined. He was not present when the subject was broached and McCaslin never told him. But when June came and the time for the double birthday celebration there was no mention of it and when November came no one spoke of using Major de Spain's house and he never knew whether or not Major de Spain knew they were going on the hunt though without doubt old Ash probably told him: he and McCaslin and General Compson (and that one was the General's last hunt too) and Walter and Boon and Tennie's Jim and old Ash loaded two wagons and drove two days and almost forty miles beyond any country the boy had ever seen before and lived in tents for the two weeks. And the next spring they heard (not from Major de

Spain) that he had sold the timber-rights to a Memphis lumber company and in June the boy came to town with McCaslin one Saturday and went to Major de Spain's office—the big, airy, book-lined, second-storey room with windows at one end opening upon the shabby hinder purlieus of stores and at the other a door giving onto the railed balcony above the Square, with its curtained alcove where sat a cedar water-bucket and a sugar-bowl and spoon and tumbler and a wicker-covered demijohn of whiskey, and the bamboo-and-paper punkah swinging back and forth above the desk while old Ash in a tilted chair beside the entrance pulled the cord.

"Of course," Major de Spain said. "Ash will probably like to get off in the woods himself for a while, where he won't have to eat Daisy's cooking. Complain about it, anyway. Are you going to take anybody with you?"

"No sir," he said. "I thought that maybe Boon——" For six months now Boon had been town-marshal at Hoke's; Major de Spain had compounded with the lumber company,—or perhaps compromised was closer, since it was the lumber company who had decided that Boon might be better as a town-marshal than head of a logging gang.

"Yes," Major de Spain said. "I'll wire him today. He can meet you at Hoke's. I'll send Ash on by the train and they can take some food in and all you will have to do will be to mount your horse and ride over."

"Yes sir," he said. "Thank you." And he heard his voice again. He didn't know he was going to say it yet he did know, he had known it all the time: "Maybe if you . . . ." His voice died. It was stopped, he never knew how because Major de Spain did not speak and it was not until his voice ceased that Major de Spain moved, turned back to the desk and the papers spread on it and even that without moving because he was sitting at the desk with a paper in his hand when the boy entered, the boy standing there looking down at the short plumpish gray-haired man in sober fine broadcloth and an immaculate glazed shirt whom he was used to seeing in boots and muddy corduroy, unshaven, sitting the shaggy powerful long-hocked mare with the worn Winchester carbine across the saddlebow and the great blue dog standing motionless as bronze at the stirrup, the two of them in that last year and to the boy anyway coming to resemble one another somehow as two people competent for love or for business who have been in love or in business together for a long time sometimes do. Major de Spain did not look up again.

"No. I will be too busy. But good luck to you. If you have it, you might bring me a young squirrel."

"Yes sir," he said. "I will."

He rode his mare, the three-year-old filly he had bred and raised and broken himself. He left home a little after midnight and six hours later, without even having sweated her, he rode into Hoke's, the tiny log-line junction which he had always thought of as Major de Spain's property too although Major de Spain had merely sold the company (and that many years ago) the land on which the sidetracks and loading-platforms and the commissary store stood, and looked about in shocked and grieved amazement even though he had had forewarning and had believed himself prepared: a new planing-mill already half completed which would cover two or three acres and what looked like miles and miles of stacked steel rails red with the light bright rust of newness and of piled crossties sharp with creosote, and wire corrals and feeding-troughs for two hundred mules at least and the tents for the men who drove them; so that he arranged for the care and stabling of his mare as rapidly as he could and did not look any more, mounted into the log-train caboose with his gun and climbed into the cupola and looked no more save toward the wall of wilderness ahead within which he would be able to hide himself from it once more anyway.

Then the little locomotive shrieked and began to move: a rapid churning of exhaust, a lethargic deliberate clashing of slack couplings travelling backward along the train, the exhaust changing to the deep slow clapping bites of power as the caboose too began to move and from the cupola he watched the train's head complete the first and only curve in the entire line's length and vanish into the wilderness, dragging its length of train behind it so that it resembled a small dingy harmless snake vanishing into weeds, drawing him with it too until soon it ran once more at its maximum clattering speed between the twin walls of unaxed wilderness as of old. It had been harmless once. Not five years ago Walter Ewell had shot a six-point buck from this same moving caboose, and there was the story of the half-grown bear: the train's first trip in to the cutting thirty miles away, the bear between the rails, its rear end elevated like that of a playing puppy while it dug to see what sort of ants or bugs they might contain or perhaps just to examine the curious symmetrical squared barkless logs which had appeared apparently from nowhere in one endless mathematical line overnight, still digging until the driver on the braked engine not fifty feet away blew the whistle at it, whereupon it broke frantically and took the first tree it came to: an ash sapling not much bigger than a man's thigh and climbed as high as it could and clung there, its head ducked between its arms as a man (a woman perhaps) might have done while the brakeman threw chunks of ballast at it, and when the engine returned three hours later with the first load of outbound logs the bear was halfway down the tree and once more scrambled back up as high as it could and clung again while the train passed and was still there when the engine went in again in the afternoon and still there when it came back out at dusk; and Boon had been in Hoke's with the wagon after a barrel of flour that noon when the train-crew told about it and Boon and Ash, both twenty years younger then, sat under the tree all that night to keep anybody from shooting it and the next morning Major de Spain had the log-train held at Hoke's and just before sundown on the second day, with not only Boon and Ash but Major de Spain and General Compson and Walter and McCaslin, twelve then, watching, it came down the tree after almost thirty-six hours without even water and McCaslin told him how for a minute they thought it was going to stop right there at the barrow-pit where they were standing and drink, how it looked at the water and paused and looked at them and at the water again, but did not, gone, running, as bears run, the two sets of feet, front and back, tracking two separate though parallel courses.

It had been harmless then. They would hear the passing log-train sometimes from the camp; sometimes, because nobody bothered to listen for it or not. They would hear it going in, running light and fast, the light clatter of the trucks, the exhaust of the diminutive locomotive and its shrill peanut-parcher whistle flung for one petty moment and absorbed by the brooding and inattentive wilderness without even an echo. They would hear it going out, loaded, not quite so fast now yet giving its frantic and toylike illusion of crawling speed, not whistling now to conserve steam, flinging its bitten laboring miniature puffing into the immemorial woodsface with frantic and bootless vainglory, empty and noisy and puerile, carrying to no destination or purpose sticks which left nowhere any scar or stump, as the child's toy loads and transports and unloads its dead sand and rushes back for more, tireless and unceasing and rapid yet never quite so fast as the Hand which plays with it moves the toy burden back to load the toy again. But it was different now. It was the same train, engine cars and caboose, even the same enginemen brakeman and conductor to whom Boon, drunk then sober then drunk again then fairly sober once more all in the space of fourteen hours, had bragged that day two years ago about what they were going to do to Old Ben tomorrow, running with its same illusion of frantic rapidity between the same twin walls of impenetrable and impervious woods, passing the old landmarks, the old game crossings over which he had trailed bucks wounded and not wounded and more than once seen them, anything but wounded, bolt out of the woods and up and across the embankment which bore the rails and ties then down and into the woods again as the earth-bound supposedly move but crossing as arrows travel, groundless, elongated, three times its actual length and even paler, different in color, as if there were a point between immobility and absolute motion where even mass chemically altered, changing without pain or agony not only in bulk and shape but in color too, approaching the color of wind, yet this time it was as though the train (and not only the train but himself, not only his vision which had seen it and his memory which remembered it but his clothes too, as garments carry back into the clean edgeless blowing of air the lingering effluvium of a sick-room or of death) had brought with it into the doomed wilderness, even before the actual axe, the shadow and portent of the new mill not even finished yet and the rails and ties which were not even laid; and he knew now what he had known as soon as he saw Hoke's this morning but had not yet thought into words: why Major de Spain had not come back, and that after this time he himself, who had had to see it one time other, would return no more.

Now they were near. He knew it before the engine-driver whistled to warn him. Then he saw Ash and the wagon, the reins without doubt wrapped once more about the brake-lever as within the boy's own memory Major de Spain had been forbidding him for eight years to do, the train slowing, the slackened couplings jolting and clashing again from car to car, the caboose slowing past the wagon as he swung down with his gun, the conductor leaning out above him to signal the engine, the caboose still slowing, creeping, although the engine's exhaust was already slatting in mounting tempo against the unechoing wilderness, the crashing of drawbars once more travelling backward along the train, the caboose picking up speed at last. Then it was gone. It had not been. He could no longer hear it. The wilderness soared, musing, inattentive, myriad, eternal, green; older than any mill-shed, longer than any spur-line. "Mr. Boon here yet?" he said.

"He beat me in," Ash said. "Had the wagon loaded and ready for me at Hoke's yistiddy when I got there and setting on the front steps at camp last night when I got in. He already been in the woods since fo daylight this morning. Said he gwine up to the Gum Tree and for you to hunt up that way and meet him." He knew where that was: a single big sweet-gum just outside the woods, in an old clearing; if you crept up to it very quietly this time of year and then ran suddenly into the clearing, sometimes you caught as many as a dozen squirrels in it, trapped, since there was no other tree near they could jump to. So he didn't get into the wagon at all.

"I will," he said.

"I figured you would," Ash said, "I fotch you a box of shells." He passed the shells down and began to unwrap the lines from the brake-pole.

"How many times up to now do you reckon Major has told you not to do that?" the boy said.

"Do which?" Ash said. Then he said: "And tell Boon Hogganbeck dinner gonter be on the table in a hour and if yawl want any to come on and eat it."

"In an hour?" he said. "It ain't nine o'clock yet." He drew out his watch and extended it face-toward Ash. "Look." Ash didn't even look at the watch.

"That's town time. You ain't in town now. You in the woods."

"Look at the sun then."

"Nemmine the sun too," Ash said. "If you and Boon Hogganbeck want any dinner, you better come on in and get it when I tole you. I aim to get done in that kitchen because I got my wood to chop. And watch your feet. They're crawling."

"I will," he said.

Then he was in the woods, not alone but solitary; the solitude closed about him, green with summer. They did not change, and, timeless, would not, any more than would the green of summer and the fire and rain of fall and the iron cold and sometimes even snow

the day, the morning when he killed the buck and Sam marked his face with its hot blood, they returned to camp and he remembered old Ash's blinking and disgruntled and even outraged disbelief until at last McCaslin had had to affirm the fact that he had really killed it: and that night Ash sat snarling and unapproachable behind the stove so that Tennie's Jim had to serve the supper and waked them with breakfast already on the table the next morning and it was only half-past one o'clock and at last out of Major de Spain's angry cursing and Ash's snarling and sullen rejoinders the fact emerged that Ash not only wanted to go into the woods and shoot a deer also but he intended to and Major de Spain said, 'By God, if we don't let him we will probably have to do the cooking from now on:' and Walter Ewell said, 'Or get up at midnight to eat what Ash cooks:' and since he had already killed his buck for this hunt and was not to shoot again unless they needed meat, he offered his gun to Ash until Major de Spain took command and allotted that gun to Boon for the day and gave Boon's unpredictable pump gun to Ash, with two buckshot shells but Ash said, 'I got shells:' and showed them, four: one buck, one of number three shot for rabbits, two of birdshot and told one by one their history and their origin and he remembered not Ash's face alone but Major de Spain's and Walter's and General Compson's too, and Ash's voice: 'Shoot? Of course they'll shoot! Genl Cawmpson guv me this un'—the buckshot—'right outen the same gun he kilt that big buck with eight years ago. And this un'—it was the rabbit shell: triumphantly—'is oldern thisyer boy!' And that morning he loaded the gun himself, reversing the order: the birdshot, the rabbit, then the buck so that the buckshot would feed first into the chamber, and himself without a gun, he and Ash walked beside Major de Spain's and Tennie's Jim's horses and the dogs (that was the snow) until they cast and struck, the sweet strong cries ringing away into the muffled falling air and gone almost immediately, as if the constant and unmurmuring flakes had already bur-

ied even the unformed echoes beneath their myriad and weightless falling, Major de Spain and Tennie's Jim gone too, whooping on into the woods; and then it was all right, he knew as plainly as if Ash had told him that Ash had now hunted his deer and that even his tender years had been forgiven for having killed one, and they turned back toward home through the falling snow—that is, Ash said, 'Now whut?' and he said, 'This way'—himself in front because, although they were less than a mile from camp, he knew that Ash, who had spent two weeks of his life in the camp each year for the last twenty, had no idea whatever where they were, until quite soon the manner in which Ash carried Boon's gun was making him a good deal more than just nervous and he made Ash walk in front, striding on, talking now, an old man's garrulous monologue beginning with where he was at the moment then of the woods and of camping in the woods and of eating in camps then of eating then of cooking it and of his wife's cooking then briefly of his old wife and almost at once and at length of a new light-colored woman who nursed next door to Major de Spain's and if she didn't watch out who she was switching her tail at he would show her how old was an old man or not if his wife just didn't watch him all the time, the two of them in a game trail through a dense brake of cane and brier which would bring them out within a quarter-mile of camp, approaching a big fallen tree-trunk lying athwart the path and just as Ash, still talking, was about to step over it the bear, the yearling, rose suddenly beyond the log, sitting up, its forearms against its chest and its wrists limply arrested as if it had been surprised in the act of covering its face to pray: and after a certain time Ash's gun yawed jerkily up and he said, 'You haven't got a shell in the barrel yet. Pump it:' but the gun already snicked and he said, 'Pump it. You haven't got a shell in the barrel yet:' and Ash pumped the action and in a certain time the gun steadied again and snicked and he said, 'Pump it:' and watched the buckshot shell jerk, spinning heavily, into the cane. This is the rabbit shot: he thought and the gun snicked and he thought: The next is bird-shot: and he didn't have to say Pump it; he cried, 'Don't shoot! Don't shoot!' but that was already too late too, the light dry vicious snick! before he could speak and the bear turned and dropped to all-fours and then was gone and there was only the log, the cane, the velvet and constant snow and Ash said, 'Now whut?' and he said, 'This way. Come on:' and began to back away down the path and Ash said, 'I got to find my shells:' and he said, 'Goddamn it, goddamn it, come on': but Ash leaned the gun against the log and returned and stooped and fumbled among the cane roots until he came back and stooped and found the shells and they rose and at that moment the gun, untouched, leaning against the log six feet away and for that while even forgotten by both of them, roared, bellowed and flamed, and ceased: and he carried it now, pumped out the last mummified shell and gave that one also to Ash and, the action still open, himself carried the gun until he stood it in the corner behind Boon's bed at the camp

—; summer, and fall, and snow, and wet and sap-rife spring in their ordered immortal sequence, the deathless and immemorial phases of the mother who had shaped him if any had toward the man he almost was, mother and father both to the old man born of a Negro slave and a Chickasaw chief who had been his spirit's father if any had, whom he had revered and harkened to and loved and lost and grieved: and he would marry someday and they too would own for their brief while that brief unsubstanced glory which inherently of itself cannot last and hence why glory: and they would, might, carry even the remembrance of it into the time when flesh no longer talks to flesh because memory at least does last: but still the woods would be his mistress and his wife.

He was not going toward the Gum Tree. Actually he was getting farther from it. Time was and not so long ago either when he would not have been allowed here without someone with him, and a little later, when he had begun to learn how much he did not know, he would not have dared be here without someone with him, and later still, beginning to ascertain, even if only dimly, the limits of what he did not know, he could have attempted and carried it through with a compass, not because of any increased belief in himself but because McCaslin and Major de Spain and Walter and General Compson too had taught him at last to believe the compass regardless of what it seemed to state. Now he did not even use the compass but merely the sun and that only subconsciously, yet he could have taken a scaled map and plotted at any time to within a hundred feet of where he actually was; and sure enough, at almost the exact moment when he expected it, the earth began to rise faintly, he passed one of the four concrete markers set down by the lumber company's surveyor to establish the four corners of the plot which Major de Spain had reserved out of the sale, then he stood on the crest of the knoll itself, the four corner-markers all visible now, blanched still even beneath the winter's weathering, lifeless and shockingly alien in that place where dissolution itself was a seething turmoil of ejaculation tumescence conception and birth, and death did not even exist. After two winters' blanketings of leaves and the flood-waters of two springs, there was no trace of the two graves any more at all. But those who would have come this far to find them would not need headstones but would have found them as Sam Fathers himself had taught him to find such: by bearings on trees: and did, almost the first thrust of the hunting knife finding (but only to see if it was still there) the round tin box manufactured for axle-grease and containing now Old Ben's dried mutilated paw, resting above Lion's bones.

He didn't disturb it. He didn't even look for the other grave where he and McCaslin and Major de Spain and Boon had laid Sam's body, along with his hunting horn and his knife and his tobacco-pipe, that Sunday morning two years ago; he didn't have to. He had stepped over it, perhaps on it. But that was all right. *He probably knew I was in the woods this morning long before I got here,* he thought, going on to the tree which had supported one end of the platform where Sam lay when McCaslin and Major de Spain found them—the tree, the other axle-grease tin nailed to the trunk, but weathered, rusted, alien too yet healed already into the wilderness' concordant generality, raising no tuneless note, and empty, long since empty of the food and tobacco he had put into it that day, as empty of that as it would presently be of this which he drew from his pocket—the twist of tobacco, the new bandanna handkerchief, the small paper sack of the peppermint candy which Sam had used to love; that gone too, almost before he had turned his back, not vanished but merely translated into the myriad life which printed the dark mold of these secret and sunless places with delicate fairy tracks, which, breathing and biding and immobile, watched him from beyond every twig and leaf until he moved, moving again, walking on; he had not stopped, he had only paused, quitting the knoll which was no abode of the dead because there was no death, not Lion and not Sam: not held fast in earth but free in earth and not in earth but of earth, myriad yet undiffused of every myriad part, leaf and twig and particle, air and sun and rain and dew and night, acorn oak and leaf and acorn again, dark and dawn and dark and dawn again in their immutable progression, and, being myriad, one: and Old Ben too. Old Ben too; they would give him his paw back even, certainly they would give him his paw back: then the long challenge and the long chase, no heart to be driven and outraged, no flesh to be mauled and bled— Even as he froze himself, he seemed to hear Ash's parting admonition. He could even hear the voice as he froze, immobile, one foot just taking his weight, the toe of the other just lifted behind him, not breathing, feeling again and as always the sharp shocking inrush from when Isaac McCaslin long yet was not, and so it was fear all right but not fright as he looked down at it. It had not coiled yet and the buzzer had not sounded either, only one thick rapid contraction, one loop cast sideways as though merely for purchase from which the raised head might start slightly backward, not in fright either, not in threat quite yet, more than six feet of it, the head raised higher than his knee and less than his knee's length away, and old, the once-bright markings of its youth dulled now to a monotone concordant too with the wilderness it crawled and lurked: the old one, the ancient and accursed about the earth, fatal and solitary and he could smell it now: the thin sick smell of rotting cucumbers and something else which had no name, evocative of all knowledge and an old weariness and of pariah-hood and of death. At last it moved. Not the head. The elevation of the head did not change as it began to glide away from him, moving erect yet off the perpendicular as if the head and that elevated third were complete and all: an entity walking on two feet and free of all laws of mass and balance, and should have been because even now he could not quite believe that all that shift and flow of shadow behind that walking head could have been one snake: going and then gone; he put the other foot down at last and didn't know it, standing with one hand raised as Sam had stood that afternoon six years ago when Sam led him into the wilderness and showed him and he ceased to be a child, speaking the old tongue which Sam had spoken that day without premeditation either: "Chief," he said: "Grandfather."

He couldn't tell when he first began to hear the sound, because when he became aware of it, it seemed to him that he had been already hearing it for several seconds—a sound as though someone were hammering a gun-barrel against a piece of railroad iron, a sound loud and heavy and not rapid yet with something frenzied about it, as the hammerer were not only a strong man and an earnest one but a little hysterical too. Yet it couldn't be on the logline because, although the track lay in that direction, it was at least two miles from him and this sound was not three hundred yards away. But even as he thought that, he realized where the sound must be coming from: whoever the man was and whatever he was doing, he was somewhere near the edge of the clearing where the Gum Tree was and where he was to meet Boon. So far, he had been hunting as he advanced, moving slowly and quietly and watching the ground and the trees both. Now he went on, his gun unloaded and the barrel slanted up and back to facilitate its passage through brier and undergrowth, approaching as it grew louder and louder that steady savage somehow queerly hysterical beating of metal on metal, emerging from the woods, into the old clearing, with the solitary gum tree directly before him. At first glance the tree seemed to be alive with frantic squirrels. There appeared to be forty or fifty of them leaping and darting from branch to branch until the whole tree had become one green maelstrom of mad leaves, while from time to time, singly or in twos and threes, squirrels would dart down the trunk then whirl without stopping and rush back up again as though sucked violently back by the vacuum of their fellows' frenzied vortex. Then he saw Boon, sitting, his back against the trunk, his head bent, hammering furiously at something on his lap. What he hammered with was the barrel of his dismembered gun, what he hammered at was the breech of it. The rest of the gun lay scattered about him in a half-dozen pieces while he bent over the piece on his lap his scarlet and stream-ing walnut face, hammering the disjointed barrel against the gun-breech with the frantic abandon of a madman. He didn't even look up to see who it was. Still hammering, he merely shouted back at the boy in a hoarse strangled voice:

"Get out of here! Don't touch them! Don't touch a one of them! They're mine!"
1942

Make-Believe

Also by Richard Collier

Nonfiction

Captain of the Queens
(with Capt. Harry Grattidge)

Ten Thousand Eyes

The City That Wouldn't Die

The Sands of Dunkirk

A House Called Memory

The Great Indian Mutiny

The General Next to God

Eagle Day

The River That God Forgot

Duce!

The Plague of the Spanish Lady

The War In The Desert
(Time-Life World War II Series)

Bridge Across the Sky

1940: The World In Flames
(U.S. title: 1940: The Avalanche)

Four From Buenos Aires
(Reader's Digest Great Cases of Interpol)

1941: Armageddon
(U.S. title: The Road To Pearl Harbor: 1941)

The War That Stalin Won
(U.S. title: The Freedom Road: 1944–1945)

The Rainbow People

Fiction

Beautiful Friend

Pay-Off in Calcutta

The Lovely and The Damned

Make-Believe

The Magic
of International Theatre

Richard Collier

Dodd, Mead & Company
New York

To the memory of
my mother
and father
*and the days when
we queued for The Pit.*

No part of this book may be reproduced in any form
without permission in writing from the publisher.
Published by Dodd, Mead & Company, Inc.
79 Madison Avenue, New York, N.Y. 10016
Manufactured in the United States of America
Designed by Erich Hobbing
First Edition

Library of Congress Cataloging-in-Publication Data

Collier, Richard, 1924–
    Make-believe: the magic of international
theatre.

    Bibliography: p.
    Includes index.
1. Theater—Great Britain—History—19th century.
2. Theater—Great Britain—History—20th century.
3. Theater—United States—History.   I. Title.
PN2594.C625   1986   792'.0941   86-4402
ISBN 0-396-08645-4

1   2   3   4   5   6   7   8   9   10

Contents

Most people are other people. Their thoughts are someone else's opinions, their life a mimicry; their passions a quotation.

—OSCAR WILDE, 1893

Roger says we don't exist. Why, it's only we who do exist. They are the shadows and we give them substance. We are the symbols of all this confused, aimless struggling that they call life, and it's only the symbol which is real. They say acting is only make-believe. That make-believe is the only reality.

—JULIA LAMBERT in
W. SOMERSET MAUGHAM'S *Theatre*, 1937

Real life is haphazard and confused. People say the wrong things. But theatre is a kind of elevated form of life—and that is where things work. In the theatre, not in life . . .

—JEAN ANOUILH, 1984

Acknowledgments

For more than thirty years I have threaded my way along the trails of the Make-Believe Jungle, eternally fascinated by the lifestyle of its inhabitants. Along the way, many of them generously took time out to satisfy my curiosity on varying aspects of their profession, revealing much that would otherwise have gone unrecorded. After all this length of time, I hope they will accept the bare mention of their names in token of my gratitude:

Ronald Adam; Julie Andrews; Michael Arlen; Richard Arlen; Mac Ashinoff (Stein Cosmetic Co, New York); Ellis Ashton; Dr. Geoffrey Ashton (Hon. Librarian, The Garrick Club, London); Sir Robert Atkins; Sir Richard Attenborough; Tallulah Bankhead; Dr. Kathleen Barker and Derek Forbes (The Society For Theatre Research, London); John Barrow (American Academy of Dramatic Arts, New York); Beverley Baxter; John Bentley; Ballard Berkeley; Aubrey Blackburn; Humphrey Bogart; Wynyard Browne; Patrick Cargill; Bonar Colleano; Peter Corneille (Green Room Club, London); George Coulouris; John Counsell (Windsor Repertory Theatre); Noël Coward; Hugh Cruttwell (Windsor Repertory Theatre); Spencer Curtis Brown; George Cuttingham (American Academy of Dramatic Arts, New York); Paul Daneman; Pauline Davies; Frances Day; Derrick De Marney; Terence De Marney; Tom Dillon (Lambs Club, New York); Maurice Willson Disher; Yolande Donlan; Melvyn Douglas; Irene Dunne; Buddy Ebsen; Alan Eisenberg (American Actors Equity); George Elliott; Douglas Fairbanks, Jr.; George Fearon; Peter Finch; Harold French; Rosalinde Fuller; Liam Gaffney; Mario Gallati (The Ivy/Caprice, London); Hermione Gingold; Lenore Grulner (American Actors Equity); Sir Alec Guinness; Stanley Hale; Margaret F. Harris ("Motley"); Signe Hasso; Jack Hawkins; Charlton Heston; George Hoare (Archivist, Theatre Royal, Drury Lane, London); W.E. Holloway; Stanford Holme (Oxford Playhouse); Robert

Holmes; Thelma Holt; Miki Hood; Judge Roger Bryant Hunting (Players Club, New York); Father Michael Hurst-Bannister (Actor's Church Union, London); Wilfrid Hyde-White; Emrys Jones; Alexis Kanner; Cecil King; Esmond Knight; Collie Knox; Margaret Leighton; Kenneth Lidstone; Sir Emile Littler; John Longden; Patrick McGoohan; Mary Mackenzie; Fred MacMurray; Colin Mabberley (Curator, The Raymond Mander and Joe Mitchenson Theatre Collection, London); Rogert Machell; Howard M. Malament (Stein Cosmetic Co, New York); Beryl Measor; Dido Milroy; Stephen Mitchell; Clifford Mollison; Henry Mollison; Elizabeth Montgomery ("Motley"); Leonard Mosley; G.H. Mulcaster; Professor A.M. Nagler (American Society for Theatre Research); Dr. Oliver Neville (Director and Principal, Royal Academy of Dramatic Art, London); Joan Newell; Beverley Nichols; Phil Nicklin; Michael Northen; Richard O'Donoghue (Administrator and Registrar, Royal Academy of Dramatic Art, London); Judy and Jack Oliphant; Enrico Olivelli; Michael Pearson; Esmé Percy; Teddy Percy; Leslie Perrins; Georgie Perrott; Wilfred Pickles; Peter Plouviez (British Actors Equity); Dennis Price; Maureen Pryor; Arthur Quin; Sir Carol Reed; Arnold Ridley; Dame Flora Robson, D.B.E.; Francoise Rosay; Hector Ross; G. Malcolm Russell; Daphne Rye (H.M. Tennent Ltd); Harvey Sabinson (League of New York Theatres and Producers); Vincent Sardi (Sardi's Restaurant, New York); Kenneth Seale ("Spotlight" Casting Directory); Athene Seyler; Alastair Sim; Hilda Simms; Harriet Slaughter (League of New York Theatres and Producers); J. Baxter Somerville (Croydon Repertory Theatre); Heather Stannard; H.C.G. "Inky" Stevens; Willard Stoker (Liverpool Playhouse); Berkeley Sutcliffe; Beatrix Thomson; Robert Lacy Thompson (Society of West End Theatre); Sophie Tucker; Peter Ustinov; Margery Vosper; George Wachtell (League of New York Theatres and Producers); Miriam Warner; John Willetts; Stephen Williams; Cecil Wilson; John L. Wilson (National Association of Theatrical Television and Kine Employees, London); Mathew Winsten; John Witty.

As always, my deepest debt is to those who worked closely alongside me throughout: to my wife, who not only typed the initial draft and kept six cats fed to bursting point but conducted much of the research, to Margaret Duff, who brilliantly carried out many key interviews, and to Hildegard Anderson and Amy Forbert, who oversaw much of my American research. My agents in London and New York, Anne McDermid and Emilie Jacobson, offered sterling support; my publisher, Allen Klots, generously granted an extension of time that helped the completed draft enormously. Elsie Couch and Ann Walker produced, as always, an impeccable typescript. In addition, I have to thank the staffs of the British Library, particularly the Department of Manuscripts, for the Lord Chamberlain's unique collection of unpublished play-texts, the London Library and the New York Public Library's Theatre Collection at Lincoln Center for their help and courtesy at all times.

Illustrations

Peggy Ashcroft in *Happy Days*.
Workroom sketch by the Motleys for *Bartholomew Fair*.
Marlon Brando and Jessica Tandy in *A Streetcar Named Desire*.
Kenneth Haigh, Alan Bates, and Mary Ure in *Look Back in Anger*.
A dresser fixes a showgirl's hair.
Diane Cilento collects her mail from the stage door keeper.
Stage hands at work.

I. The Age of "The Stare":
"Must Dress Well On and Off"

Despite his blanched, ascetic face, his curious spiderlike gait, he was an actor revered by millions. Now, on the afternoon of July 18, 1895, his hour had come. In the intimacy of the Yellow Closet, at Windsor Castle, beside the river Thames, fifty-seven-year-old John Henry Brodribb, who had rechristened himself Henry Irving, knelt, along with eighteen other recipients, to kiss the hand of his sovereign, Queen Victoria. He felt the touch of a sword on either shoulder and heard the words no actor had ever thought to hear: "Rise, Sir Henry." Then, departing from her normal custom, the Queen was moved to add, "I am very, very pleased, sir."

The Queen and the actor were far from being strangers. Since 1861, when the long twilight of mourning for her beloved consort, Prince Albert of Saxe-Coburg-Gotha, began, no playhouse had enjoyed Victoria's patronage. But from 1887 on, the seventy-year-old Queen, spurred on by her corpulent, pleasure-loving son, Albert Edward, Prince of Wales, had come increasingly to relish what she called "treats": private Command Performances given at one of the royal residences. On April 24, 1889, Irving had been in the vanguard of these clandestine revels at Sandringham, Prince Albert's seven-thousand-acre Norfolk estate—first a bravura performance of his full-blooded melodrama, *The Bells*, followed by the Trial Scene from *The Merchant of Venice*, with his longtime leading lady, Ellen Terry, as Portia.

Four years later, on March 18, 1893, he had returned to Windsor Castle's Waterloo Gallery, with a play more attuned to the monarch's taste: the *Becket* of her late poet laureate, Alfred, Lord Ten-

1

nyson. "It is a very noble play," was the Queen's unqualified verdict.

This knighthood was a landmark in theatrical history far greater than even Irving knew. "They'll knight no other actors after me," he was to prophesy, yet within a time span of sixteen years, no less than five British actor-managers were to follow in his footsteps: Squire Bancroft (1897), Charles Wyndham (1902), John Hare and Herbert Beerbohm Tree (1907), and George Alexander (1911). All five men had this in common with Irving: at one time or another, they, too, had been party to the delicious conspiracy of "treats."

Overnight, a profession deemed idle, dissolute, and drunken; in which "actress" was often an euphemism for "tart"; officially classified, until an 1824 change in Statute Law, as "rogues and vagabonds," had lost its stigma.

Few callings had ever been so universally shunned. Two years before Irving's knighthood, that founding father of the Hollywood Raj, Charles Aubrey Smith, had been entreated by his mother, "Aubrey, Aubrey . . . think of what will become of your two sisters if their brother is an actor." She spoke for the world at large. In Gainesville, Texas, twenty-two-year-old Lionel Barrymore, son of the actor, Maurice, accepted a lift in a buggy from two friendly youngsters, only to find their goodwill freezing over once his connections were revealed: "Sir, we are not allowed to be seen with show people." Touring Cornwall, in the 1880s, Philip Ben Greet (himself knighted in 1929) was banished from a lodging house with the outraged cry, "Oh, we don't take *that* sort of people here; we only take *Christians*."

Even the dear departed were denied the last sacred rites. In New York, the comedian Joseph Jefferson, who toured for more than thirty years as *Rip Van Winkle*, was given a fine rebuff by a Fifth Avenue church when he sought to bury a friend; they did not hold funeral services for actors, but a little church around the corner might oblige. From that time on, the Church of the Transfiguration on East 29th Street was by common consent the Little Church Around The Corner, the church that the profession took to its heart.

But now, as they swiftly came to recognize, actors like Aubrey Smith, and actresses, too, were acceptable in high society. When Ethel Barrymore, sister of the hapless Lionel, journeyed to England to join Irving's company in 1898, she was flanked at dinner parties by such luminaries as Lord Balfour and the writer G. K. Chesterton.

Within weeks she was on first-name terms with Millicent, Duchess of Sutherland. In New York, she watched the cup races from the deck of Mrs. John Jacob Astor's yacht; she dined at Sherry's on Fifth Avenue with that formidable trinity who ruled Newport, Rhode Island—Mrs. Mamie Stuyvesant Fish, Mrs. Tessie Fair Oelrichs, and Mrs. Oliver Hazard Perry Belmont.

"Must dress well on and off," ran a contemporary advertisement in the artistes-wanted columns of *The Stage*. "No brown paper parcels." To mark his newfound status, an actor must from now on carry his possessions in a traveling bag. "Snappy dresser on and off," actors would assure would-be employers in the New York *Dramatic Mirror*, "Complete wardrobe with dress suit and dinner clothes."

Not surprisingly, reaction set in; the despised mummers of yesterday now embarked on a memorable and monumental ego-trip. Even before his knighthood, George Alexander—a one-time city clerk, born George Alexander Gibb Samson—had pinned this high-hat notice to the call-board of his own St. James's Theatre: "Mr. Alexander, when out walking in the West End, would be obliged if the small-part actors and the extra gentlemen would refrain from acknowledging him when passing him in the street or park."

In the United States, stars of the magnitude of Maude Adams and Richard Mansfield (who was British by birth, American by adoption) toured the land in their own special eight-car trains, dining in solitude, remote from the concerns of their fellow players. In the matter of dress, they were martinets; on Maude Adams's call-boards, one notice always loomed large: "The ladies of the company are requested to wear hats and gloves in public." Mansfield was so sensitive sartorially that he once fired a player at rehearsal for wearing brown shoes with a blue suit. For an actor to accost him on the street was to court instant dismissal. John Drew, uncle of the Barrymores, was equally pernickety; known as "the Beau Brummell of Broadway," shod by Peal of London, and outfitted by Henry Poole of Savile Row, with their thirty-six royal warrants, Drew expected even the lowliest members of the company to travel in parlor cars and rest up at the best hotels.

It was all at once a world in bewildering flux. In 1881, Charles Eyre Pascoe's *Dramatic List*, a forerunner of *Who's Who In The Theatre*, had cognizance of 560 players, while listing only those 325 who had attained the West End, though census returns already put their number at 4,565. In the United States, the same pattern was emerging: 5,000 players in 1880 had swollen, by 1908, to 20,000. Yet from that time on, this make-believe jungle was to burgeon with the lushness of an Amazonian rain forest: an estimated (1984) total is 61,557 in Britain and the United States alone.

Not only Irving's knighthood had given the theatre this timely and welcome shot of adrenalin. From 1837 until Albert's death, Queen Victoria's patronage had helped, too, and there were other contributory factors: the coming of the first railway networks, ensuring a new social mobility; the onrush, from the midfifties, of the new popular press with its coverage of the latest shows. By the 1880s, the gulf separating theatre folk from London society had narrowed perceptibly; in at least two London clubs, the Garrick (on its present site since 1864) and the Beefsteak (1875), actors mingled freely with other professional men, with only the Green Room Club (1866) then barred to all save actors. Much the same pertained in New York: from 1888, the Players' Club, at 16 Gramercy Park (a brownstone house endowed to the profession by the tragedian Edwin Booth, in return for a rent-free fourth-floor suite), saw more barriers crumbling, a process which the Lamb's Club had begun in 1875.

And many new recruits to the profession—Frank Benson, Ben Webster—were the sons of eminent legal men, while others hailed from civil service, academic, or engineering backgrounds. Some, after attending major public schools, had gone on to higher education at Oxford or Cambridge. To the critic, Percy Fitzgerald, this was a new breed of actor altogether: "a gentlemanly well-dressed man . . . as little anxious to obtrude his profession as an officer or a barrister."

A case in point was the fashionable Bancroft family, who for twenty years labored single-mindedly to impose a veneer of respectability on the drama. Beginning in 1865 with a borrowed thousand pounds, the oddly named Squire Bancroft and his wife, the former Marie Wilton, leased the Queens, a run-down playhouse known locally as "The Dust Hole," on London's grimy Tottenham Street for twenty pounds a week, rechristened it the Prince of Wales, and set out to woo polite society with an art form that would become all too familiar: the drawing-room comedy. Their plays, the Bancrofts decided, should be mirrors of "real life" as the middle classes knew it: small talk, to be sure, but intelligent small talk. And if this was what the critics of the day dubbed "cup-and-saucer comedy," the cups and saucers, one man conceded, were "of the best china . . . delicately and deftly handled."

This was of a piece with all the Bancrofts' innovations at the Prince of Wales (later the Scala). They abolished the "theatrical wardrobe," a degraded species of backstage flea market for reach-me-downs; Bancroft actresses were encouraged to patronize Worth, Doucet, or Jay's, with the Bancrofts footing the bill. No longer did their players line up with the carpenters and cleaners on Saturday morning to receive their weekly salary—a routine that one rising young star, Johnston Forbes-Robertson, found so humiliating he went unpaid for three weeks in succession. When the Bancrofts reigned, a discreet tap on a dressing-room door signaled that a check was in the offing.

In the Bancroft comedies, custom-built for them by thirty-six-year-old T. W. (Thomas William) Robertson for a stipend of ten pounds a night—"cup-and-saucer" plays with monosyllabic titles like *Ours, School, Caste*—all carpets, curtains, and furniture were real, and all doors, in jungle lore, were "practicable": they could be opened and closed. The Bancrofts spent many hours in the British and Victoria and Albert Museums, poring over prints and illustrations. Thus, the high marquetry chair on which Lady Sneerwell perched in *The School For Scandal* was the genuine article, as was the saloon of the P & O liner in *The Overland Route*.

Many of these concepts—practicable scenery, and the box-set, showing the three walls and ceilings of a room—had been instituted thirty years earlier by Madame Lucy Elizabeth Vestris at her own Olympic Theatre, but until the Bancrofts' time this fashion was far from universal.

Their gamble paid off. On their opening night—April 16, 1865—only £125 of their borrowed £1,000 remained in the bank, but within three years they had repaid the loan in full. They raised the price of orchestra stalls from seven shillings to a then unheard-of ten shillings; the public—among them, the Prince of Wales, and his Danish wife, Alexandra—was willing to pay. Although the Bancrofts paid higher salaries than most, their overheads, through thrifty budgeting, never exceeded £70 a night. As early as 1878, they pioneered that time-honored middle-class institution, the Wednesday and Saturday matinée. One year later, they moved on to lusher pastures: the magnificent eighteenth-century Theatre Royal, Haymarket, flanked by Nash's six Corinthian columns, leased for £5,000 a year, with a pledge to spend £10,000 on remodeling.

By 1885, these astute entrepreneurs, after amassing close to two

5

hundred thousand pounds, elected to retire from management; their contribution to the theatre's growing prestige was complete. Both, for years to come, remained prominent West End landmarks—she, as one woman recalled her, "like a bright little robin . . . a toque with an aigrette sitting on her fuzzy fringe," and Sir Squire, his prematurely white hair contrasting with his dark moustache, seen always with a tall hat, frock coat, black-rimmed eyeglass with a black ribbon of watered silk, en route for lunch at the Garrick Club. To the end of his life—he survived until 1926—one custom never varied: a daily call at his bank in St. James's Street, to check that his balance was still in rude health.

It was Madge Robertson Kendal, sister of Tom, the dramatist, who best summed up the theatrical transition that the Victorian era had seen. As a six-year-old stage brat, cast as Little Eva in *Uncle Tom's Cabin*, Madge had been hauled to heaven with a rope around her waist at Bristol's Theatre Royal; yet thirty-two years later, she and her husband, William Hunter Kendal, had participated in the first of Queen Victoria's "treats" at Osborne, on the Isle of Wight.

"There is at last a recognised social position for the professional player," Madge Kendal, created a Dame of the British Empire in 1926, announced with pardonable smugness. "The society of the cultivated and intelligent actor is eagerly sought after."

For thirty years, the giant oak in this jungle was, and always would be, Irving, the son of a traveling salesman, initially a lawyer's clerk who had triumphed over a stammer to struggle through 428 stock company roles before he was twenty-one. His twenty-three-year lease of London's Lyceum Theatre, in partnership with Ellen Terry, a much-married, flaxen-haired actress with a brick-dust complexion, tip-tilted nose, and a wide, amused, crooked smile, had made both of them legends in their lifetimes. In playhouses as far apart as the Grand, Wolverhampton, and the Palace in Denver, Colorado—for from 1883 onward, Irving was to make nine tours of the United States—a whole generation of theatregoers spoke with awe of his unforgettable creations: the callous Dubosc, in *The Lyons Mail*, nonchalantly humming *La Marseillaise* after a cold-blooded killing; the Iago who spat out grape pips as he planned Othello's undoing; the senile old corporal, in Sir Arthur Conan Doyle's *A Story of Waterloo*, crying like a child over his broken tobacco pipe.

Yet Irving's early years had suggested no such promise. Rechristening himself at the age of eighteen after Washington Irving, the author of *Rip Van Winkle*, he had soldiered on in provincial towns for ten unremarkable years: Sunderland, Dublin, Edinburgh, five years in Manchester alone. Twice, convinced that glittering prizes awaited him, he had turned down London engagements, always holding out for larger parts, though few fellow-players shared this conviction. Once, playing Cleomenes, a Sicilian lord, in *The Winter's Tale*, his lines entirely escaped him; he fled ignominiously from the stage, followed by a storm of angry hisses. Only the faith of the comedian John Laurence Toole, a lifelong friend, brought him from the provinces to London, and it was Toole's generosity, too, that secured him his first dress suit. Irving never forgot it. "And gave me some warm underclothes, too, didn't you, Johnny?" he would recall fondly in the Garrick Club bar. "Don't forget the vest and pants!"

It was a faith that one of his first leading ladies, Ellen Terry, was far from sharing. Cast opposite Irving in David Garrick's *Katherine and Petruchio*, a potted version of *The Taming of the Shrew*, she saw not one shred of hope for him. "He was stiff with self-consciousness, his eyes were dull, his face was heavy. . . . [He] had everything against him as an actor. He could not speak, he could not walk, he could not *look*. He wanted to do things in a part but he could not do them."

The chilling, hypnotic glance that was to earn him the nickname "The Stare" was still four years distant.

It was a fond American father, the splendidly named Colonel Hezekiah Linthicum Bateman, who unwittingly gave Irving his chance. A dynamic, explosive Southern gentleman, known to his staff as "Chained Lightning," all his theatrical ambitions were vested in his three daughters, Kate, Virginia, and Isabel; in 1871, with this in view, he had taken a seven-year lease on the old Lyceum Theatre in Wellington Street, off the Strand. On March 23, Bateman made one of an audience at the Vaudeville Theatre nearby, when Irving, playing Digby Grant, a petulant windbag in the comedy *Two Roses*, took a "benefit"—a special performance that gave the bulk of the night's takings to a chosen member of the company. For his party piece, after the fall of the curtain, Irving, in full evening dress, chose to render Thomas Hood's poem, *The Dream of Eugene Aram*, the saga of a remorseful murderer and his panic-stricken attempts to conceal his victim's body.

It was a virtuoso performance. Without scenery, without proper-

7

ties or costume, Irving was living, not acting, the poem, carrying his audience on a flood tide of emotion; at the second climax, when Aram discovered that

> *A mighty wind had swept the leaves*
> *And still the corpse was bare*

the spectators erupted with violent applause. The London *Observer* commented with awe: "It was such acting as is now seldom seen."

The conniving Bateman saw his chance. To launch Isabel on a career for which she evinced little taste—her ambition, later fulfilled, was to become a nun—Bateman knew that she needed the soundest possible support, and what better support than this dark, forceful thirty-three-year-old? When he offered Irving a chance as leading man at fifteen pounds a week, which the actor readily accepted, Bateman was convinced he had found the perfect foil for Isabel.

The colonel was in error. Nobody's fool, Irving was equally nobody's foil.

Luck was with Irving. To open Isabel's autumn season, Bateman chose a vehicle titled *Fanchette*, a mishmash of a play adapted from a George Sand short story, with Irving ludicrously miscast as a lovesick peasant. Predictably, the audiences grew nightly thinner; in dudgeon, Bateman posted the closing notices and substituted a hastily cobbled-up version of *The Pickwick Papers* by James Albery, author of *Two Roses*. Although Albery's version was a sorry travesty, he had one skill in his favor: he knew how to write a part for Irving. As a result, Irving, cast as Mr. Alfred Jingle, the specious con-man who talked like a walking telegram, beaver hat cocked over one eye, resembling nothing so much as "an impudent Cockney crow," stole the show and threw the Pickwickians entirely off balance.

"Very bad indeed," noted the critic E.L. Blanchard. "I think Bateman must soon give up."

This was Irving's moment, and he seized it. For some time now he had been badgering Bateman concerning the rights of a French play, *Le Juif Polonais*, which he had secured from the translator, an eccentric, red-headed solicitor named Leopold Lewis. As a curtain raiser—a short piece offered before the main drama of the evening—he suggested that this play, which he called *The Bells*, might yet bolster *Pickwick*'s flagging fortunes.

8

It was Eugene Aram all over again, with a slight twist to the tail. The central character, Mathias, innkeeper and burgomaster of an Alsatian village, was equally a murderer, stricken by remorse. He alone knew the truth unsuspected by his family: his prosperity stemmed from the murder of a Polish Jew years earlier, a traveler whose sleigh he had intercepted, robbing the man of his gold and disposing of his body in a limekiln.

On a snowbound Christmas Eve, the night before his daughter's wedding to the local police chief, Mathias visits a country fair. He sees a mesmerist who can induce trances in his audience, probing their innermost secrets. That same night, dreaming he is before a court of law, he is horrified when the judge summons the fairground mesmerist. Mathias breaks down and is sentenced to death. On the morning of the wedding, clutching at an imaginary hangman's rope, he dies in the arms of his family.

Bateman resisted vigorously. The lanky Irving, who had scored as a character comedian, to portray an Alsatian burgomaster? The concept was absurd. To this, Irving had a short answer: hadn't his rendering of Eugene Aram on a bare stage been Bateman's sole reason for engaging him? With *Pickwick* in dire need of the kiss of life, Bateman gave in.

As rehearsals gathered pace, the company was astonished by Irving's command of the play, his sure grasp of inflections and effects. For the first time, Irving was adopting what was to become a twentieth-century commonplace: an intellectual approach to a character's psychology. To him, Mathias was no conventional villain, but a sound middle-class citizen like the bulk of the Lyceum audience: a man who, to spare his family from poverty, had succumbed to one blinding temptation and suffered agonies for the rest of his life. The phantom sleigh bells, which only Mathias hears, just as Macbeth alone sees Banquo's ghost, became a singular obsession. The crescendo of the approach, Irving reasoned, could be best achieved by a stagehand approaching from the rear, armed with a bell-strung harness such as sleigh horses wore, and jangling them until he reached the prompt corner—a desk against the inner side of the proscenium wall of the stage, on the actor's left.

On the bitter, frosty night of Saturday, November 25, 1871, there was no sense of history in the making. The stalls of the old red-and-gold theatre were half-empty. Only a ragged spatter of applause from two boxes housing family and friends greeted Irving's first appear-

9

ance, as he shook the snow from his topcoat. "It is I! It is I!"

Almost at once came the make-or-break moment: the split second when Irving must master the silent, unresponsive audience or acknowledge defeat. Mathias was now seated in the parlor of his inn, taking off his boots, putting on his shoes. At the table, a group of villagers were smoking and drinking, talking lazily. One of them noted a singular phenomenon: Never had they seen a winter so dire since the "Polish Jew's" winter.

Irving was buckling his second shoe, leaning over, his long, white, sensitive hands stretched down over the buckle. All at once the fingers were motionless. "The crown of the head suddenly seemed to glitter and become frozen," recalled Edward Gordon Craig, actor, scenic designer, and Ellen Terry's illegitimate son by the artist Edward Godwin, "and then, at the pace of the slowest and most terrified snail, the two hands, still motionless and dead, were seen to be coming up the side of the leg . . . the whole torso of the man, also seeming frozen, was gradually, and by an almost imperceptible movement, seen to be drawing up and back as it would straighten a little . . ."

Then, after an aching, twelve-second pause, Irving's voice came, deep and mellifluous: "Ah! You were talking of that?" and as he spoke the audience heard, for the first time, the regular, faraway throb of sleigh bells. At the table, the men slumped companionably, sipping their mulled wine; a thick, rich fog of tobacco smoke drifted to the rafters—and only Mathias and the Lyceum audience, bound by a dreadful complicity, listened to the bells coming nearer.

For almost an hour, the sparse audience sat in rapt silence, as if the fairground mesmerist had cast his thrall upon them, too. As the play neared its climax, Irving was seen to stagger from the curtained alcove of his bed, heedless of the urgent knocking at the door, his face seeming drained of blood, his hands clawing at his throat. "Take the rope from my neck," came the painful croaking as his family burst in. "Take the rope from my neck!" Then the pupils of his eyes literally rolled upward. He fell forward, dying in his wife's arms.

The curtain fell to a long and painful silence. Attendants were bustling to remove a woman who had fainted in the stalls. Then came a sound like an ocean rising; the mesmerist's spell was broken. Tumults of cheers brought up the curtain once more, while Irving bowed modestly, the red-headed Lewis pumped his hands in ecstasy, and Colonel Bateman led Irving back onstage, thumping him on the back.

Almost incredibly, after a lengthy interval, the curtain rose again—this time on *Pickwick*.

In his house on Gower Street, Bloomsbury, Jonas Levy, the founder and proprietor of *The Daily Telegraph*, was impatiently awaiting the arrival of his newly appointed dramatic critic, Clement Scott. A theatre buff and an inveterate first-nighter, Levy still oversaw all the paper's dramatic notices. When Scott arrived, Levy greeted him excitedly, "Tonight I have seen a great actor at the Lyceum—a great actor. There was a poor house. Write about him so that everyone shall know he is great."

All over London, forty other newspapers and periodicals were lauding Irving in the same vein. The role that he would play more than eight hundred times—the strain of which would ultimately kill him—had made him overnight, setting his feet on the long road that led to Windsor Castle.

From this time on, he was a loner. Two years earlier, on an impulse, Irving had married Florence O'Callaghan, the sulky, spoiled daughter of an Indian Army surgeon-general, and the marriage had been in deep trouble from the first. Young Mrs. Henry Irving disliked late hours as much as she disliked actors in general; when Irving brought home a friend to a frugal supper at their house in West Brompton, Florence had been known to descend from the bedroom in her dressing gown and to snap out the lights. One year earlier, past all patience, Irving had left home—returning early in 1871 when Florence begged for a reconciliation. For the sake of their year-old son, Henry Brodribb, and a second son, Laurence, born that year, Irving gave in.

In the small hours of Sunday, November 26, all this came to a head in a brougham bearing the Irvings back to West Brompton after a supper party with friends. "Well, my dear," the actor remarked, with justifiable elation, "we, too, shall soon have our own carriage and pair!"

Angry and jealous, Florence sought to wound as only she knew how. "Are you going on making a fool of yourself like this all your life?" she asked with calculated contempt.

The brougham was just then crossing Hyde Park Corner. Irving told the driver to stop. Without comment he got out, leaving Florence to journey on alone. He never returned to West Brompton, nor did he ever speak to her again.

The transformation was complete. At long last Brodribb had become Henry Irving.

Thereafter, Irving's whole life was the theatre. Except when touring, his days were divided between his top-floor bachelor apartments at 15A Grafton Street off fashionable Bond Street, the confines of the Garrick Club, and the Lyceum stage—with the Lyceum an easy winner. "It is doubtful," one American manager noted, "if there has ever been an actor so wrapped up in himself." Edward Gordon Craig agreed, "He never allowed any other thought than the stage to enter his head." Even Ellen Terry, with whom Irving for years conducted a discreet affair, deplored "his lack of enthusiasm for other people's work, or, indeed, for anything *outside his own work*." And she added, twinkling, "Were I to be run over by a steam-roller tomorrow, Henry would be deeply grieved; would say quietly, 'What a pity!'—and would add, after two moments' reflection: 'Who is there—er—to go on for her tonight?' "

Overtly a sociable man who would chat for hours over cigars and brandy, Irving found neither the time nor the need for intimate friendships. Arriving in the Garrick Club dining room around 11:45 P.M., the hour when the theatres had closed for the night, dressed in day clothes with the inevitable black spats in winter, he would stroll unselfconsciously to the desk to order his haddock or deviled kidneys. But often 3:00 A.M. found him still at the table, trading yarns with his fellows; Irving came most intensely alive after curtain fall. "I regret, sir," came his frosty rebuke to any member who departed groggily for bed, "that you are fatigued by our company."

He loved the Lyceum as he loved no other theatre, and it was in the paneled Beefsteak Room, up the back stairs, dominated by John Singer Sargent's portrait of Ellen Terry as Lady Macbeth in a blue-green dress like chain mail, that he held intimate supper parties for old friends like the Bancrofts, or visiting greats like Richard Mansfield and the French comedian, Constant-Benoît Coquelin. Each first night was the excuse for an onstage supper party with such guests as Lord Rosebery, the Liberal statesman William Ewart Gladstone, and sundry colonial prime ministers.

But after a lifetime in the jungle, Irving was adept at tooth-and-claw survival, and every Lyceum performance made this abundantly plain. A small "pin" light of steel blue always picked out Irving's features—but nobody else's—as he prowled the boards. And woe betide an actor like Norman Forbes-Robertson, whose death scene at the hands of a mob drew fervent applause in *Robespierre*. Next morning, Irving called a rehearsal "to—er—dot the i's and—er—cross the t's, me boy." But now the mob had redoubled in strength, rendering the death throes quite invisible.

Two notable innovations marked his tenure at the Lyceum: For the first time in theatrical history the auditorium lights were dimmed to secure the play undivided attention, and the stage was equipped with a false black proscenium to shut out all view of the wings. But to the bitter end he eschewed the newfangled electricity—which the Savoy Theatre had been first to adopt in 1881—always wedded to "the thick softness" of gaslight. So intense was Irving's passion for somber shadows that after witnessing the melodrama *The Silver King*, he remonstrated mildly with his fellow actor-manager, Wilson Barrett: Wasn't the scene where he descended from the train entirely too bright?

When Barrett explained, "Well, you see, it's eleven in the morning," Irving's reply was succinct: "I should have had an eclipse."

"Irving's productions," recalled one of his stage managers, Percy Nash, "were like oil-paintings . . . the boundaries lost in shadow, high-lights focussing the points of greatest interest." They were costly oil paintings, at that; in production, as in life, Irving was prodigal to the last. A good lunch at a hotel or restaurant always ended with a five-pound note for the chef and a gold sovereign for the waiter who served it, and this was but the tip of the iceberg. For the tableau curtain in the French melodrama *The Corsican Brothers*, Irving bespoke one thousand yards of crimson velvet, though only a fraction of the material was ever seen. With *Romeo and Juliet*, in 1882, he surpassed even this: sumptuous costumes, elaborate scenery and spectacular dioramas brought bills of more than £6,000. Although the bulk of Irving's offerings were foreign melodramas like *The Bells*, he doled out more than £9,000 in options for plays, few of which were ever produced.

Twenty-seven years of management netted him more than £2 million, but Irving's prophecy was not far from the truth: "I have lived keeping an army and I shall die a pauper!"

Over six feet tall and painfully thin—on tour he traveled with his own Jaeger blankets for additional warmth—Irving looked every inch an actor's actor. He made fashionable long, flowing hair, the wide-awake hat, the fur-collared overcoat; his sleeves were always cut high to show off his white, tapering fingers. His mannerisms were actor-ish, too, as even the most devoted critics had to concede. Open vowels were needlessly slurred, so that broad *o*'s and *a*'s became something like *i*'s and *e*'s. Often his delivery was strident and nasal, and Henry Austin Clapp, dramatic critic of the Boston *Evening Transcript*, spotlit other defects: a rhythmic repeated nodding of the head, a recurrent stamping of the foot. One young actor in his company, John Martin-Harvey, likened his gait to "a man trying to run quickly over a ploughed field."

Yet the high forehead, the narrow, sensitive lips, the dark, luminous eyes, and the wistful, almost feminine smile, persuaded almost every playgoer that Irving was staging a private performance for him alone.

Irving's self-appraisal, while touring America with Ellen Terry, was shot through with wry humor. "My legs, my voice, everything has been against me," he confided. "For an actor who can't walk, can't talk and has no face to speak of, I've done pretty well."

Like all the jungle's natural survivors, Irving was a stickler for perfection. When stage combats were called for, the great Victorian master of the fence, Felix Bertrand, was hired to ensure unwavering accuracy. Most probably, he saved more than one life; Irving's sole concession to electricity had been to wire up the swords, so that sparks flew frenziedly, and Bertrand, in the nick of time, had the handles insulated with rubber.

His company—whose star potential included such great Edwardian names as George Alexander, Frank Benson, and Johnston Forbes-Robertson—soon divined a sure way of gauging the duration of a rehearsal. When Irving emerged on stage, flanked by his stage manager, Harry Loveday, and his burly Irish business manager, Bram Stoker, author of *Dracula*—a trio whom the crowd artistes dubbed "The Holy Trinity"—all eyes were focused on Irving's headgear. A silk hat and an immaculate overcoat meant that Irving—"Old Hank," to the stagehands—was due at a function; this would be a mere four-hour run-through. A square bowler and an ulster was less reassuring; they would be hard at it for seven hours at least. But old clothes and a felt slouch hat spelled out the very worst, and the unspoken question then was: would the coffee stalls still be open when they broke in the small hours of the next day?

When a new play entered the repertoire, the procedure never varied. Irving would assemble the company and read the entire play aloud, indicating how he wanted each role tackled. The only ones he skipped—Ophelia, Juliet, Lady Macbeth—were those entrusted to Ellen Terry; this was a tacit avowal that Miss Terry's own interpretations would be infallible. At a later stage, Loveday would supervise rehearsals, while Irving conferred at length with Joseph Harker and Henry Hawes Craven, who designed his scenery, and Hamilton Clarke, his musical director. No one, stressed Percy Nash, would ever have dreamed of lighting a cigarette or glancing at a newspaper; though the Chief might seem to be lost in thought, he was aware of the company's every move.

"Don't walk as if you'd wetted yourself, me boy," he would tongue-lash a slovenly player, for in rehearsal Irving's humor was nearly always caustic. When he staged *The Medicine Man*, playing a moody misanthrope whose hobby was breeding caged birds, the stuffed canaries at the dress rehearsal met his approval, but not the cage. The cage was a disaster! It was too new, too tidy, above all, too *clean*. Distractedly, the property master seized up a bucket of white-wash and let fly.

Those who heard it never forgot Irving's wail of despair: "Worse and worse! It's canaries I'm breeding—*not eagles*!"

Yet so ingrained was autocracy in the Victorian way of life that Irving was revered, not reviled, by the Lyceum staff. If he was a hard taskmaster, they knew that he drove himself even harder, living every role no matter how sorely it taxed him. (As *Hamlet*, Irving would fast for twenty-four hours before each performance; as the drunken killer, Dubosc, he swigged burned brandy in the wings.) In the Bancroft tradition, he was more than generous when salaries arose. The actress Jessie Millward, who joined his company to play ingenues and to understudy Ellen Terry, had just one reservation: Would Irving be able to afford the five pounds a week she now commanded?

"Of course, I shan't give you five pounds a week," Irving remarked coolly. "For the first year I will give you twelve, and for the second year fifteen." As an afterthought he added, "I may want you to go to America and if so, of course, I shall give you more—say, twenty pounds."

15

Miss Millward was flabbergasted. Until "pounds" crept into the conversation, she had thought the great man was talking in terms of shillings.

But Irving was proverbially known as a soft touch. All through his tenure, the Lyceum was plagued with rats, a problem that Irving's overfed fox terrier, Fussie, was too lethargic to combat; a small army of tabby cats was recruited to keep them down. Thus, when Irving received a letter from an old woman, once connected with the theatre and now destitute, he saw the perfect solution: Loveday must engage her to oversee the cats.

Loveday protested; there were already three destitute old women looking after the cats. "Then," Irving chuckled, "let her look after the three old women."

Though his estrangement from Florence remained total, he was ultimately reconciled with his sons, Henry Brodribb, known always as "H.B.," and Laurence—though he was initially dismayed when both of them opted to follow in his footsteps. But all a father's warnings on the perils of the profession were in vain.

An actor much in his father's mold—tall, spare, pale, and sardonic, much given to peering quizzically through his pince-nez—H.B. even recreated four of Irving senior's roles: *Charles I*, *Louis XI*, *The Bells*, and *The Lyons Mail*, which the newly crowned King Edward VII bespoke for a command performance at Windsor. But when H.B. essayed *Hamlet*, which had been his father's greatest triumph, the old man had grave misgivings. It was with difficulty that his longtime friend, Mrs. Elizabeth Aria, a fashion diarist for the popular weeklies, persuaded him to share a box with her at the Adelphi, on London's Strand.

It was an invitation she was soon regretting. All through the performance, identifying all too keenly, Irving kept up an anguished running commentary: "No, no, my boy, that won't do . . . more emphasis, my boy . . . more emphasis . . . Christ! . . . no, no, no, not a bit like it . . . play it up, don't drop it . . . ah! That's better." To Mrs. Aria he confided in a woebegone rumble, "My God, this business of acting . . . how difficult!"

At curtain fall, Irving was all for heading home, but Mrs. Aria was adamant. H.B. had been apprised of his father's visit; he would be bitterly disappointed. Irving groaned, "What am I to say to the boy?" Mrs. Aria was tactful. "Remember he has tried very hard to please

you." Irving grew more despondent still. "That's the worst of it
. . . I know . . . um . . . he's done his best."

In H.B.'s dressing room, the conversation was desultory, to say
the least. The normally fluent Irving was at a loss for words. "A little
pale, my boy," he rambled. "Try a touch more colour . . . don't
want to start as a corpse . . . no . . . that comes later . . . been
running some weeks, I hear . . . um . . . you know your lines . . .
that's something . . ." Then, impatiently to Mrs. Aria, "Come along,
my dear, come along," before conscience assailed him: Surely the
occasion called for some profound comment on the performance as
a whole?

All of a sudden it came. "Good-bye, Harry, my boy, I was struck
today by the—um—*length* of *Hamlet.*"

As the twentieth century dawned, a new generation of saplings,
who in time would assume the mantles of Irving and Terry, was
arising in the jungle. The oldest among them were Lynn Fontanne,
daughter of a French printing-type designer, and Alfred David Lunt,
Jr., the son of a lumber merchant, both of them born in 1892, three
thousand miles apart: she in Woodford, England, he in Milwaukee,
Wisconsin.

Five years later, Katharine ("Kit"), the daughter of the stage-
struck Dr. Peter Cornell, who had renounced medicine to manage
the Star Theatre in Buffalo, was growing up in that city—eighteen
months before Violet Veitch Coward, wife of an unsuccessful traveler in pianos, gave birth to their eldest son, Noël Pierce, in Ted-
dington, England. In 1902, the daughter of another failed traveler,
this time in meat and poultry, was born—"centre stage, of course":
Helen Hayes Brown in Washington, D.C. The juveniles of this troupe
arrived when the century was young: (Arthur) John, the son of broker Frank Gielgud, in 1904, and Laurence Kerr, son of the impecunious Rev. Gerard Olivier, in 1907.

Over the years that they survived and ultimately prospered in the
jungle of make-believe, their lives were interlinked to a remarkable
degree. From the first, all of them, in common with today's 62,000
aspirants, were irredeemably, hopelessly, and shamelessly stage-
struck. "Nobody thought of any other destiny for me," Lynn was to
recall later, for at five, in the Lyceum gallery, she had to be forcibly
restrained from reciting Portia's "Quality of Mercy" speech in uni-

17

son with Ellen Terry, who was John Gielgud's "Great Aunt Nell." Soon after, a family connection led to tuition from Miss Terry herself, at her Georgian house at 215 King's Road, Chelsea; lessons that were both free—with ten shillings a week pocket money surreptitiously thrown in—and exacting. To master the art of acting, Ellen Terry avowed, a student should tackle a "big" role from the start; the thirteen-year-old Lynn was set to studying Cordelia in *King Lear*. Correction was minimal, though the line, "Oh, my dear father," prompted an immediate, "No, don't say it like that. You love him. You must say, 'Oh, my deeere father.' " By Christmas of that year, 1905, Lynn was walking on in a Christmas pantomime, *Cinderella*, at Drury Lane Theatre. She was on her way.

In Milwaukee, Alfred, who had been taken to his first theatre at the age of three, was already cramming his scrapbook with Ellen Terry portraits and constructing his own durable toy theatres, which still survive in the Museum of the City of New York, for the staging of *Rip Van Winkle* by "The Lunt Stock Company" at "Lunt's Wisconsin Theatre." Both in this and a subsequent production, *The Count of Monte Cristo*, Alfred played safe, appointing himself, for good measure, scenic designer, director, "general manager," and star.

Noël was a relatively late developer; he was all of five before Violet Coward took him to queue for *The Dairymaids* and *The Blue Moon* at the London Hippodrome. But at six, making up for lost time, he acquired a toy theatre and was soon putting on *The Forty Thieves* and *Black-eyed Susan*, aided by tinted pantomime sheets mounted on cardboard. A certified show-off, Noël's powerful treble, by the age of ten, was often heard in church anthems, though one factor galled him profoundly: Why didn't the congregation applaud? For a youngster so early in need of a fix, there was only one solution: at twelve, Noël was making his debut as Prince Mussel in *The Goldfish*, a fairy play for children at the Little Theatre.

Helen's debut as a stage brat had come three years earlier, at Washington's National Theatre; she was pushed to the fore by a "stage mother," the frustrated actress, Catherine Hayes Brown. Her act as a Gibson Girl Bathing Beauty in a sleeveless, black taffeta suit caught the attention of Lew Fields, the lanky vaudeville comedian, who promptly penned a note to the management: "If and when Helen's parents are interested in a stage career for her when older, I want to be first in line." This was a foot in the door that no stage mother could resist. Four years later, Catherine entrained for New

York to land the nine-year-old Helen the role of Little Mimi in Fields's *Old Dutch* at the Herald Square Theatre.

Soon Helen was reveling in the delicatessen sandwiches "tasting of wax and containers of never-quite-hot-enough coffee" that not only marked rehearsals but often stood in for a hot dinner at Mrs. Lewis's theatrical boardinghouse on West 45th Street. Noël, while still living with his parents, was likewise surrendering to the enchantment of an empty theatre before curtain rise: "the dim traffic noises outside . . . the thin reedy wail of a penny whistle being played to the gallery queue . . . a few exit lights left burning, casting blue shadows."

Not to be outdone, Kit, in the wings of her father's Buffalo theatre, the Star, was eavesdropping in rapture on the greats of the time: the beautiful and statuesque Maxine Elliott; Julia Marlowe, who always looked sad despite achieving her life's ambition of only playing Shakespeare; and the exotic Russian star, Alla Nazimova. At All Saint's Church School, Margaret Street, St. Marylebone, Larry was soon to demonstrate his lifelong versatility by impartially playing Maria in *Twelfth Night*, Katherine in *The Taming of the Shrew*, and Brutus in *Julius Caesar*. Ellen Terry, who sat in on this end-of-term performance, knew talent when she saw it. "The small boy who played Brutus," she noted in her diary, "is already a great actor."

Meanwhile, another talent in the making, Arthur John Gielgud, who was soon to discard the "Arthur," was devoting countless hours to *his* toy theatre, dreaming up plays with such surefire titles as *Lady Fawcett's Ruby* and *Kill That Spy*, and brazenly pilfering the canary's seed to simulate the sand for a scene in the Sahara.

Thus the stage was set; the inheritors were waiting in the wings. It was now only a question of time.

The tradition that they inherited lasted virtually unchanged until well after World War I, known then as the Great War or "the war to end all wars." As Lynn and Alfred and Noël and their peers grew up, the motive force behind the newly emerging theatre was, paradoxically, a Norwegian dramatist whose plays few theatregoers had ever seen: Henrik Ibsen, already seventy-two years old when the new century dawned, a onetime apothecary's apprentice and dramatist-in-residence at Bergen's Norske Theater, yet as far back as 1864 an exile in the sunlight of Rome.

With the advent of Ibsen a new movement was to sweep the theatres of Europe and the United States: Realism. Ibsen was eminently actable, for he took the play structures of Tom Robertson and turned them to graver purposes. His plays were taut, unromantic, topical, revolutionary—"a merciless surgery of the human soul," in the words of his greatest New York admirer, the actress Minnie Maddern Fiske. An ineffectual idealist forces a happy, if deluded family to live by "the whole truth" and wreaks havoc with their lives: *The Wild Duck*. A man strives to correct the evils of a provincial town and finds himself an outcast: *An Enemy of the People*. Such were Ibsen's underlying themes, and they were to unleash a flood tide of critical Victorian venom.

That the critics even knew of Ibsen's existence was due largely to two indomitable apostles: his translator, William Archer, the Scottish-born son of a Norwegian mother; and a contentious, red-bearded, Irish music critic named George Bernard Shaw.

The two men were strange bedfellows: Archer, sober, ponderous, the highly respected dramatic critic of the London *World*, who was wont to slumber in the stalls, furled umbrella between his knees, if trivia was on the agenda; and Shaw, the aspirant playwright lacking a stage, tramping the London streets in broken boots, the tails of his faded frock coat masking the holes in the seat of his trousers. Curiosity drew Archer to Shaw: the friendship of a man whose desk in the British Museum reading room was always piled high with the scores of Wagner's operas and Karl Marx's *Das Kapital* might be worth cultivating. Predictably, Archer's enthusiasm for the dramatist whom Shaw dubbed "Saint Henrik" proved infectious.

Archer's first translation, *Quicksands*, later *Pillars of Society*—produced for just one matinée in 1880—excited little comment. But on June 7, 1889, when an ambitious actress, Janet Achurch, staged Archer's second Ibsen play, *A Doll's House*, at the Novelty (later the Kingsway) Theatre on Great Queen Street, it was denounced as blasphemy.

Ibsen's heroine, Nora Helmer, despite eight years of marriage and two children, is still in essence a child bride. Her pompous husband, Torvald, feels that all practical knowledge is unladylike. Nora, needing money for medical expenses, had secretly forged her father's name to a note—and her father died before he could legalize the document. Threatened with exposure by one of Torvald's employees, who was under notice and desperate to keep his job, Nora tells Torvald the truth, only to be bitterly upbraided. "No man sacrifices his honour, even for one he loves," he pontificates, which prompts Nora's unforgettable retort, "Millions of women have done so."

With the blackmail threat lifted, Torvald is ready to forgive her—but Nora rejects that forgiveness. Realizing that she has been no more than a doll-wife, a pretty, patronized toy, she walks out on Torvald and her children.

The final stage direction reads, "The street door is slammed shut downstairs"—an exit that one commentator described as "the loudest slamming door in drama." Ibsen's blow for the emancipation of women and for true morality was, one critic charged, "a dreary and grossly immoral work which cuts at the very roots of family life." To Clement Scott of *The Daily Telegraph*, Nora was "a mass of aggregate conceit and self-sufficiency." Crabby old William Winter of the New York *Tribune* similarly slated Mrs. Fiske's Nora for "its rank deadly pessimism . . . injurious to the Stage and to the Public."

No dyed-in-the-wool Victorian could ever accept Nora: she was no longer the Angel in the House, content to immolate herself in marriage, but the New Woman, with a mind and will of her own.

Now a new Ibsen champion entered the lists: Jacob Thomas Grein, a boyish, disarming little Dutchman, dramatic critic and playwright, who was much taken with Archer's adaptation of Ibsen's *Ghosts*. When the Lord Chamberlain, who since 1737 had overseen all public productions (a role that was finally repealed in 1968), refused the play a license, Grein sidestepped him adroitly: a private play-producing group, the Independent Theatre Society, was set up to launch *Ghosts* on an "invitation only" basis.

The opening date—Friday, March 13th, 1891—at the Royalty Theatre in Dean Street seemed ominous.

For its time, *Ghosts* was challenging in theme. Mrs. Alving, having left her profligate husband, is persuaded by the revered Pastor Manders to return home. When she complies, she gives birth to a son, Oswald, who inherits his father's syphilis; at the onset of the final curtain, dazzled by the winter sunrise, Oswald goes quietly insane. "Mother, give me the sun."

Few plays in theatrical history ever called forth a greater torrent of vilification. To *The Daily Chronicle*, the play was "revolting, suggestive and blasphemous." "The work of a crazy foreigner," fumed *The News of the World*, "which is neither fish nor flesh, but is unmistakably foul." *The Observer* was old-maidish: "A putrid drama, the details of which cannot appear with propriety in any column, save those of a medical journal." *The Daily Telegraph* spread itself in a two-column editorial excoriating the play as "an open drain," "a loathsome sore unbandaged," "a dirty act done publicly," and "a lazar house with all its doors and windows open."

Though few opponents were more vehement than Irving himself (who charged that "his plays have abolished God, duty, the devotion of a mother to her children and the obligation of man to his fellow man") the actor was perhaps not disinterested. No admirer of Irving, Archer's criticisms had successively written off his Hamlet as "a weak minded puppy," his Macbeth as "a Uriah Heep in chain armour," and his Othello as "an infuriated Sepoy."

Yet the stalls of the Royalty Theatre—where Grein followed up *Ghosts* with a production of Émile Zola's *Thérèse Raquin*—were always packed out with literary men who were not without clout: not only novelists like Henry James, Thomas Hardy, and George Meredith, but rising playwrights like Arthur Wing Pinero, Henry Arthur Jones, and the effete Oscar Wilde, toying with his green carnation and his silver-mounted cane.

The moment was at hand when the drama, belatedly, was catching up with the novel as an adult medium, shedding what Clayton Hamilton, a lecturer on drama at New York's Columbia University, called "a girls' boarding school outlook upon life."

For more than twenty years, London and New York society had undergone a surfeit of "well-made plays"—*une pièce bien faite* (a phrase coined by a Parisian man of letters, Francisque Sarcey, who patronized the drama almost every night for forty years). Their originator was Eugène Scribe *(The Queen's Favourite, Adrienne Lecouvreur)*, author of almost four hundred such dramas, and abetted in later years by his disciples Victorien Sardou *(Madame Sans-Gêne, Diplomacy)* and Eugène Labiche *(An Italian Straw Hat)*. In a Scribe play, as with those of his acolytes, the audience was constantly agog, waiting for a secret to be uncovered, for an identity to be revealed, for a long-awaited confrontation. One British dramatist alone, Manchester barrister Sydney Grundy, was to translate untold numbers of them, yet in essence all were plots owing everything to contrivance and nothing to character—sentimental hokum played against solid Bancroft-style settings, which the contemptuous Shaw berated as "sardoodledom."

But Ibsen had paved the way for the onset of problem plays that shunned the ultraheroic and for a phenomenon unknown until now:

the Writers' Theatre. For the first time, the latest Pinero or Wilde was as big a draw as those who starred in it. The playwright was in command, and none of them more firmly so than Arthur Wing Pinero, imposing in his tall silk hat, monocle, and lavender gloves, who was in turn to be knighted by Edward VII in 1909.

A onetime actor who had served five years with Irving, Pinero at rehearsals was as fearsome a martinet as Sir Henry himself. Tall and thickset, with beetle brows, as bald as a peeled onion, Pinero would pace the stalls, hands clasped behind his back, sternly dictating every inflection, every pause. A master of stagecraft, his texts minutely indicated all stage "business." All properties and furniture must be in place from the first rehearsal, a radical departure from the norm; on casting, whatever the management, Pinero always had the final say.

Problem plays were a radical reversal of style for the Pinero who in the 1880s had first hit the jackpot with a trio of riotous farces at the Court Theatre on Sloane Square: plays like *The Magistrate*, *The Schoolmistress*, and *Dandy Dick*, which have survived well into the twentieth century. The first hint of a new Pinero out to beat the Ibsenites at their own game came with *The Money Spinner*, in which a wife with a past behind her uses her skill in cheating at cards to save her husband from an embezzlement charge—the first notable use of an antihero and antiheroine. In 1889, *The Profligate*, at the Garrick, raised more than one eyebrow with an antihero, Dunstan Renshaw, who boasted, "Oh, as to my past which you are pleased to wax mighty moral about, well—I have taken the world as I found it."

For the first time, but not the last, Pinero was attacking a convention that was anathema to him: the double standard of Victorian society. *The Profligate*'s message minced no words: A woman had a right to expect a prospective husband to be as pure as he expected her to be.

With his best-known play, *The Second Mrs. Tanqueray*, Pinero posed a knotty problem to two highly reputable managers, George Alexander of London and Daniel Frohman of New York.

"I *did* feel timorous about producing it," Frohman was to confess. "I thought that our public was not ready for a theme that indicated so radical a change in my policy." At the St. James's Theatre, George Alexander was equally diffident, and his first solution was the same as Frohman's: a tentative series of matinées to test the climate of

23

public opinion. Pinero, unusually, raised no objection, but at length both managers took their courage in their hands.

Pinero's protagonist, Aubrey Tanqueray, a widower formerly saddled with a frigid wife ("She was one of your cold sort, you know," recalls his friend Cayley Drummle, "all marble arms and black velvet") marries Paula Ray, a Woman with a Past. Retiring to Aubrey's country home, they are ostracized by their neighbors; says Cayley, "You may dive into many waters but there is *one* social Dead Sea." Paula, repenting that lurid past, sets out to win over Aubrey's daughter, the convent-bred Ellean, but when Ellean's suitor, Hugh Ardale, arrives from Paris, Paula recognizes him as a onetime paramour. Seeing that the Tanqueray home is now a house divided, Paula takes poison.

As rehearsals at the St. James's proceeded, Alexander and Pinero grew daily more despondent. To stage the play at all seemed abysmal folly; not only were Victorian audiences unused to courtesans behind the footlights, but this courtesan was largely unrepentant. Moreover, the unknown leading lady, who had been spotted by Alexander's wife, Florence, as the vamp in an Adelphi melodrama, bitterly resented Pinero's treating her as "a child who must be taught its ABC." For the first of many occasions, twenty-eight-year-old Stella Patrick Campbell, a willful Italianate beauty who had turned to the stage while her husband sought to make the family fortune in South Africa, was in a head-on collision course with a distinguished dramatist.

For "Mrs. Pat," as London and New York knew her, was openly rebellious from the first. Every suggestion was taken as a snub. She was distraught, intransigent, often in tears. The crisis point was only passed when Alexander, in the third act, required Mrs. Pat to strum a *valse* on the piano. Mrs. Pat, a skillful player, begged off; she would like time to prepare something suitable. Alexander was inflexible: "We would like to hear whether you can play." Stung by his curt manner, Mrs. Pat, as always, was prompted to show off. At the piano, her blue-and-gold prompt book hoisted in her right hand for all to see, she launched into a Bach piece for the left hand alone. Three minutes passed; then Alexander's toneless voice came from the darkened stalls. "That will do, Mrs. Campbell. We will go on with the rehearsal, please!"

But Pinero was now entirely won over. "Dear child!" he exclaimed impulsively, vaulting on stage to squeeze her arm; from this

24

moment on he was all solicitude. After one prolonged rehearsal, seeing Mrs. Pat on the point of swooning, Pinero rushed out for Brand's Beef Essence and a spoon and stood over her paternally while she swallowed it. At Mrs. Pat's request, he alone sat in on the first dress rehearsal, invisible in the dress circle and armed with a lantern, notebook, and pencil, but pledged to voice no criticism until the final curtain.

On the night of Saturday, May 27, 1893, Pinero's reputation as an international playwright hung in the balance. Everything now depended on the performance of one unknown player, who was erratic, unstable, and markedly prone to what the critic St. John Ervine called "whims and whamsies." All would be in doubt until two-thirds of the way through Act I, when Paula, in a magnificent, gold-embroidered, yellow satin cloak lined in emerald velvet, flouts convention by invading Aubrey's bachelor chambers in Albany toward midnight.

Unable to face the first-night audience, Pinero paced the length of Angel Court outside the stage door, drawing feverishly on a cigar. When the first interval was called, he hastened to his wife's box, but Myra Pinero shook her head glumly. He should go and encourage Mrs. Pat. Pinero's first call, though, was Alexander's dressing room, only to find him equally gloomy. "I think she's crumbling," was Alexander's verdict.

The wily Pinero now hastened on to Mrs. Pat. "My dear lady," he raved, seizing her by the hands, "Magnificent! If you play the second act the same way our fortunes will be made." Then, overcome, he returned to Angel Court, pacing and smoking, smoking and pacing, until the unmistakable roar of a standing ovation swept through the stage door.

Thereafter, paradoxically, save at his own first nights, the theatrical world saw little of Pinero. Only special functions now drew him to the Garrick Club; he accepted no dinner engagements. Each day, from teatime on, "Pin" was immured in his study, refusing to receive even Ellen Terry, working on until the small hours, a tray of sandwiches left at his door. Year after year the plays flowed from his pen: *The Notorious Mrs. Ebbsmith* (1895), where Mrs. Pat, as an Ibsenite freethinker, thrust a Bible into the stove—though promptly retrieving it as Victorian morality dictated; *Trelawny of the Wells* (1898), *The Gay Lord Quex* (1899); *Iris* (1901); and *His House In Order* (1906).

All of them, in Pinero's own words, "centered round our little parish of St. James's," yet his grasp of human nature was such that

25

the humblest of gallery patrons could identify with his themes and situations.

Across the Atlantic, in a five-story brownstone house on 40th Street in New York east of Park Avenue, Pinero's New World counterpart, Clyde Fitch, was also virtually a one-man play factory, often working on two plays simultaneously. Fitch, though, was far from being reclusive; whether on 40th Street or his estates near Greenwich, Connecticut, or in Westchester County, Fitch would cheerfully scribble dialogue in a room filled with chattering house guests.

A small, nervous, dark-haired man, Fitch in rehearsal was equally a martinet, and a snobbish one to boot. His constant complaint was that actors and actresses knew nothing of the manners of good society, and more than one of them—Julia Marlowe, Ethel Barrymore— was bidden to breakfast at his 40th Street home to observe the niceties of menservants in blue-and-white livery serving cutlets on plates of Delft or Spode, with vintage Tokay bubbling in Venetian spiral glasses.

His production notes, as with *His Grace de Grammont*, a four-act Charles II comedy of manners, verged on the frenetic: "The lace must be coffee-coloured—NEVER WHITE! . . . The women's hair must resemble the flappy ears of the King Charles spaniels!! . . . The pink must be *deep rose*—never pale!!"

Most of Fitch's plays—*The Climbers, The City, The Truth*—were, like Pinero's, essentially women's plays; his heroines were fearless man-tamers, elegant, fastidious, and often acquisitive besides. In play after play he satirized the parvenus, the seekers after wealth and position, and he, too, owed a debt to Ibsen: the visiting of the sins of the fathers upon the children was a recurrent theme. A prolific writer—he wrote sixty-two plays before dying of appendicitis in 1909— Fitch at times faced the problem of which first night to attend. After sitting through *The Truth* at the Criterion and responding to a curtain call, Fitch heard that the audience at the Astor was calling for him, too, following the première of *The Straight Road*. A hasty trip across the street, and Fitch delivered a second first-night speech.

As early as 1900 his schedule was that of a compulsive workaholic. After rehearsing *The Climbers* every day from 10:00 A.M. to 2:30 P.M., he went on to supervise the young Ethel Barrymore's starring debut in *Captain Jinks of the Horse Marines* until 6:00 P.M. "This is my third week of longer hours than *any bricklayer* would submit to!" he wrote pettishly to a friend, ignoring the prosaic truth: it was a rare brick-layer who pulled down $250,000 a year.

Thanks to the acumen of a gifted, resilient little Irishman, Dionysius Lardner ("Dion") Boucicault, this was a golden age for dramatists. For his most celebrated comedy, *London Assurance* (revived in London as recently as 1972), Boucicault got an outright payment of £300 in 1841, but a spell in Paris working under Eugène Scribe, where the theatres paid a standard 10 percent royalty, set him thinking. Although Irving, to the end of his life, bought plays outright, and Bancroft paid Tom Robertson a salary, Boucicault's Irish tear-jerker *The Colleen Bawn*, staged at the Adelphi in 1860—a play which twice reduced Queen Victoria to impotent blubbering—saw the turn of the tide. Far from selling his rights to provincial managers, Boucicault organized and toured three road companies of his own and cleared a handsome profit. By degrees, royalty payments became standard, and from the 1880s on dramatists were reaping rich pickings. New York's Bronson Howard netted $300,000 from one play, *Shenandoah*, and Pinero's main rival, Henry Arthur Jones, with his melodrama *The Silver King*, netted £3,398 in 1883 alone.

A tenant farmer's son who began life as a commercial traveler, Jones wrote this first melodrama, with its immortal line "O God, put back Thy universe and give me yesterday," solely to gain a footing on the London stage. All along his aim was to write the situation comedies that would secure his reputation—*The Liars, Mrs. Dane's Defence, Saints and Sinners.* Just as with Ibsen, wifely rebels loomed large in Jonesian plots.

Yet unlike Ibsen—but in tune with Pinero—Jones ultimately came down on the side of orthodoxy; his message in clear was that only those who conform can be happy. Victorian, even Edwardian society, demanded no less. *The Masqueraders,* written for Alexander and Mrs. Pat to follow up their *Tanqueray* triumph, was a case in point: at the climax the star-crossed lovers renounce their happiness at the dictates of convention. "Make this one last sacrifice," Helen Larondie begs the hero, David Remon, who is bent on seducing her married sister, Dulcie. "Keep her pure for her child."

In Jones's *The Liars,* the task of Sir Christopher Deering was to convince Lady Jessica and her lover, Edward Falkner, that their proposed elopement just "won't work"—"We're not a bit better than our neighbours, but thank God! we do pretend we are and we do make it hot for anybody who disturbs that holy pretence." Again, in *Mrs. Dane's Defence*, Sir Daniel Carteret, K.C., breaks down the front of Mrs. Dane, whom his adopted son yearns to marry—a fine cross-examination scene that reveals her as a governess caught up in a Viennese scandal. But Sir Daniel's sole justification is hidebound Victorian hypocrisy.

"The outside of the platter must be clean," he tells his old friend Lady Eastney. "The rules of the game are severe. If you don't like them leave the sport alone. They will never be altered."

A stocky red-bearded man with keen blue eyes, Jones never quite outlived his proletarian past, though he hated the lower middle classes with a passion bordering on mania. His Cockney accent was always marked. "When Mr. Jones finished reading his plays," recalls Athene Seyler, who played in the 1912 production of *The Case of Rebellious Susan*, "the stage was always knee-deep in dropped H's." Touchy to a fault, he once pursued the actor-manager Cyril Maude along Hyde Park's Rotten Row on horseback, screaming execrations against Maude's overplaying in Jones's *The Manoeuvres of Jane*. But Jones, perhaps, was always feeling his way through what one critic called "the Mayfair drama of cuckoldry," as *Rebellious Susan* made plain. When Lady Susan, happily married for six years, finds evidence of her husband's infidelity, she retaliates with a threat: an eye for an eye, a tooth for a tooth.

Jones's plan was to leave the audience guessing as to how far her retaliation went, but Charles Wyndham, for whom the play was written, would have none of that. Jones must be put in his place, and with a magisterial rebuke: "I stand bewildered at finding an author, a clean-living, clear-minded man, hoping to extract laughter from an audience on the score of a woman's impurity."

For the rules of the game were never in doubt, and the successful dramatists were those who early learned to toe the line. Society plays—what one man called "the drawing-room quietness of well-bred acting"—ruled the roost, and many actors now found a lucrative career in playing themselves. In the wake of Jones and Pinero, playwrights like Hubert Henry Davies *(The Mollusc)*, St. John Hankin *(The Return of the Prodigal)*, and William Somerset Maugham *(Lady Frederick, Mrs. Dot)* clung doggedly to one belief: playgoers had scant interest in any characters unless they lived in Mayfair, enjoyed private incomes, and dressed for dinner every evening. It was a tradition that would be long years a-dying.

One aspirant dramatist, Alfred Sutro, son of a Jewish surgeon, struggled for ten years to get a play on the boards, finally achieving it in 1904 with a drawing-room comedy, *The Walls of Jericho*. Success was assured, as his cast of twenty featured no less than ten aristocrats. On that heady first night, through his actor-manager Arthur Bourchier, Sutro, for the first time, finally met up with members of that elusive aristocracy.

Two years earlier, James M. Barrie, a frail little weaver's son from Kirriemuir, Scotland, had found himself in the hottest of water when he invaded the purlieus of Mayfair for the first and only time. In *The Admirable Crichton* Barrie pictured Lord Loam's family shipwrecked with their servants on a desert island. To everybody's surprise, Crichton, the butler, a rigid upholder of class distinction, turns out to be the man whose know-how saves the day. To society, this concept was seen as little short of heresy, though the patronage of pit and gallery kept it running. Until Jones wrote his short-lived *The Lackey's Carnival* in 1900, servants were never pictured as other than figures of fun.

Following the first night of *Crichton*, the dramatist A.E.W. Mason ran into Sir Squire Bancroft in the washroom of the Garrick Club. How, Mason asked, had he viewed the play? Bancroft shook a mournful head. "It deals, my dear Mason, with the juxtaposition of the drawing-room and the servants' hall—always, to me, a very painful subject."

Even a playwright as sagacious as Pinero came to grief with his *The "Mind-the-Paint" Girl*, a hit in New York but a disaster in Edwardian London. To the critics, the reason was plain: "Pin" had thought up the then-unthinkable, the story of a chorus girl marrying into the peerage.

Each theatre, each actor-manager, then had a policy as constant as the evening star. At the St. James's, George Alexander, with his silvery hair and impressive profile, was the glass of fashion and the mold of good form; his plays—Pinero, Wilde—were both high-minded and high-class. In his theatre, which was daily scrubbed like a battleship, a sense of Augustan calm prevailed, reinforced by stagehands in felt slippers tiptoeing over yards of thick velvet carpeting. "Our first nights were like brilliant parties," Florence Alexander was to recall as that era was ending. "Everybody knew everybody, everybody put on their best clothes, everyone wished us success."

At the Theatre Royal in the Haymarket, Herbert Beerbohm Tree featured, among others, the plays of Oscar Wilde—*An Ideal Husband* and *Lady Windermere's Fan*, both of them centering on a guilty secret—and George du Maurier's *Trilby*. It was this dramatization of the Svengali legend that helped finance the £55,000 Her Majesty's Theatre, to which Tree soon moved across the way. Tall, willowy, and resplendent, with sandy hair and a dreamy, abstracted air, Tree was to cherish his "beautiful theatre" for fully twenty years.

At the Comedy, Charles Hawtrey held sway, a sly, moustached master of duplicity with a (stage) reputation as the gayest of dogs. With his plump, orotund voice, fancy waistcoats, and gold watch chain, he was tailor-made for "the Hawtrey part" in plays like *Lord and Lady Algy* and *His Lady Friends*. The Hawtrey part was marked by the vacant stare when the hero was caught out in a fib, the contented purr when trouble was averted. "I don't want you to catch cold just because you've been making love to my wife" was a "daring" line from his *Inconstant George* that might have been lifted from any Hawtrey play.

The old Princess on Oxford Street and later the Lyric, Shaftesbury Avenue, were equally the homes of Wilson Barrett, king of all the melodrama men, with his sculpted head and a voice as tremendous as his manner. In his own play, *The Sign of the Cross*, Barrett's role was Marcus Superbus, a Roman patrician in love with a beautiful Christian girl for whom he faces the lions in the arena. Though the play had its detractors—to William Archer it was like "a Salvation Army pantomime," and his friend Shaw commented, "We may live to see him [Barrett] crucified yet"—it enabled Barrett to pay off £40,000 worth of debts and to leave a £30,000 fortune.

This was still an age when actors could rely on the tried and true, and their audiences repaid that faith. Barrett's closest rival, the virile, trumpet-tongued Lewis Waller, born William Waller Lewis, was also seen at the Lyric or at the Imperial in Tothill Street, but rarely in any other roles than *Robin Hood*, D'Artagnan in *The Three Musketeers*, or the title role in Booth Tarkington's *Monsieur Beaucaire*. But this was more than enough for the K.O.W. ("Keen On Waller") brigade, a sorority of early groupies who packed the pit and gallery cheering and screaming for minutes on end at Waller's first appearance. One groupie claimed solemnly that Waller's photograph, pinned to her berth on a transatlantic voyage, staved off all qualms of seasickness.

Early in life, Charles Wyndham, born Charles Culverwell, had favored "daring" farces adapted from the French. Later, from the profits of five plays by Henry Arthur Jones, he had built his own theatre, Wyndham's, on Charing Cross Road, subsequently building the New (now the Albery) next door and retaining control of the Criterion in Piccadilly Circus. But it was with an old faithful, *David Garrick*, that he opened Wyndham's in 1899, and it was as Garrick that his latter-day public most liked to see him; King Edward VII sat through it no less than seven times. Still playing Garrick at the age of seventy-six, the husky-voiced Wyndham seemed, in these years, to be undergoing an identity crisis. In every feminine autograph album he inscribed a favorite line from the play—"A good woman is an understudy for an angel"—and except on matinée days his afternoons were passed in an armchair beside the actor's bust at the Garrick Club. "You get more and more like Garrick every day," one malicious member took pains to assure him, then, as the old man preened, added, "And less and less like him every night."

In New York, where the heart of theatre-land was still to be found at Broadway between Thirtieth and Thirty-ninth Streets, the situation was identical. At the Empire at Broadway and 40th Street, Maude Adams, with her rippling laugh and tossing, ash brown hair, was featured in almost every play that James Barrie wrote: Lady Babbie in *The Little Minister*, Maggie Wylie in *What Every Woman Knows*, Phoebe Throssell in *Quality Street*. At the Garden Theatre at Madison Avenue and 27th Street, Richard Mansfield might be seen as Edmond Rostand's *Cyrano de Bergerac;* at the Knickerbocker, E.H. Sothern and his wife Julia Marlowe offered their sustaining diet of Shakespeare. Until his death in 1899, Augustin Daly's theatre, at Broadway below 30th Street, starred his mistress, the formidable Ada Rehan, in Pinero's *The Magistrate* and *Dandy Dick*. At the Garrick, on 35th Street, William Gillette was in his own *Sherlock Holmes*, a role he was still playing up to 1932. West of Broadway, at the Manhattan, on the present site of Gimbels department store, the red-haired Minnie Maddern Fiske, with her twinkling, electric-blue eyes, suffered the claustrophobic torments of Ibsen's Nora.

In these solid Edwardian temples, ornate with red velvet curtains, brass rails, and glittering chandeliers, conventions were as absolute as class distinctions. Evening dress was *de rigueur* in boxes, orchestra stalls, and dress circle. At matinées, ladies were expected to remove their hats. Programs, priced at two pence, featured no democratic "cast in order of appearance"; Irving's name was always at the top,

31

Ellen Terry's at the bottom. In the metropolis, prices varied little: two dollars for an orchestra stall on Broadway and ten shillings and sixpence in the Strand, where nine of London's forty-five theatres were then sited, scaled down to fifty cents or one shilling for a perch on bare boards in the gallery. For the latter, and for the pit stalls, with their inhibiting iron arms, a disorderly first-come-first-served queue was a cherished British way of life. Irving's attempt to institute a bookable pit for the Lyceum in May 1885 sparked off riots that only a posse of London bobbies could quell.

To visiting Americans the discomforts of the pit (named after the Elizabethan cockpit), sited beneath the balcony at the rear of the orchestra stalls, remained incomprehensible. Paul Kester, the Ohio-born author of *Sweet Nell of Old Drury*, was so intrigued by the little stools on which the customers perched that he promptly snapped one up, "to show the folks back there what the English people sit on to see one of MY plays!" Britons on Broadway were equally puzzled by an old New York folk custom. Since long runs were the exception rather than the rule, playgoers at the fiftieth or hundredth performances often received free gifts of painted china teapots.

These were minimal differences. In this age of transition, more and more affluent Americans were finding a kinship with the British; they were as relaxed on Piccadilly as on New York's Fifth Avenue. Fashionable Bond Street shops and hotels like London's Berkeley now took full-page space in the New York dailies, and this held equally good in the theatre world. Americans were as enamored of the works of Pinero, Jones, Barrie, and Wilde as they were of their own Clyde Fitch. Even Bernard Shaw, still a fledgling at forty-seven, was hailed as a new iconoclastic talent, though as yet unsung in Britain. It was as if the North Atlantic had mysteriously contracted its shores.

The hub of this two-way transatlantic trade centered on a third-floor suite in the newly built (1893) Empire Theatre, facing the Metropolitan Opera House. It was from here, in a theatre so spacious that its foyer measured fifty feet from entrance to ticket taker, that Charles Frohman, the younger brother of Daniel, who had secured the rights to all Pinero's plays, ruled a little empire all his own: an entourage with ten thousand employees and an annual payroll of $35 million, often with six plays in rehearsal at one time.

A shy, plump little man from Sandusky, Ohio, with the plaintive eyes of a seal and who waddled as he walked, Frohman was just as deeply involved in the theatre of Irving's day. In London, in due time, he was to control the Duke of York's, the Globe (from 1906), the Comedy, the Vaudeville, and the Empire; Baedeker noted the Savoy Hotel simply as the place where Frohman rested his head. Painfully inarticulate, speaking in a series of strangulated pauses, Frohman still had a panache and a will of his own. At thirty-six, chancing on Barrie's *The Little Minister*, then a best-selling novel, Frohman conceived this as the perfect vehicle for his newly rising star, Maude Adams. The one stumbling block: Barrie, with five novels to his credit, had absolutely no interest in becoming a playwright. Asked how he finally wrought this transformation, Frohman was characteristically laconic: "Sent him cables."

It was ultimately a profitable interchange. The three thousand performances of *The Little Minister* in America alone earned $500,000 for Barrie, $600,000 for Frohman.

On his own initiative, Frohman virtually invented the international star system; the player, rather than the play, was the thing. The first on his list was the elegant John Drew who invariably, because of a cast in his eye, played in profile. For twenty years *the* event of the fall season was the new Drew at the Empire, with Drew cast in all the plum Pinero roles, thirty plays in all. Next in line was Maude Adams, with twenty-one assignments to her credit, many of them roles dreamed up for her by Barrie. Thirdly came Drew's niece, Ethel Barrymore.

An unabashed sentimentalist, Frohman largely pinned his faith in Prince Charming and Cinderella lookalikes. Nothing distressed him more profoundly than a death scene. Despite his lifelong friendship with Fitch, with whom he met up for secret gluttonous orgies of apple and lemon-meringue pie, he turned down *The Climbers* flat; it began with a funeral and ended with a suicide. Still, he had a near-infallible instinct for a play that would hold an audience. On one London visit, Frohman was approached in great agitation by Herbert Beerbohm Tree. "Barrie," Tree warned him, "has gone completely out of his mind. He has just read me a play, and he's going to read it to you . . . he has written four acts all about fairies, children and Indians, running through the most incoherent story you've ever listened to. And what do you suppose! The last act is to be played in the tops of trees!"

And that was how, on November 6, 1905, Maude Adams opened at the Empire in *Peter Pan* in the first of 237 consecutive performances.

Frohman in rehearsal was a curious sight. Often he sat alone in the tenth row back, like a visitor to somebody else's theatre. "He talked," recalled the actress Billie Burke, "in unpunctuated telegrams"; when words failed him altogether he was reduced to making tight little stabs with his forefinger. At other times he skulked in the orchestra pit, behind the conductor's stand, busying himself with the music rack, muttering faint asides to his favorite director, Willie Seymour. "She's madder than that," he would reflect aloud, for the benefit of an actress rehearsing a quarrel scene. "She's awful mad." "Now, last act," went a typical summation to his British leading man, William Faversham. "Simple—nice—lovable—refined—sad tones in your voice—and, well, you know—you'll be tickled to death—great play—fine part."

Despite his seeming aphasia, Frohman was a master of sarcasm when the occasion arose. During rehearsals of *The "Mind-the-Paint" Girl*, when Billie Burke suffered several lapses of memory, Frohman found it necessary to reprove her. "I know my lines, Mr. Frohman," the actress protested, to which Frohman replied sadly, "I don't doubt that, Bill, but you don't seem to know Pinero's."

Even the temperamental Mrs. Pat had more than met her match. "You forget, Mr. Frohman," she reminded him majestically, "that I am a great artist." "Mrs. Campbell," Frohman assured her softly, "I will try to keep your secret."

"If I didn't keep a grip on myself, my sentiment would be the ruin of me," Frohman once confessed, yet in a celebrated, if financially disastrous repertory season at the Duke of York's, London, his choice of brand-new plays was a far cry from the spun-sugar fantasies with which his name was linked. Two plays, Shaw's discursive *Misalliance* and Harley Granville Barker's *The Madras House*, have survived until now; the third, John Galsworthy's *Justice*, changed the face of British penal history.

In cramped quarters in St. Martin's Lane, the Duke of York's was a poor choice for repertory; it lacked all accommodation for scenery. After each performance the settings for that night's play had either to be stored in the open air, at the mercy of the weather, or transported to a store across the river. But even under these adverse conditions, *Justice* burst like a starshell in the polite arena of Edwardian society.

Then best known for his novel *The Man of Property,* the first of the trilogy that formed *The Forsyte Saga,* Galsworthy, as a dramatist, forsook the drawing rooms of Bayswater Road for the office, the steelworks, and, in *Justice,* the prison cell. The acknowledged king of the Social Drama school, Galsworthy saw Society as the equivalent of the Greek fates: a man or woman might struggle, but they would not escape. For Galsworthy there were no villains, only abstract forces: Mob Law *(The Mob);* the Yellow Press *(The Show);* the Craving for Property *(The Skin Game);* and Anti-Semitism *(Loyalties).* In *Justice,* a young lawyer's clerk, William Falder, forges a check for ninety pounds to run away with a young married woman escaping from a drunken husband. He is sentenced to three years in jail—the first four months, as was then customary, served in solitary confinement. Released after two years, unable to find work, dogged by a ticket-of-leave system that keeps the police hard on his heels, Falder at last kills himself.

In one unforgettable scene, no word is spoken from first to last. As dusk gathers, Falder prowls his whitewashed cell in his stockinged feet, listening, trying vainly to peer from the barred window, using the lid of a tin as a mirror to see his own face. Then a dull banging on metal becomes audible, traveling from cell to cell, coming inexorably closer and closer. Falder hurls himself at his cell door, beating at it like a caged animal as the curtain falls.

This silent cry for help so profoundly shocked Winston Churchill, then Home Secretary, that thereafter solitary confinement was reduced to one month, and that during the hours of darkness; the ticket-of-leave system, whereby a convict granted conditional freedom must report once monthly to the police station, was abolished altogether.

On this catastrophic, if worthy season Barrie alone, as one of the backers, lost £200,000. How much Frohman lost was never known; it was a loss that, as usual, he shrugged off silently. All told, in New York, London, and Paris, he staged more than five hundred plays. "If I can produce two successes out of four I think it's fine," was his self-professed yardstick.

To the end he maintained the philosophy that perhaps only in the make-believe jungle would pass as acceptable logic: "My work is to

35

produce plays that succeed so that I can produce plays that will *not* succeed."

But in vast areas of America and the United Kingdom, a simpler breed of playgoer had neither time nor patience for sophisticated problem-plays; they hewed to an older tradition. They went to the theatre, as the critic Clayton Hamilton put it, "to be told lies about life," and for them the fit-up companies—fitting up their own scenery and playing more often in public halls than regular theatres—created a Never-Never Land far outstripping that of Barrie's *Peter Pan*.

The young Cedric Hardwicke, haunting the Alhambra in Stourbridge, Worcestershire, sampled the same kind of fare as did the young Edna Ferber, growing up in Ottumwa, Iowa—in Miss Ferber's words, "the most incredible plays and some of the worst acting in the history of the theatre." Many of the companies were legendary on their respective sides of the Atlantic: Corse Payton, billed as "The World's Worst Actor," who toured four companies across the United States and affected solid gold coins for coat buttons; the Little Allie Spooner Dramatic Company, which carved out the midwest; and Maggie Morton, the "Joan of Arc of Fit-up Management," who queened it over the Midlands and north of England. Many were "commonwealth companies"—sharing the receipts, when there were any, and thus living tenuously on credit until each Saturday night. "Where can we 'strap-up' for beer and smokes?" was always the first question at the stage door on Sunday afternoons; from then on until payday, the stagehands acted as runners to the pub opposite, bearing grubby slips of paper as IOUs.

Most of the plays were "traditional," with no author credits, a coy British euphemism for "pirated"; in 1903 this writer's uncle, Vincent Collier, was touring one such "traditional" play, *The Temptations of an Actress*, everywhere from the Conservative Hall, Dartford, Kent, to the Mechanics' Institute, Ballymena, Ireland. In the United States, with more laudable honesty, these were known as "gyp shows," for play piracy was a profession on its own; in New York and London fortunes were made in churning out typed or mimeographed copies for which the fit-ups paid in dollars or shillings. Even as late as 1950 I toured as an observer with the Peter Allen Fit-up Company through the villages of Gloucestershire, offering *The Shocking Affair of Sadie Thompson*, a drumhead version of Somerset Maugham's *Rain*.

In the United States, due to the distances involved, few fit-up companies traveled their own scenery to what they called the "tank towns"; theatres like the Concert Hall in Beaver Dam, Wisconsin, were equipped with the same standard settings for every company that arrived. A prison interior was always a "must," but not for any play remotely resembling Galsworthy's *Justice;* it stood in for Monte Cristo's dungeon in the Château d'If, for the cell where Friar Laurence gave Juliet her sleeping potion, and for the prison where Marguerite died in the arms of Faust.

On both sides of the Atlantic, Sunday was the day when the fit-ups came into their own. At British junctions like Crewe, Darlington, or Derby; at American depots like Denver, Colorado; Kansas City, Missouri; or Toledo, Ohio, the scene was much the same: a colorful panorama of frock coats and silk hats, flowing skirts and feather boas, though some traveled more informally in battered straw hats and carpet slippers or green embroidered smoking caps.

The old-time actors among them were marked out by the cigar boxes in which they stored their makeup, by their pink-rimmed shirt collars and hairlines, by vestiges of makeup they had neglected to remove in their rush to reach the pub, and by their tremendous manners, modeled, of course, upon Irving. "By my troth, if it isn't that comely wench, Daisy." "How now, Sirrah, that new mantle becomes you well." Against this clamorous backdrop, carriages were uncoupled and shunted to the sidings, awaiting the next "fish and actors" train, the only commodities rail-borne on Sundays. Reserve labels were pasted on carriage windows—*Girl Astray*, Rugby; *Her Guilty Secret*, Madison, Wis. Platforms were littered with discarded copies of the New York *Dramatic Mirror* and the buff-colored pages of the *Referee*, the profession's Sunday paper, with its columns of theatrical "cards."

On such tours as these, this wandering tribe learned strange skills: the art of smuggling fish and chips into theatre dressing rooms, forbidden as likely to taint both costumes and wigs; the skill of picking bathroom locks with hairpins, thus evading the obligatory twenty-five cents; the subterfuge, in the age before dry cleaning, of sprinkling fuller's earth on serge or suede, to arrive for the next performance as pristine as a pin.

Above all, they learned to cope with a jovial, beery audience, who in Britain greeted any delay in the curtain rise with "Up with the linen and make a beginnin'!" Strolling players like the Dublin and

Belfast Touring Company lived a hurly-burly existence from week to week; in Kilmarnock, Scotland, where the theatre lay beneath a railway arch, a potted version of *Romeo and Juliet* often contended with the doleful lowing of cattle from the shunting yards, and the roar of the 9:15 made Hamlet's soliloquy totally inaudible. At Larne, a northern Irish seaport noted for frisky sailors, Macbeth, on one memorable occasion, broke off in mid-soliloquy to stand in as chucker-out.

It was a hard and unrelenting academy, yet for the dedicated it yielded results. From theatres that seemed always to smell of sizing glue, stale talcum powder, and half-smoked cigar butts, many shining talents did emerge: E. J. (Ernie) Carpenter, for almost thirty years the dean of the American fit-up fraternity, at one time or another nurtured such hopefuls as W. C. Fields, Sophie Tucker, and Walter Huston. One of America's finest tragediennes, Margaret Anglin, the first to size up the potential of the unknown Alfred Lunt, stemmed from these unpromising beginnings. Richard Bennett, a brilliant, if bottle-happy actor, later prone to wrangle with his audience, graduated in just eight years from a fit-up role as Tombstone Jake to Maude Adams's leading man in *What Every Woman Knows*.

Another notable refugee was Laurette, the twenty-three-year-old wife of Charles A. Taylor, fit-up king of the New Third Avenue Theatre, Seattle, Washington. In the title role of *Ayesha*, a pirated version of Rider Haggard's *She*, Laurette and the property man once evolved a plan whereby Ayesha, defied by a presumptuous native, snapped her fingers in a sizzling shower of sparks so that the man fell dead. This effect, achieved by tiny metal plates attached to her hands and wires connected with the main current, so entranced the twelve-year-old Guthrie McClintic, later the driving force behind Kit Cornell, that from then on the theatre was his life.

Wearying of fit-up and fleeing to New York, Laurette, in no short order, divorced Taylor, married the playwright J. Hartley Manners, and starred for 604 performances in the role he created for her, *Peg O' My Heart*. In time, Laurette's eye alighted on another talent, still latent in the bud: the twenty-two-year-old Lynn Fontanne.

These were the exceptions. For the most part, the brave and battered brotherhood of the fit-ups struggled on year after year as best they could: scraping up the penny-a-mile tariff the railways charged for covered wagons carrying scenery, the twopence a mile for larger trucks carrying backcloths; gratefully eating, even as my Uncle Vincent was, from a communal frying pan of bacon and eggs dumped unceremoniously on a kitchen table by a lodging-house slavey; often sacrilegiously plastering the tombstones in the graveyard with their "All Next Week" posters.

On both sides of the Atlantic, those posters, a choice of more than four hundred from the Public Ledger Company of Philadelphia or David Allen & Sons of London, Belfast, and Glasgow, reflected what their public wanted: *Uncle Tom's Cabin* ("My soul ain't yours, Massa!") played for more than ninety years until it died a painless death in a tent in Wilkes-Barre, Pennsylvania, in 1930; *Lady Audley's Secret* ("Let the cold cold grave close on her"); *The White Slave* ("Rags are royal raiment when worn for virtue's sake"); above all, *East Lynne*.

All the fit-ups knew the adage: when in doubt revive *East Lynne*, always *by special request*. Sometimes, in the United States, to escape charges of plagiarism from the original novelist, Mrs. Henry Wood, it was called *New England Folks*. Always a Wednesday matinée favorite, its hoary plot was pirated in at least a dozen British versions and countless American ones. Lady Isabel, believing her husband Archibald Carlyle is unfaithful, elopes with Sir Francis Levison, leaving her infant son, Little Willie, in Carlyle's care. Carlyle remarries; Levison deserts Isabel; Isabel, disguised in dark glasses and a mobcap, returns as Willie's governess, "Madame Vine." Willie expires with Isabel at his side; Isabel in turn expires in Carlyle's arms, always to the theme music of Balfe's "Then You'll Remember Me" from *The Bohemian Girl*.

In some versions, Willie identified his mother the moment she bent over his bed and removed her goggles, crying "Mama!" as he died; this was the version that one British fit-up actress, Lydia Donovan, played more than one thousand times for a stipend of three pounds a week. In other versions there was no such recognition, giving rise to Isabel's cry, "Dead! And never called me mother!" The final stunning tableau was beyond the financial means of most fit-ups: Little Willie and Lady Isabel, side by side, enthroned on a golden cloud.

For fit-up audiences, as Charles A. Taylor, of Seattle, Washington, never tired of stressing, must be left in no doubt. Subtlety was not their dish of tea. Taylor's favorite curtain-up was a backdrop featuring the exterior of Rector's fashionable lobster palace on New York's Broadway. An old lady is selling violets. The villain enters in full evening dress, wearing an opera cape and top hat, smoking a cigar. "Buy some violets, buy some violets," begs the old lady, hurrying forward. "Get away from me, you old hag!" the villain barks, taking a sideswipe at her with his cane.

"For the rest of the evening," Taylor would declaim with indisputable logic, *"the audience is going to* HATE *that man!"*

It was the failed fit-up actress, Stella Kirby, in J. B. Priestley's finest play, *Eden End*, who summed up the sad resignation of all those players who would never make the grade: "Somehow I've never been able to do what I thought I could do. Something gets in the way. I feel it all inside, but it doesn't come out right." But this was not a heart cry that would ever be echoed latterly by Alfred or Lynn, John or Helen, Kit or Noël or Larry.

From 1896 until the last year of his life, disaster dogged Irving. The giant oak of the jungle was assailed by misfortune as the thunder and lightning raged about King Lear. In the year following his knighthood, playing *Richard III,* Irving had injured his knee and was forced to relinquish the stage for two months—a cruel reversal after he had plowed £200,000 into the Lyceum. Then in February 1898 a raging fire destroyed the Southwark, South London, depot, where most of the theatre's scenery was stored: two thousand separate pieces, the furnishings for forty-four plays, valued at £30,000, yet insured for only £6,000.

Aside from the financial loss, Irving's available repertory was now sorely restricted, but worse was to come. In October, pleurisy and pneumonia, contracted during a tour in Glasgow, again kept him from the stage for two months. But debts were mounting; to settle them he was forced to sell his interest in the Lyceum to a syndicate headed by Joseph Comyns Carr. The deal was an unhappy one. Although Irving received £26,500 in cash and £12,500 in fully paid shares, he was committed to play at least one hundred annual performances for less than his usual fee. Now, in essence, he had lost control of the theatre he loved above all else. "Henry was a changed man from the time he sold his rights," Ellen Terry noted.

There were few more triumphs ahead. "July 1899," Ellen Terry confided in her diary. "End of the London season and H. tells me that he has lost over £4,000!"

At sixty, Irving was now old beyond his years. Many years later, old-timers at the Garrick Club would recall him hunched in an armchair late one night before a dying fire, the night's return from his son Laurence's *Peter the Great* clutched in his hand, muttering dourly, "Henry Irving. Ellen Terry. Lyceum Theatre. Twenty-five pounds."

When a successful musical, *Kitty Grey,* took London by storm in 1901, Irving commented bitterly to John Laurence Toole, "Ah! Johnny, they don't want *Coriolanus,* they want 'Kitty Rubbish.'" In vain Mrs. Aria tried to comfort him on the poor showing of *Peter the Great,* despite a command performance for Queen Alexandra. "Like it? Yes they like it but they don't come," he fulminated. The painful likeness achieved years earlier by the painter John Singer Sargent in a Royal Academy portrait tormented him increasingly. Unable to bear the melancholy that was reflected there, he hacked the canvas to shreds with a knife.

July 19, 1902, was a historic occasion; for the last time Irving and Ellen Terry appeared at the Lyceum in *The Merchant of Venice.* Now the syndicate, following a run of ill luck, decided on a change of policy: the theatre was to be partly demolished and reopened as a music hall. Irving would have no part of it; he totally rejected his share in the proceeds of the sale. "I suppose you know," said his incredulous stage manager, Harry Loveday, "that you are giving away eleven thousand pounds?" Irving's jaw set hard. "The man who hasn't the courage of his conviction is not worth a damn," he rapped.

Infirmity forced him from his longtime eyrie in Grafton Street to a self-contained apartment in the Stratton Street house of the philanthropist Baroness Burdett Coutts. Sadly, he took leave of old friends before midnight; if the lift ceased running, the servants would have to carry him upstairs. Yet still, unable to afford retirement, he toured unceasingly, once more to the United States in 1904 to play *Louis XI.* The end was not far off. In the spring of 1905, playing *The Bells* in Wolverhampton, he collapsed in his hotel. The doctors diagnosed emphysema and a rapidly weakening heart. They also forbade him ever again to play *The Bells.*

In his convalescence Ellen Terry called to see him at his Wolverhampton hotel. It was their last meeting. A curious fancy crossed her mind: propped up in bed, Irving looked like a gray and beautiful tree she recalled seeing in Savannah, Georgia. His dressing gown hung on his sparse frame like gray draperies.

"What a wonderful life you've had, haven't you?" she asked her old partner, and Irving rejoined dryly, "Oh, yes, a wonderful life— of work."

Ellen was intrigued. "What have you got out of it all? You and I are getting on, as they say. Do you ever think, as I do sometimes, what you've got out of life?"

Irving stroked his chin. He smiled quizzically. "Let me see, a good cigar, a good glass of wine, and good friends." And, leaning forward, he kissed Ellen's hand.

"And the end—how would you like that to come?"

He repeated her question. Then, snapping his fingers, he said with consummate timing, "Like that!"

On Monday, October 2, 1905, his farewell tour began in Sheffield. It would amass a sizable nest egg, an escape from a poverty-stricken old age; he was determined to see it through. Waiting for cues in the wings, he fought for breath—yet when they came, his body, drilled to respond from hundreds of gaslit nights, willed him to obey. On Monday, October 9, the tour reached The Theatre Royal, Bradford; Irving played Shylock. When Gerald Lawrence, his Bassanio, quit the stage, he found Irving sitting in the wings, awaiting his first entry. Lawrence anticipated the usual query: "Well—me boy, what are they like—cast-iron?" Instead the Chief was in a strangely philosophic mood. "It's a pity," he mused, "just as one is beginning to know a little about this work of ours—it's time to leave it."

On the Tuesday night he played Becket. On the Wednesday, looking desperately ill, he left Room 20 at the Midland Hotel for a luncheon in his honor at the Town Hall, but climbing the steps, Bram Stoker noted, he resorted to an old ruse. Halting, he pointed to a local monument, posing a question as to its origins. As he listened to the answer, perhaps hearing nothing at all, he regained his breath.

On Thursday, October 12, came the moment that Stoker had dreaded: in defiance of his doctors, Irving once more played *The Bells*. In a sense, his public was to blame, for receipts always soared when Irving was featured on the billboards; in this, too, he was a legend, for youngsters who had first seen the play in repertoire thirty-four years earlier now took their own children. That night it was an agonizing performance. When the curtain fell Irving slumped in the prompt corner, battling for breath; it was ten minutes before Loveday and his faithful dresser, little Walter Collinson, could help him to his dressing room.

On Friday the 13th, again playing Becket, he seemed in better shape. Yet principals like Gerald Lawrence as King Henry II and

Edith Wynne Matthison as Rosamund de Clifford felt a strange unease; all that evening Irving's performance hovered on the threshold of death. Normally his gestures and inflections never varied, but tonight there were curious divergencies. As Becket made obeisance to the King, Lawrence felt Irving's lips brush his hand—something he had never done before. In Becket's last scene with his friend, John of Salisbury, his final line "God's will be done" became, mysteriously, "God is my judge." When the Four Knights of the Royal Household closed in on him in the North Transept of Canterbury Cathedral, Becket's last line came resonantly: "Into Thy hands, O Lord, into Thy hands." Then, alarmingly, he fell not downstage, as was his custom, but upstage, toward the choir.

Changing in his dressing room, he seemed to rally. His concern seemed more for the welfare of others than for his own. "Muffle up your throat, old chap!" he advised Bram Stoker. "It is a bitterly cold night—take care of yourself." "You ought to have a cab," he besought Loveday. "It's very cold." Then with Walter Collinson and his messenger, W. R. Shepherd, he climbed into his cab, relapsing in reverie. But, entering the Midland Hotel, he stumbled; again came that raucous air hunger, and he could gasp only, "That chair . . . !" as he subsided into it, then gracefully, like an actor conscious of the reaction from hundreds of darkened pits, slipped dying to the floor.

In London, a lighthearted supper party at the Garrick Club hosted by Tree came abruptly to an end; a telegram from Bradford had told them the worst, and the members filed silently into the night. To a young actor, Clarence Derwent, later president of American Actors' Equity, the capital, on the morning of Irving's funeral at Westminster Abbey, seemed stunned into silence. Though thousands lined the streets, every sound seemed muted. Everywhere, flags flew at half mast; black crêpe draped the pillars of the Lyceum; black bows adorned the whips of the hansom cabbies who plied the streets, their heads bared in mourning. Inside the Abbey, an enormous pall of thousands of laurel leaves dyed purple enveloped the coffin, dropping to the ground on either side.

At the Gaiety Theatre, Manchester, on the night after Irving's death, Ellen Terry somehow struggled through Barrie's *Alice Sit-By-The-Fire* until the final curtain approached. But Alice's final soliloquy cut too painfully deep: "It's summer done, autumn begun. Farewell, summer, we don't know you any more. Alice sit-by-the-fire henceforth . . . I had a beautiful husband once, black as the raven was his hair. . . ."

Then she broke down; the curtain fell; without a sound the audience filed out. An era had ended; briefly, the make-believe was now the reality.

II. Irving and After:
"Nothing Can Stop Me — Nothing!"

Long afterward, armed with the precious gift of hindsight, they could pinpoint it precisely—that magic moment when it became apparent that the only world among all available worlds was The Stage. For the nine-year-old Ralph Richardson, as a schoolboy near Brighton, it was the irresistible impulse to practice death scenes on the seashore, "to fall off groynes into the shingle, and lie asprawl, pierced with assegais or shot with arrows, torn to pieces by wild Indians." For the seventeen-year-old Guthrie McClintic, who had lost his heart to the fit-up players at Seattle's New Third Avenue Theatre, it was a surrender confirmed for all time by his first glimpse of New York's theatre district: Daly's, where Ada Rehan had reigned; the new Maxine Elliott theatre, cheek by jowl with Nazimova's on 39th Street; the spacious, brilliantly lit lobby of the Empire, where John Drew was playing in Somerset Maugham's *Smith*. For the seven-year-old John Gielgud, the moment of truth was when the curtain at the Duke of York's glowed as the footlights came up, and the first notes of the orchestra heralded *Peter Pan*.

For Kit Cornell, then aged ten, it was also *Peter Pan*—three years after its original production, but still starring Maude Adams, and now booked into her father's own Star Theatre in Buffalo. All her life the details of that day would remain preserved in her memory: the Saturday matinée, the aching vigil while she squirmed impatiently in her father's box until Alice, her mother, whispered, "Ssh! *Curtain going up!*"

For Kit, those words aroused a sudden, overpowering awe, a trepidation so great that momentarily she left her seat to hide her face in the heavy velvet entrance curtain. Then, with Maude Adams's first whisper—"Tinker Bell, Tink, are you there?"—she crept back. Three hours later, when the curtain fell, ten-year-old Katharine Cornell had achieved maturity. Her dreams of becoming a trained nurse were all behind her. She was going to be an actress.

At twelve she was ready to seize her chance, for in the summer of 1910 the Jessie Bonstelle Stock Company played a season at the Star. The dark, dynamic Miss Bonstelle was already a woman much respected by Broadway managers; often she tried out a new play for them prior to a New York opening. Long accustomed to spotting talent, she was intrigued by the awkward, slender girl, too tall for her age, with her long dark hair reaching to below her waist.

The eyes, she thought, dark, clear, and widely spaced, were not the eyes of a girl nearing her teens; they were already the eyes of a woman.

"Please," Kit asked breathlessly, after many days of trying to summon up courage, "would you mind if—may I—oh please, *could* I watch the rehearsals?" And she added, "I'll sit way in the back row and you won't even know I'm there!"

Her intensity amused Jessie Bonstelle, yet equally it impressed her. But wouldn't she rather be out playing games? Kit could not bring herself to confess the truth until Miss Bonstelle prized it gently from her: "You want to go on the stage yourself, someday, is that it?" When Kit admitted it, Miss Bonstelle did not laugh. "Hurry and grow up," was all she said, "and perhaps you can play Jo for me."

Kit was entranced. Jo, in Louisa May Alcott's *Little Women*, was then her favorite character in literature.

Thereafter her routine never varied. St. Margaret's Episcopal School was always out at 1:30 P.M. Each afternoon Kit sat in the darkened theatre, soon barely heeded by the cast, watching, fiercely absorbing every detail.

Although the plays varied from week to week, the pattern of rehearsals never did. By Tuesday afternoon, when Kit arrived, the actors had already received their next week's parts, limp little typewritten copies with pale blue covers. In these an actor meticulously noted in pencil every move the director gave him. If Jessie Bonstelle said, "On this speech, Harry, cross left," the actor duly marked the line "XL."

Plumb in the center of the stage, seated on a kitchen chair at a bare wooden table, was the stage manager. Before the rehearsal began, an attentive cast would watch him maneuver other kitchen chairs about the stage, announcing, "This is the piano" or "This is the divan." Entrances would be marked out by stage braces—two narrow slats of wood, joined together, whose function was to brace the scenery. One stage brace would be "the entrance to the garden"; another would be "the door into the drawing room."

By degrees, the bewildering jargon that would one day be Kit's *lingua franca* began to make sense. The footlights, of course, were "the foots." A small spotlight was a "baby spot." When an actress announced "Business with cup," she was signifying her awareness that at this moment she was handling a teacup. The cup itself—or a cigarette case, or anything that a player handled—was a "prop."

Backstage itself, though familiar from childhood, gradually took on a new significance as the beating heart whereby the theatre functioned. Far away above the roof of the stage, hidden from the audience, was the grid where all scenery could be lifted clear from the stage, or "flown," by pulleys; logically, this space was "the flies." Backstage was also where the "flats" were stored, painted canvas-fronted units of scenery, usually eighteen feet high by six feet wide, and here, too, were the "drops," two-hundred-pound curtains with their painted reproductions of interiors or exteriors.

At fifteen, attending the Oaksmere finishing school at Mamaroneck in Westchester County, Kit was in her element: dramatically parading the campus in a black dress, escorted by a white Russian borzoi; staging *Twelfth Night* with herself as Malvolio; organizing mime classes; not only acting in plays but producing them and writing them. "She stood out from her admiring classmates," recalled Theresa Helburn, later a guiding light of the New York Theatre Guild, "like a moon surrounded by satellites."

Yet all who were bent on survival in the jungle would receive their just portion of discouragement; Kit was no exception. Returning to Buffalo on a vacation, she met up at a social function with a stout, middle-aged actress, Miss Rose Grover, a lady who had never quite made it. Knowing nothing of Kit's ambition, the gushing Miss Grover invited her to call at her hotel.

Next day, when the secret was out, Miss Grover's demeanor changed. "I want very much to go on the stage," Kit insisted, but Miss Grover was suddenly all icy disapproval. "Don't be a fool," she derided her. "There are hundreds of girls better looking than you are, more talented, girls with experience, girls who need money, tramping Broadway, getting nowhere. Why should you want to do that?"

Hurt and bewildered, Kit could find no words; Rose Grover's bitterness was painful to see. "Look at me," she commanded. "Twenty years of my life devoted to the stage. And what have I got to show for it? . . . Think of any number of actresses who were famous only a few years ago. Where are they now? What became of them? Who knows? Who cares?"

Kit picked up her gloves and her handbag; she made ready to leave. Suddenly Miss Grover's bitterness evaporated into dull apathy. "I don't suppose I've stopped you," she said. "I don't suppose you'll take my advice. I might as well have saved my breath."

Kit was entirely composed. "No," she replied. "You can't stop me. Nothing can stop me—nothing! Perhaps I shall never be a great actress but I simply feel that I—*must* act. And nothing is going to stop me."

In a sense, she spoke for all of them.

In London, around this time, the young Lynn Fontanne met for the first time the young Noël Coward. He saw "a scraggly friendly girl with intelligent brown eyes and a raucous laugh." She saw "a boy actor with wicked eyes and a wicked sense of humour," who talked grandly of his prospects in London's West End. It was stage-door talk, for which Lynn made due allowances, for Noël, despite aspirations as a lyricist and dramatist, was not all that favored by producers; they resented both his brashness and his habit of chattering and skylarking during rehearsals while guidelines were laid down. A young revue actress, Beatrice Gladys Lillie from Toronto, Canada, who labeled herself as "lace-curtain Irish," once took the foolhardy step of introducing Noël to her producer, André Charlot.

Charlot listened in constrained silence while Noël rattled through one of his own lyrics, *Forbidden Fruit*. Then, once Noël had quit his office, he turned on Bea in cold fury. "How dare you," he said dangerously, "bring people here with no talent *whatsoever*?"

The reactions of Charles Hawtrey, who auditioned Noël to play a pageboy at two pounds per week, were much the same. Noël's one-liner, in the last act of *The Great Name*, was a remonstration with Hawtrey, who was playing the piano in the artists' room at the Queen's Hall. But like many beginners, Noël sought to make a meal of it.

"STOP that noise at once, please," he mouthed with fearsome force, then, on a note of awe, "in there"—a sweeping gesture to the left—"they're playing *The Meistersingers*." A breathless pause for effect; then, with scathing contempt, "Making such a horrible row," before ending on a note of swelling pride, "We're used to good music here!" the word "good" being stressed for essentially more than it was worth.

Though Hawtrey was later to relent, his first reaction to his stage manager was understandable: "Never let me see that boy again."

Lynn's fortune, by contrast, was set fair. Following walk-on parts in Waller's *Monsieur Beaucaire* and Tree's *Edwin Drood* for two pounds a week, eked out by penurious stints as an artist's model, she was hired by the actor Dennis Eadie—the original Falder in Galsworthy's *Justice*—for the No. 3 tour of *Milestones*, then London's biggest hit. A collaboration between the British novelist Arnold Bennett and the American playwright Edward Knoblock, *Milestones* was the story of three generations of shipowners, a "well-made" play, as solid as an Edwardian sideboard. Lynn was to play the spinster Gertrude Rhead, "twenty-one, high-spirited and independent," in Act I, "a faded acidy spinster" in Act II, "a thin shrivelled old woman of seventy-three" in Act III.

The part, and the tour that followed, was the making of her. In those years leading up to World War I, touring was an integral part of theatre life, the school in which neophytes learned their trade. In 1905, the year of Irving's death, 250 companies were touring the United Kingdom alone, with 300 more, on what was known always as The Road, across the United States. Cities like Glasgow and Chicago rated as No. 1 tours, smaller conurbations—Wolverhampton, or Canton, Ohio—were No. 2, the smallest of all—Ashby de la Zouch, or Key West, Florida—were No. 3.

This, above all, was the Great Age of the Tour, a phenomenon that was never to be repeated. At least four British companies commanded the same packed houses across the United States and Canada as they did in Britain, deliberately preserving an identical repertoire from decade to decade. As early as 1899 John Martin Harvey, a disheveled little man and a byword for pomposity, hit upon an adaptation of Charles Dickens's *A Tale of Two Cities* that he titled *The Only Way*. Two certified money spinners followed—*A Cigarette Maker's Romance*, in 1901, where the amnesiac Count Skariatine falls in love with a cigarette-factory girl, and *The Breed of the Treshams*

(1903) featuring Harvey as Lieutenant Reresby ("The Rat"), who shoulders the blame for his brother's treachery in the English Civil War.

Almost always a failure in London, Harvey on tour was a raging success, playing Sidney Carton in *The Only Way* more than four thousand times, and appropriately he and his wife Nina de Silva traveled in regal style, converting cheerless hotel suites into instant homes with whole packing cases of books, family photographs, objets d'art, and four pampered dogs. Harvey, knighted in 1921, was game to the very end; in 1938 he was still touring the youthful Sidney Carton and the dashing Lieutenant Reresby, hovering on seventy-five.

It was the same with Fred Terry—Ellen's younger brother and John Gielgud's Uncle Fred—and his wife Julia Neilsom. Six feet of swaggering charm, "Golden Fred," as his company knew him, toured just two plays of note: *Sweet Nell of Old Drury*, with Fred as King Charles II, which lasted for thirty years from 1900 on; and Baroness Orczy's *The Scarlet Pimpernel*, with Fred as Sir Percy Blakeney. Although two London flops in succession once cost Fred ten thousand pounds, he recouped it all with one six-week tour of *Sweet Nell*, and *Pimpernel* proved as lucrative. In London, critical reaction was adverse at first. "The scarlet pimpernel is a little red flower that opens in the morning and shuts at night. So should this play!" was one typical sample. Yet ultimately it clocked up one thousand London performances and almost three thousand on tour, with Fred, in the Harvey tradition, still venturing a sprightly cotillion at sixty-five.

To a man they were autocrats, and proud of it. On one occasion, at Blackpool, when Sidney Carton exchanged a farewell kiss with Lucy Manette, the galleryites were boisterous with sucking noises. At once Harvey had the curtain rung down to read them the riot act; unless they behaved they would not see Carton die. From then on they were as meek as mice. Fred Terry showed a similar mastery during World War I when a bomb from a cruising Zeppelin hit the stage-door vestibule at London's Strand Theatre, putting out every light in the house. In his familiar yellow satin suit, Fred strolled to the edge of the footlights. "Ladies and gentlemen," he announced, "we have candles. Shall we proceed?" The audience stayed put; somehow it would have seemed ill-bred to crowd for the exits.

As Lynn's tour of *Milestones* toiled from town to town, other great veterans of the road loomed large on the billboards: the recently knighted Johnston Forbes-Robertson, a melancholy, withdrawn man who confessed, "very rarely have I enjoyed myself in acting," his repertoire now scaled down to the mysterious Stranger, transforming the lives in a London boardinghouse in *The Passing of the Third Floor Back;* and Dick Heldar, the blinded artist in Rudyard Kipling's *The Light that Failed.* Following fast in his footsteps was the handsome, leonine Matheson Lang, who toured most frequently as the sinister oriental Wu Li Chiang in *Mr. Wu* and as *The Wandering Jew,* cursed with perpetual life for spitting at Christ on the road to Calvary and finally burned at the stake with satisfyingly smoky clouds of asthma powder.

It was on one Lang tour that the supreme tribute came from a gallery girl queuing at Liverpool's Royal Court: "I do love Matheson Lang! I'd go and see him anywhere—even in Shakespeare!"

Such notable companies rated rather better touring accommodation than the fit-ups could aspire to, and from 1907 on one increasingly powerful body set out to ensure that they got it: the Actors' Church Union (ACU) run by the Reverend Donald Hole from St. Anne's Rectory in Soho, London. A successor to the Church and Stage Guild, formed in 1879 to combat prejudice against the profession, Hole's organization had been initially concerned with the spiritual needs of touring players; now their temporal needs received due attention. Through the medium of 349 chaplains throughout the United Kingdom, a sizable unpaid Michelin inspectorate grew up to vet theatrical lodgings, a list that in time numbered four thousand approved addresses.

Thus in a No. 3 town like Kidderminster, Lynn could learn from her Theatrical Lodgings List (first published in 1909) that Mrs. Probert of 111 Lea Street, could offer 1sr (sitting room), 2br (bedrooms), 1cr (combined sitting and bedroom), and was also in possession of a P (piano). Moreover, Mrs. Probert, though unable to offer a B (bathroom), then a rarity, was distinguished by the ACU accolade of a ‡—a landlady undertaking to reply to every stamped and addressed inquiry, to reserve one room or set of rooms annually for the profession, and to notify the Union of any change in accommodation.

It was a much-needed innovation. Until now, all too many rooming houses—"digs" in British parlance—had offered only slovenly accommodation, dingy, stuffy little dens with poorhouse rations and primitive toilet facilities. ("Lav in pub. opp." appeared all too often in the columns of *The Stage.*) Minatory notices loomed everywhere:

PLEASE CLOSE THIS DOOR GENTLY
DO NOT LEAVE THE LIGHT BURNING
AND OBLIGE,

THE LANDLADY

More than one player would thus be stung into the retaliation of "giving her the haddock"—nailing a dried haddock beneath the flap of the dining table before leaving. Others, as a subtle warning to their successors, were content to inscribe "Quoth the raven . . ." in the hostess's visitors' book.

What the ACU sought were genuine provincial homes-away-from-home: often a riot of oilcloth, palm-leaf fans, and saddlebag chairs with antimacassars, sometimes smelling of steam laundry and onions, but offering a "combined" with good fires and all meals for seventeen shillings and sixpence a week. Thus more and more players enjoyed a robust succession of roasts, stews, and rissoles, with fish on Fridays and sausages and baked beans on Saturday. In later, more prosperous years many of them looked back with genuine nostalgia to the kindness of innumerable landladies known as "Ma." "Where are you, my brave and buxoms?" wondered the British touring manager, H. F. Maltby, recalling the friendly Mrs. Gotobed of Stoke-on-Trent. "God bless your ample bosoms and rounded rumps!"

As Lynn would later discover to her cost, no such system of vetting existed in the United States, where a typical call sheet read:

> Harp of Life Company
> Next stop Keokuk
> Company train leaves at 6:06
> Arrives 12:11
> Hotels: The New Eagle, New Globe, New American.

The intrinsic awfulness of all or any one of them was left for the company to discover.

For, improbably, just one No. 3 tour had pointed Lynn toward the big time. Once the tour ended, Dennis Eadie placed her in a new Knoblock play, *My Lady's Dress*, then, when *Milestones* was revived, cast her in her old part as Gertrude Rhead. Among the audience was Laurette Taylor, who had brought her New York hit *Peg O' My Heart* to the Globe Theatre on Shaftesbury Avenue. To Miss Taylor, Lynn's performance was a revelation. "She captured each age so completely," she recalled later, "I didn't know whether she was in real life a slender thing of eighteen or a skinny woman of eighty."

For the second time in her short career, Lynn had found herself a powerful patron. "Laurette Taylor," one society magazine noted, "is the first American actress to make a complete social conquest of London society"—not surprisingly, when Miss Taylor, sometimes warm and kind, more often cruel and imperious, had made the grade from Seattle's fit-up queen to Broadway star in seven short years.

"I've decided to form my own permanent acting company in America," she told Lynn when they met at a society reception. "Would you like to come to America and play with me?"

Lynn saw all this as tea-party persiflage. "Of course, Miss Taylor. I should love it," she answered demurely.

Some months passed, but though Lynn became part of the sycophantic Taylor ménage—to some a menagerie—backstage at the Globe, no more was said of work. Then on August 4, 1914, the cataclysm of World War I engulfed first Europe and then the world. Laurette, her nerves too fine-tuned to cope with Zeppelins, departed for New York. Lynn was philosophical. *Milestones* had seemed a breakthrough, but now it was as if *Milestones* had never been.

The cable came suddenly out of the blue at the beginning of 1916:

WILL YOU COME TO AMERICA? STARTING REHEARS
ALS NEW PLAY. COME IMMEDIATELY. SALARY 100 DOL
LARS WEEK. CABLE REPLY. FARE WILL BE SENT YOU.
LOVE LAURETTE TAYLOR.

Lynn knew no hesitation. She was burning her bridges right enough—but nothing would stop *her* either.

In Boston, Massachusetts, nineteen-year-old Alfred Lunt was in an undeniable rut. The high promise of his years at Carroll College in Waukesha, Wisconsin, when he had not only helped his widowed mother run a boardinghouse but played leads in Ibsen and Shaw and imitated the Scottish comedian Harry Lauder at Glee Club concerts, seemed very far away. After only two days of classes at Boston's Emerson College of Oratory, Alfred felt time was passing him by. One Saturday in October, 1912, he walked in to see George Henry Trader, director of the Castle Square Theatre Stock Company.

"I want to go on the stage," he told Trader hopefully.

Trader was equally direct. "Can you start rehearsing Tuesday?"

The problem was that Alfred did not conform to type. Edwardian juvenile leads were muscular, curly haired, preferably with dimpled chins. Alfred was tall, thin, and eccentric in his gait. Thus he was rarely cast for any character less than fifty years old; most often he played senile quavering grandfathers, avuncular uncles, or rascally, cackling old bankers who held the mortgage on the farmhouse. This was a phenomenon of the age on both sides of the Atlantic; in his first year at Birmingham Repertory Theatre, seventeen-year-old Harold French limped on stage week after week weighed down with beards and drooping moustaches, supported by an ebony cane, finally, at the season's end, graduating to a bathchair.

Already the steely perfectionism that became Alfred's hallmark was much in evidence. Even at Carroll College he often took three hours to make up his face, "as if he were a Rembrandt painting a portrait." So, too, was his innate professionalism; after a sixteen-hour day playing an ancient telegraph operator in William Gillette's *Secret Service* and rehearsing Lodovico in *Othello*, he would plunge into an icy bath to keep himself awake at 2:00 A.M., teeth chattering uncontrollably as he chanted his iambic pentameters. A professional was always word-perfect, and Lodovico has all of twenty-six lines.

"I became an expert in theatrical senility," Alfred would recall proudly later. "I could give you any age from forty-five upwards and come to the exact year you wanted." Yet despite this undoubted achievement, Alfred, through no fault of his own, was still denied the scope for versatility that would one day single him out.

In Washington, D.C., Helen Hayes Brown was likewise in a rut, and again through no fault of her own. As one of a troupe known as the Columbia Players, she strove with all her might to escape from child parts—Cedric in *Little Lord Fauntleroy*, the four-year-old Claudia in *The Prince Chap*—but appearances were all against her. At fifteen Helen looked all of ten years old; at twenty she was still in essence a teenager.

Nor was this surprising. The ambition of the masterful Catherine Hayes Brown dominated her life; although queen of the six hundred square feet that stretched behind the footlights, Helen was still totally innocent of the world beyond the theatre. Until she was twelve she had never played with other children. She had reached the age of twenty before she even carried a handbag. Her education was so erratic that she learned to add by counting the box-office takings.

All her life was lived backstage, where the property man made her a little proscenium stage for her dressing-room table. On a tour of one-night stands as Little Simone in *The Prodigal Husband*, even the great John Drew babied her along with the rest, bestowing on her the nauseating nickname of "Childy."

It was a beaten track that Helen hated—and never more than in her thirty-week tour of the Far West and the Deep South, which hardened actresses called "the Gum-and-Gimlet Circuit": voyeurs among the traveling salesmen used gimlet holes to spy on them undressing until the actresses plugged them up with chewing gum. Her role was the name part in the saccharine *Pollyanna*, the fable of Pollyanna Whittier, an orphan who wins all hearts and minds because she is always "glad," even in adversity. But even her triumph against all odds in Miles City, Montana, failed to reconcile Helen to Pollyanna. This was a town where Helen and her mother, glued to the window of their frame hotel, saw cowboys riding pell-mell through the streets, hallooing and shooting wildly into the air. "If they don't like your show," the theatre manager, ornate in a ten-gallon hat, reassured her, "they just shoot through the ceiling, not at you."

It was the second-act climax that Helen dreaded. Carried on with both legs broken, Pollyanna is still exulting, "I'm glad I'm alive! I'm glad I'm alive!," and all through this act there had been strange, muted trumpeting sounds, which she feared were muffled boos, drifting from the audience. At any moment, she thought, the shooting would start. But no shots resounded and the curtain finally fell to muffled applause. Peering through a peephole in the curtain, Helen saw why: the cowboys were weeping brokenly.

Thus, for the foreseeable future, yet more child parts in "stock" seemed the only option.

If this was the age of the tour, it was equally the age of the stock company—so called because the actors had originally held shares in the company and were paid according to their investment. By 1910, two thousand stock companies—the forerunners of the English repertory system—were flourishing across the United States; it was a breathless harum-scarum existence, as Kit Cornell had witnessed in Buffalo, though one that taught a multitude of players to be both practical and flexible. Given a new play per week, with a maximum of five rehearsals, they learned the trick of "winging it," propping pages of the scene in the wings and scurrying to them when minds went blank. Dress rehearsals were an unknown luxury, and scenery and props were never *in situ* until the opening night. Even so, a week afforded little time for scenic accuracy, and the dramatist Channing Pollock recalled seeing Mark Antony's tent lit by electricity, and Louis XVI chairs in Macbeth's palace.

The one drawback, as Alfred and Helen were discovering, was the tendency to typecast; the leading man was always just that, and the hierarchy scaled down through "second leads," "juveniles," "heavies," and "character men." On the distaff side it was the same: the "leading woman," the "ingenues," the "character women" cast as grandmothers, old maids, and Irish servants. Fifty parts in a season was commonplace, and one resolute actress, Victory Bateman, claimed to have learned 140,000 words in five months.

It was one such stock company—the Washington Square Players, then located at the Comedy Theatre, 108 West 41st Street, New York—that made two notable talents briefly aware of one another. A meeting had been called at the home of Lawrence Langner, a genial patent lawyer who viewed the theatre with the jubilation of a grown-up with a toy train, to discuss the possibility of forming a Theatre Guild. After much discussion, a frail, gaunt young man summed up the pros and cons in one minute flat. Impressed by his bear-trap mind, nineteen-year-old Kit Cornell asked who he was. That, she was told, was Guthrie McClintic, casting director to the producer Winthrop Ames.

Guthrie had no need to ask Miss Cornell's identity; he already knew. Kit had joined the Washington Square Players in 1916, and because of their diverse art-theatre repertoire had entirely escaped typecasting: they presented plays like *Ghosts*, Shaw's *Mrs. Warren's Profession* (banned in England until 1925), and Eugene O'Neill's *In the Line*.

It was in a long-forgotten opus called *Plots and Playwrights* that McClintic had first spotted Kit; "there was a haunting mystic quality about her like a shadow in a haze that at any moment might become clear," he recalled. Beside her name in the program, which would be duly filed in the Ames office, Guthrie wrote, "Interesting, monotonous, watch."

And theatrical history has recorded that he did.

Throughout much of World War I, Noël Coward was drifting. Such roles as came his way were largely seasonal, in the children's shows that until 1939 regularly invaded the West End at Christmas: *Peter*

Pan and *Where the Rainbow Ends*. Then, in the spring of 1916, Noël found himself briefly involved with a legend: a four-month tour of the play that the critic George Jean Nathan dubbed "that inexhaustible old heifer," *Charley's Aunt*.

Everything about *Charley's Aunt* was legendary. Inspired by a one-day visit to Oxford, the author, a touring actor named Brandon Thomas, had offered it in 1892 to W. S. Penley, a small, melancholy-faced comedian who seemed ideal to play Lord Fancourt Babberley, who, to chaperone a tea party for two college boys and their lady loves, impersonates a rich aunt from Brazil, "where the nuts come from." On the opening night, February 29, 1892, at the Theatre Royal in Bury St. Edmunds, Penley presciently wired Brandon Thomas, "Your fortune is made."

Though the play found no favor with King Edward VII, who thought the character was modeled on Queen Victoria, the king was a notable exception. On the first night at the Royalty Theatre in London, the Duke of Cambridge's equerry laughed so hysterically he fell through his stall to the floor; for sixty years thereafter, audiences somewhere in the world were reacting as hilariously on every weekday night. In Denmark, the play ran for two years. In Norway, the costume designer, who had mistakenly visited Windsor instead of Oxford, outfitted the undergraduates in bow ties and Eton collars. *Charley's Aunt* souvenirs were churned out by the truckload—dolls, penwipers, ink bottles.

In consequence, few girls were ever as closely chaperoned as *Charley's Aunt* itself. Until 1964, when the copyright expired, a producer's license could be instantly revoked if he departed one whit from the original costume: a light brown wig parted in the center, a bonnet of black lace with red roses, black silk mittens, white lace fichu, lace collars and cuffs three inches deep, a large cameo brooch, and a dress of stiff black satin—with a flat, pleated bodice set into a three-inch waistband over a black moiré silk petticoat.

It was thus a play to be treated with reverence, and since irreverence was all his life Noël's stock in trade, he was at odds from the first with the veterans of the company, all of whom had played it for years: James Page, Sidney Compton, and J. R. Crawford. Crawford, Noël noted disdainfully, "directed rehearsals with all the airy deftness of a rheumatic deacon producing *Macbeth* for a church social."

The tour was not a notable success. To Noël, *Charley's Aunt* was "that least funny of all plays," and on a salary of two pounds and

57

ten shillings a week he often made do with one meal a day. In Peterborough, during a blizzard, the company played to exactly six people. On another occasion, Noël and two others went for a picnic on the river, completely forgetting their matinée. In Chester they found, to their dismay, that their "digs" were located in a brothel. In June, to Noël's "unqualified delight," the tour came to an end— but once again there was no stampede of managers for the services of Master Noël Coward.

He was in good company. Only the sheer determination of Laurette Taylor kept Lynn in the cast of the play she had traveled three thousand miles to appear in, *The Wooing of Eve*. "My God," wailed George C. Tyler, the fat, rude little producing manager, "she's a human scarecrow, she's pigeon-toed, and they won't be able to hear her beyond the tenth row of the stalls." Equally, only the determination of the tragedienne Margaret Anglin to hire Alfred as her leading man saved him from another season enacting dodderers in Boston. The verdict of her stage manager, Howard Lindsay *(Life With Father)*, was damning. Alfred's voice was hollow, it broke badly, his movements were awkward, his shoulders stooped—"a most awkward ungainly ugly chap."

Miss Anglin, however, already saw Alfred as a member of the theatrical "400." "True, he is ugly," she agreed with Lindsay, "but it's a *handsome* ugliness, rather like that of the Vanderbilts."

The era of Ibsen and Pinero, of clinical problem-plays and the "merciless surgery of the soul," was also, by paradox, a world of wide-eyed wonder. In the New World and the Old, the appetite for spectacle—what Max Beerbohm called "gorgeous and solid scenery"—transcended all class barriers. The surge of mercantile imperialism, which gave birth to cavernous railway stations, looming exhibition halls, and department stores, was reflected in the world behind the footlights. "The theatre," noted the critic Percy Fitzgerald, "is like a gigantic peep-show."

For this was also the age of the stereoscope, the panorama, the illustrated magazine; above all, the audiences craved pictorial realism, an echo of the spectacle painting of W. P. Frith and Sir Lawrence Alma-Tadema, who designed several Irving productions. Top-hatted scene painters, like Joseph Harker, a staunch Irvingite, rode in their own carriages and even took their own curtain calls; for productions like *A Greek Slave* and *San Toy*, Harker journeyed as far afield as Athens and Tokyo. Before *Faust* was staged, he and Irving made a pilgrimage to Nuremberg, just as David Belasco journeyed all the way to Bath, Somerset, to purchase the eighteenth-century props for *Sweet Kitty Bellairs*.

Many producing managers were adherents of spectacle, but somehow Belasco, aged forty-one when the century dawned, contrived to eclipse them all. A strange, remote man with a faraway manner and blazing black eyes, who always dressed as a Roman Catholic priest, Belasco's aura was curiously forbidding; his theatre, the Stuyvesant (later the Belasco) on West 42nd Street was a sanctum cut off from all contact with the outside world. Belasco's casts lunched and even supped at the theatre, later to be dispatched home by a fleet of automobiles; once on the payroll, they became Belasco's people.

Like the press baron William Randolph Hearst, whose lifestyle was not dissimilar, Belasco had a lifelong addiction to junk; his flat on top of the Belasco Theatre, heady with incense, was crammed with relics from old churches, death masks, halberds, and Greek icons. Like Hearst, too, he reveled in panoply; visitors reached The Presence through a phalanx of liveried footmen, their passage marked, as in a Chinese temple, by the faraway striking of gongs. Vain of his prowess with women, he would proudly exhibit beds that he himself had rumpled, tokens of imaginary conquests.

If Irving was a martinet, Belasco was a tyrant. As author and adapter of more than one hundred plays and director of over three hundred, he launched his quota of stars, but he was equally swift to break them. The most glittering of all was, perhaps, Caroline Dudley Carter, at first prominent solely for her divorce from Leslie Carter, the palsied Chicago "little liver pills" millionaire, in which four corespondents had been cited. Billing her always as "Mrs. Leslie Carter" to keep her case in the public eye, Belasco featured her in such glossy spectacles as *The Heart of Maryland,* in which the red-haired divorcée swung from the clapper of a bell to prevent the tolling that would mean her lover's capture. Next he launched her as the torrid Zaza, and later still as Madame Dubarry. But in July, 1906, Mrs. Carter was guilty of most willful *lèse majesté:* she remarried without asking Belasco's permission. Belasco never spoke to her again.

In rehearsal Belasco was a sight to behold. In rage, his speech grew sibilant, resembling the hissing of a mamba on the warpath. Once, to conjure a dramatic scream from Frances Starr, Mrs. Carter's successor, he jabbed a pin into her shapely buttocks. He was habitually equipped with a one-dollar watch, which he would jump on to emphasize a point; on another impressive occasion, he grabbed a fire ax and chopped the scenery to pieces. The set was due to be scrapped anyway, but the petrified players did not know this.

Yet, for all his shortcomings, Belasco vastly improved the current standard of stage décor and lighting. As a compromise with the Ibsenites, he bought the outer trappings of a reality in which he never truly believed. For *The Easiest Way* (1908) he purchased the complete interior of a broken-down apartment—attic furniture, threadbare carpets, peeling wallpaper—and transferred them to the stage. For one scene in *The Governor's Lady* (1912) he snapped up the entire interior of a Child's restaurant; the smell of percolating coffee, drifting through the stalls, mingled with the odor of wheat cakes sizzling in batter. In truth, this realism had been pioneered in Paris back in 1887 by André Antoine's Théâtre Libre, whose banquets featured roasting geese and real barrels of wine, but Belasco brought all this to a wider public.

Though Bernard Shaw, after seeing *The Heart of Maryland* in London, ascribed Belasco's success to "a combination of descriptive talent with delirium tremens," Belasco was a supremo of the switchboard. For almost thirty years—he survived until 1931—he and his lighting expert Louis Hartmann labored to evolve new and subtler methods of illumining the stage, pioneering such innovations as the portable switchboard, the portable light bridge above the proscenium, and the "baby spot." Under Hartmann, twenty-four electricians, not the habitual two or three, worked for an entire week on lighting rehearsals alone; small wonder, when a Belasco lighting plot sometimes ran to fifty pages of text.

For his *Rose of the Rancho*, a smash-hit 1906 melodrama, Belasco achieved the stifling languor of a Californian mission by covering all the stage lights with yellow silk, thus securing the illusion of dry and scorching sunlight. *The Return of Peter Grimm* (1911), where a crotchety old man returns from the dead to atone for his past misdeeds, proved a thornier problem. More than a year of trial and error elapsed before Hartmann hit upon the solution: the footlights were abolished, amber "baby spots" lit up the faces of the main characters, with only a cold, gray light playing on the features of Peter Grimm.

"I don't want a mere moon—I want a *Japanese* moon," Belasco exploded during rehearsals of *The Darling of the Gods;* this was wholly in character. In *Madame Butterfly* (1900), which formed the basis of the Puccini opera, the transition from twilight to daybreak, when Cho-Cho-San vainly awaits Lieutenant Pinkerton's coming, took all of fourteen minutes. For *The Girl of the Golden West,* another Puccini opera, Belasco worked for three months to secure the soft changing colors of a Californian sunset over the Sierra Nevada.

In other fields besides the switchboard, Belasco was a purist. Stage directions in one of his melodramas might occupy 20 percent of the text. In his eyrie above the theatre, long nights were devoted to working out the action on four-foot models, which were more than once taken apart and reconstructed. Often a set costing $6,500 would be junked without compunction. To secure the right apparel for David Warfield as Peter Grimm, Belasco sent for fifty bolts of cloth, devoting all one summer to wrapping Warfield in different materials like a window dresser until he had hit upon one that made him look "mysterious and faraway." At times, this passion for realism verged on pedantry. In the restaurant scene of *The Governor's Lady,* Belasco threw a mammoth tantrum when a so-called jar of molasses was found to contain maple syrup.

In Europe, Belasco's closest counterpart was Max Goldmann Reinhardt, a squat, granite-faced man who dominated the Berlin stage from 1905 to 1918. From his castle at Leopoldskron, Reinhardt, in true Belasco spirit, oversaw a whole legion of actors and designers, both in Berlin's spacious Deutsches Theater and in the more intimate Kammerspiele next door. But intimacy was not truly Reinhardt's forte, as his 1905 production of *A Midsummer Night's Dream,* the first of twelve versions, made plain.

At Berlin's Neues Theater Reinhardt created an entire forest, with vast papier-mâché trees, rills, moss, grass, tiny bushes, fireflies darting above a lake, and a Puck clothed solely in grass: all this on the forty-foot revolving stage, perfected by Karl Lautenschläger of Munich in 1896, which turned on its iron shaft to reveal fresh corners of the forest with every scene. For the opening act of *Othello,* Reinhardt took poetic license in interpreting "Venice. A street"; the feuding parties met by torchlight against a background of bobbing gondolas on a section of the canal. For a garden scene in *Die Räuber* (The Robbers), Reinhardt's designer, Ernst Stern, conceived a hedge made out of canvas "flats," then set a seamstress to the weeks-long task of covering them with artificial leaves.

Such grandiose conceptions—what Lawrence Langner unkindly

called "elephantiasis of the imagination"—were in keeping with the age. When the actor-manager Oscar Asche staged *As You Like It* in 1907, it seemed only natural to contract with a Covent Garden florist to supply two thousand pots of ferns two feet high, which, with clumps of bamboo, represented the forest of Arden.

The flamboyant Sir Augustus Harris of the Theatre Royal in Drury Lane, known to his intimates as "Augustus Druriolanus," once set the young Joseph Harker to creating Charing Cross Station on stage. "Fine chance for you—platforms, lights, signals, smoke, steam! On one side, Waterloo Bridge; on the other, Houses of Parliament Clock Tower."

"But," Harker objected, "you can't see the Clock Tower from the inside of the station." "Doesn't matter a damn!" Harris scoffed. "You put it there and *they* will see it!"

Yet both Asche and Harris yielded the palm to the magniloquent Sir Herbert Beerbohm Tree, ensconced, like Belasco, in the Dome of his splendid palace of Portland stone and granite, known from Queen Victoria's death until 1953 as His Majesty's. The first London theatre to make no charge for either programs or cloakrooms, Tree treated his patrons like guests to a royal function, though his attempts to outfit his stewards in livery identical to that of Buckingham Palace were swiftly quashed by Albert Edward, then Prince of Wales. But given a stage sixty feet wide by sixty feet deep, Tree could conjure up fantasias that anticipated even Cecil B. De Mille.

Tree's passion was to regild the Shakespearean lily. At all times the stage of His Majesty's was chockablock with supernumeraries or "walking gentlemen," cavalry horses, rabbits, domestic poultry, and prize borzois. In *Much Ado About Nothing*, birds trilled unceasingly all through the scenes in Leonato's garden; in *Twelfth Night* Olivia's garden, with its broad grass terraces, was an onstage replica of a photograph from the magazine *Country Life*.

When Tree staged Louis N. Parker's *Drake*, there came a shipboard scene when Lyn Harding, as Drake, unsheathed his sword and declaimed, "I place my sword on this table. He who raises a hand against me raises a hand against Her Majesty Queen Elizabeth."

There followed a pregnant pause, but Tree detested pregnant pauses. "I want in this silence," he told his stage manager, the dapper, silver-haired Colonel Stanley Bell, "to hear the lap of waves against the ship."

The son of a German grain merchant, Julius Beerbohm, Tree (who assumed this name when the acting bug bit him) never ceased acting thereafter, whether on or off the stage. "Stay! Fairest of thy sex! I'll find my own way," was his way of greeting a parlormaid bent on announcing him, and this fustian style marred many of his performances. Triumphant when playing villains or eccentrics—Svengali, or Fagin in *Oliver Twist*—he found it almost impossible to leave well enough alone. When Irving, as Shylock, knocked at the door of his house to find his daughter Jessica gone, his first reaction was a total, frozen stillness. Tree, by contrast, stormed through the house, rushing from room to room, crying "Jessica!" and finally collapsed in hysterics as Lorenzo and Jessica were seen paddling away in a distant gondola.

When Tree's Hamlet died, an unseen flight of angels literally did sing him to his rest, once so out-of-tune that the "corpse" was heard to groan loudly. In the Brocken Scene in *Faust,* bent on eclipsing the memory of Irving's production, Tree arranged with the Carlton Hotel next door to tap the steam from their kitchens—a magnificent, swirling cloud of vapor that soaked the chorus girls to their skins.

As Richard II, Tree hit on a touch that the maladroit Shakespeare had entirely overlooked: a dog—the king's pet dog—that compounds Henry Bolingbroke's perfidy in consigning Richard to the Tower by turning and licking Bolingbroke's hand. That was the cue for Tree, his heart breaking, to leave the stage, sobbing convulsively. Tree was equally dissatisfied with Shakespeare's handling of *The Tempest;* to show a mere section of the deck, in the opening shipwreck scene, was to sell the customers short. Instead, an entire galleon under sail rocked in a sixty-foot-long tank, with roaring breakers, teeming waves, and the wind machine going full blast.

Always suspicious that Shakespeare dealt in subtleties, Tree's solution was to spell out everything with bricks. Thus when Hamlet greeted Ophelia, "Nymph, in thy orisons, be all my sins remembered," the young Prince actually discovered Polonius's daughter kneeling in prayer. In *Much Ado*, when Beatrice twitted Claudio with being "civil as an orange," no dullard could miss that point; Beatrice was brandishing an orange in her hand. Yet 220,000 Londoners witnessed Tree's *A Midsummer Night's Dream* and 242,000 his *Julius Caesar,* perhaps confirming the double-edged compliment of one London daily: "Tree made Shakespeare live for those who do not or cannot read him."

63

Always financially improvident—"Tell them we'll transfer the account," he instructed a manager when the bank refused to increase the theatre's overdraft—Tree's generosity won him the esteem of his casts. He paid for rehearsals, a custom then followed only by George Alexander, and for an astute young "super" like Donald Calthrop, later one of Britain's finest character actors, rewards could be considerable. Walking on in the first act of Tree's *The Beloved Vagabond*, Calthrop raced across the Haymarket to the Comedy for an Act II walk-on, thence to the Duke of York's as a midshipman in *The Admirable Crichton*, and finally to the Adelphi for the last act of *Mrs. Wiggs of the Cabbage Patch*.

With Tree's rehearsals, absenteeism was possible for hours at a time, since they often continued for twenty-four hours around the clock. No scene was ever played twice in the same way. Actors dozed off from sheer fatigue, but Tree never lost his temper, never tired, departing for an elaborate £10 lunch at The Carlton and sauntering back to take up the reins again. Later, food from The Carlton would arrive for the whole cast; an eager child, with his shrill, falsetto laugh, running his fingers through his sandy hair, for Tree the apogee of fun was a picnic on the stage of "my beautiful theatre." Understandably, in a building that was seldom vacated the cleaners found their work cut out. "Can you possibly," Tree asked one cleaning woman icily, "scrub with discretion?"

Trying—and trying yet again—to achieve the results he wanted, Tree would ultimately reach his goal. Sometimes his metaphors were obscure. "No, no, no!" he chided one performer. "You give me blue, and I want yellow and pink in your soul." Once, kneeling dramatically center stage, he raised his arms to heaven and cried fervently, "O God, come down from your throne and show this poor incompetent ignoramus how to play his part." When my great-aunt, Constance Collier, played Nancy to Lyn Harding's Bill Sikes in *Oliver Twist*, Tree rehearsed her and Harding in one scene up to thirty times; Sikes must hit Nancy as if he meant it. Weary unto death, Harding's foot finally slipped and he struck Constance full in the face. She groped to her feet, half-stunned, blood streaming from her mouth.

"There," said Tree, now entirely satisfied, "*that* is the effect we want."

* * *

For all his posturing, Tree, in his lifetime, gave as much back to the theatre as he took from it. On Irving's death he assumed the presidency of the Theatrical Managers' Association, as well as of the Actors' Association, an organization founded in 1891 to protect the profession from shyster impresarios who left their companies stranded. But in 1904 he further codified the whole business of survival in the jungle; in the foyer of His Majesty's he established an Academy of Dramatic Art.

Until now, most leading players had been recruited from the ranks of the amateur dramatic societies: Mrs. Pat, Alexander, even Tree himself. Despite sundry attempts to establish a training school, all of them had been short-lived. As far back as 1840, Frances Maria ("Fanny") Kelly had built a theatre, the Royalty, in Dean Street, Soho, as a training school for young actresses; the venture died a speedy death, as did Mr. and Mrs. Glovers' Musical and Dramatic Academy, also in Soho, in 1848. In 1882, a Royal Dramatic College, whose committee included the poet Matthew Arnold and the dramatist Wilkie Collins, opened its doors; three years later it closed them.

There were few other nurseries available. From 1885 to 1899, the go-ahead Miss Sarah Thorne, one of eight stagestruck brothers and sisters, took over her father's Theatre Royal, Margate, on the Kent coast, combining it with a School of Acting, "The Towers," at No. 5 Hawley Square. For a flat thirty pounds, a student underwent six months' tuition; merit was rewarded by an entrée into the theatre company at thirty shillings a week. At Sarah's School the pupils, or "pupes" as they were known, studied the rudiments of voice production, dialect, and accents, makeup, and the values of pace and of pauses. Many went on to achieve renown: the young Violet Vanburgh, soon recruited into Irving's company; the equally young Allan Aynesworth, the original Algy in Wilde's *The Importance of Being Earnest;* Ellen Terry's son, Edward Gordon Craig; and George Arliss, later a leading man to Mrs. Pat and Minnie Maddern Fiske, and later still a hardy perennial in another jungle, Hollywood.

From 1883, another solution for the novice was to tour with the exclusively Shakespearean repertoire of Frank Benson, the only actor ever to be knighted—by King George V in 1916—with a property sword, in a room behind the Royal Box at Drury Lane. Students under Benson paid a forty-pound premium for a full course of classes;

mornings in the theatre put the emphasis on deportment—walking, standing still, fencing. "Now you are a King," Benson would command a student. "Enter and sit down as a King." At nights, attired as Courtiers, Banner Bearers, Gentlemen, they found their feet in walk-on parts. Bensonians were always known for their grace of movement.

Pictured by one actor as like "a genial yet aloof El Greco monk," Benson's fetish was not spectacle but sport; even his fixture programs were designed like cricket cards. One apocryphal story told of Benson wiring his London agent, "Send a good fast bowler who can play Laertes"; the reality was not far removed. On tour, Benson could be seen every morning in running shorts, cantering through the streets of the town, running corks gripped in his hands, his knees working like pistons, his business manager panting beside him, often sweating profusely in a dark suit and starched collar. For "Pa," as his players knew him, a swim was always more exhilarating if a few inches of ice had to be broken. When Benson looked over new recruits, recalled Philip Merivale, later a Broadway star, "his first question was not 'What experience?' but 'Do you row?' "

Yet Merivale was one of several Bensonians, as they liked to call themselves, who later made their marks on Broadway and in Hollywood: among them were Clarence Derwent, Reginald Denham, Cedric Hardwicke, and Basil Rathbone. Understandably, Benson himself most excelled in parts calling for athletic prowess; his savage Caliban in *The Tempest*, hanging headfirst from a palm tree, a raw fish clamped in his jaws, never failed to win applause.

Tree's Academy, upgraded to the Royal Academy of Dramatic Art in 1921, thus filled a deep-felt need, though plainly the foyer of a busy theatre was no suitable venue for serious studies. By 1905, RADA was located on its present site: two unconverted houses at 62/64 Gower Street, in London's Bloomsbury, sharing a first-floor level that served as a stage room and a sprawling basement used as a canteen. In this hub of communal life, a buxom lady known as Hennie sold mostly sandwiches and Bourbon biscuits. It was a rare student who could afford a "plutocratic" chop.

Athene Seyler (Class of '06) recalls her own audition as unpromising; she faced an august panel composed of Sir Squire Bancroft, his eyeglass screwed truculently into place, the bald and beetle-browed Pinero, and Lena Ashwell, the creator of Mrs. Dane. After one glance at the trepidant Athene, markedly plain, she says, at seventeen, Miss

Ashwell pronounced, "I think we must tell you, first of all, that you have no obvious qualities to help you on the stage at all."

"I know what you mean, Miss Ashwell," was Athene's tactful response, "but if you hear me recite you might change your mind."

Then, even more than now, selection was a make-or-break process. A candidate must deliver two recitations of his own choosing, neither of which must be more than THREE minutes (the capitals are RADA's), although candidates showing latent promise are now encouraged to try, try again. But three minutes of Rosalind from *As You Like It* was enough to secure Athene a scholarship—equivalent to free tuition for three terms—and two years later she won the Academy's highest award, Bancroft's cherished Gold Medal, later won by such international names as Charles Laughton, Alan Badel, and Barbara Jefford. More than forty years later, Miss Seyler notched up another first: she was the first former student to be elected as the Academy's president.

When Kenneth Barnes, a onetime civil servant, took over as administrator in 1909, the balance of candidates was still uneven: four girls applied for admission to every male aspirant. Candidates, Barnes noted, fell into three groups; those with instinctive aptitude, those who were hampered by nerves and thus groping—about half the total—and those without a vestige of any kind of talent. "Don't imagine that you'll be surrounded by beautiful girls," Pinero warned Barnes, unchivalrously. "Most of the students look like damp typists!"

Not until 1910 did the students enrolled swell from sixty to one hundred, but their number enjoyed the benefit of some inspired, though unpaid onlookers. If a student seemed doubtful, advised George Bernard Shaw, set him to read a speech sight unseen; even professionals like Dennis Eadie, brilliant at a first reading, sometimes performed less surely once they had studied the part. Emotion, according to Ellen Terry, who also held an observer's role, could only be transmitted vocally through the quality of tone: "There are eleven different ways of saying 'Yes' and one of them means 'No,' " she stressed. To one student, who gave no more than a competent rendition of a speech by Juliet, Ellen commented, "Very nice, my dear! But you must remember that when Juliet said that, she was in Heaven, not in Bayswater!"

This was a belated start, considering that the American Academy of Dramatic Arts, originally the Lyceum Theatre School of Acting, at 120 Madison Avenue, the first of six locations, had been a thriving concern since 1884. Sponsored by such committed managers as Charles Frohman and Steele MacKaye, the first man to install asbestos fire curtains and fold-back seats, its innovator was Franklin Haven Sargent, a former Harvard drama teacher, a remote, stooping man with a whispering voice whose aim was to create in the United States a replica of the famous Paris Conservatoire, founded in 1786, the oldest European school of acting.

Using such skilled instructors as the young Belasco, Sargent had soon enrolled 100 pupils, the first of 4,459 alumni, in a two-year course costing two hundred dollars per annum, upped to four hundred dollars by 1904. Emphasis was laid, then as now, on "emotional involvement, psychological accuracy and simple honest communication." Sargent's successor as director, Charles Jehlinger, an intense, monkish little man who was still in harness up to 1952, rated this honesty above all other factors. "Be men and women *conversing*, not idiots pronouncing words," he stressed to such promising novices as Spencer Tracy, Rosalind Russell, and Lauren Bacall. "Do not let the 'Theatre Devil' microbe get into you."

In Hennie's basement canteen, over sugar buns and mugs of tea, their RADA counterparts traded the tips for survival learned from the lips of their elders—tips on which their very careers would soon depend. If a speech was singularly awful, deliver it as if it was a literary treasure, thus disarming an audience's animal instinct. Tell the audience you were sorry for yourself—a favorite Hawtrey axiom—"and they won't give a damn about you." If one section of an audience turned restive, lower your voice to a whisper, rather than shout; the more mannerly patrons would soon quiet the rowdy faction.

The art of the actor, George Arliss would say, was "how not to be real on the stage, without being found out by the audience." Never be seen with a walking stick, Charles Wyndham would advise, for "if you get used to it, you don't know what to do with your hands." "Don't laugh at your own jokes," Irving had always instructed the Lyceum company. "If *you* do, the audience won't."

One of their most prized mentors was Barnes's sister, Irene, who had adopted the stage name of Vanburgh; after sixteen years with the greatest of the profession, she had learned priceless lessons. An actress must give out to her audience unstintedly; this was the secret of charm that she absorbed from Ellen Terry. From Irving she had learned "the strength of stillness, the power of a silent figure." In a period play, Tree counseled, keep the head rigid; this was an era of powdered hair. Madge Kendal was unrivaled in moments of poignancy; pain was conveyed subtly by a clenched hand, a quick intake of breath, a stutter over a word. In a scene of nervousness or anxiety, Irene Vanburgh suggested, sit on the very edge of your chair.

But only time would reveal to them the most vital secret of all: acting could not be taught, merely learned. "My finest Lady Macbeth was my first," Constance Collier used to recall, "when I was only nineteen. You see, no one had taught me how difficult it was."

Behind the facade of the conventional theatre, known to every Edwardian playgoer, a new concept of acting techniques was evolving by degrees—one that would profoundly affect the world in which Helen, Noël, Kit, Lynn, and Alfred were finding their feet.

Unusually, for history, the birth of this concept can be charted with relative precision: 10:00 A.M. on a June morning in 1897. The birthplace was the Slavyanski Bazaar, a Moscow restaurant, painted in the colors of a Russian Easter egg, its high, vaulted ceiling obscured by the smoke from black Russian cigarettes. The midwives were Vladimir Nemirovich-Danchenko, thirty-eight, a drama teacher with the Moscow Philharmonic Society, and Konstantin Stanislavsky, thirty-four, a dabbler on the fringe of the theatre, the towering (six-foot-four-inch), regally handsome son of a wealthy businessman.

The two men had one thing in common: a hatred of the cloying artifice that characterized the theatre of the Czars. Acting was at as low an ebb as costume design, which recognized only three styles: "Faust," "Les Huguenots," and Molière. Mechanical actors offered no more than what both men called "rubber stamp" performances: they rolled their eyes and showed their teeth for jealousy, they tore their hair when in despair. Peasants never entered without spitting on the floor; military men clicked their spurs; aristocrats toyed with lorgnettes.

This was well enough for third-rate melodrama, but Danchenko and Stanislavsky were pinning their faith in a new dramatist whose style was quite unsuited to hollow declamation. This was Anton Pavlovich Chekhov, a thirty-seven-year-old doctor afflicted with consumption, a proud, haughty, shortsighted young man, perpetually fingering his pince-nez, who thought of himself more as a doctor than as a writer. Up to that time, the public had endorsed this verdict; Chekhov's *The Seagull*, produced one year earlier at the Alexandrinsky Theatre in St. Petersburg, had failed as dismally as his earlier full-length plays *Ivanov* and *The Wood Demon.*

Chekhov's plays called for a radically new style of acting. They lacked all "action" as older dramatists had understood it. Often the silences were as pregnant as the words the characters uttered. Thus the old methods of interpretation and setting were impossible; the stately pacing of actors with their resounding intonations, so beloved of Moscow theatregoers, would be totally irrelevant. What was called for here was ensemble playing, a rejection of the "star" and "super" system, much on the lines of the Meiningers, a remarkable theatre group from Saxe-Meiningen, Germany, who had twice visited Moscow. As pioneers of ensemble acting, their work had profoundly affected both Danchenko and Stanislavsky.

All this, and much more besides, emerged from that first meeting at the Slavyanski Bazaar—a passionate interchange of views that lasted for a marathon seventeen hours. Its upshot was that Chekhov must be persuaded, somewhat against his will, to consent to a revival of *The Seagull,* to be staged under widely divergent conditions.

To probe the inner life of a Chekhov character, the two men evolved a new approach for their company, which included Olga Knipper, later Chekhov's wife; the cast must attune themselves to the pasts of their characters, no less than their presents, to examine their motivations, even to composing imaginary life histories. This introspective approach, which came to be known as The Method, was for many years the subject of heated controversy, most especially in the United States; for nineteenth-century Moscow it was no less than revolutionary.

In this same year, a start was made in the deserted Hermitage Theatre on Karetny Row, a onetime Punch-and-Judy house, dusty, unheated, smelling of stale beer. Before rehearsals could even begin, the cast had to set to and rehabilitate the building, painting walls and carpeting the auditorium, washing the windows and hanging tulle curtains, finally building a barn for their scenery. That winter, the cold was so intense that costumes froze to the dressing-room walls. Yet against the odds they battled on. The Moscow Art and Popular Theatre, as it was christened, had become an act of faith.

On October 14, 1898—a date to go down in theatre history—its curtain rose for the first time on Alexei Tolstoy's *Tsar Feodor Ivano-*

70

vich; not until the following spring did Stanislavsky conceive the final *mise en scène* for *The Seagull,* the haunting story of the fashionable writer Boris Trigorin, who ruins the young life of Nina Zaryechny, "the seagull," for little better reason than to glean material for a short story.

On the opening night, Stanislavsky was to recall, "a gravelike silence" greeted the fall of the first-act curtain. Heavy with despair, the cast began moving to their dressing rooms. Suddenly an apocalyptic roar seemed to split the auditorium apart. To Stanislavsky's astonishment the curtain rose again; the entire audience had clambered to its feet, yelling and cheering. Overnight, Chekhov had won the acclaim that was his due.

From now until Chekhov's death in 1904, three other timeless plays followed: *Uncle Vanya, The Three Sisters, The Cherry Orchard.* Their secret, then as now, lay in their universality. "You will feel in the everyday plots of his plays the eternal longings of man for happiness, his strivings upwards," Stanislavsky wrote. "Astrov and Uncle Vanya are not simple and small men, but ideal fighters against the terrible realities." In Bernard Shaw's view, "Chekhov, in giving us Russian life, gave us the life of every country house in England, in the same way as Ibsen gave us every provincial house in the world."

Almost two thousand miles from Moscow, in the year of Chekhov's death, another intrepid band of players launched on a risky enterprise, centered around a small theatre called the Mechanics on Lower Abbey Street in Dublin, adjoining a disused city morgue. Armed with money put up by Miss Annie Horniman, the stagestruck daughter of a wealthy Victorian tea merchant, the poet William Butler Yeats bought up both theatre and morgue to create the Abbey Theatre for the Irish Players.

Under Irish law, the theatre's patent was granted not to Yeats or Miss Horniman but to a resident of Ireland: Dame Isabella Augusta Gregory, herself a gifted playwright—"a sturdy stout little figure," recalled Sean O'Casey, with a face "hardy as that of a peasant." But from the first Yeats, a dark, thin man with an unruly lock of hair, prone to chant his poetry at tea parties in a high, keening voice, spelled trouble for the Irish National Theatre.

"Differences of opinion were more prevalent than agreements at the Abbey," recalled the Englishman Ben Iden Payne, an early producer; this was a masterly understatement. Hostile to both the critics and the public, Yeats was out to ruffle as many susceptibilities as possible. Since his brief was to present only plays by Irish authors, he had soon achieved his aim.

On January 26, 1907, he raised the curtain on J. M. Synge's *The Playboy of the Western World*, the story of the braggart Christie Mahon, lionized for killing his father with a spade but later revealed as a lying coward when Old Mahon turns up alive. Not only was the play liberally peppered with swear words; it invoked God with monotonous frequency. "People here will not publicly approve of the indiscriminate use of the Holy Name on every possible occasion," tut-tutted *The Irish Times*.

That first night was a furor that Dubliners would long remember. Boos and hisses drowned out the words of the players; fistfights developed all over the house. On the second night, nationalists armed with toy trumpets sought to make the dialogue inaudible. Yeats then offered his audience the crowning insult: he called in that national symbol of oppression, the British police. The play must go on, he vowed, even if policemen stood in as chuckers-out by every row of seats. Not surprisingly the house was packed out every night; for the benefit of any Dubliners unaware of the fracas, Yeats had teams of sandwich-board men parading the city, reminding them of what they were missing.

This was a stormy start to a company whose ranks were later swelled by such masterly ensemble players as Barry Fitzgerald and his brother Arthur Shields, Sara Allgood and her sister Maire O'Neill, and Dudley Digges—most of them ultimately lost to Hollywood. But four years later, when *The Playboy* opened at New York's Maxine Elliott Theatre, the reception was stormier still. "When the Irish are looking for trouble," noted George C. Tyler, the producing manager, "any pretext will do," and to forestall that trouble Tyler had dotted the stalls with fifty plainclothesmen masquerading as drama lovers, with fifty more uniformed policemen standing guard on West 39th Street.

For all of ten minutes the first-night audience was silent—then a steady, insidious barrage of hissing began. The actors played calmly on, until a tidal wave of stink bombs and vegetables stopped them in their tracks. As the riot proceeded, one resourceful player went off to fetch a spirit lamp, and with total aplomb the ladies of the company made pots of tea and settled to drink it on stage, keeping a prudent eye open for missiles. This was the cue for Inspector McCluskey, head of the uniform squad, to alert the plainclothesmen, "All right, boys, let 'em have it!"

There followed what Tyler recalled as "the finest mass exhibition of the bum's rush in history"; the protesting patriots were pitched clean through the ticket taker's entrance into the arms of the uniformed squad, then hustled into a fleet of Black Marias en route to the night court. When the sounds of the last wagonload had died away, the curtain rang down, then rose again, and *The Playboy* once more started from scratch.

No such indecorous scenes marred the three-year season, extending from February 1904, to June 1907, at the Royal Court Theatre on London's Sloane Square, though the principles guiding them were as democratic as in Dublin or Moscow: the star players in one offering—among them Lewis Casson, Edmund Gwenn, Lillah McCarthy—might be relegated to bit parts in the next. The twin spirits of this enterprise were the playwright Harley Granville Barker, a lithe, athletic twenty-seven-year-old, and his businessman partner John Eugene Vedrenne, thirty-seven; their original intention was a series of regular matinées, with artists paid a modest one-guinea fee for each performance. But soon the Court became so popular that extra matinées and then evening performances became an integral part of the repertoire—after the theatre had closed for three weeks to install a new heating system. Initially as cold as the Moscow Arts, it had prompted a dour notice from the *Daily Mail*'s critic, headed "a Frost at the Court."

No man was more qualified as dramatist-in-residence than George Bernard Shaw, who at forty-eight, after long years in the wilderness, now came into his own. In all, the Court staged twelve of his plays, many for the first time; of 988 performances given at the theatre, 701 were of plays by Shaw. For the first time, distinguished playgoers like King Edward VII—who laughed so heartily at *John Bull's Other Island* that he broke a chair—and his premier, A. J. Balfour, exulted in a rich Shavian repertoire: *Man and Superman, You Never Can Tell, The Doctor's Dilemma, The Philanderer,* and the bewitching Ellen Terry in *Captain Brassbound's Conversion.*

This, in a sense, was paradoxical, for as dramatic critic for Frank Harris's *Saturday Review*, Shaw was the only one of his number who refused to accept that plays were primarily designed to give an audience pleasure. For Shaw, a play was "essentially identical with a church sermon"; his mission in life was to force the public, willy-nilly, to face up to unpleasant facts.

To him, Edwardian conventions existed to be overturned, which often meant the reversal of every widely accepted opinion. In *Arms and the Man*, he tilted at the Wilson Barrett–Lewis Waller tradition by creating Bluntschli, a soldier who fought solely for pay and carried no ammunition ("What use are cartridges in battle? I always carry chocolate instead!"). Other targets that drew Shavian fire were Truth, Duty, Self-Sacrifice, Virtue, and Reason, the very foundation stones of contemporary society. In essence his plays were anticapitalistic *(Widowers' Houses)*, antiromantic *(Candida)*, and antiheroic *(Caesar and Cleopatra)*. "The peace and prosperity of Victorian days," Shaw avowed, "was the peace of a lunatic living in the world of fantasy. . . . I laughed Victorianism out of existence."

For though Shaw celebrated the Will To Live as the ideal—"a race of men who are not afraid of death"—his gift of irony and his tongue-in-cheek humor always sent audiences home lighter in heart; one shrewd critic dubbed him "the laughing Ibsen." "What does govern England, pray?" demands Undershaft, the arms manufacturer, in *Major Barbara*, to which Stephen, his son, replies, "The best elements in the English national character." Undershaft is overjoyed: "Stephen, I've found your profession for you. You're a born journalist." "Martyrdom, sir, is what these people like," pronounces General 'Johnny' Burgoyne, British Army Commander in the American War of Independence, in *The Devil's Disciple*. "It is the only way in which a man can become famous without ability."

These were heady times in what later generations would call the "fringe theatre" or "off-Broadway." "We were members of a theatrical House of Lords," recalled Lillah McCarthy, years later, "all equal and all lords." No sooner had the Royal Court season ended than another venture attracted widespread critical appraisal: the theatre of Annie Elizabeth Fredericka Horniman, formerly the power behind Dublin's Abbey Theatre. Since her grandfather had pioneered the packaging of tea, Miss Horniman, described by one of her dramatists as "a withered spinster clad in rich brocade," could afford the luxury of experiment; with a company headed by Lewis Casson and his wife-to-be, Sybil Thorndike, she set up an English-style stock company in the ballroom of Manchester's Midland Hotel, later transferring it to a run-down cinema she rechristened the Gaiety.

For nine years after 1908, Miss Horniman staged some two hundred plays, at least half of them products of the newly risen "Manchester School"—plays like Harold Brighouse's *Hobson's Choice*, where Maggie, the self-willed daughter of old Hobson, the cobbler, insists on marrying her father's mousy little employee, Willie Mossop. Another that disturbed polite society profoundly was Stanley Houghton's Ibsen-oriented *Hindle Wakes*, in which Fanny Hawthorn, a spirited young mill hand, refuses to marry Alan, the mill owner's son who has seduced her, despite the outrage of both families. "You're a man and I was your little fancy. Well, I'm a woman and you were my little fancy."

In these smaller companies, the settings, too, were changing—as if the producers determinedly sought a new and streamlined simplicity, encouraging the audiences to dare to use their imagination. Cubes, steps, simple columns, and plain, dark curtains gave the effect of several levels of action. The mood of these new theatres was one of anti-illusion; the ten-minute wait to change the setting for a five-minute Shakespearean scene became a thing of the past. The pioneers of this new movement were Ellen Terry's gifted, if erratic son, Edward Gordon Craig, and Adolphe Appia, a young Swiss, who used electric lighting as the visual counterpart of music. Craig, like Belasco, scrapped the footlights, as well as sidelights from the wings; all lighting came from overhead. In the cathedral scene for his mother's *Much Ado*, only a jeweled patriarchal cross and a few arched mosaic columns were visible. Craig's aim, no less than Appia's, was one that found favor with the profession: to return the stage to the actor.

In the United States, too, new designers were arising, deeply influenced not only by Craig but by men like Fritz Erler of Munich's Künstlertheater, whose stark setting for *The Merchant of Venice* was a single column placed before a low wall, backed by the empty blue of the Venetian sky. Another newcomer, Robert Edmond Jones, a shrinking aesthete who had been psychoanalyzed by Jung, startled all New York with his designs for Ashley Dukes's *The Man Who Married a Dumb Wife:* robes of pure yellow, orange, and vermilion, accented with black, set off against a silver-and-black housefront. At the Washington Square Players, Lee Simonson, bearded and argumentative, favored "poster-like brightness—a Gothic arch, through which is seen the lemon-yellow silhouette of a medieval town." Like all of them Simonson was in revolt against "the sallow greens and soupy browns that had filtered from the walls of the academies on to the stage."

Implicitly, in these isolated outposts, war had been declared on the traditions of Irving, Tree, and Belasco; against the red curtains, the painted forests, the surprise vistas, and the painted roads that led to nowhere. But not all playgoers would react with enthusiasm to such radically avant-garde concepts. In Miss Horniman's time, two middle-aged ladies were once seen to hover indecisively outside the Gaiety, that temple of working-class realism.

"No," said one woman at last, "don't let's go in there. It's just like being at home."

III. The Twinkling Twenties:

"Can't You Say 'I Love You, Damn You'?"

At 11:00 A.M. on November 11, 1918, Londoners knew an intense disquiet. For the first time in six months, the maroons that signaled an air-raid warning boomed up from police and fire-brigade stations all over the city. Then, as the first newspaper-contents bills seen in years loomed outside Westminster Underground Station—FIGHTING HAS CEASED ON ALL FRONTS—and Big Ben, after four years of silence, tolled the hour, the city went wild.

In New York, too, it was a time for rejoicing. On this day, Fifth Avenue was closed to traffic, packed with a surging mass of men and women; from countless thousands of windows a blizzard of ticker tape and torn paper, 155 tons in all, fluttered onto the streets. Offices were half-deserted, shop doors were barred and shuttered, bearing tacked-on signs reading CLOSED FOR THE KAISER'S FUNERAL; on Morningside Heights, eight hundred Barnard College girls weaved into a snake dance, an early version of the conga. At the Little Theatre on West 44th Street, Guthrie McClintic, rehearsing *The Betrothal*, Maurice Maeterlinck's sequel to *The Bluebird*, became conscious of a racket "the like of which I had never heard"; without stopping to ask permission, his cast had piled into the street, yelling, singing, clambering onto the tops of taxicabs. At an estimated cost of ten million dead and twenty million wounded, "the war to end all wars" had officially ended.

For all those actors and managers returning from the Western Front, the jungle they had left behind had changed beyond all comprehension. Major Frank Vernon, former stage director at the Royalty Theatre, where Lynn Fontanne scored her first hit in *Milestones*, came back after four years to find that the little Royalty, once secure with takings of £800 a week, now needed a minimum of £1,500 to survive. The actor-manager Robert Loraine, who had once bought the American rights of Shaw's *Man and Superman* for £200 and parlayed them into a £40,000 fortune, was equally out of his depth. Following his discharge from the Royal Flying Corps, Loraine staged a revival of Edmond Rostand's *Cyrano de Bergerac* at the Garrick on Charing Cross Road—to find himself losing money, even when playing to capacity. Debating a move to a smaller theatre, Loraine found that its prewar rental of £200 had now upped to £600. Promptly he closed the show.

Another Flying Corps veteran, Ronald Adam, an accountant enlisted as business manager by the impresario Dion Titheradge, faced up for the first time to a world where theatres changed hands like pieces in a game of Monopoly. Titheradge had just then taken over the Vaudeville Theatre in the Strand, whose nominal owner was John M. Gatti. But Gatti, faced with overheads of £40 a week even when his theatre was "dark," had hit on a solution that now became all too common: he leased it to another entrepreneur for £80 a week, who in turn leased it to a third party for £120 a week. It was this canny soul, not Gatti, who was now charging Titheradge £180 a week.

Within four years the theatre had become a jungle such as Irving could never have envisaged. A new type of owner, who saw the theatre solely in terms of real estate, had taken possession—war profiteers, for the most part, who found backing plays a welcome way of dodging the Excess Profits Tax. Thus, the Yorkshire woolen merchant, William Gaunt, now held the Adelphi; another woolen merchant, William Cooper, had taken over the Gaiety, beloved of Edward VII. The newly knighted Sir Alfred Butt, a onetime accountant with Harrods Stores, now headed the syndicate leasing the Globe and the Queen's; the bill-posting tycoon, A. E. Abrahams, took over the Aldwych and the Garrick. Typical of these money-grubbing monopolists was the South African Joseph Leopold Sacks, a onetime fruit seller in a circus; though Sacks could neither read nor write his name, the wartime appetite for revues and musicals like *The Lilac Domino* had still won him control of five theatres, with a lilac-colored Rolls-Royce, whose klaxon played the *Lilac Domino* Waltz, as a token of his triumph.

An old-timer like Fred Terry—still prancing gamely through *The Scarlet Pimpernel*—now found to his cost that his cherished Strand

Theatre, available for £160 a week in 1915, came dear at £400 by 1929.

Although this was the golden age of the movies, the era of Mary Pickford, Douglas Fairbanks, and William S. Hart, no fewer than twenty-four Broadway theatres were to spring up between 1917 and the end of the decade. In London, one architect alone, W. G. R. Sprague, had masterminded eight theatres before the war ended; in 1930, four more opened their doors. Shows might come and go with depressing regularity, but property could only appreciate; in 1923, Daly's Theatre on Leicester Square, which Augustin Daly had built for £48,000 thirty years earlier, cost the Lancashire financier Jimmy White £200,000. Nor was there ever any shortage of aspiring backers, greedy for a quick kill—what Belasco called "theatrical Jasons seeking a Golden Fleece." Cynics in the profession had an apt adage for those who burned their fingers: "I know that my Receiver liveth."

The reign of the actor-manager was now almost done. Few of them had made old bones; Lewis Waller was no more than fifty-five when he died in 1915. Tree was the next to go, aged sixty-three, in 1917; inevitably his "beautiful theatre" was swallowed up by a syndicate. George Alexander, succumbing to pneumonia and diabetes, was only fifty-nine when he died in 1918. Only Wyndham lingered on until 1919, aged eighty-one, though his acting days were long past; that curse of all actors, a failing memory, had finally caught up with him. During the 1912 revival of *Mrs. Dane's Defence*, Athene Seyler recalls, Wyndham totally fazed Lena Ashwell during the famous cross-examination scene; the trenchant accusation, "You are Felicia Hindmarsh and your father was the vicar of Tawhampton," was mysteriously transmuted into "Your name is Letitia Fieldmouse and your father was the vicar of Wakefield."

Not surprisingly, before the end, Wyndham was frequently seen ducking into post offices to send himself telegrams, a rough and ready *aide memoire*.

The last to go was, fittingly, the most flamboyant: Charles Hawtrey, knighted in 1922 and dying in 1924, aged sixty-four. Although he had netted £100,000 from one farce, *The Private Secretary*, before the turn of the century, he splurged it all at the racetrack; Hawtrey's estate was valued at barely £1,000. To the end, his insolvency was legendary; as a veteran of two bankruptcies, his Comedy Theatre boasted three exits, the better to evade his creditors. "Now then, Mr. Hawtrey," one court official queried sternly, "when is the beginning of your financial year?" "Oh," Hawtrey answered, with a rueful smile, "every infernal day."

To the oldest stagers, this passing of an era was marked by different yardsticks. For some, it was the gradual decline of the Green Rooms, those gathering places where the cast had entertained friends before and after the play, snug, with their merry fires, club fenders, and deep green leather settees; there was no place for such grace notes in a world where theatre owners now talked bluntly of "bricks and mortar." For others, it was marked by the death of Charles Frohman on May 7, 1915, lost when a German torpedo hit the liner *Lusitania* off Kinsale Head, Ireland.

The gentle and courteous Frohman, whose word had always been his bond—never in his life had he exchanged a written contract with his artistes—went down like the "pro" he was, quoting a line from Barrie's *Peter Pan:* "Why fear death? It is the most beautiful adventure in life."

Only four years after Frohman's passing, the savage reality of the new economics became apparent. By August 7, 1919, virtually every actor in the United States was on strike.

The dispute had been more than twenty years a-building—ever since August 31, 1896, when a powerful organization, known as the Theatrical Syndicate, first saw the light of day. Ostensibly, its aim was to restore order to the chaotic system of booking plays across almost three million square miles of the United States, guaranteeing theatres that signed up thirty nonstop weeks of first-class attractions each year. On the face of it, this was an attractive proposition; whether in Columbus, Ohio, or Fort Worth, Texas, a manager would know in advance just which company would feature on his billboards each week.

Yet the system was insidious. The Syndicate could dictate what productions would appear in any given theatre at any given time—and on what terms. Armed with this power, they could—and often did—say which actors would appear in any one cast, and on what terms they should play.

Aside from the scrupulous Charles Frohman, few of the participants were true men of the theatre; like their postwar British counterparts, they were "bricks and mortar" men. Samuel F. Nirdlinger and J. Frederick Zimmerman controlled the theatres of Philadelphia, just as Henry B. Harris and his partner Isaac B. Rich held sway over Boston's theatres. Together with Marcus Alonzo Klaw, the New York booking agent, a tall, punctilious Kentuckian, and his partner, Abraham Lincoln Erlanger, a tubby, greedy man who sheltered from life behind a six-inch assault-proof door, these men had secured a tight monopoly of theatres all over the United States.

Few had any pretensions to culture. When a dramatist apologized to Erlanger for a misconceived line of dialogue, joking "Even Homer sometimes nodded," the little man was crass. "Never heard of the guy."

Not all managements fell tamely into line. Minnie Maddern Fiske defied the Syndicate from the first, and was thus forced to play Ibsen's *Hedda Gabler* in drafty, ill-lit halls and even skating rinks. The powerful Shubert brothers, the libidinous Lee, and the icy, imperious Jacob J., were in better shape to resist, since they owned or leased 193 theatres. But even the great Belasco, finding all Washington theatres barred to him, had to present Mrs. Leslie Carter in the city's leaky, cavernous Convention Hall, whose audience watched the last act sheltering beneath umbrellas.

With men like Klaw and Erlanger in the saddle, the social status of the American actor was fast slipping back to the "rogues and vagabonds" level.

There was then no limit to the free rehearsal period. One British expatriate, John Goldsworthy, on a two-year contract with the Shuberts, rehearsed for fifty-seven weeks and played for twenty-two, but was paid only for the latter period. If a play closed during rehearsals, few Syndicate members paid compensation. Often players—who were obliged to pay for all or part of their costumes—played extra matinées without pay. If a play closed on the road, even as far afield as San Francisco, no return fare was forthcoming. Early in his career, the actor-manager Otis Skinner, planning a tour of the West, was warned by a fellow player, "Don't! The plains are white with the bones of actors who have tried to get back."

Thus, on May 26, 1913, one hundred and twelve discontented spirits—among them such Broadway stars as George Arliss, Arthur Byron, and Charles Coburn—gathered in the Pabst Grand Circle Hotel on 59th Street, with one pressing aim in view: the formation of the

American Actors' Equity Association. What they sought from the producers, above all, was a standard contract, with minimum pay and basic safeguards against exploitation.

But, as yet, they had little industrial muscle, and the managers, who respected only force, knew it. "I believe that your contract is fair," the showman William A. Brady, who had promoted everything from Shakespeare to the prize fighter James J. Corbett, told one Equity member. "And when will you adopt it?" the actor wanted to know. Brady was nothing if not realistic. "When you make me."

In 1913, and for long afterward, aims were still divided: affiliation with the American Federation of Labour (AFL), thought desirable by some, was an affront to others, conscious of the status that had been theirs since Irving's knighthood. As late as 1916, the Hollywood heartthrob, Milton Sills, was vainly reassuring the wavering members, "The plumber and the engineer will not slap you on the back and call you Brother."

Still the pressures were growing. In March 1917, with Equity now 2,500 strong, George Arliss was to warn Abe Erlanger, "If you don't give the actors a standard contract there will be trouble—and I will be one of the leaders!"

Six months later, a giant step was taken: the producing managers agreed to a contract that limited unpaid rehearsals of plays to four weeks, with two weeks' pay guaranteed, no matter how short the run. If any play ran longer than a month, the management must give the company one week's notice of closing. Actresses earning less than $150 a week would be outfitted for free. And all players were guaranteed transportation, New York to New York, from this time on.

But in the spring of 1919, when the standard contract came up for revision and renewal, the Producing Managers' Association balked on one item: they refused to limit the number of paid performances to eight per week. If this issue seemed trivial, the managers had good and sufficient reasons: an Equity moving ever closer to the AFL was a threat to their autonomy. On June 24, Sam H. Harris, the PMA President, announced that the managers had now drawn up their own contracts. The actors could "take them or leave them."

At 7:15 P.M. on August 6, Equity's emergency headquarters at 160 West 45th Street had an urgent telephone call from Secretary Frank Gillmore: the strike was on.

For one man at least, this involved genuine hardship. At the Gaiety

Theatre at 46th Street and Broadway, fifty-five-year-old Frank Bacon, after seventeen years of stock in San Jose, California, had the first hit of his lifetime: as star, co-author, and part owner of his own play, *Lightnin'*. As the tipsy hotel keeper "Lightnin' Bill" Jones, whose Calivada Hotel on the California–Nevada state line proved a magnet for Reno divorcées, living six months on the Nevada side while feigning Californian residence, Bacon had delighted New Yorkers for more than a year. (His became the first play to notch up 1,291 Broadway performances.) Now, sorely perturbed, Bacon consulted with his wife, Jennie: "Mother, where do we stand?"

Jennie Bacon was never in doubt. "Frank, we've cooked over a gas-jet before now, and if we have to, we can do it again," she said.

Next day, banner headlines proclaimed LIGHTNIN' HAS STRUCK; that night the Gaiety and eleven other New York theatres were dark.

Ironically, the managers were caught totally unawares. Long lines seeking refunds formed at the box offices along the Great White Way; the ticket brokers were flooded out. Each day saw evidence of growing solidarity. Almost thirty companies in rehearsal for members of the Producing Manager's Association were called out to report to strike headquarters. Soon the ranks of the dissidents were swelled by such leading lights as John Drew, the Barrymores (Ethel, Lionel, and the up-and-coming John), along with Laurette Taylor, the comedienne Marie Dressler, and the red-nosed comic W. C. Fields. Enrolling for the first time as Equity members for modest dues of five dollars were Alfred Lunt and Lynn Fontanne.

Over the weeks, New York took the strikers to its heart. Along West 45th Street, the retail merchants took a joint decision: from now on 10 percent of their gross receipts were donated to the Equity Strike Fund. Frank Case, proprietor of the Algonquin Hotel on West 44th Street, long the profession's home-away-from-home, offered Room 2111 free of charge to Equity's publicity bureau and chipped in with free meals and a thousand-dollar check. Sam Gerson's cigar store carried the sign, STRIKING ACTORS GET YOUR CIGARETTES HERE, AND PAY WHEN YOU WIN. In the side streets off Broadway, landladies were turning a notably blind eye to overdue room rents.

On August 14, Charles C. Shay of the International Alliance of Theatrical Stage Employees (IATSE) decided that from now on the scenery could shift for itself: "You are not going to lose, but if you do go down to defeat you will have the stagehands with you." On this same day, Thomas Gamble pledged the backing of every pit orchestra: "And when the Musicians join in, there'll be a grand symphony."

There were notable dissentients. Foremost among them was George M. Cohan, actor, dramatist, and manager, who promptly resigned from the Lambs' Club, railing, "If Equity wins I'll quit the theatre business and run an elevator." As the guiding spirit behind the rival Actors' Fidelity League—"The Fidos"—virtually a PMA creation, Cohan defied the strike call to the end, stepping into the lead of *The Royal Vagabond* at the Cohan-Harris Theatre, standing his chorus eighty-five strong, not then Equity members, free dinners at the Knickerbocker Hotel. Among 1,200 players who rallied to "The Fidos" was a heartsick Helen Hayes, torn between loyalty to the profession and the debt she owed to her longtime manager, George C. Tyler.

All his life a bitter opponent of Equity, Tyler stopped at nothing to defeat them. On August 20, when the strike hit Chicago, America's second theatrical city, the one show still playing at the theatre attached to the Blackstone Hotel was Tyler's *On The Hiring Line*. Threatened with an electricians' blackout, Tyler set workmen tunneling forty feet into the basement to tap the city's Edison main cable. To transport the scenery from the New York Central yards, a squad of strikebreakers, with one rented truck, rammed the steel gates—making eight trips, engaging eight times in pitched and bloody battles with Equity loyalists.

Not all were so ruthless. When Al Woods, an affable, walleyed manager who addressed everyone regardless of sex as "Sweetheart," spotted a detachment of shivering Equity girls picketing his Eltinge Theatre in a rainstorm, he was appalled. "Hello, kids," he greeted them. "Where's your galoshes? You'll catch cold."

Fifteen minutes later an Eltinge employee was sedulously doling out overshoes.

In New York, twenty-five theatres were now dark; on September 1, Labor Day, the strike closed six Boston theatres. Then on Friday, September 5, the stagehands and musicians struck a decisive blow for Equity. Almost one thousand letters and telegrams winged across the United States, calling out the working crews of the powerful Shubert empire and closing down one hundred of their theatres. Now the losses were piling up in a way that hard-nosed theatre moguls

84

found wholly unpalatable. It was time to sue for peace.

Much earlier, the Society of American Dramatists, whose members included P. G. Wodehouse, Guy Bolton, and Augustus Thomas, had tendered their services as mediators. Now, on behalf of the managers, the genial John Golden wired Thomas, "For God's sake get in this, and help us to back-pedal."

Thomas was more than ready. At 8:00 P.M. on September 6, with Thomas in the chair, an Equity deputation headed by Frank Gillmore met up with the PMA spokesmen in the library of the St. Regis Hotel on Fifth Avenue. The six-year fight to win minimum standards—the greatest struggle in the history of legitimate theatre—was over.

It had been a long haul, at that. It had lasted for thirty days, spread to eight cities, and closed thirty-seven plays. It had stopped sixteen other shows from ever opening. All told, in round figures, it had cost those concerned $3 million.

Even so, it had been a signal victory. When Equity first entered the battle, it boasted only 2,700 members. It left the fray 14,000 strong. Its treasury, on August 6, had held a niggardly $13,500. Now, their credit balance in the Harriman National Bank stood at $120,000.

It was the kind of happy ending that always left an audience feeling good.

As the reverberations of the Actors' Strike died away, all of them were awaiting the Big Moment—that looked-for morning, which would surely come sooner rather than later, when the critics' first-night notices proclaimed that a star was born. That was the way it had happened, overnight, to Ethel Barrymore, playing in *Captain Jinks of the Horse Marines* at the Garrick on West 35th Street; approaching the stage door, she had glanced up, and there, for all to see, was her name in dazzling lights: ETHEL BARRYMORE.

Next day, as she stammered out her thanks to Charles Frohman, he waved a pudgy hand at the people passing in the street. "I didn't do it," was the way he put it. "*They* did it."

It was a moment that almost eluded Alfred Lunt. All through 1918 he had been playing George Tewkesbury Reynolds III, an Eastern fop, in Booth Tarkington's *The Country Cousin*, and the innate perfectionism that had always been part of him impressed Tarkington profoundly. Before the play opened in Chicago, Alfred had ordered a set of engraved visiting cards for George Tewkesbury Reynolds

III. At Marshall Field's department store he bought four suits such as befitted a dandy. Since Reynolds, on one occasion, lit a cigarette, Alfred shopped for a gold Cartier case, engraved G.T.R. III.

When a friend, shocked by this prodigality, remonstrated, "You could go into any five-and-dime store and buy a tin cigarette case, and who'd know the difference?" Alfred had the answer pat. "*I* would."

Such devotion to detail, Tarkington reasoned, deserved a specially tailored play, and in due time that play emerged: *Clarence*, the story of the gangling Clarence Smith, a war veteran seeking work, who was hired by an Englewood, New Jersey, householder ostensibly as a handyman but in reality as an "Admirable Crichton" to bring his adolescent children into line. Since Clarence, in civil life, had been a coleopterist who played the saxophone to beetles to test their auditory powers, the role was rich in comic scope—as was that of the teenage daughter, Cora Wheeler, "a piquant little beauty," written for Helen Hayes. "I've thought so hard about her that I've dimmed and frayed the image," Tarkington wrote to George C. Tyler. "Could you send me right away a good picture of her?"

Absorbed in the complexities of his part—the shambling gait, the falsetto crack in the voice—Alfred was far from suspecting that Helen had developed an adolescent crush on him. The Actors' Strike was looming, *Clarence* might never open, and in any case Alfred was no longer heart-whole. During a rehearsal at the New Amsterdam Theatre, Lynn Fontanne, another Tyler contract artist, had asked to be introduced to him, impressed by the "extraordinary resonance and range" of his voice. Alfred, poised on the iron staircase backstage, stepped nervously forward and tumbled headlong.

"Well," remarked the dramatist George S. Kaufman, "he certainly fell for her," and, as usual, Kaufman was right on target.

Clarence was a near-run thing, even so. On the morning of Saturday, September 6, with the strike settled, the cast reassembled—with opening night just two weeks away. Strangely, for such a flimsy play, this would prove a historic night in the theatre; in this era, when players took curtain calls following each act, the audience at the Hudson Theatre greeted the Act I curtain fall with roars of "Lunt, Lunt, Lunt!," clamoring for a curtain speech. Formerly regarded as an eccentric bag of bones, Alfred was now hailed, after one performance, as a comic virtuoso. At the evening's end he was called before the curtain twenty-five times. To Catherine Hayes Brown, it was "as wildly exciting as Armistice Day," and the comparison was apt. To vent their enthusiasm the ecstatic first-nighters not only stood on their seats but shredded their programs into confetti.

There were fewer plaudits for Helen, and she was the first to know why. "I wasn't equipped for big roles," she confessed later. "I knew that I was licked unless I did something about learning it." She was, noticed Clarence Derwent, palpably lacking in confidence; in the days when Equity permitted a seven-day probationary period, Helen would murmur gratefully as the week slid by, "I'm still with you." Her shortcomings were amply confirmed by the actress Ruth Chatterton. "You have talent," she admitted to Helen, after another disastrous first night, "but not *that* much technique." Thereafter a dramatic coach, Frances Robinson Duff, dogged Helen's every rehearsal, working to eliminate her "cute-little-girl" tricks, such as never sitting, always kneeling on a chair. But it was fully three years before Helen was cured of what one critic dubbed her "fallen archness."

Lynn's chance, by contrast, was not long in coming. Cast as another Smith, this time Dulcinea, a featherbrained Westchester County bride of three months in George S. Kaufman's and Marc Connelly's *Dulcy,* Lynn portrayed a well-meaning meddler in her husband's business affairs who comes close to bringing about disaster. "One thing that Dulcy never learned was the difference between a surprise and a shock," observed her brother, Bill. "Somebody tell me—which is higher—a heart or a spade?" Dulcy burbled, as the company settled to a game of bridge, and her dialogue was a Niagara of cliches: "Every cloud has a silver lining," and "You know, sometimes I think I would lose my head if it wasn't fastened on."

Given a player less skilled, Dulcy might have emerged as a hundred-carat suburban bore, but Lynn's hint of gentle raillery steered the play expertly to its climax. As much of a perfectionist as Alfred, she had responded to Tyler's early taunt of "pigeon toes" by learning twelve different ways in which to stand; now, as the gauche Dulcy, she turned in her toes to foster the illusion of bandy legs.

Keeping Alfred company on this fraught first night at the Frazee Theatre in August 1921, "like anxious fathers expecting twins," was a disconsolate Noël Coward, newly arrived from England with fifteen pounds (then seventy-five dollars) and a suitcase full of un-

87

wanted playscripts. With *Dulcy* assured of a respectable run (246 performances), Noël, with a clear conscience, could both congratulate Lynn warmly and tap her for a twenty-dollar loan.

This was a period in his life when he and he alone recognized the scintillating talent vested in Noël Coward. One year earlier, Noël had dashed off his first play, the amiable lightweight comedy *I'll Leave It To You*, concerning a conniving old uncle whose riches turn out to be a myth, and the American Gilbert Miller, who was fast succeeding Frohman as *the* transatlantic entrepreneur, staged a tryout at the Gaiety in Manchester. But Miller's wife, Kitty, and Hawtrey's wife, Madeleine, went to see the play and were, Noël recalled, "sadly disillusioning."

"They both stood there, shaking their heads slowly and tenderly, like china mandarins," Noël was to recall. "They were both filled and brimming over with sympathy, as though they had just been present at the greatest theatrical catastrophe of modern times."

It was thus a foregone conclusion that Miller would drop his option, and though Mary Moore (Lady Wyndham) later presented it at the New (now in Albery), the play fizzled out after five weeks.

In New York, all that autumn, Belasco, Al Woods, Abe Erlanger, and all their colleagues would in turn shake their heads, so sadly, but so definitely, "like china mandarins."

Yet for Noël, Lynn, and Alfred, this was the beginning of a lifelong friendship. Alfred and his bride-to-be were then resident at 130 West 70th Street, a theatrical boardinghouse whose landlady was Dr. Rounds. In these shabby but congenial rooms, all three allowed themselves to dream their impossible dreams. Over modest meals of delicatessen potato salad and dill pickles, they established their priorities. First Lynn and Alfred must get married. After that they must establish themselves as public idols. They would then act exclusively together. All this accomplished, Noël would write plays for them, not forgetting plum roles for himself.

But in the immediate future the only dream to be realized was on May 26, 1922, when Lynn and Alfred were married in New York's Municipal Building. It was a decision taken so suddenly, on a bench in Central Park, that Alfred, who had forgotten his wallet, had to borrow two dollars for the license fee from two witnesses he had pounced on in the corridor.

A frequent visitor to their second-floor four-room apartment at 969 Lexington Avenue was, of course, Noël—emaciated, often lacking the price of a dinner, and as woebegone as a stray cat waiting to be fed.

But Noël's Big Moment was not far off. His humor—cynical, bantering, brittle—chimed with the mood of the day. ("Coward took the fat off English comic dialogue," was the retrospective verdict of the British critic Kenneth Tynan. "He was the Turkish bath in which it slimmed.") The currency of postwar youth, on both sides of the Atlantic, was still the pursuit of pleasure, a time of mad spur-of-the-moment parties, stunts, and hoaxes, of dancing through the nights and down the days. This was the new Jazz Age of the novelist F. Scott Fitzgerald, who personified that world in the United States as did David, Prince of Wales, in England. It was the bright brash age of the nightclub and the Charleston, an age of bad manners and fashionably glib psychoanalysts, symbolized by the new "flappers," as cynical young women were called, equally at home in Palm Beach or on the French Riviera, liberal with lipstick and powder, their Eton-cropped hair fitting snugly under their cloche hats.

"There's a younger generation, knock-knock-knocking at the door," proclaimed a lyric in one Coward revue, and soon after Armistice Day that knocking became strident enough to reach the back of every London and Broadway gallery. For this younger generation was most decidedly in revolt, and as a direct consequence of that cataclysmic war; disillusioned with life, they were equally keyed up to an unnatural pitch by wartime tensions. In a blaze of unconventionality they now challenged every law that had guided their lives in the past.

Plays like Rachel Crothers's *Nice People* abounded, one of the first sympathetic studies of spendthrift young rebels—among them Kit Cornell—defying "old-fashioned" parents. Her *Mary the Third* (1923) showed Mary totally rejecting the convention of a husband as provider; even separation would be better than financial dependence. "I shall live with a man because I love him and only as long as I love him," she declared. "Anything else gives the man a horrible advantage."

Even before World War I, the determination to shock had never been far from the surface—usually with a curtain line that left the audience gasping. One of the earliest was Eugene Walter's *The Easiest Way* (1909), in which the heroine, Laura Murdock, renounces both her wealthy protector and a journalist who loves her, telling her

89

colored maid, "Dress up my body and paint up my face. It's all that they've left of me." When Annie, the maid, asks, "You goin' out, Miss Laura?" Laura replies, "Yes, I'm going to Rector's to make a hit and to hell with the rest!" That always brought them to their feet.

A dramatist in this mold was Edward Sheldon, who followed his *Salvation Nell*, the story of a prostitute who became a Salvation Army lassie, with *The Nigger*, the drama of a leading Southerner who discovered he had Negro blood. By degrees the "shock curtain" became a must. In Cosmo Hamilton's *Scandal* (1918), in which Noël was briefly glimpsed as Sir Walter Raleigh at a fancy dress party, the hero repulses the spoiled minx who has played fast and loose with him: "If you and I were the only living people on a desert island . . . I'd build you a hut at the farthest end of it and treat you as a man." In Somerset Maugham's *The Unknown* (1920), when the matriarch who had lost two sons in war challenged the vicar with, "And who is going to forgive God?" the audience applauded wildly.

Thus, to violate the prewar code, to achieve self-realization—often equated with self-pity—became a dramatic end in itself.

"The whole thing's breaking up," declared John, the hero of Miles Malleson's *The Fanatics* (1927). "The Church is losing its influence . . . what they mean by purifying society is simply forcing us back under the old rules." When his sister, Gwen, opted for a "trial marriage" with birth control, their father burst out against the "insane wickedness that I never thought I should find in a child of mine . . . trampling on everything we hold sacred." Such plays, commented George Jean Nathan, left "the net impression that everyone has been or is going to be a mother but the leading man."

Bruised youthful susceptibilities were suddenly all the rage. John Van Druten's *Young Woodley* (a school prefect falls in love with his housemaster's wife) was followed by the same author's *Diversion* (a physician gives his son poison to save him from the hangman after he has murdered his mistress). In Ernest Vajda's *Fata Morgana*—a triumphant transatlantic hit—a woman of the world seduces an eighteen-year-old student and shatters his faith in womanhood by returning to her rich husband. Rodney Ackland's *Improper People* was seen only in a club production; two star-crossed young lovers opting for suicide proved anathema to a Lord Chamberlain who had conceivably never seen *Romeo and Juliet*.

In these new "nervy" plays, noted the dramatist St. John Ervine, the commonest stage direction was "He speaks with impatience" or "with forced calmness." Thus the great roles that had rocketed an Irving or a Tree to overnight stardom were increasingly hard to find. Dialogue had become staccato. The throwaway manner was *de rigueur*. Cedric Hardwicke, who did not return to the jungle from the Western Front until 1921, found to his astonishment that "the resounding voices and broad gestures of my youth were frowned upon now. Voices were dwindling to the conversational tones of front-parlour gossip. Gestures were diminishing to the flick of ash from a cigarette, or the adjustment of shirt cuffs under a jacket."

The acknowledged master of this technique was Gerald du Maurier, knighted in 1923, a man who disliked acting and despised the theatre as intensely as Sir Johnston Forbes-Robertson. A nonacting actor, who strolled effortlessly through such roles as Raffles, the cracksman, Arsène Lupin (another cracksman), and Bulldog Drummond, du Maurier played safe for all of his sixty-one years; "Don't force it" was his cardinal principle. This passion for understatement was the motive force of his life. "Never wear a suit on stage that hasn't been at least once to the dry cleaners" was the mysterious counsel he offered the great boulevardier Sacha Guitry. Despite a lifetime of love affairs—with Ethel Barrymore and Mrs. Patrick Campbell, among others—his playing was notably devoid of passion. "Must you kiss her as though you were having steak and onions for lunch?" he rebuked one actor. "Can't you say 'I love you, damn you,' yawn, light a cigarette and walk away?"

Over two decades, many followed his example to the letter; the "matinée idols" of the twenties, for the most part, were still the idols of the thirties. One such was Owen Nares *(Peter Ibbetson, Romance)*, who devoted a whole career to dispensing blasé charm; the Nares trick of attention getting was to strike up a voluble conversation in the wings at the moment of entry, ensuring a volume of applause. When Nares was cast in *The Last Chapter* as a writer with a harem of female admirers, the producer, Reginald Denham, had hopes of shaping a performance in depth, until Nares's wife, Marie, cut in, "Owen, I've been thinking. The only way for you to play this part is to play *yourself*."

Another actor who played himself for more than fifty years was Seymour Hicks, an adroit farceur *(Vintage Wine, The Man in Dress Clothes)* who was knighted in 1935. He, too, was skilled at milking applause, in plays of his own adaptation; most often his first entry

91

was made dead center at the top of a flight of stairs, with the switch-board primed to flash on extra brackets and battens not before used. Then Hicks would stand stock-still, smiling seraphically, until the ovation died away.

Since Broadway was deficient in nurturing what Max Beerbohm once called "overtailored mimes with impeccable trouserings," British actors like Geoffrey Kerr, the blond Leslie Howard with his sad, wry smile, and A. E. Matthews ("Matty"), ambling through his roles like an amnesiac retriever who had mislaid a bone, never wanted for work in New York.

Broadway was, in fact, better supplied with *soignée* leading ladies: the tall, blond Ina Claire, dressed with classic simplicity by Chanel; the comedienne Ilka Chase; and the stately Ethel Barrymore, admirably comporting herself in Society drawing-room scenes because she was *persona grata* in so many of them. Britain's Fay Compton, wistful and elfin, and the regally handsome Gladys Cooper came later to the Broadway scene.

In London, the distaff side was ruled, with all the arrogance of a czarina, by Marie Tempest, whose cup-and-saucer comedies took the theatre back fifty years to the age of the Bancrofts. There the resemblance ended; where the Bancrofts were zealous for their players' welfare, Miss Tempest sought mainly to cow them. "She was an absolute tartar," recalls Margaret Harris, who oversaw the décor for one Tempest play. "All the actresses had to line up in the wings long before their entrances, and stand on white sheets to keep their dresses from creasing." "As delicate and elegant as a French clock," in one actor's recollection, "ticking away on some drawing room mantelpiece," she insisted that if the company rehearsed at night the males in the cast wore dinner jackets. She was respected, but never liked, in the theatre; when a provincial manager redecorated her dressing room with chintz curtains and a chintz-frilled dressing table, Miss Tempest told him brusquely, "I consider my dressing room a work place. Kindly take all this nonsense away."

Yet given the drawing power of such Tempest vehicles as *The Cat's Cradle* and *The First Mrs. Fraser*, a role in her company was always rated as a sound investment. As the comedian Leslie Henson told the young Harold French, "You'll spend every night acting with your back to the audience, but at least you'll run a year."

In a class all her own, as notorious in London as she was on Broadway, was Tallulah Brockman Bankhead. Her first London appearance—with du Maurier in a melodrama called *The Dancers* in 1923—brought forth a first-night roar of approval that lasted for eight years. It also prompted thirty-hour queues for any Tallulah show. On opening nights, the first glimpse of her petite (five-foot-three-inch) figure and her tossing waves of honey-colored hair prompted demonstrations from the gallery girls unheard since Lewis Waller's day. She was the first of the Queen Bees, and her low, throaty voice—one critic likened it to "a man pulling his foot out of a bucket of yoghurt"—provoked a perfect barrage of screams and squeals, what Leslie Howard termed "a Tallulahbaloo."

A congressman's daughter from Jasper, Alabama, named after a waterfall in the highlands of Georgia, Tallulah was the defiant younger generation incarnate. She drank immoderately, she sniffed cocaine, she smoked four packs of Craven A cigarettes a day. She was, she claimed, "as pure as the driven slush," and was thus a magnet at any party; as Mrs. Pat Campbell explained, "She's always skating on thin ice and they want to be there when it cracks." Everybody, from her current lover to her adoring fans, was "dahling" to save time, for Tallulah had her own way, even with time; she saved time in London by hiring a taxi to pilot her green Bentley to the right address.

Yet, despite her inconsequence, her magnetism saved play after play. One of the worst was *The Creaking Chair*, with Tallulah as the French wife of a crippled archaeologist, who had wedded her in Port Said to save her from white slavers. Yet the Duke of Kent saw this incredible farrago (whose Egyptian "heavy" proclaimed at the climax, "My blood is as old as the desert sand and burns as hot") fully thirty-six times. Only Tallulah redeemed Michael Arlen's *The Green Hat*, with another rebel-heroine, Iris Fenwick, whose body was, in her own words, "a house of men." Tallulah alone sustained *Scotch Mist*, whose hero, at the final curtain, promised her, "I can teach you what it means when the sun shines, when the wind blows out of heaven, calling your name; when God laughs, just because you smile."

Yet none of the old guard were writing vehicles for Tallulah—or indeed for du Maurier, Nares, or Marie Tempest. In the bar of the Garrick Club, Somerset Maugham had heard two bitterly disappointed playwrights pronounce an identical sentence: "They don't want me any more." The first was Pinero, and his tones were grim and sardonic. The second was Henry Arthur Jones, his voice baffled

93

and exasperated. The twenties would see one new Pinero play, *The Enchanted Cottage*, a vain attempt to cash in on Barrie's fantasy world, and one Jones revival, *The Liars*, with Sybil Thorndike.

One scene from a Coward revue alone demonstrated why. It pictured the contrast between a Victorian and a neo-Georgian wedding night. In the first, the young bride, innocent of the facts of life, howled wanly for her mama. In the second, the couple bounced on the bedsprings, pronouncing them satisfactory for their purpose; it was plain that the Woman with a Past had given place to the Woman with a very lively Present.

The playwrights who mirrored the new mood of disillusion were two young Americans, Philip Barry and Samuel Nathan (S.N.) Behrman, and two Britons old enough to have served in World War I, Somerset Maugham and Frederick Lonsdale.

Barry, a wealthy, cosmopolitan sophisticate, whose characters took no thought of the financial morrow, despised big business as vulgar and demeaning; no one in a Barry play stood in awe of anyone or anything. One of his earliest, *The Youngest*, showed the youngest son tearing up his elder brother's pompous Fourth of July speech—a rebellion against the convention of family oppression. In *Holiday*, his most successful play of the twenties, Johnny Case, a rising but footloose young businessman, ditches his stuffy fiancée to roam Europe, with her liberty-loving young sister in hot pursuit.

Behrman, the son of an insolvent grocer from Worcester, Massachussetts, knew poverty in his youth, but his first play, *The Second Man*, polished and epigrammatic, was an instant success. Behrman was consistently literate; "She has all the picture-book illusions of a *Saturday Evening Post* heroine" was the verdict on one mixed-up character, "but she's picked up the vocabulary of the intelligentsia." Thereafter Behrman concentrated on mirroring only the best society; in plays like *Biography*, *Rain from Heaven*, and *End of Summer*, first names were often family names—Kendall Frayne, Clark Storey—and the talk was all of boxes at the opera, well-trained servants, and well-chilled champagne. Totally identifying with the leisured and sophisticated, wryly surveying a world they had never made, Behrman, one man thought, had never quite recovered from exposure to his first duchess.

William Somerset Maugham was an old hand at the Society game; as far back as 1908, Maugham had had four West End successes running simultaneously, to a total weekly audience of thirty-five thousand. By 1919 they had netted him £186,000. Comedies like *Our Betters* and *The Constant Wife* were saturated with irony—the Scottish dramatist, James Bridie, derided them as "pee:iod plays"— yet the Society whom Maugham satirized had long sin e embraced him. "His remarks," commented the aesthete Harold A ton, "wore monocles," but though Maugham at times contrived to force a twisted smile, laughter never reached his eyes. Behrman, who visited him at his Villa Mauresque on the French Riviera when adapting a Maugham short story for the stage, judged him "the most miserable man in the world . . . embalmed in hatred."

Frederick Lonsdale, whose real name was Lionel Frederick Leonard, hated only one thing in life: dullness. "A dull dog," noted his daughter, Frances Donaldson, "was the greatest condemnation he could make of any man." Certainly Lonsdale's characters were never dull to the audiences who flocked to *The Last of Mrs. Cheyney* (Ina Claire in New York, Gladys Cooper with du Maurier in London), *On Approval, Aren't We All?* and *Spring Cleaning,* where the hero, played by A. E. Matthews, banished his wife's worthless friends by bringing a prostitute home to her dinner party. For in Lonsdale's dream world, his dukes, who employed the upper-class weapon of ridicule with searing effect, might be essentially useless, but they were always clever, elegant, and witty—never worthy but dull.

One long-forgotten piece, *The Early Worm,* somehow summed up the whole Lonsdale ethos: the hero was a duke, an intriguer, without a shred of moral conscience, the heroine an heiress with fifty thousand pounds a year. "You're not," the lady inquires suspiciously at the third act finale, "marrying me for my money?"

"No," the duke reassures her warmly, "but I'm awfully glad you've got it."

As always, the notable exception to this assembly-line production of highly varnished plays of good breeding and bad manners was George Bernard Shaw. The days were long past when Shaw's works, scribbled in penny notebooks on the open tops of omnibuses, delighted only the eclectic audiences at the Royal Court. Now, in his comfortable apartment at 10 Adelphi Terrace, or at his country retreat, Ayot St. Lawrence in Hertfordshire, he had become the guru of the age, the dramatist who created roles that actors would give their eyeteeth to play. He was still, as he liked to put it, "knocking down their sandcastles so as to make them build stone ones," but the difference now was that the public loved it.

The year 1920 saw the New York production of his own favorite, *Heartbreak House*, "a fantasia in the Russian manner" where every character from the old seadog Captain Shotover to the industrialist "Boss" Mangan represented some flaw in English society that had led to World War I. Four years later, galleryites in St. Martin's Lane, London, began queueing for the first night of *St. Joan*, with Sybil Thorndike—the play was based upon a theme suggested by Shaw's wife, Charlotte—at 5:00 A.M. To mark their appreciation, the management distributed 150 free cups of tea.

Scribbling in longhand on blocks of green-tinted water-lined paper, Shaw averaged a steady 1,500 words each morning. A lifelong vegetarian, nourished principally by lentil soup, Welsh rarebits, and curried eggs, he kept up a grueling pace; during one revival of *You Never Can Tell*, Shaw, clad in a black, homespun suit woven from his own flock of sheep, began rehearsals at 11:00 A.M., still, in the old Pinero style, acting every part, producing every passage. Toward 1:45, someone dropped the hint as to lunch. Shaw apologized. "Certainly, we'll go now," he said, "and we'll be back at a quarter past two sharp."

As a producer, Shaw showed infinite consideration. When praise was due, he gave it unstintingly; after the first rehearsal of *St. Joan* he approached Ernest Thesiger, who played the effete Dauphin, and announced solemnly, "There is one thing I want you to do about this part." Anything, Thesiger assured him. "Go home to bed and stay there until the first night," Shaw advised. "You already know as much about the part as I do."

The producer, Shaw counseled one beginner at Dublin's Abbey Theatre, must settle all stage business at the first rehearsal—who sat where, how the furniture was positioned, thus achieving "a command of the production that nothing would shake afterwards." At this juncture, the producer should be with the company onstage. Once they dispensed with scripts, he should retire to the auditorium with a large notebook and never interrupt the scene. No actor should be told more than two or three important things at any one rehearsal. Never repeat a scene time and again—"if it goes wrong it will go wronger with every repetition on the same day." And cues, Shaw stressed, should be picked up "as smartly as a ball is fielded in cricket."

"Motivation" actors received shorter shrift. After the first rehearsal of one *Candida* revival, the actor playing Eugene Marchbanks, the impassioned young poet, buttonholed Shaw with an air of mystery. "The action of your play is set in East London in 1895," he began, "so what is in my character's mind when I say this?" quoting a line of dialogue.

Shaw remained gravely courteous, but his bright blue twinkling eyes gave him away. "It is a long time since I wrote those words and I can't even remember what was in *my* mind," he confessed, "but as far as I remember I wanted to make people laugh."

It was in 1914 that Shaw's fifteen-year-old love-hate relationship with Mrs. Patrick Campbell—which dragged on in correspondence until 1939—reached a new peak of intensity at His Majesty's Theatre with the first production of *Pygmalion*, known to later generations as the nucleus of the blockbusting musical *My Fair Lady*.

Shaw had conceived the story of how the phonetics professor, Henry Higgins, molded the flower girl Eliza Doolittle into the semblance of a duchess seventeen years earlier as a vehicle for Johnston Forbes-Robertson and the young Mrs. Pat. The problem was complicated by Shaw's attitude to sex, which was essentially skittish, hiding a very real terror of his own emotions. His pseudoromantic letters to "Beatricissma" began as a salesman's ploy to induce her to play his "pretty slut." By 1913, Shaw had even descended to baby talk:

> *Who made her smile?*
> *Dis very chile*
> *With my wink and my wile*
> I *made her smile.*

To simulate submission was a fatal tactic with the willful Mrs. Pat, who was already a byword with the West End managers. Hers was a record, thought the dramatist, W. Graham Robertson, of "talent thrown away, wasted time, lost opportunities." In New York, where she played Herman Sudermann's *Magda* for George C. Tyler at the Republic Theatre, forty truckloads of tanbark had to be dumped on West 42nd Street to cushion her nerves against the clangor of the streetcars. If a bad mood seized her, she would turn her back on the audience and pull faces at her fellow players; in one performance as Ophelia she changed from a dark wig to a fair wig halfway through. When George Alexander, during the run of *The Masqueraders*, sent a message stipulating, "Mr. Alexander's compliments and will you please not laugh at him on the stage?" she replied, "My compliments to Mr. Alexander, and please tell him I never laugh at him until I get home."

Thus, despite astounding advance bookings of almost four thousand pounds, "Joey the Clown," as Mrs. Pat nicknamed Shaw, was in for a stormy rehearsal period.

Tree, cast as Higgins, often drifted offstage in midscene, missed his cues, or forgot his lines. Frequently Mrs. Pat refused to continue rehearsing until Shaw left the theatre; at other times she thumbed her nose at him, like the guttersnipe she was portraying. "That there Patrick Campbell," a stagehand confided in Philip Merivale, playing Colonel Pickering, " 'e was a lucky man!" Merivale agreed; even at forty-nine, thirty years too old for Eliza, Mrs. Pat was still a handsome woman. "I don't mean that," the stagehand retorted, " 'e got 'isself killed in the Boer War!"

Exasperated by Mrs. Pat's constant shifting of the furniture to display herself to better advantage, Shaw and the stage carpenter, before the dress rehearsal, stole into the theatre and nailed down everything lighter than the grand piano. Enraged, Mrs. Pat challenged him from the footlights, "Some day, Joey, you'll eat a pork chop—and then God help all women!"

On the first night, to Shaw's dismay, Eliza's classic reply to young Freddie's "Are you walking across the park, Miss Doolittle?"—"Walk! Not bloody likely"—saw the house laugh with such abandon that it was seventy-five seconds before the play could continue. To Shaw's fury, he discovered that although Eliza, in the finale, walks out on Higgins, offended by his cavalier treatment, Tree, once more unable to leave well alone, had contrived to toss a bouquet at her before curtain fall, a coy hint of wedding bells to come.

"My ending makes money," Tree protested. "You ought to be grateful." "Your ending is damnable," Shaw retorted, in a passion over the one play where "command of the production" had quite eluded him. "You ought to be shot."

It was Shaw, quite fortuitously, who helped to bolster the ever-recarious morale of Katharine Cornell. That was in December 1924, after Kit's first performance in *Candida* brought her photograph to the always-susceptible Shaw's attention. Something "blonde and expansive" about her name, Shaw wrote, had led him to imagine "an ideal suburban British Candida," the parson's wife who despite the ardors of a youthful suitor chooses to remain with the man who needs her most—her husband. "Fancy my feelings," wrote the enraptured Shaw, "on seeing the photograph of a gorgeous dark lady from the cradle of the human race . . . wherever that is . . . Ceylon . . . Sumatra . . . Hilo . . . or the southernmost corner of the Garden of Eden."

"If you look like that it doesn't matter a rap whether you can act or not," Shaw concluded. "Can you?"

On that score, both London and New York critics were fully in agreement: Kit *could* act. Londoners were to see her only once: as Jo in *Little Women*, the role in which Jessie Bonstelle had envisaged her all those years ago, at a special series of matinees over three months from November 1919. That triumph behind her, Kit returned once more to Detroit and Jessie Bonstelle's stock company. Almost Miss Bonstelle's first piece of news was, "I've engaged a young director named McClintic for this summer."

At long last their paths had converged—and for Guthrie, a staunch believer in fate, it was a vindication of all his premonitions. Much earlier, after glimpsing Kit in the casting office of William A. Brady, he had told the actress Olive Wyndham, "You know, it's a strange thing to say but today I saw the girl I'm going to marry."

Guthrie, though, had overlooked one trifling detail; he was already married, although separated. This was a state of affairs that took much legal wire-pulling and nominal residences across state lines to disentangle, but in the meantime, like Lynn and Alfred in New York, the two daydreamed on benches in Grand Circus Park, planning a joint future in the theatre. It was a hectic courtship, sandwiched in between the grind of rehearsals, against the tense and exciting backdrop of Detroit in the bootleg era: boats without lights, sliding across the dark water, and narrow alleys full of whispering shadows.

Kit, perhaps, only half-suspected it, but her link-up with Guthrie McClintic was to prove the making of her. Back in 1918, when she had tried out for a play starring Grace George—Mrs. William A. Brady—Miss George had been critical of her reading of the role. Kit's prompt reaction was to hand her script back to the stage man-

99

ager and flee weeping from the theatre. "There, you see," was Grace George's reaction. "She hasn't the right stuff in her."

Three years later Kit, like Helen Hayes, was still dogged by the fear that the big roles were not for her; she was content to play any part she could get. "No ambition" was the terse verdict of the producing manager, Winthrop Ames. Guthrie, by contrast, had ambition enough for both; his link with Ames was due solely to a blistering letter he had written to the courteous, remote producer, "like a Velasquez Cardinal with El Greco hands," when an underling banished him from the outer office. "I demand the right to be seen by you and not tossed into the discard because of an unfavourable report," Guthrie fumed; not long after that, he took over the underling's job.

Both, when the summer season of 1920 ended, drifted back to New York, Kit to climb the stairs of the casting agents, Guthrie to plow through scripts on Ames's behalf. On warm Sundays, they always gravitated to Mamaroneck in New York State for picnics and a swim in the Sound. On these occasions—for such was the custom in the jungle—they relaxed by reading playscripts.

Strangely, neither could ever remember the precise Sunday when Guthrie read aloud the script that changed their lives forever: *A Bill of Divorcement*, by Clemence Dane, the pen name of the British dramatist, Winifred Ashton. This story of a young girl, Sydney Fairfield, who finds that her supposedly shell-shocked father, Hilary, is a victim of inherited insanity and renounces her marriage to remain as his companion, rather than pass on the sickness, moved them both profoundly.

"I could play that girl," the "unambitious" Kit said thoughtfully, astonishing even herself.

By a strange coincidence, the Broadway rights were owned by a Scot, Allan Pollock, a onetime Broadway actor striving to make a comeback in the role of Hilary after crippling war wounds. Hearing of his struggle, a group of friends from the Players' Club had snapped up the rights and donated them as a "get-well" present. When two old ladies from Pollock's hometown, seeing the London production, at once suggested "the girl who played Jo in *Little Women*," Pollock cabled Charles Dillingham, the producing manager: "Get Katharine Cornell."

Thus 1921 was a milestone year for Kit. On September 8, one year to the day after Guthrie proposed to her on the roof of New

York's Pennsylvania Hotel, they were married at Coburg, Ontario. Almost at once she plunged into rehearsals—concentrating on the subtle hand gestures to suggest instability, the flash of terror in her dark eyes when she first learned of the family taint.

Unhappily, the play's director, Britain's Basil Dean, disliked her from the first. One of a new breed of producer, born out of an economic climate where there was no margin between "smashes" and "flops," Dean was a closet sadist, whose "frightening toothy smile," as the Canadian Raymond Massey put it, was dreaded by his casts. A world away from the courteous guidance of Shaw, Dean laid down every inflection, every tone, every mood. One leading man was so cruelly flayed by his tongue that he fainted on the stage; with only a cursory glance, Dean slipped on his jacket and announced, "I think we will break for lunch." Often he would start a twelve-hour dress rehearsal at midnight. No detail was ever too trivial for Dean; during rehearsals for Maugham's *East of Suez* he and the actor Henry Kendall indulged in a thirty-minute shouting match over the footlights about how to tie a shoelace, prompting Maugham, in the stalls, to chuckle balefully, "I see Basil is burning the Kendall at both ends!"

This was the producer who now subjected Kit to days of continuous terror, convinced that she would lose the part. "*Must* you walk like Henry Irving?" he snapped at her during every rehearsal. Only Guthrie's solicitude and supportiveness in their first home, a three-story apartment at 23 Beekman Place, on the East River, saw her through to the tryout in Philadelphia.

Even so, the play's success trembled in the balance. The first night—October 10, 1921, at the George M. Cohan Theatre—saw four other more spectacular openings; only three first-string critics attended, two of them to damn it with faint praise. On the second night, the house took only two hundred dollars. In two weeks the play was due to close.

Then the critic who made or broke attended the sparsely filled Wednesday matinée: the overweight (three-hundred-pound) epicene Alexander Woollcott of *The New York Times*, known to his friends as "Acky-Wacky." "Seeing himself as a kind of Paul Revere," in Guthrie's words, "he, figuratively speaking, got on his horse" to bully and cajole all New York's critics that *Bill* was a "must" for next Sunday's dramatic pages.

Thus Woollcott wrought the miracle. From Monday, the box office was taking $1,200 a night; by the second week the theatre was nearing capacity; by the third, they were playing to standees. Quite suddenly Kit became "the critics' pet," and Guthrie was now known, to his rueful amusement, as "Mr. Cornell."

The way to *Candida*—which was to feature in Kit's repertoire for more than twenty years—lay ahead.

About this time, two impecunious young men ventured for the first time into the outskirts of the jungle. At seventeen, Laurence Kerr Olivier, dark and intense, blessed with "a voice with an edge like a Saxon battle-axe," prepared to transmute the talent that had so electrified Ellen Terry into a tangible asset. Strangely enough, it was his father, the Reverend Gerard Olivier, who crystallized this decision. When his beloved elder brother, Dickie, left for India to work on a tea plantation, Laurence conceived a wild desire to join him.

"Don't you be a fool, Kim," his father replied, using the family nickname. "You are going on the stage."

It was the one encouraging paternal word that Larry, as the entire profession knew him, could ever recall. Until now, his father had seemed an unfeeling martinet, bent on piffling economies; at his insistence the entire family, all five of them, shared the same bath water. Now the vicar of Letchworth, in Hertfordshire, he was still outwardly as remote as ever, but Olivier senior, like Catherine Hayes Brown, had once nourished a secret passion for the stage. As a youngster, he had dreamed of being an opera singer until his mother forbade all thoughts of "that monstrous profession." At Oxford he had joined the University Dramatic Society (O.U.D.S.); even when he finally opted for holy orders, he was known as a dramatic and resonant preacher.

Then Ellen Terry's verdict, backed by the enthusiasm of Sir Johnston Forbes-Robertson, rekindled that desire on his son's behalf. At All Saint's Church School, St. Marylebone, Father Geoffrey Heald, who had all along coached Larry, had valuable contacts with Sybil Thorndike and Elsie Fogerty, a short, plump lady known for her broad-brimmed hats and brown fur tippet. Since 1906, she had run the Central School for Speech Training and Dramatic Art in dingy classrooms sited at balcony level in London's Albert Hall.

For his audition in June 1924, Larry had chosen the "Seven Ages of Man" speech from *As You Like It*, with magnificent gestures to match. When it was the soldier's turn,

102

Full of strange oaths and bearded like the pard
Jealous in honour and quick to quarrel . . .

Larry launched into a spirited shadow-duel across the stage, until a cool voice from the auditorium checked him: "I don't think we need *that*!" Yet he showed promise enough to qualify for a year's free tuition, with a bursary of fifty pounds, one of six young men enrolled along with more than seventy girls, among them the seventeen-year-old Peggy Ashcroft.

In that crowded year of tuition, verdicts on his prowess were mixed. One instructor, the veteran Bensonian Henry Oscar, reported that Larry always erected "an invisible wall of discomfort" between himself and his audience. Athene Seyler, though, invited to judge the best students in a scene from *The Merchant of Venice*, was struck by his latent power, though his facial expressions were hard to discern; "his beard grew almost up to his nose, to meet bushy eyebrows, and he had put on sideburns." Nonetheless Larry—along with a bearded Peggy Ashcroft, as Clerk of the Court—carried off the diplomas.

Another trepidant beginner, twenty-year-old John Gielgud, received equally mixed verdicts. As one of four male students out of thirty studying under Lady Benson, the wife of Sir Frank, his gait attracted comment on the first day. "Good heavens," Constance Benson cried out, "you walk exactly like a cat with rickets!" At RADA, where John put in an extra year's tuition, Athene Seyler had similar misgivings. "He played a comedy part as badly as one could conceive," she recalls, "yet all along, one felt there was *something* there."

John had, in fact, given himself a fixed time limit: If he hadn't succeeded by the age of twenty-five, he would follow his parents' wishes and study architecture. But here the family connection stood him in good stead. His second cousin, Phyllis Neilson-Terry, Uncle Fred's daughter, was just then launching a fifteen-week tour of J. B. Fagan's melodrama *The Wheel*. In the time-honored beginner's tradition, John was hired for a walk-on part and as assistant stage manager (ASM).

This was a lowly, though essential calling, followed at a later date by such novices as Humphrey Bogart, Margaret Leighton, Kirk Douglas, and John Osborne. It was the ASM's job to see that the stage was cleared for rehearsals, then to supervise its resetting for the evening show. It was his or her duty to check that props were

103

in position, to mark the lighting cues in the prompt copy, and to be "on the book"—holding the prompt script—for most of the show. Each weekday night it was he or she who lowered and raised the "iron," as the safety curtain was known. On tour, following a Saturday night show, the ASM supervised the stagehands in "getting out"—removing the scenery from the theatre—prior to the Sunday afternoon ritual of "getting in" at the next town.

It was a job John performed conscientiously enough, though he never sought to dramatize it as Larry did during a charity show staged by Edith Craig, Ellen Terry's daughter, at Letchworth. This function baffled his father's old housekeeper, Amy Porter, who demanded, "But tell me, Master Laurence, what do you *do?*" Master Laurence could milk a part for all it was worth, even then. "When you are having tea during the interval," he explained, "and you hear a bell summoning you back to your seat, *you'll know that my finger is on that bell!*"

In the approved tradition, both youngsters now took pains to enroll in a repertory company. John made for J. B. Fagan's company at the Oxford Playhouse, where the cast numbered, among others, Flora Robson, Alan Napier, and two men later famed as directors, Tyrone Guthrie and James Whale. Larry joined the Birmingham Repertory Company, in Station Street, whose players then included Ralph Richardson, Cedric Hardwicke, and Peggy Ashcroft. Despite his unprepossessing appearance—a thatch of hair that jutted forward in a widow's peak, and ill-fitting suits cast off by an elderly uncle—he was soon esteemed as a fifteen-pound-a-week character juvenile. In swift succession he played the roistering Tony Lumpkin, Chekhov's futile Uncle Vanya, Monsieur Parolles in *All's Well that Ends Well*, and the lead in Alfred Lord Tennyson's *Harold*, a three-thousand-line part that even Irving had deemed "quite impossible," though Larry memorized it within a week.

This was a feat beyond John and the company at Oxford; faced with a new role each Monday—Valentine in Congreve's *Love for Love* and young Marlow in *She Stoops to Conquer*—and doubting the prompter's promptitude, he and the others resorted to the old stock-company trick of pinning their lines around the stage. The system was not foolproof. Once, in *Oedipus*, a local super planted both feet and a spear on the crucial sheet of paper and Jocasta had to give him an unmaidenly shove, then kneel as if overcome by grief. On another occasion Raymond Massey, guesting in *Captain Brassbound's*

Conversion, upset an entire bottle of ink over the last three pages of dialogue.

These contretemps called for a resourcefulness that Larry mastered early on. Cast in a one-act curtain raiser at Brighton Hippodrome opposite the veteran actress Ruby Miller, his role was that of a youngster so smitten by the charms of a famous actress that he invades her dressing room. On the first night, forgetting the thick wooden bar that held the "flats" together in old-time sets, Larry hit the stage face first—then, playing perfectly in character, advanced across the boards on his knees, exclaiming, "Madame! You were *wonderful*! You *are* wonderful!" Convinced that this was part of the business, the audience remained totally absorbed.

In striking contrast to the United States, where, by 1926, Equity listed only 257 stock companies still holding out, this was the golden age of British repertory. Although Miss Horniman, her company depleted by wartime call-ups, closed down in June 1917, the Liverpool Repertory Company had opened as early as 1911 under the fearsome Basil Dean, and two years later Barry Jackson had opened Britain's premier repertory company at Birmingham.

A tall, fey, youthful-looking man, who drove through the city streets in an electric brougham steered with a tiller, Jackson was heir to the Maypole Dairies' fortune, a chain of prosperous grocery stores, and thus could afford to experiment. "Are you interested in Bernard Shaw?" were his first words to Cedric Hardwicke. "You won't like it here if you aren't." But Jackson's passion for innovation shocked even the egocentric Shaw. "Mr. Jackson, are your wife and children provided for?" was his awed inquiry when Jackson proposed staging his "metabiological pentateuch" *Back to Methuselah,* which demanded the presence of a patient and attentive audience for two long nights on end. When Jackson was adamant, Shaw entered into rehearsals with gusto; in the Garden of Eden scene, where an emerald serpent coiled around a mustard yellow tree trunk, with a purple rock and a lemon yellow sky, he stepped in to coach Edith Evans as to just how the serpent should hiss.

By 1950, more than one hundred repertory companies would be established in Britain, many of them valuable nurseries of versatility. At Northampton, Errol Flynn was, predictably, a chivalrous Prince Donzil in the Christmas pantomime *Jack and the Beanstalk,* but he went on to tackle roles in *The Devil's Disciple, A Doll's House,* and *Pygmalion.* At the Festival in Cambridge, the first theatre to abolish the proscenium, the footlights, and the drop curtain, players like Robert Donat and Maurice Evans learned their trade; Hull was to yield up Colin Clive, Sebastian Shaw, and Robert Newton.

Conditions were not always propitious. Rusholme Repertory, run by an undertaker, Arthur Belt, in an old tramway depot outside Manchester, nourished the talents of Broadway stalwarts like George Coulouris and Robert Coote, but business was sometimes less than brisk; the sight of hearses parked outside the theatre proved off-putting to the faint-hearted. At Sheffield, where Donald Wolfit was an early talent, the stage was so cramped that exits were made into an outside passage, with two umbrellas permanently on tap for rainy days.

At the least, Rex Harrison, who served his time at Liverpool along with Diana Wynyard, Michael Redgrave, and Hugh Williams, summed up with customary nonchalance, "rep" served one invaluable purpose: it taught you, early in life, "to stop people coughing their hearts out on damp Wednesday afternoons."

For most of this rising generation, the names of Sarah Bernhardt and Eleonora Duse were little more than imperishable legends. Only John was lucky enough to have seen them both, when a schoolboy: Bernhardt, with an air of "indomitable gallantry," playing a wounded *poilu* of eighteen, dying on the battlefield; Duse in *Ghosts*, "like some romantic Spanish empress." As a student at the American Academy, Guthrie had waited three times at the stage door of the Globe to see Bernhardt emerge swathed in chinchilla, an ardent fan paying silent homage. To Kit she was a figure of mystery, glimpsed briefly in the wings of her father's theatre.

Yet on March 26, 1923, when Sarah died at her Paris home, 56 Boulevard Pereire, everything about her was already enshrined in theatrical lore.

Her passion for detail, for a start. On one occasion in London, Mrs. Pat, visiting her dressing room, watched with impatience as Sarah, by degrees, transformed herself for her son Maurice's play, *La Mort de Cléopâtre*, staining both fingertips and palms dusky red with henna. "Why do you take so much trouble?" Mrs. Pat asked. "What you are doing will never show from the front." "I shall see it," Sarah replied. "I am doing it for myself. If I catch sight of my hand, it will be the hand of Cleopatra."

"On the stage to be natural is good, but to be sublime is always better" was her watchword, for the approval of the Beloved Monster, as she called her audience, was always foremost in her mind.

Although she had entered the Comédie-Française, France's foremost theatre, as far back as 1862 at the age of eighteen, she was a demon for work until the end. The dramatist W. Graham Robertson once remonstrated with Maurice, the assistant director of her Théâtre Sarah Bernhardt: was it really necessary for Sarah to sandwich in extra matinées every week? "Well," replied Maurice, thoughtfully, "what *is* mother to do in the afternoons?" The young Sacha Guitry, who played with her in Edmond Rostand's *L'Aiglon*, one of her classic roles, recounted with wonder that rehearsals took up to six months. At sixty-six, she still played two five-act plays a day, before traveling all night in her private train—often on 25,000-mile trips across the United States.

Journeys to the United States were a prime necessity for "Sally B," as Ellen Terry called her, since money "dribbled through her fingers like sand"; all told she crossed the Atlantic eleven times in search of precious dollars. One year before her death, she confided in her grandson, the dramatist Louis Verneuil, that she had earned $9 million, yet still she must sell jewelery and raise loans to support an eight-strong retinue. If her great roles—Scribe's *Adrienne Lecouvreur*, Racine's *Athalie, La Dame aux Camélias*—were part of history, so, too, was her prodigality; even in winter, her suite at the London Carlton was piled high with roses. Heedless of the express post, she would dispatch her long-suffering secretary, Pitou, to deliver a letter by hand to the other end of France, paying his fare there and back. Distrustful of banks and bankers, she never wrote a check in her life; all her fortune was stored in an old chamois leather bag or in small suitcases. When funds ran out, it was high time for another world tour.

Although her every role was performed in French, often to audiences with no knowledge of that language, Sarah could net forty thousand pounds from one tour of the United States alone. Much later Lee Shubert, who handled her American bookings, was to recall, "English she couldn't talk, English she couldn't pronounce, but boy, could she count in English!"

At 56 Boulevard Pereire, where rumor had it that she both learned her lines and received her lovers in a silk-lined coffin, she lived like an uncrowned queen. Seated on a thronelike chair, dressed always in white, she dominated a dinner table graced by such renowned figures as Rostand, Sardou, and the explorer Pierre Loti. At dinner parties, when an unseen orchestra played behind a heavy curtain, she would fly into paroxysms of fury if the chef had used thyme instead of tarragon.

To the very end, her public treated her like a queen—even after her right leg, injured in a shipboard fall in 1896, turned gangrenous and was amputated in 1915. At first her Beloved Monster must remain content with excerpts, until Verneuil cleverly constructed full-length plays like *Daniel*, where Sarah could remain immobile. Then the public all over again took her to its heart. When a theatrical paper requested a first-night Parisian audience to bring one flower by way of tribute, the stage was piled higher than a haystack; it took ten minutes to remove the bouquets. In Madrid in 1921, five thousand people greeted the arrival of her train; at the Estacion del Norte, one thousand coats were spread across the booking hall, a symbolic red carpet for those who had the honor to carry her.

Long ago, the profession had accorded her the ultimate accolade: Sarah was a trouper. Even two months before her death, she told Alexander Woollcott of another tour she was planning of the United States—nothing exhausting, she was too old for that, just an itinerary of twelve cities between New York and San Francisco. At seventy-eight, she was as beset by first-night nerves as she had ever been. "My God, my God! If only the theatre would burn down!" she would agonize, half an hour before facing her Beloved Monster again. Yet at curtain-up, like every trouper, she was eternally hopeful that on this night she would truly master the role, that "God," as she put it, "would be there."

At sixty-four, Italy's Eleonora Duse was a player of another caliber—remote where Sarah was immediate, muted where Sarah was vibrant. She was a stage brat from the age of four; at fourteen she was already playing Juliet, the age that Shakespeare had envisaged. In roles like Sudermann's *Magda* and Rebecca West in Ibsen's *Rosmersholm*, her work delighted such diverse personalities as Chekhov and Shaw—who, even so, admitted that "Duse without her genius would be a plain little woman of no use to any manager."

Unlike Sarah, whose histrionics in her declining years were often exaggerated—"chewing the scenery," the profession called it—Duse was, in her own words, "the slave of a temperament which does not allow me, alas, simply to 'play' my parts but, much against my will, forces me to suffer with the beings I am forced to represent."

When life grew intolerable, as in her torrid affairs with Arrigo Boito, Verdi's librettist, and the raunchy poet Gabriele D'Annunzio, Duse took refuge in her career. "If I speak of *art*," she confessed once, "I become calm. As soon as I speak of *life*—my throat tightens." When she died on April 21, 1924, at the Schenley Hotel in Pittsburgh, on her fourth and last tour of the United States, *The New York Times* struggled in vain to sum up her contribution to the drama. "The major part of Duse's art lay in a thing which no one could see or adequately describe," their editorial concluded. "The thing for which we have only the poor, hackneyed word 'spirit'."

The playwright Bayard Veiller perhaps came closer. Duse had reigned before her time, foreshadowing a style of subtle underplaying that would soon be typified by Larry and Noël, John and Kit, Alfred, Lynn, and Helen, "in her methods more modern than tomorrow."

Seven months after Duse's death, on November 25, 1924, Noël's Big Moment dawned in an improbable setting—a drafty, converted drill hall, now the Everyman Theatre, in the North London suburb of Hampstead, which was staging his play *The Vortex*. For thirty years thereafter, Noël was the golden boy of theatre-land.

It had been an uphill road, even so. Those autumn months in New York in 1921, when only the bounty of Lynn and Alfred had saved him from going hungry to bed, were indelibly impressed on his memory: the bug-ridden studio apartment in Washington Square, the long hours of tramping the city streets, the packets of bacon supplied on credit by an Italian grocer. Even London in 1922 was little better—a bleak vista of pawnshops, broker's men, and mortgages on his beloved piano. At times he was so poor, he later admitted to scooping up the pennies left under the plates for teashop waitresses.

Then, during the long run of the revue *London Calling*, of which he was featured player, part-author, and composer, Noël dashed off two highly controversial plays, *The Vortex* and *Fallen Angels*. It was *The Vortex* that struck the fancy of Norman Macdermott, the Everyman's director, who at once put it into production.

Then, as so often happened in the jungle, the money ran out. Without two hundred pounds, Macdermott explained, the play would have to be abandoned. It was with trepidation that Noël approached the one source from whom he had not yet borrowed money: the dapper, best-selling novelist Michael Arlen. Over lunch at The Ritz—or dinner at the Embassy Club, the accounts afterward varied—Noël broached his problem with Arlen, who asked no details of play or title, set no terms for repayment, or even expressed a desire to read the script. Instead he wrote out a check for two hundred pounds and continued his blow-by-blow account of a new short story that *he* was planning.

The Vortex, which swiftly transferred to the Royalty, naturally offered Noël his meatiest part to date: he had written it for himself. Nicky Lancaster, despairing at the promiscuities of his flighty mother, Florence, develops an addiction to cocaine, only revealed in a last act reminiscent of the Closet Scene in *Hamlet*. At the climax, Noël sweeps the makeup bottles from her dressing table, urging, "Promise you'll be different," and Florence wanly agrees to try.

The choice of theme was curious, since Noël, a certified homosexual, was incapable of loving any woman other than his mother. "All that open plumbing absolutely revolts me," he once told a heterosexual friend. One of his first acts, when *The Vortex* was a smash hit in New York, was to buy Goldenhurst, a farm near Aldington, Kent, as a country home and a retreat for his mother.

The first play on a London stage ever to assault the sanctity of motherhood, *The Vortex* was a grave affront to the old guard in society. *The Sunday Express*, in what the profession knew as a "money notice," accused Noël of "shovelling up the ordure of an unprincipled smart set, exposing their nasty souls, bedizening their ugly manners."

Noël's understudy at this stage of his career was the young John Gielgud, much perturbed when a kindly soul knocked on his door to announce that several in the audience had asked for their money back when they knew of Noël's absence. Later John, whose career was marking time, was indebted to Noël for another second-fiddle role, as his understudy in Margaret Kennedy's *The Constant Nymph*.

Noël was at once smart enough to fuel the public's sense of outrage. He posed for a photograph of himself in bed wearing a Chinese silk dressing gown, in a scarlet bedroom decorated with nudes, wearing an expression of "advanced degeneracy." He followed up *The Vortex* with *Fallen Angels*, another Tallulah vehicle, which provoked violent protests all over again. "Drunken young married women, both confessing to immoral relations with the same man," cried the *Daily Express* in dudgeon.

Now Noël's lifestyle changed beyond recognition. He became the darling of the Smart Set. He was, he admitted, "a bad celebrity snob," reveling in the company of Douglas Fairbanks and Mary Pickford. He was lionized at weekend parties, in houses filled with "tennis racquets, young people in flannels . . . and huge truculent cakes." He socialized at Deauville with the financier Sir James Dunn and Lady Diana Cooper, in an ambience of "champagne, beautifully-gowned women, high powered gambling, obsequious *maîtres d'hotel*, moonlit terraces." Each night his dressing room was so crammed with sycophantic well-wishers that Waugh, his dresser, only cleared the room by announcing the arrival of a mythical Lady Biddle's car. Noël himself surveyed London with quiet satisfaction from the windows of his new Rolls-Royce.

Contemporary reactions to him were mixed. The dramatist George Middleton saw him as "a tall slim no-stomachy young fellow, with a puckery smile, and eyes as alert and nervous as his hands." Evelyn Waugh found him to be "simple, friendly, with no brains and a theatrical manner." Virginia Woolf tended to be dismissive; in her words, he was "as clever as a bag of ferrets, as trivial as a perch of canaries."

Yet no one could deny his industry. In the years that followed, plays came as facilely from his pen as from a latter-day Pinero's: *Hay Fever*, "a comedy of bad manners," written for Marie Tempest in 1925 and still in repertoire today; and *Easy Virtue*, in which the Broadway star Jane Cowl took London by storm. But too many were long-forgotten light-weights: *The Queen Was in the Parlour*, starring Madge Titheradge; and *This Was a Man*, banned by the Lord Chamberlain because a husband laughs uproariously when learning of his wife's adultery. In 1927 came *The Marquise*, a period comedy, again for Marie Tempest, and *Home Chat*, a vehicle for Madge Titheradge.

"I do not think he will ever quite fulfil his great promise if he does not curb his versatility," was Marie Tempest's evaluation. "He is spending his gifts too lavishly."

At Daly's Theatre, on November 24, 1927, almost three years to the day that the public had acclaimed *The Vortex*, Miss Tempest's prophecy was fulfilled. Noël's long love affair with his public now suffered a very decided setback.

The play, *Sirocco*, was far from his best, a trifling affair of an Italian artist seducing a married English woman in Florence. Yet three factors seemed to augur in its favor: it was a Coward first night, a Basil Dean first night, and an Ivor Novello first night. Though Novello, at thirty-four, had only six years' stage experience, his pulling power at the cinema box office had made him an international name.

"It was probably," Noël recalled later, "the bloodiest failure in the history of the English theatre"—and this was no overstatement. Only an oppressive stillness prevailed throughout Act I. In Act II, Novello's love scene with his leading lady, Frances Doble, was greeted with raucous mirth and sucking sounds from the gallery; from then on, catcalls punctuated almost every line. The last act was total chaos; few lines were even heard. The gallery, pit, and upper circle hooted and yelled; the stalls, the boxes, and the dress circle shushed and tut-tutted.

When Noël took the stage at the final curtain call, the gallery booed him and the company for fully seven minutes—an atmosphere not ameliorated by Frances Doble's tremulous curtain speech, rehearsed for a kindlier reception: "Ladies and gentlemen, this is the happiest night of my life." This understandable faux pas only provoked fresh screams and yahooing. "In all my years on the London and Broadway stage, I never saw such an opening night," recalls George Coulouris, who was in the cast. "The audience were really terrifying."

As Noël walked to his car from the stage door, a hostile crowd showered him with spittle; next day his evening coat was dispatched to the cleaner.

It wasn't that Noël was unused to failure; *This Was a Man* had played its third act in New York to an almost empty house. But in New York the sound of failure was the sound of tip-up seats snapping back as the audience filed out; in London it was the boorish execrations of galleryites out for blood, a fate known in the profession as "getting the bird." "Bears now being protected by law," Max Beerbohm reflected, as far back as 1901, "dramatists are baited in their stead." It was a reception such as had greeted Lynn and Laurette Taylor at the London premiere of *One Night in Rome*, a phenomenon that always shocked Americans to the core. To the Broadway dramatist George Broadhurst, it was "like a steamer's foghorn when icebergs were about." Another dramatist, Bayard Veiller, had never heard "anything as terrifying as this sound."

For the foreseeable future Noël and the public were not on speaking terms. After the first night of his hit musical, *Bitter Sweet*, he deliberately took no curtain call. When vociferous gallery girls at the stage door demanded the reason, Noël had the short answer: "I only come on when you boo."

The year 1924 was likewise a momentous one for the Lunts. After *Clarence* and *Dulcy*, both had been acclaimed as "gifted grotesques, sure to shine in the sideshow but doomed never to achieve prominence in the Main Tent." But from the outset both were determined to put those stereotypes behind them, and they hit on the one sure way to secure roles to show them both to maximum advantage. Five years after its inception, they threw in their lot with the Theatre Guild, a postwar successor to the Washington Square Players.

The Guild's aims were avowedly noncommercial. They catered to a subscription audience, which at first numbered 135 doughty souls. After leasing the shabby old Garrick Theatre on West 35th Street from Otto Kahn, the Wall Street banker and philanthropist—who generously waived the rent—they set out on the course that they pursued for more than twenty years: to star the play and feature the players, to concentrate on works of real value, on plays that had something to say. The Guild did not pander to the Tired Businessman.

These intrepid idealists were led by the patent lawyer Lawrence Langner; his executive secretary, Theresa Helburn, small, dark, and volatile; the producer Philip Moeller, slim and aesthetic; and the actress Helen Westley, an ample lady who fell in and out of love with the speed of a sleight-of-hand artist. Volatile and voluble in their dissentions—and there were many of these each Thursday night at Henri's crowded French restaurant on West 45th Street—each of them fought their individual corner with passion. They lost Marc Connelly's *The Green Pastures*, encapsulating the black plantation workers' view of Heaven, after Helen Westley, with the fervor of Lady Macbeth, trumpeted, "I won't do a play in which God smokes a cigar!" (It ran five years and won the Pulitzer Prize.) On the credit side, they snapped up Sidney Howard's *They Knew What They Wanted* after twelve managers had turned it down; this, too, won a Pulitzer Prize, the Guild's first. The Guild would try anything once. Theresa Helburn even hit on the idea of casting Mae West, that all-time sex symbol, as the brothel owner in Shaw's *Mrs. Warren's Profession*, but Miss West graciously bowed out. "I feel I owe it to my boys," she told Theresa Helburn, "not to play the part of a mother."

This fervid and mildly eccentric ambience might have been created solely to accommodate the Lunts—from this time on they were always "the Lunts." Although Alfred now commanded $500 per week and Lynn was priced at $750, the impoverished Guild could then offer only $250 a week between the two of them. Lynn and Alfred shrugged this aside. The Guild had a mission. With the Guild they could do Shakespeare and Shaw and plays that New Yorkers had never seen, for the Guild, unlike the Provincetown Players in Greenwich Village, who sponsored rising American dramatists like Eugene O'Neill, specialized largely in European fare. The Lunts' first Guild undertaking was the Hungarian Ferenc Molnár's *The Guardsman*, in which a famous actor tests his actress wife's fidelity by masquerading as a flirtatious officer of the Russian Guards.

Now, at long last, day in and day out, they could indulge their insatiable quest for perfection. They dipped into Lynn's savings for a trip to Budapest, for how could they possibly play Hungarians without visiting Hungary? In Budapest they met a Russian doorman who had been an officer under the czar; Alfred sketched his uniform and had a replica tailor-made in London. As the Actor he wore a wig, since he had shaven his head, the better to suggest a military mien. In Paris, Lynn bought a white Paul Poiret evening gown for one thousand dollars; in Act II, the flirtation scene, the Actress must look especially dazzling. They arrived back in New York with no more than the cab fare to their apartment—but now they were "in character."

From the first, Philip Moeller directed them with the loosest of reins. He was discovering what many directors would discover after him: the one way to direct the Lunts was to let them direct themselves. When he objected to Alfred's black uniform, insisting, "You can't play comedy in black," Lynn came right back at him: "You can play comedy in a burlap bag inside a piano with the cover down *if* the lines are funny and the audience can hear them."

At times there were flashes of temperament. The Lunts were forever polishing one scene, which the Guild directors ordered to be cut. Stalking to the footlights, Alfred delivered a resonant rebuke: "Playing light comedy for you is like feeding a soufflé to a horse!"

These were halcyon days for the Lunts, and for the Guild besides; *The Guardsman* became the first play to make them real money. After five weeks at the Garrick it moved uptown to the Booth to play for forty more. Now they reveled in the challenge of role after role. On the roof of 969 Lexington Avenue, Alfred was spotted by bewildered fellow tenants pinning a damp, blue uniform onto a clothesline. Weeks later the uniform was still there, scorched by heat waves, soaked with rain, with Alfred returning at intervals to lambaste it with a rattan rug beater. Shaw had described Captain Bluntschli in *Arms and the Man* as "in a deplorable plight, bespattered with mud and blood and snow," and Alfred was no man to ignore a stage direction. To provide the blood, he gouged his thumb with a needle.

Five years after the Lunts joined the Guild, the subscription level had soared to sixty thousand. Now their salary, too, had soared: $750 a week with a small percentage of the gross. They moved to a handsome triplex apartment on 30th Street. Still they rang the changes, twenty-five plays in all: Jennifer Dubedat and her amoral husband, Louis, in *The Doctor's Dilemma*, Higgins and Eliza in *Pygmalion*. Ironically, many Guild directors after *The Guardsman* saw them as the epitome of worldly sophistication, totally unsuited to play Juvan, a neurotic student who leads a serfs' revolt, and Stanja, a peasant girl, in Franz Werfel's *The Goat Song.*

"The Lunts," said Theresa Helburn firmly, "can play anything— *anything*," and Miss Helburn was right. For seven weeks *The Goat Song* played to standing room only.

Never at any time were they tempted to rest on their laurels. That was not the Lunts' way. In the throes of a divine dissatisfaction they sought—in the twenties and for all their lives—to be more real than reality. They dared to play with their backs to the audience. In *Caprice*, a Viennese offering—the first play in which Londoners would see them—they experimented with overlapping dialogue, dovetailing their lines without the audience missing a word.

For Alfred, his body seemed to exist primarily as a vehicle to convey the underlying truth of a character. As a middle-aged roué in *Caprice*, he decided that he must physically gain fifty pounds; padding was not for Alfred. He gorged himself on rich desserts, cream sauces, and two loaves of bread a day, for Alfred was a gifted cook. As the lean and tormented tycoon in S.N. Behrman's *Meteor*, he shed, by contrast, forty pounds: his diet was limited to black coffee for breakfast, more black coffee and toast for lunch, lean lamb chops and pineapple for dinner.

Behrman, who first encountered the Lunts in 1927 when the Guild staged *The Second Man*, was fascinated by their technique. On the top floor of the Guild headquarters, where they rehearsed in a converted ballroom, he heard overtones that he hadn't even known were there. Alfred's details, he thought, "were like the observations of a great novelist." As the sophisticated Mrs. Kendall Frayne, Lynn had one line regarding a character who bored her: "He never has anything interesting to say." As she developed the part, it became, "He never has anything interesting to say—never—never—never—never—never": as Behrman put it, "a perfectly graduated diminuendo of 'nevers,' conveying an endless vista of boredom."

As incomparable judges of what to underscore, what to throw away, their command over an audience was absolute. The patrons divided, Lynn said once, into those who surrendered gloriously to the magic and those who remained like wary children, determined to resist the conjuror's wiles.

"Her hands," enthused one radiant matinée matron. "Oh, what lovely hands she has."

"Ah," replied her friend, meaningly, "but are they her own?"

When the Lunts espoused the Theatre Guild they were, perhaps, more astute than they knew. No Guild offering ever remotely smacked of an earlier mold; no Guild producer ever typecast the Lunts. Unlike their contemporaries, they steered clear of "vogue" plays. For as the twenties gathered pace, managements on both Shaftesbury Avenue and Broadway were forced to play increasingly safe; the spiraling economics of the decade decreed it so. Plays that had been mounted for $3,000 around 1909 now cost up to $20,000 to open, perhaps to show a $50,000 loss.

Thus Noël's *The Vortex*—224 performances in London, 157 in New York—with its attack on motherhood was just the tip of the iceberg. Between 1923 and 1934, by one estimate, at least fifty Oedipus-oriented dramas were devoted to savaging the Mother who reduced her children to psychic impotence; for the best of Freudian reasons, the Mother had become the fashionable "heavy" of the twenties. In *Apron Strings*, a priggish young man consulted his dead mother's wishes bequeathed in a trunk full of letters laying down instructions for every occasion; told to treat his bride reverently, he was unable to consummate his marriage until a friend got him drunk. *Conquest* pictured a son avenging his father's death by ruining his mother's lover on the stock market. "Mother fixation," joked the writer William Bolitho, "is the most dreaded disease of the times, supplanting the old bogies of constipation, smallpox and appendicitis."

The most sibylline of all stage mothers was the awful Mrs. Phelps in Sidney Howard's *The Silver Cord*, although the whining, insidious Mrs. Hallam in Rose Franken's *Another Language* ran her close. Mrs. Phelps stops at no insinuations, no lies, no threats of suicide, both to break off her younger son's engagement and break up her elder son's marriage. When the boy's hysterical fiancée attempts suicide in an icy pond, the mother screeches at her sons, bent on rescue, to get their coats or they will catch pneumonia. At the close the elder son leaves, reconciled with his wife; the younger collapses sniveling at his mother's knees.

British matriarchs were usually titled, like Caroline, Lady Beresford in *No Way Back*, who weaned her daughter on to drugs, leading to the girl's suicide, or Lady Gaynes in *The Iron Woman*, who had ruled her late husband's mills and her offspring with a rod of iron. The Act II curtain saw the speedy dissolution of her family; "My daughter a harlot and my son a thief!" she cried in understandable outrage, just as the butler announced, "The American ambassador, m'lady." All this proved too much for the "iron woman," who collapsed on the carpet, as the butler told the parlormaid, "like a mighty oak stricken by lightning."

It was small wonder that at least one critic, Robert Littell of *The New York World*, lamented, "There ought to be a closed season during which playwrights are not allowed to paint mothers black and then shoot them."

Instead, in both London and New York, it was open season on the entire female sex. The Bitch Woman (like the cold, house-proud Harriet Craig in *Craig's Wife*, whose husband finally walked out, charging, "I have no wife to leave, for you neither loved nor honoured me") trod hard on the Heavy Mothers' heels. Of these Kit Cornell had more than her share—strange casting for a girl who eschewed lipstick, disliked jewelery, traveled third class on British trains, and drove herself to the theatre in a battered old Dodge.

Even so, anxious to escape typecasting, Kit played Suzanne Chaumont, created in London by Edith Evans, in *Tiger Cats*—"a horrible woman—the most horrible I have ever known"—who derides her neurologist husband for his failure to lavish luxuries on her. "Do you realise I'm the only woman of our set who hasn't got a motorcar, nor a long rope of pearls?" she demands, before flaunting her adultery with a Rumanian oil baron. *Tiger Cats* ended with the husband again

117

totally enslaved, on his knees before the "horrible" Suzanne, who wheedles, "Say that you'll give me everything—your whole life— your world—your existence."

Faced with the unrealities of Iris March Fenwick in Michael Arlen's *The Green Hat*, with her "thousand carnal Calvaries," Kit's novel solution was to smile quietly when she came to the worst lines of all. Iris's husband, "Boy," has committed suicide on their wedding night after discovering that he had contracted syphilis. " 'Boy' died— he died for—purity," Iris tells his assembled family, to which Gerald, her brother, retorts, "Say it again, Iris, it's good to hear that word on your lips, like a flower in hell." In such moments, Kit smiled more fixedly than ever, as if to say, "That's the worst nonsense I can think of. A catch phrase that I know is bunky and you know is bunky."

A harder role by far was the Malayan rubber planter's wife, Leslie Crosbie, in Somerset Maugham's *The Letter*, a Gladys Cooper part. In the final scene Leslie reveals that the man she claimed to have shot to defend herself from rape was in truth her lover, who had spurned her for a Chinese woman. "My retribution is greater," she told her interlocutors, "with all my heart I still love the man I killed." "I had to fight every minute against the antagonism of the audience," Kit was to recall.

The psychological climate was now ripe for a dramatist contemporary with Ibsen but never seen in London until now: the misogynistic Swede, August Strindberg, who lived unhappily with three successive wives, making their lives and his own a hell. As presented by the actor-manager Robert Loraine, Adolf in *The Father* struggles with his wife Laura for the possession of their child; the predatory Laura, to gain her ends, instills a doubt in his mind that he is not the father at all. As a result, Adolf is driven insane and lured into a straight jacket by his old nurse, the only woman he had ever trusted.

One year after this, in 1928, Loraine followed *The Father* with Strindberg's *The Dance of Death*, the triangle story of Edgar, an army officer sunk in a rut, his vengeful wife, Alice, and her lover, Curt— culminating in Edgar's wild, boastful dance, cut short by a paralytic stroke, with Alice hissing exultantly over his body, "Is he dead, is he dead?"

But Cinderella was also alive and well, in many venues apart from British pantomime, and Kit Cornell had her share of these roles, too:

the put-upon Shirley Pride in Clemence Dane's *The Way Things Happen*, who allows herself to be seduced to save the son of the house from prison; the crippled Lalage Sturdee in *The Outsider*, who yearns for a rich, complete life. "I don't want a good man's love," she tells her scandalized father, a Harley Street physician, "I want a young man's passion," and to this end she pins her faith on an "outsider" like herself, Anton Ragatzy, a bone-setter branded as a charlatan by organized medicine. After a year strapped to the vibrating Ragatzy Rack, he commands her, "Walk! Walk, I tell you. Look at me. Come to me." And Lalage walks, as the audience always knew she would, into his outstretched arms.

Both Kit and Guthrie were always dubious that playgoers would swallow this instant miracle, but a crippled Cinderella proved to be "one of those gift-of-the-gods parts that you can't go wrong on." When Lalage rose shakily from her couch, many of the audience were seen to faint with great abandon.

Yet as Bernard Shaw was to point out, "The golden rule is that there is no golden rule." The success of Eden Phillpotts's bucolic comedy *The Farmer's Wife* (one thousand London performances) and Frank Bacon's *Lightnin'* in New York provoked a flood tide of what Britain's Nigel Playfair called "Lumpshire plays," few of which even recovered their costs. Larry was involved in Barry Jackson's six-month tour of *The Farmer's Wife*, as Richard Coaker, a cider-sipping rural swain—"Your voice is so sweet as a chime of bells, I reckon"—and thus inevitably graduated to John Hardy, a midwestern farmer's son in Crane Wilbur's *The Stranger Within*. "No country lout but a thinker, ever thirsting for knowledge," ran the reassuring stage direction.

John, who shared the farmhouse with his paralyzed father Mark, "a living dead man," and his brothers Simon, a hypocritical lay preacher, and Andrew, a half-wit, falls heavily for Molly, a soubrette stranded by a train wreck; he marries her and fathers a son. In Act II, watched only by the catatonic Mark, Simon attempts to rape Molly, and the baby is dropped on its head—fatally. In Act III, with Molly accused of infanticide, she clears herself at the eleventh hour by wheeling old Mark center stage and appealing to heaven, "Give the old man a voice, dear Christ . . . Granddad, you saw it all, tell them." Choking and spitting and gurgling, the old man finally gulps out "Yes!"—at which point Larry often swung away from the footlights, apparently swooping with emotion, in reality convulsed with giggles.

Although Phillpotts scored with other rural comedies—*Yellow Sands,
Devonshire Cream*—the bulk of these bumpkin sagas failed to please.
Notorious among them were *If Four Walls Told*, with dialogue like
"Nigh on sixty-four year ago come next Michaelmas"; Clemence
Dane's *Granite*, mirroring fraught passions in a lighthouse; and *The
Squall*, accorded a unanimous thumbs-down by both London and
New York. Set in a farmhouse near Granada, where Nubi, a gypsy
girl, wreaks havoc with the menfolk, the characters, for no discernible reason, conversed mainly in pidgin English. Nubi's first arrival,
and her greeting, "Me Nubi. Nubi good girl. Nubi stay here," proved
too much for *Life* magazine's critic, Robert Benchley. Tiptoeing up
the aisle, he announced sepulchrally, "Me Bobby. Me bad boy. Me
go."

Many a dramatist followed Rudyard Kipling's injunction to take
up the white man's burden—and none more successfully than Leon
Gordon, whose *White Cargo* achieved 821 performances in London,
864 on Broadway. Gordon's West African rubber planters were bur-
dened for the most part by the battle against "mammy-palaver"—
miscegenation—as symbolized by the sensuous coffee-colored maiden,
Tondeleyo. Young Langford, the newcomer, who wears tropical whites
and vows to shave daily, predictably makes an honest woman of her,
to the chagrin of Weston, the cynical station agent. "Sanctify it with
the church, if you like, but it's still mammy-palaver." Weston is
conveniently on hand when the girl, wearying of wedded bliss, tries
to poison Langford and tips the poison down her own gullet. Langford departs for England on a stretcher, to be succeeded by another
immaculate newcomer, who is "not going to let the loneliness or
anything like that get me," a cue for the obligatory "shock curtain,"
Weston's "You poor bloody fool!"

Few players in the twenties suffered more acutely from "vogue"
plays than the young John Gielgud. After succeeding Noël in *The
Constant Nymph*, his star potential was evident—and sure enough, in
June 1928, his name appeared for the first time in lights outside the
Globe Theatre. "A comedy with a catch in it," *Holding Out the Apple*
(which the author, Betty Wynne-Bower, was rash enough to finance
herself) was part of the "Bright Young Things" cycle; Vera, the
flippant young heroine, who stays in bed for a fortnight, is thought
to be pregnant, whereas the "dearest Philip" to whom she had written, saying she could not "hide it any longer," was her dentist, about
to replace a tooth knocked out in a hockey game.

As the family doctor, John's repartee was much on this level throughout:

Doctor: Take another tablet.
Vera: I haven't much faith in them.
Doctor: That's of no consequence. I'm not a Faith healer.

Some nights later, the lights that spelled out JOHN GIELGUD suffered an eclipse.

In 1922 two Broadway successes—*The Bat* and *The Cat and the Canary*—prompted an onrush of what George Jean Nathan called "frightwig melodramas," a world of sliding panels, sudden blackouts, piercing shrieks, and sinister Orientals like Dr. Chan Fu, with his deaf-mute servant, in *The Silent House,* and Yuan Sing in Matheson Lang's *The Chinese Bungalow,* whose designs on white women prompted such fine xenophobic lines as "You Oriental fiend!" Thus, by August 1928, John had moved up the street to the Shaftesbury as Captain Vernon Allenby of Scotland Yard in *The Skull,* set in a deserted church near Greenwich, Connecticut, and featuring a woman escapee from an asylum, a silly-ass reporter, an organ played by unseen hands, and a Cockney sexton with a clubfoot. In the end Professor Vaughan, a supposed psychic medium, was revealed as Captain Allenby, John as "the hideous grinning gaping human skull," Leslie Austin, who hooted like an owl to announce his murders, "the most looked-for international crook."

By November John had moved to the Strand in *Out of the Sea,* a J. M. Barrie lookalike set near Land's End, site of the lost kingdom of Lyonnesse, whose heroine, convinced she was Isolde reincarnated, greatly shocked John, her lover, by stabbing her husband with a bronze bodkin and pushing him off the cliff. "You are like some wild thing to me now!" was John's pained reaction. "Not a woman but some strange wild thing out of the sea!"

Come Christmas, and John was yet again seeking work, or, as the profession always politely termed it, "resting."

Of all the young aspirants, none waged a harder battle to develop her potential than Helen Hayes. She had, she confessed later, to learn how to use herself "as Heifetz learned to use that violin," and this was only a part of her struggle. After much heart searching, she finally resigned from the maverick Actors' Fidelity League and enrolled in the ranks of Equity along with Alfred and Lynn. Thus,

121

after seven years, her long partnership with George C. Tyler was irrevocably severed. "I am through," Tyler told her, his plump little face white with anger. "You belong to the Union now."

For the first time in her life she dared to defy her mother, for Helen had fallen in love with a man Catherine Hayes Brown always designated disparagingly as "that tramp!" It began at a late-afternoon studio party, hosted by the then-famous illustrator, Neysa McMein. As always at parties Helen was the perfect wallflower, gravitating to a corner, hoping not to be noticed, pretending to laugh at the barbed witticisms of Alexander Woollcott, though mostly their significance escaped her. Suddenly "a beautiful young man" towered above her, offering a bag of peanuts. When Helen accepted, he smiled and said, "I wish they were emeralds."

The courtship of Charles MacArthur, newspaper man and some-time dramatist, and Helen Hayes Brown was long and checkered. MacArthur, in the words of his friend and collaborator Ben Hecht, was a man who "walked backward through life looking at the day he was twenty-one." He was charming, feckless, irresponsible, and often in his cups—an irresistible combination to the shy and sheltered Helen. Like many newspapermen, his hands and collar were frequently inky and Catherine Hayes Brown saw good reason to carp. The remark about emeralds particularly irked her. "He probably heard someone else say that," she gibed, "and seeing how green you were, just threw it up at you."

Since Helen shared a three-room apartment at Park Avenue and 35th Street with her mother and the actress Jean Dixon, the courtship presented problems. It was hardly a setting in which to entertain a beau. Thus they took train trips up to Nyack, New York, for long walks along the riverbank. They rode the ferry to Staten Island, with Charlie reciting Edna St. Vincent Millay's "Recuerdo."

> *We were very tired, we were very merry—*
> *We had gone back and forth all night on the ferry;*
> *And you ate an apple, and I ate a pear,*
> *From a dozen of each we had bought somewhere;*
> *And the sky went wan, and the wind came cold,*
> *And the sun rose dripping, a bucketful of gold.*

In all this time, Helen was battling with her mother, not only over the attentions of "that tramp" but over acceptance of the role that the Theatre Guild had offered her—Cleopatra in Shaw's *Caesar and Cleopatra*. Helen, like Lynn, could now command $750 a week; the Guild could only offer $350, an insulting pittance, her mother scoffed. But Helen was adamant; this was a role she had to play, a chance to leave all those wearisome ingenues behind her.

Her resolution did her credit. At the Guild's new theatre on West 52nd Street, Helen not only occupied the star dressing room but, in that ebullient month of April 1925, took fifty curtain calls for her rendering of Shaw's voluptuous little vixen. Yet this triumph only served to further postpone her marriage. Now that she was a star in her own right, MacArthur was determined to score a success equal to hers.

At first she resisted William A. Brady's offer of an eight-week revival of Barrie's *What Every Woman Knows;* for all the actresses of that generation, Maude Adams was deemed a hard act to follow. Every audience would judge you by those famous lines in Act I: "[Charm's] a sort of bloom on a woman. If you have it you don't need to have anything else; and if you don't have it doesn't much matter what else you have." But finally she took the plunge. No one would dare offer her a part as an ingenue or even as a flapper after this.

For just this reason, Helen had two years earlier spurned a flapper comedy co-authored by the veteran showman George Abbott, *Norma's Affair.* When Abbott produced a new version, retitled *Coquette*, Helen at first refused to read it, despite her mother's enthusiasm. *Coquette*, Mrs. Brown pointed out, was now a tragedy, but Helen was skeptical. "How can they make a good tragedy out of a bad comedy?"

Coquette was not a good tragedy, but a steamy melodrama of the Deep South, fixed in an ethos where, as the heroine, Norma Besant, says, "Whenever a relation of ours kills somebody he is a wonderful man defending the honour of pure womanhood." When Norma sets her cap at Michael, a youngster from the wrong side of the tracks, barred from the Country Club for not owning a dinner jacket, the young man seduces her—"We're as good as man and wife now." To avenge Norma's honor, Dr. Besant shoots Michael. When a jury acquits him, Norma shoots herself.

The play's outcome was always in doubt. The producing manager, Jed Harris, born Jacob Horowitz in Lemberg, Austria, was Broadway's answer to Basil Dean—a man with a terrible instinct to

123

quarrel and wound, whose venom was a legend. His low, icy voice and gleaming, dark brown eyes set in a pale ivory face were the bane of a whole generation of actors. In his teens his orthodox Jewish parents had wondered if he was possessed of a *dybbuk*, the spirit of a dead person wronged in life, forever seeking revenge. His casts were sure of it.

Four days before the opening in Atlantic City, with Abbott directing, Harris attended his first rehearsal. Almost at once the storm broke. Although Helen's first entrance came five minutes after curtain-up, it was two hours before Harris had finished dissecting every move, restressing inflections, analyzing every nuance. Although her first line was a simple "hello" to her brother Jimmy, Harris checked her at once. "What are you going to do with that 'hello'?" came his sibilant query. Helen went dangerously quiet, replying, "Just nothing."

Halfway through her next speech he stopped her again, with a long dissertation on the inner meaning of the lines. Then Helen boiled over. "I didn't know this was Euripides!" she screamed. "I thought it was a simple play about plain people! I won't go on until you get out of here!"

From then and till the dress rehearsal, Harris was in the invidious position of a manager barred from his own production. Yet all along Helen felt that the Act II curtain, in which Norma tamely submits to her father's decision, was psychologically at fault. "The bottom dropped out of your play from then on," she told Abbott flatly. "If I get bad criticisms in Philadelphia, I'll not open in New York in this play."

It was then that Harris's perverted genius saved the day, as would happen time and again on Broadway. On the opening night, the Act II curtain fell on a hate-crazed Norma, beating her fists on the couch and screaming "I hope he hangs! I hope he hangs!"—an ending that Harris had contrived after an all-night session in Atlantic City that brought Philadelphia's mainliners to their feet.

"Now what do you think of it?" Catherine Hayes Brown asked triumphantly. Charles MacArthur was scathing. "I still think it stinks." But the dramatist Sidney Howard charted its future to perfection: "It will run two years in New York."

It was as well that MacArthur, in tandem with Ben Hecht, now achieved a tangible success of his own: the breezy, rip-roaring drama of Chicago newspaper life, *The Front Page*. Poised on the fire escape of the Times Square Theatre, the two authors glumly sweated it out, with Helen—granted a night off from *Coquette*—bringing them a summary bulletin of success after each act. Now Charlie could, in honor, propose formally on the fire escape; on August 17, 1928, they were at last married.

It was ironic that Helen heard clearly the applause in the Times Square Theatre but not that which resounded for her at the Maxine Elliott. All her life, stage fright had rendered her hearing strangely selective; always she heard her fellow actors on stage, but to every sound emanating from the audience she was stone deaf.

"The lock that opens the door to public approval," George Arliss once warned, "has a very tricky combination which is frequently stumbled upon only by chance." In 1928, the year that he came of age, Laurence Kerr Olivier became acutely aware of this.

For four years now, a small clutch of dramatists had been pronouncing that life in the trenches in World War I had been an unmitigated hell. The first play to proclaim this undeniable truth was Maxwell Anderson's and Lawrence Stallings' *What Price Glory?*— never seen on Shaftesbury Avenue—which opened at the Plymouth in New York in September 1924. Nine months earlier, its British counterpart, *Havoc* by Harry Wall, a Yorkshire solicitor, scored a triumph at the Haymarket, though destined to fold on Broadway; one character actor, Richard Bird, as "The Babe," a shell-shocked young officer, took thirty-five curtain calls. One year later, *Tunnel Trench*, the only play to suggest that Germans were also human beings—an unpopular contention in 1925—failed to draw.

This was the climate when Larry, in December 1928, was offered two weekend performances by the Incorporated Stage Society, a successor to J. T. Grein's Independent Theatre, in a new war play, *Journey's End*, at the Apollo Theatre.

No play more cogently illustrated the perennial climate of uncertainty that reigned in the make-believe jungle. It was a first play by a young traveling rep for the Sun Life Insurance Company, R. C. (Robert Cedric) Sherriff, written for a rowing club's amateur dramatic society. Moreover, it was a play without women, set in the trenches before St. Quentin in the spring of 1918—so palpably box-office poison. Larry's role, that of Captain Dennis Stanhope, a nerve-racked battalion commander fighting a losing battle against hard liquor, appealed to him only marginally.

"There is nothing but meals in it," he complained to the producer, John's old colleague at the Oxford Playhouse, James Whale, who, with the superior wisdom of a former prisoner-of-war, properly put him in his place. "That's all there was to think about in Flanders during the War," he retorted curtly.

Too young and callow to discriminate between the first-rate and the meretricious, Larry's desires, at this stage of his career, centered primarily on money and fame. His whole being revolted passionately against the years of genteel poverty, the half-sandwich wolfed at Maida Vale coffee stalls that had so often served him for supper, the humiliating memories of the shared bath water and the cast-off suits. His sole reason for accepting Stanhope was the hope that Basil Dean, known to be casting for his own dramatization of P. C. Wren's Foreign Legion melodrama, *Beau Geste*, would visit the Apollo and select him for the title role.

In this era, *Beau Geste* was still permeated with the sweet smell of success. As a best seller it would ultimately run into fifty-one editions. As a silent film it had propelled Ronald Colman, a handsome, competent British actor with a pencil-line moustache, to overnight Hollywood stardom. The fact that the plot defied credibility cut little ice with Larry. To save his aunt, Lady Brandon, from disgrace—she has secretly sold the Blue Water diamond to protect her tenantry, unknown to her cruel husband—Michael "Beau" Geste steals the substitute, writes a faked confession, and joins the Foreign Legion. He is soon joined by his twin brother, Digby ("Small Geste") and their younger brother, John ("Very Small Geste"). Two of them at length die gloriously in Fort Zinderneuf, leaving John to clear Beau's name.

To win Dean's approval Larry had even grown a lip-line moustache like Colman's, oiled his curly hair into a gigololike lacquer, and industriously plucked his eyebrows. A Hollywood idol was there for the casting.

On Sunday, December 10, 1928, only one factor marred Larry's keen sense of anticipation: he was sharing a dressing room with Maurice Evans, cast as the hero-worshiping young Lieutenant Raleigh, and Evans was known to be the only other contender for Beau. The embarrassment heightened perceptibly after the Act III climax, when Dean, entering the dressing room along with a colleague, instructed Evans curtly, "Leave the room, d'you mind?"—in Larry's words, "the most vulgarly unkind thing I had as yet witnessed."

Then, wasting no time, Dean asked Larry directly, "Well, would you like to play it?"

Since the pay was thirty pounds a week, Larry assented on the spot. Stanhope could go to the devil.

Whale and Sherriff were now in a quandary. Although the play's agent, the highly savvy Spencer Curtis Brown, announced that every West End manager was battling for the rights, only one man was, in fact, remotely interested—Maurice Browne, a forty-seven-year-old British actor, founder of the Little Theatre Movement in the United States, who hadn't even seen the play. A midnight phone call from the poet, Harold Monro, had alerted him that this was a play he must not miss.

Browne himself was without funds, but a weekend visit to two wealthy philanthropists, Dorothy and Leonard Elmhirst, who had purchased Dartington Hall near Totnes in Devon as a center for promoting rural industries, changed all that. With the four-hundred-pound loan that they advanced—repaid within three weeks—Browne was able to secure an option, though he still found Curtis Brown, his sights set on bigger game, "as friendly as a Chicago blizzard."

The terms were onerous, even so; within ten days Browne must engage a cast and a director, secure a West End theatre, and open within four weeks. But still one problem loomed larger than any: with Larry out of the running, who could carry the crucial role of the tortured Stanhope?

The one man who seemed right for the part, as Whale and Sherriff conceived it, was Colin Clive, a young graduate from Hull Repertory, but his reading was as inept as could be. He stumbled fatally over his lines, in need of constant prompting; at one point, as temperamental as Stanhope himself, he offered to give up the part. It was Sherriff who hit on the solution. Since Stanhope drove himself on with whisky, why didn't Clive, although he never drank at rehearsals, stretch a point and treat himself to two stiff whiskies before the afternoon rehearsal?

Though Clive fought the suggestion—it was fatal for an actor to get a name for drink—ultimately he agreed. That afternoon, following perhaps three whiskies, he was a man transformed. The drink had freed him from his inhibitions; from then on the words flowed perfectly, without restraint.

Larry, in the meantime, was fast realizing what every London critic would stress on the morning of January 31, 1929: that *Beau Geste* was a very bad play indeed. Beau's persiflage ("Pish! Also tush! And pshaw! Also Tut twice") was only marginally less embarrassing than his heroics ("Stout Fella! I'm for it all right. Bled white . . . God, I'm going blind!"). During rehearsals things went repeatedly and disastrously wrong. The Foreign Legion uniforms that Dean had bought from the French Government were so acrid with sweat that even repeated fumigation failed to sweeten them.

The opening night was a debacle. In the climax at the fort, Jack Hawkins, as John, firing wooden bullets from a Maxim gun on a low trajectory, struck showers of splinters from the stage; those in the front stalls dived energetically for cover. When John gave Beau his Viking funeral, pouring petrol onto a pile of sand, choking clouds of smoke filled the theatre, and a newly enlisted fireman, who had not seen the dress rehearsals, sent the vast iron-and-asbestos safety curtain crashing down. When the cast at last assembled to take their bows, the theatre was empty; the audience had fled.

One month later, Dean had registered a £24,000 loss, and "Stout Fella" was once more looking for work.

Meanwhile *Journey's End* was enjoying a worldwide bonanza. The film rights were sold for $80,000. Within a year of its opening it had been presented by seventy-six companies in twenty-five languages, including Japanese; forty companies were performing it in Germany alone. The New York run extended to 485 performances, but the London Savoy topped that with 594. Since Stanhope was the role of a lifetime, it was Colin Clive who went on to Hollywood stardom.

For Larry, only four more disastrous flops followed, including *The Last Enemy*, in which he was cast—by a management who had plainly seen *Journey's End*—as a nerve-racked young airman, "rather more than halfway to a nervous breakdown." His dialogue inspired neither him nor his audience: "Try and crowd all the vices of a lifetime into a few months! Fun they call it . . . By God, Cynthia, it's like a mouthful of ashes."

As the 1930s dawned, Larry had put his worst foot forward with a vengeance.

John Gielgud, like the Lunts before him, at last saw the light. Across the river, in the smoky confines of the Waterloo Road, stood the Old Vic (more properly the Royal Victoria Theatre), which until the 1960s was the nearest thing England had to a national theatre. Since 1912, the controlling spirit had been Lilian Mary Baylis, an intensely religious lady. "O God, send me a good actor—and cheap!" she was wont to pray on her knees, center stage, at times of stress. "Are you pure, dear boy?" she often asked newcomers. "I'm not narrow minded but I won't have anything going on in the wings." Afflicted by a stroke that lent a strange Cockney twang to her speech, her aim in life was single-minded: to stage every play in the Shakespearean repertory, and to stage it to perfection.

The older generation of "Vic" actors was slowly phasing out; their attitude was less dedicated than those who would follow. (Esmond Knight, hired for walk-ons in 1925, recalls one of them, musing, "Can't make up me mind whether to play Mercutio and get home early, or the Friar and keep me trousers on!") Under Lilian, the Vic would soon emerge as the true cradle of English drama—the theatre that lured stars like Edith Evans and Sybil Thorndike away from the West End to play the truly testing roles, stiffened at all times by a nucleus of connoisseurs' actors: Ernest Milton, Baliol Holloway, Marie Ney, Ion Swinley. Pay was negligible—no more than twenty pounds a week, even in the late thirties—and conditions were often primitive. All the actresses shared one tin washbasin; on matinée days the wings reeked of the steak and tomatoes or kippers that Lilian was frying up on her gas ring in the prompt corner.

Thus in September 1929, when John crossed Waterloo Bridge to the Vic, where he had once walked on as a student, he was, in a very real sense, coming home.

IV. A Genus Surveyed:
"All These Strange Tatterdemalions..."

On Thursday, July 19, 1951, Larry—who four years earlier had become "Sir Larry"—was one of a group of dignitaries clustered beneath the Irving Statue in Charing Cross Road. As a gift to the citizens of London, Westminster City Council had just created the Irving Garden, an expanse of lawns and flower beds flanked by low railings, and it was Larry's lot to declare it officially open.

Irving, he told the assembled company, had "brought dignity to the theatre and integrity to the actor." In insisting upon discipline at work, and decent accommodation to carry out that work, he had proved himself "the actor's friend." "He died two years before I was born," was Larry's touching confession, "yet I am as conscious of him as if I had served as a member of his company."

At first glance, the analogy was farfetched. In Irving's theatre, that faraway world of gaslight and tall silk hats, a rigid formality had prevailed; first names were almost never used, and no union muscle limited the rigors of rehearsal periods. In Larry's theatre, by contrast, overtime payments were mandatory beyond an eight-hour day, first names were as freely traded as "darlings" between both sexes, rehearsals were commonly conducted in T-shirts and slacks, and pub sandwiches stood in for Irving's habitual 4:00 P.M. dinner hour.

Yet the fundamentals had not changed; beneath the surface, the genus actor was much as it had ever been. Stepping backward in time, Larry and all those present on that July Thursday—Dame Sybil Thorndike, her husband, Sir Lewis Casson, and Richard Attenborough—would have been perfectly at home in Irving's Green Room, capping anecdotes, trading shop, recalling all those nights when the audience had been "cast-iron, me boy," those rarer nights when "God was there." The bond had been forged; nor would the passing years weaken it.

Self-absorption was always a way of life, a truism as self-evident in Larry's day as in Irving's. "They have one common denominator," David Belasco maintained, "they are all adult children," and Somerset Maugham concurred. "I found it a frustrating and maddening world," he summed up, "full of childish people—charming but childish. I adored them, but they often needed . . . spanking"—and here Willie would spread his hands ruefully—"and how does one go about spanking, say, Ethel Barrymore?"

Not all were as self-centered as Maurice Moscovitch, the celebrated Jewish player, who once billed himself on a tour of Europe as "The Greatest Actor in the World"; it was merely that all outside events were related to their own private concerns. On the night of Queen Victoria's death, Lewis Waller's business manager, William Mollison, found him in his dressing room distraught, weeping uncontrollably, "She's dead, Bill, she's dead!" Mollison strove to comfort him, but Waller was inconsolable. "It's the receipts, Bill," he sobbed. "The receipts are bound to drop."

As the epicenters of their own universe, they were puzzled rather than wounded when instant recognition was not their due. On a tour of Dublin, Wilson Barrett was overcome by the warmth of his audience until a property man disillusioned him; a political patriot named Barrett had just been hanged, "and they're after taking you for a relation." George Alexander was equally perturbed when a woman guest at a luncheon party knew neither his name, his profession, nor even of his theatre. "What sort of parts do you play?" she inquired, to which Alexander retorted tersely, "Lovers." "Oh, do be careful," the lady implored him, "my husband's at the next table, and he's terribly jealous."

To his credit, Alexander told the story that night to his assembled company, concluding, "Let none of us on the stage imagine that we're universally well-known. We're not."

The British actor Herbert Standing was heartbroken when his wife died—but even sadder when he found his portrait beneath her pillow. "It doesn't do me justice," he lamented. "Forever the Great Actor must be a poseur," Lionel Barrymore used to chuckle. "To the very last second of his life it must be pose and posture." Thus

Guthrie McClintic noted that Mrs. Leslie Carter always spoke of herself in the third person, as if surveying herself from the outside with an eye to the effect.

Frank Beard, the manager of Truefitt and Hill's world-famous hairdressing establishment on Old Bond Street, recalls that Sir Ralph Richardson, a regular client, once asked to be shown a walking stick. To Beard's surprise, Sir Ralph neither tested the stick for length nor for weight; instead, crooking it over his arm, he slowly stalked the length of the salon, trying out the image in each mirror.

"He wasn't looking for a walking stick at all," Beard reasons. "He was looking for a 'prop'."

Outwardly confident, like precocious children, their public stance—what Sir Richard Attenborough once described to me as "the teeth-and-smiles routine"—often masked a deep-rooted insecurity. Even at the height of their drawing power, the Lunts balked at a $35-a-day suite at Boston's Ritz-Carlton; the $15 a day charged by the more modest Copley-Plaza was consonant with their budget. It was the same with Britain's Jack Hawkins; when he reached £26,000-a-year stardom, a friend suggested he must soon put his two sons, aged two and four, down for a public school. In all seriousness, Hawkins replied, "But that's years away and I might not be able to afford it. I'm quite prepared to face complete professional desolation a year from now."

At times, this constant need for reassurance was almost a physical craving. When she bemoaned that the critics "say I look all right and I have this that and the other, but that I am always Ethel Barrymore," Irving laid a long, delicate hand on hers and consoled her, "See to it that they never say anything else." Even a run of luck was often counted too good to last, so that the current engagement was always the final one. "I'm coining it in before my teeth drop out. It's as simple as that," was Peter O'Toole's philosophy at the peak of stardom.

"You want to be at your very best, and how can you be sure that you're going to be at your very best every night in the week?" was how Kit Cornell summarized the eternal dilemma. And always there was the fear of the up-and-comers making ready to supplant them. Thus Lynn, while agreeing to assist the Theatre Guild in their search for new faces, conscientiously tested a clutch of applicants, then reported with quiet satisfaction, "Not a particle of talent in this group—thank God."

Their relationship with their audience was always ambivalent, at best. All of them, in their heart of hearts, shared the reservations of Richard Mansfield, akin to those of Bernhardt. "That monster waiting there every night has to be fed," was how Mansfield put it. "It is my sweetheart when I love it and my cold and freezing enemy when its face is stone." To John Gielgud, it was "that unpredictable seductress out front, that benevolent Medusa." Larry had even been known to arrive early in the theatre, to lean against the safety curtain, shouting, "You bastards, you bastards"—but only on first nights and meaning, of course, the critics.

Sometimes the tributes of the public proved bewildering. How, wondered Frederick Valk, did one deal with an excitable stranger who burst into his dressing room during a London matinée of *The Merchant*, announcing, "The only thing wrong with Shylock was that he needed mothering!" How, pondered Moira Lister, did one react to a comment like that overheard from a soldier in the audience: "Well, she could pee in my soup any day." After a spell of years, Miss Lister decided to class this as a compliment.

Occasionally there were ructions between actors and their public. Robert Loraine was so incensed by audience chatter that he once cut short a Shavian sermon to berate a lady who had dropped her tea tray. (When she made to pick it up, her friend restrained her, cautioning, "No, no, dear, Mr. Loraine wouldn't like it.") Few were as uninhibited as John Barrymore during the flu epidemic that coincided with Tolstoy's *Redemption* in 1918. Heaving a five-pound sea bass among the coughers and wheezers in the front stalls, Barrymore trumpeted, "Busy yourselves with *this*, you damned walruses, while the rest of us proceed with the libretto."

Yet there were always happier occasions: the magic moments when players and their audience briefly became a divine entity. "The right audience is the greatest stage director in the world," Otis Skinner once avowed, and that was the way it was at Greenwall's Theatre in Fort Worth, Texas, when ankle-deep mud delayed the arrival of Mansfield's scenery train until 7:45 P.M., the hour of curtain-up.

But the theatre, the mayor assured Mansfield, was packed; if necessary, the audience would wait all night to see him play *Cyrano de Bergerac*. The actor was dubious, but only three people, whose train left at midnight, asked for their money back. The first curtain rose at 10:30 P.M.; Cyrano expired as dawn was breaking, at twenty minutes before three in the morning.

As the jungle's population thrived and multiplied—more than 3,000 on Shaftesbury Avenue by 1932, and 8,500 on Broadway, but only 4,000 in work—the inhabitants needed to be tough indeed. It was the kind of toughness, pronounced Broadway's Billy Rose, "compounded of ego, energy and a white flame in the vitals . . . the kind of toughness that shrugs off walking to save car fare, sorry-you're-not-the-type, leave-your-name-and-address, and the other assorted kicks in the slats." The kind of toughness, in fact, that enabled the young Peggy Ashcroft, playing Strindberg's *Fraulein Elsa* in 1932, not only to endure a 2:00 A.M. tongue-lashing from the Russian producer Theodore Komisarjevsky ("I will wring a good performance out of her if it's the last thing I do!") but, two years later, to marry him.

Resilience was likewise a "must," the kind that led Broadway's William Collier senior to remark of a show that opened on Thursday and closed on Saturday, "The play was a success but the audience was a failure." Such resilience prompted Fay Compton, forced to dress in the manager's office on a run-down provincial tour, to urge every telephone caller, "Don't miss Fay Compton—she's marvellous."

Above all, in that most hackneyed of backstage phrases, they needed to be troupers: "The Show Must Go On" was a precept that they had absorbed along with their alphabet. Ill health was something that afflicted lesser breeds; the British actress, Mary Mackenzie, played the first night of one short-lived play stricken with polio, unable to raise her arms above her waist. Madge Kendal, after mistakenly swallowing poison instead of medicine in Philadelphia, played for three weeks on a diet of egg whites beaten up in champagne. Mansfield somehow managed the dance routines of the sprightly Prince Karl Heinrich in *Old Heidelberg* with his ankle in a plaster cast, just as Peggy Ashcroft played an Old Vic matinée of *Caesar and Cleopatra* after breaking her toe on an iron counterweight. Cathleen Nesbitt once won a round of applause after collapsing on her curtain line in Edgar Wallace's *The Case of the Frightened Lady;* no one in the audience knew that she had survived three acts battling viral pneumonia.

Their traditions demanded no less. When her cast broke rehearsals to dive for cover during a World War I Zeppelin raid, Lilian Baylis upbraided them, "I am ashamed of you all. If you have to be killed, at least die at your job."

Those at the peak of the profession cultivated perfectionism-plus. The bywords, of course, were Alfred and Lynn; as a degraded has-been in Durrenmatt's *The Visit,* Alfred wore not only a shabby old suit, but socks darned at the toe and heel, though he was never required to remove his shoes. Lynn, after working on a line for eight months in *Reunion in Vienna,* finally got her laugh on the 264th night. But others, at all times, took infinite pains to submerge themselves in a part. Tree, a nonsmoker, could stomach thick black cigars when playing a financier in *Business Is Business;* as Count d'Orsay in *The Last of the Dandies,* he habitually cut friends of whom he felt the Count would have disapproved. When Cathleen Nesbitt vanished from her lunchtime haunts, her friends soon learned the reason; cast as a prostitute in Lonsdale's *Spring Cleaning,* she had found a small café in Greek Street, Soho, patronized solely by ladies of the town.

To those outside the profession, this meticulous approach was always a source of wonder. One Harley Street physician was entirely nonplussed when Peter Finch, who was boning up on Mercutio, entered his consulting room armed with the text of *Romeo and Juliet.* "If I'm dying with a sword in my gut," he wanted to know, "how should I deliver this speech?"

The cultivation of a role might call for hours of patient observation. Barry Fitzgerald, selected for "Captain" Jack Boyle in Sean O'Casey's *Juno and the Paycock,* an Abbey, Dublin, production, spent weeks roaming the quays of the Liffey, studying weather-beaten salts. As the tormented hero in *Detective Story,* Ralph Bellamy sat for hours in friendly station precincts, studying the ways of plainclothes men; as Franklin D. Roosevelt in *Sunrise at Campobello,* he spent weeks among paralytics. When Lionel Barrymore played Guiseppe, an Italian organ grinder in *The Mummy and the Hummingbird,* he was duly coached by the genuine article—to the delight of his sister, Ethel, but to the total disgust of her escort, a Roman count. "He's *not* an Italian," he complained furiously. "He is a *Sicilian.*"

It was, of course, never too late to get a performance exactly right. On a night in 1940, touring *Twelfth Night,* Helen called Charles MacArthur long distance to announce in ecstasy, "Charlie, I did it! I *was* Viola tonight!" Not unreasonably MacArthur was overcome with laughter; the show was closing next day.

Through all these vicissitudes, it was essential to be clinical, standing as far apart from one's performance as the coolest of critics, cultivating what Alfred called "an outside eye and an outside ear."

Ellen Terry, as Juliet, was one case in point, carefully adjusting the safety pins that held her kerchief in place as she sank to her knees in tears before Friar Laurence. In a later age, James Mason was typical; after a death scene that reduced even the stage hands to silent awe, he called abruptly to an electrician, "That fifth light on Number Two batten needs bringing up if I'm to be shown to full advantage."

It was imperative to be resourceful. Britain's Claude King, later a pillar of the Screen Actors' Guild in Hollywood, flummoxed by a door that came away in his hand while touring in *The Silver King*, tucked it smartly under his arm and exited with aplomb. It was in this tradition that John, playing the Graveyard Scene in *Hamlet* and finding that Yorick's skull had rolled out of reach, skipped thirty lines of the speech and brought Ophelia's funeral procession scurrying from the wings like tumblers.

Robert Speaight, playing Booth in John Drinkwater's *Abraham Lincoln*, showed similar acumen; realizing he had forgotten his revolver, he stepped into the box to stab Lincoln in the back with an imaginary knife, thus altering the course of American history. Yet by common consent the palm for improvisation went to Otto Kruger, Kit Cornell's leading man, in Clemence Dane's *Will Shakespeare*. "I shall write a play about two lovers who lived in Verona," he told Kit, as Mary Fitton, at which the curtain was to fall. But the ASM was pursuing his own Dark Lady up a side alley; the curtain stayed obstinately up. Then, as Kit "turned to stone," Kruger went manfully on, "It will be called *Romeo and Juliet*," a cue for the Balcony Scene, but no curtain fall came with its conclusion. "Then I shall write a play called *Hamlet*," Kruger ad-libbed desperately, "and I shall have my hero say 'To be or not to be,' " a cue for further soliloquy. Before he had time for Lear's curse or Othello's death throes, the curtain mercifully came down.

More than most other professionals, they were confronted all their lives with the same adverse factors. To Henry James, a bitterly disappointed dramatist, the theatre was always "an unholy trade." Even Sir Seymour Hicks, who enjoyed fifty years as a successful farceur, had to admit that it was "a damned exacting mistress." Few of its hardships were restricted to beginners; they could recur even after a successful twelve months' run. "Don't go on the stage unless you want your heart broken," Edith Evans would warn hopeful aspirants, for all too soon they would learn what Kenneth Barnes at RADA impressed on Margaret Lockwood and the class of 1933: "Only one of all of you here will ever make a name, or win a place in the eyes of the public."

Even Sir Alec Guinness, as he once told this author, was reduced to roaming the London streets with only half a crown (twelve pence) in the world; he, like Larry, had known the penury of dining on coffee-stall sandwiches and learned, in the dramatist Leonard Merrick's words, "to disguise privation under well-cut clothes, to smile in the Strand and break your heart in private."

Thus the Bodega in Bedford Street, off the Strand, "The Actors' Mile," was a mecca for hard-up actors anxious to punish the free cheese, as was the bar of the Knickerbocker Hotel at Broadway and 42nd Street, with its mouth-watering free lunch counter: sardines, pumpernickel, cottage cheese, and ripe olives. Yet all this presupposed the price of a beer: ten cents. Lacking even this sum, Henry Fonda lived for three weeks on a box of wild rice.

In this often-frugal world, no story was more widely circulated than that of the Hysons' Christmas Eve, with its poignant undertones of an O. Henry short story.

Carl Hyson and his actress wife, Dorothy Dickson, were "resting" at the time they checked into Frank Case's Algonquin Hotel on New York's West 44th Street. To sample the hotel's menu was quite beyond them. On Christmas Eve, as on every day in that week, they smuggled in their sliced ham, rye bread, and pickles from the next-door delicatessen, then, since this *was* Christmas, phoned room service for a pot of coffee and a single order of mashed potatoes in order to avail themselves of knives and forks. Later, wondering just what tip was feasible, they summoned the waiter and asked for the check.

"Check?" the waiter echoed. "There is no check. Don't you know that Mr. Case plays host to everyone in the hotel on Christmas Eve?" Blissfully unaware of the salt that he was rubbing into the wound, he marveled, "You ought to see the dinner *some* of the guests are eating."

A world whose inhabitants walked a perpetual tightrope through life developed certain skills to a fine art, most especially the art of the alibi. Certain conventions prevailed. It was accepted, as the late Peter Bull noted, that a show never closed down because nobody wanted to see it. The weather was "too hot" or "too cold" or "nobody was in town." In London, the advent of the Ideal Home Exhibition was bound to help; in New York, business would pick up after Labor Day. There was never any question of one's talents going unrecognized; it was merely a matter of coming to terms. In that bow-windowed alcove of the Green Room Club overlooking Leicester Square, known as "Boozers' Bay," Harold French heard the alibis time and again: "I'm looking for a part that's up my street" or "I've had the offers but they won't pay my money." In the Lamb's, New York, the refrain was identical: "I'm holding out for Broadway."

The alibis, of course, deceived nobody, least of all the agents to whom they wrote endless letters—"perfectly willing to tour," while perfectly willing to do nothing of the sort—or paid almost daily visits. In New York, creaking elevators took them to the crowded outer office of the Packard Theatrical Agency, where the kindly Mrs. Ada Humbert might find something on her books; a player willing to settle for stock called on Wales Winter. In London those opting for a similar compromise—five pounds a week in repertory—made for Cambridge Circus and the office of Miss Miriam Warner, a lady never seen with her hat off or her shoes on, known affectionately, through the adjacent neon sign boosting a virility pill, as the Duchess of Damaroids Corner. Other flights of hard, stone stairs led to the Leicester Place offices of Akerman May and to the Garrick Street office of Herbert Blackmore, an agent since Irving was a juvenile, with his piercing eyes and the hard, sharp voice that barked out, "What experience? Nothing today!"

Those were the words that always cast a chill, as painful as the dreaded "Next, please!" that echoed from the darkened stalls when auditions were in progress. Few in the profession had any faith in their efficacy. "I saw a clever young man at Cambridge last night," Harcourt Williams, the Old Vic producer, enthused to his secretary. "Anthony Quayle. Know anything about him?" "Yes," the girl replied sweetly. "You turned him down at an audition two days ago."

When the great Lee Shubert hired Margaret Sullavan without even a reading, he justified his choice. "You have a voice like Ethel Barrymore." "What I have," countered Miss Sullavan with dignity, "is a bad case of laryngitis."

Even the visible token of one's name in flashing lights was rarely a guarantee that the wolves would remain at bay; it was a come-day, go-day, God-send-payday world. When one Wilson Barrett play opened to glowing notices, the queue outside his Princess Theatre stretched for yards along Oxford Street—a line not of patrons seeking stalls but of creditors seeking something on account. As late as 1933, Ethel Barrymore's home in Mamaroneck was plunged into darkness; the feckless lady had failed to pay her electricity bills. When the bailiffs moved in on Edgar Wallace, the dramatist borrowed two shillings from the broker's man, staked it at the races, won £130, and redeemed his home. As an insurance for the future, Wallace—who died bankrupt in 1932—bought his own theatre, Wyndham's, to stage his own melodramas, and from then on made free of the box office till on his way to Ascot races.

For newcomers to the jungle, the first yardsticks of success seemed incredibly far away: the daily breakfast in bed that was Alfred's dream; the belted camel-hair coat, which testified to Larry's thirty pounds a week in *Beau Geste*; the spatter of applause, led by the Savoy Grill waiters, that so heartened John; the reserved table at Signor Abel's Ivy Restaurant, off St. Martin's Lane, or the good front table downstairs at Sardi's on West 44th Street ("the A-group on the east wall," as Tyrone Guthrie put it).

For almost all the profession, these exclusively theatrical and literary watering holes filled a deep-felt need. Among their own kind, immured from a hostile world, they felt a rare security: the knowledge of being pampered and appreciated, the gratification of dining cheek by jowl with the greats of the profession. Some restaurants had begun as modestly as their own clientèle. In 1921, The Ivy, facing the St. Martin's and Ambassador's Theatres, was a one-room café, with a linoleum floor, paper napkins, and no liquor license. Abetted by his restaurant manager, Mario Gallati, Abel bought the lease of the next-door building and took on a first-class chef. Soon the showman Charles B. Cochran became a regular patron, along with the French actress Alice Delysia; Noël, Tallulah, Pinero, and Galsworthy followed suit. Even in 1928, when the restaurant was entirely rebuilt and swarmed with workmen, the regulars remained resolutely loyal; during one rainy lunchtime, Marie Tempest was seen impassively finishing her steak under a raised umbrella.

With the instinctive sixth sense of a fine restaurateur, Mario often gauged when times were tough; at such moments, the bill bore Mario's signature and the stamp "With the compliments of the management." This was equally a tradition, from the day in 1927, when Vincent Sardi senior moved his restaurant to its current location at

234 West 44th Street. "You just sign the bill and pay when you can," he told the indigents gently. Sardi's was rich in such traditions: the six hundred-plus portraits lining the walls, initiated by a Russian refugee, Alexander Gard, and later continued by others; the specialty dishes like Crabmeat Sardi (with asparagus) and *Boccone Dolce* (meringue, whipped cream, strawberries, and bitter chocolate), relished by Kit Cornell and the columnist Walter Winchell; the standing ovation that still greets a first-night triumph, introduced in 1950 for Shirley Booth in William Inge's *Come Back, Little Sheba*. When fortune smiled, Sardi's patrons repaid that long-standing credit with interest; not for nothing was the hatcheck girl, Renée Carrol, celebrated as the richest in the United States.

Few players chose to rest their heads anywhere but Frank Case's two hundred-room Algonquin Hotel farther up West 44th Street; for Larry and Ralph Richardson, no less than Charlton Heston and Orson Welles, this was their chosen haven. For ten years after 1918, its Round Table, whose habitués included Alexander Woollcott, Dorothy Parker, Robert Benchley, Robert E. Sherwood, and George S. Kaufman, drew its full complement of gawkers; the celebrated Rose Room was most generally known as the "Don't Look Now" room. Since Case also extended generous credit, he was at one point saddled with $80,000 worth of debts, but in due time the celebrities both stayed faithful and paid in full. To the perpetually insecure regulars, it was infinitely reassuring to be part of an exclusive world, where the chef, Otto Schmuck, and the maître d', George Jacques, knew that Helen would opt for corned beef hash, while John Barrymore favored terrapin in Amontillado, that Irish stew was always Herbert Marshall's choice, and that Ben Hecht craved minute steak with garlic sauce.

Life in the theatrical clubs differed markedly from that of more staid venues. Although the Lamb's, again on West 44th Street, was named after the British essayist, Charles Lamb, the ambience was at all times frolicsome; stray pigeons were known to perch for hours on the Club's mantelpiece, unmolested by the Club's cat, Thomas C. Lamb III, who was more responsive to a pewter mug of beer at a rough-hewn oak table in the bar. Chimpanzees were freely admitted, if accompanied by their trainers, and Presidents of the United States, besides; Raymond Massey, fully made up as Abraham Lincoln, would drop in after a matinee, in time succeeded by Ralph Bellamy, wearing leg braces as FDR.

Every club treasured mementos of the profession, like sacred tribal totems; the Players prized Mark Twain's pool cue as dearly as the Green Room in London prized the clock that tolled the hours while Pinero composed his "well-made" plays. On the main staircase leading to the Garrick Club bar stands the chair from the Midland Hotel, Bradford, on which Irving "breathed his last," as the plaque puts it—a gift from Sir Seymour Hicks, whose portrait, along with that of Leslie Howard, gazes benignly down from the walls.

In time, the luckiest in the jungle might see the pipe dreams of the profession come true: membership of one or more of these clubs, regular work, the first-night Sardi's ovation, international recognition. But there were many other bogeys with which they contended for all their working lives. "I wouldn't give a nickel for an actor who isn't nervous," David Belasco used to say, and all of them were prey to first-night nerves, retching dismally, as Peter Finch told me, over the dressing-room washbasin. With Sir Alec Guinness, fear took on a subtler guise: a crippling pain in his knee in the week before opening was followed by the symptoms of a nasty head cold on the first night. For Margaret Leighton, every first night was "like being in a dark tunnel, walking over treacle." Charles Laughton was seized by a recurrent phobia—his clothes would fall off, leaving him naked the moment he faced an audience. Both age and experience were quite immaterial. On the first night of Robert Morley's play *Short Story*, Marie Tempest, aged seventy-one, shook so badly with nerves that her teacup had to be glued to its saucer. "After one thousand performances," mourned Eva Le Gallienne, "it just gets worse every year."

The reasons were not hard to find. All of them were anticipating first-night disasters that had become part of jungle lore: the doors that wouldn't shut, the matches that wouldn't strike, the drawers that wouldn't open. Each generation had its own dire examples, and in the twenties the opening night of *The Garden of Allah* at the Theatre Royal, Drury Lane, ranked high on the list: the realistic "sand storm" that sent a whirling torrent of bran over the front six rows of the stalls. At the Century in New York, a crew of 150 stagehands had rehearsed for three days to ensure perfection, but the end result was the same: James Buchanan "Diamond Jim" Brady, the super railroad salesman, was only one of many first-nighters who strode from the theatre bespattered from head to foot with farina.

Sometimes a show could survive such disasters. Constance Collier

141

and her leading man, John Barrymore, had the flats representing an opera house collapse on them at the first night of *Peter Ibbetson,* but the play ran two years. The same held good with Leslie Howard, as the gentleman-convict on the run in Galsworthy's *Escape;* after missing his cue for a scene where he hid under a lady's bed, he had to crawl on stage through a hole that the carpenter sawed in the scenery.

But as often, a first-night disaster spelled just that at the box office. When Johnston Forbes-Robertson played *Caesar and Cleopatra* at the New Amsterdam in New York, the meticulous Shaw had specified one scene in which Caesar must eat dates. On the first night, the effect was totally ruined; a date embedded in his upper plate rendered the actor speechless, and he tumbled offstage in mid-sentence to extricate it. The play failed dismally. Elaborate stage effects were a sure way of giving hostages to fortune. In Act II of *The Orchard Walls,* staged by Henry Sherek in London, three coaches of the Dunkirk ferry, with honeymooners aboard, were seen departing Victoria Station. This was ten minutes after curtain-up, but on the opening night the first coach moved a yard, then stopped dead. When the curtain, in due course, rose on Act III, the mystified audience had been deprived of thirty minutes of explanatory dialogue.

Under such emotional stress, the list of those who took to the bottle to anesthetize their fears understandably embraced many of the topmost stars. In Britain, the most notable casualty was Henry Ainley, with the profile of a Greek god, unemployed and unemployable after 1932, though piteously begging to play even a butler. "I drink too much and I'm getting very old," he told the teenage Harold French; that was in 1916, when Ainley was thirty-seven. Ten years later he was drinking so heavily that his voice went completely while essaying *Macbeth;* in 1930, halfway through a Royal Command Performance of *Hamlet,* his memory went blank. From then on, Ainley's mellifluous voice was heard only on the radio.

The same problem afflicted John Barrymore, so far gone in liquor he often retired to the wings to vomit; as early as 1914, the curtain was rung down on him as he lurched incomprehensibly about the stage in *The Yellow Ticket* at the Eltinge. Another flawed talent was Britain's Wilfrid Lawson, prone to ring up managers and abuse them at 2:00 A.M.; on one occasion he and his fellow toper, Richard Burton, attended a matinée of a play where Lawson made a late entrance. Time passed, but he made no move toward his dressing room. Finally he told Burton confidentially, "You'll like this bit. This is where I come on."

Laurette Taylor was one who fought a quasisuccessful battle to overcome her craving, sometimes taking to her heels in sheer terror at the sight of a liquor-store window. Tragically, this was a fight that Jeanne Eagels could not win. Here was an actress who never smoked nor drank until she won the role of Sadie Thompson, the prostitute, in Somerset Maugham's *Rain*, yet toward the end of the two-year run she was passing out cold in her dressing room. In *Her Cardboard Lover*, opposite Leslie Howard, she went fast asleep in midscene; the tour was a fearsome cycle of missed performances and bottles hurled from hotel windows, culminating at the last in an eighteen-month Equity suspension. On the day the ban was lifted, October 4, 1929, Jeanne Eagels died, aged thirty-five—with no trace of the $2 million that her talents had netted her.

The only player forced into semiretirement though she faced no alcoholic problems was Mrs. Patrick Campbell, and for one good reason: with her, it was the management and fellow players who suffered the emotional stress. "I am a *tour de force* but I am forced to tour," was how Mrs. Pat put it, and with truth; at times she was on the road for four years at a stretch, esteemed only by her griffon, Pipsi, and a succession of Pekingese—Kweilli, Moonbeam, and Pinky Panky Poo. No West End or Broadway manager could endure an actress who behaved, in Woollcott's words, "like a sinking ship firing on her rescuers." Drifting back and forth across the Atlantic, she was at length reduced to teaching debutantes how to enunciate. Three years before Mrs. Pat's death in 1940, Eva Le Gallienne noted in her diary: "Poor old woman! She's made a point all her life of being spectacularly nasty to everyone, and now she's quite alone."

To the denizens of the jungle, the critics could prove a mixed blessing. Britain's acerbic James Agate (*The Sunday Times*) was a much-feared man; told that he was slumbering through the first night of *The Improper Duchess*, the author, J. B. Fagan, begged, "Don't wake him. Agate's always very good when he's asleep." Broadway critics, too, were skilled at drawing blood, notably Dorothy Parker (*The New Yorker*), who claimed that Katharine Hepburn in *The Lake* "ran the gamut of emotion all the way from A to B," and summed up another doomed offering, "*House Beautiful* is play lousy." Even John Mason

143

Brown (*The New York Post*), more tolerant than most, recorded sadly, "Tallulah Bankhead barged down the Nile last night as Cleopatra and sank."

Yet faced with an unsung talent, the critics were as eager to make as to break. Woollcott had early entered the lists on Kit's behalf; when London's tiny Gate Theatre, by Charing Cross, so small that the actors were forced to dress on the stage, put on Georg Kaiser's Expressionist drama, *From Morn to Midnight*, Agate's rave review urging playgoers to go *now*—"It is no use bringing a tube of oxygen after the patient is dead"—even included the club theatre's telephone number. Twenty-four hours later the run was sold out.

Failing memory was to plague many of them as the years wore on; as the nurse in *Romeo and Juliet*, John noted, his Great-Aunt Ellen cleverly feigned deafness, enabling the rest of the cast to whisper her lines in her ear. But Ellen's memory had always been her weak point; at the time of Irving's death, rehearsing *Alice Sit-By-The-Fire*, J. M. Barrie had exploded, "It doesn't matter what you say, dear lady, but for God's sake say something!" Many a young ASM who later rose to eminence spent hours each evening "on the book," crouched in the property fireplace, "feeding" the amnesiacs their lines—as did Leonard Sachs for Edmund Gwenn in Galsworthy's *The Skin Game*, and Hollywood's George Cukor for Ethel Barrymore in *The Constant Wife*. Afterward Maugham was in no way appeased when Miss Barrymore flung her arms around his neck, consoling him with, "Darling, I've ruined your play but don't worry, it will run for two years," though, in fact, it did just that.

Runs of this duration could prove a problem, condemning the players to what Kenneth Macgowan called "the squirrel-cage wheel of the same monotonous lines." As a young actor who trod that wheel for almost eighteen months following Noël's departure from *The Constant Nymph*, John's feelings were mixed: it was useful for making money, for establishing one's name with the public, for perfecting one's timing, yet it was still an eternal battle to conceal one's inner boredom. There was inevitably a fatal tendency to sneak in "improvements" ("I always looked in to take them out," Larry noted in his producing days) so that the original focus of a play was lost. After four months out of New York, Reginald Denham found to his horror that his production of *The Two Mrs. Carrolls* now ran twenty minutes longer; Elisabeth Bergner was repeating every line two, even three times, so that "Darling, must you go to Monte Carlo?" became

Ellen Terry as Portia in The Merchant of Venice: *Lyceum, London, 1902.*

Sir Henry Irving: A generation knew him as "The Stare."

Sir Charles Wyndham and his wife, Mary Moore, in David Garrick: *Criterion, London, 1886.*

George Alexander and Mrs. Patrick Campbell in Pinero's The Second Mrs. Tanqueray: *St. James's, London, 1893.*

Sir Herbert Beerbohm Tree as Svengali in Trilby: *Haymarket, London, 1895.*

A 1903 programme featuring the author's uncle, Vincent Collier.

PROGRAMME.

EACH EVENING AT 8 O'CLOCK.

"Temptations of an Actress."

COMEDY-DRAMA in Four Acts.

Henery Bunston	...	...	... Mr. FRED BAINES
Capt. Gerald Wilton	...	...	Mr. ROY G. HEWLAND
Capt. Horace Garside	...	...	Mr. VINCENT COLLIER
The Hon. Reginald Softer	...	Mr. F. E. ACHER-SMITH
Joseph Hodson	...	...	Mr. C. T. CHAPMAN
Horatio Wilkins	...	...	Mr. HERBERT SPENCER
John ...	...	...	Mr. HENRY HARVEY
Helena Lennox	...	...	Miss EVA NEVILLE
Mrs. Wilkins	...	...	Miss MINNIE SINCLAIR
Bridget	..	...	Miss ELAINE FENTON
		AND	
Violet	...	...	Miss EDITH HERON-BROWN

Act I. ... ... **Grand Hotel, Northbridge**
JEALOUSY.

Act II. ... ... **Bunston's Lodgings**
LOVE AND WAR.

Act III. ... ... **Green Room, Theatre Royal,**
THE RIVALS **Northbridge**

Act IV. ... ... **An Old Manor House**
THE TEMPTOR'S POWER.

Stage Manager ... *Mr. FRANK RIDLEY.*

Sir Johnston Forbes-Robertson and his wife, Gertrude Elliott, in The Passing of the Third Floor Back: *St. James's, London, 1908/Maxine Elliott, New York, 1909.*

Extra women making up at His Majesty's, London, in Beerbohm Tree's time.

The White Man's Burden: Mary Clare (Tondeleyo), Brian Aherne (Langford), and Franklin Dyall (Weston) in White Cargo: *Playhouse, London, 1924/Greenwich Village, New York, 1923.*

War Is Hell: Richard Bird as the shell-shocked subaltern assaults his C.O., Leslie Faber, in Havoc: *Haymarket, London/Maxine Elliott, New York, 1924.*

The Heavy Mother: Noël Coward and Lilian Braithwaite in The Vortex: *Royalty, London, 1924/Henry Miller, New York, 1925.*

Sir Charles Hawtrey with His Lady Friends: *St. James's, London, 1920. On his left, Athene Seyler.*

Helen Hayes playing the little-girl role of Little Simone in The Prodigal Husband *with John Drew: Empire, New York, 1914.*

Helen Hayes at last came of age as the contrary Norma Besant in Coquette, *seen here with Elliot Cabot and Charles Waldron: Maxine Elliot, New York, 1927.*

Brian Aherne (Robert Browning) and Katharine Cornell (Elizabeth Moulton-Barrett) in The Barretts of Wimpole Street: Empire, New York, 1931.

Helen Hayes as the young queen in Victoria Regina: Broadhurst, New York, 1935.

Gertrude Lawrence and Noël Coward (Amanda and Elyot) in Act One of Coward's Private Lives: *Phoenix, London, 1930/ Times Square, New York, 1931.*

Katharine Cornell as Lalage with Lionel Atwill (Ragatzy) in The Outsider: *Forty-Ninth Street, New York, 1924.*

Katharine Cornell, with Edith Evans as the Nurse, in Romeo and Juliet: *Martin Beck, New York, 1934.*

Lynn Fontanne (Irene) and Alfred Lunt (Harry Van) in Robert E. Sherwood's Pulitzer Prize winner, Idiots Delight: *Shubert, New York, 1936.*

The Lunts as Jupiter and Alkmena in Amphitryon 38: *Shubert, New York, 1937/ Lyric, London, 1938.*

The Lunts as Sir John Fletcher and Olivia Brown in Terrence Rattigan's Love in Idleness: *Lyric, London, 1944/Empire, New York, 1946, retitled* O Mistress Mine.

John Gielgud as the patriarch Noah in André Obey's play of that name: New, London, 1935.

John Gielgud as Hamlet with Leslie Banks (Claudius) and Marian Spencer (Gertrude): Haymarket, London, 1944/1945.

*Laurence Olivier as the ma-
levolent Richard III at the
New Theatre, London,
1944/Century New York,
1946.*

*Laurence Olivier as Othello
at the Old Vic and Chichester
Festival Theatre, 1963/1964.*

Laurence Olivier as Archie Rice in John Osborne's The Entertainer: *Royal Court and Palace, London, 1957/Royale, New York, 1958*

John Gielgud (the seedy Spooner) and Ralph Richardson (the alcoholic Hirst) in Harold Pinter's No Man's Land: *Old Vic and National, London, 1975/1976.*

Peter Bull, Timothy Bateson, Paul Daneman, and Peter Woodthorpe in Samuel Beckett's Waiting for Godot: *Arts and Criterion, London, 1955.*

Peggy Ashcroft as Winnie, up to her neck in it in Beckett's Happy Days: *National Theatre at the Old Vic, London, 1975.*

BARTHOLOMEW FAIR

QUARLOS
ESMOND KNIGHT

BLACK FELT HAT.
BLACK AND WHITE UNCURLED
OSTRICH FEATHERS.
PEARL EARRINGS.

WHITE ORGANDY COLLAR AND
CUFFS. WITH WHITE MACRAMÉ
LACE EDGING. WHITE
LAWN UNDER SLEEVES.

STIFF CRIMSON SATIN
SUIT. THE WAIST
CUT MUCH HIGHER
THAN NATURAL
WAIST LINE
MELON SHAPED
BREECHES ON
STIFF INTERLINING.
BLACK VELVET POINTS
(WITH SILVER TAGS)
AND GARTERS (WITH
SILVER FRINGE)

CRIMSON WOOL. OR
DULL NYLON TIGHTS.
BLACK SUEDE BOOTS
WITH SPURS AND
SPUR GUARDS.
BLACK SUEDE GLOVES
TRIMMED WITH SILVER.
BLACK SUEDE SWORD
BELT.

CLOAK. (CIRCULAR)
BLACK. SMOOTH CLOTH.
HEAVY ENOUGH TO BE
UNLINED. EDGE
CUT. WITH NO HEM

BLUE MOIRÉ OR TAFFETA
SASH.

Workroom sketch by the Motleys for a production of Bartholomew Fair: Old Vic, London, 1950.

Marlon Brando and Jessica Tandy in A Streetcar Named Desire: *Ethel Barrymore, New York, 1947.*

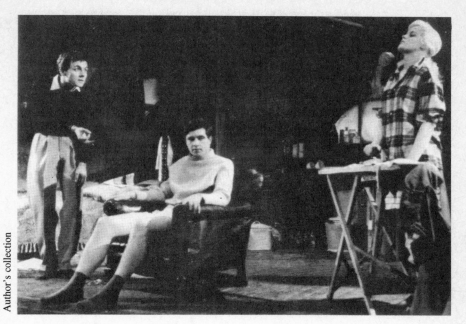

Kenneth Haigh, Alan Bates, and Mary Ure in John Osborne's Look Back in Anger: *Royal Court, London, 1956/Lyceum, New York, 1957.*

Dresser Pansy Alcott fixes the hair of showgirl Maisie Hiatt backstage at the London Hippodrome.

Actress Diane Cilento books in with the stage door keeper at the Duke of York's during the run of Clifford Odets's The Big Knife.

Stage hands at work at London's Scala Theatre.

"Darling—darling—darling. Must you go to Monte Carlo? Must you? Must you? Please don't."

Some combated the ennui with elaborate practical jokes, like du Maurier in *The Last of Mrs. Cheyney*, peopling the breakfast table in Act III with jumping cups and saucers, clockwork mice, and trick apples that squeaked piteously. But others, like Tree, who yearned to play a different role each night, were too despondent for such tomfoolery, and Leslie Howard was foremost amongst them. "Can't you hold out any hope of business falling off?" he would ask the management almost nightly.

To be typecast in a long run was an even sorrier fate. Some—the less dedicated—surrendered to it, seeing a meal ticket for life, but others, the true perfectionists, fought it valiantly, even risking long months out of work. Thus Charles Laughton, scoring as a pickpocket in Molnar's *Liliom*, was at once offered thirty pounds a week to play another pickpocket. Laughton, courageously, held out until the part of a fat old general cropped up—only to be wooed, when the play closed, with the offer of another fat old general. More and more of them grew to hate what John Mason Brown called "the stencil of their success." "I hate the Flora Robson part," Dame Flora told me frankly. "The management have only to see a tin of weedkiller in the script and they send it to me." Dame Edith Evans conceived a similar loathing for Wilde's Lady Bracknell. "I've played her everywhere except on ice and under water," she once exploded.

Yet in the last resort the public shouldered the blame; the few failures that the greats of the profession recorded came when they chose an unfamiliar role. Du Maurier once essayed a paralyzed violinist in *Fame;* the public stayed resolutely away. Wyndham's fans refused to accept him as a society roué in *Bellamy the Magnificent*, or even as the ugly Cyrano de Bergerac. Waller was an abysmal failure as Romeo, for the K.O.W.'s saw his death as sheer sacrilege. As for Hawtrey, with his moustache shaved off for a costume play, *Mr. George*, the sense of outrage at the Vaudeville was almost tangible. Only when he allowed it to grow again did his public forgive him.

Upstaging—moving up on an actor's lines, forcing him to turn away from the audience—was a cardinal sin, practiced by many old-timers, to the despair of their juniors. A past mistress at this, the veteran British actress Nancy Price once contrived to outsmart that other veteran, Mrs. Pat, during a production of Ibsen's *John Gabriel Borkman* at the little "Q" Theatre, beside the Thames near Richmond.

On the first night Mrs. Pat's big scene was well-nigh invisible; Miss Price had bribed the electrician to focus the spot on her. At curtain fall, Mrs. Pat, exiting in fury through the fireplace, was heard to declaim in tones of thunder, "Electrician! I want a word with you!"

It was Mrs. Pat, starring in G. B. Stern's *The Matriarch* in London, who heard with incredulous rage that her role in the forthcoming Broadway production had gone to Constance Collier. Her revenge was sweet, if not short. On the New York first night, the entire cast, frozen with dread, heard that Mrs. Pat was in the front row. At curtain rise, understandably, Constance dried up altogether.

Promptly, a sepulchral whisper was heard from the stalls—"The line, I seem to remember, goes something like this"—which was why *The Matriarch* very soon vacated the Longacre Theatre on 48th Street.

At the height of Irving's eminence, actors—"all these strange tatterdemalions between whom there was no atom of love lost," noted the manager Charles Brookfield—addressed each other as "Laddie," and Larry was thus hailed on an early engagement in 1925. Yet this strange jargon persisted even into Larry's time. A theatre was never open or closed; it was "lit" or "dark." An actor never stumbled over his lines, he "fluffed"; he never forgot his dialogue, he "dried." Nor did he succumb to giggles on stage: he "corpsed." A play never caught the public fancy; it was a "smash" or a "hit" or a "wow." Likewise a play never failed; it "flopped" or "bombed" or was a "turkey." Often the "turkey" was playing to "paper"—free seats—or in the United States, where passes came in twos, to "Annie Oakleys," after the famous markswoman who shot two holes in a card tossed in the air. Some plays featured "money actors," those who only spoke up resonantly when a paying audience was out front, although even these actors were never paid: "the ghost walked on Friday."

The superstitions of Irving's time were equally valid in Larry's. No trouper ever whistled in a dressing room, failed to pick up pins, or passed another player on the stairs. It was fatal to start rehearsals on a Friday. It was helpful if it rained on the day of a first night; it augured well if the dress rehearsal went badly.

The play's last line must never be spoken until the first night; thresholds were invariably crossed on the left foot. Equally, there were taboos against umbrellas, peacock's feathers, palms, and wearing green or lavender. No one ever quoted from that ill-starred play

146

Macbeth, and at times there was logic to support this: at the Old Vic in 1934, four actors cast in the role fell ill within a single week, and a 1954 tour in Dublin saw an attempted suicide and an electrocution, while the company manager broke both legs.

Cats featured largely in this idolatrous litany, often with diametrically opposed beliefs. Hawtrey attributed the entire success of *The Private Secretary* at the Globe to a black cat's presence; Tree blamed the failure of *The Happy Island,* at His Majesty's, on a black cat giving birth to kittens. Lester, the cat at the Knickerbocker Theatre in New York, was said to be infallible in spotting a "turkey," notably Basil Dean's production of *Hassan,* a costume drama with music by Delius. Disdainful of bribes—liver, sardines, whiting, and even salmon—Lester steadfastly boycotted all Dean's rehearsals. When an important daily headlined KNICKERBOCKER CAT KNOCKS DELIUS OFFERING, the wiseacres nodded their heads. "Three weeks at the outside," they prophesied, and once again Lester had it right; *Hassan,* savaged by the press, ran three weeks to the hour.

Above all, what truly linked Irving's age with Larry's was the eternal preoccupation with striking a truer note; more than once, when the curtain had fallen, Irving would start the scene all over again, "hammer and tongs . . . until we got it right for tomorrow night." So it was, to a lesser degree, with Larry, who all his life had felt "as though I had served as a member of his company."

On a night in the summer of 1964, playing his triumphant *Othello* at the Chichester Festival Theatre, his fellow players—Maggie Smith, Frank Finlay, Joyce Redman—were conscious of a performance transcending all the others. That night they huddled uneasily in the wings, as if in the presence of real tragedy. After his last call, Larry strode to his dressing room, through two lines of fellow actors applauding vigorously, ignoring them all, slamming the door. One of the company made bold to knock, inquiring, "What's the matter, Larry? It was *great!*"

At once Larry's voice boomed back through the door, "I know it was great, damn it, but I don't know how I did it, so how can I be sure I can do it again?"

147

V. The Turbulent Thirties I:

"Do You Realise That the Whole World Has Gone to War?"

As 1930 dawned, the statistics conveyed only a fraction of the crisis. Two months earlier, on Black Tuesday, October 29, 1929, the Wall Street crash had wiped out two million investors, together with the brokers who had financed them and the banks from whom they had borrowed. Overnight, the United States had become a world of grinding depression, of bread lines and "Brother, Can You Spare A Dime?," a world in which 8,700,000 Americans vainly sought work, where 6,000 apple sellers peddled their wares at five cents apiece on the sidewalks of New York and eked out their days in grim collections of shacks called "Hoovervilles."

It was a world where 40,000 New Yorkers could no longer afford the telephone—and likewise a world where cigarette consumption had jumped to 125 billion. The hit tune of the day was "Life Is Just A Bowl Of Cherries"—cold comfort for 3,000,000 British unemployed in the ghost towns of the industrial north, for the 250,000 living below the poverty line.

In the make-believe jungle, as George Bernard Shaw pointed out, the hard economics were antic, to say the least; either a theatre was making so much profit that waste was not worth eliminating, or losing so much money that no economy could arrest the process. And all through the thirties the costs went nowhere but up. By the end of the decade, a show could cost $45,000 to stage, a London theatre needed £900 a week to stay open—yet 70 percent of all plays were outright failures. One Broadway producer, Joseph Verner Reed, after a four-year run of hard luck, pulled out altogether, and others only clung on by their fingernails. On Maugham's lavishly staged *East of Suez*, which ran for 209 performances, Basil Dean showed a final profit of fifteen shillings and twopence (seventy-seven pence).

Thus the $64,000 question—more urgent than ever in this climate of economic malaise—was: What did the paying public want?

In September 1930, at London's newly opened Phoenix Theatre, the answer was patently that they wanted to laugh immoderately—at the nonstop bickering of Elyot (Noël Coward) and Amanda (the beautiful Gertrude Lawrence) in Noël's witty battle royal of the sexes, *Private Lives*. Though Gertie was known primarily as a revue star, one musical disaster had persuaded her to broaden her range, opening on Broadway in the Viennese comedy *By Candlelight*, which prompted an instant cable from her old friend Noël: LEGITIMATE AT LAST, WON'T MOTHER BE PLEASED?

A comparatively modest three-thousand-pound production, jointly financed by Noël, Gertie, and Charles Blake Cochran, the comedy derived from the cat-and-dog battles staged in most public places by Viscount Castlerosse, the gossip columnist, and his wife, Doris Delavigne. First conceived in the small hours of the morning in a bedroom at the Imperial Hotel, Tokyo—a vision of Gertie in a white Molyneux dress on a terrace in the south of France resolutely refused to go away—it was completed in a few days with an Eversharp pencil while convalescing from flu in the Cathay Hotel, Shanghai. Gertie at first was of two minds as to its merits. NOTHING WRONG THAT CAN'T BE FIXED was her first cabled reaction, prompting Noël to cable back that the only thing that was going to be fixed was her performance.

An unlikely participant in this four-handed romp, along with Adrienne Allen (Mrs. Raymond Massey), was the twenty-three-year-old Larry as the hidebound Victor, at first prone to quibble over the fifty-pound salary until Noël rejoined briskly, "Look, young man, you'd better be in a success for a change!" Since this was the sum he needed to set the seal on his marriage to the actress Jill Esmond, Larry gave in.

As a result he was lost to the theatre for almost two years; a triumphant run at the Times Square Theatre, New York, led directly to a Hollywood contract with R.K.O. Pictures for him and his bride. Although few then assessed him as more than a promising juvenile, Noël was shrewder. "That young man," he told John Mills, "unless something goes radically wrong, will, before long, be acknowledged as our greatest actor."

That *Private Lives* should have taken the fancy of such jaded first-nighters as Schuyler Parsons, the art dealer, and Jules Glaenzer, the head of Cartier, New York, was in itself a notable achievement. More than ever before, Broadway and Shaftesbury Avenue were, as the jungle had it, "two thoroughfares divided by a common language." Between 1910 and 1939 only eighteen plays—most of them old standbys like *White Cargo*, *Journey's End*, *Peg O' My Heart*, and *The Bat*—won approval on both sides of the Atlantic.

The reason was partly temperamental. London audiences liked to savor their first acts, like a glass of vintage port; in the nervy atmosphere of Depression Broadway, audiences demanded an instant shot in the arm, action within the first five minutes. Comical spinsters, gouty colonels, and embittered young poets, so beloved of British dramatists, were entirely alien to them. Similarly, few American dramatists, save for Robert E. Sherwood and Elmer Rice, were much concerned with Europe.

The vogue plays of the twenties were already old hat. "Lumpshire" had become a no-go area. Sliding panels slid no longer, killed by modern psychodramas like Patrick Hamilton's *Rope* (on Broadway, *Rope's End*), the story of two young degenerates who killed for kicks. Moreover, the new vogues arising found no meeting of minds across the Atlantic. Lovable (i.e., scatterbrained) Families might be in fashion, but the "adorable" Garth-Bander family of Hampstead, squabbling their way through 799 nights of *George and Margaret*, were loved on Broadway to the tune of 86 performances. The equally "enchanting" Sycamore family of New York, opting out of the rat race to embrace ballet dancing and firework making in Kaufman and Hart's *You Can't Take It With You*, stayed the course for 837 performances, grossed £160,000, spawned four road companies, and won a Pulitzer Prize. London love-hated it for exactly ten showings, then the hatred won out.

The trauma of the Depression, more deeply felt on Broadway, evoked a new breed of Protestant playwrights: Elmer Rice, Sidney Howard, Clifford Odets, and Lillian Hellman, whose venal Hubbard family in *The Little Foxes* was condemned as "people who ate the earth." A Communist for exactly eight months, Odets centered all his plays *(Golden Boy, Waiting for Lefty, Till The Day I Die)* on the theme "What shall it profit a man, if he shall gain the whole world, and lose his own soul?" "Go out and fight so life shouldn't be printed on dollar bills" was the older generation's advice to the new in his *Awake and Sing*. But only those plays that lampooned capitalism, like

Kaufman and Hart's *Once in a Lifetime,* a send-up of Hollywood, struck a chord in London. "I hate to go into the playwrights' room," confessed the producer's secretary. "It always scares me—those padded walls and the bars on the windows."

The truth was that a deep gulf had divided Europe from the United States ever since U.S. Senator Henry Cabot Lodge had sabotaged President Woodrow Wilson's campaign to join the foundering League of Nations. Few had ever forgiven Britain and France, their onetime allies, from reneging on their debts after World War I. Thus, in February 1933, when Adolf Hitler became Führer and Chancellor of the German Third Reich, three years later to reoccupy the demilitarized Rhineland; and again, in 1935, when Italian troops under Benito Mussolini invaded Ethiopia, these were not seen as American concerns. "There are no Genghis Khans or Xerxes marching against our Western nations," stressed the idol of the isolationists, the aviator Colonel Charles A. Lindbergh.

Few of the plays stressing that war was a hell that must never happen again were consequently ever seen on Broadway. Their tone, if strident at times, was undeniably sincere. In Channing Pollock's *The Enemy,* where the real enemy was seen as hate, Pauli, the heroine, rejoiced in the death of her infant son, who would never grow up to be cannon fodder ("Not *my* baby! He won't answer your trumpets!"). And Mrs. Morris, the working-class matriarch in *Moloch,* slipped her son an overdose rather than see him enlist in World War II.

For the most part, the mood was one of total disenchantment, a sense that World War I had been all in vain. Maugham's *For Services Rendered* closed on the embittered spinster, Eva, mocking her father's patriotism with a satiric chanting of "God Save The King." *Dark Horizon* brought down its curtain on the inhabitants of a block of flats succumbing to a gas attack. In *The Unknown Warrior,* The Soldier avows that "because politicians don't have to go over the top and government is always in the hands of the old, there will always be wars, wars and still more wars." In the far-sighted *Wings Over Europe,* the Secretary of State for War, confronted with a young scientist who had invented the atom bomb, shot him stone-cold dead in the Cabinet Council Room at No. 10 Downing Street. His ultimatum—that war should be outlawed or he would bring the world to an end—was deemed to be simplistic.

The few American dramatists to ponder this dilemma played to phantom houses. Sidney Kingsley's *Ten Million Ghosts* died after one performance. Irwin Shaw's *Bury The Dead*, showing six soldiers who refused to be buried until they had aroused the living to war's futility, fared little better. Elmer Rice's *Judgement Day*, echoing the sham Reichstag fire trial, by which Hitler sought to discredit the Communists, was written off as "intemperate" by Brooks Atkinson of *The New York Times*—but in all Europe, for fear of Nazi reprisals, only Britain and Norway dared to stage it.

As so often happened, the incomparable Lunts were the exceptions that proved the rule.

After all the plans they had hatched at Dr. Rounds's rooming house back in 1921, they were to appear only once with Noël, in his own *Desire For Living*, at the Ethel Barrymore Theatre. Lynn was cast as the beautiful and sparkling Gilda, who slept alternately with Otto (Alfred), a poor painter who achieved renown, and Leo (Noël), a struggling playwright who equally gained fame. In one key speech, Leo summed up this quaint *ménage à trois*, with its covertly homosexual implications: "The actual facts are so simple. I love you. You love me. I love Otto. Otto loves you. Otto loves me. There now! Start to unravel from there."

But it was one year later, with their discovery of the dramatist Robert Emmet Sherwood, that Alfred and Lynn finally overcame the public reluctance to recognize the threat of war.

Sherwood's first Lunt vehicle, *Reunion in Vienna*, a nostalgic comedy of the fading aristocrats haunting that city's Hotel Sacher, was lightweight stuff from the author of *The Road To Rome*, Sherwood's first play, described by *The New Yorker* as "a hymn of hate against militarism." Then, in 1935, Alfred's desire to play a song-and-dance man meshed curiously with Sherwood's ambition to write a play denouncing war, Fascism, and the worldwide munitions market. On a trip to Budapest, Sherwood dropped in on a cabaret, the Club Arizona, and chanced upon a stranded American vaudeville act—six dancers and a hoofer, hoping to work their way back to the States. On another European trip, he heard of a hotel in Harbin, Manchuria, where a strange mix of nationalities, people without passports or hope, constantly scanned the sky awaiting the bombers that would start the next war.

That was the genesis of *Idiot's Delight*, in which Alfred, as Harry Van, stranded like the Budapest hoofer with six chorus girls known as "Les Blondes," met up in the cocktail lounge of the Hotel Monte Gabriele in the Italian Alps with an assorted group of travelers, including Irene (Lynn in a blond wig, with a page-boy bob), the mistress of a munitions manufacturer—a girl with whom Harry had shared a brief idyll in Omaha, Nebraska, back in 1926. (In England, Foreign Office appeasers of the Fascist régimes converted the locale to "the Hotel Loda on a mountain peak in the Continent of Europe.")

The role brought out all Alfred's craving to go one better. He soaked up the tricks of the trade from Milton Berle, master of ceremonies at the Paradise Cabaret on Broadway. The veteran chanteuse Sophie Tucker coached him in the art of nightclub singing. For an hour before each performance, he plastered his hair and face with grease, before wiping it off—to achieve the pasty-faced complexion of a stranger to fresh air.

The beginnings were far from propitious. At the dress rehearsal in Washington, D.C., almost nothing went right. A distinguished cast that numbered such later Hollywood reliables as Sydney Greenstreet, Thomas Gomez, Edgar Barrier, and Richard Whorf, both fluffed their lines and missed their cues. The Wagnerian sound effects that ended the play—air-raid sirens, whistling bombs, the thunder of wings—were woefully bungled. Finally, at 3:00 A.M., Alfred's patience snapped: the superstition that a lamentable dress rehearsal betokened a first-night hit was not for him. In the attention-getting tradition of Belasco, he seized his champagne glass and smashed it against the piano. His eyes were cold and baleful.

"We will now," he said meaningly, "*start* to rehearse. From the beginning. Places, please." And from then on the cast of thirty-five, plus fourteen stagehands and assorted technicians, worked until they literally dropped at 8:00 A.M.

The result was sheer triumph. Somehow Sherwood had contrived to strike the note that all the earlier dramatists had striven for and failed to find. When Irene asked Harry, "Do you realise that the whole world has gone to war? The *whole world!*" as they faced only annihilation huddled by the piano in the deserted cocktail lounge with bombs raining down, his reply spoke for millions of bewildered citizens: "I realise it. But don't ask me why. Because I've stopped trying to figure it out."

"Because we are the little people," Irene answered, "and for us the deadliest weapons are the most merciful."

On their next date, Pittsburgh, their fame had preceded them. Though the entire city was engulfed by floods, with all trains canceled and the telephone dead, their audiences were so anxious to see the Lunts—and the Lunts to gratify that wish—that they played to sparse houses of one hundred people, many of whom had arrived by rowboat.

At the Shubert in New York, there was the same empathy: from March 1936 on, *Idiot's Delight* notched up three hundred performances. Sherwood, who won the Pulitzer Prize, henceforth explained the secret of his success: "It's really quite simple. I just write plays for the Lunts." Only Alfred was still uneasy. For him, a hit show was judged by the number of standees, and thus a single empty seat conjured up visions of the poorhouse. Finally, the press representative, Russel Crouse, recalled a dummy in the basement that had stood in for the crippled General Mannon, bound to his wheelchair, in Eugene O'Neill's *Mourning Becomes Electra*. Outfitting the General with modern clothes, he stood him up at the back of the house.

Alfred was elated. "There was one standee," he told Crouse, after the show, "who was so interested in the play, why, he hardly moved during the whole performance. Most gratifying."

On any matinée afternoon in 1933, passers-by in London's theatre-land beheld a curious sight. Toward 5:00 P.M., as the theatres emptied, a young man strode determinedly toward Seven Dials, his brown trilby hat pulled low over his eyes, the collar of his camel-hair overcoat turned up, followed by a long crocodile of twenty or more hallooing fans. When he passed inside the door of No. 7 Upper St. Martin's Lane, the bulk of them dispersed, but a few took up vigils in doorways across the street, hopeful of intercepting their quarry once he emerged. Others, often teenage schoolgirls, crowded into phone boxes to call Temple Bar 5175, in the giggling hope that The Voice would answer. Day and night, thirty-year-old John Gielgud was under siege by his fans.

As if at the stroke of a magician's wand, John had become a cult figure. From the window of his flat he could see the crowds coiled like serpents around the New Theatre, where his smash hit *Richard of Bordeaux* was playing to packed houses. White harts, the emblem of the unhappy Richard II, whose misfortunes the play chronicled, arrived by every post—made up into posies, embroidered on handkerchiefs, stenciled on cigarette boxes.

To the media of the day, this was a flash-in-the-pan success, but in reality John had more than worked his passage. From September

1929 on, along with such talented players as Martita Hunt, Adèle Dixon, Donald Wolfit, Gyles Isham, and Leslie French, he had transformed the Old Vic from what the actress Veronica Turleigh called "the graveyard of talent" into what was perhaps London's most exciting theatre. George Coulouris, who was briefly at the Vic in 1926, recalls it as "full of terrible character actors . . . a mediocre audience laughing dutifully at the same hoary jokes"—yet within three years that verdict was outdated. In that first season, stretching himself to the utmost, John tackled, among other roles, Romeo, Richard II, Marc Antony, Macbeth, and Hamlet.

In these brief but formative months the Vic cast its spell. John surrendered unreservedly to the gloomy old auditorium, with its stalls shrouded in dust sheets, and its grimy lincrusta pillars; to the mysteries of Wardrobe, where Mr. Orlando Whitehead presided over serried ranks of crowns and armor and black velvet robes; to the excitement of snatched lunches at the "Wellington" pub or Waterloo Station buffet, and the heated arguments that ensued as the company gobbled their sausage rolls and sandwiches. And so, in 1930, a second season lured John back, to play, among other parts, Prospero in *The Tempest*, Antony, Benedick, and, at twenty-six, the youngest King Lear ever seen.

It was thus almost inevitable that Bronson Albery, the son of the playwright, should invite him to do *Richard of Bordeaux*—first tried out at the Little Arts Theatre on two successive Sunday nights—for a regular run at his New Theatre. A first play by Gordon Daviot, the pen name of Elizabeth Mackintosh, a shy Scottish physical training instructor, *Richard* was to launch John, slim and ascetic with his violoncello voice, as the newest matinée idol. Some playgoers came to view what James Agate called his "exquisite Gielgudry" more than forty times.

Given such a success, it was a foregone conclusion that Albery, in 1934, should invite him to do a series of seasons at the New, virtually as an actor-manager—the closest thing to a permanent London company since Tree's death in 1917.

It was as distinguished a company as the capital had ever seen. Gwen Ffrangcon-Davies, an enchanting Anne of Bohemia in *Richard of Bordeaux*, followed on as Mary Stuart in Gordon Daviot's *Queen of Scots*. Peggy Ashcroft, a radiant Juliet, was next Nina in *The Seagull* to Edith Evans's actressy Irina Arkadina; Miss Evans also scored as Juliet's Nurse and as the sinister gypsy woman, Agatha Payne, in

Hugh Walpole's *The Old Ladies*. Some players—Leon Quartermaine, George Howe—had found their feet years earlier; others were still groping. When his twenty-year-old understudy asked him honestly as to his chances of survival, Ballard Berkeley, the leading man in the thriller *Queer Cargo* at the Piccadilly, was markedly plainspoken: "Look, your hair's going, you've got just a faint Cockney accent, you've got holes in your wretched shoes and you don't know how to walk—your chances are very slim."

John, however, saw latent talent where Berkeley saw none, and two months later the understudy, Alec Guinness, his Cockney accent ironed out by the Fay Compton Studio, began his long career of certified eccentrics as the foppish Osric in John's revival of *Hamlet*.

Predictably, there were failures. *The Old Ladies*, adapted from Walpole's story by Rodney Ackland, petered out within weeks. An ambitious four-thousand-pound production of Emlyn Williams's *Spring 1600*, featuring the Globe Theatre in Shakespeare's time, sank without a trace. Yet in 1937, with a company augmented by Anthony Quayle, Michael Redgrave, Angela Baddeley, and Carol Goodner, John, as manager of the Queen's Theatre, was on altogether surer ground. His Richard II, his Shylock, his Joseph Surface in *The School for Scandal*, and his stern Lieutenant-Colonel Alexander Vershinin in Chekhov's *The Three Sisters* won him ever-greener laurels.

But not only gifted players were flocking to his banner; producers were equally tugged by the Gielgud lodestone. Theodore Komisarjevsky, a bald, six-foot veteran of the Imperial and State Theatres, Moscow, and an old friend of John's, was an early adherent. A silent, brooding man, content to let his casts feel their way through both "sitting" and "standing" rehearsals, "Komis" almost always came up with one pithy but penetrating comment that said it all. When Martita Hunt rehearsed a scene as Charlotta, the German governess in *The Cherry Orchard*, Komis heard her to the end, patted her on the shoulder, and murmured just one word: "Irony."

Michel St.-Denis, a plump, flamboyant, pipe-smoking recruit from the Parisian La Compagnie des Quinze, was a man much preoccupied with nuances, though hampered by limited English. Esmond Knight, who played Orsino in his *Twelfth Night*, still complains, "He befuddled me so much with high-falutin' ideas that I had no more idea on the first night than at the first rehearsal." John, though, who submitted to his direction in André Obey's *Noah* and *The Three Sis-*

ters, admired his unquenchable idealism. On the last night of *Noah*, St.-Denis paid what for him was a supreme tribute: "At last you are beginning to find the way to play the first act."

John's reputation for simple but telling stage design and costumes rested largely on the shoulders of three shy and sheltered girls from Queen Anne's Studios, an art school off the King's Road, Chelsea: the sisters Margaret and Sophia Harris and their friend Elizabeth Montgomery. As fans of John's from his Old Vic seasons, they had first submitted sketches of him in various poses, which John bought and paid for. Next came a commission to design the costumes for an Oxford University Dramatic Society (O.U.D.S.) production of *Romeo and Juliet*, which John produced with Peggy Ashcroft and Edith Evans as guest stars.

From the first they worked under the joint trademark of Motley, taken from Jacques's observation in *As You Like It*, "Motley's the only wear." "We wanted to get rid of all the brocade and rabbit fur and make things cleaner and clearer," Margaret Harris recalls, and to this end they embarked on a formidable program of research. They spent hours in the National Gallery, not to admire the techniques of the artists but to study the placing of seams. Determined to avoid the cliché of tinsel and bright gilt braid, they experimented cease- lessly. For John's 1934 *Hamlet* they used scenery canvas painted with dyes and metallic paints for the costumes; bands of velveteen were the only trimmings. For *The Merchant*, at a total cost of ninety pounds, they used costumes of unbleached calico and dish rags, with designs adapted from Italian brocades drawn freehand, then painted with dyes.

"As a producer John was always fizzing with ideas," says Margaret Harris. "The problem was to sort out the most valuable ones." But Motley, too, was prolific with ideas. At their studio in Garrick Yard off St. Martin's Lane, Chippendale's former workshop, which in time became an unofficial Green Room Club for John's company, they learned such dodges as how to "age" materials with pumice stone, wire brushes, candle grease, and fuller's earth. They concentrated on significant details, in the style of Gordon Craig and Appia before them, such as the buttress and the single window that represented Conway Castle in *Richard of Bordeaux*. They became adept at point- ing up character through minute details of costume; in *The Three Sisters* they designed a uniform with its collar cut too low for the gawky Tusenbach (played by Michael Redgrave in gold-rimmed

157

spectacles) and one cut too high for John, to emphasize Vershinin's martinet aspect.

This was the true spirit of make-believe that divined that velveteen looked more velvety than velvet, that paper doilies made splendid lace cuffs, that plastic jerkins (in a later era) looked more leathery than leather, and that woven string sprayed with aluminum paint made superb chain mail.

This greater sophistication in stage setting was made possible largely by the marked progress in the field of stage lighting. Even in the twenties, striking effects had been achieved by rotating perforated screens before colored lanterns, so that dawn, twilight, and sunset came that much closer to reality. But in 1935, when twenty-four-year-old Frederick Bentham, a researcher for the Strand Electric and Engineering Company, perfected his Strand Light Console, based on a Compton organ console, the result was revolutionary. From this time on, an operator could use the organ's stops to preselect the dimmers, the pedals to regulate the motor speed, and the keys to raise or lower the lighting level.

As a result the art of makeup was turned upside down. Even in the twenties, Esmond Knight recalls, the makeup standards at the Old Vic were "balletic—dark blue eyebrows, the nostrils outlined with red, the mouth outlined with black." "Youngsters became old men by dint of crimson lake shadows"; the "blue for a working-class chin," mandatory in Irving's day, when makeup was referred to as "mask building," still prevailed. Now the foresight of Ludwig Leichner, a onetime Wagnerian opera singer who, from 1873, had perfected a range of standard grease paints from No. 1 (palest flesh color) to No. 20 (white) was finally vindicated. The players of John's company "built masks" no longer.

This very real breakthrough at the New and the Queen's might have been cause for intense self-esteem, but in the jungle, as John discovered, there were always those skilled at deflation. About this time, responding to an invitation from Lilian Baylis, he marched into her office in full West End style, trilby cocked jauntily, new yellow gloves held negligently in his hand. They chatted for a while before John said grandly, "I should simply love to come down some time and act and produce again for you at the Vic, but of course I'm awfully busy for the next month or two."

Her eyes fixed firmly on his fast-receding hairline, Lilian cut him briskly down to size. "Oh no, dear," she said sweetly. "You play all the young parts you can while you're still able to!"

Noël Coward was no stranger to poverty. Despite his affluence in the thirties—an average of one thousand pounds a week during the run of *Private Lives*—he never forgot his humble origins, like those of Gertrude Lawrence, daughter of a hard-drinking music hall artist. One of his favorite stories was that of the white fox fur that in the course of a single month was borrowed by nineteen separate actresses seeking work at auditions. Yet in the summer of 1931, Noël was appalled by the hardships besetting his profession.

As always, Noël was in the height of fashion, and the fashion, at the onset of the thirties, was to vie with the newly emergent talking pictures—usually with signal lack of success. *Sexton Blake*, at the Prince Edward, called for a car to be demolished by a train at a level crossing. *The Flying Fool*, at Prince's, featured a passenger plane hitting the control tower at Croydon Airport and bursting into flames. Briefly, the revolving stage was in its element; the German Max Hasait's new revolve offered nineteen scene changes in Edward Knoblock's adaptation of Vicki Baum's *Grand Hotel*, while the newspaper melodrama *Late Night Final* at the Phoenix (*Five Star Final* on Broadway) made do with nine. Noël, as was his wont, topped all of them. His thirty-thousand-pound production of *Cavalcade* at the Theatre Royal in Drury Lane, a patriotic saga of one London family, the Marryots, from the Boer War to the present day, featured twenty-three scene changes, aided by six hydraulic lifts, forty-three speaking parts, and four hundred nonspeakers.

It was these crowd auditions that hit Noël the hardest—"they lay heavily on my conscience for a long while." Hour after hour, day after day, he and the producing manager Charles Blake Cochran sat at a long table, set against the lowered Drury Lane safety curtain, while more than a thousand "out-of-works" trooped past them. Some of them had played important parts on this very stage, yet all were in desperate need of the thirty shillings a week that was the limit of Cochran's budget. The old women, Noël thought, were the most pathetic—a shade too dressy, prone to hedge over salary, then caving in suddenly before it was too late with "Very well, I'll take it."

At Noël's level, it was hard to realize that this was symptomatic of the profession. Nowhere outside the jungle could such a lemminglike rush toward self-destruction have made sense: three thousand members of the profession in 1932 had swollen to four thousand a year later. Yet at any one time only two and a half percent were in regular work; in the capricious thirties any play running longer than six months was a box-office miracle.

What all these storm-tossed players needed was a protective umbrella—something that the Actors' Association (A.A.), in existence since 1891, had notably failed to provide. In 1919, they had sought both rehearsal payments and a minimum salary of three pounds a week; in 1921, by now five thousand strong, they delayed the curtain rise for twenty minutes on a long-forgotten play called *Emma* at the St. James's until the manager, May Palfrey, agreed to pay extra for evening performances. (Until then *Emma* had played matinées only.) Yet the A.A.'s Valentine Standard Contract, named after the actor Sydney Valentine, guaranteed no rehearsal pay for any actor earning more than six pounds a week. Even actors earning less rehearsed the first two weeks for free.

All through the twenties and thirties, salaries had remained almost static. As World War I ended, an average actor worked for thirty-five weeks a year for an annual increment of seventy-five pounds. As a character actress touring with the Ben Greet company in 1922, Flora Robson had drawn three pounds a week. Six years later, George Coulouris, cast in such leads as Yank in Eugene O'Neill's *The Hairy Ape* at Terence Gray's Cambridge Festival Theatre, earned four pounds a week—the same stipend that Michael Redgrave was earning at Liverpool Repertory Theatre in 1934.

Week after week, *The Stage* carried headline stories of companies stranded in the provinces, forced to appeal to the police for funds to return to the capital. In the West End, on an average, every six weeks saw a failure to pay salaries—or the management would slyly offer to carry on, given a 20 percent salary cut. Finally, on December 1, 1929, a mass meeting of actors and actresses at the Duke of York's Theatre called for action that their American counterparts had taken ten years earlier: the setting up of British Actors' Equity Association.

Just as in New York, there was a very real fear of Bolshevik influence, until the affable and apolitical matinée idol Godfrey Tearle agreed to stand in as president, and Marie Tempest presided over the Savoy Hotel luncheon that witnessed the drawing up of the Equity Standard Contract. But the true motive power behind Equity was their honorary adviser, the silver-haired Alfred Wall of the London Trades council, a union man to his bones. At the Trade Union Club, on the corner of New Oxford Street, Wall ran into the dockers' leader, Ben Tillett, who was highly skeptical. "I hear you're going to organise the actors; you'll never bloody well do anything with that sort!" Wall was fully determined. "Oh, won't I? Well, I ruddy well will."

And Wall made good his boast. From 1933 on, Equity became a closed shop. No manager could compel an artist to work with non-members of Equity. By degrees, more and more players, for an entrance fee of five shillings and annual dues graded according to income, took refuge with Equity, battling for a modest rehearsal pay of two pounds a week. "The prime concern then was for actors earning less than ten pounds," says the present general secretary, Peter Plouviez. "If you earned more than that you were on your own."

As the ranks of the profession swelled alarmingly, others saw further need for codification. To cast a play, West End managers like Cochran, Alban Limpus, and E. P. Clift spent hours poring over thousands of portraits submitted by the agents of the day. Then, in August 1927, W. Keith Moss, a canny stage director, hit on the novel concept of publishing the photographs in book form, setting up the *Spotlight* Casting Directory at Palace House, Shaftesbury Avenue. (In New York, Equity established The Players' Guide, though with fewer details.) Moss's idea bore fruit; the first issue, a 115-page *vade mecum*, featured 356 players, but by 1932 more than 800 of them, for annual fees of twenty pounds (full page) to two pounds, ten shillings (one-eighth of a page) were taking space in *Spotlight*.

Thus Larry's best friend in the theatre world, Denys Blakelock, could list not only his telephone number and details of six recent productions but notify managers that he had a baritone voice, played the piano, dived and ice skated, and had six dialects at his command, North Country, American, Irish, Scottish, and Welsh being marked with an asterisk for "fluency or exceptional ability." Since *Spotlight* was graded strictly by categories, Blakelock was cast among "Juvenile Men," along with Maurice Evans, Rex Harrison, and Ralph Richardson. Accordingly, Flora Robson was a "Leading Woman," Sara Allgood a "Feature Woman," Cedric Hardwicke a "Character Man," and Brian Aherne a "Leading Man."

All told, since the photographs rarely featured makeup, it was a system destined to save both managements and players time and trouble. When the hard-pressed Broadway manager Gilbert Miller attended the first night of Eden Phillpotts's *Yellow Sands* at the Haymarket, London—one year before *Spotlight* was launched—he was greatly impressed by the spry old Cedric Hardwicke, plainly pushing seventy and wholly deserving of a life contract. On reaching New York he cabled his London agent to this effect.

But the agent knew better. HARDWICKE ONLY THIRTY-FIVE STOP THINK AGAIN was the cable he sent to Miller, and, as Hardwicke was to record sadly, Miller did.

The actor-manager Otis Skinner, that veteran of a thousand-and-one-night stands, was the first to sound the tocsin, as far back as 1926. "The Road is no more," he said. "It is dead, dead as Marley's ghost," and this was no alarmist verdict. By 1928 Broadway boasted 70-plus playhouses, but across the length and breadth of America the theatres had shrunk from 1,520 in 1910 to 634 in 1925. More and more the movies had taken over legitimate houses; the soaring costs of railroad travel had eaten into managerial profits. Thus a city like Denver, Colorado, counted itself fortunate to see five plays a year; Charleston, South Carolina, was lucky to see one play every two years.

To revive The Road against all economic logic called for a monumental act of faith—yet in 1933, despite the odds, Kit Cornell achieved just that.

It began, improbably, aboard a liner in the Panama Canal, as Kit sailed back to Los Angeles following a tour of another sultry melodrama, *Dishonoured Lady*. Seated on deck beside her secretary, Gertrude Macy, Kit read for the first time another play that was to alter the entire course of her life: Rudolph Besier's *The Barretts of Wimpole Street*. The story of Elizabeth Moulton-Barrett, a sofa-bound invalid tyrannized by her Victorian father, Edward, the play told of how the love of the poet Robert Browning restored her health, enabling her and her cocker spaniel Flush to flee with Browning to a new life in Italy.

The fact that twenty-eight managements had so far turned it down was no obstacle to Kit. Given a cast of seventeen, it was a perfect vehicle for Guthrie to direct and for her to present in her first venture into management—and it was primarily as a vehicle for his talents that she cabled for and secured the rights.

Over breakfast in their Beekman Place apartment, Guthrie, though duly grateful, was adamant on one point: "You've got to play Elizabeth." But with all the urgency at her command, Kit resisted this. Elizabeth bored her. She was there for all of five acts, tied to the sofa, "feeding" her brothers, "feeding" her father, "feeding" Browning. Elizabeth was not for her. But with all the urgency at *his* command, the persuasive Guthrie finally won out.

The play, with Charles Waldron from *A Bill of Divorcement* as Barrett and Britain's debonair Brian Aherne as Browning, was not without its problems. Though the Broadway first night at the Empire Theatre went well, presaging a run of 370 performances, Kit had soon developed what she called "sofa neck." The strain of keeping rock-still in one position for almost three hours demanded constant orthopedic treatment for her agonized neck muscles.

To contemplate a grueling journey in such a role on The Road, now so long defunct, somehow savored of a very special kind of masochism.

The idea grew by degrees through the buffet suppers that Kit and Guthrie always gave each Sunday night, when theatrical greats like Sidney Howard, Margalo Gillmore, and George Gershwin yarned and chatted against a background of white marble mantelpieces and red brocade curtains. At heart both Guthrie and the company press agent, Ray Henderson, were hundred-carat romantics, who thought of a great star not as one who ruled on Broadway or in London but one who was forever arriving by train, scenery and costumes in tow, from some hazy, mysterious distance.

The logistics of Kit's tour in the winter of 1933–1934 were to pass into theatrical annals. All told, she was touring a company of sixty-four carloads of actors, technicians, costumes, and properties, for besides *The Barretts* and *Candida*, she had added *Romeo and Juliet* to her repertoire, with Basil Rathbone as Romeo and Orson Welles as Mercutio. In 29 weeks on the road they covered 16,853 miles, giving 225 performances in 74 cities and 31 states, grossing around $650,000, and playing to 500,000 people. But logistics were only a fraction of that saga.

They opened up mildewed and cobwebby opera houses, which had stood dark for so long that the guy ropes broke as they swung the scenery into place, and startled rats ran along the footlight troughs during the performance. In Emporia, Kansas, they played in a schoolhouse without running water; the local hospital had to provide pails of warm water so that the cast could wash. Often, as in Nashville, Tennessee, they played inside a church.

Acoustics were at times so bad that they had to scream to make themselves heard. In Colorado Springs, the theatre had only two dressing rooms; the company dutifully lined up in turns to use the mirrors. In Oakland, California, they played in a basketball stadium; in Memphis, in an abandoned temple. In Amarillo, Texas, a sand storm compelled Kit and Aherne in *The Barretts* to play their first tender love scene entirely in dumb show.

Yet all of them were conscious of seeing an America of which Broadway never dreamed, and Cornelia Otis Skinner, who followed in the same tracks, would recall with aching affection "the bright undulating wheat fields of Iowa . . . the mountains of Oregon with their fairy tale forests . . . the white herons fluttering up from the Florida bayous . . . the V-shaped flocks of geese flying south along the great rivers."

It was Christmas Eve, 1933, en route to Seattle, Washington, Guthrie's hometown, that saw the peak point of Kit's grand tour. In Washington State, it had then rained for twenty-three days and nights; as darkness fell, their train was inching slowly through driving rain, a long, long way from Seattle. Nine o'clock, ten o'clock came and went, but not until 11:15 P.M. did the company finally clamber wearily onto the platform at Seattle. And here news awaited them, much like that which had greeted Mansfield almost forty years earlier at Fort Worth. The house was sold out. And the audience was waiting.

It was then Kit had a brainstorm. An audience of this caliber deserved just that much more in the way of entertainment. They deserved an almost unprecedented treat—a peep behind the scenes. Thus the curtain should be rung up forthwith. At midnight on Christmas Day, it was the stagehands who received the first rounds of applause as they swung the walls of No. 50 Wimpole Street into place, with their portières and rich valances. Intrigued, the audience watched the stocky Jimmy Vincent, the stage manager, stretch luxuriously out on the sofa, to assume all the languorous postures that Kit would later adopt. Simultaneously the wardrobe mistress, Johanna Kling, was unpacking onstage, and the players, in dripping raincoats, lined up "like charity boys at a handout" to collect *écru* pantaloons, flowered waistcoats, and ruffled shirts. Then a warning bell rang, the house lights dimmed, and at 1:05 A.M. precisely the play began.

It was only when Act I ended that a great lassitude seized Kit. She had to eat. En route to her dressing room at 2:00 A.M., she beseeched the attendant Guthrie, "Get me an egg." But this posed a problem. The kitchens of the Olympic Hotel opposite had long closed down. The patient audience, in their vigil, had consumed every morsel of food available at the lunch wagon and the drugstore. It was thus up to a local boy to make good, and Guthrie, hastening through the dripping darkness, began to hammer on doors—unavailingly—that long ago had housed his fellow scholars. Finally an upstairs window creaked open and a sleepy, feminine voice was heard to wonder who could be calling at this God-forsaken hour. McClintic strove to spirit her mind back some twenty-eight years. Did she remember Guthrie, who had been with her at Lincoln High School and lived nearby on Beacon Hill? She supposed she did—and what then?

"Well," Guthrie stammered, his voice falsetto with embarrassment, "can you let me have an egg?" (It was recorded that she could, and she did.)

Kit's pioneering work was not in vain. Although Ibsen's plays had not been written with a public address system in view, Eva Le Gallienne took *Hedda Gabler* and *The Master Builder* thirty thousand miles across America, playing one hundred towns in forty-two states in the space of six months. Ethel Barrymore, in the same spirit, toured Sheridan's *The School for Scandal* for eighty-five weeks. The Lunts, too, took *Idiot's Delight* and *The Seagull* to the Deep South, playing their delicate comedy in boxing stadiums built to seat seven thousand, dressing in gymnasium locker rooms, playing in semidarkness every time the fuses blew, which was often.

"We were all so tired we could hardly stagger out of our dressing-rooms," Alfred reminisced of one such occasion, and Lynn agreed wholeheartedly: "You know it's this kind of thing that makes trouping worth while."

VI. The Turbulent Thirties II:
"All Acting is Giving and Receiving"

By 1935, the year that du Maurier died, his cheeks pathetically stained with iodine to simulate rude health, it was said with authority that the theatre, too, was dying. To some it had gone out in glory as far back as 1905. "Irving," wrote James Agate, "impressed me as so utterly outstanding and pre-eminent that all the other actors I have ever seen have seemed to be practising some other profession." Actresses, too, had died with Bernhardt, "a creature half-sylph, half-rainbow . . . [who] unveiled for me the ecstasy of the body and the torture of the mind."

Yet in March 1935, King George's Jubilee year, *The Theatre World* was exulting, "The stage is set for a varied and interesting spring season. . . . London will have a splendid list of entertainments to offer to the thousands of potential playgoers."

The truth, as Larry discovered on returning to England after almost two years in the salt mines of Hollywood, lay somewhere in between, with theatrical life, as always, generating the sense of a nonstop ride on a Coney Island roller coaster.

In Hollywood, despite the resurrection of Beau Geste's lip-line moustache, Larry had entirely failed to dent the Ronald Colman image. In mercifully forgotten "turkeys" like *Friends and Lovers*, *Westward Passage*, and *The Yellow Passport*, he conveyed little more than a specious nothingness. But the theatre, too, presented pitfalls. Back in England, in the spring of 1934, his role as a self-righteous prig in S. N. Behrman's short-lived *Biography* was too reminiscent of his part in *Private Lives*. His swaggering Bothwell in Gielgud's *Queen of Scots*, a part undertaken at eight days' notice, was, one critic opined, "more Hollywood than Holyrood."

Ironically, both in London and on Broadway, he scored most tellingly in homosexual roles—in Keith Winter's *The Rats of Norway* and Mordaunt Shairp's *The Green Bay Tree*. As Steven Beringer, a master at a boy's preparatory school in *The Rats*, Larry depicted a young man vainly trying to reciprocate the love of Tilly, the music mistress, though irresistibly drawn to Sebastian (Raymond Massey), a tortured soul who had fought a losing battle against his carnal desire for Jane (Gladys Cooper), the headmaster's wife. As Julian in *The Green Bay Tree*, he was caught up in a spiritual tug of war between Mr. Dulcimer (James Dale), the epicene sybarite who had adopted him, and Leonora (his wife, Jill Esmond), who ultimately lost out— "I hope I shan't meet you one day in Piccadilly with a painted face, just because you must have linen sheets!"

In Larry's long career the play was especially notable for his one encounter with the venomous Jed Harris, who singled him out as a scapegoat from the start. Unlike Helen Hayes, who had fought Harris tooth and nail and won, Larry submitted painfully to warped sarcasms, to the grinding, thirty-hour rehearsals called by "the most hurtful, arrogant, venomous little fiend that anyone could meet, let alone be asked to work with." On the opening night at the Cort on West 48th Street, Harris could not resist implanting one last *banderilla* as the actor waited tensely in the wings. "Good-bye, Larry," he breathed. "I hope I never see you again."

But revenge in the jungle, although many years a-festering, would nonetheless prove sweet. In 1944, when Larry launched his triumphant *Richard III*, his portrayal was modeled exclusively on the unspeakable Harris. "I thought of the most venal person I knew," he confessed at the time. "I based my make-up and performance on him."

This sure approach to homosexual roles was all the more remarkable given Larry's hundred-carat heterosexuality; from 1935 on he was to become increasingly involved with twenty-four-year-old Vivien Leigh, a beautiful and rising star whose instability was to become a byword, herself married to the barrister Leigh Holman. So ambitious was Vivien to become Larry's equal on the stage, so certain that she and Larry were soul mates, that Jill Esmond's visit to Vivien's Mayfair flat, begging her to give Larry up, became by degrees a reversal of roles. How did Larry like his shirts ironed? Vivien wanted to know. Did he favor a three-minute egg? "Jill felt," one friend of the family remarked, "as though Vivien was some kind of housemaid who was taking over from her."

Vivien's hero-worship had survived even such unpromising performances as *Biography* and *Queen of Scots*. By 1935, when Larry and John staged a controversial revival of *Romeo and Juliet* at the New, alternating Romeo and Mercutio, with Peggy Ashcroft as their mutual Juliet, he was ensconced as the romantic figure behind all her fantasies.

At this stage of Larry's career, Vivien was perhaps one of the few to perceive that inside the matinée-idol persona that Larry so sedulously cultivated, an outstanding classical actor was struggling to emerge. Certainly few critics of the day shared her enthusiasm for his Romeo, which he played, despite Gielgud's wintry disapproval, with a false nose. "I think of him as a boy practically with conkers in his pocket," he justified himself to John, and this was of a piece with his concept of Romeo as a gauche, tongue-tied boy groping for words. "One wanted over and over again to stop the performance and tell the actor he couldn't just rush this or that passage," one critic complained. Another commented sourly, "He plays Romeo as though he were riding a motor-bike."

Belatedly, in 1937, sanity prevailed; his bank balance bolstered by a £500-a-week film contract with Alexander Korda, Larry realized that it was now or never. For £20 a week, like John before him, he joined Lilian Baylis's Old Vic to play a full-length version of *Hamlet* under the formidable direction of the tall, thin, patrician Tyrone "Tony" Guthrie, whose personality one actress likened to that of "a popular slightly scratchy schoolmaster." "Never mind, dear," Guthrie would console a player who fumbled an interpretation, "astonish us in the morning."

It was a decision that Larry himself viewed with more than a leavening of doubt. Supposing his Hamlet went the same ignominious way as his Romeo? He was twenty-nine years old—but was he big enough, talented enough, to carry an entire Old Vic season on his own shoulders?

History would vindicate Larry's choice, but in January 1937 only one thing was certain. His new venue assured him of one factor vital to any rising player: he was playing the right parts in the right place at the right time. For if the nineties had been the era of Writers' Theatre, the thirties, as a legacy of the twenties, was the age of Directors' Theatre.

All of them—Stanislavsky, Komisarjevsky, St.-Denis—were autocrats, egotists who unflinchingly called their own tune. Approached by the Theatre Guild to stage a New York production on the lines of the Moscow Art Theatre, Stanislavsky, unabashed, stipulated a two-year rehearsal period. To such men, brilliant innovations came naturally; as the war clouds gathered over Europe, the Mercury Theatre of the boy-wonder Orson Welles staged *Julius Caesar* in modern dress, with Caesar and Marc Antony (George Coulouris) in the black shirts of Mussolini's Fascists and Brutus (Welles) with the sports jacket and floppy tie of a Greenwich Village intellectual. In rehearsal they were often devastating, like Sir Robert Atkins, who from 1936 on set his personal stamp on the Open Air Theatre in London's Regent's Park. "Scenery by God, words by Shakespeare," Atkins annihilated one hapless player, "then *you* come on."

Few, however, were more profoundly autocratic than Guthrie himself. Older players found his methods less than congenial. Athene Seyler still recalls with distaste her 1933 season at the Vic, when her rendering of Madame Ranevsky in *The Cherry Orchard* was cut short by a bellow: "Listen, dear, we don't want any Athene Seyler tricks here!" ("He *shouted*," is how Miss Seyler remembers this singular breach of etiquette, "and from the back of the stalls.") Older playgoers were equally wary of what a later generation would know as "gimmickry." For *Much Ado*, in the Vic season of 1934–1935, Guthrie's disciple, Henry Cass, staged the low comedy scenes before a backdrop of "roofs and chimney pots with cats dangling watches and a general air of Micky Mousery." In the Church Scene, Alec Clunes as Friar Francis was dressed, for no discernible reason, as a high priest of the Greek Orthodox Church.

Guthrie's 1938 *Hamlet*, with Alec Guinness in the lead, featured lounge suits, flannels, and trilby hats; the Graveyard Scene was played under raised umbrellas, with the cast attired in seamen's jerseys and gumboots. The Play Scene was done in full Edwardian court dress, with trains, feathers, and long white gloves for the ladies. His *Troilus and Cressida* was likewise given an Edwardian bias, with Helen of Troy playing the piano in a hobble skirt. His *Henry VIII* dissolved abruptly into knockabout comedy, with courtiers both dodging incontinent pigeons and recoiling from imaginary puddles.

If this was scarcely Shakespeare as Irving and Terry had envisaged it, at least every Guthrie gimmick made news.

The Hamlet with which he launched Larry's Old Vic debut was no exception. From the first the producer had pondered the question, Was Hamlet's paralyzing dilemma motivated by jealousy of Claudius, the husband of his mother, whom the young prince loved in an unnatural way? This was the Freudian interpretation, based on the psychoanalyst's study of the Oedipus complex, which Guthrie urged on Larry, who seized upon the concept with enthusiasm. In the Closet Scene, with Dorothy Dix as Gertrude, his playing was both passionate and tempestuous; on the line "O that this too, too *sullied* flesh would melt," he impulsively wiped his mother's kiss from his face, as if it were a loathsome insect.

Many spectators, though, resented his emphasis on the physical—"There is more to acting than gymnastics" one critic objected—and these were to include both Alec Guinness (Osric) and Michael Redgrave (Laertes). Guinness found himself outraged by "the gymnastic leaps and falls"; at the climax Hamlet leaped twelve feet through the air to kill Claudius. Redgrave thought Larry "a bad Hamlet—too assertive and too resolute." Neither man could divine that this Hamlet, with its emphasis on virility and panache, was in effect a way of wooing Vivien Leigh, who was seldom absent from the stalls—what Kenneth Tynan was later to call a "long-distance Valentine."

Other roles were swift to follow—a bawdy slapstick-oriented Sir Toby Belch in *Twelfth Night*, a laudably subdued Henry V—so that Larry was at length emerging as a Shakespearean actor whom critics and public could take seriously. He was finally perceiving a vital truth of the jungle: "Less can be More."

At this stage in theatrical history, few British directors or actors were much concerned with Stanislavsky's hotly debated Method, "perhaps," as Phyllis Hartnoll suggests, "because good English actors, like good actors everywhere, were already Method actors without realising it." The one director to succumb heavily to the lure, Harley Granville-Barker, with his passion for nuances nowhere indicated in the text, found his casts unresponsive. Once, when he had baffled Dennis Eadie to the point of frenzy with his emphasis on "inner meanings," Sir James Barrie called sarcastically from the stalls, "Do ye not think, when ye walk upstage there . . . ye could convey that ye had a brother in Shropshire who's awfu' fond o' reading Shelley?"

Others were equally dismissive. When a beady-eyed seeker after truth asked the urbane Godfrey Tearle, "Sir, does Hamlet sleep with Ophelia?" Tearle went straight to the point. "Well, she always did when I was on Number One tour, me boy."

Tyrone Guthrie, although no Method adherent, had a marked affinity for Freud. When *Othello* was chosen to open the second half of the Old Vic's season in February 1938, Guthrie at once contacted Dr. Ernest Jones, who had done much to explain Freud's precepts to the English, in quest of theories. Happy to expound on the subject, Jones invited Guthrie to his house in Regent's Park, along with Larry, cast as Iago. The one man kept strictly in the dark was Othello himself, played by Ralph Richardson.

Jones's theories, once formulated, were far from conventional. For him the clue to the play was not Iago's hatred of Othello. He was not envious of the Moor, nor did he love Desdemona. The key to his character was that he adored Othello, with a homosexual passion that he could barely acknowledge to himself.

Thus, in Act III, when Othello and Iago planned Cassio's death, they were really enacting a subconscious love scene, with Othello's "Now art thou my lieutenant" matched by Iago's fervent "I am your own for ever." As they left Jones's house Larry was seized by sudden misgivings. "I don't think we dare tell Ralphy."

Nor did they, just then. All through rehearsals, although Larry adopted a conventionally mincing gait, the bluff, no-nonsense Richardson seemed totally oblivious. But at the dress rehearsal the die was finally cast. At the appropriate moment Larry seized Richardson in a fond embrace and kissed him resoundingly.

Richardson's next line did not emerge. Disentangling himself from Larry's arms, he made for the footlights. "Tony!" he called imperiously. "What was the meaning of that?" Guthrie, unusually, was momentarily at a loss. "Well, Ralph," he extemporized, "we didn't want to tell you sooner but . . . well, Ralph, I never *believe* Iago onstage somehow . . . Larry and I talked it over . . . Well, Ralph, there's no other explanation. Iago is a poof."

"He's a poof, Ralph," Larry chimed in loyally. "He has to be," but abruptly he was addressing an empty stage; Richardson was heading for the wings. "Where are you going?" both Larry and Tony cried in unison.

"I," Richardson replied with monumental hauteur, "am going home—and staying there until both you lads have come to your senses."

Two days later, when he finally agreed to return, the kiss, by mutual consent, was out—but on the opening night, and on all the nights that followed, the audience was totally mystified by a smiling, affectionate, pouting, nonmalevolent Iago who seemed to belong to quite another play.

All through the 1930s Larry was learning the economics of theatrical life the hard way. His first venture into management, along with the gargantuan (230-lb.) Broadway producer Gilbert Miller, the natural successor to Charles Frohman, seemed assured of success. Had not Miller been the presiding genius behind such international hits as *Journey's End, Berkeley Square,* and *The Late Christopher Bean?*

Moreover, Larry, after breaking an ankle through more unbridled acrobatics in George S. Kaufman's and Edna Ferber's *Theatre Royal,* had astutely snapped up Keith Winter's *Ringmaster,* in which he played Peter Hammond, an embittered cripple dominating the world of his Devonshire guest house from a wheelchair.

The opening night only confirmed this belief. At the climax of the play, when Hammond, realizing that all his victims had walked out on him, toppled from his chair, crying "I can't be alone! I can't be alone!" Larry, for the first time in his life, saw an audience rise to its feet and cheer him. Later, in his dressing room, there was the quiet sense of total euphoria as Miller, his first visitor, inquired briskly, "What are we going to do with all this money we're going to make?"

This was on Monday, March 11, 1935. On Saturday, March 16, *Ringmaster* sank quietly and without trace.

To a veteran like Miller who, in the forty years after 1916 was to present almost two hundred plays, such quirks of fortune were merely the luck of the draw, but to Larry, even after ten years' trouping, the fickleness of a first-night audience that gave the same uproarious ovation to both flops and hits was for long a disturbing phenomenon.

Yet all through the thirties the dressing rooms of Shaftesbury Avenue buzzed with such horrendous tales. At the Criterion Theatre on Piccadilly Circus in November 1936, the dress rehearsal of *French Without Tears,* a new comedy by a novice playwright, Terence Rattigan, went so disastrously that the infuriated producer, Harold French, promptly called for a repeat. As this proceeded the author's agent,

172

A.D. Peters, slipped backstage, anxious to sell his £500 stake in the play for a cut-price £100. From a cast that included Rex Harrison, Kay Hammond, Trevor Howard, and Jessica Tandy, there were no takers. Two days later, following a riotous first night, Rattigan was dragged swooning from his refuge at the back of the dress circle to face hysterical acclaim, a curtain that narrowly missed braining him, and an ultimate profit of £23,000.

Star names, the strident fanfare of advance publicity, made not one iota of difference. One month after *French Without Tears* embarked on its phenomenal run (1,039 performances), all the omens looked good for Charles Blake Cochran's *The Boy David*, Sir James Barrie's first play in sixteen years. Not only was the beloved Viennese Elisabeth Bergner, who had captivated London in Margaret Kennedy's *Escape Me Never,* cast in the star role, but Bergner herself had virtually commissioned the play, the story of the young David who slew Goliath, while taking tea in Barrie's Adelphi flat. "The combination," Cochran recalled later, "seemed to me irresistible," and if more were needed, Godfrey Tearle had been signed as Bergner's leading man, the painter Augustus John was to design the sets, William Walton was composing the incidental music, and Reinhardt's right-hand man, Ernst Stern, had charge of the costumes.

Certainly the canny Scots who packed out the King's Theatre, Edinburgh, on the night of Saturday, November 21, 1936, fully endorsed Cochran's faith. Dazzled by the ninety-foot arc of a cyclorama backcloth forty feet high, by the lights of sixty-one spot lanterns and fifty-three flood lanterns, powered by three-quarters of a mile of cable, they accorded Bergner and her leading man sixteen curtain calls.

On the strength of this, Herbert Smith (head of the long-established Keith Prowse ticket agency), along with his opposite numbers at Lacon and Ollier, Lashmar, and Leader, clinched the crucial deal on which the play's future would hinge: buying up the bulk of the stalls, dress circle, and upper circle for the first six weeks of the run at His Majesty's, London. (One month earlier, seeing no future for *French Without Tears,* Smith had made no deal at all.)

Yet on December 14, 1936, half an hour after curtain-up at His Majesty's, Cochran "knew the play was doomed . . . we had drawn a so-called sophisticated audience with their thumbs turned down" against biblical whimsy. "Waves of dislike and even hate," recalled Peter Bull, one of the cast, "came wafting over the footlights." Next

173

morning, given dismissive press notices, the West End "libraries," as the ticket agencies were known, were in a dilemma. After buying seats for six weeks, they could not give them away.

Predictably, it was only when Cochran, after losing one thousand pounds a week for seven weeks on end, posted the closing notices that the box office was besieged by patrons now willing to pay any price for a seat.

In this maverick world, where failure and success operated as haphazardly as the spin of a roulette wheel, one man's prejudice often proved another man's profit. For no known reason, Hugh "Binkie" Beaumont, who controlled the powerful H.M. Tennent management, was allergic to plays about schoolteachers; when Emlyn Williams's autobiographical *The Corn is Green* arrived on his desk, the saga of how the Welsh teacher Miss Moffat befriended the young miner Morgan Evans, Beaumont sent it posthaste back to its author. This proved the heaven-sent chance for a newcomer to the managerial ranks, thirty-one-year-old Stephen Mitchell, who at once put it into production with Williams and Dame Sybil Thorndike. Ten years later, when Beaumont summarily rejected Rattigan's *The Browning Version*, another schoolroom play, Mitchell was once more the beneficiary.

On Broadway the same indeterminate conditions prevailed. When *Tobacco Road*, Jack Kirkland's adaptation of Erskine Caldwell's novel of illiterate and incestuous white trash in Georgia, opened at New York's Masque Theatre, the press was lukewarm; failure was just around the corner. Only when the star, Henry Hull, volunteered a salary cut did the management dig in its toes—until word-of-mouth notices of the play's sexual shenanigans drew a nightly audience of voyeurs. Thus nursed to success, *Tobacco Road* clocked up what in 1933 was Broadway's longest run: 3,182 performances.

It was thus not surprising that the lottery-loving thirties, the era of the Irish Sweep and the numbers racket, became the Age of the Angel—a term that from 1925 on came to denote the backers who floated the shows.

London "angels," for the most part, were small investors who hedged their bets, usually making part of a syndicate up to fifteen strong, rarely venturing more than £100, expecting at best 40 percent of the profits, if forthcoming. In time they came to accept, though reluctantly, that nothing was so moribund as a play that had died; a £1,500 set would fetch at most £200, a glamorous £80 gown would retail at £10—with luck.

The bigger investors were as wary. Unlike most gamblers, they had an unerring sense of when to quit the table. The diamond magnate Barney Barnato, said to be worth a conservative £20 million, staked £1,000 on the thriller *Ten Minute Alibi* (878 performances), but backed no other play. Sir Auckland Geddes, a former director of recruiting in World War I, "angeled" the antiwar play *The Enemy* out of pacifist convictions but let well alone thereafter. The industrialist Stephen Courtauld was equally a one-play man. His sole flutter was Dodie Smith's Scottish guesthouse comedy *Touch Wood*.

Those who took the maximum risk at times came disastrously unstuck. Although "Madame Estelle" was London's wealthiest and most sought-after clairvoyant, her crystal ball clouded over when it came to show business; virtually all her savings were ventured on a 1935 failure called *Murder in Motley*. On the final Saturday night, her cast was more than a little embarrassed to find her paying them off, not with checks or five-pound notes but with florins, shillings, and pence— all the coins she had been able to scrape together.

The motives of angels were manifold. When the distiller Daniel K. Weiskopf was forced into retirement by Prohibition, he put his considerable fortune at the disposal of the producing managers Archie and Edgar Selwyn, and found his crock of gold regularly replenished. Guy George Gabrielson, Speaker of the New Jersey Senate, thwarted of an acting career when his family sent him to law school at Harvard, took his revenge by backing Samson Raphaelson's successful high comedy *Accent on Youth*.

On Broadway the angel stereotype, as pictured by P.G. Wodehouse—"a little group of fat rich men with tight lips and faces carved out of granite"—was fast fading, given the stringent economic climate. Typical of the new breed emerging as the thirties closed was Jacob Stewart Seidman, a teetotal, vegetarian certified public accountant, who from 1935 on proved himself a man with a system, a wily operator who backed two plays a year out of two hundred offered, choosing only those that seemed surefire on the basis of the script rather than casting. Often plowing in 40 percent of the capital in return for 20 percent of the profits, Seidman's best-known hits then included *Three Men on a Horse*, *Room Service*, and *Lady in the Dark*.

What Seidman and his fellow angels sought were solid, upbeat, middle-class offerings that were long on entertainment and short on social comment. Marxist analyses, they rationalized, sold only balcony seats; angels sought to fill the stalls and the circle. George Sklar's *Stevedore*, an indictment of racism in Louisiana, was not for the angels, any more than the Communist-oriented dramas *(Steel, They Shall Not Die)* of John Wexley. They fought shy of the plays of Clifford Odets, with their dominant matriarchs and unemployed fathers demeaned to ciphers by the Depression, and equally of John Howard Lawson *(The Pure in Heart, Success Story),* who denounced "crazy people all hopped up with crazy ideas, selling bad stocks, passing bad cheques, chasing money. . . ." It was from just such a rat race that the angels had emerged unscathed.

Seidman's closest rival, Howard S. Cullman, a prosperous tobacco merchant known on Broadway as the "Angel of Mercenary," was bitten by the bug in 1938, staking a paltry $5,000 on *Life with Father*, which returned him $110,000, a 2,000 percent profit, in no short order. Like most angels, Cullman—*Arsenic and Old Lace*, Maurice Evans's *Macbeth*—looked eagerly for Hollywood sales (*Abe Lincoln in Illinois* went for $250,000) and calculated he could afford four flops, at $1,500 each, to every hit. A hit would bring a minimum of $20,000 profit.

When envious Wall Street friends begged him for tips, Cullman had one unfailing answer. "Just put your dough into plays where Katharine Cornell or Helen Hayes is playing the lead," he counseled. "Brother, you can't miss."

Cullman's recipe for success, had she known of it, would have astonished Helen Hayes. With part of her being she had almost bidden farewell to the theatre. The birth of her daughter, Mary, in 1931, had been followed by almost two years' exile in Hollywood, on a weekly $3,500 contract with Metro-Goldwyn-Mayer. Although her films had been more prestigious than Larry's (Sinclair Lewis's *Arrowsmith*, with Ronald Colman, Ernest Hemingway's *A Farewell to Arms,* with Gary Cooper), Helen found herself pining for more permanent things: her gracious old home at Nyack, New York, with its terraces and rose gardens sloping down to the Hudson River.

By her own estimation, Helen's claim to theatrical fame was still modest. When a radio program billed her as the First Lady of the American Theatre, to the mortification of both Kit and Lynn, Helen hastened to explain that her sponsor was Lipton's Tea: "They had a lot of tea to sell in the Midwest and it would help them if I had some sort of reputation."

Finally, in 1933, she broke free from the glitter of Hollywood, spurning a $85,000-a-year offer from Paramount Pictures, and returned to her first love, Broadway.

This was an age when costume chronicles were all the rage (*The Barretts; The Rose Without a Thorn*, featuring Henry VIII; *Charles the King*, celebrating the melancholy Charles I; *Clive of India*), and it was Helen's lot to be offered the most challenging role of all: the ill-starred Mary Stuart in Maxwell Anderson's blank-verse drama *Mary of Scotland*.

It was the first historical character that she had ever portrayed, and from the outset she saw complications; fair haired and just on five feet high, she had been cast as the tallest woman (six feet) in English history. "I'm nothing like Mary Stuart," she reflected, staring despairingly in her bedroom mirror. "How *can* I go out there and make the audience see what I feel?" The solution, fortuitously, was provided by Mae West, herself as petite as Helen, yet who nonetheless achieved her voluptuous carriage with the aid of four-inch heels and two-inch soles. From the first rehearsal, Helen learned to queen it in identical footwear.

Supported by a strong cast—Helen Menken (Elizabeth I), Philip Merivale (Bothwell), and George Coulouris, who recalls her as "good, steady, reliable and simple-minded beyond belief," as Lord Burghley—Helen achieved her first, and she imagined her last, success in a costume role.

She had reckoned without the peripatetic Gilbert Miller, who on a fleeting visit to London in May 1935 had witnessed a remarkable play, *Victoria Regina*, by the dramatist Laurence Housman at London's Little Gate Theatre. Since the Lord Chamberlain's regulations forbade the portrayal of recently deceased characters, the play was staged to a subscription audience only, for a profit of exactly five pounds. But in New York, of course, the censor's writ did not run, and Miller secured the rights.

He also secured the services of the unknown young American amateur (cast as Prince Albert) whose sole experience, despite a creditable German accent, had been a six-line walk-on in the Gate's previous production, *Chicago*. Thus six months later Vincent Price was to find himself as Helen's leading man, adapting his voice, as to the manor born, to the acoustics of New York's Broadhurst Theatre, which seated more than 1,100 playgoers.

But just as Kit had stubbornly resisted Elizabeth Moulton-Barrett, Helen fought against Victoria. "Oh, how dark brown!" was a friend's reaction when Helen first broached the title, and this precisely mirrored the actress's own feelings. Charles MacArthur, duly consulted, had no feeling for the play at all. For weeks the manuscript gathered dust around the Nyack house, unwanted and unread.

At length Miller called Helen urgently from his Rockefeller Plaza office. "Have you read it?" he demanded. "If you haven't you must at once because I'm going to lose my rights to this. There is some kind of hassle going on and it's imperative that you read it."

With little enthusiasm, Helen retired to the garden, and by degrees became so engrossed in the script that the sudden onset of neighbors coming to view her flower beds sent her scampering to the bathhouse attached to the swimming pool, there to lock herself in and complete her reading sitting on the floor. She emerged, once her neighbors had departed, "passionately in love with the play and that role."

Yet there were complications. Of the nine vignettes that Miller had selected from Housman's thirty-two, the last three dealt with Victoria in her dotage—scenes from which Helen fought shy. To her *Victoria Regina* was the love story of a little princess and her German prince, and the play should end with Albert's death, the end of a great love story. Miller only shrugged. "If you feel that way," he said, "maybe it would be better if you talked to Housman," and, as an afterthought, offered to pay her expenses for the trip to London.

It was a fruitless journey. At sixty-eight, Housman, with an ego to rival the 150-foot Albert Memorial in Kensington Gardens, was in no mood to be taught his trade by an unknown American actress. Without pausing for breath, he proceeded to act out scenes that Helen already knew by heart. The final scenes, he stressed, had been his main reason for writing the play. If the play was not done with those scenes, it would not be done at all. He knew Americans would flock to the theatre if only to hear the play read aloud. "Anyone," he said, "could act it."

"He behaved like an old bully," Helen told Miller wrathfully. "A road-company Shaw."

Diction posed another problem. Since Helen's accent was decidedly American, she took comfort in the belief that Victoria, whose mother had been Mary Louise Victoria of Saxe-Coburg-Gotha, had spoken with a faintly guttural intonation, a cover for her Americanese. Once again, Miller's impeccable connections secured her an invitation to meet the Marchioness of Milford Haven, over tea at Kensington Palace.

But on the problem of pronunciation, the Marchioness proved unhelpful. "Vy," she replied, "my grandmutter spoke chust as gut Anglish as I do."

Throughout rehearsals Helen struggled to conjure up the old queen in vain. Come the premiere in Baltimore, and she was still struggling, knowing that she was "awful, like an amateur in a high-school production." Then one night, as she lay courting sleep, a mental picture of Grandmother Hayes marched before her vision—the Irish grandmother who, as a child, had cheered the young queen's wedding procession, who, for ten years after the queen's death, had still clung to the bonnet with the black egret that had been high Victorian fashion. From this moment on there were no doubts; this was how the old queen should be played, most especially at the climax, on June 20, 1897, the occasion of her Diamond Jubilee, when the crowds had hailed her open carriage, "Go it, Old Girl! You've done it well! You've done it well!"

"Oh, I hope it's true! I hope it's true!" Victoria reminisced as the last slow curtain descended. "Albert! Ah! If only you could have been there!"

When ex-Queen Ena of Spain visited the United States and saw the play, she was dumbfounded. Over tea she asked Helen, "How did you ever learn my grandmother's every mannerism, gesture, idiosyncrasy of behaviour and speech?" Helen found it difficult to explain that she was merely re-creating her own grandmother, another old lady but possessed of the same indomitable spirit.

This was to be her greatest role, played for 517 performances on Broadway, for more than 950 across the United States. For in 1937, the year that the Lord Chamberlain finally assented to grant the play a British license, on the hundredth anniversary of Victoria's accession—at the behest, it was said, of King Edward VIII—Helen, like Kit, took *Victoria Regina* on the road for the best part of a year.

It was a properly regal procession, with red carpets, ermine cloaks at each first night, and the mayor of each city meeting the company train on arrival. In Des Moines, Iowa, ten thousand citizens witnessed her performance; in Washington, D.C., the Roosevelts gave her a special White House dinner along with the secretary of state, Cordell Hull. Yet Helen, as vulnerable as most players, remembered most vividly the closing night in Pittsburgh, a night when the seething crowd of admirers showed its Janus face.

Intent on catching the midnight train back to Nyack, Helen joined the cast assembled onstage for Miller's champagne and caviar party for just one glass—then fled from the stage door of Nixon's Theatre to the sanctuary of her car. It was a schedule too tight to sign autographs for all that milling crowd, and abruptly their bitterness and disappointment spilled over.

As the car backed away from the theatre, away from *Victoria Regina,* her greatest triumph, the chanting was painfully audible as the Beloved Monster gave tongue: "You stink! You stink! You stink!"

In London, the night of Tuesday, May 17, 1938, was one to confound the pessimists. After four years' absence, the Lunts were returning to Shaftesbury Avenue with their latest offering, S.N. Behrman's adaptation of Jean Giraudoux's Grecian satire, *Amphytrion 38.* Their return was indisputable proof that the theatre was alive and well.

At the Lyric Theatre, where the opening was timed for 8:30 that night, there was a palpable air of bustle and excitement. As early as 9:00 A.M., the stage-door keeper, the painfully deaf Mr. Charles Keogh, who whiled away his days engrossed in the plays of Shakespeare, opened up the padlocked front of the house doors that gave onto Shaftesbury Avenue; within the hour, the box-office staff under C.J. Roberts would arrive to deal with the first of "the doors," tickets sold for that evening's performance. Meanwhile, at the Cadogan Square house of the playwright Edward Knoblock, which they had rented for the summer, Lynn and Alfred awoke and breakfasted late, as was their custom.

The play itself was in essence a cobweb, the story of Alkmena (Lynn), a loyal Grecian wife who, over three acts, refuses to betray her husband even with the lascivious god Jupiter himself (Alfred). Yet their attention to detail was as singular as it had always been. Lynn, after learning that this had been customary among Grecian women, had let her fingernails grow to mandarin length and painted them white; at the Lyric, her dressing table, under the care of her London dresser, Bessie Porter, featured several bottles of attar of roses from Floris, the Jermyn Street perfumier, an aroma that helped Lynn "feel" Grecian.

Toward 6:30 P.M., Charles Keogh (his little cubbyhole crammed, despite his deafness, with cages of singing canaries) handed two keys to Jules Johnson, Alfred's dresser, who served as the star's valet at the Lunts' country home in Genesee Depot, Wisconsin: one key to the Lyric's Wardrobe Department, where Johnson would collect Alfred's toga and beard, and one to the Number One "star" dressing room. Johnson was at least ninety minutes ahead of the other dressers, who clocked on at the statutory thirty-five minutes before curtain-up, but Alfred, ever a stickler for meticulous makeup, would arrive by 7:00 P.M. at the latest. On his dressing table, in a prominent position, Johnson had arranged the silver-pig salt shaker that a woman first-nighter had presented to Alfred four years earlier during the London run of *Reunion in Vienna,* a good-luck charm that he had treasured ever since.

All over London, as the soft May dusk thickened, the theatre world was coming alive. As the crowds of pitgoers, with a pleasant tingle of expectation, settled on their stools, a unique fraternity was already making a clamant bid for their attention, vying with the rumble of traffic and the cries of news vendors; namely, the buskers of London. Estimated at 150 strong, theirs was an exclusive and precarious vocation, inherited from their Italian forebears: to entertain the theatre queues in the brief hour before 8:00 P.M., when the crowds filed into the playhouses.

Most regulars greeted their acts as old familiars, mindful of the first time that Frank Bates had launched his paper-tearing act, a kind of primitive origami, or Billy Wilton, working perilously in the midst of Shaftesbury Avenue traffic, began his high-pitched yodeling and imitations of chickens and dogfights. Rivaling both in their popularity were the itinerant violinist Leo Morest, with his perky monkey, Stanley, and Roy Jackson, onetime skipper of an American rum-runner, who treated the crowds to stentorian renderings of Kipling's "If." Stern tradition laid down that no busker worked a queue for more than ten minutes before collecting his earnings—known as "bottling"—though takings, at best, were modest enough. A five-shilling "bottle" was commonly reckoned to be the most a busker could pull down.

By 7:45 P.M., the stage-door keepers were keeping a sharp eye

181

open, more than justifying their stipend of two pounds fifteen shillings a week. At the Old Vic, across the river, Bob Robertson noted Larry's hasty entry for one of the last performances of *Coriolanus*, but Robertson, like Mr. Keogh at the Lyric, was concerned with more than "booking in" the first comers and doling out mail. His nostrils were primed for the telltale smells of fish and chips and oranges, both forbidden in dressing rooms lest the odor penetrate to the stalls.

For C.J. Roberts and his staff in the Lyric's box office, this was the peak point of their day. Since the Lunts' first nights were always a sellout, the only seats officially changing hands were those booked in advance, what the trade called COBOs (collect at box office), but there were still the unlooked-for hassles of double bookings and lost tickets with which to contend. At 6:30 P.M., two hours before the show, the day's cash had been counted up; at 8:00 P.M., when the box office closed, it would be checked all over again before locking up. Then it would be time for a pint, for bemoaning the stupidity and rudeness of many patrons (with schoolteachers taking priority), and the iniquity of the Sale or Return system, whereby the "libraries" clung onto unsold tickets that the theatre could have allocated.

Since the movie-minded thirties still favored multiple sets, the backstage staff at several theatres were tonight stretched to capacity. Some of the stagehands, like Jimmie Hester at the old Lyceum, where Sir Seymour Hicks's *Money Talks* was playing, had been almost thirty years on the job, beginning their apprenticeship the hard way by sweeping the stage. Since the Hicks's vehicle involved seven scene changes, from the ornate Louis XVI furniture of a Paris apartment to a corset factory, Hester and his mates would also qualify for "heat and burden" money, overtime paid in excess of the one shilling and five pence per hour laid down by their union, NATKE (National Association of Theatrical and Kine Employees). Yet the Lyceum, like the nearby Vaudeville, whose *Toss of a Coin* involved scene changes from Brighton Pier to a French gaming casino, was lucky; the proximity of Covent Garden Market ensured that a hard core of brawny fruit-and-vegetable porters (all enrolled in NATKE) was always on call each evening.

Most porters, in time, became seasoned professionals, with the two injunctions known to all stagehands springing readily to their lips: "Clear, please!" a warning to the actors to disperse, and "Strike!" which signaled the dismantling of a set.

182

Many plays then running—*The Island*, a drama of garrison life with Godfrey Tearle at the Comedy, and St. John Ervine's *Robert's Wife*, with Edith Evans and Owen Nares, at the Globe—called for elaborate byplay with food and drink, and the ASMs of the day were adept in this singular aspect of make-believe. Thus, on Miss Evans's opening line "Ouf, I'm tired. Anne, bring the sherry," ASM Madge Whiteman had a decanter of cold tea standing by in the wings. For the numerous rounds of drinks demanded in *The Island*, stage manager Nona Saffel would ring the changes on ginger ale, brown sugar solutions, and water tinted with cochineal. In the cocktail-party scene of *Money Talks*, mashed prunes stood in for caviar canapés; more substantial meals would be bread or cereal soaked in hot gravy.

At 8:00 P.M., the darkened side streets teemed with scurrying figures, soon swallowed up by sundry stage doors; these were the "beginners" of the evening, with barely enough time to discard their day clothes and don costumes and makeup. At varying distances, the callboy's voice rose and fell through the echoing corridors: "Half-hour, please! Half-hour, please!"

At the Lyric, Bessie Porter was toiling up steep flights of iron stairways toward Wardrobe, in quest of the first of the white silk-jersey costumes designed for Lynn by the Russian Valentina. En route, she exchanged a time-honored joke with some stagehands; a dresser, forever ascending to Wardrobe, stood as much in need of an oxygen cylinder as a stagehand, working in total darkness, of a miner's lamp.

In his dressing-room mirror, Alfred thoughtfully surveyed the beard of lustrous golden ringlets that transformed him into Jupiter. "It makes me look," he observed, dead-pan, "as if I had swallowed Shirley Temple."

Soon after 8:00 P.M. Shaftesbury Avenue was experiencing what, even for 1938, amounted to a sizable traffic jam; by taxi, private car, and sleek limousine furnished by Godfrey Davis, the inveterate first-nighters were arriving. The men, without exception, wore black ties and dinner jackets, though white tie and tails were *de rigueur* if a supper dance was planned. The women, for the most part, wore long evening dresses, evening jackets with sumptuous fur collars, and clutched mesh or diamanté evening bags. Theirs was a small, tight world where, as *The Daily Telegraph*'s W. A. Darlington noted, "nobody knows everybody, but everybody knows somebody . . .

the stalls at any one first night look exactly as they did on the immediately preceding first night."

Thus the vulgarian department-store owner Gordon Selfridge would be on hand to exchange greetings with the Sapphic Lady Mendl, whose hair, according to fancy, might be dyed lilac or parakeet green; the Marchioness of Headfort, the former Gaiety girl, Rosie Boote, was a never-failing presence; Sir Milsom Rees, for twenty-six years laryngologist to the Royal Family, would nod politely, to the handsome young Lord Lurgan and to Sir Louis Sterling, the music publisher. Swooping nimbly through the crowd, forever in quest of fresh celebrities, was Sibyl, Lady Colefax, the interior decorator, whose appetite for poets, politicians, and royalty was both ardent and totally indiscriminate.

As they sauntered unhurriedly toward the stalls and dress circle, smiling, chattering, bowing graciously, all were oblivious of the callboy's backstage cry, by now high-pitched with urgency: "Quarter-hour, please! Quarter-hour, please!"

One privileged bystander, the Lunts' cherished friend, the seventy-one-year-old dramatist W. Graham Robertson, was already backstage, swaddled by a comfortable armchair in the wings. Minutes earlier, he had watched with amusement as Alfred and Richard Whorf (Mercury) took up their precarious positions on a papier-mâché thundercloud above Mount Olympus, noting their uneasy interchange. "How do you feel?" came Alfred's hollow whisper.

"Feel?" Whorf whispered back. "I feel I've lost my voice. Supposing I can't speak?"

At this moment, from the prompt corner, the stage manager called, "Set your lights!" to the electrician perched above him on an elevated platform; the switches clicked home and a blaze of colored light flooded the scene. Twenty-two feet above stage level, the flymen, in their gallery, stood by the curtain winch, eyes alert for the stage manager's "go" signal.

"You *must* speak," Jupiter was urging Mercury. "Gawd—I'm afraid I'm going to be sick."

"You can't be sick," Mercury objected. "There goes the curtain."

Now the house lights had dimmed. Unconscious of all that backstage anguish, the audience settled tranquilly in their seats. A play was born.

*   *   *

More than three thousand miles from Shaftesbury Avenue, in a host of venues across the United States, the drama was gaining fresh impetus from a relatively new institution: the summer theatre. From the Rocky Mountains to the Atlantic seaboard, in barns, garages, warehouses, and churches, the stars of tomorrow—playwrights, actors, directors, scene designers—were year by year gaining an apprenticeship that larger cities would be slow to bestow.

The time was fast waning when such downbeat descriptions as Straw Hat, Red Barn, and Cow Shed Theatre had summed up Broadway's attitude to this new growth. New York managers like Lawrence Langner and John Golden had come to see distinct advantages in this new-style summer repertory—economic advantages, above all. In summer theatre, eight to ten plays could be staged for no more than one thousand dollars apiece, the price of one modest New York production. Many communities asked a modest rental of no more than five hundred dollars for the entire season. Front-rank players like Ethel Waters, Tallulah Bankhead, and Miriam Hopkins were glad to play for derisory sums—a weekly average of one thousand dollars—if only to escape the bogey of typecasting.

Although the Elitch Gardens Theatre of Denver, Colorado, had paved the way as far back as 1891, the movement had been slow to catch on; the thousand-seater Lakewood Theatre at Skowhegan, Maine, was not established until early in the 1920s, followed by the Berkshire Playhouse at Stockbridge, Massachusetts, and the Cape Playhouse at Dennis, in the same state. But from such obscure beginnings many freshly minted talents would emerge. In the summer of 1931 the Playhouse in Ivoryton, Connecticut, brought forth the lively, freckle-faced Katharine Hepburn, though still painfully raw and much in need of guidance, and the shambling Buddy Ebsen, soon bound for Broadway and Hollywood.

In those pioneering days, enthusiasm was as much a necessity as talent. When the University Players Guild opened up at Falmouth, Massachussetts, in 1928, the director, Bretaigne Windust, abruptly called a halt to rehearsals, explaining logically, "We can't put on a play without a theatre. Go on, help work on it, we've got to get it finished." From then on, recalls Josh Logan, then a bright-eyed twenty-year-old, he, Henry Fonda, and Fonda's first wife, Margaret Sullavan, worked almost nonstop for seventy-two hours, building scenery and installing seats.

185

By 1936, fully thirteen summer-stock companies had been established, from the Westchester Playhouse at Mount Kisco to the Maverick Players in Woodstock, New York; at Mount Kisco, in the summer of that year, the locals could delight in such acknowledged talents as Burgess Meredith in *Liliom*, Peggy Wood in *The Taming of the Shrew*, and Vincent Price and Mildred Natwick in *Elizabeth the Queen*. The festival spirit, born at Bayreuth in 1876 and fostered both at Salzburg (from 1920) and Malvern, Worcestershire (from 1929), was slowly gaining ground in America. Twenty years on, some three hundred summer theatres would be grossing $7 million each season, catapulting some fifty new players toward Broadway and at least eight new plays.

The ambience was a far cry from the Great White Way. Gnats and cockchafers were as strongly lured to the glare of the footlights as playgoers, all of whom bought programs to stand in as both fans and mosquito-swatters in the sticky heat. Casts commonly attended rehearsals in slacks or swimming trunks, to old-timers like Ethel Barrymore a painful departure from tradition, who similarly found it an odd sensation to approach the stage door across an open country meadow.

Cornelia Otis Skinner, making a round of summer theatres as the diva Cavallini in Edward Sheldon's *Romance* in 1938, descried an aura of "slap-happy optimism" that irked her. Whoever had hired the men's dress suits had neglected to think of the pumps, and thus the young, fee-paying students, attired as elegant dandies in the crowd scenes, ambled through the first night in swallow-tail coats, ruffled shirts, and bare feet. In her love scene with Donald Cook as the pure young clergyman, both swooned throughout, though not with guilty passion; the stagehands had neglected to remove a dead mouse from inside their velvet love seat.

Some players, bored to extinction by the rural round, did little more than go through the motions. When William Redfield played the summer circuit in *Arms and the Man* as late as 1953, he was disturbed that the great Marlon Brando, cast as Sergius, made an effort on an average of twice a week—and threw away every other performance. After a matinee in Framingham, Massachusetts, a delegation of angry matrons intercepted Redfield at the stage door, complaining, "We'd like you to tell him that we're not a bunch of yokels. Does he think we can't see that he's laughing at us while we sit out there?"

When Redfield passed on this remonstration, Brando was totally indifferent. "Man, don't you get it? This is *summer stock*!"

Given the British climate, only two examples of summer theatre were ever recorded: that of the pioneer venture at Frinton-on-Sea, Essex, still in existence after fifty years; and that of Peter Bull at Perranporth, Cornwall, which ran for three seasons from 1936. This was a shoestring operation with a vengeance, based on an ancient Women's Institute building, leased for four pounds a week, seating only 145, with a stage no more than six feet deep. None of the cast—which included Robert Morley, fiercely ambitious to limp heavily and wield a swordstick as the hero in Patrick Hamilton's *Rope*—was ever paid a penny. With a total capital of ninety pounds, Bull could offer his players only free housing and food, with a share of the profits (if any) at the season's end. Since no funds even existed to hire scenery, they were reduced to spiriting the furniture out of their digs, *Mon Repos*, then smuggling it back again after each performance.

No American summer theatre was ever reduced to quite those straits. At the best times, in the best places, they played a warm and intimate role in the communities they served. At the Clinton Playhouse in Clinton, Connecticut, the impresario Charlotte Buchwald Harmon regularly gave box-office space to up to seven babies whose sitters had failed to arrive, changing diapers and warming bottles, as well as walking pet dogs and parking cars. Though often faced with temperamental stars, Mrs. Harmon catered imperturbably to Mischa Auer's craving for herrings in sour cream three times a day, and Van Heflin's need for the hot tea spiked with 150-proof Demerara rum that soothed his vocal chords. When the electric power cut out, grateful patrons, entering into that community spirit, would sprint for their cars and switch on the headlights so that the show could go on.

"Summer theatre," Mrs. Harmon would acknowledge freely, "is a crazy business, but I can't help myself—I'm simply crazy about it."

The year 1939, when World War II could plainly no longer be averted, was a time to take stock. The veterans among them, Lynn, Helen, Noël, and Alfred, had been learning their craft when the carnage of the Western Front was still an inconceivable nightmare. Kit had studied with the Washington Square Players even before the United States entered that "war to end all wars." Even John and

Larry, the juvenile leads, had now amassed some thirty years' experience between them.

So what had they learned that was enduring and valid in these interim years? What guidance could they offer to the beginners, whose feet were poised tentatively on the first rungs of the rickety ladder that led to stardom?

Not all actors had it in their power to follow Tyrone Guthrie's advice and play Hamlet, Benedick, and Romeo in their formative years; John had achieved it, but Larry was never to essay Benedick. Yet both stars, as beginners often noted, themselves set more store by relaxation—"an art," John observed acidly, "never taught at drama schools." "Relax your feet!" was Larry's constant injunction. "And always have more breath than you need!"

Tension in young players, while understandable, was a weakness to be conquered at all costs. "Relax. That's all you have to do—just relax," Ethel Barrymore once counseled a nervous bit-player. "It will all be the same in a hundred years." And the bit-player Spencer Tracy was to follow that counsel to perfection for the rest of his natural life.

Teamwork, such as the Moscow Art Theatre and the Abbey in Dublin had pioneered, was an integral part of the approach. "Good acting," Dame Edith Evans put it to Peter Finch, "is like a good tennis match. An actor, like a tennis player, can only play his best game with players of his own class." John was of like persuasion. "Be a good partner," he would stress, "and learn to listen. Don't pounce on cues or drop your voice at the end of a line," a tip passed on to him by his Uncle Fred. "All acting is giving and receiving," was Dame Flora Robson's main tenet, or, as a young New York graduate, Rod Steiger, put it, "Acting isn't acting—it's interacting." Back in 1933, Konstantin Stanislavsky had expressed this to perfection: "If your feelings don't reach even your partner who is standing beside you, how do you expect them to reach that absent-minded restless spectator, way off in the twentieth row?"

All were profoundly wary lest artificiality creep in. To an earlier generation Shakespeare had proved a particular pitfall, with players lapsing all too easily into the pompous and pretentious. Even the veteran Old Vic producer Harcourt Williams was pulled up on this count by Margaret Carrington, the elocution teacher who had helped John Barrymore interpret Hamlet. "Why do you assume that particular voice when you are speaking Shakespeare?" she asked Williams. "Do you do anything else besides Shakespeare?"

When Williams revealed that he often told stories to children, instancing an excerpt from Hans Christian Andersen's *The Tinder Box*, Mrs. Carrington promptly pounced. "But that's your real voice— that's the voice you ought to use in Shakespeare."

Not all were wholly agreed on how best to achieve results. Essentially it was a question of temperament. Alfred, like John, noted the producer Peter Brook, was "a brilliant improviser," who arrived at a role by intuition, by trial and error. Lynn followed Larry's example, working from her mind, meticulously, slowly, putting pieces together as a whole.

An imaginative actor, maintained Theodore Komisarjevsky, worked from "the inside," unlike a stagey actor inventing grimaces and movements before a mirror. Helen was only partly in agreement. Whether the character was Norma in *Coquette* or Queen Victoria, she first saw the role as someone quite apart from herself, living in her own integrated world. "*She* does that," Helen would analyze, never "*I* do that." Only much later in rehearsals would this illusory character be related to Helen Hayes.

For a profession that traded in emotion they were at all times chary of emotionalism as such. "Emotion can play a big part in acting," Alfred would agree, "but it must always be *controlled emotion*," and John supported this to the hilt. For him, emotion must be felt only at the first rehearsal, to be stored away like a precious keepsake, to be studied at intervals and drawn on discreetly. It was a lesson he had early on absorbed from Sybil Thorndike.

As a sometime instructor at RADA, Dame Sybil outlined this same technique to the student Flora Robson. As Andromache in *The Trojan Women*, Miss Robson burst out with a loud "Oh God!" when the death of her baby son was mooted. Dame Sybil checked her; the line must be whispered, for more tragic news yet was in store for Andromache. Once it was broken, Dame Sybil gave her pupil her head. "Now!" she said. "Now the audience knows what is going to happen, and you can break your heart!"

The lesson was implicit to them all; an audience could cope with only one climax.

At all times the players at the top threaded delicately across a tightrope that veered between overplaying and underplaying. Ultra-emotional performances, known to the profession as "ham acting" after the hog's lard once used as greasepaint by third-rate players, was excused by Noël, for one. "All acting worth the name is 'ham,' " he insisted, and Dame Marie Tempest tended to agree: "Cover up the 'ham' but don't take it away."

In the final analysis, all that they had absorbed was so much instinctive as to almost defy definition. Once, when a student asked Alfred intensely, "What is technique?" the great man was totally nonplussed.

"I haven't the slightest idea," he had to confess. "I'll go home and ask my wife."

VII. The Theatre at War:
"Every Night Something Awful"

On Monday, September 4, 1939, the London theatre took a giant step backward in time. One day earlier, a quavering radio declaration by Prime Minister Neville Chamberlain had signaled that Britain was honoring her pledge to Poland, invaded by Germany on September 1; for the second time in twenty-one years, Great Britain and Germany were at war.

Since Chamberlain's Cabinet envisaged a mass air assault on the capital, with anything up to 600,000 fatalities, London's forty-three theatres, for the first time since the Puritan interregnum of 1642, were now dark and silent.

Within days came a partial relaxation; the imposition of a 6:00 P.M. curfew now permitted any playhouse to stage up to six weekly matinées. Yet in the capital all but five theatres stayed dark. It was young John Gielgud's company, in the relatively safe northern suburb of Golders Green, who reaped the rewards; at the local Hippodrome, *The Importance of Being Earnest*, with John and Edith Evans, took over one thousand pounds in its first five performances, nearly two thousand pounds in the next full week.

Since almost 400,000 men had been called to the colors, the British from the first were resolved on one thing: the troops would not go short of entertainment. As far back as the Munich Crisis of 1938, when Germany had swallowed up Czechoslovakia, the energetic Basil Dean, who had done much for troop entertainment in World War I, had resolved on a positive plan of campaign. In that war, Dean recalled, the troops had endured much more than the squalor of the trenches; they had suffered an endless round of talentless amateurs, unfunny comics, and brats from dancing academies, ubiquitous in

191

camps and hospital wards, to the very real pain of their captive audience.

At one hospital, the entertainers had arrived to find the patients had taken to the woods; only the resource of a patient regimental sergeant major had contrived to round them up. "Men," he said, "I sympathise with you, but play the game. They like doing it, don't let's spoil their enjoyment." As seasoned veterans, the soldiers saw no option but to surrender.

To Dean, all this had served as a dreadful warning for the future. By Sunday, September 3, he was organized for action. Backed by, among others, Sir Seymour Hicks as Leader of the Stage, RADA's Sir Kenneth Barnes as General Secretary, Jack Buchanan as Chief of Revue, and Colonel Stanley Bell, Tree's former stage director, as Chief of Equipment, Dean made public that, as from September 11, he was setting up headquarters at the Theatre Royal, Drury Lane, London's most famous playhouse. His organization would be known as Entertainments National Service Association (ENSA), which the troops, with dour anticipation, at once christened "Every Night Something Awful."

Two weeks to the day, on September 25, all the talent that Dean could at first muster ventured timorously into a blacked-out England that had relapsed into the pitch darkness of the seventeenth century. Twelve seaside concert parties, their seasons abruptly cut short by fear of a seaborne invasion, sallied forth to such anonymous whistle stops as Ludgenhall, Burscough, and Winterbourne Gunner, offering such sprightly titles as *Bubbles*, *Sunny Smiles*, and *Hullo, Happiness*.

The legitimate drama proved more of a problem. Nominated by British Actors' Equity as the logical head of the Drama Section, Henry Oscar, that veteran Bensonian who had seen little hope for Larry in his student days, moved into the windowless Dressing Room No. 6, flanked by a secretary, a typewriter, two alumni of the Croydon Repertory Company, Hamilton Price and Edmund Bailey, as assistants, plus an asthmatic electric fan for ventilation.

From the first their stumbling block was not suitable plays but suitable actors. Since ENSA's rates of pay were minimal, agents did not steer clients their way. Many personable juveniles of the thirties—Frank Lawton, Guy Middleton, Hugh Williams—had enlisted in the King's Royal Rifle Corps when war broke out. Larry was in the United States, where he had first toured with Kit Cornell in

192

S.N. Behrman's *No Time for Comedy* and married Vivien Leigh, whose fame as Scarlett O'Hara in *Gone With The Wind* had already eclipsed her husband's, before returning in 1941 to enlist as a lieutenant in the Royal Naval Volunteer Reserve. Alec Guinness and Michael Redgrave were likewise absorbed by the navy. Though Oscar sent James Mason on tour in the leading roles in *Eight Bells*, a merchant navy melodrama, and *Heroes Don't Care*, a send-up of polar exploration, he was perpetually strapped for talent, often forced to rely on early casualties of the fray.

Once, when Dean commented sourly on the low standards of a company, Oscar retorted, "What can you expect? The leading man has only got one arm, also he's going deaf." On another occasion, struggling to recruit for six plays in one morning, Oscar had a call from the stage-door keeper: "There's a man to see you, sir. Says he's an actor."

Speaking not as a racist but as a hard-pressed casting director, Oscar replied desperately, "Tell him, if he's white he's got the job!"

Yet in time those who trod the ENSA trail found themselves part of a world they had known only by hearsay. Hitherto, pampered by attentive dressers, flatteringly lit by Bentham Light Consoles, steered through the evening by vigilant callboys and ASMs, they now plunged overnight into the world of fit-up, into the punishing stock-company routine that Irving had known. Far from the theatre taking a retrograde step, the players, in many crucial ways, were rediscovering old roots.

One such pioneer was Private Griffith Jones, who had exchanged the comforting security of partnering John in *Richard of Bordeaux* and Larry in *The Rats of Norway* for the rigors of "Stars in Battledress." "Now I know the full and glorious life those barnstorming troupers lived in the past," he wrote to a friend, in ecstasy. "One of the most successful shows of our winter season was presented on a duck-board stage in a drenched marquee which had been pitched in a swamp of a field. Two oil lamps served as footlights to illuminate a stage that was cut in two by the central post supporting the tent. Who cared?"

Reflecting that he had once played opposite Elisabeth Bergner in *Escape Me Never* for 230 consecutive performances at the Apollo in London and the Shubert in New York, Jones concluded unchivalrously, "I often wonder how I endured it."

For all such pioneers were facing, for the first time in their lives, a totally new audience: an audience conditioned to the pace and amplified dialogue of a movie, who found a play the strangest of art forms. To refrain from comment was beyond them. If a maid drew the curtains in a darkened country house she was greeted with hilarious cries of "Mind the black-out." If a character ordered coffee in a café scene, ribald shouts compared the prices in the YMCA to those of the local services canteen.

Often a hard-pressed entertainments officer went before the curtain at the outset to explain what Act I was all about. In the interval, to stop them stampeding out, he explained what Act II had in store. Yet, as Dean was to point out, any cast that had performed Noël's *Private Lives* on a billiard table, with table tops laid athwart it, supported by beer crates at the outer ends, was a cast that had earned its accolade as troupers.

But as 1939 gave place to 1940, the twilight calm of the Phoney War set in. Once more, forty-three theatres were back in business— a marked contrast to Manhattan's twenty-four—with 8:30 P.M. as the normal opening time, a newly relaxed curfew of 11:00 P.M., and a welcome drop in prices, with twelve shillings and sixpence front stalls reduced to ten shillings and sixpence. Purists, however, detected a regrettable lowering of standards; even in the stalls, lounge suits were now as prevalent as dinner jackets.

On September 7, 1940, all this was ended. Around 5:00 P.M. on that tranquil Saturday, the air-raid sirens wailed; for the first time the city was under attack. Hundreds of German bombers struck the dockland area, which burned with a dry and terrible crackling. At the New Theatre in St. Martin's Lane where Sutton Vane's *Outward Bound* was playing, it fell to the star, Terence de Marney, to get the biggest unintentional laugh of that night. As one of a group of passengers aboard a ghostly liner, bound nobody knew where, it was de Marney, as young Mr. Prior, who voiced his realization to the others: "We're dead—we're all dead, I tell you!"

Hysterical laughter and the whistle of bombs brought the performance to a chaotic close.

By November 3, the bombs had rained on the city for fifty-seven nights. Theatregoing became an affair of matinées, even morning performances; Rex Harrison and Lilli Palmer who brought *No Time for Comedy* to the Theatre Royal, Haymarket, where it ran for a year, never once played an evening performance in all that time. Most often it was Harrison's lot to step from character and announce, "Ladies and gentlemen, an air-raid warning has sounded.

Those who wish to leave the theatre . . ." followed by instructions on how to reach the nearest shelters. (Later a lighted panel before the footlights assumed this function.)

In true the-show-must-go-on tradition, the play then proceeded—but, Harrison noted, "it was like having nobody there . . . the people out front seemed to be frozen stiff, listening not to us but to the planes."

Surprisingly, few theatres suffered physical damage. Three were hit beyond repair on the night of April 16, 1941, when 450 bombers attacked the capital: the little Royalty, in Dean Street, the site of Fanny Kelly's first dramatic academy; the Shaftesbury (now a fire station) in the avenue of that name; and the Little in the Adelphi. The Queen's, damaged in the autumn blitz, was to reopen in July 1959.

In the smoky aftermath of one such night, Gielgud had the uncanny experience of seeing a fragment of his former life unfold like a tableau before his eyes. A bomb had struck the Motleys' old workshop in Garrick Yard, and the overalled Heavy Rescue men, toiling in the debris, had merrily donned the black felt three-cornered hats that had featured in his 1934 production of *Hamlet*. At the top of the ruined staircase, flapping like a standard in the stiff morning breeze, was the scarlet cloak that he had worn as Richard II.

Yet from a passive acceptance of discomfort and disrupted routine, Londoners were changing by degrees to a stubborn refusal to be subjugated. Lunchtime concerts at the National Gallery, with artists like the pianist Myra Hess, had become the daily norm, but by mid-October 1940 the city was witnessing a phenomenon unique in contemporary history: lunchtime Shakespeare.

The concept was the brainchild of a thirty-eight-year-old classical actor Donald (later Sir Donald) Wolfit, who had been part of John's Old Vic season in 1929. Early that autumn he hit upon the idea of renting the Strand Theatre for a nugatory ten pounds a week. His company of twelve stalwarts, including the veteran actress Cathleen Nesbitt, was paid three-guineas-a-week expenses; his repertoire was an hour-long (1:00 P.M. to 2:00 P.M.) symposium of Shakespearean excerpts—the Sleepwalking Scene from *Macbeth*, the Casket Scene from *The Merchant of Venice*. Only the theatre's stalls were used, and the audience paid one-shilling-a-head admission.

On the first day, October 13, they played to an audience of sixty-one. On the next day, following a direct hit by a bomb on the rear of the theatre, they arrived to find the dressing rooms in ruins and the stage ankle-deep in dust and soot. But as troupers they were not deterred; they changed on the stage before curtain-up and the show went on.

By the end of the month Wolfit was playing to audiences of one thousand a week, and *The Daily Express*'s appropriate headline was SHAKESPEARE BEATS HITLER. Ever ingenious, Wolfit had even been prompted to add the Graveyard Scene from *Hamlet;* the stage door, which had been blown clean into the street, would make a perfect bier for Ophelia.

As the blitz continued unabated, a new organization sprang up with the need of civilians in mind: the miners, the factory workers, and all those evacuated from the bomb-stricken cities. All modern wars spawn acronyms, and thus CEMA (The Council for the Encouragement of Music and the Arts) was no exception, guided from the first by three doughty spirits, Dame Sybil Thorndike, her husband Lewis Casson, and Tyrone Guthrie, who, now that the Old Vic had become a hostel, was a man at liberty.

It was Casson, a Welshman, who conceived a passion to tour the villages of South Wales in the autumn of 1940, though his choice of play for the first tour, *Macbeth*, at first disconcerted CEMA's organizers. "Good Lord!" they exclaimed, "poor miners!" But Casson was unrepentant. "I know the Welsh people," he avowed, "and they like a tragedy."

Since Guthrie was involved, this was a *Macbeth* with a difference. To begin with, the dramatist Lionel Hale had written a prologue pointing up the play's contemporary relevance: "You needn't always think of dictators in terms of concentration camps and tanks and aeroplanes . . . what Macbeth wanted, what all such people want, is power. This is a play about a tyrant, a dictator." With Sybil doubling as Lady Macbeth and the First Witch, and a cast attired in the kilts and tam o'shanters of the 1745 Rebellion, their rendering was riotously received.

"At the end they went wild and lifted the roof with their clapping," Sybil wrote home, echoing Griffith Jones. "This is the theatre we like best—getting right in amongst people."

There followed ten weeks of one-night stands, thirty-seven in all, before they returned to London for the first wartime Old Vic season at the New, but by the autumn of 1941 they had returned to Wales, reveling in an audience that was in no way shy of expressing its emotions. Each day brought fresh surprises—like the luncheon where a church dignitary introduced Sybil as "a famous member of the oldest profession in the world." In the Rhondda Valley, they stayed, for the most part, with "the wonderfully hospitable" families of the miners.

The biggest surprise was that *The Medea* of Euripides far, far outstripped Shaw's *Candida* in popularity. *Candida,* to the Welsh, was frivolous and insubstantial, but *The Medea* was entirely to their taste. "This is the play for us," one miner told Sybil, "it kindles a fire," while another remarked, "There's no light pastry about this. It's good solid meat." Villagers walked miles from one valley to another to see the play again, and given this heady acclaim, Sybil was mindful to exercise restraint. "I mustn't wail too loud," she remarked, as Medea prepared to mourn her children offstage. "They can't see me, and they'll think it's a siren."

Toward December 1942, when CEMA's tour of the valleys finally came to an end, a new mood was evident in the theatre. Following December 7, 1941, when the Japanese attack on Pearl Harbor plunged the United States into World War II, it was as if the "special relationship," on which Churchill and Roosevelt liked to dwell, was mirrored simultaneously on Broadway and Shaftesbury Avenue. Not since the days of Charles Frohman had servicemen and their girlfriends, with money to burn, queued at the box office on both sides of the Atlantic for precisely the same attractions: plays that stressed the blessings of democracy, like Lillian Hellman's antifascist *Watch on the Rhine* and *Tomorrow the World,* with a small boy infected by the virus of Hitlerism; farces like *My Sister Eileen* and *Arsenic and Old Lace;* "family plays" like *Life with Father;* fast-paced satires like *The Man Who Came to Dinner.* A notable hit with audiences of all persuasions was Noël's hilarious *Blithe Spirit,* concerning the two wives of Charles Condomine, one living (Ruth), the other dead but still kicking (Elvira), summoned back to earth by the eccentric medium, Madame Arcati.

Long runs were now the order of the day, an omen for the future. *The Man Who Came to Dinner* ran for more than 700 performances in London and New York, *Arsenic and Old Lace* for more than 1,300.

All this, though gratifying for the casts involved, still fell short of the magical rapport of front-line theatre. Thus Emlyn Williams took the other-worldly preoccupations of *Blithe Spirit* to the little play-

197

house below Monte Cassino, at a time when the ground around the Italian monastery was being contested yard by bloody yard. One company, which included the young Donald Sinden, played half an hour of *French Without Tears* to an RAF audience who remained totally oblivious; all were busy counting the engine throb of returning fighters. Other companies played in the enormous Roman amphitheatre of Leptis Magna, one hundred miles outside Tripoli, where every word could be heard in each one of the seven thousand seats. ENSA's Major Nigel Patrick even secured the use of the National Theatre of Athens, provided he maintained the tradition of "only the spoken word." This was honored, though the company, John Longden, Geoffrey Keen, and Faith Brook spoke not the words of Aeschylus or Aristophanes but of the comedy thriller *Someone at the Door*.

No one found the strolling player's life more stimulating than John Gielgud. On a five-month around-the-world ENSA tour of *Hamlet* and *Blithe Spirit* he faced, for the first time, audiences who were ignorant of the plots of either play. In Madras, like any chorus boy, John shared a tiny dressing room with eleven other actors, and pitted his mellifluous voice against the tumult of the monsoon. Arriving in Cairo on the unpopular King Farouk's birthday, he found his first *Hamlet* abruptly canceled; the King of Denmark's murder, it was feared, might give Farouk's many enemies ideas.

In all, "Mr. Gogo," as the Egyptians called him, gave eight performances of *Hamlet* at Cairo's white, gold, and crimson Royal Opera House, but only after its ebullient director, Soliman Bey Naguib, had secured a personal guarantee from the Students' Committee of the Nationalists: positively they would not burn down the Opera House until John had departed.

After her historic revival of The Road in the thirties, it was inevitable that Kit Cornell should contribute some wartime statistics of her own.

Many American units had gone overseas sponsored by USO (United Service Organizations, Inc.), but Kit's was a tour organized by the American Theatre Wing, which gave away one thousand Broadway tickets a day to men in uniform and had already sent Frank Fay, along with his illusory rabbit *Harvey,* to the Pacific. Asked to choose a play and a company for a front-line tour of Italy, France, and Holland, Kit chose *The Barretts*, with Guthrie McClintic doubling as producer and the family doctor, Brian Aherne as her leading man, and a Yorkshire terrier masquerading as the cocker spaniel, Flush. In the summer of 1944, Unit 319, as the company was known, took to the high seas.

Weighed down with tins of insecticide, musette bags, steel helmets, and canteens, they finally disembarked in Naples. At the barracks in Caserta, a taste of their new life awaited them: the sign in every toilet read, TAKE IT EASY—PLUMBING DELICATE. More pertinently, they found the U.S. Army had the gravest doubts as to the wisdom of their choice. To keep the love scenes intact was just to ask for trouble; give the GI a love scene and hell always broke loose. As for Papa Barrett, the GIs, if they stayed at all, would stay to shoot him. "It is your duty," boomed a militant major, "to make every man who leaves the theatre . . . better able to turn a knife in the guts of a German."

On August 25, 1944, with all this advice unheeded, their own baptism of fire took place in the Teatro Garibaldi at Santa Maria, a dusty, biscuit-brown town up the line from Caserta.

As with so many battles, the worst part was the anticipation. It was true as each of her five brothers bent to kiss the reclining Elizabeth, smacking sounds were audible, and there were cries of "Pass it around." Papa Barrett's first entrance, in austere Victorian black, was usually a cue for trepidant silence, though McKay Morris, Kit's choice for the role, heard ominous rumbles of "Who does he think he is, a top sergeant?" The love scenes came and went, but without the storms they had feared, for as Kit consoled the nervous Aherne, "It's just a release—it's just an expression of their own loneliness!"

Afterward, at Kit's insistence, all the GIs who wanted to come were allowed backstage to voice their appreciation. "It's like a letter from home," one soldier told Margalo Gillmore, summing up what so many had felt.

McKay Morris was prouder than he had ever been, even after his years with Belasco. "They didn't love me," he said triumphantly. "They hissed me. God bless them."

Next day the army newspaper *Stars and Stripes*, which circulated all over the Italian peninsula, endorsed them with a banner headline: LONG-HAIRED DRAMA MAKES HIT WITH GI'S.

Thus their fame traveled ahead of them, to Foggia, Lecce, Bari, and Rome, to audiences consisting not only of Americans but Poles, Yugoslavs, South Africans, Russians, and Britons. After Rome they played Siena and then in Florence and Montecatini to General Mark

Clark's Fifth Army. Their last Italian performance, in Leghorn, was their seventy-eighth in seventy-nine days; from here they flew on to Marseilles.

And now, in Aix-en-Provence, they faced their greatest challenge of all, for the ship that carried their scenery and costumes had beached on a rock off Corsica. In the hospital at Aix the stage was a raised platform approached by three steps; there was no curtain. For the first and only time Elizabeth was dressed in a shirt and army blouse instead of a trailing gown, making do with Kleenex in lieu of a lacy handkerchief, and Robert Browning wore a trench coat, not a cape. When Act II ended, he and Elizabeth sauntered offstage arm in arm.

Thereafter, with scenery and costumes restored to them, they played Dijon, Vittel, on the very fringe of the Battle of the Bulge, Versailles, Paris, Maastricht and Heerlen in the Netherlands, and, their last date of all, Reims. No evening in the theatre, they knew now, could ever be quite the same again.

It was a GI's remark, overheard in Montecatini, that Kit and Guthrie always treasured as the most cherished compliment. "Didn't I tell you," he was remarking to a buddy, as they left the theatre, "that it'd be better than a whore-house?"

VIII. The Age of Olivier:

"Acting Great Parts ... It's a Dangerous Game"

In 1944 the Age of Olivier was dawning, and it was possible even then to spotlight its beginning. On Tuesday, August 15, Larry and his old friend Ralph Richardson, after collecting their mail from the Opera House in Manchester, where they had opened the previous night in *Arms and the Man*, were en route to their quarters at the Midland Hotel. On an impulse, Richardson bought a copy of that day's *Manchester Guardian* from a newsstand, turning, as is an actor's wont, to the reviews. To Larry's supreme mortification, he read over his companion's shoulder, "Mr. Ralph Richardson is a brilliant Bluntschli; Mr. Laurence Olivier, on the other hand . . ." After six years' absence from the London stage, Larry's confidence was at its lowest possible ebb. "Oh God!" he told himself, "I really can't go on with this . . . I shall do no good to these people or to myself if I stay on."

It was another old friend, Tyrone Guthrie, who was to change both his mind and the entire course of his life. That night, as the two men met up beneath the Opera House canopy, Guthrie commented gently, "Liked yer Sergius." Larry was stung. "Oh, thank you very much," he rejoined acidly. When Guthrie pursued this, persisting, "But don't you love Sergius?" Larry came close to losing his temper. The pompous Major Sergius Saranoff, as pictured by Shaw, "half tragic, half ironic," possessed by "mysterious moodiness," was a role with which he had never been able to come to terms. "How could you love a *bloody awful part* like that?" he demanded belligerently.

"Oh, I see," Guthrie replied. "Well, of course, unless you learn to love him, you'll never be any good in it, will you?"

This was a turning point in Larry's career, for what was at stake was not only the Olivier future but the fate of a newly resurrected Old Vic company—with Larry and Richardson released from the Navy to join Sybil Thorndike, Harcourt Williams, Margaret Leighton, and Joyce Redman in an all-star season at the New Theatre in London, a showcase of British talent at its brightest and best.

"By the end of the week," Larry recounted later, "I was loving Sergius so much I was the hit of the show, and when we opened in London I got the best notices."

As the summer of 1945 brought V-E Day to Europe, those rapturous notices never ceased. His Justice Shallow in *Henry IV, Part II*, whom one critic likened to "a dried seed-pod of a man," was a world away from his braggart, headstrong Hotspur; his smiling, melancholy Dr. Astrov in *Uncle Vanya* was in striking contrast to his unctuous, skittering Mr. Puff in Sheridan's *The Critic* and to his blinded, bleeding Oedipus, whose howl of torment was based upon memories of an ermine trapped in the snow. All these were characters whom Larry had "learned to love," and in the first postwar season of 1945 to 1946, Broadway came to love them, too.

Older critics now harked back to his prewar years at the Vic, and the subtleties that even then had been apparent: his convulsive retch at the moment of Coriolanus's banishment, and how his Henry V, commiserating with Sir Thomas Erpingham on the eve of Agincourt, had mused:

> *A good soft pillow for that good white head*
> *Were better than a churlish turf of France . . .*

It was the pause after "turf," with "of France" thrown in as a contemptuous afterthought, that had somehow pointed up the old knight's hard lot.

All these had been portents of greatness, now coming to fruition after seven years, which would culminate, in 1947, in his knighthood.

Yet toward the end of 1944, he had already received a rarer and more personal tribute. One night, in his dressing room at the New, making up as the malevolent Richard III, an ornate sword arrived as a gift: one of the most famous weapons in theatrical history. Originally it had been the property of the nineteenth-century tragedian Edmund Kean, who had used it when he played Richard III; in

1877, when Irving first essayed the role, it had passed to him. Ultimately, although he had never been cast as Richard, it had been acquired by Gielgud. Now, in relinquishing the weapon, John was not only paying homage to Larry's striking performance but, many critics felt, acknowledging his supremacy as Britain's finest Shakespearean actor.

In those postwar years London had need of such rich theatrical fare. In the cold, gray capital the citizens faced up, in 1947, to their eighth consecutive year of stringent rationing of food, fuel, shoes, and clothing. In most shop windows the operative word was "No": "No coal," "No cigarettes," "No meat." In the unheated theatres, playgoers and dramatic critics, of whom this author was one, huddled in their overcoats and kept on their gloves; their womenfolk wore not the dainty satin sandals of prewar days but fur boots. In a country whose government was preoccupied with such tempting Socialist Utopias as the nationalization of the Bank of England, fuel and power, inland transport, and iron and steel, the citizens hungered for glamour—for such moments as the unveiling of Christian Dior's New Look, with its tiny hats and vast billowing skirts, on February 12, 1947, and the electric first night of *Oklahoma* at Drury Lane on April 30.

Theatricality was thus much in vogue, and few dramatists came more theatrical than forty-one-year-old Christopher Fry, a onetime schoolmaster, who burst upon the West End scene with a pyrotechnic force in 1948. A man of dazzling verbal virtuosity, of striking and immediate metaphors, Fry was in a very real sense the literary equivalent of Dior's New Look. Critics were often at a loss to fathom the plots of such Fry epics as *The Lady's Not for Burning*, a fifteenth-century frolic that featured Thomas Mendip, a world-weary soldier yearning to be hanged, and Jennet, an alleged witch who did not want to burn. But with Fry what counted was the language, as when Alizon in *The Lady* described the spring sunshine:

> . . . *the trees were as bright as a shower of broken glass* . . .
> *I've an April blindness. You're hidden in a cloud of crimson catherine-wheels* . . .

In Fry's *The Firstborn*, Anath said of Moses, much in her thoughts, "He has stood all day under my brain's stairway." When a scream was heard, as a slave on the pyramids fell to his death, the rich image Fry gave to Anath was: "It is only a scare of birds in the air: And a pair of women with their nerves uncovered."

Fry's renown did not survive beyond the fifties, but in his day he claimed some notable adherents. Following a triumphant season at the Theatre Royal, Haymarket, where he had staged *Love for Love*, *Hamlet*, Maugham's *The Circle*, and *The Duchess of Malfi*, John now set his sights distinctly high. When Terence Rattigan offered him the role of Andrew Crocker-Harris, the embittered schoolmaster in *The Browning Version*, a role that both Maurice Evans and Eric Portman were proud to play, John responded: "Ye-es. Of course, my public have come to expect the first rate of me," then, as Rattigan glowed gently, "therefore I feel they would hardly accept me in the second rate." Yet John was more than ready to star as Thomas Mendip in *The Lady*, both at London's Globe and the Royale in New York, spewing out his ennui and disgust:

> *Since opening-time I've been*
> *Propped up at the bar of heaven and earth, between*
> *The wall-eye of the moon and the brandy-cask of the sun,*
> *Growling thick songs about jolly good fellows*
> *In a mumping pub where the ceiling drips humanity . . .*

Equally, Larry was drawn to Fry's second play, *Venus Observed*, casting himself as the urbane, elderly Duke of Altair, amateur astronomer and connoisseur of women, who invited three of his former mistresses to witness an eclipse of the sun from his observatory. In 1949, when Larry took a four-year lease of George Alexander's beautiful old St. James's Theatre from Gilbert Miller, *Venus Observed* was his first choice, one of almost a score of plays he was to present over the next ten years—involving him in a routine so nonstop that from now on he wore two wristwatches, one showing London time, the other New York time.

This hectic schedule was in many ways an anodyne, for all was far from well with his marriage to Vivien Leigh. On the glittering surface, all was as it should be: a beautiful seventeenth-century town house, Durham Cottage, near Chelsea Hospital; a sumptuous country home, Notley Abbey, at Thame, in Buckinghamshire—whose dining room, with its mighty baronial table, Capo di Monte dinner service, and Brussels lace tablecloths reminded the actress Yolande Donlan of an Orson Welles set from *Citizen Kane*. Yet increasingly it was a question of divergent lifestyles. Vivien, a born hostess, adored entertaining; her dream was to resurrect, at the St. James's, something of the glamour that Florence Alexander had mourned, with white ties and tails *de rigueur* for opening nights. Larry, tired after an evening's performance and always short on small talk, longed to slip quietly away home, anything rather than put on a dinner jacket and socialize.

The problem had been compounded, in the summer of 1949, by Larry's involvement, along with Hugh "Binkie" Beaumont, of H. M. Tennent in a new play in which Vivien was to star, *A Streetcar Named Desire*. A Pulitzer Prize winner, which had run three years on Broadway, *Streetcar* had both confirmed the glowing talent of Britain's Jessica Tandy and created a Broadway meteor overnight in the person of twenty-four-year-old Marlon Brando. Yet as producer Saul Colin put it frankly, "Larry's first mistake was getting involved with *Streetcar*. His second was letting Vivien get involved."

The author Thomas Lanier Williams III, who had rechristened himself Tennessee, was essentially a poet of the dispossessed. His was a world of lonely people—*Night of the Iguana, Cat on a Hot Tin Roof, Sweet Bird of Youth*—people morbid and maladjusted, unable to face up to reality. Like the homosexual Williams himself, a one-time waiter, elevator operator, and cinema usher, they drifted through life as lost souls, as three-time losers. Blanche du Bois in *Streetcar*, who arrives at her sister Stella's squalid New Orleans apartment, was just such a character. The last of an impoverished Southern plantation family, who claims to have quit her job as a schoolteacher in Laurel, Mississippi, she has in truth been run out of town for prostitution. Stung by her refined and uppity airs, her brother-in-law Stanley Kowalski, a redneck laborer, first exposes her pretensions, then rapes her ("We've had this date with each other from the beginning!"). For the male chauvinist Stanley had clearly seen the warning signs: he must either destroy or be dethroned.

For some years now the unstable Vivien's ambitions to top Larry's successes in roles like Oedipus had been insatiable; as the lead in Sophocles's *Antigone*, who was buried alive in a cave, she identified so closely with the role she came close to cracking. In the spring of 1949, mental lapses several times caused her to miss out on a performance. All through rehearsals of *Streetcar*, Larry, as director, saw the distinction between Vivien and Blanche blur increasingly. On more than one night after the play opened, she failed to return home, intent on casual pick-ups, as Blanche would have been.

Though under such intense pressure, the marriage was somehow to survive for eleven more years.

In this same era John and Helen were grappling with another Tennessee Williams opus, the playwright's first Broadway hit, *The Glass Menagerie*. In essence Helen's problem was exactly the reverse of Vivien's: try as she might, she could not identify with the fussy, genteel Amanda Wingfield, forever meddling with the lives of her son, Tom, and her crippled daughter, Laura, who was so immersed in her collection of glass animals she was unable to respond to Jim, the "gentleman caller" her mother foisted upon her.

To Helen, who had learned to stand up and fight, the frail, futile Wingfields were anathema—and only the urging of Laurette Taylor, who had made a triumphant Broadway comeback in the role after six years of alcoholic oblivion, persuaded her to do the play as her one and only London appearance. But Helen's lack of empathy with Amanda was only the beginning. John, assigned as producer, was notorious for his daily changes of mind, a failing that at times had infuriated both Noël and Larry; given his head, he would and did change the moves of the cast every day until the dress rehearsal.

It was small wonder that after the final run-through at Brighton's Theatre Royal, Helen, suffering from a painful attack of fibrositis, summoned John, Williams, and the supporting cast to her dressing room to announce ominously, "At this point in the making of a play, I know if it will go or won't go." And so saying, she solemnly shook her head.

But though Helen was right—her performance, in Williams's words, was "pancake flat," and the play petered out in London after two months—she had far from done with Amanda.

In 1956 a desperate plea from the New York City Center put her in the tightest of spots: unless she agreed to play *The Glass Menagerie* for two weeks, as a form of collateral, the bank would foreclose on the Center's loan. So Helen could only comply. Four years later, with Amanda mercifully forgotten, Lawrence Langner, urged by the State Department to organize a global goodwill theatre tour, once more came up with *The Glass Menagerie*.

"He was really a lawyer by profession," Helen would explain ruefully, "and I was just a poor actress with a shamed face and a prejudice"—an actress, moreover, who was condemned to play Amanda in twenty-nine countries from Europe to South America, always hat-ing her quite as intensely as Larry had hated Sergius on the first night of *Arms and the Man*.

Midway through the 1950s, all these leading lights faced a crisis, just as much as they had ever done as juveniles in their twenties. The question now was, In which direction were they going? Were they to resign themselves to being "old hat"—or did they make the supreme effort to be, in that much-vexed phrase, "with it"?

Some were happier to be without it. When Williams's *Cat on a Hot Tin Roof* opened on Broadway, Noël did his utmost to persuade the British diseuse, Joyce Grenfell, to pay it a visit. "You *should* go," he urged her. "Such things go on in real life." Miss Grenfell was far from persuaded. "So does diarrhoea, but I don't fancy paying a lot of dollars to go and watch it."

It was noticeable that neither agents nor managements were offering the pick of the new mainstream playwrights to the Lunts—perhaps because as the British critic Ivor Brown put it, "Now on both sides of the Atlantic we have stool tragedies, not throne tragedies . . . it is the clerk, not the king, who inspires the tragedian." Long before 1945, the Lunts, polished and imperturbable, somehow suggested the throne, not the stool.

The consummate architect of the "stool tragedy" was Arthur Miller, a tall, lean, born-again Ibsenite, who in 1947 at the age of thirty-one reaped his first dramatic reward with *All My Sons*, the story of Joe Keller, a self-made factory owner whose shipment of faulty cylinder heads caused the death of more than twenty combat fliers—perhaps even his own son Larry. But even the central irony of Keller's tragedy, a man whose crime against other men's sons had also doomed his own, was eclipsed by Miller's pathetic, vulgar Willy Loman, the chief protagonist of *Death of a Salesman*, in 1949.

In Loman, Miller encapsulated the dark side of the American Dream, the naïve belief that "a man can end with diamonds here on the basis of being liked!" Willy's was the tragedy of Mr. Average, who never quite made it, "the man way out there in the blue, riding on a smile and a shoeshine. And when they start not smiling back— that's an earthquake. And then you get yourself a couple of spots on your hat and you're finished." Willy could never acknowledge, as his son Biff challenged him, that he was "a dime a dozen." To the end, Willy's idol was the eighty-four-year-old Dave Singleton who "died the death of a salesman in his green velvet slippers, in the smoker of the New York, Newhaven and Hartford." To the end he barely realized, as his wife Linda foresaw, "that a terrible thing is happening to him. So attention must be paid." For to be not only "liked" but "well liked" was all that Willy's mind could encompass.

"Why didn't Elia Kazan [the producer] give us a crack at *Death of a Salesman?*" Alfred complained, but the question was, in a sense, rhetorical. The Lunts' last commitment to serious theatre had been in 1940, when they played in Robert E. Sherwood's tragedy of the Russian invasion of Finland in *There Shall Be No Night;* three years later in London, with Russia now an "ally," the action had been shifted to Germany's invasion of Greece. Their longest run, Terence Rattigan's *Love in Idleness*, rechristened *O Mistress Mine* for Broadway, in which they played for almost four years, was essentially a reprise of *The Guardsman* and *Caprice:* a beautiful widow's affair with a war minister was interrupted by the return of her seventeen-year-old Marxist son from Canada. In short, the Lunts were seducing each other on stage all over again—with such erotic fervor that one dowager whispered to a matinée companion, "It's nice, my dear, to know they're really married, isn't it?"

"You could," Alfred confessed around 1960 to Lewis Funke of *The New York Times*, "call us old hat," and it was irrefutable that managements were now doing just that. The role of Joe Keller had gone to Ed Begley, a gnarled exponent of tough, proletarian drama; Willy Loman fell to Lee J. Cobb, a product of New York's left-oriented Group Theatre.

A new tone of voice was being heard across the footlights, and it was pitched to a register beyond the inner ear of many older players. Kit Cornell increasingly took refuge in revivals *(The Barretts, Candida*, Maugham's *The Constant Wife)*; one of her few innovations was to star as Mrs. Pat Campbell, with her old sparring partner, Brian Aherne, as George Bernard Shaw, in Jerome Kilty's *Dear Liar*. As far back as 1937, Shaw had complained to Edith Evans that Kit found the lead in his play *The Millionairess* "too unamicable for her worshippers even if she could act it," and with the years Kit played increasingly safe. After Guthrie McClintic's death in 1961, all her old reservations were once more apparent until her own death in 1974. "I couldn't do anything after that," she admitted sadly. "He always gave me the security I needed."

Noël was not only out of tune with the new demotic mood, but positively reveled in being so. "The war brought about an enormous change in everything and much of it I deplore," he told the playwright William Marchant. "I refuse categorically to acknowledge that anything is different even when it stares me in the face." This flight against the face of accepted opinion became more apparent as the years went by. In Noël's 1947 drama *Peace in Our Time*, which showed a Britain under the yoke of Nazi occupation, the sole collaborator was a left-wing intellectual, editor of a highbrow magazine called *Forethought*, who deplored the "jingoistic platitudes" of King and Country—a strange aberration considering the role of the left wing in European Resistance. His *Relative Values* (1951) concluded with a toast to "the final inglorious disintegration of the most unlikely dream that ever troubled the foolish head of man—Socialist Equality."

More and more, Noël, like an overzealous museum curator, was becoming the self-appointed guardian of his own work. Even the most obscure provincial tours of his plays were subject to his own personal approval on casting. Once, when a pair of leading players loafed self-indulgently through a Coward matinée, he rampaged backstage to castigate their performance as "a triumph of never-mind over doesn't-matter." When the manager Henry Sherek revived *Private Lives* in 1951, twenty-one years after its first opening, he thought one of Elyot's lines dated the play badly. (Asked by Amanda whose yacht was moored close by, Elyot replied "The Duke of Westminster's, I expect. It usually is," but Bendor, second Duke of Westminster, was no longer page-one news.) Accordingly, Sherek transferred the yacht's ownership to the film stars Michael Wilding and Stewart Granger. But at Brighton's Theatre Royal, Coward viewed this minor change as near-heresy. "I insist that you replace my original line," he yelled at Sherek, visibly quaking with fury.

Even the flimsiest of his revivals were treated as holy writ. When *Fallen Angels* again saw the light of day in 1949, the scene in which two young married women drank themselves paralytic while waiting for the same French lover struck both leading ladies, Hermione Gingold and Hermione Baddeley, as having a distinct aroma of mothballs. Thus they and the producer, Willard Stoker, agreed to camp it up. Few of them, in consequence, ever forgot the first night of the pre-London tour at the Theatre Royal in Plymouth.

Minutes after the final curtain, Noël was onstage, flushed and tense with anger, flanked by five apprehensive players and a notably unruffled Hermione Baddeley. "Tell us the worst, Noël darling," she purred with sublime complacency, a cue for Coward to let fly. "The

209

worst?'' he exploded. "The whole evening was bloody from beginning to end! You all ought to be deeply ashamed of yourselves.''

It was strange, thought the producing manager, Peter Daubeny, "to observe how this great master of his craft . . . could show momentary weakness, could temporarily lose all sense of proportion.'' Yet this was only symptomatic of how The Master was losing his touch. Played in London as an all-out send-up, *Fallen Angels* ran for almost three hundred performances, but Noël was not there to see it. He had sailed for Jamaica, nursing his grievance, resenting a world that was passing him by.

For by 1949, the days when everything Noël wrote had been eagerly snapped up had long gone. Like any beginner, he was forced to descend into the marketplace to peddle his wares. His *South Sea Bubble*, an evanescent fable of a Socialist governor in the South Seas, though completed in 1949, took seven years to reach the West End— successively turned down by John Clements and Kay Hammond, and Diana Wynyard, violently condemned by Larry, and rejected by sundry managements, until finally accepted as a vehicle for Vivien Leigh.

At this stage of his career, everything that Noël hated most in life was embodied in the plays of John James Osborne, a splenetic twenty-seven-year-old who had learned his craft through taxing years as a small-part player and ASM. Osborne's *Look Back in Anger*, launched at the Royal Court in Sloane Square, that longtime seedbed of dissent, on May 8, 1956, predictably became the mouthpiece of a new generation: the era of the Angry Young Man. Its antihero, Jimmy Porter, was, in one critic's phrase, "a self-flagellating solitary in self-inflicted exile," living in a run-down attic flat in a drab Midlands town, earning his living by running a sweet-stall, and constantly railing at his upper-middle-class wife, Alison, whose background he could never forgive.

"I suppose people of our generation aren't able to die for good causes any longer," Jimmy exploded. "We had all that done for us, in the thirties and forties, when we were still kids. There aren't any good brave causes left. If the big bang does come and we all get killed off, it won't be in aid of the old-fashioned grand design. It'll just be for the Brave New nothing-very-much-thank you."

All this, noted one critic, Harold Rosenberg, enshrined "the vision of injured being . . . the always ready impulse for indignation and blame," the first outcry from postwar youth, an angry, classless, grade-school intelligentsia, whose ethos was the bedsitter and the bus stop. Even in an earlier play, *Epitaph for George Dillon*, Osborne had experimented with Jimmy Porter's prototype, a self-conscious proletarian who condemned all "phoniness" and deplored "good taste"—forever, as Kenneth Tynan put it, "the sick sad oyster that could not produce the pearl."

As the spokesman for disaffected youth, Osborne was equally acceptable on Broadway, where *Look Back* ran for 407 performances, though producing manager David Merrick took no chances. When business waned, he hired an out-of-work actress for $250 to burst on stage from the second row and slap Kenneth Haigh, who was repeating his London triumph as Jimmy, resoundingly across the face. By Merrick's calculation, the play's run was thus extended by a further seven months.

Although Osborne's adherents liked to claim that he had killed the well-made plays of Coward and Rattigan stone-dead, this was far from the truth. *Look Back* was itself a well-made play, with three finite acts and a single attic room as setting. What Osborne had done was to focus on the have-nots of life, along with other playwrights of his generation: Harold Pinter *(The Homecoming, The Caretaker)*, master of the obscure motive, the uncertain background, and the indeterminate fate; Shelagh Delaney *(A Taste of Honey, The Lion in Love)*; and the Utopian Socialist Arnold Wesker *(Chicken Soup with Barley, Roots)*. What Clement Scott of *The Daily Telegraph* had called, in the 1890s, "the drama of the dustbin," the critics of the new generation called "the kitchen-sink drama."

Some traditionalists in the theatre found them deeply distasteful. "Praise was only praiseworthy when applied to plays with a message," complained Edith Evans's secretary, Jean Batters, "plays which made the audience feel guilty rather than jolly." "I went to one of Mr. Osborne's plays in which there was a death and an accident, so I left," Athene Seyler recalled in 1984. "I don't enjoy plays about misfortune. Then I went to see Mr. Pinter's *No Man's Land* and I couldn't follow a word of it. So I haven't been to the theatre since."

Many such playwrights in the fifties incurred the wrath of the older critics, notably France's Jean Anouilh (often translated by Christopher Fry), whose *Ardèle* was denounced as "one long wallow of unedifying lechery" and "as distasteful and offensive a play as ever saw a stage." In Anouilh's plays *(Colombe, Ring Around the Moon)*, the tragic and the ludicrous, the realistic and the romantic went hand

211

in hand, though his basic preoccupations were the same as Miller's or Williams's: the tyranny and corruption engendered by money, a yearning for lost innocence. Another hobbyhorse was the contamination vested in togetherness, as in *The Waltz of the Toreadors*, where General Saint-Pé described life as like "one long family luncheon—boring, like every other meal with the family, but necessary."

A marked austerity of setting now dominated many of these new dramas—and even Shakespearean productions. Lear and the Fool now played on a bare stage, with no attempt to create a blasted heath. "Half a dozen actors," as Michael Booth noted, "represent the Coronation Procession of Henry V; there are no cheering crowds, no scattering of flowers, no painted or built-up streets of London." Actors moved in an empty space, defined and limited by light; spectacle was totally absent.

Nonconformist dramas called for nonconforming actors, and in Britain these were not slow to emerge, in time to be hailed on Broadway as well. All of them were a far cry from the well-bred deportment and Waterford-crystal accents of du Maurier and Owen Nares. Most hailed from the provinces, like Albert Finney, a bookmaker's son from Salford, Lancashire, and Peter O'Toole, another bookmaker's son from Dublin; the callow Tom Courtenay, son of a house painter, came from the grimy back streets of Hull. Unlike their elders, these new-wave players rejected the trappings of stardom, the Bentley convertibles and the well-groomed, well-publicized personal appearances. Finney, after a smash hit in Osborne's *Luther*, betook himself to Glasgow's Citizens' Theatre, for twenty-five pounds a week, to act in Luigi Pirandello's *Henry IV* and to direct Pinter's *The Birthday Party*. Alan Bates, who supported Haigh in *Look Back* in London and New York, cheerfully passed up Hollywood offers to play in Pinter's *The Caretaker*.

A tragic exception was Richard Jenkins, the Welsh miner's son who took the name of a benefactor, Philip Burton, scored triumphantly at the Old Vic in parts as varied as Caliban, Hamlet, and Othello, but all too soon succumbed to the lures of Hollywood and hard liquor.

All these newcomers were entering a theatre increasingly given over to the avant-garde. The guru of the age was the German Bertolt Brecht, who viewed make-believe as the Antichrist; such plays as his *Mother Courage* and *The Good Women of Setzuan* called instead for "audience alienation," whereby the actor, far from carrying the spectators with him, must never hide the fact that he was performing. Songs, placards, and even documentary film were all drawn upon further to dispel the illusion.

In such plays, mankind seemed lost and alone in a terrifying present, oblivious to either a past or a future. Within that present, anything was possible. In Samuel Beckett's *Endgame,* the parents, Nagg and Nell, passed their stage lives in dustbins; Roberta II, the heroine of the Rumanian Eugène Ionesco's *Jack,* possessed only nine fingers but had three noses. In Ionesco's *Amédée,* a corpse offstage grew so hideously that a gigantic foot smashed into the set at the climax. In Rochelle Owens's *Futz,* the hero fornicated with a pig.

All this, in fact, harked back to 1896, when Alfred Jarry's *Ubu Roi,* presented at the Théâtre de L'Oeuvre in Paris, outraged the audience with its use of masks, cardboard horses slung around the actors' necks, and frequent cries of *"Merde."* Jarry, his detractors noted, died in a lunatic asylum, but his work gained fresh impetus in 1938 when another French surrealist, Antonin Artaud, propounded the Theatre of Cruelty. Artaud, in turn, died in an asylum, but his concept of the cruelty of the cosmos, "where the sky can still fall in on our heads," found an echo in the fifties in the plays of Ionesco, Beckett, and Jean Genet.

Often, in a style reminiscent of a medieval morality play, the characters of these playwrights had no names of their own but were stereotypes: A Logician, A Grocer's Wife. At times, their identities were tentative at best; in Ionesco's *Rhinoceros,* a satire on the herd instinct, the citizens of the town turned one by one into rhinoceroses and even took over the TV channels. In Genet's *The Balcony,* a comment on wish fulfillment, the regulars of Madame Irma's brothel expressed their fantasies by dressing up and acting the parts of bishops, judges, and generals. Came the revolution and they all took up these roles in real life, with a plumber as Chief of Police.

Few writers plumbed the depths of nihilism more profoundly than Samuel Beckett, an Irish-born dramatist resident in Paris, whose *Waiting for Godot* was first seen in London, in translation from the French, in 1955. It was now that Beckett, all unwittingly, created what Martin Esslin, in 1962, dubbed the Theatre of the Absurd: a group of playwrights—Beckett, Ionesco, Pinter—bound by the common belief that man's life is meaningless and that human beings cannot communicate.

Certainly Beckett, as a playwright, posed more questions than he

213

answered. In a bleak landscape, featuring only a gaunt tree, rocky ground, and a discarded oil drum, two tramps, Vladimir and Estragon, waited for a mysterious Mr. Godot, who was going to restore their fortunes. Presently a shepherd boy arrived to tell them that Mr. Godot would not be coming, followed by the arrival of Pozzo, a master, and Lucky, his slave. On the following night, Lucky returned leading his master, now blind. At the end of the day, both tramps agreed on departure.

"Well, shall we go?" Vladimir asked. "Yes, let's go," Estragon replied. But when the curtain fell, neither had moved, nor would they ever do so.

In Britain, where *Godot* drew much acclaim, critics and playgoers alike pondered its multiple meanings. (Broadway playgoers were in no mood to ponder; to them *Godot* was a no-no.) Did the tramps, inseparable to the end, represent the two sides of Man's nature? Were Pozzo and the feeble-minded Lucky symbolic of Mammon and the Intellect in decay? Why did the characters' names all suggest different nationalities? Was Godot, one critic was emboldened to ask Beckett, actually God? "If you like," was Beckett's courteous, if ambivalent reply.

Vladimir and Estragon had at least an illusory freedom of movement, something that Beckett increasingly denied his characters as time went on. Nagg and Nell never left their dustbins. Winnie, in *Happy Days*, was buried up to her waist in earth, finally up to her chin, though never ceasing her prattling stream-of-consciousness monologue: "Sometimes I am wrong. But not often. Sometimes all is over, for the day, all done, all said, all ready for the night, and the day not over, far from over, the night not ready, far, far from ready. But not often."

Not until *Breath*, in 1970, did Beckett achieve the ultimate: the cry of a newborn baby was followed by a man's death rattle, and in exactly thirty seconds the play was over.

Another dramatist verging on the nihilistic was Edward Albee *(Tiny Alice, A Delicate Balance)*, a dramatist who in works like *Who's Afraid of Virginia Woolf?* used words like deadly weapons. A savage ritual dance, which never involved the emotions, *Woolf* showed one night of scabrous conflict between George, an ineffectual college professor, and his bitch-wife, Martha, who inveighed against "the sewer of this marriage . . . the sick nights and the pathetic stupid days . . . the derision and the laughter." For both audience and cast,

Woolf emerged as a marathon so arduous that Uta Hagen and Arthur Hill, who played both in New York and London, were relieved on matinée days by special standbys: Elaine Stritch and Shepperd Strudwick in New York, Constance Cummings and Jerome Kilty in London.

Yet, like it or not, this bleak miasma of austerity and disillusionment was the mood of the moment, and, at fifty the youngest of Irving's successors, Larry was still percipient enough to sense it. The fastidious John had rejected *Endgame* out of hand ("It nauseates me. I hate it and I won't play it"), but Larry was canny enough to swim with the tide rather than against it. His first viewing of *Look Back in Anger* had deeply disappointed him, but when Arthur Miller arrived in London, along with his then wife, Marilyn Monroe, who was to star with Larry in the film of Rattigan's *The Sleeping Prince*, Larry was persuaded to pay a second visit with the Millers in tow.

At the end of Act I, Miller turned to Larry in genuine bewilderment. "God, Larry, you're wrong," he declared. "'This is great stuff.''

Soon after, Larry was once more at the Royal Court, this time to visit Osborne's dressing room, where the actor was cast in Nigel Dennis's *Cards of Identity*. Congratulating him both on his work and on *Look Back*, Larry asked boldly, Would Osborne ever consider writing a play with him in mind? Osborne was so dumbfounded he could scarcely take it in. Did Larry really mean it? he asked on more than one occasion.

To the old guard in the theatre, the news that Larry really did— and that Osborne had accepted the commission—came as a bombshell. This was a partnership akin to an ardent nuclear disarmer giving his daughter in wedlock to an atomic scientist. That Britain's foremost actor-knight, a pillar of the Establishment, that privileged minority in whom all wealth and power and influence was vested, a public-school boy and a member of the Garrick Club, should align himself with Osborne, the young working-class radical, a barmaid's son, who was capable of describing the British Royal Family as "the gold filling in a mouthful of decay," was to them profoundly shocking.

The role that Osborne had created for Larry—who was prepared to play it for fifty pounds a week at the Royal Court—in no way reassured them. For in this new play, *The Entertainer*, Larry would be seen as Archie Rice, a broken-down, third-rate music hall artist, a self-pitying, gin-sodden womanizer who for twenty years had been cheating on his income tax. Moreover, this seedy showman patently represented Britain in decline, for one scene in Archie's twice-nightly nude revue showed Patriotism as Britannia, naked save for her helmet. "Look at my eyes," Archie commanded his daughter Jean in a maudlin and drunken moment. "I'm dead behind these eyes. I'm dead, just like the whole inert, shoddy lot out there. It doesn't matter because I don't feel a thing, and neither do they. We're just as dead as each other."

Yet word came from rehearsals that Larry was reveling in the role, perhaps his greatest outside the classics: he might have been born to the natty check suit and the tip-tilted gray bowler, the rakish, black bow tie. Meticulous as always, he had done his fieldwork at the crumbling old Collins's Music Hall in Islington, one of the few surviving bastions of an art form that was as dead as vaudeville in the United States. And by degrees it was as if all his life he had been uttering not the rolling periods of Shakespeare but Archie's desperate, forced, bonhomous patter:

> Archie Rice is the name. Archie Rice. Mrs. Rice's favourite boy. We're going to entertain you for the next two and a half hours, and you've really had it now. All the exit doors locked . . . I've played in front of them all! "The Queen"; "The Duke of Edinburgh"; "The Prince of Wales" and the—what's the name of that other pub? . . . I've taken my glasses off. I don't want to see you suffering. . . .

In a sense Larry was seeking a new challenge, an escape through a character who bore no remote resemblance to himself. His marriage was now close to breaking point, complicated by the fact that Vivien Leigh was deeply infatuated with Peter Finch, the Australian actor whose London career Larry had launched back in 1949, in James Bridie's *Daphne Laureola*, with Edith Evans. Increasingly, Vivien's bouts of manic depression tore him apart. He was, she maintained, to the end "her beautiful, shining, brilliant, darling Larry"—yet when the madness seized her, she would awaken and savage him in the small hours, slashing at his eyes with a wet facecloth. To escape, Larry was forced to take a furnished room in a mews nearby, but in September 1957, when *The Entertainer* transferred to the Palace, Shaftesbury Avenue, the inevitable happened. A new actress, twenty-eight-year-old Joan Plowright, replaced Dorothy Tutin as Archie's daughter Jean. When the run ended, she and Larry had fallen in love.

It was a clandestine arrangement at first. A furnished room in Walton Street, Chelsea, provided by George Devine, artistic director of the Royal Court, was their only meeting place. Yet Larry's resolution was hardening. "You can reach a point," he said once, "where it's like a life raft that can hold only so many. You cast away the hand grasping it because it's both of you. Two instead of one. Then you go on living and there you are, with it, knowing what has happened, remembering its details. Yet what else is there to do?"

It was a question that permitted only one answer. What Larry did, in 1960, was to leave Durham Cottage forever.

In London, the story was not slow to break. In March 1960, still "with it" in his choice of plays, Larry was rehearsing Ionesco's *Rhinoceros* along with Joan Plowright, in a church hall in Maida Vale, under the majestic direction of Orson Welles. One afternoon, a young man dressed as a curate sauntered across the hall, then vanished. Minutes later, as Larry "dried" on a line, the press representative, Virginia Fairweather, heard an unmistakable click from the recesses of a curtain. At a nod from Welles, two ASMs tiptoed to the rear, emerging with a struggling cameraman who had sneakily reversed his collar. Oblivious to his voluble swearing, Welles coolly removed the film from the camera, challenging him, "Go right ahead and sue, you bum."

But now the witch hunt was on in earnest. When the cast moved to the Royal Court, a glint of light from the dress circle flushed out another photographer; *Rhinoceros* was rehearsing under siege. All the main entrances were locked, even the women cleaners were vetted, and Larry was presented with a special key to a side entrance. Finally, on Sunday, May 15, 1960, the news became worldwide. From New York, where she was playing in Giraudoux's *Duel of Angels*, Vivien announced that she was regretfully giving Larry his freedom to marry Joan Plowright. "Oh, Jesus Christ," was her husband's numbed reaction.

Despite all this personal publicity, which he loathed, this was Larry's greatest testing time as an artist. Even before the split with Vivien, he had been tackling what he called the "cannibal" roles with the Shakespeare Memorial Company at Stratford-upon-Avon: *Macbeth* (with Vivien as his Lady), Titus Andronicus (with Vivien as

Lavinia), and Malvolio. As the monstrous Titus, he played in Paris, Vienna, Belgrade, Zagreb, and Warsaw. Back at Stratford, as Coriolanus, he plummeted in a terrifying backward death fall down a flight of stairs.

Once, describing the consuming effect of such roles, Larry's analysis was Irving-oriented: "You give them all you've got and the author says to you 'You've given all you've got? Good. Now, more. Good. Now, more, damn you. *More! More!*' Until your heart and guts and brain are pulp and the part feeds on you. Acting great parts devours you. It's a dangerous game."

But from March 1961 on—the year that he and Joan Plowright were married quietly in Wilton, Connecticut—acting great parts was only the tip of the iceberg. In that same month Larry was offered a momentous appointment, the directorship of a new Festival Theatre at Chichester, in Sussex. This was the concept of an optician and ex-mayor of the cathedral city, Leslie Evershed-Martin, who had seen a TV program featuring Tyrone Guthrie's Festival Theatre at Stratford, Ontario, and was ambitious to follow suit.

Although John sniffily dismissed the project as a "harum-scarum idea," to Larry it offered rich potential. This was to be a spacious hexagonal amphitheatre, seating 1,360, in Chichester's Oaklands Park, a cross between a theatre-in-the-round (first pioneered at the University of Washington, Seattle, in 1932) and the traditional Elizabethan playhouse, with the stage flanked by the audience on three sides. This, in turn, would be the proving ground for a long-awaited National Theatre, an idea first mooted by David Garrick in the eighteenth century, later espoused by such unlikely bedfellows as Irving and Shaw, twice shelved because of successive world wars but now a dream within an inch of becoming reality. Until the ultimate National Theatre building was completed, the company would commute between Chichester and Lilian Baylis's beloved Old Vic.

To function as actor, director, and administrator would tax Larry's ability and stamina to the utmost, though few other players could have called upon the services of Sir Michael Redgrave, Dame Sybil Thorndike, Sir Lewis Casson, Fay Compton, Athene Seyler, and Nicholas Hannen. Only his choice of plays, in 1962, seemed antic: such justly forgotten Jacobean museum pieces as Beaumont and Fletcher's knockabout *The Chances* and John Ford's melodrama *The Broken Heart*.

It was a program that prompted *The Observer*'s Kenneth Tynan to query, "Who put the hex on the hexagon?" and it was scarcely co-incidence that Tynan, not long after, became the National Theatre's first literary adviser. In Tynan's earthy summary, "They would probably rather have me on the inside pissing out than on the out-side pissing in."

Larry's choice of Tynan—a passionate Brechtian and a dedicated anti-Establishment Socialist—was of a piece with his determination to avoid such damning and untrendy labels as "staid" and "predict-able." His first directors, John Dexter and William Gaskill, had both trained under George Devine at the Royal Court. None of the play-ers who had featured in his award-winning Shakespearean films, *Hamlet, Henry V, Richard III*—John Laurie, Norman Wooland, Es-mond Knight—became part of the National Theatre company. "We all tried to get into the National," as Esmond Knight recalls, "but none of us succeeded." Instead, the players were once again Royal Court material, who had all made their mark in working-class plays: Albert Finney, Colin Blakely, Frank Finlay, and Robert Stephens.

But all old friends were by no means forgotten. John, whose for-tunes had fluctuated since the year when he yielded up the sword, had achieved his high triumph in *The Ages of Man*, a solo Shake-spearean recital, which both filled the cavernous 1,400-seater 46th Street Theatre in New York and opened the rebuilt Queen's on Shaftesbury Avenue. In all he was to tour this for seven years, in locations as far apart as Israel and the USSR. Yet he was still four times Larry's guest at the National—in Molière's *Tartuffe*, as Oedi-pus, as Prospero in *The Tempest,* and finally as the rumpled dropout Spooner to Ralph Richardson's alcoholic Hirst in Pinter's enigmatic *No Man's Land.* Two years later came John's theatrical swan song.

Another old friend was Noël, to whom Larry, in the autumn of 1964, accorded a signal honor: he became the first contemporary playwright to have a revival of his work, the classic comedy *Hay Fever,* staged at the National Theatre. Although a tax exile in Ja-maica since 1956, Noël willingly returned to England to take charge of the production, enchanted to be working with "a cast that could play the Albanian telephone directory." Larry had never forgotten the debt he owed to Noël: his first big West End success in *Private Lives.*

Yet it was far from a happy occasion. Even so gifted a cast, with Dame Edith Evans in the old Marie Tempest role and such embry-onic talents as Derek Jacobi, Maggie Smith, Robert Stephens, and

Lynn Redgrave, needed time to settle in, but Noël, touchy to a fault, demanded word-perfection from the first rehearsal. At seventy-six, Edith Evans's memory was no longer her best friend, and Noël harassed her without mercy. Although he claimed to possess no more than "a talent to amuse," a line from a lyric in his own *Bitter Sweet*, it was rather a talent to abuse that the cast at the National witnessed.

Cicely Courtneidge, who was simultaneously playing Madame Arcati in a musical version of *Blithe Spirit*, felt the same. "He's cruel as hell," she maintained, "and I'm no good when people are cruel to me. I don't think it's necessary to be like that."

The climax came before the opening night in Manchester, when Edith, far from well, retired to bed at the Midland Hotel, unable to face the dress rehearsal. Noël was without pity. He stormed into her room, berating her for her lack of professionalism, pouring scorn on her beliefs as a Christian Scientist, finally forcing her to go through the rehearsal despite her near-swooning condition. Edith was ready to throw in the part. "I've got enough money," she wept despairingly. "I've got a home. Why should I be insulted?" It was only Larry, who took time off to be present in Manchester, constantly at her side, that saw her through this calamitous week.

Those close to Noël knew that his time was almost done. Three years later, when *Hay Fever* was revived yet again, with Celia Johnson and Roland Culver, he was so frail he needed a taxi to cover the two hundred yards from The Ivy to the Duke of York's. In the Savoy Grill, the waiters noted that it took him a full two minutes to hobble, escorted by aides, from his table to the door. In these years he spent much of his time in bed, dependent on a wheelchair for locomotion, refusing to give up a single one of his forty cigarettes a day. In November 1972, at a party given in his honor in the ballroom of Claridge's Hotel, it was only Larry's arms that saved him from toppling at the moment he reached the piano stool for a last recital of his lyrics. Six months later he was dead.

Larry's time was almost done, too; the problem was that he refused to acknowledge it. His manifold illnesses began in the summer of 1967, soon after his brilliant Edgar, a parade-ground martinet on a marital battlefield, in Strindberg's *The Dance of Death;* the doctors diagnosed cancer of the prostate gland. Larry resolved to fight it. Undergoing chemotherapy at St. Thomas's Hospital—the nearest to the Old Vic—he still conducted rehearsals of *The Three Sisters* from his bed. Then thrombosis developed in his right leg, until it weighed twenty pounds more than the other. Next came myositis, a muscular-inflammation disease, leaving him so weak that he could not stand. Still he fought back with the rage and fury of a Lear, emerging from hospital after sixteen weeks instead of the nine months anticipated, though surgery for a fibrous tissue on his kidney had still to be undergone.

For there were yet more "cannibal" roles to be tackled: a painfully human Shylock, in the Irving tradition, in 1970, the year that he became the first actor ever to take his seat in the House of Lords; and a monumental James Tyrone in Eugene O'Neill's epic *Long Day's Journey Into Night* a year later.

"I can no longer be a stage actor," he conceded after that, "because I don't feel I've got the power or the physical attributes."

In London and New York the Age of Olivier was at last ending, so to whom did he plan to surrender the sword? His answer was quite uncompromising: "To no one. It's mine."

Yet the theatre in which Larry and John, Helen and Noël, Lynn and Alfred and Kit had grown up was undeniably changing. There were developments that Irving would have barely recognized, many that he would have little relished.

To a new generation, Larry and John would soon be familiar only as faces on a TV screen, or in cameo character roles in blockbuster movies: Larry as Lord Marchmain in the widely acclaimed TV series "Brideshead Revisited," John as the Master of Trinity in *Chariots of Fire*, Charles Ryder's father in "Brideshead," or Lord Urwin in *Gandhi*. Alfred and Lynn, like Kit and Helen, would scarcely be visible at all, retiring to the obscurity that most, outside the jungle, call home, secure with their selective memories of triumphant first nights.

The theatre they were leaving behind was one where many of the old intimacies were lacking. Tannoys had long replaced the piping treble of the callboy. An entire lighting plot could now be programmed by computer, reducing the lighting staff of a theatre like London's Prince of Wales from thirty to three. In New York, few theatres—the Helen Hayes, the Lunt-Fontanne—now seated less than one thousand playgoers. Vast complexes, like the National in London, which finally opened under Sir Peter Hall in 1976 and encompasses three playhouses and dressing rooms for 150 players, were a far cry from the homely cooking smells of Lilian Baylis's time.

221

"It's just a factory here," confesses John Willetts, the National's deputy wardrobe master. "You don't get the theatre atmosphere. I miss the West End feeling."

On Broadway, union tyrannies, notably those of IATSE (International Alliance of Theatrical Stage Employees) were to prove a perennial headache to the successors of Gilbert Miller and Al Woods, men like David Merrick, Arnold Saint-Subber, and Alexander Cohen. A one-man show, like John's *The Ages of Man*, would still demand a minimum of eight stagehands. Even a nonmusical show required four musicians on tap; after midnight all would be on "golden time," double pay. A property man might handle an unlit lamp, but once lit it required the services of an electrician besides. And pay scales (£160 a week for a London carpenter as against $658 in New York) account for a marked discrepancy in seat prices: A West End stall still retails for £12, a comparable seat on Broadway for $32.50.

British repertory was as dead as stock in the United States; in its place arose the new subsidized community theatres, "regional" rather than "repertory," with bars, restaurants, roomy foyers housing art exhibitions, and runs of three to four weeks the norm. Summer theatres, from the fifties on, became a strictly commercialized routine, with packagers guaranteeing to deliver ready-made, smoothly rehearsed companies from big star to bit player to the summer theatre chain: Vivian Blaine in *Call Me Madam*, followed by Burgess Meredith in *The Remarkable Mr. Pennypacker*.

On both sides of the Atlantic, costs were to escalate with each passing decade. "Up to ten years ago," recalls the producing manager Stephen Mitchell *(The Corn Is Green, Separate Tables)*, "it was possible to put on a good straight play for £10,000. Now it's closer to £100,000." Martin E. Gottlieb, who in 1974 staged *Same Time Next Year*, featuring only two characters in a single motel-room set, agrees. His original mounting cost was $230,000—"but," he stressed in 1984, "it would cost $800,000 to put it on Broadway today." Corporate investors—Britain's Lord Grade, ABC, Columbia-Warner— thus became more common than once-avid "angels."

Regional and off-Broadway tryouts, at theatres like the Cherry Lane, were to replace the traditional out-of-town tryouts at Atlantic City or New Haven; costs were once again the reason. By the sixties, only thirty-five British theatres were classified as No. 1 for the use of touring companies. Sheer expense made pre-London tours an increasing rarity; the plays of the post-Olivier age were "tried on the dog" at Watford or Guildford. It was in the sixties, too, that the Actors' Church Union finally dispensed with that once-indispensable *vade mecum,* "The Theatrical Lodgings List."

Yet as Larry and John, surveying the rising generation, would testify, one vital quality is still undiminished: perpetual and unquenchable optimism. In their youth, neither player could have envisaged a population explosion that would see 31,000 players enrolled in British Actors' Equity, with more than 10,000 of them taking space in the *Spotlight* Casting Directory. It was a situation so potentially disastrous that in March 1983 Equity instituted a controlled-entry system, whereby only provisional membership was granted to players until they had worked outside the West End for fully thirty weeks.

But still, it seemed, there was no stopping them. In the United States, where no controlled entry exists, 30,000 Equity members— 80 percent of them unemployed at any time—earn a median average of $8,000 a year. But the old dreams will not be denied. None of them—the bit players, the dressers, the ASMs, the box-office managers, the doorkeepers—would bemoan with Jimmy Porter that "there aren't any good brave courses left." For them the make-believe jungle is always the best and bravest cause of all.

It was Kit Cornell's favorite story that perhaps best summed up that irresistible magic. A forlorn old actor-laddie and his wife were on their way back to their theatrical rooming house. It was sleeting, and their bags were heavy. Ahead of them stretched a bleak prospect: a frugal supper of an egg fried over a gas jet, a 4:00 A.M. call for their next date in the sticks. Suddenly a limousine full of high-society nabobs swept by: women with furs and jewels, men in starched shirts and opera hats.

"Looks pretty wonderful, doesn't it?" was her wistful comment.

"Yes," he had to admit, "looks wonderful. But"—and this was the clincher—"*they* can't act."

Bibliography

Abbott, George A. *"Mister Abbott."* New York: Random House, 1963.

A'Beckett, Arthur. *Green Room Recollections.* London: Simpkin, Marshall, Hamilton, Kent, 1896.

Adam, Ronald. *Overture and Beginners.* London: Victor Gollancz, 1938.

Adam, Ruth. *What Shaw Really Said.* London: Macdonald, 1966.

Adams, Samuel Hopkins. *Alexander Woollcott.* London: Hamish Hamilton, 1946.

Adlard, Eleanor, ed. *Edy: Recollections of Edith Craig.* London: Frederick Muller, 1949.

Agate, James. *The Amazing Theatre.* London: George Harrap, 1939.

————. *Buzz-Buzz!* London: William Collins, 1918.

————. *The Contemporary Theatre: 1926.* London: Chapman and Hall, 1927.

————. *Ego.* London: Hamish Hamilton, 1935.

————. *My Theatre Talks.* London: Arthur Barker, 1933.

————. *Red Letter Nights.* London: Jonathan Cape, 1944.

————. *A Short View of the English Stage, 1900–1926.* London: Herbert Jenkins, 1926.

————. *Those Were the Nights.* London: Hutchinson, 1947.

Albanesi, E.M. *Meggie Albanesi, by her Mother.* London: Hodder and Stoughton, 1928.

Alexander, Martha. *Behind the Footlights.* London: John Murray, 1954.

Allen, David Rayvern. *Sir Aubrey.* London: Elm Tree Books, 1982.

Alltree, George W. *Footlight Memories.* London: Sampson Low, Marston & Co., 1932.

Alpert, Hollis. *The Barrymores.* London: W.H. Allen, 1965.

Anderson, James R. *An Actor's Life.* London: Walter Scott Publishing Co., 1902.

Anderson, Jean. *Late Joys At The Player's Theatre.* London: T.V. Boardman, 1943.

Anderson, John. *The American Theatre.* New York: The Dial Press, 1938.

Anderson, Maxwell. *Off Broadway.* New York: William Sloane, 1947.

"Angel With A System," *Fortune.* New York: March, 1948.

Archer, Charles. *William Archer: Life, Work and Friendships.* London: George Allen and Unwin, 1931.

Archer, William. *About the Theatre.* London: T. Fisher Unwin, 1886.

————. *English Dramatists of Today.* London: Sampson Low, Marston, Searle and Rivington, 1882.

————. *Henry Irving, Actor and Manager.* London: Field and Tuer, 1883.

————. *Masks or Faces?* London: Longmans Green, 1888.

Aria, Mrs. Elizabeth. *My Sentimental Self.* London: Chapman and Hall, 1922.

Bibliography

Arliss, George. "Realism On The Stage." *The Atlantic Monthly*, Boston, April 1923.
———. *Up the Years from Bloomsbury*. Boston: Little Brown, 1927.
Arnott, James Fullarton, and John William Robinson. *English Theatre Literature, 1559–1900*. London: The Society for Theatre Research, 1970.
Arthur, Sir George. *From Phelps to Gielgud*. London: Chapman and Hall, 1936.
———. *Sarah Bernhardt*. London: William Heinemann, 1923.
Asche, Oscar. *Oscar Asche: His Life, By Himself*. London: Hurst and Blackett, 1929.
Ashwell, Lena. *Myself A Player*. London: Michael Joseph, 1936.
———. *The Stage*. London: Geoffrey Bles, 1929.
Atkinson, Brooks. *Broadway*. London: Cassell, 1970.
Austin, H.W. "Bunny," and Phyllis Konstam. *A Mixed Double*. London: Chatto and Windus, 1969.

Bablet, Denis. *Edward Gordon Craig*. Translated by Daphne Woodward. London: William Heinemann, 1966.
Baddeley, Hermione. *The Unsinkable Hermione Baddeley*. London: William Collins, 1984.
Bakeless, Katherine Little. *In the Big Time*. Philadelphia: J.P. Lippincott, 1953.
Baker, H.B. *History of the London Stage*. London: George Routledge, 1904.
Baker, Michael. *The Rise of the Victorian Actor*. London: Croom Helm, 1978.
Balmforth, Ramsden. *The Problem Play and Its Influence on Modern Thought and Life*. London: George Allen and Unwin, 1928.
Bancroft, George Pleydell. *Stage and Bar*. London: Faber and Faber, 1939.
Bancroft, Marie and Squire. *The Bancrofts*. London: John Murray, 1919.
———. *Empty Chairs*. London: John Murray, 1925.
Bannister, Winifred. *James Bridie and His Theatre*. London: Rockliff, 1955.
Baring, Maurice. *Sarah Bernhardt*. London: Peter Davies, 1933.
Barker, Felix. *The Oliviers*. London: Hamish Hamilton, 1953.
Barker, Harley Granville. *The Exemplary Theatre*. London: Chatto and Windus, 1922.
Barkworth, Peter. *About Acting*. London: Secker and Warburg, 1980.
Barnes, Clive. "Britain's New Actors—Rougher, Tougher, Angrier." *The New York Times Magazine*, October 6, 1963.
Barnes, Eric Wollencott. *The High Room*. London: W.H. Allen, 1957.
Barnes, J.H. *Forty Years On The Stage*. London: Chapman and Hall, 1914.
Barnes, Sir Kenneth. *Welcome, Good Friends*. London: Peter Davies, 1958.
Barrett, Wilson. *On Stage for Notes*. Edinburgh: William Blackwood, 1954.
Barrymore, Diana, and Gerold Frank, *Too Much, Too Soon*. London: Frederick Muller, 1957.
Barrymore, Ethel. *Memories*. New York: Harper, 1955.
Barrymore, John. *Confessions of an Actor*. Indianapolis: Bobbs-Merrill, 1926.
Barrymore, Lionel, and Cameron Shipp. *We Barrymores*. London: Peter Davies, 1951.
Batters, Jean. *Edith Evans: A Personal Memoir*. London: Hart-Davis Macgibbon, 1977.
Bax, Peter. *Stage Management*. London: Lovat Dickson, 1936.
Baxter, Beverley. *First Nights and Noises Off*. London: Hutchinson, 1949.
Beaumont, Cyril W. *Flash-Back*. London: C.W. Beaumont, 1931.

Bibliography

Beerbohm, Max. *Around Theatres*. London: Rupert Hart-Davis, 1953

———. *More Theatres, 1898–1903*. London: Rupert Hart-Davis, 1969.

———, ed. *Herbert Beerbohm Tree*. London: Hutchinson, 1920.

Behrman, S.N. *Tribulations and Laughter*. London: Hamish Hamilton, 1972.

Beiswanger, George. "Of Thee I Sing: Twenty-Five Years of American Playwriting." *The Theatre Arts Monthly*, New York, November 1941.

Belasco, David. "About Acting." *The Saturday Evening Post*, Philadelphia, September, 24, 1921.

———. "About Play Producing." *The Saturday Evening Post*, Philadelphia, January 10, 1920.

———. "Making Dreams Come True." *The Saturday Evening Post*, Philadelphia, May 4, 1929.

———. "Stage Art—New and Old." *The Saturday Evening Post*, Philadelphia, March 20, 1920.

Belden, K. D. *The Westminster Theatre*. London: Westminster Productions, 1965.

Belfrage, Bruce. *One Man In His Time*. London: Hodder and Stoughton, 1951.

Bell, Mary Hayley. *What Shall We Do Tomorrow?* London: Cassell, 1962.

Bell, Stanley, Norman Marshall, and Richard Southern. *The Essentials of Stage Planning*. London: Frederick Muller, 1949.

Benchley, Nathaniel. *Robert Benchley*. London: Cassell, 1956.

Bennett, Jill, and Suzanne Goodwin. *Godfrey: A Special Time Remembered*. London: Hodder and Stoughton, 1983.

Benson, Lady (Constance). *Mainly Players*. London: Thornton Butterworth, 1926.

Benson, Sir Frank. *My Memoirs*. London: Ernest Benn, 1930.

Bentham, Frederick. *Stage Lighting*. London: Sir Isaac Pitman, 1950.

Bentley, Eric. *Bernard Shaw*. Norfolk, Conn.: New Directions Books, 1947.

———. *The Modern Theatre*. London: Robert Hale, 1948.

Bernard, Oliver P. *Cock Sparrow*. London: Jonathan Cape, 1936.

Bernhardt, Lysiane. *Sarah Bernhardt: My Grandmother*. Translated by Vyvyan Holland. London: Hurst and Blackett, 1949.

Bernhardt, Sarah. *My Double Life: Memoirs*. London: William Heinemann, 1907.

Berton, Thérèse, and Basil Woon. *Sarah Bernhardt As I Knew Her*. London: Hurst and Blackett, 1923.

Bester, Alfred. "A Thousand Curtains Rise." *Holiday*, Philadelphia, September 1957.

Bevan, Ian. "Chaperoning Charley's Aunt." *John Bull*, London, October 20, 1951.

Billington, Michael. *The Guinness Book of Theatre Facts and Feats*. London: Guinness Superlatives, 1982.

Bingham, Madeleine. *"The Great Lover": The Life and Art of Herbert Beerbohm Tree*. London: Hamish Hamilton, 1978.

———. *Henry Irving and the Victorian Theatre*. London: George Allen and Unwin, 1978.

Bishop, George W. *Barry Jackson and the London Theatre*. London: Arthur Barker, 1933.

Blakelock, Denys. *Round The Next Corner*. London: Victor Gollancz, 1967.

Bloom, Claire. *Limelight and After*. London: Weidenfeld and Nicolson, 1982.

Bloomfield, Roderick, ed. *Heard In The Wings*. London: Stanley Paul, 1972.

Bibliography

Blow, Sydney. *The Ghost Walks on Fridays*. London: Heath Cranton, 1935.

————. *Through Stage Doors*. Edinburgh: W. and R. Chambers, 1958.

Bolitho, Hector. *Marie Tempest*. London: Cobden-Sanderson, 1936.

Booth, J.B. *Master and Men: Pink 'Un Yesterdays*. London: T. Werner Laurie, 1926.

————. *Old Pink 'Un Days*. London: Grant Richards, 1924.

————. *Palmy Days*. London: The Richards Press, 1957.

————. *Pink Parade*. London: Thornton Butterworth, 1933.

Booth, Michael. *English Melodrama*. London: Herbert Jenkins, 1965.

————. *Victorian Spectacular Theatre, 1850–1910*. London: Routledge and Kegan Paul, 1981.

Boyd, Alice Katharine. *The Interchange of Plays Between London and New York, 1910–1939*. New York: King's Crown Press, Columbia University, 1948.

Brady, William A. *Showman*. New York: E.P. Dutton, 1937.

Brambell, Wilfred. *All Above Board*. London: W.H. Allen, 1976.

Brandon-Thomas, Jevan. *Charley's Aunt's Father*. London: Douglas Saunders/ Macgibbon and Kee, 1955.

Brandreth, Gyles. *Great Theatrical Disasters*. London: Granada, 1982.

————. *John Gielgud: A Celebration*. London: Pavilion/Michael Joseph, 1984.

Brereton, Austin. *H. B. and Laurence Irving*. London: Grant Richards, 1922.

————. *The Lyceum and Henry Irving*. London: Launce and Bullen, 1903.

————. *Sir Henry Irving*. London: Anthony Treherne, 1905.

Brian, Dennis. *Tallulah, Darling!* London: Sidgwick and Jackson, 1980.

Bridie, James. *One Way of Living*. London: Constable, 1939.

Brighouse, Harold. *What I Have Had*. London: George Harrap, 1953.

Broadbent, R.J. *Stage Whispers*. London: Simpkin, Marshall, Hamilton, Kent, 1901.

Broadhurst, George. "Some Others and Myself." *The Saturday Evening Post*, Philadelphia, October 16, 1926–March 5, 1927.

Brookfield, Charles H.E. *Random Reminiscences*. London: Thomas Nelson, 1911.

Brooks, Cleanth, and Robert B. Heilman. *Understanding Drama*. London: George Harrap, 1946.

Brough, J. Ainsley. *The Secrets of Making Up*. London: The Star Music Publishing Co., 1914.

Brough, Jean Webster. *Prompt Copy*. London: Hutchinson, 1952.

Brown, Catherine Hayes. "Mary, This Is Your Mother." *The Saturday Evening Post*, Philadelphia, November 4–December 30, 1939.

Brown, Ivor. *Parties of the Play*. London: Ernest Benn, 1928.

————. *Shaw In His Time*. London: Thomas Nelson, 1965.

————. *The Way of My World*. London: William Collins, 1954.

Brown, John Mason. *Dramatis Personae*. London: Hamish Hamilton, 1963.

————. *Seeing Things*. New York: McGraw Hill, 1946.

————. *Two On The Aisle*. New York: W.W. Norton, 1938.

————. *Upstage*. New York: W.W. Norton, 1930.

————. *The Worlds of Robert E. Sherwood*. London: Hamish Hamilton, 1965.

Browne, Maurice. *Too Late To Lament*. London: Victor Gollancz, 1955.

Bull, Peter. *I Know the Face, But. . . .* London: Peter Davies, 1959.

————. *I Say, Look Here!* London: Peter Davies, 1965.

————. *Life is a Cucumber*. London: Peter Davies, 1973.

Burke, Billie, and Cameron Shipp. *With a Feather on my Nose*. London: Peter Davies, 1950.

————. *With Powder on my Nose*. New York: Coward-McCann, 1959.

Burnand, Sir Francis C. *Records and Reminiscences*. 2 vols. London: Methuen, 1904.

Burns, Mary. *Theatricality*. London: Longmans, 1972.

Burton, Percy, and Lowell Thomas. *Adventures Among Immortals*. New York: Dodd, Mead, 1937.

"Buskers of London." *Picture Post,* London, December 3, 1938.

Calthrop, Dion C. *My Own Trumpet*. London: Hutchinson, 1935.

Calvert, Adelaide. *Sixty-Eight Years on the Stage*. London: Mills and Boon, 1911.

Campbell, Beatrice Stella (Mrs. Patrick). *My Life and Some Letters*. London: Hutchinson, 1922.

Carpenter, Charles A. *Bernard Shaw and the Art of Destroying Ideals*. Madison, Wis.: University of Wisconsin Press, 1969.

Carr, Alice Comyns. *Reminiscences*. Edited by Eve Adams. London: Hutchinson, 1926.

Carson, William G.B. *Dear Josephine*. Norman, Okla.: University of Oklahoma Press, 1963.

Carter, Huntly. *The New Spirit in the European Theatre, 1914–1924*. London: Ernest Benn, 1925.

Case, Frank. *Do Not Disturb*. New York: Frederick A. Stokes, 1940.

————. *Feeding the Lions*. New York: The Greystone Press, 1942.

————. *Tales of a Wayward Inn*. New York: Garden City, 1940.

Castle, Charles. *Noël*. London: W.H. Allen, 1972.

Catling, Patrick Skene. "We Few, We Happy Few: The Royal Academy of Dramatic Art." *The Sunday Telegraph Magazine*, London, November 25, 1984.

Charques, R.D., ed. *Footnotes to the Theatre*. London: Peter Davies, 1938.

Chase, Francis, Jr. "Angel With The Midas Touch." *The Saturday Evening Post*, Philadelphia, July 7, 1956.

Chase, Ilka. *Past Imperfect*. Garden City, N.Y.: Doubleday, Doran, 1943.

Cheney, Sheldon. *Stage Decoration*. London: Chapman and Hall, 1928.

————. *The Theatre*. London: Vision Press, 1953.

Chiari, J. *Landmarks of Contemporary Drama*. London: Herbert Jenkins, 1965.

Child, Harold H. *A Poor Player*. Cambridge: The University Press, 1939.

Chisholm, Cecil. *Repertory*. London: Peter Davies, 1934.

Chisman, Isabel, and Hester Emilie Raven-Hart. *Manners and Movements In Costume Plays*. London: H.F.W. Deane, 1934.

Churchill, Allen. *The Great White Way*. New York: E.P. Dutton, 1962.

Churchill, Sarah. *Keep On Dancing*. London: Weidenfeld and Nicolson, 1981.

Clapp, H.A. *Reminiscences of a Dramatic Critic*. Boston: Houghton Mifflin, 1902.

Clarence, O.B. *No Complaints*. London: Jonathan Cape, 1947.

Clark, Barrett H., and George Freedley, eds. *A History of Modern Drama*. New York: D. Appleton-Century, 1947.

Clunes, Alec. *The British Theatre*. London: Cassell, 1964.

Bibliography

Clurman, Harold. *All People Are Famous*. New York: Harcourt, Brace, Jovanovich, 1974.

———. *The Fervent Years*. London: Dennis Dobson, 1946.

Coad, Oral Sumner, and Edwin Mims, Jr. *The American Stage*. New Haven: Yale University Press, 1929.

Cochran, C.B. *Cock-a-Doodle-Doo*. London: J.M. Dent, 1941.

———. *I Had Almost Forgotten*. London: Hutchinson, 1932.

———. *Secrets of a Showman*. London: Hutchinson, 1929.

———. *Showman Looks On*. London: Guild Books, 1949.

Coffin, Charles Hayden. *Hayden Coffin's Book*. London: Alston Rivers, 1930.

Cohan, George M. *Twenty Years on Broadway*. New York: Harper, 1925.

Cohen, David, and Ben Greenwood. *The Buskers*. Newton Abbot: David & Charles, 1981.

Colbourne, Maurice. *The Real Bernard Shaw*. London: J.M. Dent, 1949.

Cole, Marian. *Fogie: The Life of Elsie Fogerty, CBE*. London: Peter Davies, 1967.

Cole, Toby. *Acting: A Handbook of the Stanislavsky Method*. New York: Crown, 1958.

——— and Helen Krich Chinoy. *Directing the Play*. London: Vision Press/Peter Owen, 1954.

Collier, Constance. *Harlequinade*. London: John Lane, 1929.

Collier, Richard. "Countrymen's Theatre." *Bandwagon*, London, September–October 1951.

———. "A First Night Every Night." *John Bull*, London, January 14, 1950.

———. "Girl Who Is Wanted In Two Million Homes." *The Sunday Chronicle*, London, February 17, 1952.

———. "Hotel That Lives on Variety." *John Bull*, London, October 1, 1949.

———. "Masks and Faces." *Town and Country*, London, February 1947.

———. "New Deal for Playgoers." *The Sunday Chronicle*, April 13, 1952.

———. "Pepping Up Panto." *John Bull*, London, November 23, 1950.

———. "Peter Pan: This Show Must Never Change." *The Sunday Chronicle*, London, December 23, 1951.

———. *The Rainbow People*. New York: Dodd, Mead, 1984.

———. "Secrets of A Woman With Four Faces: Hermione Gingold." *The Sunday Chronicle*, London, May 4, 1952.

——— and Terence De Marney. "The Truth About Show Business." *The Sunday Graphic*, London, October 10–November 22, 1953.

——— and Captain Harry Grattidge. *Captain of the Queens*. New York: E.P. Dutton, 1956.

Collins, Horace. *My Best Riches*. London: Eyre and Spottiswoode, 1941.

Compton, Fay. *Rosemary: Some Remembrances*. London: Alston Rivers, 1926.

Connell, Brian. *Knight Errant*. London: Hodder and Stoughton, 1955.

Constanduros, Mabel. *Shreds and Patches*. London: Lawson and Dunn, 1947.

Cook, Dutton. *On The Stage*. 2 vols. London: Sampson Low, Marston, Searle and Rivington, 1883.

Cook, Judith. *Director's Theatre*. London: George Harrap, 1974.

Cooper, Courtney Ryley. "The Villain Still Pursued Her." *The Saturday Evening Post*, Philadelphia, April 8, 1933.

Bibliography

Cooper, Gladys. *Gladys Cooper: An Autobiography*. London: Hutchinson, 1931.

Cordell, Richard A. *Henry Arthur Jones and The Modern Drama*. New York: Ray Long and Richard R. Smith, Inc., 1932.

Cornell, Katharine, and Alice Griffin. "A Good Play Will Always Find a Good Audience." *The Theatre Arts Monthly*, New York, May 1954.

———— and Ruth Woodbury Sedgwick. *I Wanted to Be an Actress*. New York: Random House, 1939.

Corson, Richard. *Stage Make-Up*. New York: Appleton-Century Crofts, 1949.

Cotes, Peter. *No Star Nonsense*. London: Rockliff, 1949.

Cottrell, John. *Laurence Olivier*. London: Weidenfeld and Nicolson, 1975.

Counsell, John. *Counsell's Opinion*. London: Barrie and Rockliff, 1963.

Courtneidge, Cicely. *Cicely*. London: Hutchinson, 1953.

Courtneidge, Robert. *I Was an Actor Once*. London: Hutchinson, 1930.

Courtney, W.L. *The Idea of Tragedy*. London: Archibald Constable, 1900.

Coward, Noël. *Future Indefinite*. London: William Heinemann, 1954.

————. *Present Indicative*. London: Theatre Book Club, 1950.

Craig, Edward Gordon. *Henry Irving*. London: J.M. Dent, 1930.

————. *Index To The Story of My Days*. Cambridge: Cambridge University Press, 1981.

Cronyn, Hume. "Dear Diary." *The Theatre Arts Monthly*, New York, July 1961.

Cross, Farrell. "Broadway's Merry Lambs." *Coronet*, New York, June 1961.

Croxton, Arthur. *Crowded Nights—And Days*. London: Sampson Low, Marston, 1934.

Cullman, Marguerite. "How an 'Angel' Picks a Play." *The Theatre Arts Monthly*, New York, April 1963.

Culver, Roland. *Not Quite a Gentleman*. London: William Kimber, 1979.

Curtis, Anthony, ed., *The Rise and Fall of the Matinée Idol*. London: Weidenfeld and Nicolson, 1974.

Dale, James. *Pulling Faces for a Living*. London: Victor Gollancz, 1971.

Daly, Frederick. *Henry Irving in England and America*. London: T. Fisher Unwin, 1884.

Daly, J.F. *The Life of Augustin Daly*. New York: Macmillan, 1917.

Dare, Phyllis. *From School to Stage*. London: Collier & Co., 1907.

Darlington, W.A. *The Actor and His Audience*. London: Phoenix House, 1949.

————. *I Do What I Like*. London: Theatre Book Club. 1950.

————. *Six Thousand and One Nights*. London: George Harrap, 1960.

————. *Through the Fourth Wall*. London: Chapman and Hall, 1922.

Darlow, Michael, and Gillian Hodson. *Terence Rattigan*. London: Quartet Books, 1979.

Daubeny, Peter. *My World of Theatre*. London: Jonathan Cape, 1971.

————. *Stage By Stage*. London: John Murray, 1952.

Dean, Basil. *Mind's Eye*. London: Hutchinson, 1973.

————. *Seven Ages*. London: Hutchinson, 1970.

————. *The Theatre at War*. London: George Harrap, 1956.

Delderfield, Eric. *Cavalcade By Candlelight*. Exmouth, Devon: The Raleigh Press, 1950.

Delderfield, R.F. *Bird's Eye View*. London: Constable, 1954.

Bibliography

Denham, Reginald. *Stars in my Hair*. London: T. Werner Laurie, 1958.

Denison, Michael. *Overture and Beginners*. London: Victor Gollancz, 1973.

Dent, Alan. *Mrs Patrick Campbell*. London: Museum Press, 1961.

———. *Nocturnes and Rhapsodies*. London: Hamish Hamilton, 1950.

———. *Preludes and Studies*. London: Macmillan, 1942.

———, ed. *Bernard Shaw and Mrs Patrick Campbell: Their Correspondence*. London: Victor Gollancz, 1952.

Derwent, Clarence. *The Derwent Story*. New York: Henry Schuman, 1953.

Desmond, Florence. *Florence Desmond*. London: George Harrap, 1953.

Deutsch, Hermann B. "Memoirs of a Spear Bearer." *The Saturday Evening Post*, Philadelphia, May 23, 1936.

Devlin, Diana. *A Speaking Part: Lewis Casson and The Theatre of his Time*. London: Hodder and Stoughton, 1982.

Dickinson, Thomas H. *The Contemporary Drama of England*. Boston: Little, Brown, 1917.

———. *Playwrights of the New American Theatre*. New York: Macmillan, 1925.

Disher, Maurice Willson. *Blood and Thunder*. London: Frederick Muller, 1949.

———. *The Last Romantic*. London: Hutchinson, 1948.

———. *Melodrama: Plots that Thrilled*. London: Rockliff, 1954.

Dixon, Ella Hepworth. *As I Knew Them*. London: Hutchinson, 1930.

Doherty, Edward J. *The Rain Girl: The Tragic Story of Jeanne Eagels*. Philadelphia: Macrae Smith, 1930.

Donaldson, Frances. *The Actor Managers*. London: Weidenfeld and Nicolson, 1970.

———. *Freddy Lonsdale*. London: William Heinemann, 1957.

Donaldson, William. *Great Disasters of the Stage*. London: Weidenfeld and Nicolson, 1984.

Donisthorpe, G. Sheila. *Show Business*. London: Fortune Press, 1943.

Donland, Yolande. *Shake the Stars Down*. London: Hodder and Stoughton, 1976.

Donohue, J.W., ed. *The Theatre Manager in England and America*. Princeton: Princeton University Press, 1971.

Drake, Fabia. *Blind Fortune*. London: William Kimber, 1978.

Dressler, Marie. *Life Story of an Ugly Duckling*. London: Hutchinson, 1925.

——— and Mildred Harrington. *My Own Story*. London: Hurst and Blackett, 1935.

Drew, Edwin. *Henry Irving: On and Off Stage*. London: Henry J. Drane, 1907.

Drew, John. *My Years on the Stage*. New York: E.P. Dutton, 1922.

Druxman, Michael B. *Basil Rathbone*. New York: A.S. Barnes, 1975.

Dukes, Ashley. "The Mechanics of 'Grand Hotel.' " *The Theatre Arts Monthly*, New York, November 1931.

———. "The Scene in Europe." *The Theatre Arts Monthly*, New York, March 1936.

———. *The Scene is Changed*. London: Macmillan, 1942.

———. *The World to Play With*. London: Oxford University Press, 1928.

Du Maurier, Daphne. *Gerald: A Portrait*. London: Victor Gollancz, 1934.

Dunbar, Janet. *Flora Robson*. London: George Harrap, 1960.

Duncan, Barry. *The St. James's Theatre*. London: Barrie and Rockliff, 1964.

Dundy, Elaine. *Finch, Bloody Finch*. London: Michael Joseph, 1980.

Dunkel, Wilbur Dwight. *Sir Arthur Pinero*. Chicago, Ill.: University of Chicago Press, 1941.

Bibliography

Duval, Elizabeth R. "Every Barn's a Stage." *The New York Times Magazine*, June 28, 1940.

Dyas, Aubrey. *Adventures in Repertory*. Northampton: The Repertory Players, 1948.

Earl, Marjorie. "Constance Collier, Star Who Coaches Stars." *John Bull*, London, November 3, 1951.

Eaton, Walter Prichard. "Tryout in New Haven." *The Theatre Arts Monthly*, New York, Summer 1948.

Edwards, Anne. *Vivien Leigh*. London: W.H. Allen, 1977.

Eells, George, and Stanley Musgrove. *Mae West*. London: Robson Books, 1984.

Elder, Eleanor. *Travelling Players: The Story of the Arts League of Service*. London: Frederick Muller, 1939.

Ellis, Mary. *Those Dancing Years*. London: John Murray, 1982.

Emil-Behnke, Kate. *Speech and Movement on the Stage*. London: Oxford University Press, 1930.

Engel, Lehman. *The Critics*. New York: Macmillan, 1976.

England, John. *Across My Path*. Weybridge, Surrey: Pennant Publishing Co., 1975.

English, Arthur, ed. *Anecdotes of the Theatre*. London: Grant Richards, 1914.

Ervine, St. John. *Bernard Shaw: His Life, Work and Friends*. London: Constable, 1956.

———. *The Theatre in my Time*. London: Rich and Cowan, 1933.

Eustis, Morton. "The Actor Attacks His Part." *The Theatre Arts Monthly*, New York, October 1936–March 1937.

———. *B'Way Inc!* New York: Dodd, Mead, 1934.

———. "A Generation of Lost Plays." *The Theatre Arts Monthly*, New York, July 1938.

———. "On The Road With The Lunts." *The Theatre Arts Monthly*, New York, June 1939.

———. "Scene Designing as a Business." *The Theatre Arts Monthly*, New York, July 1934.

———. "Summer Theatre—1936 Model." *The Theatre Arts Monthly*, New York, June 1936.

———. "The Summer Theatres." *The Theatre Arts Monthly*, New York, June 1933.

Evans, Gareth Lloyd. *The Language of Modern Drama*. London: J.M. Dent, 1977.

Fagan, Elizabeth ("The Stage Cat"). *From The Wings*. London: William Collins, 1922.

Fairbrother, Sydney. *Through an Old Stage Door*. London: Frederick Muller, 1939.

Fairweather, Virginia. *Cry God for Larry*. London: Calder and Boyars, 1969.

Farber, Donald C. *Producing on Broadway*. New York: DBS Publications, 1969.

Faulkner, Trader. *Peter Finch*. London: Angus and Robertson, 1979.

Fawkes, Richard. *Fighting for a Laugh*. London: Macdonald and Janes, 1978.

Fecher, Constance. *Bright Star*. London: Victor Gollancz, 1971.

Felheim, Marvin. *The Theatre of Augustin Daly*. Cambridge, Mass.: Harvard University Press, 1956.

Fenston, Joe. *Never Say Die*. London: Alexander Moring, 1958.

Ferber, Edna. *A Peculiar Treasure*. New York: Doubleday Doran, 1939.

Bibliography

Fernald, John. *The Play Produced*. London: H.F.W. Deane, 1933.

Findlater, Richard. *Lilian Baylis, The Lady of the Old Vic*, London: Allen Lane, 1975.

————. *The Player Kings*. London: Weidenfeld and Nicolson, 1971.

————. *The Player Queens*. London: Weidenfeld and Nicolson, 1976.

————. *The Unholy Trade*. London: Victor Gollancz, 1952.

Fitch, Clyde. *Clyde Fitch and His Letters*. Edited by Montrose J. Moses and Virginia Gerson. Boston: Little, Brown, 1924.

Fitzgerald, Percy. *Henry Irving: Twenty Years at the Lyceum*. London: Chapman and Hall, 1893.

————. *The World Behind The Scenes*. London: Chatto and Windus, 1881.

Flanagan, Hallie. *Shifting Scenes of the Modern European Theatre*. London: George Harrap, 1929.

Flexner, Eleanor. *American Playwrights, 1918–1939*. New York: Simon and Schuster, 1938.

Forbes, Bryan. *Ned's Girl*. London: Elm Tree Books, 1977.

————. *That Despicable Race*. London: Elm Tree Books, 1980.

Forbes-Robertson, Diana. *Maxine Elliott*. London: Hamish Hamilton, 1964.

Forbes-Robertson, Sir Johnston. *A Player Under Three Reigns*. London: T. Fisher Unwin, 1925.

Forbes-Winslow, D. *Daly's*. London: W.H. Allen, 1944.

Forman, Robert. *Scene Painting*. London: Sir Isaac Pitman, 1951.

Forsyth, James. *Tyrone Guthrie*. London: Hamish Hamilton, 1976.

Fraser, M.F.K. *The Alexandra Theatre*. Birmingham: Cornish Bros., 1948.

Freedley, George. *The Lunts*. London: Rockliff, 1957.

French, Harold. *I Swore I Never Would*. London: Secker and Warburg, 1970.

————. *I Thought I Never Could*. London: Secker and Warburg, 1973.

Frohman, Daniel. *Daniel Frohman Presents*. New York: Lee Furman, 1935.

————. *Encore*. New York: Lee Furman, 1937.

————. *Memories of a Manager*. London: William Heinemann, 1911.

Fromm, Herbert. *Bernard Shaw and the Theatre in the Nineties*. Lawrence, Kan.: University of Kansas, 1967.

Fuerst, Walter René, and Samuel J. Hume. *Twentieth-Century Stage Decoration*. 2 vols. New York: Dover Publications, 1967.

Funke, Lewis. "Always in the Wings—The Shakes." *The New York Times Magazine*, May 17, 1964.

————. "First Night Flutters." *The New York Times Magazine*, January 6, 1952.

———— and John E. Booth. *Actors Talk About Acting*. New York: Random House, 1961.

Gagey, Edward M. *The San Francisco Stage*. New York: Columbia University Press, 1950.

Gaige, Crosby. *Footlights and Highlights*. New York: E.P. Dutton, 1948.

Gallati, Mario. *Mario of the Caprice*. London: Hutchinson, 1960.

Gay, Maisie. *Laughing Through Life*. London: Hurst and Blackett, 1931.

Gielgud, John. *Distinguished Company*. London: William Heinemann, 1972.

————. *Early Stages*. London: Falcon Press, 1953.

————. *Stage Directions*. London: William Heinemann, 1963.

Bibliography

———. "The Urge to Act—An Incurable Fever." *The New York Times Magazine*, February 14, 1960.

Gielgud, Kate Terry. *Kate Terry Gielgud: An Autobiography*. London: Max Reinhardt, 1953.

Gilder, Rosemond. "The Actor as Biographer: Wilfrid Lawson." *The Theatre Arts Monthly*, New York, December 1937.

———. "The American Theatre, 1916–1941." *The Theatre Arts Monthly*, New York, February 1941.

———. "In the Service of Comedy." *The Theatre Arts Monthly*, September 1938.

Gill, Brendan. *Tallulah*. London: Michael Joseph, 1973.

Gill, Maud. *See The Players*. London: Hutchinson, 1938.

Glover, J.M. *Hims, Ancient and Modern*. London: T. Fisher Unwin, 1926.

———. *Jimmy Glover and His Friends*. London: Chatto and Windus, 1913.

———. *Jimmy Glover His Book*. London: Methuen, 1911.

Godfrey, Philip. *Back-Stage*. London: George Harrap, 1933.

Golden, John C., and Viola Brothers Shore. *Stage-Struck John Golden*. New York: Samuel French, 1930.

Goldman, Emma. *The Social Significance of the Modern Drama*. Boston: Richard G. Badger, 1914.

Goldstein, Malcolm. *The Political Stage*. New York: Oxford University Press, 1974.

Goodwin, Nat C. *Nat Goodwin's Book*. Boston: Richard G. Badger, 1914.

Gordon, Max, and Lewis Funke. *Max Gordon Presents*. New York: Bernard Geis Associates, 1963.

Gordon, Ruth. *Myself Among Others*. New York: Atheneum, 1971.

Gorelik, Mordecai. *New Theatres For Old*. London: Dennis Dobson, 1947.

Gottfried, Martin. *Jed Harris: The Curse of Genius*. Boston: Little, Brown, 1984.

Graham, Joe. *An Old Stock Actor's Memories*. London: John Murray, 1930.

Granville, Wilfred. *A Dictionary of Theatrical Terms*. London: André Deutsch, 1952.

Graves, George. *Gaieties and Gravities*. London: Hutchinson, 1931.

"Green Grows The Theatre." *The Theatre Arts Monthly*, New York, Fall 1948.

Green, Roger Lancelyn. *Fifty Years of Peter Pan*. London: Peter Davies, 1954.

Greenwall, Harry. *The Strange Life of Willy Clarkson*. London: John Long, 1936.

Grey, Elizabeth. *Behind the Scenes in the Theatre*. London: J.M. Dent, 1969.

Grossmith, George. *"G.G."* London: Hutchinson, 1933.

Gruver, Bert. *The Stage Manager's Handbook*. New York: Harper, 1953.

Guitry, Sacha. *If I Remember Right*. Translated by Lewis Galantière. London: Methuen, 1935.

Guthrie, Tyrone. *A Life in the Theatre*. London: Hamish Hamilton, 1960.

———. *Theatre Prospect*. London: Wishart, 1932.

Haddon, Archibald. *Green Room Gossip*. London: Stanley Paul, 1922.

———. *Hullo, Playgoers*. London: Cecil Palmer, 1924.

Hageman, Maurice. *Hageman's Make-Up Book*. Chicago, Ill.: The Dramatic Publishing Co., 1898.

Hamilton, Bruce. *The Light Went Out*. London: Constable, 1972.

Hamilton, Clayton. *Studies in Stagecraft*. London: Grant Richards, 1914.

Hamilton, Cosmo. *Unwritten History*. London: Hutchinson, 1924.

Bibliography

Hapgood, Elizabeth Reynolds, ed. and trans. *Stanislavsky's Legacy*. London: Max Reinhardt, 1958.

Hapgood, Norman. *The Stage in America, 1897–1900*. New York: The Macmillan Company, 1901.

Harding, Alfred. *The Revolt of The Actors*. New York: William Morrow, 1929.

Hardwicke, Sir Cedric. *Let's Pretend*. London: Grayson and Grayson, 1932.

────── and James Brough. *A Victorian in Orbit*. London: Methuen, 1961.

Hare, Robertson. *Yours Indubitably*. London: Robert Hale, 1956.

Harker, Joseph. *Studio and Stage*. London: Nisbet & Co., 1924.

Harmon, Charlotte Buchwald. "Confessions of a Strawhat Impresario." *The New York Times Magazine*, June 16, 1957.

────── and Maurice Zolotow. "Summer Theater is Crazy!" *The Saturday Evening Post*, Philadelphia, August 20, 1955.

Harris, Radie. *Radie's World*. London: W.H. Allen, 1975.

Harrison, Elizabeth. *Love, Honour and Dismay*. London: Weidenfeld and Nicolson, 1976.

Harrison, Rex. *Rex*. Boston: G.K. Hall, 1976.

Hart, Moss. *Act One*. London: Secker and Warburg, 1950.

Hartman, John G. *The Development of American Social Comedy from 1787 to 1936*. Philadelphia: University of Pennsylvania, 1939.

Hartmann, Louis. *Theatre Lighting*. New York: D. Appleton, 1930.

Hartnoll, Phyllis M. *The Oxford Companion to the Theatre*. Oxford: Oxford University Press, 1983.

Harvey, Sir John Martin. *The Autobiography of Sir John Martin-Harvey*. London: Sampson Low, Marston & Co., 1933.

──────. *The Book of Martin Harvey*. London: Henry Walker, 1930.

Harwood, Ronald. *All The World's a Stage*. London: Secker and Warburg/British Broadcasting Corporation, 1983.

──────. *Sir Donald Wolfit, C.B.E.* London: Secker and Warburg, 1971.

──────, ed. *A Night at the Theatre*. London: Methuen, 1982.

Hatton, Joseph. *Henry Irving's Impressions of America*. 2 vols. London: Sampson Low, Marston, Searle and Rivington, 1884.

Hawkins, Jack. *Anything for a Quiet Life*. London: Elm Tree Books, 1973.

Hawtrey, Sir Charles. *The Truth At Last*. London: Thornton Butterworth, 1924.

Hayes, Helen. "Just Living." *The Ladies Home Journal*, Philadelphia, April 1936.

────── and Sandford Dody. *On Reflection*. New York: M. Evans & Co., 1968.

────── and Lewis Funke. *A Gift of Joy*. New York: M. Evans, 1965.

Hayman, Ronald. *John Gielgud*. London: Heinemann, 1971.

──────. *The Set-Up*. London: Eyre Methuen, 1973.

──────. *Techniques of Acting*. London: Methuen, 1969.

──────. *Theatre and Anti-Theatre*. London: Secker and Warburg, 1979.

Hayward, Brooke. *Haywire*. London: Jonathan Cape, 1977.

Hazzard, John E., and Robert Gordon Anderson. "Troupers All." *The Saturday Evening Post*, Philadelphia, April 13, 1929.

Heather, Stanley. *That Struts and Frets*. Ilfracombe, Devon: Arthur H. Stockwell, 1972.

Hecht, Ben. *Charlie*. New York: Harper, 1957.

————. *A Child of the Century*. New York: Simon and Schuster, 1954.

Heilman, Robert B. *The Iceman, The Arsonist and The Troubled Agent*. London: George Allen and Unwin, 1973.

Helburn, Theresa. *A Wayward Quest*. Boston: Little, Brown, 1960.

"Helen Hayes Picks The 10 Most Memorable Performances." *Collier's*, New York, September 22, 1951.

Hellman, Lillian. *Pentimento*. Boston: Little, Brown, 1973.

Helvenston, Harold. "West Coast Audiences." *The Theatre Arts Monthly*, New York, July 1933.

Heppner, Sam. *"Cockie."* London: Leslie Frewin, 1969.

Heston, Charlton. *The Actor's Life*. New York: E. P. Dutton, 1978.

Hethmon, Robert H., ed. *Strasberg at the Actors Studio*. London: Jonathan Cape, 1966.

Hewitt, Barnard. *Theatre U.S.A.—1668–1957*. New York: McGraw Hill, 1959.

Hiatt, Charles. *Ellen Terry and Her Impersonations*. London: George Bell, 1898.

————. *Henry Irving: A Record and Review*. London: George Bell, 1899.

Hibbert, H.G. *A Playgoer's Memories*. London: Grant Richards, 1920.

Hickman, Charles. *"Directed By."* Bognor Regis, Sussex: New Horizon, 1981.

Hicks, Seymour. *Between Ourselves*. London: Cassell, 1930.

Himelstein, Morgan. *Drama Was A Weapon*. New Brunswick, N.J.: Rutgers University Press, 1963.

Hirschfeld, Al. "Angel Auditions." *Holiday*, Philadelphia, January 1951.

————. "You'll Never See *This* Show." *Holiday*, Philadelphia, February 1951.

Hobbs, William. *Techniques of the Stage Fight*. London: Studio Vista, 1967.

Hobson, Harold. *Indirect Journey*. London: Weidenfeld and Nicolson, 1978.

————. *Verdict at Midnight*. London: Longmans Green, 1952.

Hole, Rev. Donald. *The Church and the Stage*. London: The Faith Press, 1934.

Holloway, David. *Playing The Empire*. London: George Harrap, 1979.

Home, William Douglas. *Half Term Report*. London: Longmans Green, 1954.

————. *Mr Home Pronounced Hume*. London: William Collins, 1979.

Hopkins, Arthur. *How's Your Second Act?* New York: Samuel French, 1931.

Hornblow, Arthur. *A History of the American Theatre*. 2 vols. Philadelphia: J.B. Lippincott, 1919.

Houghton, Norris. *Advance From Broadway*. New York: Harcourt, Brace, 1941.

Houseman, John. *Run-Through*. New York: Simon and Schuster, 1972.

Howard, J. Bannister. *Fifty Years A Showman*. London: Hutchinson, 1938.

Howard, Keble. *My Motley Life*. London: T. Fisher Unwin, 1927.

Howard, Leslie. *Trivial Fond Records*. Edited by Ronald Howard. London: William Kimber, 1982.

Howard, Leslie Ruth. *A Quite Remarkable Father*. London: Longmans, 1961.

Howard, Ronald. *In Search of My Father*. London: William Kimber, 1981.

Hoyt, Edward P. *Alexander Woollcott: The Man Who Came To Dinner*. London: Abelard-Schuman, 1968.

Hoyt, Harlowe R. *Town Hall Tonight*. Engelwood Cliffs, N.J.: Prentice-Hall, 1955.

Hubert, Philip G., Jr. *The Stage as a Career*. New York: The Knickerbocker Press, 1900.

Hunt, Morton M. "Panic in the Wings." *Cosmopolitan*, New York, January 1953.

Bibliography

Hurlbut, Gladys. *Next Week—East Lynne!* New York: E.P. Dutton, 1950.
Hutchison, Percy. *Masquerade.* London: George Harrap, 1936.
Hutton, Laurence. *Curiosities of the American Stage.* New York: Harper, 1891.

Irving, Laurence H. *Henry Irving.* London: Faber and Faber, 1951.
———. *The Successors.* London: Rupert Hart-Davis, 1967.
Isaac, Winifred F.E.C. *Ben Greet and the Old Vic.* London: Privately printed, 1966.
Isaacs, Edith J.R. "Type Casting." *The Theatre Arts Monthly*, New York, February 1933.

James, Henry. *The Scenic Art.* Edited by Allen Wade. London: Rupert Hart-Davis, 1949.
James, Judith. *Mother Signed The Contract.* London: Peter Davies, 1957.
Jasen, David A. *The Theatre of P.G. Wodehouse.* London: B.T. Batsford, 1979.
Jeans, Ronald. *Writing for the Theatre.* London: Edward Arnold, 1949.
Jerome, Jerome K. *Stage-Land.* London: Chatto and Windus, 1889.
Jones, Doris Arthur, ed. *The Life and Letters of Henry Arthur Jones.* London: Victor Gollancz, 1930.
Jones, Henry Arthur. *The Renascence of the English Drama.* London: Macmillan, 1895.

Kahn, E.J., Jr. "Abe Burrows: What He Does to Earn $2,000 A Day." *McCalls*, Dayton, Ohio, February 1965.
Kane, Whitford. *Are We All Met?* London: Elkin Matthews and Marrot, 1931.
Kanin, Garson. *Remembering Mr Maugham.* New York: Atheneum, 1966.
———. *Tracy and Hepburn.* New York: The Viking Press, 1971.
Kavanagh, Peter. *The Story of the Abbey Theatre, Dublin.* New York: The Devin-Adair Company, 1950.
Kemp, T.C. *Birmingham Repertory Theatre.* Birmingham: Cornish Bros., 1943.
Kendal, Dame Madge. *Dame Madge Kendal, by Herself.* London: John Murray, 1933.
Kendall, Henry. *I Remember Romano's.* London: Macdonald, 1960.
Keown, Eric. *Peggy Ashcroft.* London: Rockliff, 1955.
Kerr, Fred. *Recollections of a Defective Memory.* London: Thornton Butterworth, 1930.
Kerr, Walter. *Pieces At Eight.* London: Max Reinhardt, 1958.
Kiernan, Thomas. *Olivier.* London: Sidgwick and Jackson, 1981.
Kingston, Gertrude. *Curtsey While You're Thinking. . . .* London: Williams and Norgate, 1937.
Kinne, Wisner Payne. *George Pierce Baker and the American Theatre.* Cambridge, Mass.: Harvard University Press, 1954.
Kitchin, Laurence. *Mid-Century Drama.* London: Faber and Faber, 1960.
Knight, Esmond. *Seeking the Bubble.* London: Hutchinson, 1943.
Knoblock, Edward. *Round The Room.* London: Chapman and Hall, 1939.
Komisarjevsky, Theodore. *The Costume of the Theatre.* London: Geoffrey Bles, 1931.
———. *Myself and the Theatre.* London: William Heinemann, 1929.
——— and Lee Simonson. "Settings and Costumes of the Modern Stage." *The Studio*, London: Winter 1933.
Koster, Donald N. *The Theme of Divorce in American Drama, 1871–1936.* Philadelphia: University of Pennsylvania, 1939.

Bibliography

Kramer, Dale. *Heywood Broun*. New York: A.A. Wyn, 1949.

Kronenberger, Louis. "Show Business." *Holiday*, Philadelphia, April 1949.

Krows, Arthur Edwin. *Play Production in America*. New York: Henry Holt, 1916.

Krutch, Joseph Wood. *The American Drama Since 1918*. London: Thames and Hudson, 1951.

Lanchester, Elsa. *Charles Laughton and I*. London: Faber and Faber, 1938.

Landa, M.J. *The Jew in Drama*. London: P.S. King, 1926.

Landis, Jessie Royce. *You Won't Be So Pretty (But You'll Know More)*. London: W.H. Allen, 1954.

Landstone, Charles. *I Gate-Crashed*. London: Stainer and Bell, 1976.

Lane, Janet. "Take a Deep Breath." *Collier's*, New York, October 9, 1937.

Lane, Margaret. *Edgar Wallace*. London: The Book Club, 1939.

Lane, Yoti. *The Psychology of the Actor*. New York: The John Day Company, 1960.

————. *Stage Make-Up*. London: Hutchinson, 1960.

Lang, Matheson. *Mr Wu Looks Back*. London: Stanley Paul, 1941.

Langner, Lawrence. *The Magic Curtain*. London: George Harrap, 1952.

Laver, James. *Costume in the Theatre*. London: George Harrap, 1964.

————. *Museum Piece*. London: André Deutsch, 1963.

Laye, Evelyn. *Boo, To My Friends*. London: Hurst and Blackett, 1958.

Lazenby, Walter. *Arthur Wing Pinero*. New York: Twayne Publishers, 1972.

Leavitt, Richard, ed. *The World of Tennessee Williams*. London: W.H. Allen, 1978.

Le Gallienne, Eva. *At 33*. London: John Lane, The Bodley Head, 1934.

————. "Back to the Road." *The Christian Science Monitor Magazine*, Boston, November 30, 1940.

————. *With a Quiet Heart*. New York: The Viking Press, 1953.

Lemon, Richard. "Anne Bancroft: 'Hey, Ma, I Can Do That!' " *The Saturday Evening Post*, Philadelphia, November 20, 1965.

Lesley, Cole. *The Life of Noël Coward*. London: Jonathan Cape, 1976.

Letters of An Unsuccessful Actor. London: Cecil Palmer, 1923.

Leverton, W.H., and J.B. Booth. *Through the Box-Office Window*. London: T. Werner Laurie, 1932.

Levy, E. Lawrence. *Birmingham Theatrical Reminiscences, 1870–1920*. Birmingham: J.G. Hammond, 1922.

Lewis, Philip C. *Trouping: How the Show Came to Town*. New York: Harper and Row, 1973.

Lillie, Beatrice, John Philip, and James Brough. *Every Other Inch a Lady*. London: W.H. Allen, 1973.

Lion, Leon M. *The Surprise of My Life*. London: Hutchinson, 1948.

Lister, Moira. *The Very Merry Moira*. London: Hodder and Stoughton, 1969.

Little, Stuart W., and Arthur Cantor. *The Playmakers*. London: Max Reinhardt, 1970.

Littlewood, S.R. *Dramatic Criticism*. London: Sir Isaac Pitman, 1939.

Lockwood, Margaret. *Lucky Star*. London: Odhams Press, 1954.

Logan, Joshua. *Josh: My Up and Down, In and Out Life*. London: W.H. Allen, 1977.

Loos, Anita. *A Girl Like I*. London: Hamish Hamilton, 1967.

Loraine, Winifred. *Robert Loraine: Soldier, Actor, Airman*. London: William Collins, 1938.

Bibliography

Lyons, Leonard. "Never Marry an Actress." *The Saturday Evening Post*, Philadelphia, August 21, 1954.

McCall, Margaret, ed. *My Drama School*. London: Robson Books, 1978.

McCallum, John. *Life With Googie*. London: Heinemann, 1979.

MacCarthy, Desmond. *The Court Theatre*. London: A.H. Bullen, 1907.

McCarthy, Lillah. *Myself and My Friends*. London: Thornton Butterworth, 1933.

McClintic, Guthrie. *Me and Kit*. Boston: Little, Brown, 1955.

MacFall, C. Haldane. *Sir Henry Irving*. Edinburgh, T.N. Foulis, 1906.

MacGowan, Kenneth. *Footlights Across America*. New York: Harcourt, Brace, 1929.

Machen, Arthur. "The Benson Company." *The Theatre Arts Monthly*, New York, September 1931.

Mackail, Denis. *The Story of J.M.B.* London: Peter Davies, 1941.

Macqueen-Pope, W. *Back Numbers*. London: Hutchinson, 1954.

———. *Carriages at Eleven*. London: Hutchinson, 1947.

———. *The Footlights Flickered*. London: Herbert Jenkins, 1959.

———. *Ghosts and Greasepaint*. London: Robert Hale, 1951.

———. *Haymarket, Theatre of Perfection*. London: W.H. Allen, 1948.

———. *An Indiscreet Guide to Theatreland*. London: Muse Arts, 1947.

———. *Ladies First*. London: W.H. Allen, 1952.

———. *Pillars of Drury Lane*. London: Hutchinson, 1955.

———. *Shirtfronts and Sables*. London: Robert Hale, 1953.

———. *St. James's, Theatre of Distinction*. London: W.H. Allen, 1958.

———. *Theatre Royal, Drury Lane*. London: W.H. Allen, 1945.

Magarshack, David. *Chekhov, The Dramatist*. London: John Lehmann, 1952.

Malevinsky, Mose L. *The Science of Playwriting*. New York: Brentano's, 1925.

Maltby, H.F. *Ring Up the Curtain*. London: Jarrolds, 1928.

Mander, Raymond, and Joe Mitchenson. *The Lost Theatres of London*. London: Rupert Hart-Davis, 1968.

Maney, Richard. "End of the Run for the Empire." *The New York Times Magazine*, March 15, 1953.

———. "No Feuds Like Show Feuds." *The New York Times Magazine*, March 26, 1961.

Marchant, William. *The Privilege of His Company*. London: Weidenfeld and Nicolson, 1975.

Marcosson, Isaac F., and Daniel Frohman. *Charles Frohman: Manager and Man*. London: John Lane, 1916.

Marinacci, Barbara. *Leading Ladies*. London: Alvin Redman, 1961.

Marker, Lise-Lone. *David Belasco: Naturalism in the American Theatre*. Princeton: Princeton University Press, 1975.

Marsh, Edward Owen. *Jean Anouilh*. London: W.H. Allen, 1953.

Marshall, Audrey. *Fishbones into Butterflies*. London: Chatto and Windus, 1964.

Maschwitz, Eric. *No Chip on my Shoulder*. London: Herbert Jenkins, 1957.

Mason, A.E.W. *Sir George Alexander and the St James's Theatre*. London: Macmillan, 1935.

Mason, James. *Before I Forget*. London: Elm Tree Books, 1981.

Massey, Raymond. *A Hundred Different Lives*. London: Robson Books, 1979.

Bibliography

Matthews, A.E. *Matty.* London: Hutchinson, 1953.

Matthews, J. Bache. *A History of the Birmingham Repertory Theatre.* London: Chatto and Windus, 1924.

Matthews, James Brander. *Rip Van Winkle Goes to the Play.* New York: Charles Scribner's, 1926.

Matthison, Arthur L. *Less Paint, More Vanity.* London: Heath Cranton, 1937.

Maude, Cyril. *Behind the Scenes with Cyril Maude.* London: John Murray, 1957.

Maude, Pamela. *Worlds Away.* London: John Baker, 1964.

May, Robin. *Theatremania.* London: Vernon and Yates, 1967.

———, ed. *The Wit of the Theatre.* London: Leslie Frewin, 1969.

Mayer, Sylvain. *Reminiscences of a K.C., Theatrical and Legal.* London: Selwyn and Blunt, 1924.

Melvill, Harald. *Designing and Painting Scenery for the Theatre.* London: The Art Trade Press, 1948.

Melville, Lewis. *Not All the Truth.* London: Jarrolds, 1928.

Menken, Helen. "Don't Envy Me!" *Woman's Home Companion*, Springfield, Ohio, July 1923.

Middleton, George M. *These Things are Mine.* New York: The Macmillan Co., 1947.

Miller, Ruby. *Believe Me or Not!* London: John Long, 1933.

———. *Champagne from my Slipper.* London: Herbert Jenkins, 1962.

Mills, Sir John. *Up in the Clouds, Gentlemen Please.* London: Weidenfeld and Nicolson, 1980.

Millward, Jessie, and J.B. Booth. *Myself and Others.* London: Hutchinson, 1923.

Minney, R.J. *The Bogus Image of Bernard Shaw.* London: Leslie Frewin, 1969.

Mitchell, Yvonne. *Actress.* London: Routledge and Kegan Paul, 1957.

Moderwell, Hiram Kelly. *The Theatre of Today.* New York: Dodd, Mead, 1927.

Moffat, Graham. *Join Me in Remembering.* Camps Bay, Cape Province: Privately printed, 1955.

Moore, Eva. *Exits and Entrances.* London: Chapman and Hall, 1923.

Moore, Mary. *Charles Wyndham and Mary Moore.* London: Privately printed, 1925.

Mordden, Ethan C. *The American Theatre.* New York: Oxford University Press, 1981.

More, Kenneth. *More or Less.* London: Hodder and Stoughton, 1978.

Morehouse, Ward. "Broadway After Dark." *Collier's*, New York, February 16, 1952.

———. *George M. Cohan, Prince of the American Theater.* Philadelphia: J.B. Lippincott, 1943.

———. *Matinée Tomorrow.* New York: Whittlesey House, 1949.

———. "Portrait of a Producer: Gilbert Miller." *The Theatre Arts Monthly*, New York, July 1956.

Morley, Malcolm. *Margate and its Theatres, 1730–1965.* London: Museum Press, 1966.

Morley, Sheridan. *Sybil Thorndike: A Life in the Theatre.* London: Weidenfeld and Nicolson, 1977.

———. *A Talent to Amuse.* London: William Heinemann, 1969.

Morris, Clara. *Life on the Stage.* London: Isbister, 1906.

Morris, Lloyd. "He Built a Theatre, Stars and a Legend." *The Theatre Arts Monthly*, New York, November 1953.

———. *Incredible New York.* New York: Random House, 1951.

Bibliography

Morse, Frank P. *Backstage with Henry Miller*. New York: E.P. Dutton, 1938.

Morton, Cavendish. *The Art of Theatrical Make-Up*. London: Adam and Charles Black, 1909.

Morton, Frederic. "Straw-Hat Circuit." *Holiday*, Philadelphia, July 1959.

Motley [Margaret F. Harris, Audrey Sophia Harris, Elizabeth Montgomery]. *Designing and Making Stage Costumes*. London: Studio Vista, 1964.

————. *Theatre Props*. London: Studio Vista, 1975.

Mozart, George. *Limelight*. London: Hurst and Blackett, 1938.

Munro, C.K. *Watching a Play*. London: Gerald Howe, 1933.

Nagler, A.N. *A Source Book in Theatrical History*. New York: Dover Books, 1952.

Napier, Frank. *Noises Off*. London: Frederick Muller, 1936.

Nares, Owen. *Myself and Some Others*. London: Duckworth, 1925.

Nathan, George-Jean. *Another Book on the Theatre*. New York: B.W. Huebsch, 1915.

————. *George-Jean Nathan Presents*. New York: Alfred Knopf, 1917.

————. *Since Ibsen*. New York: Alfred A. Knopf, 1933.

Neagle, Anna. *There's Always Tomorrow*. London: W.H. Allen, 1974.

Neilson, Julia. *This for Remembrance*. London: Hurst and Blackett, 1941.

Nesbitt, Cathleen. *A Little Love and Good Company*. Owings Mills, Md.: Stemmer House, 1977.

Nethercot, Arthur. *Man and Superman: The Shavian Portrait Gallery*. Cambridge, Mass.: Harvard University Press, 1954.

Newton, H. Chance. *Crime and the Drama*. London: Stanley Paul, 1927.

————. *Cues and Curtain Calls*. London: John Lane, 1927.

Nicholson, Nora. *Chameleon's Dish*. London: Paul Elek, 1973.

Nicoll, Allardyce. *The Development of the Theatre*. London: George Harrap, 1948.

————. *Late Nineteenth Century Drama*. Cambridge: Cambridge University Press, 1959.

————. *World Drama; From Aeschylus to Anouilh*. London: George Harrap, 1976.

Noble, Peter. *Ivor Novello: Man of the Theatre*. London: The Falcon Press, 1951.

O'Casey, Sean. *Mirror in my House*. 2 vols. New York: The Macmillan Co., 1956.

O'Connor, Garry P. *Ralph Richardson*. London: Hodder and Stoughton, 1982.

Oenslager, Donald. *Stage Design*. New York: The Viking Press, 1975.

Olivier, Lord. *Confessions of an Actor*. London: Weidenfeld and Nicolson, 1982.

O'Malley, Frank Ward. "Putting the Hearse in Rehearsals." *The Saturday Evening Post*, Philadelphia, February 14, 1920.

Orme, Michael. *J.T. Grein*. London: John Murray, 1936.

Osborne, John. *A Better Class of Person*. London: Faber, 1981.

Ould, Herman. *John Galsworthy*. London: Chapman and Hall, 1934.

Owen, Harrison. *The Playwright's Craft*. London: Thomas Nelson, 1940.

Paine, Albert Bigelow. *Life and Lillian Gish*. New York: The Macmillan Co., 1932.

Palmer, John. *The Future of the Theatre*. London: G. Bell, 1913.

Palmer, Lilli. *Change Lobsters—and Dance*. London: W.H. Allen, 1976.

Parker, Louis N. *Several of My Lives*. London: Chapman and Hall, 1928.

Patch, Blanche. *Thirty Years with G.B.S.* London: Victor Gollancz, 1951.

Bibliography

Payne, Ben Iden. *A Life in a Wooden O.* New Haven: Yale University Press, 1977.

Paxton, Sydney. *Stage See-Saws.* London: Mills and Boon, 1917.

Pearson, Hesketh. *Beerbohm Tree.* London: Methuen, 1956.

———. *Bernard Shaw.* London: Methuen, 1961.

———. *Hesketh Pearson.* London: Heinemann, 1965.

———. *The Last Actor Managers.* London: Methuen, 1950.

———. *Modern Men and Mummers.* London: George Allen and Unwin, 1921.

Peile, F. Kinsey. *Candied Peel.* London: A. and C. Black, 1931.

Pellizzi, Camillo. *English Drama.* Translated by Rowan Williams. London: Macmillan, 1935.

Pemberton, Brock. "Angels Over Broadway." *The New York Times Magazine*, October 22, 1944.

Pemberton, T. Edgar. *Ellen Terry and Her Sisters.* London: C. Arthur Pearson, 1902.

———. *The Kendals.* London: C. Arthur Pearson, 1900.

———. *A Memoir of Edward Askew Sothern.* London: Richard Bentley, 1889.

———. *Sir Charles Wyndham.* London: Hutchinson, 1904.

Pepperburg, Roy L. "Noises Off-Stage." *The Christian Science Monitor Magazine*, Boston, July 6, 1938.

Perry, George Sessions. "Darnedest Thing You've Seen." *The Saturday Evening Post*, Philadelphia, March 1, 1952.

Pertwee, Roland. *Master of None.* London: Peter Davies, 1940.

Peters, Margot. *Mrs Pat.* London: The Bodley Head, 1984.

Phillips, Norman. "Greatest Gambler in Show Business." *John Bull*, London, June 21, 1952.

Pilbrow, Richard. *Stage Lighting.* London: Studio Vista, 1970.

Playfair, Giles W. *My Father's Son.* London: Geoffrey Bles, 1937.

Playfair, Sir Nigel. *Hammersmith Hoy.* London: Faber and Faber, 1930.

Pogson, Rex. *Miss Horniman and the Gaiety Theatre, Manchester.* London: Rockliff, 1952.

Poirier, Normand. "A Miracle on Broadway." *The Saturday Evening Post*, Philadelphia, April 25, 1964.

Pollock, Channing. *The Footlights Fore and Aft.* Boston: Richard G. Badger, 1911.

———. *The Harvest of My Years.* Indianapolis: Bobbs-Merrill, 1943.

Pollock, Walter Herries. *Impressions of Henry Irving.* London: Longmans Green, 1907.

Power-Waters, Alma. *John Barrymore: The Authorised Life.* London: Stanley Paul, 1942.

Preston, Harry. *Memories.* London: Constable, 1928.

Price, Nancy. *Each in His Own Way.* London: Frederick Muller, 1960.

———. *Into an Hour Glass.* London: Museum Press, 1953.

Prideaux, Tom. *Love or Nothing: The Life and Times of Ellen Terry.* London: Millington Books, 1976.

Priestley, J.B. *Particular Pleasures.* London: Heinemann, 1975.

———. *Theatre Outlook.* London: Nicholson and Watson, 1947.

Rahill, Frank. "Dion Boucicault and Royalty Payments for Playwrights." *The Theatre Arts Monthly*, New York, November 1939.

————. *The World of Melodrama*. Philadelphia: Pennsylvania State University Press, 1967.

Redfield, William. *Letters from an Actor*. London: Cassell, 1967.

Redgrave, Michael. *The Actor's Ways and Means*. London: William Heinemann, 1953.

————. *In My Mind's Eye*. London: Weidenfeld & Nicolson, 1982.

Reed, Joseph Verner. "Apologia of a Producer." *The Theatre Arts Monthly*, New York, February 1934.

Reed, Rex. *Do You Sleep in the Nude?* London: W.H. Allen, 1969.

Rees, Terence. *Theatre Lighting in the Age of Gas*. London: The Society for Theatre Research, 1978.

Reeve, Ada. *Take it for a Fact*. London: William Heinemann, 1954.

Reynolds, Ernest. *Modern English Drama*. London: George G. Harrap, 1950.

Rice, Elmer. *The Living Theatre*. London: Heinemann, 1960.

————. *Minority Report*. London: Heinemann, 1963.

Ridge, C. Harold. *Stage Lighting*. Cambridge: W. Heffer, 1928.

Rigg, Diana. *No Turn Unstoned*. London: Elm Tree Books, 1982.

Roberts, Vera Mowry. *The Nature of Theatre*. New York: Harper and Row, 1971.

Robertson, W. Graham. *Time Was*. London: Hamish Hamilton, 1931.

Robins, Elizabeth. *Both Sides of the Curtain*. London: William Heinemann, 1940.

Robinson, Lennox. *Curtain Up*. London: Michael Joseph, 1942.

Robyns, Gwen. *Light of a Star*. London: Leslie Frewin, 1968.

Roose-Evans, James. *Experimental Theatre from Stanislavsky to Today*. London: Studio Vista, 1970.

Rose, Billy. *Wine, Women and Words*. London: Reinhardt and Evans, 1949.

Rosenthal, Jean. "Native Son—Backstage." *The Theatre Arts Monthly*, New York, June 1941.

Rossi, Alfred. *Astonish Us in the Morning: Tyrone Guthrie Remembered*. London: Hutchinson, 1977.

Rowell, George. *The Victorian Theatre*. London: Oxford University Press, 1956.

———— and Anthony Jackson. *The Repertory Movement: A History of Regional Theatre in Britain*. Cambridge: Cambridge University Press, 1984.

Rueff, Suze. *I Knew Sarah Bernhardt*. London: Frederick Muller, 1951.

Ruhl, Arthur. *Second Nights*. New York: Charles Scribner, 1914.

Russell, Charles Edward. *Julia Marlowe*. New York: D. Appleton, 1926.

Rutherford, Margaret, and Gwen Robyns. *Margaret Rutherford*. London: W.H. Allen, 1972.

Saddlmyr, Ann, ed. *Letters to Molly: J.M. Synge and Maire O'Neill*. Cambridge, Mass: The Bellknap Press, 1971.

Saintsbury, H.A., ed. *We Saw Him Act*. London: Hurst and Blackett, 1939.

Sala, George Augustus. *Living London*. London: Remington, 1883.

Salberg, Derek. *My Love Affair with a Theatre*. Luton, Beds.: Cortney Publications, 1978.

Saunders, Peter. *The Mousetrap Man*. London: William Collins, 1972.

Sayler, Oliver. *Our American Theatre*. New York: Brentano's, 1923.

Schalit, Leon. *John Galsworthy: A Survey*. London: William Heinemann, 1929.

Bibliography

Scott, Clement. *The Drama of Yesterday and Today*. 2 vols. London: Macmillan, 1899.

———. *From "The Bells" to King Arthur*. London: John Macqueen, 1897.

———. *Thirty Years at the Play, and Dramatic Table Talk*. London: Railway and General Automatic Library, 1892.

Scott, Marion. *Chatauqua Caravan*. New York: D. Appleton-Century, 1939.

Selden, Samuel, and Hunton D. Sellman. *Stage Scenery and Lighting*. New York: Appleton-Century Crofts, 1959.

Seyler, Athene, and Stephen Haggard. *The Craft of Comedy*. London: Frederick Muller, 1943.

Sharpe, Robert Boies. *Irony in the Drama*. Chapel Hill, N.C.: University of North Carolina Press, 1959.

Shaw, George Bernard. *Our Theatres in the Nineties*. 3 vols. London: Constable, 1932.

Shaw, Martin. *Up to Now*. London: Oxford University Press, 1929.

Sherek, Henry. *Not In Front of the Children*. London: William Heinemann, 1959.

Sheringham, George, and James Laver. *Design in the Theatre*. London: "The Studio," 1927.

Sherriff, R.C. *No Leading Lady*. London: Victor Gollancz, 1968.

Sherson, Erroll. *London's Lost Theatres*. London: John Lane, The Bodley Head, 1925.

Shore, Florence Teignmouth. *Sir Charles Wyndham*. London: John Lane, 1908.

Short, Ernest. *Sixty Years of Theatre*. London: Eyre and Spottiswoode, 1951.

———. *Theatrical Cavalcade*. London: Eyre and Spottiswoode, 1942.

Sievers, W. David. *Freud on Broadway*. New York: Heritage House, 1955.

Simonson, Lee. *The Stage is Set*. New York: Harcourt, Brace, 1933.

Simpson, Harold. *Excursions in Comedy*. London: Besant, 1929.

Sims, George R. *My Life: Sixty Years Recollections of Bohemian London*. London: Eveleigh Nash, 1917.

Sinden, Donald. *A Touch of the Memoirs*. London: Hodder and Stoughton, 1982.

Singer, Kurt. *The Charles Laughton Story*. London: Robert Hale, 1954.

Skinner, Cornelia Otis. *Bottoms Up!* London: Constable, 1955.

———. *Happy Family*. London: Constable, 1950.

———. *Life with Lindsay and Crouse, 1976*. Boston: Houghton, Mifflin, 1976.

Skinner, Otis. *Footlights and Spotlights*. Indianapolis: Bobbs-Merrill, 1924.

———. "One Thousand and One Night Stands." *The Saturday Evening Post*, Philadelphia, July 24, 1926.

Smedley, Constance. *Crusaders: Reminiscences*. London: Duckworth, 1929.

Smith, C. Ray, ed. *The Theatre Crafts Book of Make-Up, Masks, and Wigs*. London: White Lion, 1974.

Smith, Dodie. *Look Back with Astonishment*. London: W.H. Allen, 1979.

———. *Look Back with Mixed Feelings*. London: W.H. Allen, 1978.

Sothern, E.H. *My Remembrances: The Melancholy Tale of "Me."* London: Cassell, 1917.

Southern, Richard. *The Seven Ages of the Theatre*. London: Faber and Faber, 1962.

Speaight, Robert. *The Property Basket*. London: Collins and Harvill Press, 1970.

Spence, E.F., K.C. *Bar and Buskin*. London: Elkin Matthews and Marrot, 1930.

Spitzer, Marian. "Ten-Twenty-Thirty." *The Saturday Evening Post*, Philadelphia, August 22, 1925.

Bibliography

————. "What Do They Do With All Their Money?" *The Saturday Evening Post*, Philadelphia, January 26, 1924.

Sprigge, Elizabeth. *Sybil Thorndike Casson*. London: Victor Gollancz, 1971.

Squire, Tom. "Broadway Bits." *The Theatre Arts Monthly*, New York, February 1936.

Stanford, Derek. *Christopher Fry*. London: Peter Newill, 1951.

Stanislavsky, Konstantin. *An Actor Prepares*. Translated by Elizabeth R. Hapgood. New York: Theatre Arts, 1936.

————. *My Life in Art*. Translated by J.J. Robbins. London: Geoffrey Bles, 1945.

Stanton, Sanford E. *Theatre Management*. New York: D. Appleton, 1929.

Steen, Marguerite. *A Pride of Terrys*. London: Longmans, 1962.

Stern, Ernst. *My Life, My Stage*. Translated by Edward Fitzgerald. London: Victor Gollancz, 1951.

Stevens, Thomas Wood. *The Theatre from Athens to Broadway*. New York: D. Appleton, 1932.

Stewart, Hal D. *Stagecraft*. London: Sir Isaac Pitman, 1949.

Stiefel, Milton. "The Summer Theatre Looks About." *The Theatre Arts Monthly*, New York, 1941.

Stoker, Bram. *Personal Reminiscences of Henry Irving*. 2 vols. London: William Heinemann, 1906.

Stoker, H.G. *Straws in the Wind*. London: Herbert Jenkins, 1925.

Stokes, Sewell. *Monologue*. London: Hutchinson, 1934.

————. *Without Veils*. London: Peter Davies, 1953.

Stott, William, and Jane Stott. *On Broadway*. London: Thames and Hudson, 1979.

Strauss, Theodore. "Dudley Digges." *The Theatre Arts Monthly*, New York, October 1941.

"Straw Hat Circuit." *The Theatre Arts Monthly*, New York, August 1954.

Stuart, Pauline. *Theatre Procedures and Practice*. Banbury, Oxon: British Theatre Institute, 1982.

Sutro, Alfred. *Celebrities and Simple Souls*. London: Duckworth, 1933.

Swaffer, Hannen. *Really Behind the Scenes*. London: George Newnes, 1929.

Swears, Herbert. *When All's Said and Done*. London: Geoffrey Bles, 1937.

Tarkington, Booth. *On Plays, Playwrights and Playgoers*. Edited by Alan S. Downer. Princeton: Princeton University Library, 1959.

Taubman, Howard. *The Making of the American Theatre*. New York: Coward McCann, 1967.

Taylor, Dwight. *Blood and Thunder*. London: Michael Joseph, 1963.

Taylor, John Russell. *Alec Guinness: A Celebration*. London: Pavilion/Michael Joseph, 1984.

————. *Anger and After*. London: Methuen, 1962.

————. *The Rise and Fall of the Well-Made Play*. London: Methuen, 1967.

Taylor, W. Buchanan. *Shake the Bottle*. London: Heath Cranton, 1942.

————. *Shake It Again*, London: Heath Cranton, 1943.

Teichmann, Howard. *George S. Kaufman: An Intimate Portrait*. London: Angus and Robertson, 1973.

————. *Smart Alec*. New York: William Morrow, 1976.

Tellegen, Lou. *Women Have Been Kind*. London: Jarrolds, 1932.

Bibliography

Terkel, Studs. *Hard Times*. London: Allen Lane, 1970.

Terriss, Ellaline. *Ellaline Terriss, by Herself*. London: Cassell, 1928.

———. *Just a Little Bit of String*. London: Hutchinson, 1955.

Terry, Ellen. *The Story of My Life: Memoirs*. London: Victor Gollancz, 1933.

Thesiger, Ernest. *Practically True*. London: William Heinemann, 1927.

Thomas, A.E. "Going on the Stage, Sir?" *The Saturday Evening Post*, Philadelphia, April 6, 1929.

Thomas, Augustus. *The Print of My Remembrances*. New York: Charles Scribner, 1922.

Thompson, Alan Reynolds. *The Dry Mock: A Study of Irony in the Drama*. Berkeley: University of California Press, 1948.

Thorndike, Russell. *Sybil Thorndike*. London: Theatre Book Club, 1950.

——— and Sybil Thorndike. *Lilian Baylis*. London: Chapman and Hall, 1938.

Tomkinson, Constance. *What a Performance!* London: Michael Joseph, 1962.

Towse, John Ranken. *Sixty Years of the Theatre*. New York: Funk and Wagnalls, 1916.

Trader, George Henry. "Grandpa's Odyssey." *The Christian Science Monitor Magazine*, Boston, July 20, 1938.

Tree, Herbert Beerbohm. *Thoughts and Afterthoughts*. London: Cassell, 1915.

Trewin, J.C. *Alec Clunes*. London: Rockliff, 1958.

———. *Benson and the Bensonians*. London: Barrie and Rockliff, 1960.

———. *Edith Evans*. London: Rockliff, 1954.

———. *The Gay Twenties*. London: Macdonald, 1958.

———. *Paul Scofield*. London: Rockliff, 1956.

———. *Robert Donat*. London: William Heinemann, 1968.

———. *Sybil Thorndike*. London: Rockliff, 1955.

———. *The Theatre Since 1900*. London: Andrew Dakers, 1951.

———. *The Turbulent Thirties*. London: Macdonald, 1960.

Trewin, Wendy. *All On Stage*. London: George Harrap, 1980.

Truax, Sarah. *A Woman of Parts*. New York: Longmans Green, 1949.

Trussler, Simon. *The Plays of John Osborne*. London: Victor Gollancz, 1969.

Tunney, Kieran. *Tallulah—Darling of the Gods*. London: Secker and Warburg, 1972.

Tyler, George C. "Not that it Matters." *The Saturday Evening Post*, Philadelphia, January 13–March 10, 1934.

Tynan, Kenneth. *Alec Guinness*. London: Rockliff, 1953.

———. *Curtains*. London: Longmans, 1961.

———. *He That Plays the King*. London: Longmans Green, 1950.

———. *The Sound of Two Hands Clapping*. London: Jonathan Cape, 1975.

———. *Tynan Right and Left*. Longmans, 1967.

Valk, Diana. *Shylock for a Summer*. London: Cassell, 1958.

Vanburgh, Irene. *To Tell My Story*. London: Hutchinson, 1948.

Vanburgh, Violet. *Dare to be Wise*. London: Hodder and Stoughton, 1925.

Van Druten, John. *Playwright at Work*. London: Hamish Hamilton, 1953.

———. *The Way to the Present*. London: Michael Joseph, 1938.

———. *The Widening Circle*. London: William Heinemann, 1957.

Van Vechten, Carl. *The Merry-go-Round*. New York: Reynal and Hitchcock, 1941.

Bibliography

Verneuil, Louis. *The Fabulous Life of Sarah Bernhardt*. Translated by Ernest Boyd. New York: Harper, 1942.

Vernon, Frank. *The Twentieth-Century Theatre*. London: George Harrap, 1924.

Wagner, Leopold. *How to Get on the Stage and How to Succeed There*. London: Chatto and Windus, 1899.

———. *Roughing It on the Stage*. London: Iliffe, 1895.

———. *The Stage with the Curtain Raised*. London: Privately printed, 1880.

Walbrook, H.M. *Nights at the Play*. London: W.J. Ham-Smith, 1911.

———. *A Playgoer's Wanderings*. London: Leonard Parsons, 1926.

Wallace, Irving. "King of Melodrama." *Collier's*, New York, December 6, 1964.

Ward, A.C., ed. *Specimens of English Dramatic Criticism*. London: Oxford University Press, 1945.

Ward, Eric. *A Book of Make-Up*. London: Samuel French, 1930.

Warre, Michael. *Designing and Making Stage Scenery*. London: Studio Vista, 1966.

Weaver, William. *Duse*. London: Thames and Hudson, 1984.

Webster, Margaret. *Don't Put Your Daughter on the Stage*. New York: Alfred A. Knopf, 1972.

Whistler, Laurence. *The Initials in the Heart*. London: Rupert Hart-Davis, 1964.

Whiting, John. *On Theatre*. London: Alan Ross, 1966.

Williams, Bransby. *An Actor's Story*. London: Chapman and Hall, 1909.

———. *Bransby Williams*. London: Hutchinson, 1954.

Williams, Emlyn. *Emlyn*. London: The Bodley Head, 1973.

———. *George*. London: Hamish Hamilton, 1961.

Williams, Harcourt. *Four Years at the Old Vic*. London: London, Putnam, 1935.

Williams, R. Gillespie. *The Technique of Stage Lighting*. London: Sir Isaac Pitman, 1947.

Williams, Tennessee. *Memoirs*. London: W.H. Allen, 1976.

Williamson, Audrey. *Contemporary Theatre*. London: Rockliff, 1956.

———. *Old Vic Drama*. London: Rockliff, 1948.

——— and Charles Landstone. *Bristol Old Vic*. London: J. Garnet Miller, 1957.

Wilson, A.E. *East End Entertainment*. London: Arthur Barker, 1954.

———. *Edwardian Theatre*. London: Arthur Barker, 1951.

———. *The Lyceum*. London: Dennis Yates, 1952.

———. *Playgoer's Pilgrimage*. London: Stanley Paul, 1948.

Wilstach, Paul. *Richard Mansfield: The Man and the Actor*. London: Chapman and Hall, 1908.

Winsten, Stephen. *Days with Bernard Shaw*. London: Hutchinson, 1948.

Winter, William. *The Life and Art of Richard Mansfield*. 2 vols. New York: Moffat, Yard, 1910.

———. *The Life of David Belasco*. 2 vols. New York: Moffat, Yard, 1918.

Wise, Arthur. *Weapons in the Theatre*. London: Longmans, 1968.

Wodehouse, P.G. *Over Seventy*. London: Herbert Jenkins, 1957.

Wolfit, Donald. *First Interval*. London: Odham's Press, 1954.

Wood, Joan. *The Casting Couch*. London: Paul Elek, 1975.

Wood, Peggy. *Actors—and People: Both Sides of the Footlights*. New York: D. Appleton, 1930.

Bibliography

————. *A Splendid Gypsy: John Drew*. New York: E.P. Dutton, 1928.

Woollcott, Alexander. *Enchanted Aisles*. New York: G.P. Putnam, 1924.

————. "Miss Kitty Takes to the Road." *The Saturday Evening Post*, Philadelphia, August 18, 1934.

————. *Shouts and Murmurs*. New York: The Century Co., 1922.

————. *While Rome Burns*. London: Arthur Barker, 1934.

Index

Index

250

Index

Index

Index

Index

254

Index

Index

Index

Index

MAKE-BELIEVE

Richard Collier

When, on July 18, 1895, at Windsor
Castle, Queen Victoria knighted Britain's leading actor, Henry Irving, a
landmark in theatrical history had been
reached. A profession that had once
been officially classified as being com-
possed of "rogues and vagabonds" had
overnight lost its stigma, as five more
actor-managers were to follow in Irving's footsteps. With the dawn of the
twentieth century, a new generation,
who in time would assume the mantles
of Irving and his frequent partner Ellen
Terry, was arriving on the scene of this
world of make-believe. Among them
were seven in particular who rose to
become representatives of the best of
their age: Lynn Fontanne, Alfred Lunt,
Katharine Cornell, Noël Coward,
Helen Hayes, John Gielgud, and Laurence Olivier.

This book tells the stories of their
careers, their difficult beginnings, how
they have related to their audiences, the
qualities needed for survival, their chal-
lenges. It is in essence the story of a
tribe, focussing not only on the actors
and actresses but examining as well the
entire infrastructure that makes up this
world: the "angels" like Howard S.
Cullman and Princess Indira of Kapur-
thala; the faithful dressers like Irving's
Walter Collins, in whose arms the actor
died; the understudies; the assistant